Oxford Studies in European Law
General Editors: Paul Craig and Gráinne de Búrca

EU COUNTER-TERRORIST POLICIES AND FUNDAMENTAL RIGHTS

EU Counter-Terrorist Policies and Fundamental Rights

The Case of Individual Sanctions

CHRISTINA ECKES

OXFORD
UNIVERSITY PRESS

OXFORD
UNIVERSITY PRESS

Great Clarendon Street, Oxford, OX2 6DP,
United Kingdom

Oxford University Press is a department of the University of Oxford.
It furthers the University's objective of excellence in research, scholarship,
and education by publishing worldwide. Oxford is a registered trade mark of
Oxford University Press in the UK and in certain other countries

First published 2009

Published in the United States of America by Oxford University Press
198 Madison Avenue, New York, NY 10016, United States of America

British Library Cataloguing in Publication Data
Data available

Library of Congress Control Number: 2009040541

ISBN 978–0–19–957376–9

Meinen Eltern

PREFACE

This book is an updated, revised, and extended version of my doctoral thesis, defended at King's College London on 21 February 2008. Back when I started my PhD in September 2003, European sanctions against private individuals were a new and interesting yet unexplored phenomenon. At that time, the only consideration of such sanctions was in the form of an order of the Court of First Instance (CFI) whereby the Court had rejected an application for interim relief for failure to establish 'urgency'. Today, six years later, the CFI and the European Court of Justice (ECJ) have given several landmark judgments in relation to individual sanctions and nearly every legal scholar interested in European law has come across individual sanctions at one point or another. Individual sanctions are a counter-terrorist policy that raises so many constitutional questions, including questions surrounding the protection of human rights, that they undoubtedly deserve in-depth treatment. While the amount of academic work on this subject has exploded in the past years, this book makes its contribution by comprehensively analysing case-law on individual sanctions and addressing fundamental questions arising from the adoption of individual sanctions.

I am indebted to many people who have contributed to this book in various ways. The first person I would like to thank is my PhD supervisor Piet Eeckhout. Not only do I owe him gratitude for his invaluable comments and his generous support during the process of writing my doctoral thesis, but he was also the person who encouraged me to apply for funding for a PhD project when I was doing my master's degree at the College of Europe in Bruges. For all their time and advice during my time in London, I would further like to thank Andrea Biondi and Itai Rabinowitz.

Without the full funding of the Centre of European Law at King's College London I would not have been in the position to write a doctoral thesis. Further financial support has then enabled me to turn my thesis into this book. A research grant of the School of Law at the University of Surrey, Guildford, allowed me to spend the summer of 2008 at the Max-Planck Institute in Heidelberg and at the European University Institute in Florence.

I am greatly indebted to Deirdre Curtin for giving me the opportunity to revise and extend my PhD thesis into this book. Further, I have benefited substantially from the supportive and stimulating research environment at the Amsterdam Centre of European Law and Governance at the University of Amsterdam (ACELG).

At various stages this book has been subject to critical scrutiny which has been extremely fruitful. I am grateful to Marise Cremona and Takis Tridimas, my PhD examiners, who engaged closely with my writing and gave me insightful comments and suggestions that contributed to the final version of this book. I further wish to thank Ester Herlin-Karnell, Stephan Hollenberg, Joana Mendes, Ronald van Ooik, Itai Rabinowitz, Jan-Herman Reestman, Anniek de Ruijter, and Jure Vidmar for reading and commenting on earlier drafts.

Finally I owe the greatest gratitude to my parents, Margret and Norbert Eckes, to whom I dedicate this book, for raising me in a supportive environment that enabled me to make my own choices in life and for their particular support in those moments where it was most needed.

Christina Eckes
Amsterdam, The Netherlands

CONTENTS

Table of Cases xvii
Abbreviations xxxiii

Introduction **1**

1. European Sanctions against Individuals: Classification and Origins **12**

Introduction 12
1. Traditional Sanctions Light? 15
2. Two Different Types of European Sanctions against Individuals 22
3. The UN Side of the Game 23
3.1 UN Lists of Terrorist Suspects – Resolutions 1267, 1333 and 1390 24
3.1.1 Listing 24
3.1.2 Delisting 31
3.1.3 Exemptions and Qualifications 36
3.2 The General Call to Fight Terrorism – Resolution 1373 37
3.3 Concluding Remarks 40
4. European Sanctions against Individuals 43
4.1 European Sanctions Implementing UN Sanctions 44
4.2 Autonomous European Sanctions 46
5. National Implementation 52
6. Individual Sanctions as One Way to Fight Terrorism 57
6.1 The International Fight against Terrorism 57
6.2 The European Union's Counter-Terrorist Policy 64
6.2.1 Terrorism as a European Problem 64

6.2.2 Individual Sanctions as Part of the European Union's Fight against Terrorism 69
7. The Effectiveness of Individual Sanctions and Other Counter-Terrorist Measures 72
Conclusions 76

2. The Legal Basis of Community Sanctions: Moving Competences from One Pillar to Another? 78

Introduction 78
1. The Legal Basis of Community Measures 81
1.1 Listing Practice under the European Treaties 81
1.2 Articles 301 and 60 EC as the Legal Basis for Individual Sanctions 82
1.3 Articles 301, 60, and 308 EC as a Joint Legal Basis: the Healing Power of Article 308 EC 90
1.3.1 Articles 301 and 60 EC as a Partial Legal Basis 91
1.3.2 Article 301 EC as a Bridge to the TEU 92
1.3.3 Article 308 EC in Opinion 2/94 93
1.3.4 The Missing Boundaries of Community Competence 96
2. CFSP versus PJCC 100
3. Uneven Partners, Each Striving for Dominance: the Binding Force of Union Law on the Community 105
4. Power Balance between the EU and its Member States 114
4.1 Community Law 115
4.2 Union Law 117
5. Treaty of Lisbon 121
Conclusions 124

3. The Right of Access to Justice 127

Introduction 127
1. A Union of Law 129
2. The Relevance of the ECHR for EU Law 133
3. The Right of Access to Justice under the Convention 138
3.1 Scope of the Convention Rights – Distinction Between Articles 6 and 13 ECHR 138
3.2 Article 6 ECHR 139
3.2.1 Excluded by Nature 140
Administrative Measures 140
Political Question Doctrine 141
International Cooperation 145
3.2.2 Criminal Charge 150
Classification of the Proceedings in Domestic Law 151
Nature of the Offence or Conduct in Question 155
Severity of Any Possible Penalty 157
Conclusion – a Criminal Charge? 164
3.2.3 The Determination of Civil Rights and Obligations 166
Case-law of the ECtHR on Civil Rights 166
Practical Consequences of being Listed and Sanctioned 170
Direct Impact on the Rights of Those Listed 172
Determination 173
3.2.4 Application of Article 6 ECHR 176
3.2.5 Independent and Impartial Tribunal 177
3.3 Article 13 ECHR 180
Conclusions 183

4. Limits of Fundamental Rights in the Face of Terrorism **185**

Introduction 185
1. Duty to Protect 187
2. Terrorism as Exceptional Circumstances 189
3. Case-law of the European Court of Human Rights 196
   3.1 Non-Disclosure of Evidence 197
   3.2 Terrorism 200
4. The House of Lords on Terrorism 201
5. Terrorism Jurisprudence in Non-EU Member States 206
   5.1 US Courts 206
   5.2 Supreme Court of Israel 215
Conclusions 217

5. Judicial Review of European Sanctions Giving Effect to UN Lists of Terrorist Suspects **221**

Introduction 221
1. Individual Rights Lost in Hierarchy 223
2. From the Standpoint of International Law 228
3. From the Standpoint of European Law 234
   3.1 The Binding Force of Security Council Resolutions 234
      3.1.1 International Fruit Company 235
      3.1.2 Articles 297 and 307 EC 242
      3.1.3 National Measures 244
   3.2 The Prevailing Force of Security Council Resolutions 245
      3.2.1 International Fruit Company 245
      3.2.2 State Sanctions under Review 246
      3.2.3 Review of Individual Sanctions 250
      3.2.4 Autonomy of the European Legal Order 253
      3.2.5 Amending the European Treaties? 259

4. Between a Rock and a Hard Place: Determining the Status of Security Council Resolutions 261
4.1 A European *Solange*-Approach 263
4.2 The Constitutionalization of the UN – Work in Progress? 268
4.2.1 *Rechtsstaatsprinzip* 269
4.2.2 Limits of Actions by the Security Council 272
4.2.3 Effectiveness 274
4.2.4 Primacy 278
4.3 A Compromise on Substance rather than Forum 279
5. The European Legal Order in Context 282
5.1 The Strasbourg Court 282
5.1.1 Protection from Community Law 282
5.1.2 Primacy of Security Council Resolutions 284
5.2 National Courts 288
5.2.1 Primacy of Security Council Resolutions in National Law 288
5.2.2 Reviewing Individual Sanctions 290
5.3 Interplay between the Different Courts 295
Conclusions 298

6. Protection from Autonomous European Sanctions: Community Law and Union Lists 303

Introduction 303
1. Protection from Community Acts Giving Effect to Union Lists 306
1.1 Rights of Defence 308
1.1.1 Right to a Fair Hearing 308
1.1.2 Access to Information 320
1.2 Obligation to State Reasons 322
1.3 Judicial Review 324
2. Protection from Union Lists: the Status Quo 327
3. Review of Union Law 333

3.1 Indirect Review 334
3.2 The Principle of Wider Jurisdiction 338
3.2.1 The Mandate of the EU courts and its Limits 339
3.2.2 *Les Verts* 340
3.2.3 Attempts to Extend the Powers of the EU courts under the Union Pillars 345
3.3 Preliminary Ruling Procedure 347
3.4 Direct Actions against Union Lists of Terrorist Suspects 351
3.5 Rights of Defence 353
3.6 Obligation to State Reasons 354
3.7 Concluding Remarks 356
4. The European Legal Order in Context 357
4.1 The European Court of Human Rights 357
4.2 National Courts 358
4.2.1 Advocate-General Mengozzi's Opinion in *Segi* 358
4.2.2 The European Arrest Warrant Judgments 362
4.2.3 Lists of Terrorist Suspects in National Courts 365
4.3 Interplay between the Different Courts 367
Conclusions 368

7. What are the Alternatives? Adoption and Review 372

Introduction 372
1. Adopting Autonomous European Sanctions in Compliance with Procedural Rights 375
1.1 Reform of the Autonomous European Sanctions Regime 375
1.2 Further Necessary Changes to the Autonomous Listing Procedure 380
1.2.1 Legislative Changes 380
1.2.2 Institutional Changes 383

1.2.3 Procedural Changes 384
1.2.4 Concluding Remarks 386
1.3 Reviewable Listing Criteria 387
1.4 Disclosure of Information 391
2. European Sanctions against Individuals Giving Effect to UN Lists of Terrorist Suspects 393
3. Judicial Review of European Sanctions against Individuals 396
3.1 Role of the Judiciary 397
3.2 The Struggle for the Last Word 400
3.3 Political Solutions – or a Right to Diplomatic Protection? 405
4. Proportionality of Individual Sanctions 408
Conclusions 417

Conclusions **420**

Bibliography 436
Index 463

TABLE OF CASES

Decisions of the International Court of Justice:

ICJ, Case concerning Armed Activities on the Territory of the Congo (Democratic Republic of the Congo v Rwanda) (Jurisdiction), judgment of 3 February 2006, ICJ Reports 2006 . . . . . 191, 262

ICJ, Legal Consequences of the Construction of a Wall in the Occupied Palestinian Territory, (Advisory Opinion), ICJ Reports 2004, 134–203 191

ICJ, Legality of the Threat or Use of Nuclear Weapons Case (Advisory Opinion), ICJ Reports 1996, 66 191

ICJ, Application of the Convention on the Prevention and Punishment of the Crime of Genocide, Order of 13 September 1993 (Further Requests for the Indication of Provisional Measures), ICJ Reports 1993, 4 272

ICJ, Nicaragua v United States of America, ICJ Reports 1984, judgment of 26 November 1984 233

ICJ, Legal Consequences for States of the Continued Presence of South Africa in Namibia (South West Africa) notwithstanding Security Council Resolution 276 (1970), Order No. 1 of 26 January 1971 (Advisory Opinion), ICJ Reports 1971 262

ICJ, North Sea Continental Shelf Cases, Judgment of 20 February 1969, ICJ Reports 1969, 4 229

ICJ, Certain Expenses of the United Nations, ICJ Reports 1962, 151 229

Dissenting Opinion of Judge Sir Robert Jennings, Lockerbie (Preliminary Objections), ICJ Reports 1998 . . . . . 269, 274

Dissenting Opinion of President Schwebel, Lockerbie (Preliminary Objections), ICJ Reports 1998 273–4

Dissenting Opinion of Judge Weeramantry, East Timor (Portugal v Australia), Judgment of 30 June 1995, ICJ Reports 1995, 155 274

Dissenting Opinion of Judge Skubiszewski, East Timor (Portugal v Australia), Judgment of 30 June 1995, ICJ Reports 1995, 251 274

Decisions of other International Courts and Tribunals

ICTR, The Prosecutor v Kanyabashi, decision of 8 June 1997 251

ICTY, The Prosecutor v Tadic, appeal decision of 2 October 1995, ILM 35 (1996) 250

Inter-American Court of Human Rights, Velásquez Rodríguez Case, Inter-Am Ct HR, Ser C, No. 4 (1988) 187

Decisions of the Court of First Instance

Case T-85/09, Kadi v Commission, pending, [application of 26 February 2009, OJ 2009 C 90/37] 221, 403

Case T-45/09, al Barakaat v Commission, pending, application OJ 2009 C 153/39 . . . . . 221, 403

Case T-284/08, People's Mojahedin Organization of Iran v Council (OMPI III), judgment of 4 December 2008, not yet reported 4, 7, 10, 19, 43, 48, 51, 128, 142–3, 178, 190, 198, 280, 307–8, 310, 312, 319–20, 322, 324, 326, 373, 375, 377–8, 382, 385, 392, 396, 400, 403, 428, 431

Case T-341/07, Sison v Council, pending [application of 10 November 2007, OJ 2007 C 269/58] 4, 400, 403, 428

Case T-256/07, People's Mojahedin Organization of Iran v Council (OMPI II), judgment of 23 October 2008, not yet reported; appeal pending: Case C-576/08 P People's Mojahedin Organization of Iran. 4, 7, 10, 43, 51, 74, 128, 142–3, 155, 190, 280, 307, 310–12, 316–19, 322, 324, 326, 373, 375, 377–8, 382, 389, 392, 396, 400, 402–3, 428, 431

Case T-138/06, Nasuf v Council, pending [application of 15 July 2006, OJ 2006 C 165/30]. 7, 46, 238, 290

Case T-137/06, Abdrabbah v Council, pending [application of 15 July 2006, OJ 2006 C 165/30]. 7, 46, 238, 290

Case T-136/06, Sanabel Relief Agency v Council, pending [application of 15 July 2006, OJ 2006 C 165/30] 7, 46, 238, 290

Case T-135/06, al-Faqih v Council, pending [application of 15 July 2006, OJ 2006 C 165/29]. 7, 46, 238, 290

Case T-474/04 Pergan Hilfsstoffe für industrielle Prozesse v Commission [2007] ECR II-4225 168–9

Case T-299/04, Selmani v Council and Commission, order of 18 November 2005, not published in the ECR 7

Case T-253/04, Kongra-Gel and others v Council [2008] ECR II-46. 307

Case T-49/04, Hassan v Council and Commission [2006] ECR II-52; appealed: C-399/06 P, Hassan v Council and Commission, OJ 2006 C 294/30 . . . . 7, 22, 46, 128, 223–4, 245, 290, 304

Case T-327/03, al-Aqsa v Council [2007] ECR II-79 (summ.pub.) 7, 307

Case T-259/03, Nikolaou v Commission [2007] ECR II-99 (summ.pub.) 353

Joined Cases T-110/03, T-150/03 and T-405/03, Jose Maria Sison v Council [2005] ECR II-1429. . . . . 150, 321, 354, 364,

Case T-47/03, Jose Maria Sison v Council and Commission [2007] ECR II-73 (summ.pub.) 4, 7, 10, 43, 51, 59, 110, 165, 196, 304, 307–8, 310–12, 319–21, 324, 328, 354, 373, 386, 391, 400, 402–3, 428

Case T-47/03 R, Jose Maria Sison v Council and Commission [2003] ECR II-2047 . . . . 7, 10, 51

Case T-338/02, Segi and others [2004] ECR II-1647 . . . . 7, 10, 50–1, 80, 123, 128, 143, 156, 175–6, 305, 328–30, 333, 335, 338, 340, 360, 369, 384, 429

Case T-333/02, Gestoras Pro Amnistía and Others v Council, not published in the ECR; upheld in: Case C-354/04 P, Gestoras Pro-Amistia, judgment of 27 February 2007, not yet reported 7, 10

Case T-253/02, Chafiq Ayadi v Council [2006] ECR II-2139; appealed: C-403/06 P, Ayadi v Council, OJ 2006 C 294/32 . . . . 7, 22, 31, 44, 46, 59, 81, 128, 172, 223–5, 238, 245, 290, 304, 313, 352, 407–8

Case T-229/02, Kurdistan Workers' Party, Kurdistan National Congress v Council (PKK) [2005] ECR II-539 . . . . 51, 143, 157, 224, 307–8, 385

Case T-228/02, Organisation des Modjahedines du peuple d'Iran v Council and UK (OMPI I) [2006] ECR II-4665 . . . . 4, 7, 10, 20, 43, 51, 59, 71, 128, 142–3, 154, 165, 179, 184, 190, 196, 198, 220, 280, 306–8, 310–12, 319–22, 324–7, 333, 340, 355, 358, 373, 375, 377-378, 382, 391–2, 396, 400–2, 428, 431

Joined Cases T-22/02 and T-23/02, Sumitomo Chemical and Sumika Fine Chemicals v Commission [2005] ECR II-4065 168

Case T-318/01, Omar Mohammed Othman v Council and Commission, judgment of 11 June 2009, not yet reported 196, 221, 396, 404

Case T-315/01, Yassin Abdullah Kadi v Council and Commission [2005] ECR II-3649 . . . . . 17, 20, 23, 46, 78–9, 81, 83, 87, 90, 91, 92, 93, 96, 99, 100, 106, 107, 110, 114, 128, 140, 148, 174, 181, 219, 221, 223–5, 227, 233–5, 242–3, 245, 250–3, 261–2, 264, 267, 273, 275, 278, 281, 287, 290–1, 296–7, 299, 304, 312–15, 395, 403–4, 407, 423, 427

Case T-306/01, Ahmed Ali Yusuf and Al Barakaat International Foundation v Council and Commission [2005] ECR II-3533 . . . . . . 2, 7, 22, 46, 78–9, 81, 83, 89–93, 96, 100, 107, 110, 114, 128, 148, 171, 179, 181, 221, 223–26, 233, 243, 250–2, 267, 271, 275, 278, 287, 290, 297, 299, 304, 307, 312–14, 328, 390, 404, 420, 423, 427

T-306/01 R, Aden and others v Council and Commission [2002] ECR II-2387 . . . . 7, 33–4, 45, 53, 224, 226, 404,

Case T-198/01, Technische Glaswerke Ilmenau v Commission [2004] ECR II-2717 .... 310, 317

Case T-177/01, Jégo-Quéré [2002] ECR II-2365 219

Case T-19/01, Chiquita [2005] ECR II-315 245

Joined Cases T-377/00, T-379/00, T-380/00, T-260/01 and T-272/01, Philip Morris International and Others v Commission [2003] ECR II-1 175

Case T-372/00 Campolargo v Commission [2002] ECR II-223 312

Case T-211/00, Aldo Kuijer [2002] ECR II-485 354

Case T-189/00 R, Invest Import und Export and Invest Commerce v Commission [2000] ECR II-2993 .... 310, 313–14, 320

Joined Cases T-222/99, T-327/99 and T-329/99, Martinez and Others v Parliament [2001] ECR II-2823 129

Case T-14/98, Heidi Hautala MEP [1999] ECR II-2489 .... 353, 355

Case T-277/97 Ismeri Europa v Court of Auditors [1999] ECR II-1825 .... 309, 353

Case T-183/97, Micheli and Others v Commission [2000] ECR II-287 354

Case T-89/96 British Steel v Commission [1997] ECR II-835 .... 320, 391

Case T-212/95, Officimen v Commission [1997] ECR II-1161 174

Case T-184/95, Dorsch Consult [1998] ECR II-667 .... 235, 250

Case T-174/95, Svenska Journalistförbundet [1998] ECR II-2289 353

Case T-346/94, France Aviation v Commission [1995] ECR II-2841 .... 310, 314–15, 317

Case T-260/94, Air Inter v Commission [1997] ECR II-997 308

Decisions of the European Court of Justice:

Case C-340/08, M (FC) and Others, pending [OJ 2008 C 260/8] 20, 37, 171, 295

Case C-403/06 P, Ayadi v Council, pending [application of 27 September 2006, OJ 2006 C 294/32] 22, 46, 290, 352, 407

Case C-399/06 P, Faraj Hassan v Council and Commission, pending [application of 25 September 2006, OJ 2006 C 294/30] 22, 46, 128, 290

Case C-301/06 Ireland v Parliament and Council (Data Retention Directive), judgment of 10 February 2009, not yet reported 66, 80, 99,

Case C-117/06, Gerda Möllendorf and Christiane Möllendorf-Niehuus [2007] ECR I-8361 .... 167, 171, 233, 295

Case C-440/05, Commission v Council (Ship Source Pollution) [2007] ECR I-9097 .... 92, 108

Cases C-402/05 P and C-415/05 P, Kadi and al Barakaat, judgment of 3 September 2008, not yet reported 21, 23, 34, 46, 78, 79, 81, 83, 86, 88, 93, 94, 98, 99, 100, 108, 110, 111, 124, 128, 141–2, 144, 148, 181, 184, 196, 215–16, 219, 221, 224, 226–7, 233, 244, 247, 251–5, 257–8, 261–4, 266–7, 273, 276, 280, 287, 290–1, 296–8, 300–2, 304–5, 321, 328, 337, 373–4, 391, 393–7, 403–5, 411, 416, 418, 421, 424, 431

Case C-303/05, Advocaten voor de Wereld VZW v Leden van de Ministerraad [2007] ECR I-3633 . . . . 118, 120

Case C-266/05 P, Sison v Council [2007] ECR I-1233 321

Case C-229/05 P, PKK and KNK v Council [2007] ECR I-439 . . . . 143, 162, 174, 307–8, 385

Case C-91/05 Commission v Council (ECOWAS) [2008] ECR I-3651 . . . . 92, 108, 111, 335–6

Case C-28/05 Dokter and others [2006] ECR I-5431 308

Case C-355/04 P, Segi v Council [2007] ECR I-1657 . . . . 7, 10, 50–1, 102, 104, 112–13, 123, 128–9, 131–3, 135, 138, 172, 219, 284, 298, 305–6, 330–4, 337, 339, 343–50, 352–3, 355–62, 368, 384, 429, 433–4

Case C-354/04 P, Gestoras Pro Amnistía and others v Council [2007] ECR I-1579 330

Case C-351/04, Ikea Wholesale Ltd v Commissioners of Custom & Excise [2007] ECR I-7723 249

Case C-341/04 Eurofood IFSC [2006] ECR I-3813 320

Case C-540/03, EP v Council [2006] ECR I-5769 . . . . 132, 355

Case C-459/03, Commission v Ireland (MOX) [2006] ECR I-4635 . . . . 254, 256

Case C-209/03, Dany Bidar [2005] ECR I-2119 89

Case C-176/03, Commission v Council (Environmental Crime case) [2005] ECR I-7879 . . . . 92, 96, 108, 153–4, 335–6

Case C-160/03, Spain v Eurojust [2005] ECR I-2077 345

Case C-131/03 P, RJ Reynolds Tobacco Holdings Inc v Commission [2007] ECR I-7795 175

Case C-105/03, Pupino [2005] ECR I-5285 . . . . 103, 107–8, 111, 119, 149, 173, 339, 347, 352, 358, 362–3

Case C-456/02, Trojani [2004] ECR I-7573 89

C-377/02, Van Parys [2005] ECR I-1465 . . . . 245, 248

Case C-263/02 P, Jégo-Quéré & Cie SA [2004] ECR I-3425 219

Case C-200/02, Kunqian Catherine Zhu Chen [2004] ECR I-9925. . . . . . . 89, 136, 296

Case C-138/02, Collins [2004] I-2703. 89

Case C-93/02 P, Biret International v Council [2003] ECR I-10497 248

Case C-224/01, Köbler [2003] ECR I-10239 . . . . 131, 352

Case C-339/00, Ireland v Commission [2003] ECR I-11757. 311

Case C-317/00 P(R), 'Invest' Import und Export and Invest Commerce v Commission [2000] ECR I-9541. 313

Case C-112/00, Schmidberger [2003] ECR I-5659 . . . . 136, 344

Joined Cases C-20 and C-64/00, Booker Aquaculture Ltd and Hydro Seafood GSP Ltd v The Scottish Minister [2003] ECR I-7411. . . . 296, 310

Case C-60/00, Carpenter [2002] ECR I-6279. . . . . 136, 296

Case C-50/00 P, Unión de Pequeños Agricultores v Council (UPA) [2002] ECR I-6677. . . . . 132, 219, 346–8, 361

Case C-424/99, Commission v Austria [2001] ECR I-9285. . . . . 132, 136, 350

Case C-413/99, Baumbast [2002] ECR I-7091 . . . . 89, 136, 296

Case C-315/99 P, Ismeri Europa v Court of Auditors [2001] ECR I-5281 . . . . 309, 353

Case C-184/99, Rudy Grzelczyk [2001] ECR I-6193 89

Case C-122 and C-125/99 P, D v Council [2001] ECR I-4319. 344

Case C-1/99, Kofisa Italia [2001] ECR I-207 132

Case C-462/98 P, Mediocurso v Commission [2000] ECR I-7183 310

Case C-376/98, Germany v Parliament and Council [2000] ECR I-8419 99

Case C-224/98, d'Hoop [2002] ECR I-6191. 89

Case C-78/98, Shirley Preston and others [2000] ECR I-3201 350

Case C-437/97, Evangelischer Krankenhausverein Wien v Abgarenberufungskommission Wien and Wein & Co HandelsgesmbH v Oberösterreichische Landesregierung [2000] ECR I-1157 94

Case C-378/97, Wijsenbeek [1999] ECR I-6207. 89

Case C-185/97, Coote v Granada Hospitality, [1998] ECR I-5199 136

Case C-274/96, Bickel and Franz [1998] ECR I-7637. 89

Case C-170/96, Commission v Council (Airport Transit Visa case) [1998] ECR I-2763 335

Case C-149/96, Portugal v Council, [1999] ECR I-8395. . . . . 245, 248

Case C-85/96, Martinez Sala, [1998] ECR I-2691. 89

Case C-309/95, Commission v Council [1998] ECR I-655 . . . . 320, 391

Case C-177/95, Ebony Maritime, [1997] ECR I-1111. 247

Case C-124/95, Centro-Com [1997] ECR I-81. . . . . 238, 242, 247–8

Case C-122/95, Germany v Council [1998] ECR I-973 254–5

Case C-84/95, Bosphorus Airways [1996] ECR I-3953 ...... 136, 247–8, 252, 286, 414

Case C-57/95, France v Commission (Re Pension Funds Communication) [1997] ECR I-1627................................ 332

Case C-32/95, Commission v Lisrestal [1996] ECR I-5373.................... 310

Case C-83/94, Leifer [1995] ECR I-3189................................ 335

Case C-70/94, Werner [1995] ECR 1-3189 335

Case C-13/94, P v S [1996] ECR I-2143.................................. 136

Opinion 2/94, ECHR [1996] ECR I-1759 .... 82, 93–6, 256, 340, 344, 423

Opinion 1/94, re WTO Agreement [1994] ECR I-5267 237

Case C-360/93, Parliament v Council [1996] ECR 1145...................... 255

Case C-280/93, Germany v Council [1994] ECR I-4973...................... 246

Cases C-133/93, 300/93 and 362/93, Crispoltoni [1994] ECR I-4863 410

Case C-188/92, Textilwerke Deggendorf v Germany, [1994] ECR I-833 .... 219, 348

Case C-135/92 Fiskano v Commission [1994] ECR I-2885.................... 308

Opinion 1/92, EEA Agreement [1992] ECR I-2821 256

Case C-327/91, France v Commission [1994] ECR 3641 255

Case C-314/91, Weber v Parliament [1993] ECR I-1093 129

Case C-97/91, Oleificio Borelli v Commission [1992] ECR I-6313.... 132, 350–1, 385

Case C-47/91, Italy v Commission [1992] ECR I-4145....................... 174

Opinion 1/91, Draft Treaty on European Economic Area [1991] ECR I-6079 .... 254, 256

Case C-269/90, Technische Universität München, [1991] ECR I-5469 .... 309, 315, 322

Case C-159/90, Society for the Protection of Unborn Children Ireland Ltd v Grogan [1991] ECR I-4685 410

Case C-71/90, Spain v Council [1992] ECR I-5175 334

Case C-70/90, Spain v Council [1992] ECR I-5159 334

Case C-63/90 and C-67/90, Portugal and Spain v Council [1992] ECR I-5073 334

Joint Cases C-6 and 9/90, Francovich and Bonifaci v Italy [1991] ECR I-5357 94

Case C-260/89, Elliniki Radiophonia Tileorassi AE [1991] ECR I-2925.......... 344

Case C-213/89, R v Secretary of State for Transport ex parte Factortame Ltd [1990] ECRI-2433 94

Joint Cases C-143/88 and C-92/89, Zuckerfabrik Süderdithmarschen und Zuckerfabrik Soest [1991] ECR I-415............................ 166

Case C-331/88, R v Minister of Agriculture, Fisheries and Food and Secretary of State for Health, ex p Fedesa and others [1990] ECR I-4023 410

Case 114/88, Delbar [1989] ECR 4067 . . . . . 90, 92

Case 70/88, Chernobyl I [1990] ECR I-2041 132

Case C-49/88 Al-Jubail Fertilizer Company (Samad) and Saudi Arabian Fertilizer Company (Safco) v Council [1991] ECR I-3187 308–9

Case 5/88, Wachauf v Bundesamt für Ernährung und Forstwirtschaft [1989] ECR 2609 . . . . . 296, 310, 344

Case C-2/88, Zwartveld [1990] ECR I-3365 370

Case 374/87, Orkem [1989] ECR 3283 136

Case 242/87, Commission v Council (Erasmus) [1989] ECR I-1425 90

Joined Cases 97/87 to 99/87, Dow Chemical Ibérica and Others v Commission [1989] ECR 3165 278

Case 46/87, Hoechst v Commission [1989] ECR 2869 . . . . . 174, 344

Case 222/86, UNECTEF v Heylens and Others [1987] ECR 4097 . . . . . 88, 132, 355

Case 45/86, Commission v Council [1987] ECR 1493 91

Case 12/86, Demirel v Stadt Schwäbisch Gmünd [1987] ECR 3719 255

Case 314/85, Foto-Frost [1987] ECR 4199 . . . . . 115, 129, 297, 330, 347, 359–60

Case 234/85, Keller [1986] ECR 2897 278

Case 59/85, NL v Reed [1986] ECR 1283 84

Case 53/85, AKZO Chemie v Commission [1986] ECR 1965 174

Case 234/84, Belgium v Commission [1986] ECR 2263 308

Case 222/84, Johnston [1986] ECR 1651 . . . . . 88, 131–2, 136, 344,

Case 44/84, Hurd v Jones (Her Majesty's Inspector of Taxes) [1986] ECR 29 334

Case 294/83, Parti Ecologiste and 'Les Verts' v Parliament [1986] ECR 1339 . . . . . 129-133, 232, 306, 339–42, 370

Case 63/83, Kirk [1984] ECR 2689 136

Case 14/83 Von Colson and Kamann v Land Nordrhein-Westfalen [1984] ECR 1891 347

Case 294/81, Control Data [1983] ECR 911 322

Case 283/81, CILFIT [1982] ECR 3415 . . . . . 83–4, 362

Case 60/81, IBM v Commission [1981] ECR 2639 174–5

Case 44/81, Germany v Commission [1982] ECR 1855 341

Case 150/80, Elefanten Schuh GmbH v Jacqmain [1981] ECR 1671 83

Case 812/79, Burgoa [1980] ECR 2787 243

Case 155/79, AM&S [1982] ECR 1575 . . . . 153, 344

Case 44/79, Hauer v Rheinland-Pfalz [1979] ECR 3727 . . . . 136, 166, 344, 410

Case 230/78, Eridania [1979] ECR 2749 166

Case 45/76, Comet v Produktschap [1976] ECR 2043 350

Opinion 1/76, Draft Agreement on the establishment of European Laying-up Fund for Inland Waterway Vessels [1977] ECR 741 239

Opinion 1/75, Understanding on a Local Cost Standard [1975] ECR 1355 237

Case 181/73, Haegeman v Belgium [1974] ECR 449 255

Case 8/73, Hauptzollamt Bremerhaven v Massey Ferguson [1973] ECR 897 98

Case 4/73, Nold [1974] ECR 491 . . . . 136, 166, 322, 344

Cases 21-24/72, International Fruit Company [1972] ECR 1219 . . . . 223, 235–6, 245, 248, 427

Case 25/70, Köster [1970] ECR 1162 166

Case 22/70, Commission v Council (ERTA) [1971] ECR 263 . . . . 132, 239, 332

Case 11/70, Internationale Handelsgesellschaft [1970] ECR 1125 410

Case 45/69, Boehringer [1970] ECR 769 153

Case 56 and 58/64, Grundig [1966] ECR 299 153

Case 6/64, Costa v ENEL, [1964] ECR 585 . . . . 268, 276, 278

Case 26/62, van Gend, [1963] ECR 1 . . . . 232, 268, 276, 279, 302

Cases 17 and 20/61, Klöckner-Werke AG and others/ECSC High Authority [1962] ECR 325 409

Case 19/61, Mannesmann AG/ECSC High Authority [1962] ECR 357 409

Case 18/57, Nold [1958] ECR 41 . . . . 136, 166, 322, 344

Decisions of National Courts:

Belgium

Tribunal de première instance de Bruxelles, Fourth Chamber, Nabil Sayadi and Patricia Vinck v Belgian State, judgment of 11 February 2005 . . . . 28, 181

Cyprus

Supreme Court of Cyprus, Judgment of 7 November 2005 (Case 294/2005) 362

Czech Republic

Czech Constitutional Court, Judgment of 3 May 2006 (Case 66/04) 362

Denmark

Danish Supreme Court, Carlsen v Rasmussen, Case I 361/1997 . . . . 114, 116

England and Wales

House of Lords, R (Al-Jedda) v Secretary of State for Defence (Justice and another intervening) [2007] UKHL 58; [2008] 1 AC 332 . . . . 223, 275, 285, 288–9, 293

House of Lords, R (Al-Skeini) v Secretary of State for Defence (The Redress Trust Intervening) [2007] UKHL 26; [2008] 1 AC 153 288

House of Lords, Secretary of State for the Home Department v MB; Same v AF, decisions of 31 October 2007, [2007] UKHL 46 202–4

House of Lords, Secretary of State for the Home Department v JJ [2007] 3 WLR 642, HL 202

House of Lords, Secretary of State for the Home Department v E [2007] 3 WLR 720, HL 202–3

House of Lords, R (Quark Fishing Ltd) v Secretary of State for Foreign and Commonwealth Affairs [2006] 1 AC 529 288

House of Lords, A (FC) and others; X (FC) and others v Secretary of State for the Home Department (Belmarsh detainees case), judgment of 16 December 2004, [2004] UKHL 56, [2005] 2 AC 68, [2005] 2 WLR 87, [2005] HRLR 1 . . . . 186, 189, 191–5, 202, 397–8, 400, 416, 426, 435

House of Lords, Roberts v Parole Board [2005] UKHL 45, judgment of 7 July 2005 393

House of Lords, A and Others v Secretary of State for the Home Department [2005] UKHL 71 (Torture Evidence case) 205–6, 426

House of Lords, R (on the application of M) v HM Treasury [2008] UKHL 26. . . . . 37, 295

Court of Appeal, A, K, M, Q, G v HM Treasury [2008] EWCA Civ 1187. . . . . 34, 54, 292, 297, 394, 407

Court of Appeal, M, A, MM v HM Treasury [2007] EWCA Civ 173 . . . . 36, 171, 294–5

Court of Appeal, Secretary of State for the Home Department v AF and Others [2008] EWCA Civ 1148 204

High Court, A, K, M, Q & G v HM Treasury [2008] EWHC 869 (Admin) 292, 394, 407

High Court, M, A, MM v HM Treasury [2006] EWHC 2328 (Admin). 36, 171, 261, 279, 294–5

High Court, Secretary of State for the Home Department v AH [2008] EWHC1018 (Admin). 204

High Court, Secretary of State for the Home Department v AF [2008] EWHC 689 (Admin), [2008] 4 All ER 340 204

High Court, Secretary of State for the Home Department v AE (Rev 1) [2008] EWHC 585 (Admin) 204

High Court, Secretary of State for the Home Department v AF [2008] EWHC 453 (Admin). 204

High Court, Secretary of State for the Home Department v AN [2008] EWHC 372 204

High Court, Secretary of State for the Home Department v AE [2008] EWHC 132 (Admin) 204

France

Conseil d'Etat, M Hamssaoui, judgment of 9 June 1999 367

Conseil d'Etat, Case 190384, Mr and Mrs Forabosco, of 9 June 1999 367

Germany

German Constitutional Court, Treaty of Lisbon, judgment of the Second Senate of 30 June 2009, 2 BvE 2/08; 2 BvE 5/08; 2 BvR 1010/08; 2 BvR 1022/08; 2 BvR 1259/08; 2 BvR 182/09. . . . . 115, 362, 399

German Constitutional Court, Aviation Security Act, judgment of 15 February 2006, 1 BvR 357/05, 115 BVerfGE 118 188

German Constitutional Court, EAW decision, of 18 July 2005 (2 BvR 2236/04) on the German European Arrest Warrant Law. 118, 144, 261, 362–5

German Constitutional Court, Banana decision, of 7 June 2000, EuZW 2000, pp 702 et seq 182, 258, 263–4

German Constitutional Court, Alcan decision, of 17 February 2000, EuZW 2000, 445. . . . . 182, 258, 263

German Constitutional Court, Maastricht decision, of 12 October 1993, BVerfGE 89, 155; for a translation see: Brunner v European Union Treaty, 57 CMLRev 1994. . . . . 114–17, 119–21, 182, 258, 263-265, 364

German Constitutional Court, Solange II-decision, BVerfGE 73, 339. . . . . 137, 182, 258, 263–5, 279, 297, 427, 435

German Constitutional Court, Solange I-decision, BVerfGE 37, 271. . . . . 263–5, 279, 297, 427, 435

German Constitutional Court, public warnings against youth sects and poisoned wine, decisions of 26 June 2000, BvR 670/91 and BvR 558/91 and 1428/91 . . . . 261, 365

VG Ansbach, 1st Chamber, judgment of 14 December 2006, AN 1 K 06.30883 . . . . 175, 261, 275, 279

Israel

Supreme Court of Israel, HCJ 769/02 [2006] HCJ 769/02, Public Committee against Torture in Israel et al v Government of Israel et al, 13 December 2006 .... 187, 215–16, 426

Supreme Court of Israel, HCJ 8276/05, Adalah – The Legal Center for Arab Minority Rights in Israel v The Minister of Defense (unpublished)... 409

Poland

Polish Constitutional Court, Judgment of 27 April 2005, No P 1/05 362

Switzerland

Swiss Supreme Court, Youssef Mustapha Nada v Staatssekretariat für Wirtschaft [2007] 1A.45/2007 .... 35, 53, 128, 223, 261, 291–2, 297, 405–6,

United States of America

US Supreme Court, Boumediene v Bush (2008), 128 S Ct 2229.................................. 210, 212–14, 415

US Supreme Court, Yaser Esam Hamdi v Rumsfeld et al, 542 US 507; 124 S Ct 2633; 159 L ed 2d 578; 2004 US LEXIS 4761; 72 USLW 4607; 2004 Fla L Weekly Fed S 486 .... 207–9, 211, 415

US Supreme Court, Hamdan v Rumsfeld 548 US 557 (2006).............. 212, 415

US Supreme Court, Rasul v Bush, 28 June 2004, 124 S Ct 2686 (2004) 207

US Supreme Court, Mathews v Eldridge, 424 US 319, 335; 96 S Ct 893 208

US Supreme Court, Odah v US, 11 March 2003, ILM 42 (2003) 207

US Supreme Court, Claiborne Hardware Co, 458 US at 932 391

US Supreme Court, Healy v James, 408 US 169, 186–7 (1972)................ 391

US Supreme Court, US v Robel, 389 US 258, 265–66 (1967)................. 391

US Supreme Court, Elfbrandt v Russell, 384 US 11, 19 (1966)................ 391

US Supreme Court, Apotheker v Secretary of State, 378 US 500, 510–12 (1964) 391

US Supreme Court, Scales v US, 367 US 203 (1961) 390

US Supreme Court, Korematsu v US, 323 US 214 (1944) 141

US Supreme Court, Marbury v Madison, 1 Cranch 137, 177, 2 L Ed 60 214

US District Court for the District of Columbia, Re Guantanamo Detainee Cases, judgment of 31 January 2005, 355 F Supp 2d 443 (DDC 2005)................................. 207–8, 210–12, 415

US District Court for the District of Columbia, Khalid v Bush, 355 F Supp 2d 311..................................... 208–9

Decisions of the European Court of Human Rights and the European Commission of Human Rights:

ECtHR, Botmeh and Alami v UK, application no 15187/03, 7 June 2007, (2008) 46 EHRR 31 .... 196–8, 285, 288–9, 293

ECtHR, Behrami v France; Saramati v France, Germany and Norway, (2007) 45 EHRR 10 . . . . 223, 284–7, 405

ECtHR, Beric and Others v Bosnia and Herzegovina, application nos 36357/04, 36360/04, 38346/04, 41705/04, 45190/04, 45578/04, 45579/04, 45580/04, 91/05, 97/05, 100/05, 101/05, 1121/05, 1123/05, 1125/05, 1129/05, 1132/05, 1133/05, 1133/05, 1169/05, 1172/05, 1175/05, 1177/05, 1180/05, 1185/05, 20793/05 and 25496/05, admissibility decision of 16 October 2007. . . . . 287, 405

ECtHR, Gejic v Germany, application no 31446/02, 28 August 2007 405

ECtHR, Kasumaj v Greece, application no 6974/05, 5 July 2007 405

ECtHR, Kafkaris v Cyprus, application no 21906/04 120

ECtHR, Lindon, application nos 21279 & 36448/02 168

ECtHR, Markovic and others v Italy, application no 1398/03, judgment of 14 December 2006. . . . . 144–5, 166

ECtHR, Bosphorus Hava Yollari Turizm veTicaret AS v Ireland, application no 45036/98, (2006) 42 EHRR 1 . . . . 127–8, 134–6, 138, 146, 149–50, 2234, 233, 253, 282–4, 286–7, 290, 296, 357, 368

ECtHR, Segerstedt-Wiberg v Sweden (2006) 44 EHRR 14 200–1

ECtHR, Brinks v The Netherlands (2005) 41 EHRR SE 76. 200

ECtHR, Kadlec and Others v Czech Republic, application no 49478/99, judgment of 25 May 2004 139

ECtHR, Dostál v Czech Republic, application no 52859/99, judgment of 25 May 2004 139

ECtHR, E.H. v Finland, application no 60966/00, judgment of 16 March 2004 139

ECtHR, Dowsett v UK (2004) 38 EHRR 41 196–7

ECtHR, Al-Nashif v Bulgaria (2003) 36 EHRR 655 200

ECtHR, Segi and others vs all 15 MS, application no 6422/02, judgment of 23 May 2002 . . . . 127–8, 135, 153, 160–2, 169, 175, 357–8, 367

ECtHR, Atlan v UK (2002) 34 EHRR 33. 196–8

ECtHR, Bankovic, application no 52207/99, judgment of 12 December 2001 146

ECtHR, Markass Care Hire ltd v Cyprus, No. 51591, judgment of 23 October 2001 174

ECtHR, Erdem v Germany (2001) 35 EHRR 383 . . . . 187, 200

ECtHR, Kilic v Turkey (2001) 33 EHRR 58 187

ECtHR, Phillips v UK, application no 41087/98, judgment of 5 July 2001 162–3

ECtHR, Prince Hans Adam II of Liechtenstein v Germany [GC], application no 42527/98, ECHR 2001 VIII 148

ECtHR, Lauko v Slovakia, application no 4/1998/907/1119 151

ECtHR, Z and Others v UK, application no 29392/95, ECHR 2001-V 166

ECtHR, Marshall v UK, application no 41571/98, 10 July 2001 193

ECtHR, Kudla v Poland, application no 30210/96, judgment of 26 October 2000 139

ECtHR, Rotaru v Rumania, application no 28341/95, 4 May 2000 . . . . 161, 381

ECtHR, Jasper v UK, judgment of 16 February 2000, application no 27052/95 . . . . 196–8, 322

ECtHR, Rowe v UK (2000) 30 EHRR 1 196–8

ECtHR, Fitt v UK (2000) 30 EHRR 480 196–8

ECtHR, Matthews v UK, application no 24833/94, judgment of 18 February 1999 . . . . 148, 182, 233

ECtHR, Waite and Kennedy v Germany, ECHR 1999-I 148, 196

ECtHR, Zana v Turkey (1999) 27 EHRR 667 . . . . 179, 196

ECtHR, Osman v UK, Reports 1998-VIII, 3124, judgment of 28 October 1998 . . . . 187, 195

ECtHR, Malige v France, 28 September 1998 157

ECtHR, Tinnelly and McElduff v UK, 27 EHRR 249, judgment of 10 July 1998 . . . . 144, 196

ECtHR, Incal v Turkey (1998-IV), 1547 179

ECtHR, United Communist Party of Turkey and Others v Turkey, judgment of 30 January 1998, Reports, 1998-I. 148

ECtHR, Hertel v Switzerland, judgment of 25 August 1998 415

ECtHR, Saunders v the United Kingdom, Reports 1996-VI, 2064, judgment of 17 December 1996. 162

ECtHR, Hamer v France, judgment of 7 August 1996, RJD 1996-III, no 13. 151

ECtHR, Chahal v United Kingdom, judgment of 15 November 1996, (1996) 23 EHRR 413. 325

ECtHR, Allenet de Ribemont v France, judgment of 10 February 1995, Series A, no 308 (1996) 22 EHRR 582. 163–4

ECtHR, Aksoy v Turkey (1996) 23 EHRR 553 193

ECtHR, Murray v UK (1995) 19 EHRR 193 200

ECtHR, Jacubowski v Germany (1995) 19 EHRR 64 415

ECtHR, Vereinigung Demokratischer Soldaten Österreichs and Gubi v Austria (1995) 20 EHRR 56. 415

ECtHR, Fayed v United Kingdom, (1994) 18 EHRR 393. . . . . 170, 174

ECtHR, Schuler-Zgraggen v Switzerland, judgment of 24 June 1993 141

ECtHR, Esbester v UK, application no 18601/91, judgment of 2 April 1993 180

ECtHR, Brannigan and McBride v UK (1993) 17

EHRR 539 193

ECtHR, Open Door Counselling Ltd & Cublin Well Woman Centre v Ireland (1993) 15 EHRR (1) 244, Series A Vol 246-A 410

ECtHR, Edwards v UK (1993) 15 EHRR 417 . . . . . 196, 198

ECtHR, Hadjianastassiou v Greece, judgment of 16 December 1992, Series A, No 252-A, 16 EHRR 219 151

ECtHR, Helmers v Sweden, judgment of 29 October 1991, Series A no 212, 15 EHRR 285 . . . . . 168, 176

ECtHR, Demicoli, application no 13057/87, judgment of 27 August 1991, (1991) ECHR 37 . . . . . 151, 154, 158–61, 177–9, 396

ECtHR, Fox, Campbell and Hartley v UK, Series A no 182 (1990); (1991) 13 EHRR 157 199

ECtHR, Weber, Series A no 177, judgment of 22 May 1990 154

ECtHR, Kamasinski v Austria, application no 9783/82, Series A 168, judgment of 19 December 1989 151

ECtHR, Soering v UK, application no. 14038/88, judgment of 7 July 1989 . . . . . 147–8, 394

ECtHR, Brogan and Others, judgment of 29 November 1988, Series A no 145-B 199

ECtHR, Price v UK, application no 12402/86, 14 July 1988, 55 DR 224 166

ECtHR, Leander v Sweden (1987) 9 EHRR 433 . . . . . 180, 200

ECtHR, Feldbrugge v The Netherlands, judgment of 29 May 1986 141

ECtHR, Deumeland v Germany, judgment of 29 May 1986 141

ECtHR, F v UK, application no 11862/85, of 18 July 1986 168

ECtHR, AGOSI v UK, 24 October 1986, Series A no 108 167

ECtHR, Council of Civil Service Unions v Minister of Civil Service [1985] AC 374 144

ECtHR, Campbell and Fell, judgment of 28 June 1984, Series A no 80 151

ECtHR, Malone v the United Kingdom, judgment of 2 August 1984, Series A no 82 201

ECtHR, Sporrong and Lönnroth v Sweden, judgment of 23 September 1982, Series A no 52 . . . . . 141, 166–7, 361

ECtHR, Klass v Germany, judgment of 6 September 1978, application no 5029/71, (1978) ECHR 4 . . . . . 161, 180–1, 196, 199–200

ECtHR, Ireland v United Kingdom (1978) 2 EHRR 25 . . . . . 189, 193, 398

ECtHR, Agee v UK, application no 7729/76 (1977) 169

ECtHR, Engel and Others, judgment of 8 June 1976, Series A no 22 151

ECtHR, Golder v UK, of 21 February 1975, Series A no 18, 1 EHRR 524 . . . . 139, 168–9, 394

ECtHR, Ringeisen, series A no 13, judgment of 16 July 1971 . . . . 140, 166

ECtHR, Delcourt, judgment of 17 January 1970, series A no 11 . . . . 139, 394

ECtHR, The Greek case (1969) 12 Yearbook ECHR 1 193

ECtHR, ISOP v Austria, application no 808/60, Yearbook V (1962), 108 169

ECtHR, Lawless v Ireland (No 3), application no 332/57, judgment of 1 July 1961 . . . . 189, 193, 413

ECommHR, Tolstoy Miloslavsky, Commission report of 17 January 1994, A.316-B, p 8 168–9

ECommHR, Al Fayed and Others, Commission report of 7 April 1993, A.294-B, p 6 169

ECommHR, M & Co v Germany, application no 13258/87, Commission decision of 9 February 1990, Decisions and Reports (DR) 64 . . . . 138, 148, 253

ABBREVIATIONS

AG	Advocate-General
AQO	Al-Qaida and Taliban (United Nations Measures) Order 2006
ATCSA	Anti-Terrorism, Crime and Security Act 2001
CCP	Common Commercial Policy
CFI	Court of First Instance
CFSP	Common Foreign and Security Policy
COREPER	Permanent Representatives Committee
CTC	Counter-Terrorism Committee
CTITF	Counter-Terrorism Implementation Task Force
DTA	Detainees Treatment Act of 2005
EAW	European Arrest Warrant
EC	European Community
ECHR	European Convention on Human Rights
ECJ	European Court of Justice
ECommHR	European Commission of Human Rights
ECR	European Court Reports
ECtHR	European Court of Human Rights
EEA	European Economic Area
EP	European Parliament
EPC	European Political Co-operation
EU	European Union
Europol	European Police Office
FATF	Financial Action Task Force
FRY	Federal Republic of Yugoslavia
GATT	General Agreement on Tariffs and Trade
GCC	German Constitutional Court
GG	Grundgesetz (German Constitution)
HMT	Her Majesty's Treasury
ICC	International Criminal Court
ICCPR	International Covenant on Civil and Political Rights
ICJ	International Court of Justice
ICTR	International Criminal Tribunal for Rwanda
ICTY	International Criminal Tribunal for the former Yugoslavia
JHA	Justice and Home Affairs
KFOR	Kosovo Force
PJCC	Police and Judicial Cooperation in Criminal Matters

POAC	Proscribed Organisations Appeal Commission
RAF	Red Army Faction
SC Res	Security Council resolution
SIS	Schengen Information System
TACT	Terrorism Act 2000
TEU	Treaty on European Union
TEU (Lisbon)	Treaty on European Union after the Treaty of Lisbon has entered into force
TFEU	Treaty on the Functioning of the European Union
TO	Terrorism (United Nations Measures) Order 2006
UDHR	Universal Declaration of Human Rights
UK	United Kingdom
UN	United Nations
UNC	UN Charter
UNMIK	UN Mission in Kosovo (UN interim administration for Kosovo)
US	United States of America
VCLT	Vienna Convention on the Law of Treaties
WTO	World Trade Organization

INTRODUCTION

> But it really doesn't matter whom you put upon the list,
> For they'd none of 'em be missed – they'd none of 'em be missed![1]

In the context of counter-terrorist sanctions against private individuals this quote sounds shockingly drastic, but even in the European Union (EU) it is not as fictional as one would like to believe. Today, individuals are publicly listed as terrorists in legal instruments adopted by the European institutions without a direct means to challenge these listings. Others find their entire financial belongings frozen but do not know the case against them. The latter have access to the courts but even the EU courts do not have access to sufficient information to rule on the merits. They can only annul the measures for breaching procedural rights.

Counter-terrorist sanctions against private individuals adopted both by the United Nations (UN) and by the EU combine two factors that have justified extraordinary fundamental rights restrictions in other contexts: first, they are based on international cooperation and secondly, they form part of the fight against terrorism. It is not disputed that fundamental rights can be legitimately restricted for these two reasons. However, this does not justify compromising the very core of procedural and judicial protection.

This book examines the complex institutional and substantive issues arising from the EU's practice of listing and sanctioning private individuals who are suspected of supporting terrorism. It provides a comprehensive analysis of the two types of counter-terrorist sanctions adopted within the EU: those giving effect to UN lists of terrorist suspects and those giving effect to autonomous European lists.

In more detail, the book seeks to demonstrate that in the area of individual sanctions, procedural and judicial protection both from Community (first pillar) and Union (second and third pillar) measures has fallen below the standard required by EU law and by the European Convention on Human Rights (ECHR). European sanctions against individuals continue to infringe the fundamental rights of those targeted. While the European

[1] No 5a: Song (Ko-Ko & Chorus), 'As someday it may happen that a victim must be found', Lord High Executioner of Titipu in *The Mikado of Japan* by W S Gilbert and Arthur Sullivan.

Court of Justice (ECJ) has in principle confirmed that all Community sanctions are subject to full judicial review irrespective of whether they give effect to UN or EU lists,[2] in practice individuals do not (yet) have the necessary procedural rights at their disposal. In particular, the relevant information on which the listings are based is not shared with the parties or even with the courts. Further, procedural and judicial protection from terrorist listings in the second and third pillar (Union lists) remains very limited. The book argues that independent judicial review, but also procedural protection, take an exceptionally important role in the area of counter-terrorist policies where it is crucial to ensure the proportionality of far-reaching fundamental rights restrictions in the individual case.

Beyond this, individual sanctions endanger the foundations and the functioning of the European legal order. The Court of First Instance (CFI)'s rulings on individual sanctions[3] seriously challenged the autonomy and effectiveness of the EU, by allowing the Security Council to determine directly the content of European law.[4] On appeal the ECJ defended the constitutional foundations of the European legal order;[5] yet, the relationship between the European legal order and the UN Charter requires further definition.

Individual sanctions further threaten the *internal* functioning of the European legal order. First, they have exacerbated the risk that measures adopted by the Union under the second and third pillar influence action by the Community under the first pillar. This remains relevant despite a certain approximation of the three pillars of the EU, because the division of powers between the EU institutions and the Member States is different between the Community pillar and the Union pillars. Further, the Union pillars continue to offer less transparency, less democratic legitimacy, and less judicial control than the first pillar. Under the Lisbon Treaty this problem continues to exist with regard to measures adopted under the Common Foreign and Security Policy (CFSP). Secondly, national constitutional courts could decide to challenge the supremacy of European law

[2] Cases C-402/05 P and C-415/05 P, *Kadi and al Barakaat*, judgment of 3 September 2008, not yet reported.

[3] Case T-306/01, *Ahmed Ali Yusuf and al Barakaat International Foundation v Council and Commission* [2005] ECR II-3533; Case T-315/01, *Yassin Abdullah Kadi v Council and Commission* [2005] ECR II-3649.

[4] 'European law' refers in the present book to acts adopted under the three pillars of the European Union. 'Union law' refers to acts adopted under the second and third pillar and 'Community law' to acts adopted under the first pillar.

[5] Cases C-402/05 P and C-415/05 P, *Kadi and al Barakaat* (n 2 above).

as a reaction to the EU's current practice of adopting individual sanctions by which – it is submitted – the EU acts ultra vires and infringes the fundamental rights of those sanctioned. This would not only challenge the position of the ECJ but also in the last instance endanger the existence of the European legal order in its current form.

The EU adopts two different types of sanctions against private individuals. Both are adopted as a consequence of UN Security Council resolutions dealing with terrorism. The main difference is the level at which those listed and sanctioned are identified.

Under the first sanctions regime (UN-based sanctions regime) individuals are identified as terrorist suspects at the UN level and under the second sanctions regime (autonomous European sanctions regime) individuals are identified at the European level.

From a European point of view this translates into a difference in discretion exercised by the European institutions. Where those listed are directly identified by the UN Security Council – or, to be more precise, a UN Sanctions Committee – the EU institutions do not have the least margin of discretion. The Sanctions Committee precisely determines who will be targeted, while the European institutions simply reproduce the UN lists. By contrast, where the UN Security Council generally calls upon the UN member states to fight the financing of terrorism, the European institutions follow this call by adopting autonomous European lists of terrorist suspects. Here, they exercise discretion in the process of identifying who is placed on these lists.

Individual sanctions giving effect to UN lists of terrorist suspects highlighted that the fears of anti-globalisation campaigners are not entirely unfounded. Individual sanctions became an example of how opening domestic legal orders – both at the national and at the European level – to international cooperation can strip individuals of fundamental rights that were considered to be well-established both in the common traditions of the Member States[6] and in the EU. In the first instance, those sanctioned were denied full judicial protection. Only after nearly seven years, the ECJ annulled the measures on appeal. However, the individuals in question remain listed and sanctioned without access to the information that

[6] 'Member States' is used throughout this book to refer to the EU Member States, while 'member states' refers to the UN member states.

supports the allegation that they are involved with terrorism. The adoption procedure of European sanctions giving effect to UN lists is currently being reformed.[7] However, the basic problem is likely to subsist: the European institutions do not have access to the relevant information on which the UN listing is based.

The CFI has repeatedly annulled Community sanctions under the autonomous European sanctions regime and the Council has reformed the autonomous adoption procedure with the intention to comply with the CFI's rulings. However, a series of successful challenges by the same applicants[8] demonstrate that those sanctioned still do not have the necessary procedural rights and that the Council continues to conceal relevant information from the EU courts.

Under both sanctions regimes, European sanctions against individuals are adopted pursuant to Articles 301, 60, and 308 EC. The procedure is determined by Article 301 EC, which requires a policy decision under the CFSP before a Community regulation can be adopted. Hence, European sanctions against individuals consist of lists of terrorist suspects adopted under the Union pillars and the actual economic sanctions adopted under the Community pillar. The Union lists are drawn up in common positions adopted either under the second pillar alone (UN-based sanctions regime) or on a combined basis of second and third pillar provisions (autonomous European sanctions regime). The additional legal basis in the third pillar[9] allows the Member States to assist each other with police and judicial cooperation when they gather the information used to identify those allegedly involved in terrorism. In a second step, the Community then adopts EC regulations that contain detailed restrictive measures, such as asset freezes and travel bans, and which are directly applicable within the national legal orders of the EU Member States.

From the perspective of the individual the effects of the two sanctions regimes are very similar. Under both regimes, there is a public allegation

[7] See the latest Commission proposal for amending the existing sanctions regulation (Reg 881/2002/EC) of 22 April 2009, COM(2009) 187 final, 2009/0055 (CNS).

[8] OMPI: Case T-228/02, *Organisation des Modjahedines du peuple d'Iran v Council and UK (OMPI I)* [2006] ECR II-4665; Case T-256/07, *People's Mojahidin Organization of Iran v Council (OMPI II)*, judgment of 23 October 2008, not yet reported; appeal pending: Case C-576/08 P *People's Mojahedin Organization of Iran* and Case T-284/08, *People's Mojahedin Organization of Iran v Council (OMPI III)*, judgment of 4 December 2008; and *Sison:* Case T-47/03, *Jose Maria Sison v Council and Commission* [2007] ECR II-73 (summ pub); see also: application of 10 November 2007 in Case T-342/07, *Sison* [2007] OJ C 269/58.

[9] Police and Judicial Cooperation in Criminal Matters (PJCC).

that the person is involved in terrorism. This allegation is adopted in the name of the EU. Under both regimes, those sanctioned find all their financial assets frozen and are prevented from obtaining any new financial means. Only the stigmatizing effect of the public allegation is different depending on whether the European list is simply a copy of an existing UN list or whether the European list is the first public allegation that the person supports terrorism. In the latter case the destructive effects on the reputation of the individual are considerably stronger. Yet, in the former case, the EU equally lends its name and credibility to the allegation. The European institutions carry a responsibility for their actions even when these actions are meticulously predetermined by narrowly construed Security Council resolutions.

European sanctions against individuals raise many questions. Can European legal instruments depart from the human rights standards that have thus far been guaranteed in the EU, because these measures are required by the international security framework? Can the EU recognize Security Council resolutions as binding within the European legal order without submitting them to any form of scrutiny?[10] Do individual sanctions change the division of competences between the EU and the EC? If at all, at what level could individuals be legitimately identified as supporting terrorism? What are the roles of the national courts and of the European Court of Human Rights (ECtHR) in providing protection from individual sanctions?

This book argues that the Union is not competent to adopt lists of terrorist suspects, nor is the Community competent to freeze the assets of individuals. Article 301 EC allows the Community 'to interrupt or to reduce, in part or completely, economic relations with one or more third countries'. The Community cannot adopt sanctions against private individuals (including European citizens) that have the effect of punitive measures. Adding the residual competence norm Article 308 EC cannot change this conclusion.

Irrespective of the question of competences, the EU courts have the mandate to provide judicial protection from Union lists and Community sanctions under both sanctions regimes. The absence of a provision clearly

[10] Discussing this question under the label of 'open network approach': Martin Nettesheim, 'UN Sanctions Against Individuals: A Challenge to the Architecture of European Union Governance', *CML Rev*, 44 (2007), 567, p 567 et seq; more in the abstract: Christoph Möllers, 'European Governance: Meaning and Value of a Concept', *CML Rev*, 43 (2006), 313, 2006, p 313 et seq.

conferring jurisdiction on the EU courts for Union lists of terrorist suspects is not surprising in light of the fact that the Union indeed does not have the competence to adopt those measures. Yet, the lack of competence of the institutions can only be interpreted as an additional argument supporting the need for judicial review. Where acts are potentially adopted ultra vires it is even more pressing that they are subject to the control of the courts. The EU courts further have the mandate to ensure that the *acquis communautaire* is not encroached upon by obligations arising from lists of terrorist suspects adopted under Union law. In addition to protecting the rights of individuals they must protect Community law. Any other interpretation amounts not only to a violation of the fundamental rights of those listed, but also threatens the division of competences between the EU and the Member States and ultimately the entire legal order of the EU.

The discussion allows conclusions as to the level at which the identification of terrorist suspects must take place. Contrary to the perception of many international lawyers,[11] the general call of the Security Council that member states must fight terrorism is, from the perspective of the individual, less of a threat than specific UN terrorist lists. The latter directly identify terrorist suspects at the UN level and compel the UN member states to take actions against these persons. The adoption of terrorist lists must be confined to levels of governance where individuals can avail themselves of effective judicial remedies, clearly outlined in law. This excludes at the moment both the UN level and the Union level – despite the fact that a coherent interpretation of EU law allows for judicial review of Union lists. Therefore, if individual sanctions were to be adopted at the European level at all, it would have to be for the Community to identify those who are allegedly supporting terrorism.

Some limitations must be expressed. First, this book only deals with sanctions against *private* individuals. This excludes sanctions placed on individuals because of a political function that they have in the government of a country.[12] The terms 'individual sanctions' and 'sanctions against individuals' are used to indicate all restrictive measures targeting private persons, be it natural or legal persons. Secondly, this book deals with *European* sanctions only. By adopting sanctions against individuals the Security Council has started to take decisions that directly concern individuals.

[11] See eg: Matthew Happold, 'Security Council Resolution 1373 and the Constitution of the United Nations', *Leiden Journal of International Law*, 16 (2003), pp 593-610, in particular p 607 et seq.

[12] Or one of their family members.

However, UN sanctions are here discussed only to the extent that they are relevant for the examination of European sanctions. Also, judicial review of Security Council decisions is considered only in as far as this is necessary for the examination of European sanctions against individuals.

The core and starting point of this book is a critical analysis of the case-law of the CFI[13] and the ECJ[14] on individual sanctions. The book provides a comprehensive analysis of the involved legal issues and collates the specific literature on the subject, while placing it at the same time within the broader literature on these issues. Conclusions are drawn about how the EU courts should provide fundamental rights protection and suggestions are made about how the adoption procedure of individual sanctions could comply with general principles of EU law.

This book contains seven chapters, an introduction and conclusions. The first chapter distinguishes the two types of European sanctions against individuals and places them in the international legal context. This includes a brief discussion of the Security Council resolutions that led to the adoption of European sanctions against individuals. The chapter introduces the adoption procedure and the different regulatory measures used to adopt sanctions against individuals in the EU. It further places individual sanctions in the context of other counter-terrorist policies at the international, European, and national level. Finally, the chapter introduces differing assessments of the effectiveness of counter-terrorist sanctions against individuals.

Chapter 2 argues that the European Community does not possess the competence to adopt individual sanctions. This differs from the understanding of the CFI, the ECJ, and Advocate-General Maduro in the case of

[13] Eg: Case T-306/01 R, *Aden* [2002] ECR II-2387; Case T-306/01, *Yusuf* (n 3 above); Case T-315/01, *Kadi* (n 3 above); Case T-47/03 R, *Jose Maria Sison v Council and Commission* [2003] ECR II-2047; Case T-338/02, *Segi and others* [2004] ECR II-01647 (upheld in Case C-355/04 P, *Segi v Council* [2007] ECR I-1657); Case T-228/02, *OMPI I* (n 8 above); Case T-256/07, *OMPI II* (n 8 above); Case T-284/08, *OMPI III* (n 8 above); Case T-333/02, *Gestoras Pro Amnistía and Others v Council*, not published in the ECR (upheld in: Case C-354/04 P, *Gestoras Pro Amnistía and others v Council* [2007] ECR I-1579; Case T 299/04, *Selmani*; Case T-49/04, *Hassan v Council and Commission* [2006] ECR II-52; Case T-253/02, *Chafiq Ayadi v Council* [2006] ECR II-2139; Case T-327/03, *al-Aqsa v Council* [2007] ECR II-79 (summ pub); Case T-47/03, *Sison* (n 8 above); further cases are pending: T-138/06, *Nasuf*; T-137/06, *Abdrabbah*; T-136/06, *Sanabel Relief Agency*; T-135/06, *al-Faqih*.

[14] Cases C-402/05 P and C-415/05 P, *Kadi and al Barakaat* (n 2 above); Case C-355/04 P, *Segi* (n 13 above).

Kadi.[15] The two courts constructed competence on the joint legal basis of Articles 301, 60, and 308 EC. Advocate-General Maduro even found Articles 301 and 60 EC sufficient. Both views are contrary to the clear wording of Article 301 EC which refers to 'third countries'. Although a Community competence to adopt counter-terrorist sanctions against individuals might be politically desirable, it is at present *contra legem*. Yet, Article 301 EC does not allow for the adoption of sanctions against private individuals; and, since there is no Community objective that would require the adoption of individual sanctions, this cannot be solved by adding Article 308 EC. Finally, it is argued that endorsing the unlawful adoption of individual sanctions by the Community endangers the relationship of cooperation between the EU courts and the courts of the Member States.

Chapter 3 demonstrates that those listed and sanctioned by the EU have a right of access to justice both under the ECHR and according to the general principles of EU law. The notions of 'criminal charge' and 'determination of civil rights and obligations' in Article 6 ECHR are applied to Union lists of terrorist suspects and Community regulations freezing the assets of those singled out by the Union. This allows the conclusion that individual sanctions have sufficient similarity to criminal law for them to require strict judicial safeguards, irrespective of their qualification under Article 6 ECHR.

Chapter 4 considers to what extent terrorism creates exceptional circumstances that justify the limitation of fundamental rights beyond what is justified by ordinary principles of law. It discusses the case-law of the ECtHR and of a selection of national courts concerning restrictions in the fight against terrorism. This includes the case-law of US courts on the detentions in Guantanmo Bay, the decisions of the House of Lords on the detentions in Belmarsh prison and on the admissibility of third party torture evidence, as well as the decisions of the Israeli Supreme Court on 'preventative strikes' or 'targeted killings'. Although both the specific situations and the counter-terrorist policies that these courts have examined are very different from individual sanctions, the discussion demonstrates the importance that courts attach to judicial review and in particular to the review of proportionality in the face of terrorism.

Chapter 5 argues that the EU courts have jurisdiction to review Community instruments adopting sanctions against those listed by the UN

[15] Case T-315/01, *Kadi* (n 3 above); Cases C-402/05 P and C-415/05 P, *Kadi and al Barakaat* (n 2 above) and AG Maduro in the same cases.

Sanctions Committee. This was confirmed by the ECJ in the *Kadi* and *al Barakaat* appeal.[16] It is further submitted that judicial deference to the Security Council is, in any event, inappropriate for measures as narrowly construed as individual sanctions. The ECJ was right in avoiding to imply that a *Solange* approach (similar to the approach of the German Constitutional Court towards Community law) is even thinkable. The CFI's suggestion to reduce the substantive standard of judicial protection to *jus cogens* is rejected as both undesirable and contrary to European law as interpreted by the ECJ. Security Council resolutions do not bind the EU and do not enjoy primacy *within* the European legal order. Review on the basis of *jus cogens* (far below the standard of the ECHR and EU law) could lead national courts to defend their national legal orders against fundamental rights intrusions by 'externally imposed' European law.

Chapter 6 examines procedural and judicial protection from autonomous European sanctions against individuals. Those sanctioned by the Community still lack effective rights of defence. In particular their right to a fair hearing is split between the national authorities taking a decision that justifies the listing at the European level, eg a decision to instigate investigations, and the Council taking the actual listing decision without reviewing the factual grounds of the (prior) national decision. As a matter of principle, it makes sense to provide for a hearing where the actual decision is taken. However, in the adoption procedure of individual sanctions the decision-making process is artificially split and the discretion of the European institutions does not extend to substance. At the same time, the European institutions attach far-reaching adverse consequences to the decision of the competent national authorities. Limiting the hearing at the European level in this situation to the *existence* of a decision in separate national proceedings, deprives those listed of effective procedural protection against the European listing.

Further, Chapter 6 argues that the European legal order obliges the EU courts to review lists of terrorist suspects adopted under Union law.[17] The CFI entirely rejected reviewing Union lists on their merits. It restricted its control to the purely technical question of whether there was a norm in the EC Treaty reserving restrictive measures against individuals to

[16] Cases C-402/05 P and C-415/05 P, *Kadi and al Barakaat* (n 2 above).

[17] The Union pillars are the second and third pillar, dealing with the CFSP and PJCC respectively; as opposed to the first or Community pillar.

the Community.[18] This limited review was not considered sufficient by the ECJ.[19] Instead, the ECJ offered national courts the possibility to seek a preliminary ruling (on the merits of the case). However, this solution is not entirely satisfactory either. It does not offer full judicial protection to the individual. Further, the solution suggested by Advocate-General Mengozzi[20] that national courts should review Union law on the basis of the general principles of EU law is discussed and likewise rejected. The introduction of a provision clearly stating that the EU courts must review all Union law directly changing the legal position of the individual would be desirable.[21] Yet, already *de lege lata* the European legal order as a whole vests the EU courts with the mandate to review Union lists of terrorist suspects. Indeed besides preliminary rulings, judicial review is possible under the Union pillars in form of: (1) direct review of compliance with procedural rights; (2) indirect review of whether Union law encroaches upon Community competences; as well as (3) direct review based on the principle of wider jurisdiction.

Chapter 7 assesses the reform of the autonomous European sanctions regime after the annulments of the CFI.[22] It considers what further changes are desirable to ensure sufficient procedural and judicial protection. The role of the judiciary is discussed in controlling the executive in the fight against terrorism. The chapter concludes by examining the proportionality of individual sanctions.

The Conclusions wrap up the discussion and summarize the findings. Community sanctions should be distinguished from Union lists of terrorist suspects. Despite repeated annulments by the EU courts of Community sanctions the European institutions continue to list and sanction individuals. The institutions have introduced limited procedural changes. However, as the repeated successful challenges of the same applicants show, individual sanctions continue to infringe the procedural and judicial rights of those listed. Because of lack of information the EU courts have not so far reviewed the well-foundedness of a single decision to list and sanction someone as a terrorist. They annul Community measures for breaching procedural rights. By contrast, the EU courts have not so far

[18] Case T-338/02, *Segi* (n 13 above).

[19] Case C-355/04 P, *Segi* (n 13 above).

[20] AG Mengozzi in C-354/04 P, *Gestoras Pro Amnistia* and C-355/04 P, *Segi* (n 13 above).

[21] See Art 275(2) of the Treaty on the Functioning of the European Union.

[22] Case T-228/02, *OMPI I*; Case T-256/07, *OMPI II*; Case T-284/08, *OMPI III*; Case T-47/03, *Sison* (all n 8 above).

annulled any of the Union listings. Those included on Union lists remain in a 'legal protection limbo'[23] without full access to justice. Hence, despite the repeated acknowledgement that 'the systematic violation of human rights undermines true national security and may jeopardize international peace and security,'[24] those targeted by sanctions against individuals continue to be effectively deprived of their rights. The European institutions remain largely free to draw up Union lists of terrorist suspects without legal scrutiny. This is irrespective of whether they identify those persons themselves, or whether they lend their name and credibility to the UN lists of terrorist suspects.

[23] Ramses A Wessel, 'The UN, the EU and *Jus Cogens*', *International Organizations Law Review*, 3 (2006), p 1.

[24] 'The Siracusa Principles adopted by the International Commission of Jurists on the limitation and derogation provisions in the ICCPR, 36' *Int Comm J Rev* 47 (50) (1986), para 32.

1

European Sanctions against Individuals: Classification and Origins

Introduction

A plethora of counter-terrorist measures was adopted at the international,[1] European,[2] and national level[3] after the attacks on New York, Washington DC, and Philadelphia on 11 September 2001. Based on considerable political support, these counter-terrorist measures have imposed far-reaching long-term restrictions on human rights. More recently, however, the political atmosphere has changed: today there is increasing pressure on states and international organizations to return to the previously existing human rights standards. The end of fighting terrorism no longer justifies all means.

Lists of terrorist suspects are one means used in the fight against terrorism. The United Nations (UN), the European Union (EU), and some states[4] keep lists of private individuals, groups, and organizations that they suspect to support international, regional or national terrorism. Besides the public stigmatization as terrorists, these persons, groups, and organizations are then typically made subject to sanctions in the form of asset freezes and travel bans. The UN lists are given effect at the domestic level. The actual

[1] See eg Implementation of the UN Global Counterterrorism Strategy, 42nd Conference on the United Nations of the Next Decade, Sponsored by The Stanley Foundation, 8–13 June 2007.

[2] See Doron Zimmermann, 'The European Union and posy 9/11 Counterterrorism: A Reappraisal', *Studies in conflict and terrorism*, 29 (2006), pp 123–45 and below.

[3] See the country reports at: Christian Walter, 'Terrorism as a Challenge for National and International Law: Security Versus Liberty', Max-Planck-Institut für Ausländisches Öffentliches Recht und Völkerrecht (Springer, 2004), see also for an overview of the UK's counter-terrorist measures: HM Government, Countering International Terrorism: The United Kingdom's Strategy, July 2006, Cm 6888.

[4] See below; eg the United States of America (US) and the United Kingdom (UK).

sanctions are adopted either by the UN member states, or in the case of those states that are both members of the UN and the EU, by the EU.

When individuals are listed at the UN level this directly impacts on the rights of individuals. UN sanctions require the UN member states to freeze the financial resources of particular individuals without leaving these states any scope of discretion. The UN sanctions against individuals lead to an increasingly close interaction between the different layers of law (international, European, and national), both at the implementation stage and at the judicial review stage. And, although individual responsibility is a development that can be witnessed more broadly under international (criminal) law, a comparison between individual sanctions and international criminal responsibility before international tribunals or the International Criminal Court (ICC) should not omit that international tribunals and the ICC are set up as judicial bodies with the greatest intention of impartiality, not political judgment.

This first chapter places individual sanctions among other counter-terrorist efforts made both internationally and domestically. It examines the nature of individual sanctions and introduces their adoption procedure. Further, it gives an overview of counter-terrorist activities at the UN, the European, and the national level. Later chapters will then turn to specific issues concerning individual sanctions and discuss the consequences of the interaction of these three layers of law. Chapter 5 will, for instance, examine to what extent the protection from individual sanctions giving effect to UN lists of terrorist suspects[5] depends on the relevance of international law for judicial review in domestic courts. Since domestic courts – both at the EU and national level – are called upon by individuals to protect their rights, much depends on how these courts place themselves in the larger structure of overlapping layers of international, European, and national law. At the same time, all individual sanctions, irrespective of the level at which they originate, raise difficult questions of how to fight terrorism effectively without violating human rights.

The structure of Chapter 1 is as follows. Section One identifies critical differences between state sanctions and individual sanctions. Individual sanctions do not constitute decisions of foreign policy, but resemble criminal law. Because of their direct legal effects on those listed and sanctioned the adoption and enforcement mechanisms of state sanctions are in many regards inappropriate–in particular, because they do not offer the

[5] See in particular Chapter 5, Section 3.

necessary procedural rights. Section Two gives an overview of the two UN sanctions regimes and explains how they lead to the adoption of two different types of European sanctions. Section Three explains the two UN sanctions regimes in more detail. The first UN sanctions regime is adopted under Resolutions 1267,[6] 1333,[7] and 1390.[8] This is the regime where the UN identifies terrorist suspects and obliges the UN member states to sanction them. The listing and delisting procedures and the possibilities to apply for humanitarian exemptions are briefly described. The second sanctions regime is adopted under Resolution 1373.[9] Under this second regime, it is for the UN member states to draw up lists of alleged terrorists. Finally, questions are raised concerning the legitimacy of adopting individual sanctions at the UN level, in particular regarding the lack of procedural rights. Section Four addresses how individual sanctions are adopted under EU law, including the range of different instruments used. The analysis distinguishes between the two sanction regimes. Section Five examines the implementation of both UN Security Council resolutions and European law measures under national law. Particular attention is paid to the sharing of tasks between the EU and its Member States. Section Six places individual sanctions in the wider context of the fight against terrorism at the UN level, at the EU level, and at the national level. It introduces other counter-terrorist policies and examines to what extent individual sanctions complement these policies. Moreover, it delineates in what way individual sanctions differ from other counter-terrorist measures. Finally, Section Seven briefly addresses the effectiveness of asset freezes. Prima facie it appears that the 'assault on terrorist finances'[10] has not slowed down the occurrence of terrorist attacks since 2001;[11] even though the hypothetical number of attacks if no attempts had been made to reduce terrorist finances is, of course unknown.

[6] S/RES/1267 (1999), of 15 October 1999.

[7] S/RES/1333 (2000), of 19 December 2000.

[8] S/RES/1390 (2002), of 16 January 2002.

[9] S/RES/1373 (2001), of 28 September 2001.

[10] Phil Williams, 'Warning indicators and Terrorist Finances', in JK Giraldo and HA Trinkunas (eds), *Terrorism Financing and State Responses: A Comparative Perspective* (Stanford: Stanford University Press, 2007), p 74.

[11] Besides the attacks in Madrid in March 2004 and in the UK in July 2005, terrorist attacks were carried out in Pakistan, Tunisia, Morocco, Qatar, Jordan, Indonesia (including the bombing in Bali in October 2002, in which over 190 people were killed), Turkey, Egypt, Saudi Arabia, Yemen, and India (including the attacks in November 2008, in which over 170 people were killed).

1. Traditional Sanctions Light?

Sanctions have undergone great changes since the UN adopted the first sanctions against South Rhodesia in the period from 1965 to 1979.[12] Originally adopted as blunt instruments aimed at putting economic pressure on states as a whole, sanctions became increasingly sophisticated in who they target. First, comprehensive trade embargoes exempted trade with humanitarian goods. Then, trade embargoes changed to asset freezes and travel bans against leading regimes, government officials, and their families and supporters. Today, a specifically designed Sanctions Committee draws up lists of private individuals suspected to support Al-Qaida or the Taliban (UN Sanctions Committee).

Over time, comprehensive state sanctions were reconsidered because of their limited effectiveness and the massive collateral damage to human rights that they caused amongst entire populations.[13] The limited effectiveness of state sanctions was to some extent attributed to enforcement difficulties.[14] Moreover, while the leading classes find sophisticated ways of circumventing trade embargoes, usually the wider population suffers most. The most widely used negative example of ineffective state sanctions continues to be the sanctions against Iraq.[15]

[12] Malcolm Shaw, *International Law* (Cambridge: Cambridge University Press, 2003), p 1125, for more details: Jericho Nkala, *The United Nations, International Law and the Rhodesia Independence Crisis* (Oxford: Clarendon Press, 1985).

[13] See on this matter eg: Robin Geiss, 'Humanitarian Safeguards in Economic Sanctions Regimes: A Call for Automatic Suspension Clauses, Periodic Monitoring, and Follow-Up Assessment of Long-Term Effects', *Harvard Human Rights Journal*, 18 (2005), p 183 et seq; Erika de Wet, 'Human Rights Limitations to Economic Enforcement Measures under Article 41 of the United Nations Charter and the Iraqi Sanctions Regime', *Leiden Journal of International Law*, 14 (2001), pp 289–91; Matthews Craven, 'Humanitarianism and the Quest for Smarter Sanctions', *European Journal of International Law*, 46 (2002), p 46 et seq; Lutz Oette, 'A Decade of Sanctions against Iraq: Never Again! The End of Unlimited Sanctions in the Recent Practice of the UN Security Council', *European Journal of International Law*, 13 (2002), p 93 et seq.

[14] Richard W Parker, 'The problem with Scorecards: How (and How not) to Measure the Cost-Effectiveness of Economic Sanctions', *Michigan Journal of International law*, 21/2 (2000), p 235; Lisa L Martin and Jeffrey Laurenti, *The United Nations and Economic Sanctions: Improving Regime Effectiveness* (New York: United Nations Associations of the United States of America, 1997).

[15] Abbas Alnasrawi, *Iraq's burdens: Oil, Sanctions and Underdevelopment* (Westport: Greenwood Press, 2002); Richard Garfield, 'Morbidity and Morality among Iraq's Children from 1990 to 1998: Assessing the impact of Economic Sanctions', *Occasional Paper Series University of Notre Dame*, 16/3 (1999).

Originally, sanctions against individuals were designed to address the shortcomings of state sanctions. The first sanctions against individuals were aimed at the political elites of countries that were or would have earlier been targeted by state sanctions. Later, the nature of individual sanctions changed with the change of what is thought to constitute a 'threat to the peace' within the meaning of Article 39 UN Charter. Today, they aim to affect those who are personally contributing to the situation that the sanctions intend to change – either the political situation in a specific country or terrorism. In many ways, individual sanctions avoid the problems of state sanctions. They do not deprive entire populations of access to basic goods. Hence, they do not have the same 'collateral damage.' Additionally, individual sanctions were strengthened through the introduction of new enforcement mechanisms. To ensure the highest effectiveness, the Security Council created two committees that monitor individual sanctions and make suggestions for improvement.[16]

Some definitions are in order. The 'sanctions' examined in this book are coercive measures directed against individuals and legal entities. By way of comparison, reference is made to sanctions against states, which are sometimes also called embargoes or trade sanctions. In international law the term 'sanction' is sometimes also used for 'counter-measures' or 'acts of retorsion'. These measures however do not fall within the scope of this book. The terms 'individuals' or 'persons' refer to both natural and legal persons, except for where otherwise indicated. Finally, although 'fundamental rights' and 'human rights' can be distinguished based on whether rights are guaranteed by a state (fundamental rights) or whether they pertain to a person because of her quality as person (human rights)[17] both terms are used interchangeably in this book. By tendency, 'fundamental rights' is used more widely in the discussion of the domestic context (European law and national law), while the term 'human rights' is more often used in the discussion of international law.

[16] The 1267 Sanctions Committee (UN Sanctions Committee) and the Counter-Terrorism Committee, see n 54 below.

[17] See on the distinction between human rights and fundamental rights: Francisco Rubio Llorente, 'Mostrar los derechos sin destruir la Unión', in: Eduardo García de Enterría and Ricardo Alonso García (eds), *La encrucijada constitucional de la Unión Europea* (Madrid: Civitas, 2002), pp 120–2.

The impact that individual sanctions have on human rights is subject to an ongoing debate. On the one hand, the terms 'smart sanctions'[18] or 'intelligent sanctions' reflect the assessment of a considerable number of both academics[19] and policy makers[20] that sanctions against individuals are a better choice than state sanctions. On the other hand, the term 'blacklisting'[21] is used to indicate arbitrariness and lack of judicial control over procedure by which the individuals and entities are identified. Both terms are avoided in this book. Instead, the (value neutral) terms 'sanctions against individuals' and 'individual sanctions' are used.

It is perilous to see individual sanctions as a 'light version' of state sanctions.[22] They also violate human rights, only in a different way. Individual sanctions are a unique example of how singularized private individuals are directly made subject to binding unilateral decisions of an international organization. Security Council resolutions in combination

[18] Eg: Case T-315/01, *Yassin Abdullah Kadi v Council and Commission* [2005] ECR II-3649, para 90; David Cortright and George A López, *Smart Sanctions: Targeting Economic Statecraft* (Lanham: Rowman & Littlefield, 2002), focusing on sanctions against political elites and drawing the conclusion that the effectiveness of sanctions depends less on whether they are comprehensive or targeted, but more on whether they are seriously enforced; Frank Meyer, 'Lost in Complexity: Rechtsschutz gegen Smart Sanctions in der EU', *Zeitschrift für Europarechtliche Studien* (2007), pp 1–69.

[19] Michael Brzoska, *Smart Sanctions: The Next Stops. The Debate on Arm Embargoes and Travel Sanctions within the Bonn-Berlin Process* (Baden-Baden: Nomos, 2001), see in particular in this book: Cortright and López, ibid, p 20 et seq.

[20] House of Lords, Select Committee on Economic Affairs, 2nd Report of Session 2006–07, 'The Impact of Economic Sanctions', Vol I: Report, Published 9 May 2007, Chapter 5: 'Targeted Financial Sanctions on Individuals and Groups; the United Nations, the IMF, the Swiss Federal Office for Foreign Economic Affairs'.

[21] Eg: Iain Cameron, 'Report to the Swedish Foreign Office on Legal Safeguards and Targeted Sanctions', http://resources.jur.uu.se/repository/5/PDF/staff/sanctions.pdf (2002), p 34, identifying 'at least one very likely violation of the ECHR, namely the right of access to court' and stating that 'business property rights may be violated'; opposed by: Göran Lysén, 'Targeted UN Sanctions: On the Issue of Legal Sources and their Application and also some Procedural Matters', Swedish Institute of International Law, Uppsala University, http://www.hotel.uu.se/webbtjanster/hotell.php, 2003), p 9, claiming that the 'Security Council acted legally'; more general to UN sanctions against individuals and the threat they constitute for human rights: Gernot Biehler, 'Individuelle Sanktionen der Vereinten Nationen und Grundrechte', *Archiv des Völkerrechtes*, 41 (2003), pp 169–81; Peter Gutherie, 'Security Council Sanctions and the Protection of Individual Rights', *New York University Annual Survey of American Law*, 60 (2004), p 491; Erika de Wet and André Nollkaemper, 'Review of the Security Council by Member States' in Vera Gowlland-Debbas (ed), *National Implementation of Non-Military Security Council Sanctions: A Comparative Study* (Leiden: Brill Publishers, 2004).

[22] Compare the criticism at: Biehler, 'Individuelle Sanktionen der VN und Grundrechte' (n 21 above), p 169.

with lists of individuals drawn up by the UN Sanctions Committee target individual persons and oblige the UN member states to sanction them without any room for discretion.[23] At the same time, only states continue to have the status of legal subjects at the UN level; and, only states are able to take legally relevant action from the perspective of the UN Charter.[24] This discrepancy between the effects that international law has on individuals' rights and their possibilities of legal redress violates the human rights of those individuals that are the subject of international sanctions. Yet beyond this, it also sacrifices well-established rights standards on the altar of security and international cooperation, and changes the rights-based system of states purporting to govern under the rule of law.

Individual sanctions and state sanctions are so dissimilar that they should be considered distinct in nature. While the difference between the threat posed by a terrorist organization and the threat posed by a state has been highlighted repeatedly,[25] the necessary changes in the adoption procedure of counter-terrorist sanctions as opposed to state sanctions have received less attention. A terrorist organization and its supporters are not bound by the same web of civil responsibility that constrains private and public actors in international society; yet, it is not protected by these constraints either.

There are strong economic and political reasons *not* to sanction a recognized actor of international law. Multilateral state sanctions must strike a balance between the political interests of the sanctioning states. General trade sanctions risk further harming not only the economy of the sanctioned state but also the economy of the sanctioning state; they require a genuine economic sacrifice.[26] The impact on their own economy is decisive for states when determining whether to adopt state sanctions.[27] The deterring force is greater, the stronger the economic ties between the

[23] Security Council resolutions are not intended to have direct legal effect. UN member states are to ensure compliance via their own national legislation. However, the naming of individuals does have a direct impact on their rights.

[24] See Chapter 5, Section 4.

[25] See eg: Ruth Wedgewood, 'Responding to Terrorism: The Strikes against Bin Laden', *Yale Journal of International Law*, 24 (1999), p 559.

[26] Esa Paasivirta, 'Human Rights, Diplomacy and Sanctions: Aspects to 'Human Rights Clauses' in the External Agreements of the European Union' in Jarna Petman and Jan Klabbers (eds), *Nordic Cosmopolitanism: Essays in International Law for Marti Koskenniemi* (Boston, Mass: Nijhoff, 2003), p 174.

[27] As Margaret Thatcher put it in the discussion on sanctions against South Africa: '[W]e came to the conclusion that [sanctions] would harm the people who put them on far more than they would harm South Africa.', BBC, on 17 October 1987, cited by: Margaret P Doxey, *International Sanctions in Contemporary Perspective* (London: Macmillan, 1996), p 106.

two states are. Yet, the impact of the sanctions on the targeted state also grows with the economic relevance of the sanctioning state for the former's economy. The EU's practice of sanctioning states has, for instance, been criticized for lack of coherency and consistency. Not only a state's human rights record but also its trade balance with the EU influences the decision.[28] Sanctioning terrorist suspects, by contrast, does not usually create a conflict of interests or raise the same foreign policy concerns. Economically, sanctions against terrorist suspects do not impact significantly on the sanctioning state and politically, they are (to a varying degree) in the interest of all states. This is particularly true for the executive branch, which increases the powers over its subjects by adopting individual sanctions.[29]

As a consequence, it is easier to reach a consensus to target an alleged terrorist than to target a country. This is exemplified by the adoption of sanctions by the EU. While the decision to impose trade sanctions against third states is the result of complicated negotiations between the governments of the 27 Member States, autonomous sanctions against private individuals are usually adopted in the Council as an 'A-point' in written procedure.[30] This is also to some extent reflected in the much greater support for Resolution 1373 (second sanctions regime) than for Resolutions 1267, 1333, 1390 (first sanctions regime).[31] Under the first sanctions regime it is the UN, or indeed the countries represented in the Security Council, which decide who is a terrorist suspect for all the UN member states. The second sanctions regime allows each UN member state to identify their own terrorist suspects. This allows all member states to target their own personae non grata. Individual sanctions appear to be a possible form of action in which the political gains are maximized while minimizing

[28] Iain Cameron, 'Rapports: European Court of Human Rights. January 2005 – March 2006', *European Public Law*, 13 (2008) and 'UN Targeted Sanctions, Legal Safeguards and the European Conventions on Human Rights', *Nordic Journal of International Law*, 72 (2003), pp 28–9 citing Clara Portela, *The Efficacy of Sanctions of the European Union: When and why do they work?*, EU Institute Florence, unpublished PhD (2008).

[29] Concluding that this is the reason why despite all human rights concerns the listing procedure has been changed so little since its introduction: Spiegel, issue No 14/2006, p 43.

[30] The European Union's failures to act in a unified manner in the face of various foreign policy crises in the 1990s have been extensively discussed (Baches Sergio Opi and Ryan Floyd, 'A shaky Pillar of Global Stability: The Evolution of the European Union's Common Foreign and Security Policy', *Columbian journal of European Law*, 9 (2003), p 300). By contrast, changing the list of individuals threatened under a specific resolution passes usually painless (see below and also the discussion at: Case T-284/08, *People's Mojahedin Organization of Iran v Council* (*OMPI III*), judgment of 4 December 2008, not yet reported, para 27 et seq).

[31] See below at 2.2.

the economic sacrifice on the part of the sanctioning state.[32] They can also be adopted where the political will to make an economic sacrifice is missing.

The impact on the target also differs considerably from state sanctions to individual sanctions. Sanctioned states are usually much less dependent on the sanctioning states, even where the latter are great economic powers. States are sovereign entities with their own resources and complex economic relations with a multitude of other states. Individuals, by contrast, even though they might have ties with a number of states, are usually dependent on the economic structures in their home country, such as banks or other companies. Where for instance, European sanctions are targeted at individuals residing in the EU, their participation in economic life is completely blocked. They might no longer be able to satisfy even their basic needs, such as nutrition.[33] Sanctioned states on the other hand will try to reduce the impact by trading with states that either do not implement or insufficiently enforce the embargo.

Further, the adoption procedure differs greatly. The interruption of economic relations with a state is a highly political decision, typically taken after intense discussion on the international stage. It commonly follows a diplomatic exchange during which the targeted state has the opportunity to take a position on its alleged wrong-doings. Usually, the targeted state can demonstrate compliance with international law in order to avoid being sanctioned.[34] This stands in sharp contrast with the adoption procedure of individual sanctions: the listing of an individual at the UN level was originally neither communicated to the affected person,[35] nor is the individual listing subject to public debate.

At the European level, changes have been introduced in response to the annulments by the Court of First Instance (CFI)[36] and by the European

[32] Gary Hufbauer, Clyde Schott, and Kimberly Ann Elliott, *Economic Sanctions Reconsidered* (Washington DC: Peterson Institute, 1985), p 3; Michael Malloy, *United States Economic Sanction: Theory and Practice* (The Hague: Kluwer Law International, 2001), p 20 et seq.

[33] Following SC Res 1452 Community measures provide for Humanitarian exceptions or authorise member states to grant such exceptions; these exceptions were implemented in Art 2a of Regulation 881/2002, a preliminary request for the interpretation of Art 2a is currently pending before the ECJ: Case C-340/08, *M (FC) and Others*, OJ [2008] C 260/8; see also Section 3.1.3 below.

[34] State sanctions intend to change the behaviour of states (Christoph Ohler, 'Die Verhängung von smart sanctions durch den UN-Sicherheitsrat: Herausforderung für das Gemeinschaftsrecht', *EuR*, 2006).

[35] Iain Cameron, 'European Union Anti-Terrorist Blacklisting', *Human Rights Law Review*, 4 (2004); see however below the changes introduced by SC Res 1822.

[36] See eg: Case T-315/01, *Kadi* (n 18 above) and Case T-228/02, *Organisation des Modjahedines du peuple d'Iran v Council and UK (OMPI I)* [2006] ECR II-4665.

Court of Justice (ECJ),[37] including that those listed are now provided with a statement of reasons.[38] However, those targeted by European sanctions that give effect to UN lists do not have the opportunity to make their views known, either at the UN or at the European level.

Finally, a more technical difference, but perhaps the most relevant one, is the importance of identifying the target. When state sanctions are adopted no identification is necessary. In the case of leading government officials the identification is based on their function, which is comparatively easy. However, when the targeted person is a private individual who has allegedly given financial support to terrorism, the unequivocal identification – besides all human rights concerns – is not only absolutely crucial for the effectiveness of the sanction, but also very difficult.[39] The traditional mechanisms, in which state sanctions are adopted, are not equipped to identify alleged terrorists organized in loose networks. Additionally, this strips individual sanctions from a limitation inherent in the nature of state sanctions. While state sanctions or even sanctions adopted against political leaders still have a territorial connection, sanctions against private individuals are not even subject to a geographical limitation. The group of people who could potentially be targeted is open ended, and the criteria on the basis of which someone is identified as a terrorist suspect, either at the UN or at the domestic level, are not clearly defined.[40]

For all these reasons it is very difficult to compare individual and state sanctions with regard to their impact on fundamental rights. Comprehensive state sanctions have had devastating effects on entire populations. Individual sanctions as a counter-terrorist policy target roughly 1,000 persons at the UN and at the EU level together. Yet, any comparison is likely to disregard the particular and immediate impact on the legal position of those who are subject to individual sanctions and herewith the similarities between individual sanctions and criminal law.[41] Because of these differences and because of the difficulties in identifying terrorist

[37] Cases C-402/05 P and C-415/05 P, *Kadi and al Barakaat*, judgment of 3 September 2008, not yet reported.

[38] See Chapter 7, Section 1.1.

[39] Peter Fitzgerald, 'Compliance Issues Associated with Targeted Economic Sanctions,' in House of Lords, Select Committee on Economic Affairs, 2nd Report of Session 2006–07, 'The Impact of Economic Sanctions', Vol II: Evidence (2007), p 151; Steven Dewulf and Didier Pacquée, 'Protecting Human Rights in the War on Terror: Challenging the Sanctions Regime Originating from Res 1267 (1999)', *Netherlands Quarterly of Human Rights*, 24/4 (2006), p 616 et seq; see Section 7 below for effectiveness and error rate.

[40] See below Section 3.1.1; compare also Chapter 7, Section 1.3 on the listing criteria within the EU.

[41] See Chapter 3, Section 3.2.2 for the similarities with criminal law.

suspects, individual sanctions cannot legitimately be adopted pursuant to the same rules as state sanctions.

2. Two Different Types of European Sanctions against Individuals

European sanctions against private individuals can be divided into two groups: sanctions adopted against individuals listed at the UN level and sanctions giving effect to autonomous European lists. This distinction reflects the difference between the two sanction regimes of the UN.

The most important formal difference is who identifies the alleged terrorists. Under the first regime, individuals are publicly named as terrorist suspects at the UN level before the EU takes action. Here, the European institutions do not take a discretionary decision, but merely copy the UN lists into European legal instruments and impose sanctions. Under the second regime, the EU Council decides name by name who is publicly alleged to have supported terrorism and should be targeted by restrictive measures. The effects on the listed individual are initially the same: all their financial assets are frozen and their travel is restricted. For effective judicial protection, however, the origin of the listing continues to be relevant.

European sanctions that give effect to UN lists were originally considered to fall outside of the jurisdiction of the EU courts. The CFI rejected reviewing EC regulations because this would entail an indirect review of the underlying UN lists.[42] In the appeal decision, the ECJ repealed the CFI's judgments and ruled that European law measures must be subject to full judicial review. In practice, however, access to the information on the basis of which the listing decisions were taken is significantly more difficult in the international context. Additionally, the obligations of the Member States to give effect to the UN listings remain in place irrespective of the ECJ's rulings.

[42] Case T-306/01, *Ahmed Ali Yusuf and al Barakaat International Foundation v Council and Commission* [2005] ECR II-3533 and Case T-315/01, *Kadi* (n 3 above); Case T-49/04, *Hassan v Council and Commission* [2006] ECR II-52, summ pub; Case T-253/02, *Ayadi v Council* [2006] ECR II-2139; see also: Cases C-402/05 P and C-415/05 P, *Kadi and al Barakaat* (n 37 above) and the pending appeals: Case C-399/06 P, *Hassan*, OJ 2006 C 294/30; Case C-403/06 P, *Ayadi*, OJ 2006 C 294/32.

For sanctions that give effect to autonomous European listings a greater problem lies in the particularities of the European legal system and in the limited competences of the EU courts under the Union pillars. European lists of terrorist suspects are drawn up under the Union pillars, where the EU courts have either no direct jurisdiction at all (second pillar) or no jurisdiction for direct actions by individuals (third pillar).[43]

Each of the two types of sanctions deals with a different form of terrorism. The UN Sanctions Committee lists 'international terrorists' associated with Al-Qaida or the Taliban.[44] The EU Council lists predominantly 'national and regional terrorists' like ETA, those allegedly involved in terrorism in Northern Ireland, the PKK (the Kurdish Workers Party), the Palestinian Islamic Jihad and the terrorist wing of Hamas. Not all of those identified as terrorist suspects by the EU Council are also listed outside of Europe.[45]

3. The UN Side of the Game

As of 24 March 2009, the list of terrorist suspects administered by the UN Sanctions Committee contained 507 entries (396 individuals and 111 entities). This can be compared with 482 entries at the end of 2007 with approximately US$85 million in assets frozen in 36 states.[46] At the end of 2005, 466 names (347 individuals and 119 entities) were listed and a total of US$93.4 million in assets were frozen in 34 states (belonging to 205 individuals and 118 entities).[47] The first report the Monitoring Team issued on 23 August 2004 only made reference to 'some millions of dollars of assets'

[43] See Arts 46 and 35 TEU.

[44] See Section 3.1.1 below on the listing criteria.

[45] Compare the UK lists of terrorist groups, at: http://security.homeoffice.gov.uk/legislation/current-legislation/terrorism-act-2000/proscribed-terrorist-groups (listing as of 20 March 2009: 46 international terrorist organizations, 14 Northern Irish terrorist organizations, and two organizations for glorifying terrorism) with the US lists of terrorist groups, at: http://www.state.gov/s/ct/list/index.htm (listing as of 20 March 2009: 44 'foreign terrorist organizations') and with the most recent EU lists of terrorist suspects in Council Common Position 2009/67/CFSP of 26 January 2009, OJ L 23/37–42 (listing 59 persons and 47 groups and entities).

[46] Eighth Report of the Analytical Support and Sanctions Monitoring Team, UN Doc S/2008/324 (14 May 2008), para 23, p 12 and para 47, p 19.

[47] Fourth Report of the Analytical Support and Sanctions Monitoring Team, UN S/2006/154 (10 March 2006), para 61, p 19. The Team notes that no state has informed the Committee or the Team that they have located and frozen assets belonging to any of the 23 individuals or one entity added to the List since June 2005 (para 62).

that were reported to be frozen by the UN member states.[48] However, the Monitoring Team has also repeatedly concluded that the lack of information suggests that the overall total of reported frozen assets is inaccurate and that states have frozen a greater amount of money.[49]

3.1 UN Lists of Terrorist Suspects – Resolutions 1267, 1333, and 1390

3.1.1 Listing

Sanctions against individuals as a counter-terrorist policy have been part of the Security Council's sanctioning practice for the past decade.[50] They have incited much discussion concerning whether and to what extent the UN Security Council is bound by human rights guarantees, and what the consequences would be if the Security Council was found to act ultra vires.[51] It is controversial whether the adoption of individual sanctions is actually covered by the Security Council's mandate under the UN Charter.[52] And, although these questions remain outside the scope of this book, it is useful to keep this controversy in mind when discussing European measures adopted in order to implement UN sanctions against individuals.

[48] First report of the Analytical Support and Sanctions Monitoring Team appointed pursuant to resolution 1526 (2004) concerning Al-Qaida and the Taliban and associated individuals and entities, UN S/2004/679, para 6, p 4.

[49] Sixth report of the Analytical Support and Sanctions Monitoring Team, UN S/2007/132 (8 March 2007), para 39.

[50] See for an overview of the development of the Security Council sanctioning practice: Inger Österdahl, *Threat to Peace* (Uppsala: Iustus, 1998), pp 45–84; Vera Gowlland-Debbas, 'Sanctions Regimes under Article 41 of the UN Charter' in Vera Gowlland-Debbas (ed), *National Implementation of Non-Military Security Council Sanctions: A Comparative Study* (Leiden: Brill Publishers, 2004), pp 1–31. The discussion focuses on the kind of measures taken, while the competence of the Security Council for such actions do not seem to be questioned in principle: Nico Krisch, 'The Rise and Fall of Collective Security: Terrorism, US Hegemony, and the Plight of the Security Council' in Christian Walker, Silja Vöneky, Volker Röben and Frank Schokopf (eds), *Terrorism as a Challenge for National and International Law: Security versus Liberty?* (Berlin, Heidelberg: Springer, 2003), p 4.

[51] See eg: Erika de Wet and André Nollkaemper, 'Review of Security Council Decisions by National Courts', *German Yearbook of International Law*, 45 (2002), pp 166–202; Erika de Wet, *The Chapter VII Powers of the United Nations Security Council* (Oxford: Hart Publishing, 2004); Iain Cameron, 'Protecting Legal Rights: On the (In)Security of Targeted Sanctions' in Peter Wallensteen and Carina Staibano (eds), *International Sanctions: Between Words and Wars in the Global System* (London: Routledge, 2005), pp 181–206.

[52] In favour: Ohler, 'Die Verhängung von smart sanctions durch den UN-Sicherheitsrat: Eine Herausforderung für das Gemeinschaftsrecht' (n 34 above).

Following the attacks on US embassies in Nairobi and Dar-e-Salaam in 1998 the UN Security Council had, in a series of resolutions,[53] requested the Taliban regime in Afghanistan to extradite Usama bin Laden, to close all the terrorist training camps, and to cease providing sanctuary for terrorists on its territory. After the Taliban ignored all requests for cooperation the Security Council unanimously approved Resolution 1267. Resolution 1267 reinforced these requests and called upon all states, inter alia, to freeze the funds and other financial and economic resources either directly belonging to the Taliban, or from which they might benefit in any way. At the institutional level, Resolution 1267 established the Al-Qaida and Taliban Sanctions Committee,[54] whose task it is to manage and monitor the implementation of the sanctions imposed. The Sanctions Committee's composition is identical to that of the Security Council.

A series of UN resolutions followed Resolution 1267 and reinforced the obligations of the UN member states.[55] The UN Sanctions Committee has continued to administer the lists of those allegedly supporting terrorism. Resolution 1333 instructed the Sanctions Committee to maintain, in addition to the Taliban list, an updated list of individuals and entities associated with Usama bin Laden.[56] It further imposed travel bans on Taliban officials of a certain rank.[57] Resolution 1390 renewed the Taliban and Al-Qaida lists and extended travel and arms embargo sanctions to the listed persons. Furthermore, while Resolution 1333 – despite the fact that it extended to individuals associated with Usama bin Laden, who are not directly linked to Afghanistan – still referred to Afghanistan, Resolution 1390 had no longer any connection with a territory or state.[58] Slowly, what started as sanctions against Afghanistan, melted into the broader framework of the response to terrorism.[59] Resolutions 1267 and 1333 predated the terrible attacks on New York, Washington DC, and Philadelphia on 11

[53] UN Security Council documents: S/RES/1189, of 13 August 1998; S/RES/1193, of 28 August 1998; and S/RES/1214, of 8 December 1998.

[54] First called the 1267 Committee; since September 2003 officially titled 'The Al-Qaida and Taliban Sanctions Committee', see: UN Security Council document SC/7865, of 4 September 2003.

[55] SC Res 1333 (19 December 2000); SC Res 1390 (16 January 2002); SC Res 1455 (17 January 2003); SC Res 1526 (30 January 2004); SC Res 1617 (29 July 2005); SC Res 1735 (22 December 2006); SC Res 1822 (30 June 2008).

[56] SC Res 1333, para 8.

[57] ibid, para 14.

[58] The same was already true for SC Res 1373.

[59] Gowlland-Debbas, 'Sanctions Regimes under Article 41 of the UN Charter' (n 50 above), p 15; see also Section 3.2 below.

September 2001, while Resolution 1390 was adopted thereafter. However, the sanctions regime introduced by Resolution 1373 appears to be a more direct response to the attacks of 11 September 2001,[60] than the rather small changes to the sanctions regime under Resolutions 1267 and 1333.

Sanctions adopted in Resolution 1390 apply for an unlimited period of time, since – despite the review mechanism – by default they remain in place.[61] This last novelty is particularly regrettable since it is a step backwards. Time limits had just been introduced for state sanctions[62] as a response to the ongoing criticism of their legality.[63] What had been considered necessary from a humanitarian point of view in the context of state sanctions has hence been reversed with regard to individual sanctions.

On 8 March 2001 the UN Sanctions Committee published the first list of individuals subjected to the freezing of funds pursuant to Resolutions 1267 and 1333. The list has been constantly reviewed and extended ever since. The Al-Qaida section of the list in particular has undergone numerous amendments. Before, the Al-Qaida and Taliban sanctions against individuals were all limited to senior officials of the targeted regime and their immediate families.[64] The scope of the sanctions regime under Resolutions 1267, 1333, and 1390 by contrast is unlimited with regard to the number of potential subjects. They set up a sanctions regime of 'global reach,'[65] which targets individuals other than incumbents of government or their immediate families without any logically inherent limitation to the circle of people that can be declared targets. Under these circumstances the matter of identifying the target and deciding if the gathered evidence is sufficient, plays an even more decisive role. The Taliban and Al-Qaida lists are adopted pursuant to the guidelines of the Sanctions Committee;[66] these guidelines determine the details of

[60] See the discussion below.

[61] Para 3 of SC Res 1390 foresees a review after 12 months. The two outlined options between which the Security Council is charged to decide, however, is to let them continue or to improve them. This results in a default position in which the sanctions continue. The decision to terminate it must be actively taken and conform to the 'parallelism of forms' rule which asks for the same legal form to terminate a measure in which it has been set up, if not provided differently.

[62] Introduced for the first time in SC Res 1298 (2000).

[63] Oette, *A Decade of Sanctions against Iraq: Never again! The End of Unlimited Sanctions in the Recent Practice of the UN Security Council* (n 13 above), p 94.

[64] Eg SC Res 1127, para 4 a; with respect to travel bans SC Res 1343, para 7 a.

[65] Dewulf and Pacquée, *Protecting Human Rights in the War on Terror: Challenging the Sanctions Regime Originating from Res 1267 (1999)* (n 39 above), p 609.

[66] Guidelines of the Committee for the conduct of its work, adopted on 7 November 2002, as amended on 10 April 2003, 21 December 2005, 29 November 2006 and 12 February 2007 ('Guidelines'); at: http://www.un.org.

the listing procedure. The Sanctions Committee decides in principle by consensus, which constitutes an exception to Article 27(3) UNC.[67] The open-ended circle of potential targets vests the UN Sanctions Committee, which decides on the listings, with unprecedented powers. At the same time, despite the potential scope and impact of its decisions, the UN Sanctions Committee takes a purely administrative role. The names and the appending information have been submitted to the Sanctions Committee by UN member states. The designating state does not share the information that justifies proposing the listing of a certain person to the Sanctions Committee.[68] Hence, the Sanctions Committee lists the proposed person without being in the position to judge whether the evidence that the person is indeed involved in terrorism is sufficient and convincing.

With regard to the information required to support a proposal of a particular name the guidelines refer to Resolution 1617.[69] In comparison to earlier listing practice under Resolution 1267,[70] Resolutions 1526 (2004) and 1617 brought considerable improvements as regards the amount of identifying information provided by the designating state to the Sanctions Committee and by the Sanctions Committee to the implementing member states.[71] Resolutions 1617 (2005) further defines '"associated with" Al-Qaida, Usama bin Laden or the Taliban' as including:

- participating in the financing, planning, facilitating, preparing, or perpetrating of acts or activities by, in conjunction with, under the name of, on behalf of, or in support of;
- supplying, selling or transferring arms and related materiel to;
- recruiting for; or
- otherwise supporting acts or activities of;

  Al-Qaida, Usama bin Laden or the Taliban, or any cell, affiliate, splinter group or derivative thereof;[72]

[67] Article 27(3) UNC: Decisions of the Security Council on all other matters shall be made by an affirmative vote of nine members including the concurring votes of the permanent members; provided that, in decisions under Chapter VI, and under para 3 of Art 52, a party to a dispute shall abstain from voting.

[68] Iain Cameron, 'The European Convention on Human Rights: Due Process and United Nations Security Council Counter-Terrorism Sanctions', Report to the Council of Europe, of 6 February 2006, http://www.coe.int/; see also Bardo Fassbender, 'Targeted Sanctions and Due Process', study commissioned by the United Nations, 20 March 2006 (final), http://www.un.org/law/counsel/Fassbender_study.pdf.

[69] Guidelines (n 66 above), para 6(c) and (d).

[70] See on the old procedure: de Wet and Nollkaemper, *Review of Security Council Decisions by National Courts* (n 51 above), pp 166–202.

[71] SC Res 1526, para 17 and SC Res 1617, paras 2 and 4

[72] SC Res 1617, para 2 and 4; reaffirmed by SC Res 1822, para 2.

As becomes clear from this 'definition', the criteria for being listed on the Al-Qaida or Taliban lists remain very broad. It is interesting to consider at what level of suspicion or at which stage of an investigation a UN member state is obliged to submit a listing suggestion to the Committee.[73]

The information on the basis of which listings are proposed can vary: they can include public sources, such as company registers or newspaper reports, but also secret intelligence material.[74] Overall, there is little transparency concerning the evidence required, the sources of information and the advance consultation with other states.[75] So far, most suspects appear to have been listed on the initiative of the US.[76] Until 2006, Germany had presented about 15 listing requests.[77] Each member of the Security Council can object within five working days.[78] This strict time limit makes it nearly impossible for states to verify any of the information given or to compare it with their already existing intelligence. Reflecting the spirit of the listings the question is: 'how one is protected against being included in the list',[79] rather than why one is included. In the UK context, it was appositely observed that 'there is something distasteful about a process which begins by convicting someone and then proceeds to inquire whether there is a case against them.'[80]

[73] See the discussion at: Communication No 1472/2006, *Nabil Sayadi and Patricia Vinck*, Views adopted on 29 December 2008.

[74] Cameron, *The European Convention on Human Rights: Due Process and United Nations Security Council Counter-Terrorism Sanctions* (n 68 above), p 5.

[75] Larissa van der Herik and Nico Schrijver, 'Section Two: Human Rights Concerns in Current Targeted Sanctions Regimes from the Perspective of International and European Law' inThomas J Biersteker and Sue E Eckert, 'Strengthening Targeted Sanctions through Fair and Clear Processes', White Paper prepared by the Watson Institute Targeted Sanctions Project, Brown University 30 March 2006, p 28.

[76] Eric Rosand, 'The Security Council's Efforts to Monitor the Implementation of Al Qaeda Taliban Sanctions', *American Journal of International Law*, 98 (2004), p 749; Cameron speaks of 'rubber stamping US anti-terrorist blacklists' (Cameron, *UN Targeted Sanctions, Legal Safeguards and the European Convention on Human Rights* (n 28 above), p 166); Ohler, 'Die Verhängung von smart sanctions durch den UN-Sicherheitsrat: Eine Herausforderung fur das Gemeinschaftsrecht' (n 34 above).

[77] Spiegel, issue No 14/2006, p 43.

[78] Guidelines (n 66 above), para 4(b); this period was extended; before objections had to be brought within 48 hours.

[79] August Reinisch, 'The Action of the European Union to Combat International Terrorism' in: Andrea Bianchi (ed), *Enforcing International Law Norms Against Terrorism* (Oxford: Hart Publishing, 2004), p 119 et seq, at 131.

[80] Lord Archer of Sandwell, in UK Terrorism Act: 21 New Proscribed Organizations, abstract from the House of Lords debate on 27 March 2001, available at http://www.statewatch.org/news/2001/oct/01proscribed.htm.

The UN lists of terrorist suspects are published on the internet.[81] Originally, these lists only set out the names, aliases, of those listed. Since the adoption of Resolution 1822 in 2008 the Al-Qaida and Taliban Sanctions Committee makes accessible a 'narrative summary of reasons' for those listed[82] and notifies the member state where the listed person 'is believed to be located'.[83] This member state is then obliged to inform in a timely manner the listed person and to provide those listed with the publicly releasable portion of reasons.[84]

Pursuant to Resolution 1363 the Secretary General established a monitoring group on Afghanistan. The group has the task of monitoring the implementation of the measures under Resolutions 1267 and 1333. It informs about violations and makes recommendations on how to address them. In its first report, adopted on 14 January 2002, the monitoring group recommended that the asset freezing 'be maintained and monitored for full compliance'.[85] In its second report, adopted on 19 September 2002, the monitoring group even suggested that 'much greater use'[86] be made of the listing practice of the UN. Even though the monitoring group acknowledged that it became increasingly difficult to identify additional funds and resources and 'that the task is further complicated by the lack of sufficient identifying information',[87] it did not address the implicated matters of human rights protection or recommend any monitoring in this respect. In 2004 the monitoring group was replaced by the 'Analytical Support and Sanctions Monitoring Team' (Monitoring Team). The Monitoring Team assists the UN Sanctions Committee more broadly in monitoring the implementation of individual sanctions.[88]

In the more recent reports the Monitoring Team recalled on several occasions the 'need to accord with other obligations under international law, including human rights law.'[89] It also addressed specifically that

[81] Available at: http://www.un.org/sc/committees/1267/consolist.shtml.

[82] SC Res 1822, para 13; see also below.

[83] ibid, para 15.

[84] ibid, para 17; see for examples of the narrative summary: http://www.un.org/sc/committees/1267/narrative.shtml.

[85] Report of the Monitoring Group on Afghanistan pursuant to resolution 1363 (2001), S/2002/65, para 53.

[86] Second report of the Monitoring Group established pursuant to Security Council resolution 1363 (2001) and extended by resolution 1390 (2002), S/2002/1050, summary, p 3.

[87] ibid.

[88] See SC Res 1526 (2004), paras 6 and 7 and Annex to SC Res 1526, SC Res 1617 (2005), para 20, SC Res 1735 (2006), para 32, and SC Res 1822 (2008), para 39.

[89] See eg: S/2008/324, para 15.

compliance by the member states depends on whether they perceive individual sanctions not only as an effective tool in the fight against terrorism, but also as a legitimate means.[90] The Monitoring Team moreover suggested setting up an automatic review mechanism (on which however the Sanctions Committee failed to reach a consensus).[91] Yet, the responsibility of the Monitoring Team is in principle limited to monitoring the effective implementation of individual sanctions.

The protection of human rights in the fight against terrorism has been addressed more generally at the UN level. The post of 'the Special Rapporteur on the promotion and protection of human rights and fundamental freedoms while countering terrorism' (Special Rapporteur) was created. This Special Rapporteur specifically addressed the lack of fundamental rights protection from UN sanctions against individuals.[92] He examined the practice of placing individuals and entities on terrorist lists, including the procedure of the UN Sanctions Committee,[93] and stated clearly that at present the necessary procedures do not exist at the international level and 'if there is no proper or adequate international review available, national review procedures – even for international lists – are necessary.'[94] The Special Rapporteur more specifically suggested that (1) precise definitions should be used for placement on lists; that (2) reviews take place after reasonable periods (6 or 12 months), in order to ensure that sanctions remain temporary and preventive, rather than permanent and akin to criminal punishment; and (3) certain procedural guarantees should be utilized for those placed on lists, including proper notice, the right to judicial review (whether

[90] See in particular the Sixth report of the Analytical Support and Sanctions Monitoring Team, UN S/2007/132 (8 March 2007): 'The List can be most useful, and attract most support, when it is recognized as a fair reflection of the threat as perceived by the international community at large. The greater the number of States that submit names, the more representative the List becomes, and the more States are likely to take notice and implement the sanctions with vigour and commitment. It is clear that an inadequate List is likely to result in inadequate or half-hearted implementation of the measures.' (para 14); 'some States believe are insufficiently in tune with human rights concerns or too inflexible to allow for the speedy addition or removal of names' (para 16); 'There is a sense in certain Member States that the List is not a useful operational tool in counter-terrorist work. This lack of confidence in the List is unfortunate as it is in fact potentially one of the most useful operational tools in the whole panoply of international measures against Al-Qaida-related terrorism.' (para 17).

[91] Sixth Report, ibid, para 39.

[92] Robert K Goldman, 'Report of the Independent Expert on the Protection of Human Rights and Fundamental Freedoms while Countering Terrorism', E/CN 4/2005/103, paras 30–41.

[93] See UN General Assembly, A/61/267, 16 August 2006, paras 30–41.

[94] ibid, para 39.

at the national or international level), the right to a remedy if wrongly listed, and the right to humanitarian exemptions, where appropriate.

In conclusion, the UN Sanctions Committee lists private individuals who are suspected of supporting terrorism in a closed procedure, without clear evidentiary requirements. These lists are publicly available and contain an official statement that those named are involved in terrorism. The Security Council refers to these lists in binding resolutions adopted under Chapter VII of the UN Charter and compels the UN member states to act upon them by imposing asset freezes and travel bans against those listed.

3.1.2 Delisting

From 1999 to 2002 no mechanism at all existed to remove someone once placed on the list. The UN Sanctions Committee acted under an aura of infallibility. In 2002 the guidelines of the Sanctions Committee first introduced a delisting procedure. However, despite considerable improvements the delisting procedure has always been, and still is, based on diplomatic protection.[95] It is not an effective remedy directly available to the individual person. Until December 2006 those listed did not even have the formal right to submit information on their case to the Sanctions Committee. They were forced to rely entirely on their national governments to act as agents for them.

According to the guidelines of the Sanctions Committee, the affected individual can – and always could after the introduction of the delisting procedure in 2002–petition their government of residence or citizenship.[96] The petitioned government can then turn to the designating government firstly to seek additional information and secondly to ask it to submit a delisting request. The guidelines stipulate that '[i]f [...] the petitioned government wishes' it may submit a delisting request.[97] Hence, the requesting government is at the unlimited discretion of the petitioned national government to pursue or drop the delisting request. It is not even bound to decide according to its best judgment of the situation, disregarding diplomatic sensitivity.[98] The delisting procedure appears to be based on the assumption that the government of the listed individual is aware of the origin of the proposal. This appears to allow the conclusion

[95] Enrico Milano, 'Diplomatic Protection and Human Rights Before the International Court of Justice: Re-fashioning Tradition?', *Netherlands Yearbook of International Law* (2004), pp 85–142, compares human rights and diplomatic protection and analyzes the unexpected revival of the latter.

[96] Guidelines (n 66 above), para 8(e).

[97] Guidelines (n 66 above), para 8(e)(iii)

[98] See however for the EU Member States: Case T-253/02, *Ayadi* (n 42 above).

that there must be some form of record, stating which country made the proposal to list a particular person. If this was not the case those countries that are not represented in the UN Sanctions Committee could not proceed according to the guidelines. Nonetheless, if there is such a record it is not publicly available.

While the possibility to request diplomatic protection from the government of residence/citizenship continues to exist under the new rules, UN Resolutions 1730[99] and 1735[100] introduced changes aiming to improve the participation of the individual and the influence of the particular state that requests a delisting. Resolution 1730 established an administrative body within the Security Council Secretariat, the so-called 'focal point'. Amongst other tasks, the focal point receives delisting requests from petitioners;[101] identifies repeated requests;[102] informs the petitioners on the general procedure for processing their request;[103] and forwards the requests to the designating government(s) and to the government(s) of citizenship and residence.[104] Finally, it informs the petitioners of the decision of the Committee whether or not to grant the delisting petition.[105] Those listed by the Sanctions Committee can for the first time directly address a body at the UN level with their delisting requests.[106]

The introduction of the focal point appears to be a reaction to the widespread criticism of the existing system. It allows individuals to directly submit their petition to the UN and thereby reduces their dependency on their state of residence/citizenship. Still, the focal point is a purely administrative body that is not involved in the ultimate decision on the merits of delisting requests. It cannot even place the request on the Sanctions Committee's agenda for discussion. The request is placed on the agenda only if either the designating state or the state of residence/citizenship recommends delisting.[107] There are no transparent requirements on how to deal with a delisting request submitted by a listed individual, nor is there an obligation for the Sanctions Committee to review such a request at all. The establishment of the focal point is an

[99] S/RES/1730 (2006), of 19 December 2006.

[100] S/RES/1735 (2006), of 22 December 2006.

[101] Annex attached to SC Res 1730 (2006), para 1.

[102] ibid, paras 2, 3.

[103] ibid, para 4.

[104] ibid, para 5.

[105] ibid, para 8.

[106] SC Res 1730, para 1; Guidelines (n 66 above), para 8(d).

[107] ibid, para 8vi(a).

improvement, but it should not be overrated. It acts as a mailbox receiving and forwarding requests of individuals, but it has no influence on the delisting itself. The focal point cannot be regarded as a hearing mechanism at the UN level.

Originally, only the designating government or the government of residence/citizenship could start a re-examination. Now, three months after the request was forwarded to these governments, any member of the Sanctions Committee can require the Sanctions Committee to deal with the request if the former did not react.[108] Nonetheless, if the designating government does not agree to the delisting, it appears nearly impossible to achieve removal; in particular if the suggesting government is one of the permanent members of the Security Council. The decision to remove a person from the list is taken in a silent non-objection procedure. This requires that none of the members of the Sanctions Committee – identical to those in the Security Council[109] – object. Hence, the designating government, which just refused to file a delisting request, must at least not vote against the delisting.

So far, only very few individuals have been successful in their efforts to be delisted,[110] and there is only limited evidence of states taking action for their citizens. One illustrative example is the delisting of three Swedish citizens:[111] Abdirisak Aden, Abdi Abdulaziz Ali, and Yusuf Ahmed Ali.[112] They appeared on the UN list for the first time on 9 November 2001.[113] The Swedish government approached the Sanctions Committee and the US for further information. After receiving information on the listing, the Swedish government declared this information to be insufficient to confirm the accusation.[114] Sweden's intelligence agency drew the conclusion that there was not enough information to trigger prosecution and Sweden's

[108] ibid, para 8vi(c).

[109] Article 2(a) of the Guidelines (n 66 above).

[110] On 2 December 2008, one individual and nine entities had been removed from the Taliban section of the list and 13 individuals and 15 entities from the Al-Qaida section, see: http://www.un.org/sc/committees/1267/removed.shtml.

[111] More in general on the national sanctioning practice in Sweden: *Statens Öffentliga Utredninga, Internatinalla Sanktioner: Betänkande av Sanktionslagutredningen* (Stockholm: SOU, 2006); Fredrik Stenhammar, 'Swedish State Practice 2004–05: United Nations Targeted Sanctions', *Nordic Journal of International Law*, 75 (2006), pp 317–20.

[112] See Case T-306/01 R, *Aden and others v Council and Commission* [2002] ECR II-2387 and Case T-306/01, *Yusuf* (n 42 above).

[113] Press Release SC/7206.

[114] Statement by Margareta Linderoth, Supreme Commander at the Swedish Security Police in *Dagens Eko* of 14 December 2001.

ambassador to the UN publicly declared that the information that Sweden received from the US was 'unconvincing'.[115] The apparently unsatisfactory evidential standard raises concerns regarding the legitimacy and autonomy of the UN, which relies on unscreened information of its member states. The credibility of this 'decision-making' authority is called into question. On 22 January 2002 the Swedish government requested the revision of the UN sanctions list.[116] The Sanctions Committee refused to remove the concerned individuals on 5 February 2002.[117] Abdi Abdulaziz Ali and Abdirisak Aden were removed on 26 August 2002, after nearly one year on the Al-Qaida section of the UN list of terrorist suspects.[118] After five years, Ahmed Ali Yusuf was finally also removed from the list on 24 August 2006.[119] The appeal in the case of al-Barakaat, filed together with Yusuf's appeal, was decided by the ECJ on 3 September 2008.[120] Yet, despite the ruling in the appellants' favour their names remain listed and their assets remain frozen.[121] A period of time that may seem like an eternity to the targeted person is very short in international relations.[122]

Several courts have commented on the delisting procedure in proceedings against domestic measures implementing UN sanctions. Most prominently, the ECJ remarked in *Kadi* and *al Barakaat* that the delisting procedure before the Sanctions Committee is 'still in essence diplomatic and intergovernmental' and does not amount to effective judicial protection (irrespective of the improvements under Resolutions 1730, 1735, and 1822).[123] The UK Court of Appeal held even more explicitly that the UN Sanction Committee's delisting procedure 'does not begin to achieve fairness for the person who is listed'.[124] The Swiss Supreme Court examined the improvements under Resolutions 1730 and 1735 (not yet those under Resolution 1822) and concluded that the delisting procedure still suffers

[115] Sweden's Foreign Affairs Ministry in the *Wall Street Journal* 6 May 2002, CNN.com WORLD 22 February 2002.

[116] Ministry of Foreign Affairs Press Release of 22 January 2002 www.regeringen.se.

[117] UN Document S/AC.37/2002/13 (2002).

[118] 9 November 2001–26 August 2002; Press Release SC/7490.

[119] Press Release SC/8815.

[120] Cases C-402/05 P and C-415/05 P, *Kadi and al Barakaat* (n 37 above).

[121] Chapter 5, n 27 and accompanying text; Chapter 7, Section 3.2.

[122] SC Res 1822.

[123] Cases C-402/05 P and C-415/05 P, *Kadi and al Barakaat* (n 37 above), paras 322–3.

[124] Court of Appeal, *A, K, M, Q, G v HM Treasury* [2008] EWCA Civ 1187, para 114.

from serious shortcomings.[125] Yet, the Swiss Supreme Court also held that the *listing* procedure does not violate *jus cogens*.[126]

The UN Human Rights Committee considered a violation of the fair trial guarantees in Article 14(1) of the International Covenant on Civil and Political Rights[127] in the case of two Belgians who were listed following a request by the Belgian government.[128] The Committee found that the listed individuals in question 'did have an effective remedy, within the limits of the jurisdiction of the State party'.[129] It accepted 'the assertion of the State party' that they could take the state party to court and 'obtained an order requiring it to submit a delisting request to the Sanctions Committee'.[130] This particular case is exceptional because the authors of the complaint were listed based on the request by their own government, which–following the court order–also filed a delisting request. However, considering the fact that despite Belgium's delisting request the authors remained listed the result might surprise. Irrespective of whether individuals have an effective remedy within a national jurisdiction to compel their government to file a delisting request, the request itself is not an effective remedy against the listing at the UN level. This is where the effectiveness of the remedy ends.[131]

In the delisting procedure, the Sanctions Committee remains *iudex in causa sua*. Apart from a number of recommendations,[132] no procedural standards of examination have been established–nor clear criteria that have to be met to be removed from the list. Instead of providing for an effective remedy the delisting procedure at the UN level is based on a reversal of the presumption of innocence. It does not provide an effective remedy.

[125] Swiss Supreme Court, *Youssef Mustapha Nada v Staatssekretariat für Wirtschaft* [2007] 1A.45/2007, para 7.4.

[126] ibid.

[127] Article 14(1) ICCPR: 'All persons shall be equal before the courts and tribunals. In the determination of any criminal charge against him, or of his rights and obligations in a suit at law, everyone shall be entitled to a fair and public hearing by a competent, independent and impartial tribunal established by law. [...]'

[128] Communication No 1472/2006 (n 73 above).

[129] ibid, para 10.9.

[130] ibid.

[131] Compare Chapter 7, Section 3.3.

[132] SC Res 1735 (2006), para 14 sets out that the Committee 'may consider, among other things,' whether the individual or entity was placed on the list due to a mistake of identity, or whether the individual or entity no longer meets the criteria of being listed, especially whether the individual is deceased or whether the individual or entity has severed all association with Al-Qaida, Usama bin Laden, the Taliban and their supporters, including all individuals and entities on the list.

3.1.3 Exemptions and Qualifications

More than 20 months after the Sanctions Committee drew up the first list of terrorist suspects on 8 March 2001, Resolution 1452[133] introduced the possibility to request humanitarian exemptions. It provides for partial exceptions to the freezing of assets when such money is deemed to be necessary for basic expenses to satisfy essential human needs, such as 'foodstuffs, rent or mortgage, medicines [...], taxes, insurance premiums, and public utility charges [...]'.[134]

The exemption procedure established by Resolution 1452 is a further example of the underlying concept of representation of the individual by their government of citizenship/residence. The latter may notify the Sanctions Committee of its intention to introduce an exemption. The Sanctions Committee can then deny this exemption within three working days.[135] The individual concerned has no say in the process at all. Further, the possibilities for legal persons to qualify for an exemption remain entirely unclear.[136]

Humanitarian exemptions are considered to have been introduced as a consequence of the political pressure exercised by individual states through political channels at the UN.[137] Already before Resolution 1452 there was evidence of member states allowing for humanitarian exemptions on a unilateral basis.[138] These unilateral exemptions appear to demonstrate that some states are aware of the implications of individual sanctions for human rights. They made a timid attempt to improve the conditions of those listed, both by trying to introduce changes at the UN level and by deviating from the UN sanctions regime. At the same time, there is evidence of states applying the sanctioning regime, including the exemption procedure 'deliberately draconian'.[139] For example, the UK Treasury had interpreted the UN sanctions regime to cover social security benefits paid to the spouses

[133] S/RES/1452 (2002), of 20 December 2002.

[134] SC Res 1452, para 1(a).

[135] See SC Res 1452, para 1(a), SC Res 1735, para 15, and para 9(a) of the Guidelines (n 66 above); the period was extended from 48 hours to three working days.

[136] Van der Herik and Schrijver, *Section Two: Human Rights Concerns in Current Targeted Sanctions Regimes from the Perspective of International and European Law* (n 75 above), p 31.

[137] Compare the statement by Anna Lindh, Ministry of Foreign Affairs Press Release of 22 August 2002 and 20 December 2002, www.regeringen.se.

[138] See Section 5 below.

[139] High Court, *M, A, MM v HM Treasury* [2006] EWHC 2328 (Admin), para 64; Court of Appeal *M, A, MM v HM Treasury* [2007] EWCA Civ 173, para 17; see also Chapter 5, Section 5.2.2.

of those listed and required the spouses to apply for humanitarian exemptions to receive the payments. The UK Court of Appeal agreed with the Treasury's interpretation, but Appellate Committee of the House of Lords disagreed and suggested submitting a preliminary ruling request to the ECJ.[140]

3.2 The General Call to Fight Terrorism – Resolution 1373

Besides listing individuals as terrorist suspects at the UN level, the Security Council has also called upon its member states to fight terrorism in a more decentralized way. Resolution 1373 obliges the UN member states inter alia to identify terrorist suspects and to freeze their financial resources.

After the attacks of 11 September 2001 a new chapter on sanctions against individuals was opened. On 12 September 2001 the UN Security Council adopted Resolution 1368 defining the terrorist acts of 11 September to be a threat to peace under Article 39 UN Charter.[141] This was much criticized for being ambiguous and contradictory.[142] Yet, despite the criticism, Resolution 1368 had enormous consequences. It opened the gate to a whole new set of measures, including Resolution 1373, which stipulates 'that all States shall [...] prevent and suppress the financing of terrorist acts'. The latter resolution created the Counter-Terrorism Committee (CTC) and imposed an obligation – besides criminalizing the financing of terrorism – to freeze and seize funds associated with terrorism.[143] The most important difference between Resolution 1373 on the one hand and Resolutions 1267, 1333, and 1390 on the other, is that the former does not contain an annexed list. The CTC is not mandated to draw up lists of terrorist suspects. It only assists and monitors the UN member states'

[140] Report from the Appellate Committee of 30 April 2008, at: *R (on the application of M) v HM Treasury* [2008] UKHL 26; currently pending: Case C-340/08, *M (FC) and Others*, OJ [2008] C 260/8.

[141] SC Res 1368, adopted on 12 September 2001 stipulates in its second recital its determination to combat terrorism acts as a threat to international peace and security. In its first paragraph it refers to the 11 September attacks.

[142] Antonio Cassese, 'Terrorism is Also Disrupting Some Crucial Legal Categories of International Law', *European Journal of International Law*, 12 (2001), p 993 (996): The preamble of SC Res 1368 recognises the right of self-defence whereas the operative part declares the attacks to be a threat to peace only and not an armed attack, the latter of which is the precondition for a right of self-defence. There is a perceivable wavering between the desire to take action collectively and a resignation of the unilateral action of the United States of America.

[143] SC Res 1373, para 1.

listing activities. However, Resolution 1373 might be the most sweeping sanctioning measure ever adopted by the Security Council.[144]

Resolution 1373 does not fit into the pattern of earlier sanctions resolutions.[145] Presumably, the potential group of targeted individuals had been at least somewhat limited by the requirement that those listed were 'associated with' the Taliban or Al-Qaida. Resolution 1373 dropped this last – albeit weak – restriction. It supplies the member states with new options for action, but fails to confine its scope of application. They are required to 'prevent and suppress the financing of terrorist acts,'[146] but at the UN level there is not even a uniform definition of what constitutes 'terrorism'.[147] This makes Resolution 1373 open to unilateral interpretation in the light of national interests. All measures taken to implement it, including European sanctions against individuals, have to be seen against this background. It is further remarkable that while the measures in Resolutions 1333 and 1390 were made subject to review after a period of 12 months,[148] Resolution 1373 does not require review after a predefined period.

The Security Council was much criticized for adopting Resolution 1373.[149] It is considered to be a new and more principled exercise of power,

[144] It was considered to be evidence that the Security Council assumes the role of a legislator: Gilbert HE Guillaume, 'Terrorism and International Law', *Grotius Lecture at the British Institute of International and Comparative Law, 13 November 2003* ; Paul C Szasz, 'Notes and Comments: The Security Council starts Legislating', *American Journal of International Law*, 96 (2002), p 901; Clementine Olivier, 'Human Rights Law and International Fight against Terrorism: Could Security Council Regulations Impact on States' Obligations under International Human Right Law?' NJIL, 73 (2004), p 399: 'the Security Council is not supposed to legislate', 'there exists a border-line between enforcement and law-making'.

[145] Gowlland-Debbas, *Sanctions Regimes under Article 41 of the UN Charter* (n 50 above), p 6.

[146] SC Res 1373, para 1(a).

[147] Jean-Marc Sorel, 'Some Questions About the Definition of Terrorism and the Fight Against Its Financing', *European Journal of International Law*, 14 (2003), p 366 et seq; Stefan Oeter, 'Terrorismus und Menschenrechte', *Archiv des Völkerrechts*, 40 (2002), p 424 et seq; but see also the 'working definition' in the Report of the High-level Panel on Threats, Challenges and Change, entitled 'A more secure world: our shared responsibility', UN doc A/59/565, 2 December 2004, available at: http://www.un.org/secureworld/; see below more broadly on the UN's fight against terrorism.

[148] SC Res 1390, para 3, even if by default the sanctions remain in place, see Section 3.1.1 above.

[149] Krisch, 'The Rise and Fall of Collective Security: Terrorism, US Hegemony and the Plight of the Security Council' (n 50 above), p 10; Olivier, *Human Rights Law and International Fight against Terrorism: Could Security Council Regulations Impact on States' Obligations under International Human Right Law?* (n 144 above), p 399; Nico Krisch and Jochen Frowein, 'Chapter VII: Action with respect to the Peace, Breaches of the Peace and Acts of Aggression. Introduction' in Bruno Simma (ed), *The Charter of the United Nations: A Commentary* (Oxford: Oxford University Press, 2002), p 708.

which is, according to many, incompatible with the Security Council's mandate to act in response to specific situations rather than imposing general guidelines.[150] At the same time, this new development was welcomed by some authors as equipping the Security Council with a new effective tool to fight terrorism.[151]

There are many reasons to question the Security Council's competence to pass Resolution 1373. The Security Council could indeed be criticized for having assumed the role of a 'world legislator' by declaring the International Convention for the Suppression of the Financing of Terrorism binding on all UN member states.[152] The Security Council's powers under Chapter VII of the UN Charter are confined to specific situations and for the time until the threat to peace and security has ceased to exist.[153] The adoption of general rules for an unlimited period of time is not obvious under Chapter VII.[154] However, it must be conceded that classical international law-making processes, the adoption of treaty law and the establishment of customary law, appear inadequate for a quick and detailed response to terrorism.[155] The UN Charter is subject to dynamic interpretation and state practice has an influence on the actual reading of the Charter. Nonetheless, it should be reiterated that only 15 member states

[150] Nicolas Angelet, 'Vers un renforcement de la prévention et la répression du terrorisme par de moyens financiers et économiques?' in Karine Bannelier et al (eds), *Le droit international face au terrorisme: après le 11 septembre 2001* (Paris: Pedone, 2003), p 219 et seq; Matthew Happold, 'Security Council Resolution 1373 and the Constitution of the United Nations', *Leiden Journal of International Law*, 16 (2003), p 593 et seq; José Alvarez, 'Hegemonic International Law Revisited', *American Journal of International Law*, 97 (2003), p 875 (calling SC Res 1373 an opportunistic choice of measure).

[151] Very positive: Szasz, *Notes and Comments: The Security Council starts Legislating* (n 144 above), p 905: 'this new tool will enhance the United Nations and benefit the world community'.

[152] Another example of the Security Council's legislative activity is SC Res 1540 of 28 April 2004. It also relates to terrorism and addresses the possession of weapons of mass destruction by private actors.

[153] Krisch and Frowein, 'Chapter VII: Action with respect to the Peace, Breaches of the Peace and Acts of Aggression. Introduction' (n 149 above), p 708.

[154] ibid, p 709.

[155] Pierre-Marie Dupuy, 'The Law After the Destruction of the Towers', *European Journal of International Law, Series on Legal Responses to 'The Attack on the World Trade Center'* (2002); Andrea Bianchi, 'Enforcing International Law Norms Against Terrorism: Achievements and Prospects' in Andrea Bianchi (ed), *Enforcing International Law Norms Against Terrorism* (Oxford: Hart Publishing, 2004), p 515; Jonathan Charney, 'Universal International Law', *American Journal of International Law*, 87 (1993), p 529 et seq.

are represented in the Security Council,[156] while the UN currently has 191 members.[157] For this development to become a modification of the norms of the UN Charter through practice, it must continue to go unchallenged.[158] In this regard, some authors suggested that the General Assembly could be given the task of ratifying *ex post* the Security Council's 'legislation' to increase its legitimacy.[159]

3.3 Concluding Remarks

The two UN sanctions regimes are assessed and contrasted in very different ways. Some authors consider Resolution 1373 to be 'the next step', constituting a counter-terrorist policy that is 'no longer limited in time or in scope', applicable 'to all states of the world regardless of a specific conflict'.[160] They criticize the increasing powers of the Security Council. Other authors regard the evolution from Resolutions 1267 and 1333, drawing up a centralized list, to the more general 'legislative' Resolution 1373, as a reaction to member states' resistance and human rights concerns.[161]

When evaluating the threat to fundamental rights resulting from individual sanctions some authors exclusively focus on Security Council resolutions that directly list a group of persons, without a single reference to Resolution 1373,[162] while others mention the Resolution 1373 sanction regime[163] but

[156] Krisch and Frowein, *Chapter VII: Action with respect to the Peace, Breaches of the Peace and Acts of Aggression. Introduction* (n 149 above), p 709: '...action by the SC is immediately supported only by 15 members and therefore cannot claim to represent the view of the whole international community.'.

[157] See also below the General Assembly's criticism of the UN sanction regimes.

[158] There has been considerable resistance to earlier sanctioning regimes under SC Res 1267 and 1333: see for example the proceedings in Sweden: Per Cramér, 'Recent Swedish Experience with Targeted UN Sanctions: The Erosion of Trust in the Security Council' in Erika de Wet and André Nollkaemper, *Review of the Security Council by Member States* (Antwerp: Intersentia, 2003), pp 85–106.

[159] Bianchi, *Enforcing International Law Norms Against Terrorism: Achievements and Prospects* (n 79 above), p 518; Szasz, *Notes and Comments: The Security Council starts Legislating* (n 144 above), p 903.

[160] Krisch, *The Rise and Fall of Collective Security: Terrorism, US Hegemony, and the Plight of the Security Council* (n 50 above), p 6.

[161] De Wet and Nollkaemper, *Review of Security Council Decisions by National Courts* (n 51 above), p 201.

[162] SC Res 1267, 1333, and 1390: Biehler, 'Individuelle Sanktionen der Vereinten Nationen und Grundrechte' (n 21 above), p 169.

[163] Cameron, 'Protecting Legal Rights: On the (In)Security of Targeted sanctions' (n 51 above), p 200; Cameron, 'Report to the Swedish Foreign Office on Legal Safeguards and Targeted Sanctions' (n 21 above), p 48.

discuss it separately with emphasis on the human rights situation at the domestic implementation level.[164] Some of the fundamental rights concerns obviously shift away from the UN level to the domestic level when the identification of those listed takes place under the Resolution 1373 regime. A decentralized sanctioning regime similar to Resolution 1373 was even thought to have 'major advantages from the perspective of legal safeguards'.[165]

Resolutions 1267, 1333, and 1390 oblige the UN member states to adopt restrictive measures against a clearly determined group of people. The UN directly identifies particular persons who will be affected. A review mechanism exists, but by default the measures remain in force indefinitely. The identification procedure remains obscure and delisting decisions depend on the will of those states who decided on the listings in the first place. The UN Sanctions Committee exercises a purely administrative function when adopting the list of terrorist suspects. It does not take informed decisions, but vests routinely the decisions of individual states with universal validity for all UN member states. Empowered by the Security Council the Committee's decisions on who must be targeted have binding force. In light of the fact that the circle of potential targets is neither geographically, nor temporarily limited and extends to ordinary citizens, the impact of the Security Council's actions can hardly be overestimated. Resolutions 1267, 1333, and 1390 were considered to empower states to limit human rights in an unprecedented form.[166]

Resolution 1373, by contrast, remains at a more general level. It obliges member states to take actions that they previously had to consent to in international conventions in order to be bound.[167] The Security Council assumed with Resolution 1373 an unprecedented quasi-legislative function.

[164] Cameron, *European Union Anti-Terrorist Blacklisting* (n 35 above).

[165] Cameron, *Protecting Legal Rights: On the (In)Security of Targeted sanctions* (n 51 above), p 200; Cameron, *Report to the Swedish Foreign Office on Legal Safeguards and Targeted Sanctions* (n 21 above), p 48.

[166] Biehler, 'Individuelle Sanktionen der Vereinten Nationen und Grundrechte' (n 21 above), p 169.

[167] In particular, it imposed on all states certain obligations specifically selected from those imposed by the International Convention for the Suppression of the Financing of Terrorism, UN Doc A/RES/54/109 of 9 December 1999, which at that time had not passed the necessary number of ratifications for it to enter into force (only four ratifications and 46 signatures).

It expanded its powers by creating a new general form of binding rules. In the past the Security Council adopted sanctions against states, governments or elite groups in possession of governmental powers. It carried out executive tasks, rather than legislative tasks.

Most situations discussed in the Security Council are highly contentious. The discussion takes place behind closed doors.[168] Its decisions are of widely felt consequences. The Security Council is equipped to take 'prompt and effective action'[169] in response to international crises. This role as a 'policeman'[170] is what disqualified the Security Council in the eyes of some authors to reflect on general guidelines for the approach to comprehensive situations.[171] Resolution 1373 could be seen as a more far-reaching limitation of the sovereignty of UN member states.

When the Security Council directly lists terrorist suspects it exercises an executive function: it strikes a limited circle of persons with clearly formulated repressive measures. In this respect listing individuals as terrorist suspects is in closer compliance with the spirit of the UN Charter. However, these legal instruments are of the same quality as national law, both as concerns the detail and the subject matter (criminal law) of these instruments. At the time when the UN Charter was adopted, no one thought of these or similar instruments ever being passed at the UN level. It is too simple to argue in favour of lists of terrorist suspects at the UN level only because from the point of view of the member states they impose less far-reaching obligations. They pierce the sovereignty of states differently in that they immediately change the legal position of a state's citizens. Moreover, despite the criticism that Resolution 1373 limits state sovereignty further than any other resolution before, the general perception is that the political support of Resolution 1373 is 'significantly greater' than

[168] See for examples and reflection on the Council procedures: Sydney D Bailey and Sam Daws, *The Procedure of the UN Security Council* (Oxford: Clarendon Press, 1998).

[169] Article 24 UN Charter.

[170] See the Statement of the representatives of the United States, UNCIO VI, p 29, Doc 1006 I/6 and the report of the Committee I/1, UNCIO VI, p 453, Doc 944 I/1/34 (1).

[171] Olivier, 'Human Rights Law and International Fight against Terrorism: Could Security Council Regulations Impact on States' Obligations under International Human Right Law?' (n 144 above), p 408: '... for these very reasons, this makes the Council a totally inappropriate legislative and law-creating body'.

for sanctions directly targeted by the UN.[172] The quality and quantity of reporting by the UN member states has 'increased dramatically'.[173]

Resolution 1373 creates a comprehensive obligation to criminalize the support of terrorism. The actual identification of terrorist suspects takes place at the national and regional level, where it can be made subject to judicial review.[174] Hence, those sanctioned have the opportunity to challenge directly the allegation to have supported terrorism. Leaving aside institutional considerations and taking the perspective of the affected individual, Resolution 1373 does not go a step further; on the contrary, it takes a step back. It limits the direct effects of Security Council action on the person's legal position. From a human rights point of view this is a welcome development. Resolution 1373 does not have an immediate impact on the legal position of the individual.

4. European Sanctions against Individuals

Sanctions against individuals adopted under European law reflect the two UN sanctions regimes: on the one hand, Resolutions 1267, 1333, and 1390 targeting particular individuals related to the Taliban and Al-Qaida and, on the other, Resolution 1373 calling more generally for a fight against terrorism and in particular the financing of terrorism. Under the first sanctions regime the EU reproduces the UN lists and adopts restrictive

172 Curtis A Ward, 'The CTC and Targeted Sanctions' in Peter Wallensteen and Carina Staibano (eds), *International Sanctions – Between Words and Wars in the Global System* (London: Routledge, 2005), p 173; David Cortright and George A López, 'A Sanctions Coordinator: Options for Enhancing Compliance' in Peter Wallensteen and Carina Staibano (eds), *International Sanctions: Between Words and Wars in the Global System* (London: Routledge, 2005), p 70.

173 Thomas J Biersteker, Sue E Eckert, Aaron Halegua and Peter Romaniuk, 'Consensus from the Bottom Up? Assessing the Influence of the Sanctions Reform Processes' in Peter Wallensteen and Carina Staibano (eds), *International Sanctions: Between Words and Wars in the Global System* (London: Routledge, 2005), p 25; see 'Letter dated 15 July 2003 from the Chairman of the Security Council Committee established pursuant to Resolution 1373 (2001) concerning counter-terrorism addressed to the President of the Security Council', S/2003/710, p 2.

174 See eg the series of challenges before the CFI: Case T-228/02, *OMPI I* (n 36 above); Case T-256/07, *People's Mojahidin Organization of Iran v Council (OMPI II)*, judgment of 23 October 2008, not yet reported; appeal pending: Case C-576/08 P, *People's Mojahedin Organization of Iran*; Case T-284/08, *OMPI III* (n 30 above); Case T-47/03, *Jose Maria Sison v Council and Commission* [2007] ECR II-73 (sum pub); see also Chapter 6 for more detail on these cases.

measures against those listed, while under the second sanctions regime the EU draws up its own lists of terrorist suspects.[175]

Both types of European measures are based on a joint legal basis of Articles 301, 60, and 308 EC. The two-tiered procedure is set out in Article 301 EC. First, the Council adopts a 'strategic decision' to adopt individual sanctions in a common position or joint action under the second pillar (Common Foreign and Security Policy (CFSP)). This CFSP instrument is then implemented by a Community regulation. In practice the decision to adopt sanctions has so far always been taken in a common position. The actual operational measures, such as asset freezes and travel bans, are adopted in the following EC regulations. The latter are directly applicable and constitute the immediate legal basis for national implementation measures; they leave no discretion to national authorities. Member States then adopt under national law so-called 'secondary sanctions' imposing criminal charges for the infringement of the Community measures. They further use third pillar mechanisms in order to assist each other in the gathering of information and to exchange information that may lead to a listing at the European level.

4.1 European Sanctions Implementing UN Sanctions

The first EU instruments containing sanctions against individuals were adopted to implement Resolutions 1267 and 1333.[176] Considering that action by the Community was necessary, the Council adopted restrictive measures. The first individual sanctions were adopted not only pursuant to the same procedure but also on the exact same legal basis as sanctions against states, namely Articles 60 and 301 EC. Later in EC Regulation 881/2002, Article 308 EC was added. The changes in the first sanctions regime adopted under Resolutions 1267, 1333, and 1390 are reflected in the European legal instruments implementing them. The CFI acknowledged in this regard that EC Regulation 881/2002 brought about 'a distinct change in the [...] legal position' of those sanctioned as compared to their legal position under the earlier EC regulations.[177] The Court pointed in

[175] Apart from the here examined counter-terrorist sanctions the EU has adopted sanctions against the Transnistrian leadership in Moldavia as a measures targeted at a non-state entity (CP 2008/160/CFSP, 25 February 2008 [2008] OJ L 51, 26.2.2008, p 23). These measures will however not be discussed in this book.

[176] Common Position 2002/402/CFSP; EC Regulations 337/2000 and 467/2001.

[177] Case T-253/02, *Ayadi* (n 42 above), paras 71–9 (77).

particular to the different titles,[178] preambles[179] and material provisions,[180] but also to the fact that Regulation 881/2002 had a more extensive temporal scope.

The CFSP common positions required by Article 301 EC for adopting restrictive measures under the first pillar contain an exact copy of the UN lists. They are adopted pursuant to Article 15 TEU.[181] The EC regulations implementing these common positions then either contain the (identical) list itself,[182] or rely on Commission regulations[183] to set out the circle of persons affected.

The amendments to the UN lists are not automatically incorporated into European law. They have to be implemented by domestic European legislation. So far, however, the Commission has faithfully copied every single amendment of the UN lists of terrorist suspects. In challenges to individual sanctions the institutions have not denied 'the applicants' claim that they did not check whether the names on the list drawn up by the Taliban Sanctions Committee had been included justifiably'.[184] On the contrary, they stated 'that they are under a mandatory duty' to adopt sanctions against the individuals listed by the UN Sanctions Committee.[185]

[178] While Reg 467/2001 adopts measures 'prohibiting the export of certain goods and services to Afghanistan, strengthening the flight ban and extending the freeze of funds and other financial resources in respect of the Taliban of Afghanistan', Reg 881/2002 speaks of 'imposing certain specific restrictive measures directed against certain persons and entities associated with Usama bin Laden, the Al-Qaida network and the Taliban'.

[179] The preamble of EC Regulation 467/2001 refers to SC Res 1267 and 1333 only, which are both limited to measures against Usama Bin Ladin and the Taliban. The preamble of EC Regulation 881/2002, on the other hand, contains additional references to SC Res 1373 and 1390. The latter reiterates the broad obligations of the UN Member States set out in the former, to take certain actions 'with regard to any member of the Taliban and the Al-Qaida organisation, but also with regard to those who are associated with them and have participated in the financing, planning, facilitation, preparation or perpetration of terrorist acts'.

[180] In particular the extension of the freezing measures to 'economic resources'.

[181] Eg: Common position 2002/402/CFSP of 27 May 2002 concerning restrictive measures against Usama bin Laden, members of the Al-Qaida organisation and the Taliban and other individuals, groups, undertakings and entities associated with them and repealing Common Positions 96/746/CFSP, 1999/727/CFSP, 2001/154/CFSP and 2001/771/CFSP, OJ 2002 L 139/4.

[182] Compare the different consolidated versions of Council Regulation (EC) No 881/2002 of 27 May 2002 imposing certain specific restrictive measures directed against certain persons and entities associated with Usama bin Laden, the Al-Qaida network and the Taliban from 27 May 2002 to 5 August 2006.

[183] Eg: Commission Regulation (EC) No 639/2007 of 8 June 2007 amending for the 78th time Council Regulation (EC) No 881/2002, OJ L 148/5.

[184] Case T-306/01 R, *Aden* (n 112 above), para 70.

[185] ibid.

Therefore, it can be assumed that the European institutions did not exercise any form of scrutiny, nor did they usually possess or attempt to obtain the information on which the sanctioning decision is based.[186]

The CFI has given a series of judgments on the legality of European sanctions giving effect to UN lists of terrorist suspects.[187] It denied jurisdiction because of the UN origin of the measures. The ECJ however has repealed the CFI's rulings on appeal.[188] Further actions are pending both before the CFI[189] and before the ECJ.[190]

In principle, the ECJ confirmed in *Kadi* and *al-Barakaat* that European sanctions giving effect to UN lists of terrorist suspects infringe the procedural rights of those listed and sanctioned.[191] Even though this might not place the European institutions under an immediate legal obligation to re-examine all listings, the European sanctioning procedure would have to be changed in order to avoid a series of successful challenges by those whose listing is tainted with the same procedural defects. Following the ECJ's ruling the institutions have introduced changes to the listing procedure.[192] Yet, under the UN-based sanctions regime the institutions simply implement the decisions of the UN Sanctions Committee. It remains doubtful whether they are actually in the position to offer effective procedural protection – in particular, whether they have access to the necessary information.

4.2 Autonomous European Sanctions

The general obligation to freeze financial assets of terrorist suspects under Resolution 1373 was implemented by the EU Council in Common

[186] See also the discussion in Chapter 7, Section 2.

[187] Cases T-306/01, *Yusuf* (n 42 above) and Case T-315/01, *Kadi* (n 18); Cases T-49/04, *Hassan* (n 42 above) and Case T-253/02, *Ayadi* (n 42 above).

[188] Cases C-402/05 P and C-415/05 P, *Kadi and al Barakaat* (n 37 above).

[189] Case T-135/06, *Al-Faqih v Council*, application of 15 July 2006, OJ 2006 C 165/29; Case T-136/06, *Sanabel Relief Agency*, application of 15 July 2006, OJ 2006 C 165/30; Case T-137/06, *Abdrabbah*, application of 15 July 2006, OJ 2006 C 165/30; Case T-138/06, *Nasuf*, application of 15 July 2006, OJ 2006 C 165/30; all pending.

[190] Case C-399/06 P, *Hassan* (n 42 above); Case C-403/06 P, *Ayadi* (n 42 above); see Chapter 2 on the competence to adopt individual sanctions and Chapter 5 on the relationship between European law and international law.

[191] Cases C-402/05 P and C-415/05 P, *Kadi and al Barakaat* (n 37 above); see also Chapter 5, Section 1.

[192] See also Chapter 7, Section 2.

Position 2001/931/CFSP[193] and EC Regulation 2580/2001.[194] The European instruments autonomously identify those subject to so-called restrictive measures (sanctions) in an annex. Common Position 2001/931/CFSP is a cross-pillar instrument based on Article 15 TEU (second pillar) and Article 34 TEU (third pillar). It provides for measures in all three pillars. In the first pillar the common position initiates concrete measures, like the freeze of funds by the Community (Articles 2, 3); in the third it calls upon the Member States to exchange information (Article 4). More generally, it stipulates a definition of 'terrorist act' (Article 1), which is applicable across all three pillars.[195] Finally, the common position serves as a CFSP decision within the meaning of Article 301 EC and allows the Community to adopt individual sanctions against those listed in its annex.

This list has been updated in numerous common positions.[196] In the beginning, amendments to the list were discussed in an ad hoc forum set up

[193] OJ 2001, L 344/93, of 27 December 2001.

[194] OJ 2001, L 344/ 70, of 27 December 2001.

[195] The general definition of a terrorist act was taken up by Framework Decision 2002/475/JHA, OJ 2002 L 164/3.

[196] 27 times between 27 December 2001 and 15 June 2009: Council Common Position 2009/468/CFSP of 15 June 2009, OJ 2009 L 151/45–50; Council Common Position 2009/67/CFSP of 26 January 2009, OJ 2009 L 23/37–42; Council Common Position 2008/959/CFSP of 16 December 2008, OJ 2008 L 338/77–78; Council Common Position 2008/586/CFSP of 15 July 2008, OJ 2008 L 188/71–76; Council Common Position 2008/347/CFSP of 29 April 2008, OJ 2008 L 116/55–55; Council Common Position 2008/346/CFSP of 29 April 2008, OJ 2008 L 116/53–54; Council Common Position 2008/586/CFSP of 15 July 2008; Council Common Position 2007/871/CFSP of 20 December 2007, OJ 2007 L 340/109–14; Council Common Position 2007/448/CFSP of 28 June 2007, OJ 2007 L 169/69–74; Council Common Position 2006/1011/CFSP of 21 December 2006, OJ 2006 L 379/129–30; Council Common Position 2006/380/CFSP of 29 May 2006, OJ 2006 L 144/25–9; Council Common Position 2006/231/CFSP of 20 March 2006, OJ 2006 L 82/20–4; Council Common Position 2005/936/CFSP of 21 December 2005, OJ 2005 L 340/80–4; Council Common Position 2005/847/CFSP of 29 November 2005, OJ 2005 L 314/41–5; Council Common Position 2005/725/CFSP of 17 October 2005, OJ 2005 L 272/28–32; Council Common Position 2005/427/CFSP of 6 June 2005, OJ 2005 L 144/54–8; Council Common Position 2005/220/CFSP of 14 March 2005, OJ 2005 L 69/59–63; Council Common Position 2004/500/CFSP of 17 May 2004, OJ 2004 L 196/12–16; Council Common Position 2004/309/CFSP of 2 April 2004, OJ 2004 L 99/61–4; Council Common Position 2003/906/CFSP of 22 December 2003, OJ 2003 L 340/77–80; Council Common Position 2003/651/CFSP of 12 September 2003, OJ 2003 L 229/42–5; Council Common Position 2003/482/CFSP of 27 June 2003, OJ 2003 L 160/100–3; Council Common Position 2003/402/CFSP of 5 June 2003, OJ 2003 L 139/35–8; Council Common Position of 12 December 2002, OJ 2002 L 337/93–6; Council Common Position of 28 October 2002, OJ 2002 L 295/1–4; Council Common Position 2002/462/CFSP of 17 June 2002, OJ 2002 L 160/32–5; Council Common Position 2002/340/CFSP of 2 May 2002, OJ 2002 L 116/75–7.

by COREPER,[197] known as the 'clearing house', which consists of representatives of the Member States and the Commission. In June 2007, the Council established a permanent Working Party (CP 931 WP) and introduced some basic procedural safeguards.[198] However, the basic procedure has not changed. Names are added based on a proposal from one of the Member States,[199] after preparation first in the ad hoc forum and now in the Working Party. The Council takes the final decision on any listing. The process also continues to take place without consultation of the European Parliament, which expressed regret over the Council's failure to consult it.[200] A unanimous decision of the Council is required in order to amend the list.[201] Article 1(6) of Common Position 2001/931/CFSP provides every six months for a revision of the list, while the process of removing a specific name is not explicitly outlined. Therefore, according to the general amendment rules, it requires unanimity, which gives one Member State the power to keep the sanction system indefinitely in place with regard to a specific person. The listing practice of terrorist suspects in CFSP decisions reflects the political consensus surrounding individual sanctions. Usually, the competent national authorities conduct an investigation and decide whether to propose a specific name to the other members of the Working Party. After a proposal is made the representatives have two weeks to consult other governmental officials. The formal decision is then taken in the Council by written procedure if there are no objections (A-point).

In the case of *OMPI III*[202] the applicant alleged that the voting process within the Council on draft Community decisions containing lists of terrorist suspects was irregular. The allegation was based on a statement of the UK Minister of State to the House of Lords, in which he explained that the UK abstained during the vote on a new Council decision instead of opposing it, because the vote took place with regard to the 'total list with all terrorist organisations on it'.[203] The Minister of State explained that

[197] French acronym of the Permanent Representatives Committee.

[198] Council Document 10826/07 on the fight against the financing of terrorism–implementation of Common Position 2001/931/CFSP, of 21 June 2007, Annex II; see Chapter 7, Section 1.1 for more detail.

[199] Member States are divided over how to go about adding a name proposed by a third country (http://www.europarl.eu.int/comparl/libe/elsj/newsletter/2002_06/default_en.htm).

[200] Parliament Resolution adopted on 7 February 2002: http://www3.europarl.eu.int/omk/omnsapir.so/calendar?APP=PDF&TYPE=PV2&FILE=p0020207FR.pdf&LANGUE=EN.

[201] The Ministry of Foreign Affairs: Finland and Terrorism: http://formin.finland.fi/doc/eng/policies/repterro.htm.

[202] Case T-284/08, *OMPI III* (n 30 above), para 27 et seq.

[203] ibid, para 28.

voting against the new list as a whole would make its adoption impossible, which would lead to 'the unpalatable situation that either the old list would be retained..., or we would have been left with no listed terrorist organisations in Europe'.[204] Assuming that the Minister's explanations before the House of Lords correctly reflect the voting practice, this means that at least at the voting stage Member States are not in the position to oppose an individual listing. In the proceedings before the CFI however, the Council submitted that (assumingly before the voting stage) 'each member of the Council has the right to express itself on all of the entries on the list individually and to indicate its position in relation to all or any of those entries.'[205] The CFI rejected the applicant's plea for lack of objective evidence.[206] The Court further added that Member States received an extension for commenting on new information concerning a particular listing. This indicated – in the Court's view – that the Member States retained the possibility to oppose this listing.[207]

Common positions adopting autonomous European lists of terrorist suspects are cross-pillar instruments based on a combined legal basis of Articles 15 and 34 TEU. The legal basis in the third pillar is necessary because of the exchange of information and mutual assistance with investigations where the lists are autonomously drawn up on the basis of information provided by the EU Member States. Article 4 of Common Position 2001/931/CFSP stipulates that Member States shall afford each other particular assistance with regard to the persons listed in the annex. Council Decision 2003/48/JHA[208] provides for third pillar measures strengthening police and judicial cooperation in respect to groups, organisations and individuals in order 'to combat terrorism in accordance with Article 4 of Common Position 2001/931/CFSP'. However, mutual cooperation appears already useful and necessary prior to the listing pursuant to Article 1(4) of Common Position 2001/931/CFSP. At this stage, Member States already assist each other with their investigations.

Regulation 2001/2580/EC implements the CFSP aspects of Common Position 2001/931/CFSP. It is based on Articles 301, 60 and 308 TEC.

[204] ibid; see also Art 249(2) EC

[205] ibid, para 31.

[206] ibid, para 33.

[207] ibid, para 34.

[208] Council Decision 2003/48/JHA of 19 December 2002 on the implementation of specific measures for police and judicial cooperation to combat terrorism in accordance with Art 4 of Common Position 2001/931/CFSP, OJ 2003, L 16/68–70.

Recital 15 stipulates that the persons and groups listed in Resolutions 1267 and 1333 are not covered by this regulation. Hence, if the UN subsequently listed someone already on an autonomous European list, the person would automatically fall within the sanctions regime under Resolution 1267. The list of persons, groups, and entities to whom Community asset freezes apply has so far been contained in a separate Council decision pursuant to Article 2(3) of the Regulation.[209] In June 2009, the Council adopted the first Council *regulation* to implement Article 2(3) of Regulation 2580/2001/EC.[210] The regulation is 'binding in its entirety and directly applicable in all Member States'.[211]

In principle, the adoption mechanism and the instruments used to adopt sanctions giving effect to European lists is the same as the mechanism and instruments used to adopt sanctions based on UN lists. There are only two formal differences. First, the common positions containing autonomous lists are based on Articles 15 *and 34 TEU*; they combine second *and* third pillar elements. Secondly, the EC regulations implementing them are applicable to a list of persons adopted in a *Council* decision (now regulation),[212] rather than a *Commission* regulation.[213]

The Community law instruments copy CFSP lists and freeze the assets of those listed. However, Common Position 2001/931/CFSP sets out that some of those listed in the common position should not be made subject to Community asset freezes, but remain subject to operational measures under the third pillar only.[214] Consequently, the lists adopted in the CFSP

[209] See for the most recent decision: Council Decision 2009/62/EC of 26 January 2009 implementing Art 2(3) of Regulation (EC) No 2580/2001 on specific restrictive measures directed against certain persons and entities with a view to combating terrorism and repealing Decision 2008/583/EC, OJ 2009 L 23/25–9.

[210] For the first regulation: Council Regulation 501/2009/EC of 15 June 2009 implementing Art 2(3) of Regulation (EC) No 2580/2001 on specific restrictive measures directed against certain persons and entities with a view to combating terrorism and repealing Decision 2009/62/EC, OJ 2009 L 151/14–16.

[211] ibid; and Art 249(2) EC.

[212] See Art 2(3) of Council Regulation EC/2580/2001, of 27 December 2001, OJ 2001 L 344/70.

[213] Eg: Commission Reg EC/2062/2001 of 19 October 2001 amending, for the third time, Regulation EC/467/2001, OJ 2001 L 277/25; Commission Reg EC/553/2007 of 22 May 2007 amending for the 77th time Council Regulation (EC) No 881/2002 imposing certain specific restrictive measures directed against certain persons and entities associated with Usama bin Laden, the Al-Qaida network and the Taliban, and repealing Council Regulation (EC) No 467/2001, OJ 2007 L 131/16.

[214] For example: Case T-338/02, *Segi and others* [2004] ECR II-01647; Case C-355/04 P, *Segi v Council* [2007] ECR I-1657; See Chapter 3 and 6 for more detail.

common position and those in the legal instruments adopted under the Community pillar are not always identical. Judicial protection from autonomous European lists of terrorist suspects adopted under the Union pillars remains difficult where no Community law measures are taken with regard to the person seeking protection.[215] Particularly, when the Council adopts sanctions based on autonomous European lists of terrorist suspects, it acts in different functions at the same meeting on the same date. It adopts measures against the same list of people[216] in all three pillars: CFSP common positions, measures in the area of Police and Judicial Cooperation in Criminal Matters (PJCC) and EC regulations. Here, the legal consequences attached to the choice of pillar in which the measure is adopted appear particularly arbitrary in view of the fact that the stigmatizing effect of being publicly labelled as a terrorist suspect is the same. The CFI has given judgment in a series of cases challenging the legality of autonomous sanctions, including listings both in EC Council decisions[217] and in common positions.[218] The ECJ has ruled on an appeal against the CFI's decision to deny judicial review of common positions entirely and allowed for preliminary rulings.[219]

The autonomous European sanctions regime provides for the possibility of making an application for humanitarian exemptions pursuant to Article 5(2) of Regulation 2580/2001. The applications have to be made to the competent authorities of the Member States.[220]

[215] See Chapter 6.

[216] Some measures are not applied to all those listed.

[217] Case T-284/08, *OMPI III* (n 30 above); Case T-256/07, *OMPI II* (n 174 above); appeal pending: Case C-576/08 P, *People's Mojahedin Organization of Iran*; Case T-228/02, *OMPI I* (n 36 above); Case T-229/02, *Kurdistan Workers' Party, Kurdistan National Congress v Council (PKK)* [2005] ECR II-539; Case T-47/03, *Sison* (n 174 above); Case T-47/03 R, *Jose Maria Sison v Council and Commission* [2003] ECR II-2047.

[218] Case T-338/02, *Segi* (n 214 above).

[219] Case C-355/04 P, *Segi* (n 214 above); see Chapter 6 for more details on protection from autonomous European sanctions.

[220] See for more detail: Notice for the attention of the persons, groups and entities on the list provided for in Art 2(3) of Council Regulation (EC) No 2580/2001 on specific restrictive measures directed against certain persons and entities with a view to combating terrorism (see Annex to Council Decision 2009/62/EC of 26 January 2009), OJ C 20/24–5.

5. National Implementation

UN member states have given effect to Security Council Resolutions 1267 and 1333 either through legislation or directly through executive orders.[221] The approach differs largely depending on whether the member state implements the resolutions following the procedures for asset freezes in the national, mostly criminal, context or whether they are implemented on the same legal basis as international state sanctions. The difference in choice of procedures reflects the hybrid nature of individual sanctions, containing both elements of criminal law and of international policy decisions. The report of the Monitoring Team identifies three different methods of implementation: based on specialized laws for automatic implementation, through ad hoc executive decisions, or based on the existing criminal codes.[222]

Those countries that apply the legal provisions adopted for state sanctions usually vest a high political figure with the powers to adopt Security Council sanctions by orders.[223] Countries using specialized laws for automatic implementation replace the judicial order usually required for the freezing of assets with the decision of the Security Council and administrative authorities are directly allowed to proceed with the freezing order.[224]

[221] For the implementation of SC sanctions resolutions see above all: Gowlland-Debbas, *Sanctions Regimes under Article 41 of the UN Charter* (n 50 above); and: Gutherie, *Security Council Sanctions and the Protection of Individual Rights* (n 21 above), p 516; on the effects of UN Security Council resolutions in national law more in general: Eric Stein, 'Application and Enforcement of International Organization Law by National Authorities and Courts' in Stephen Schwebel (ed), *The Effectiveness of International Decisions* (Leyden: Sijthoff, 1971), p 68; Vera Gowlland-Debbas, 'Comments' in Harry Post (ed), *International Economic Law and Armed Conflict* (Dordrecht: Nijhoff, 1994), p 165; Ricardo Pavoni, 'UN Sanctions in EU and National Law: The Centro Com Case', *ICLQ*, 48 (1999), pp 582–612.

[222] Dewulf and Pacquée, 'Protecting Human Rights in the War on Terror: Challenging the Sanctions Regime Originating from Res 1267 (1999)' (n 39 above), p 614.

[223] For the purpose of example some non-European countries: Commonwealth of the Bahamas Report on UN Security Council Resolution 1455, p 3, UN Doc S/AC.37/2003/(1455)/43 (2003); Report of Canada on UN Security Council Resolution 1455 (2003), pp 2–4, UN Doc S/AC.37/2003/(1455)/20 (2003), Report of Australia on Security Council Resolution 1455 (2003), pp 5–6, UN Doc S/AC.37/2003/(1455)/13 (2003).

[224] See at: Gutherie, *Security Council Sanctions and the Protection of Individual Rights* (n 21 above), p 517 referring to the Report of the Argentine Republic on the implementation of Security Council resolution 1455 (2003), para 4, UN Doc S/AC37/2003/(1455)/29 (2003).

Human rights concerns are repeatedly highlighted in the national reports to the UN Sanctions Committee.[225] Yet, they do not appear to have incited significant disobedience. Nonetheless, a number of countries have made efforts to delist individuals and to reform the UN listing procedure.[226] Further, some UN Member States derogated from the wording of the UN sanctions resolutions and introduced humanitarian exceptions on a unilateral basis. In Sweden, for instance, individual sanctions adopted in EC regulations are announced in government regulations[227] in accordance with the *1996 Act on Certain International Sanctions*.[228] The Act specifies that a prohibition may not be applied to property that is intended exclusively for the personal use of the owner.[229] This general guarantee of a minimum level of income to sustain the necessities of life has always been in place in Sweden, even before Resolution 1452 introduced exceptions to Resolution 1267.[230] The granting of welfare benefits may comply with national Swedish law;[231] yet, before Resolution 1452 was adopted it was contrary to the UN sanctions regime. Nonetheless, granting exemptions for basic necessities of life concerns a different question and must be

[225] Report of the Czech Republic in Fulfilment of United Nations Security Council Resolution 1455 (2003) S/AC.37/2003/(1455)/59, para 6; Report of the Republic of the Fiji Islands to Security Council Committee Al-Qaida and Taliban Resolution 1267, S/AC.37/2004/(1455)/39, paras 3 and 6; Report of the United Republic of Tanzania Pursuant to Security Council Resolution 1455 (2003), S/AC.37/2005/(1455)/10, para 3.

[226] See eg: Swiss Supreme Court (Schweizer Bundesgericht), *Youssef Mustapha Nada v SECO*, Staatssekretariat für Wirtschaft, judgment of 14 November 2007, 1A.45/2007/daa, para 8.3; for Germany: Spiegel, issue No 14/2006, p 43; see for the Swedish efforts to delist *Yusuf* and Al Barakaat: Stenhammar (n 111 above), pp 317–20.

[227] SFS nr: 2001:126, 2001:576, 2001:1271: Tillkännagivande om EG-förordningar med anledning av lagen (1996:95) om vissa internationella sanktioner.

[228] SFS nr: 1996:95: Lag om vissa internationella sanktioner.

[229] ibid, para 8.

[230] Alternative report to 'Comments by the Government of Sweden on the Concluding Observations of the Human Rights Committee' (CCPR/CO/74/SWE) by The Swedish NGO Foundation for Human Rights and The Swedish Helsinki Committee for Human Rights www.humanrights.se/svenska/Follow-up%20report%20HRC%202.pdf; see also for Switzerland: Thomas Meerpohl, *Individualsanktionen des Sicherheitsrates der Vereinten Nationen: Das Sanktionsregime gegen die Taliban und Al-Qaida vor dem Hintergrund des Rechts der VN und der Menschenrechte* (München: Herbert Utz Verlag, 2008), p 262.

[231] Questioned by the applicants in Case T-306/01 R, Aden (n 112 above), para 98.

regarded separately from the listing itself. The listing itself, irrespective of certain exemptions, has an enormous impact on fundamental rights.

In the UK freezing orders are adopted under the national framework legislation for sanctions (section 1 of the 1946 United Nations Act). The powers were introduced to give effect to Security Council resolutions. Sanctions are adopted through orders in Council rather than statutes. This excluded any parliamentary debate on the issue. At the time the 1946 United Nations Act was adopted the only sanctions that the legislator could foresee were generally applicable legislation dealing with the situation in a country (trade embargoes). Today, the Security Council adopts sanctions against individualized persons. The implementation of Security Council resolutions on the basis of this framework law, irrespective of the content or legal nature of the implementing act, raises concerns both with regard to the human rights situation, but also with regard to the division of competences in the national legal system.[232] The executive is in principle empowered to give effect to any Security Council resolution without requiring the support of Parliament.

Another example of a country giving effect to UN sanctions against individuals based on general framework legislation for sanctions is Germany. Article 24(1) of the German Constitution (GG) allows the transfer of sovereign rights to international organizations.[233] The transfer of sovereign rights is commonly interpreted to allow international organizations to exercise jurisdiction with direct effects within the German legal order.[234] However, Article 24 GG is not applicable to the UN. Even resolutions adopted under Chapter VII of the UN Charter are not considered to have direct effect within the German legal order.[235] Sanctions

[232] See: *A, K, M, Q, G v HM Treasury* [2008] EWCA Civ 1187, paras 128–9; see by analogy the discussion of the shift in competence in the European Union resulting from the adoption of individual sanctions on the legal basis for state sanctions.

[233] Comments to Art 24 in: Theodor Maunz, Günter Düring, and Roman Herzog, *Kommentar zum Grundgesetz* (München: Beck Verlag, 2005).

[234] Until 1992 the direct applicability of EC law was based on Art 24(1) of the German Constitution; see today: Art 23.

[235] Jochen Frowein, 'Implementation of Security Council Resolutions taken under Chapter VII in Germany' in Eibe Riedel (ed), *German Reports on Public Law* (Baden-Baden: Nomos, 2002), p 11.

against individuals are adopted based on the Foreign Trade Act,[236] which does not contain a specific provision for restrictive measures against individuals but usually serves to adopt state sanctions. This is also the reason why the Foreign Trade Act does not provide for a procedural mechanism of participation for individuals.

In the EU Member States, Security Council resolutions imposing sanctions are not directly implemented at the national level. It is the EU that adopts sanctions in order to comply with the Member States obligations under the UN Charter. It does so pursuant to the above-described procedure in Article 301 EC.[237] The adopted EC regulations are directly applicable in the national legal order. Hence, while UN sanctions resolutions are not usually considered self-executing at the national level,[238] Community law implementing UN sanctions resolutions becomes directly part of the national legal order. Only for certain subject matters is it accepted that the Member States adopt complementary national measures. For instance with regard to state sanctions, this is the case with trade in weapons under Article 296 EC.[239]

For individual sanctions, the Member States have so far adopted criminal and administrative punishment in case of violation of the sanctions prohibitions (so-called secondary sanctions). Non-compliance or violation includes any form of assistance, such as holding and transferring funds, or facilitating travel for those listed. In Germany, by way of example, secondary sanctions are adopted pursuant to section 34(4), (7) and (8) of the Foreign Trade Act. They consist of criminal charges complementing the primary sanctions adopted at the European level. The precise content of the elements of the offence are identified by a reference to the relevant EC regulation. Although secondary sanctions are currently adopted by the Member States, it cannot be ruled out that the Community adopts criminal

[236] Außenwirtschaftsgesetz, in combination with the specific regulation for foreign trade (Außenwirtschaftsverordnung); criminal sanctions for infringing sanctions rules are based on s 34 of the Foreign Trade Act.

[237] See Section 4.1 above.

[238] Antonio Cassese, *International Law* (Oxford: Oxford University Press, 2005), p 232 et seq.

[239] Frowein, *Implementation of Security Council Resolutions taken under Chapter VII in Germany* (n 235 above), p 13 with further references.

sanctions for the violation of the European sanctions regime at some point in the future.[240]

Moreover, some EU Member States adopted additional national laws for the exchange of data under the third pillar of the European Union. Germany for instance adopted an emergency measure on 9 January 2002,[241] which aims more generally to address the 'new threat' of international terrorism. Under this law the competences of the national secret service units[242] were broadened and restrictions on data collection were loosened. Under the new law, the secret services are enabled to request any desired information from all financial institutions. They can start an investigation without any particular requirements: there is no need for a primary suspicion,[243] nor do the secret service units have to give any reason for their action; and even *ex-post* judicial review is not always available.[244] Following a decision of the Council of the Interior and Justice, section 129b was inserted in the German penal code. It extends the investigational powers to foreign associations and furnishes the Ministry with the discretionary power to start an investigation. This is a controversial amendment in light of the historical separation of powers between executive and police forces in Germany.

In conclusion, the UN member states implement UN sanctions against individuals largely pursuant to pre-existing procedures, which were either introduced to adopt state sanctions or belong in the field of criminal law. Yet in a number of states, additional legislation has been adopted to vest the state with additional (mainly investigative) powers in the fight against terrorism. In principle, the EU Member States do not implement UN sanctions against individuals at the national level. They only adopt complementary criminal sanctions. Restrictive measures against those listed by the UN are adopted at the European level. While UN resolutions are not usually self-executing in the national legal orders of the EU Member States, individual sanctions in the EU are adopted by way of directly applicable EC regulations.

[240] See on the legality of EC criminal measures: Ester Herlin-Karnell, 'Commission v Council: Some Reflections on Criminal Law in the First Pillar', *European Public Law*, Vol 13(1) (2007), pp 69–84.

[241] Gesetz zur Bekämpfung des internationalen Terrorismus, BGBl 2002 I, 361ff.

[242] Bundesverfassungsschutz, militärischer Abschirmdienst (MAD), Bundesnachrichtendienst.

[243] Anfangsverdacht.

[244] Articles 1–6 Antiterrorismusgesetz.

6. Individual Sanctions as One Way to Fight Terrorism

6.1 The International Fight against Terrorism

The Security Council's role in fighting international terrorism did not begin with 11 September 2001,[245] but it has dramatically accelerated since. This is the result of an evolution in the nature of terrorism. Its complexity, sophistication, and reach have made it a truly international concern. Numerous counter-terrorism measures have been agreed at the UN level, including most prominently 'The United Nations Global Counter-Terrorism Strategy' of 8 September 2006.[246] This document is the first agreement of the UN member states on a common strategic framework bringing together all the counter-terrorist activities of the UN. An annexed plan of action divides counter-terrorist measures into four groups according to their operational intent: (1) measures to address the conditions conducive to the spread of terrorism; (2) measures to prevent and combat terrorism; (3) measures to build states' capacity to prevent and combat terrorism and to strengthen the role of the UN system in this regard; (4) measures to ensure respect for human rights for all and the rule of law as the fundamental basis of the fight against terrorism. The Global Counter-Terrorism Strategy also reflects the more recent development of interlinking the international fight against terrorism with other issues, such as anti-money laundering policy;[247] the fight against illicit production and trafficking of drugs;[248] and the prevention of conflicts, rather than addressing it as a problem in isolation. The Global Counter-Terrorism Strategy fleshes out the practical work of the

[245] Shaw, *International Law* (n 12 above), p 1048 et seq; see eg SC Res 731, referring to 'acts of international terrorism that constitute threats to international peace and security'. The same is true for the General Assembly [See eg: International Convention against the Taking of Hostages, GA res. 34/146 (XXXIV), 34 UN GAOR Supp (No 46) at 245, UN Doc A/34/46 (1979); Declaration on Measures to Eliminate International Terrorism, A/RES/49/60, 84th plenary meeting 9 December 1994; Convention for the Suppression of the Financing of Terrorism (n 167 above) and the Council of Europe (see the European Convention on the Suppression of Terrorism, 1977, but compare also the Protocol amending the Convention adopted by the Committee of Ministers of the Council of Europe in February 2003).

[246] See also: Implementation of the UN Global Counter-Terrorism Strategy (n 1 above); see for an overview of the UN action to counter terrorism: http://www.un.org/terrorism/strategy-counter-terrorism.shtml.

[247] See the work of the FATF below; but also: Concepcion Verdugo-Yepes, 'Enhancing International Cooperation in the Fight Against the Financing of Terrorism', *Journal of Global Change and Governance*, Vol 1(3), p 1 et seq.

[248] SC Res 1817 (2008); SC Res 1822 of 30 June 2008.

Counter-Terrorism Implementation Task Force (CTITF).[249] The CTITF was established by the Secretary-General in July 2005 with the task of ensuring overall coordination and coherence in the counter-terrorism efforts of the UN system.[250]

International terrorism has repeatedly been classified as a threat to international peace and security, not only by the Security Council[251] but also by the General Assembly[252] and independent investigators.[253] This classification allows the Security Council to take action under Chapter VII of the UN Charter. Sanctions against private individuals are adopted under Chapter VII.

Individual sanctions are but one means in the comprehensive counter-terrorist strategy of the international community. They consist predominantly of asset freezes, which are aimed at cutting the financial support for terrorist activities and form consequently part of the fight against the *financing* of terrorism. Another key instrument in the fight against the financing of terrorism is the Convention for the Suppression of the Financing of Terrorism.[254] This convention requires states to take appropriate measures for the identification, detection, and freezing or seizure of funds used for the commission of terrorist acts.[255] It also requires states to make it a punishable offence to collect or provide funds for use in such terrorist acts. All the EU Member States have ratified and implemented the convention. It takes a criminal law approach to terrorism and was even considered 'the way forward in effective criminal law cooperation in this field' that would make the recourse to individual sanctions in the present form unnecessary.[256] At present however individual sanctions and measures under the Convention for the Suppression of the Financing of Terrorism are adopted in parallel. While the former start at a preventive

[249] http://www.un.org/terrorism/cttaskforce.shtml.

[250] See the positive appraisal of the CTITF's work by the General Assembly at: A/RES/62/272 of 15 September 2008.

[251] See eg the general statement on the problem of terrorism in SC Res 1566 (8 October 2004); but also: SC Res 1624 (2005), and more recently: 2nd recital of SC Res 1822 (2008).

[252] General Assembly Resolution (A/RES/60/288), of September 2006, 60th session, The United Nations Global Counter-Terrorism Strategy.

[253] Report of the High-level Panel on Threats, Challenges and Change (n 147 above), paras 145–64.

[254] UN Doc A/RES/54/109 of 9 December 1999.

[255] Terrorist acts are understood to be those acts covered by an attached list of anti-terrorist Conventions or any other act intended to cause death or serious injury to a civilian or any other person not active in hostilities during an armed conflict in order to intimidate a population or compel a government or international organisation to do or abstain from doing something.

[256] Iain Cameron, 'Respecting Human Rights and Fundamental Freedoms and EU/UN Sanctions: State of Play', October 2008, Study requested by the European Parliament's Subcommittee on Human Rights, EXPO/B/DROI/2008/34, p 34.

stage and are partially thought of as preventive[257] or precautionary[258] measures only, the latter rely largely on prosecution. Yet, the distinction is more complicated. Disastrous terrorist attacks have sowed the seed of great fear among the general public of many countries. Great fear, however, inevitably leads to calls for preventive measures. Punishing the perpetrators after the fact appears no longer sufficient; preventing the next disaster from occurring is necessary.[259] Yet, just because the evidentiary standard for the adoption of individual sanctions is set lower than for criminal measures this does not prevent them from having punitive effects comparable to criminal charges.[260] Further, traditional criminal law also provides the means for preventive action against crime.

At the international level the Financial Action Task Force (FATF) is the only body dedicated solely to attacking financial crime.[261] Established as early as 1989, the FATF's original mandate focused on assisting states in fighting money-laundering and more generally in preventing the use of their financial systems for criminal purposes.[262] Since 2001 the FATF has engaged in assessing counter-terrorist financing regulations. By October 2004 it had adopted nine Special Recommendations on Terrorist Financing.[263] These

[257] Erin Miller, 'The Use of Targeted Sanctions in the Fight Against International Terrorism: What about Human Rights?' in American Society of International Law, *An Imperial Security Council? Implementing Security Council Resolutions 1373 and 1390. Proceedings of the Annual Meeting* (Washington DC: American Society of International Law, 2003), vol 97, p 48; see also the interpretation of the CFI at: Case T-228/02, *OMPI I* (n 36 above), para 130 and Case T-47/03, *Sison* (n 174 above), para 177.

[258] In later rulings the CFI used the term 'precautionary measures', see eg Case T-253/02, *Ayadi* (n 42 above), para 135.

[259] See in the midst of the Cold War: John Lord O'Brian, *National Security and Individual Freedom* (Cambridge: Harvard University Press, 1955), pp 24–5.

[260] See Chapter 3.

[261] FATF Annual Report 2007–08, of 30 June 2008. The Financial Action Task Force (FATF), established in July 1989, is an inter-governmental policy-making body whose purpose is inter alia to combat money laundering and terrorist financing.

[262] See: Alexander Kern, Rahul Dhumale and John Eatwell, *Global Governance of Financial Systems – The International Regulation of Systemic Risk* (Oxford: Oxford University Press, 2005), Chapter 2: Global Governance and International Standard Setting, p 67 et seq on the work of the FATF.

[263] The Nine Recommendations on Terrorist Financing relate to: (1) Ratification and implementation of UN instruments (in particular the UN International Convention for the Suppression of the Financing of Terrorism and SC Res 1373); (2) Criminalizing the financing of terrorism and associated money laundering; (3) Freezing and confiscating terrorist assets; (4) Reporting suspicious transactions related to terrorism; (5) International co-operation; (6) Alternative remittance (registering actors in informal money or value transfer networks); (7) Wire transfers; (8) Non-profit organizations; (9) Cash couriers; See also the Forty Recommendations (on money-laundering), both available at: http://www.fatf-gafi.org.

recommendations specifically refer to the ratification of the International Convention for the Suppression of the Financing of Terrorism, the implementation of Resolution 1373, and the freezing of assets.[264] They attach considerable value to asset freezes as a means of fighting the financing of terrorism. Major criticism has been voiced against the lack of accountability and legitimacy in FATF's decision-making processes.[265] Although stated as voluntary codes of good practice the FATF recommendations have become effectively mandatory,[266] and the FATF is largely considered effective in ensuring compliance with its standards.[267] However, a report prepared by IMF Monetary and Financial Systems and Legal Departments and the World Bank in 2005 found that overall compliance is better for the money laundering recommendations than for the special recommendations on terrorist financing.[268] All 25 assessed countries showed weakness on freezing terrorist assets and on instituting a legal requirement for reporting transactions where terrorist financing is suspected. Yet, the majority of countries had adopted measures to give effect to the UN sanctions regime under Resolution 1267.[269] Hence, a centralized authoritative listing mechanism, such as the sanctions regime under Resolution 1267,[270] appears to hold the advantage of a higher compliance rate.

Such a mechanism also holds remarkable disadvantages. Freezing assets is subject to an inherent conflict between the necessity to act fast and in secret to ensure the effectiveness and the requirements of a certain transparency which could ensure judicial and public control. In order to avoid time lapses that would render freezing measures futile individual sanctions

[264] ibid; the FATF developed a formalized policy for sanctioning states that do not comply.

[265] ibid, p 74.

[266] Kern, Dhumale and Eatwell, *Global Governance of Financial Systems – The International Regulation of Systemic Risk* (n 262 above), p 68.

[267] ibid and Supplementary information to 'Anti-Money Laundering and Combating the Financing of Terrorism: Observations from the Work Program and Implications Going Forward', staff report prepared by IMF Monetary and Financial Systems and Legal Departments and the World Bank, Financial Sector Vice-Presidency, 31 August 2005, p 10, available at: www.imf.org/external/np/pp/eng/2005/083105.htm; more critical: Concepcion Verdugo-Yepes, 'Enhancing International Cooperation in the Fight Against the Financing of Terrorism', *Journal of Global Change and Governance*, Vol 1(3), p 10.

[268] Supplementary information to 'Anti-Money Laundering and Combating the Financing of Terrorism', IMF Monetary and Financial Systems and Legal Departments and the World Bank, ibid; discussed by: Jean-Francis Thony and Cheong-Ann Png, 'FATF Special Recommendations and UN Resolutions on the Financing of Terrorism: A Review of the Status of Implementation and Legal Challenges faced by Countries', *Journal of Financial Crime*, Vol 14(2) (2007), pp 150–69.

[269] ibid, p 10.

[270] For more details, see above Section 3.1.1.

are in practice approved largely automatically at the domestic level after they have been agreed at the UN level.[271] It is difficult to see how effective human rights protection could be easily materialized at the UN level without hindering the tasks of the Security Council. Hence, any mistake made at the international level is transposed to the domestic level, notwithstanding that the speed of adoption and the underfunding and understaffing of some of the UN bodies involved in counter-terrorism policy,[272] contribute to a considerable mistake rate.[273]

In more recent years the debate on counter-terrorist policies has shifted from instruments and methods to fight terrorism to the impact on human rights both of terrorism[274] and of counter-terrorist policies.[275] For instance, the terminology has changed. The term 'war on terror' originally coined by the Bush administration[276] was at the very beginning widely used. Today it is almost rejected in unison. Further developments are that the Council of Europe complemented the 1977 Convention on 15 July 2002 with 'Guidelines on Human Rights and the Fight against Terrorism'.[277] In these guidelines the Committee of Ministers specifically addressed issues like the prohibition of arbitrariness,[278] legal certainty, and

[271] Luis Hinjosa Martinez, 'Las Sanciones del Consejo de Seguridad Contra al Qaeda y los Talibanes: Son realmente inteligentes?', *REDI*, vol LVIII (2006), p 744.

[272] See the example of CTITF at: Implementation of the UN Global Counterterrorism Strategy (n 1 above), pp 4 and 34.

[273] See both the criticism and the improvements of the listing procedure at: Eighth Report of the Analytical Support and Sanctions Monitoring Team, UN Doc S/2008/324 (14 May 2008), para 27, see also below.

[274] Implementation of the UN Global Counterterrorism Strategy (n 1 above), p 3; Human Security Brief 2007, Featuring A Special Report – Dying To Lose: Explaining The Decline In Global Terrorism, Human Security Report Project, Simon Fraser University, Canada.

[275] See above all: Conor Gearty, *Can Human Rights survive?* (Cambridge: Cambridge University Press, 2006).

[276] See for a legal critique of the term 'war on terror': Mary Ellen O'Connell, *International Law and the Global War on Terror*, Cours et travaux/Institut des Hautes Etudes Internationales de Paris (Paris: Pedone, 2007).

[277] Guidelines on human rights and the fight against terrorism adopted by the Committee of Ministers on 11 July 2002 at the 804th meeting of the Ministers' Deputies.

[278] Guideline II–Prohibition of arbitrariness: All measures taken by states to fight terrorism must respect human rights and the principle of the rule of law, while excluding any form of arbitrariness, as well as any discriminatory or racist treatment, and must be subject to appropriate supervision.

proportionality of counter-terrorism measures,[279] and the right to a fair hearing.[280]

More particularly in the context of individual sanctions the shift of attention towards human rights can be seen in the Reports of the Monitoring Group/Monitoring Team.[281] While the earlier reports focused on increasing the effectiveness of individual sanctions, the later reports address more frequently human rights concerns.[282] Further, while the General Assembly in the '2005 World Summit Outcome' emphasized the importance of sanctions as a policy tool, referring both to state and to individual sanctions,[283] it also expressed its concern for the procedural rights of those targeted by individual sanctions. It called

[279] Guideline III (2): When a measure restricts human rights, restrictions must be defined as precisely as possible and be necessary and proportionate to the aim pursued. See also Guideline IX (4).

[280] Guideline IX–Legal proceedings: 1. A person accused of terrorist activities has the right to a fair hearing, within a reasonable time, by an independent, impartial tribunal established by law. 2. A person accused of terrorist activities benefits from the presumption of innocence. 3. The imperatives of the fight against terrorism may nevertheless justify certain restrictions to the right of defence, in particular with regard to: (i) the arrangements for access to and contacts with counsel; (ii) the arrangements for access to the case-file; (iii) the use of anonymous testimony. 4. Such restrictions to the right of defence must be strictly proportionate to their purpose, and compensatory measures to protect the interests of the accused must be taken so as to maintain the fairness of the proceedings and to ensure that procedural rights are not drained of their substance.

[281] Compare: S/2007/132, 8 March 2007–Sixth Report of the Analytical Support and Sanctions Monitoring Team; S/2006/750, 20 September 2006–Fifth Report of the Monitoring Team pursuant to resolutions 1526 (2004) and 1617 (2005); S/2006/154, 10 March 2006–Fourth Report of the Monitoring Team pursuant to resolution 1526 (2004); S/2005/572, 9 September 2005–Third Report of the Monitoring Team pursuant to resolution 1526 (2004); S/2005/83, 15 February 2005–Second Report of the Monitoring Team pursuant to resolution 1526 (2004); S/2004/679, 25 August 2004–First Report of the Monitoring Team pursuant to resolution 1526 (2004); S/2003/1070, 2 December 2003–Second Report of the Monitoring Group pursuant to resolution 1455 (2003); S/2003/669, 8 July 2003 and S/2003/669/Corr.1, 17 July 2003–First Report of the Monitoring Group pursuant to resolution 1455 (2003); S/2002/1338, 17 December 2002–Third Report of the Monitoring Group pursuant to resolution 1390 (2002); S/2002/1050, S/2002/1050/Corr.1 and S/2002/1427, 20 September 2002–Second Report of the Monitoring Group pursuant to resolution 1390 (2002); S/2002/541, 15 May 2002– First Report of the Monitoring Group pursuant to resolution 1390 (2002); S/2002/65, 15 January 2002–Report of the Monitoring Group on Afghanistan pursuant to resolution 1363 (2001).

[282] See pp 29 and 30 above.

[283] General Assembly, 2005 World Summit Outcome, A/RES/60/1, of 24 October 2005, para 106.

upon the Security Council, with the support of the Secretary-General, to ensure that fair and clear procedures exist for placing individuals and entities on sanctions lists and for removing them, as well as for granting humanitarian exemptions.[284]

The Security Council by contrast '[e]ncourages the Committee *to continue* to ensure that fair and clear procedures exist for placing individuals' on the terrorist list 'and for removing them as well as for granting humanitarian exemptions'.[285] Other more recent developments include the work of the 'Special Rapporteur on the Promotion and Protection of Human Rights and Fundamental Freedoms while Countering Terrorism'. He welcomed the General Assembly's call for fair procedures and highlighted a number of 'basic principles' and 'procedural guarantees.'[286]

The intensified counter-terrorist activities of the international community reflect a widely shared agreement that 'something needs to be done' to counter international terrorism. The fight against the financing of terrorism, including individual sanctions, is a logical response: terrorists need money to plan and execute terrorist attacks.[287] At the same time, the nature of terrorist financing has changed: terrorist groups become less and less reliant on state sponsorship, but use alternative, illegal sources of money.[288] The shift to a more integrated counter-terrorist strategy is a sensible reaction to this development.

Whether individual sanctions are an adequate, necessary, and proportionate tool in this strategy is a different matter. It is not sufficient to argue that the financing of terrorism needs to be stopped. The use of individual sanctions as a policy tool requires particular justification – even more so when taking into account the controversial effectiveness of asset freezes[289] and the far-reaching restriction they impose on human rights. Indeed, as will be examined in the following chapters, drawing up lists of terrorist suspects and freezing their assets continues to reduce procedural rights beyond what is traditionally accepted by many international, European, and national human rights standards.[290]

[284] ibid, para 109.

[285] SC Res 1822, para 28 (emphasis added).

[286] Goldman, Report of the Independent Expert (n 92 above); see also above.

[287] Williams, 'Warning Indicators and Terrorist Finances' (n 10 above); although terrorist attacks are cheap.

[288] SC Res 1373, para 4; Jeanne K Giraldo and Harold A Trinkunas, *Terrorism Financing and State Responses: A Comparative perspective* (Stanford, California: Stanford University Press, 2007).

[289] See below. [290] See Chapters 5, 6 and 7.

6.2 The European Union's Counter-Terrorist Policy

Within the European Union the pace of adopting counter-terrorist policies has equally accelerated. Even though multilateral counter-terrorist activity within Europe also pre-dates 2001[291] the increased momentum started with the European Council's 'Action Plan' to fight terrorism on 21 September 2001.[292] In the present context the assessment of the numerous measures adopted by the European Union in its fight against terrorism can be no more than cursory. The overview is given to demonstrate that within the EU's counter-terrorist policies individual sanctions are part of a bigger picture. The intention here is to highlight some of the particularities of the EU's counter-terrorism policy, but also the specific problems that the European Union faces when fighting terrorism.

6.2.1 Terrorism as a European Problem

The European Union is in a difficult position. Most of the powers and capabilities in the field of counter-terrorism continue to remain with the Member States, the discussion is dominated by national threat perception, and much of the political discourse takes place at the national level.[293] Further, the threat of terrorism is perceived very differently from one Member State to the next. A divide is identifiable between the west and the east of the EU and between countries that have experienced internal terrorism and those that have not.[294] All Member States not only participate

[291] See TREVI (Terrorisme, Radicalisme, Extremisme, Violence Internationale), an independent consultative forum; but see also: the Schengen Agreement (although not exclusively intended to counter terrorism, it led to the establishment of the Schengen Information System (SIS), which is a comprehensive computerized repository on persons and goods considered to constitute a threat to society); see more broadly: Martin Trybus and Nigel White (eds), *European Security Law* (Oxford: Oxford University Press, 2007).

[292] Compare documents adopted only in September and October 2001: Conclusions of JHA Council Meeting of 21 September 2001, SN 3926/6/01; Solana: Joint EU-US statement on terrorism, 20 September 2001; Conclusions and Plan of Action of the Extraordinary European Council Meeting on 21 September 2001, SN 140/01, endorsed by the European Parliament on 4 October 2001; Conclusions, General Affairs Council Meeting of 17 October 2001; and Declaration, European Council Meeting of 19 October, SN4296/2/01.

[293] Jörg Monar, 'Common Threat and Common Response? The European Union's Counter-Terrorism Strategy and its Problems', Government and Opposition, Vol 42, No 3 (2007).

[294] Eurostad, but also: Portela 'The Efficacy of Sanctions of the European Union: When and why do they work?' (n 28 above).

in the European counter-terrorist policies but have some sort of national counter-terrorist policy, and all Member States have views on what should be done to address the threat of terrorism. Their support for individual sanctions depends on their assessment both of its value as such (effectiveness, human rights concerns, etc), and of its value in relation to their own national counter-terrorist concerns.[295]

Against these odds the EU has made a strong appearance as a security actor in the area of counter-terrorist policy. In December 2003, the *European Security Strategy* identified terrorism as the first of five key threats to European interests.[296] Also, the EU has put into place a quite comprehensive 'Counter-Terrorism Strategy', supported by an 'Action Plan'.[297] The 2005 Counter-Terrorism Strategy defines four headings for EU action: Prevent (radicalization and recruitment); Protect (citizens and infrastructure); Pursue (terrorists across borders); and Respond (to the consequences of terrorist attacks).[298] However, the key document remains the Action Plan against terrorism of 2001 that has been updated several times.[299] The most well-known legal instruments are the framework decisions of 13 June 2002 on combating terrorism and on the European Arrest Warrant,[300] but the EU's counter-terrorism strategy goes much further. In 2007, the Commission adopted a package containing a series of proposals fleshing out the EU's legal framework to counter terrorism. The

[295] See for counter-terrorist policies more in general: Monar, *Common Threat and Common Response? The European Union's Counter-Terrorism Strategy and its Problems* (n 293 above).

[296] Council of the European Union, 'A Secure Europe In A Better World–The European Security Strategy', http://www.consilium.europa.eu/showPage.asp?id=266&lang=en&mode=g; see also: Becher (2003), pp 345–59.

[297] Conclusions and Plan of Action, 21 September 2001 (n 292 above).

[298] Presidency and CT Co-ordinator, 'The European Union Counter-Terrorism Strategy', Brussels, 30 November 2005, 14469/4/05 REV 4.

[299] See for the latest developments: http://ec.europa.eu/justice_home/fsj/terrorism/fsj_terrorism_intro_en.htm.

[300] Council Framework Decision 2002/475/JHA of 13 June 2002 on combating terrorism OJ L22/6/2002, 164/3; see also: Council Framework Decision 2008/919/JHA of 28 November 2008 amending Framework Decision 2002/475/JHA on combating terrorism, OJ L 330/21–3; Council Framework Decision 2002/584/JHA of 13 June 2002 on the European arrest warrant and the surrender procedures between Member States, OJ 2002, L 190/1; see also the legal challenges against the national implementation measures: Chapters Two, Five and Six. Both framework decisions are coherent with traditional legislative responses to terrorism: Yonah Alexander and Allan S Nanes (eds), *Legislative Responses to Terrorism* (Dordrecht: Martinus Nijhoff Publishers, 1986); David Charters (ed), *Democratic Responses to International Terrorism* (London: Cavendish Publishers, 1991).

Commission proposed in particular measures to criminalize terrorist training, recruitment and public provocation to commit terrorist offences,[301] the prevention of the use of explosives by terrorists[302] and the use of airline passenger information in law enforcement investigations.[303] Another recent tool in the fight against terrorism is the Data Retention Directive.[304] It harmonizes the rules on how long telecom operators and internet providers must retain data. The directive is a good example for first pillar *Community* activity relating to terrorism that leads to controversy not only because of its impact on fundamental rights but also because it goes beyond (traditional) Community competences into the area of crime prevention and prosecution.[305] The fight against terrorism has also become one of the central objectives in the creation of the Area of Freedom, Security and Justice.[306] The post of the EU Counter-terrorism Coordinator was created.[307] Finally, numerous bodies with broader objectives

[301] IP/07/1649: Fight Against Terrorism: stepping up Europe's capability to protect citizens against the threat of terrorism; COM (2007) 649 final: Communication from the Commission to the European Parliament and the Council–Stepping up the fight against terrorism; COM (2007) 650 final: Proposal for a Council Framework Decision amending Framework Decision 2002/475/JHA on combating terrorism; adopted on 28 November 2008: Council Framework Decision 2008/919/JHA, ibid.

[302] COM (2007) 651 final: Communication from the Commission to the European Parliament and the Council on enhancing the security of explosives.

[303] COM (2007) 654 final: Proposal for a Council framework decision on the use of Passenger Name Record (PNR) for law enforcement purposes.

[304] Directive 2006/24/EC, OJ 2006 L105/54; the directive was adopted given the Declaration on Combating Terrorism adopted by the European Council on 25 March 2004, '[b]ecause retention of data has proved to be such a necessary and effective investigative tool for law enforcement in several Member States, and in particular concerning serious matters such as organised crime and terrorism...' (Recitals 8–9).

[305] Case C-301/06, *Ireland v Parliament and Council (Data Retention Directive)*, judgment of 10 February 2009 (confirming that Art 95 EC was the appropriate legal basis) and the constitutional complaint against the national implementation measure pending before the German Constitutional Court, interim decision: 1 BvR 256/08.

[306] The Hague Programme: Strengthening Freedom, Security and Justice in the European Union, Council document of 3.3.2005, OJ 2005 C 53/1; see also: Communication from the Commission to the Council and the European Parliament – The Hague Programme: Ten priorities for the next five years The Partnership for European renewal in the field of Freedom, Security and Justice, Brussels, 10.5.2005, COM(2005) 184 final; Douglas-Scott (2004).

[307] The EU Counter-terrorism Coordinator is generally perceived as lacking teeth, see eg: Zimmermann, 'The European Union and Post-9/11 Counterterrorism: A Reappraisal, Studies in Conflict & Terrorism' (n 2 above), pp 133–4.

contribute to the fight against terrorism, such as the European Border Agency (Frontex)[308] and the European Police Office (Europol).[309]

The EU has also focused on fighting the *financing* of terrorism. Examples of legislative instruments are the Council framework Decision on the Execution of Orders Freezing Property or Evidence of 22 July 2003, and more famously, the so-called Third Money Laundering Directive of 26 October 2005.[310] In contrast to asset freezes, these instruments target 'illegal money' only. The money used to finance terrorist attacks, however, comes both from legal and illegal sources (despite a certain shift towards the latter).[311] The Third Money Laundering Directive explicitly includes the financing of terrorism within its scope. This is in principle in line with the FATF approach and the Nine Special Recommendations.[312] However, the definition of terrorism in the Third Money Laundering Directive also displays a 'unique' European approach. It specifically targets cross-border cash movements[313] and follows the Council Framework Decision on combating terrorism,[314] rather the UN Convention for the Suppression of the Financing of Terrorism.[315]

[308] Council Regulation 2007/2004, of 26 October 2004, establishing a European Agency for the Management of Operational Cooperation at the External Borders of the Member States of the European Union, OJ 2004 L 349/1. The six tasks of Frontex were to coordinate operational cooperation, train national border guards, do risk analyses, develop research, assist member states with technical and operational facilities, and organise joint return operations.

[309] See the reference to Europol in Conclusions and Plan of Action, 21 September 2001 (n 292 above): 'Member States will share with Europol, systematically and without delay, all useful data regarding terrorism. A specialist anti-terrorist team will be set up within Europol as soon as possible and will cooperate closely with its US counterparts…'; Europol and the United States of America have since concluded two agreements on the exchange of personal data (available at: www.europol.europa.eu), which have raised many concerns of data protection.

[310] Council Framework Decision 2003/577/JHA of 22 July 2003 on the execution in the European Union of orders freezing property or evidence, OJ L196/45, 2.8.2003 and Directive 2005/60/EC of the European Parliament and of the Council of 26 October 2005 on the prevention of the use of the financial system for the purpose of money laundering and terrorist financing, OJ L 309/15, 25.11.2005.

[311] See Section 6.1 above.

[312] See n 263 above; see also: Valsamis Mitsilegas and Bill Gilmore, 'The EU legislative framework against money laundering and terrorist finance: a critical analysis in the light of evolving global standards', *International and Comparative Law Quarterly* 56 (2007), pp 119–41.

[313] See eg: Steve Peers, 'EU Responses to terrorism', *International and Comparative Law Quarterly* 52 (2003), pp 227–43.

[314] Council Framework Decision 2002/475/JHA of 13 June 2002 on combating terrorism (n 300 above).

[315] Convention for the Suppression of the Financing of Terrorism (n 167 above) and text accompanying n 245 above.

The EU has to some extent succeeded in Europeanizing[316] a threat that is usually presented either as a national or global one. Terrorism became an *internal* security problem of the Union.[317] Yet, the EU's counter-terrorist policy is based on a combination of internal and external measures.[318] This creates problems with regard to the (partial) separation between internal and external activities in the existing pillar structure of the EU. The fight against terrorism is now not only addressed within the second and third pillar, but has also become a consideration when the Community takes action.[319] Cross-pillar acts, such as individual sanctions, raise particular problems of competences, democratic legitimacy and judicial protection.[320]

Overall, the fight against terrorism in the European Union is judged to be more successful at the legislative and institutional level than at the operational level.[321] Part of the problem is that the EU's response to terrorism is based on cooperation and coordination rather than on integration. Its success depends even after a particular instrument is agreed at the European level on the continuous will of the Member States to take action, and the Member States are better in agreeing politically than in implementing their decisions. This reflects the particular nature and the limited competences of the European Union.[322] It also explains why measures like the Data Retention Directive are adopted under the Community pillar (with better enforcement mechanisms), despite their objective of fighting terrorism. Individual sanctions take a particular position in this respect.

[316] Monar, 'Common threat and common response? The European Union's Counter-terrorism Strategy and its Problems' (n 293 above) pp 293–6.

[317] The attempt to Europeanize the treat of terrorism can be seen in the first more substantial legislative act in the fight against terrorism: the Framework Decision on Combating Terrorism, of 13 June 2002 (n 300 above). The strongly worded preamble describes terrorism as a threat to the fundamental values that the EU is founded on, the political, constitutional and socio-economic foundations of the EU and its member states.

[318] See eg: Report on the Implementation of the European Security Strategy – Providing Security in a Changing World, Approved by the European Council held in Brussels on 11 and 12 December 2008 and drafted under the responsibilities of the EU High Representative Javier Solana, S407/08, p 4.

[319] Directive 2006/24/EC (n 304 above), recitals 8, 9 and 10.

[320] See Chapters 2 and 6.

[321] August Reinisch, 'The Action of the European Union' (n 79 above); Monar, *Common threat and common response? The European Union's Counter-terrorism Strategy and its Problems* (n 293 above) (example of the 2002 Framework Decision on Combating Terrorism); Zimmermann, *The European Union and Post-9/11 Counterterrorism: A Reappraisal, Studies in Conflict & Terrorism* (n 2 above), p 130.

[322] Similar with regard to earlier counter-terrorist activities: Peter Chalk, *West European Terrorism and Counterterrorism. The Evolving Dynamic* (Basingstoke: Palgrave Macmillan, 1996), p 117.

They are agreed under the Union pillars but adopted in directly applicable Community regulations without any further need for implementation.

6.2.2 Individual Sanctions as Part of the European Union's Fight against Terrorism

A Report on the Implementation of the European Security Strategy approved in December 2008[323] attests the European Union 'progress' in countering terrorism overall, but–and this is highly relevant for individual sanctions–it also points out that '[f]urther work on terrorist financing is required, along with an effective and comprehensive EU policy on information sharing, taking due account of protection of personal data'.[324]

In 2003, the Council of the European Union drafted guidelines for the adoption of sanctions.[325] These guidelines describe sanctions 'as part of an integrated, comprehensive policy approach which should include political dialogue, incentives, conditionality' but also as a last resort the use of coercive measures.

The EU is said to have adopted a criminal justice counter-terrorist model.[326] This reflects the convictions of a number of Member States that have always taken a more integrated view on terrorism[327] that is in line with the approach the international community has moved to more recently.[328] Terrorism is believed to be closely interlinked with other criminal activities, such as illegal immigration, drug trafficking and organized crime more generally. Dealing with it as a separate problem is therefore perceived as inefficient. Further, the criminal justice model appears more palatable to EU Member States than allowing the EU to interfere with even more politically sensitive internal security matters. Sanctions against individual are in

[323] Report on the Implementation of the European Security Strategy (n 318 above), p 4.

[324] ibid.

[325] Council of the European Union, Guidelines on implementation and evaluation of restrictive measures (sanctions) in the framework of the EU Common Foreign and Security Policy, 3 December 2003 Doc 15579/03; see also: Council of the European Union, Basic Principles on the use of restrictive measures (sanctions), 7 June 2004, Doc 10198/1/04.

[326] Critical: Zimmermann, *The European Union and Post-9/11 Counterterrorism: A Reappraisal, Studies in Conflict & Terrorism* (n 2 above), pp 125 and 134; suggesting a criminal justice model: Cameron, 'Respecting Human Rights and Fundamental Freedoms and EU/UN Sanctions' (n 256 above).

[327] See on the different views of selected EU Member States: Ariane Chebel d'Appollonia and Simon Reich, *Immigration, Integration, and Security, America and Europe in Comparative Perspective* (Pittsburgh: University of Pittsburgh Press, 2008).

[328] See Section 6.1 above.

this context to some extent an exception. Even thought the European Union also draws up autonomous lists of terrorist suspects based on cooperation in criminal matters in the third pillar, individual sanctions address terrorist financing and other support in isolation. Indeed, the Council attempts to pass these sanctions off as preventive administrative measures rather than as part of criminal law.[329] Additionally, individual sanctions that give effect to UN lists of terrorist suspects are unrelated to the Member States' cooperation in the third pillar.

By way of conclusion, sanctions against private individuals suspected to support terrorism form a cornerstone of the EU's counter-terrorism strategy.[330] They complement a wide range of other measures adopted to fight the financing of terrorism and terrorism itself. Fighting terrorism at the EU level has great advantages, but it also suffers from considerable drawbacks. National agencies continue to be reluctant to share intelligence on terrorism,[331] even though considerable efforts have led to some progress on this issue.[332] Also, the coordination of counter-terrorism policy between the UN and the EU has improved.[333]

Counter-terrorist policy at the national level differs greatly, including among the EU Member States. By way of example, in Germany the counter-terrorist discourse takes an international perspective. Although it enacted legislation as a response to the terror activities in the late sixties and seventies[334] Germany introduced the first general law with the objective to fight international terrorism in early 2002.[335] Many more

[329] See Chapter 3.

[330] Guild (2008), pp 173–93.

[331] See eg: Magnus Ranstorp (Director of the Centre for the Study of Terrorism and Political Violence, St Andrews), 'The European Terror Challenge', available at: http://news.bbc.co.uk/2/hi/europe/3563713.stm.

[332] Report on the Implementation of the European Security Strategy, 2008 (n 318 above).

[333] See also Chapter 7 on the proportionality of individual sanctions.

[334] Including the three 'Anti-Terror-Gesetze': Gesetz zur Ergänzung des Ersten Gesetzes zur Reform des Strafverfahrensrechts vom 20. Dezember 1974, Bundesgesetzblatt (BGBl.) 1974 I, 3686; Gesetz zur Änderung des Strafgesetzbuches, der Strafprozessordung und des Strafvollzugsgesetzes, der Bundesrechtsanwaltsordnung und der Strafvollzugsgesetzes vom 18. August 1976, BGBl. 1976 I, 2181; Gesetz zur Änderung der Strafprozessordung vom 14 April 1978, BGBl. 1978 I, 497.

[335] Gesetz zur Bekämpfung des internationalen Terrorismus, 9 January 2002 (Terrorismusbekämpfungsgesetz), Bundesgesetzblatt (BGBl.) I 361, 3142.

legal instruments have followed since.[336] These measures are partially adopted in order to implement counter-terrorist policies agreed at the European level,[337] but they also originate in part from the national discourse.

In the UK by contrast, counter-terrorist policy is developed predominantly in a national discourse. Since early 2003 the UK has developed a long-term, 'co-ordinated, multi-agency, and international approach to the disruption of terrorist activity.'[338] The key pieces of the legislative framework that give the UK government the powers to combat terrorism are: the Terrorism Act 2000 (TACT), the Anti-Terrorism, Crime and Security Act 2001 (ATCSA), the Prevention of Terrorism Act 2005, and the Terrorism Act 2006. The Terrorism Act 2000 made it illegal for certain terrorist groups to operate in the UK and extended proscription to include international terrorist groups, like Al-Qaida. The Prevention of Terrorism Act 2005 introduced control orders.[339] The Terrorism Act 2006 made it a criminal offence directly or indirectly to encourage the commission, preparation, or instigation of acts of terrorism or to disseminate terrorist publications. It also broadened the basis for proscribing organisations to include those that promote or encourage terrorism.[340] In the UK, although prosecution remains the preferred way of responding to persons involved in terrorist activity, other options for taking disruptive action have been introduced as well, including the deportation on grounds of national security or unacceptable behaviour, control orders, freezing and seizing financial assets, and proscription of organisations.

[336] Jutta Limbach speaks of an 'unbroken line of political activism in the fight against terrorism' ('Human Rights in Times of Terror – Is Collective Security the Enemy of Individual Freedom?', *Göttingen Journal of International Law*, 1 (2009), 19); for a more provocative journalistic account: Heribert Prantl, *Der Terrorist als Gesetzgeber. Wie man mit Angst Politik macht* (Droemer Knaur 2008); see for an overview of the legislative activity in the immediate aftermath of 11 September 2001 the report of the Counter Terrorist Committee S/2002/11 of 2 January 2002.

[337] Gesetz zur Neuregelung der Telekommunikationsüberwachung und anderer verdeckter Ermittlungsmaßnahmen sowie zur Umsetzung der Richtlinie 2006/24/EG, 21 December 2007, BGBl. I, 3198, implementing: Directive 2006/24/EC (n 304 above).

[338] See: Countering International Terrorism: The United Kingdom's Strategy (n 3 above).

[339] See cases in Chapter 4.

[340] See the case of Case T-228/02, *OMPI I* (n 36 above) in Chapters 6 and 7.

7. The Effectiveness of Individual Sanctions and Other Counter-Terrorist Measures

Assessing the effectiveness of individual sanctions is an even greater challenge than assessing the effectiveness of state sanctions. The latter typically aim at changing the political situation in a particular country, be it a regime change or preventing (further) human rights violations. The former are intended to fight the insufficiently defined phenomenon of terrorism. Individual sanctions are further only one means in the comprehensive counter-terrorist efforts of the international community and of the European Union. This makes it additionally difficult to identify them in isolation either as a complete success or as a complete failure. Finally, the reporting practice under the UN sanctions regime is slow and incomplete. Against this background, it is not surprising that assessments of the effectiveness of individual sanctions remain tentative.[341]

Difficulties are, for instance, noticeable in the assessment of the amount of funds frozen under the different sanctions regimes. For the UN Taliban and Al-Qaida regime this was at the end of 2007 approximately US$85 million.[342] However, the Monitoring Team acknowledged that 'the true figure of frozen assets' is not known.[343] Irrespectively, it evaluated the overall success of the policy of freezing assets as positive. The Monitoring Team pointed out that 'the quantity of assets frozen is not the sole determinant of the value of the assets'.[344] It emphasized that the asset freezes also serve as a general deterrent. They restrict 'the ability of Al-Qaida-related terrorists to run extensive networks, training camps and social programmes for the

[341] Mr Anthonius de Vries, the EU's sanctions coordinator in the late 1990s, acknowledged that evidence of the effectiveness of individual sanctions is 'unavailable', at: House of Lords, Select Committee on Economic Affairs, 2nd Report of Session 2006–07, The Impact of Economic Sanctions, Volume II: Evidence, Published 9 May 2007, p 166; see also: Giraldo and Trinkunas, 'Terrorism Financing and State Responses: A Comparative perspective' (n 288 above); Parker 'The Problem with Scorecards' (n 14 above); Swiss Federal Office for Foreign Economic Affairs, 2nd Interlaken Seminar on Targeting United Nations Financial Sanctions, 29–31 March, 1999, pp 101–15. See also more generally on the effectiveness of counter-terrorist measures: Human Security Brief 2007, Featuring a Special Report – Dying To Lose: Explaining The Decline In Global Terrorism, Human Security Report Project, Simon Fraser University, Canada, see in particular Overview and Chapter 1, pp 1–21, available at: http://www.humansecuritybrief.info/.

[342] See above for comparisons to earlier years; Eighth Report of the Analytical Support and Sanctions Monitoring Team (n 46 above), para 23, p 12 and para 47, p 19.

[343] Sixth report of the Analytical Support and Sanctions Monitoring Team, UN S/2007/132 (8 March 2007), para 52

[344] ibid, para 55.

families of supporters, especially across borders'.[345] Individual sanctions further serve the broader aim of having a symbolic value in that they send the message that financial support of terrorism will not be tolerated.

By contrast to the Monitoring Team's assessment, the UK House of Lords Select Committee appears to consider the amount of money frozen as an important indication of the effectiveness of the measures. It observed that:

> [t]he evidence suggests that the amounts of money frozen are so small both in absolute terms and relative to the probable resources of the targets, that it is doubtful whether asset freezes are effective as a means of inhibiting or changing the behaviour of those who are targeted.[346]

The Committee further pointed out that 'just because ... [individual sanctions] are labelled as targeted, this does not necessarily mean that they are hitting their targets'.[347] The Committee continued by pointing out that the efforts made to improve targeting were inadequate. Overall however, the Committee also concluded that the findings do not mean that individual sanctions should be abandoned and that they may be effective 'when the target wishes to avoid the stigma of illegitimacy'.[348]

The National Commission on Terrorist Attacks on the US (9/11 Commission)[349] is overall critical of the effectiveness of individual sanctions. It considers their impact as highly limited. Further, although most scholars focus on the impact on human rights rather than on the effectiveness of individual sanctions, those who do examine the latter reach even more critical conclusions.[350] Iain Cameron evaluated the impact on stopping terrorist groups from obtaining financing as being 'most likely zero'.[351]

The different assessments demonstrate a further difficulty. Effectiveness should be measured against clear policy goals. The effectiveness of

[345] ibid, paras 53–4.

[346] House of Lords, Select Committee on Economic Affairs, 2nd Report of Session 2006–07, The Impact of Economic Sanctions, Volume I: Report, Published 9 May 2007, Chapter 5: Targeted Financial Sanctions on Individuals and Groups, p 26, para 68.

[347] ibid, p 24, para 64.

[348] ibid, p 26, para 69.

[349] National Commission on Terrorist Attacks on the US, The 9/11 Commission Report, 2004, http://govinfo.library.unt.edu/911/report/911Report.pdf, p 382.

[350] Eg: Cameron, 'Respecting Human Rights and Fundamental Freedoms and EU/UN Sanctions' (n 256 above), p 34; Martinez, *Las Sanciones del Consejo de Seguridad Contra al Qaeda y los Talibanes:¿ Son realmente inteligentes?* (n 271 above), p 738; Giraldo and Trinkunas, *Terrorism Financing and State Responses: A Comparative perspective* (n 288 above).

[351] Cameron, ibid, p 34.

individual sanctions in general and asset freezes in particular hinges consequently on whether or to what extent these measures meet their objectives. The narrowest direct objective of individual sanctions is to prevent terrorists from receiving (financial) support. This appears also to be the understanding of the CFI. In the case of *OMPI II* the Court argues that the prime consideration in the decision of whether a person remains listed should not be the person's recent conduct but whether the assets belonging to that person would be used to finance terrorism.[352] In contrast to the CFI, both the Monitoring Team and the House of Lords Select Committee appeared to have a broader understanding of the objectives of individual sanctions. They include the overall deterring effects of the sanctions regime and the impact on the behaviour of those sanctioned. The lack of a clear definition of what individual sanctions intend to achieve may explain some differences in appraisal.

Finally, it is impossible to judge whether the freezing of US$85 million is a sign of effectiveness or not. It depends on whether these funds would have otherwise been used to finance terrorist activities, and on what share US$85 million constitute of the total amount of funds available to 'terrorists'. Also, it should be kept in mind that committing a terrorist act is – in the end – a cheap enterprise.[353]

While the contribution of individual sanctions to reducing the financial support of 'terrorism' is extremely difficult to appraise, it is easier to assess the practical effectiveness of the UN sanctions regime. This is also the focus of the Monitoring Team. In its Sixth report of 8 March 2007 the Monitoring Team suggests a two-level effectiveness examination: first, whether the state has the *legal, administrative, enforcement, and political means* in place to implement the sanctions and, second, how the state *implements the sanctions in practice*.[354] The speed, quality, and quantity of investigation and information on terrorist financing have a major impact on the effectiveness of measures in practice. One problem is that a significant number of listed names had insufficient identifiers to allow (effective) enforcement action.[355] Yet again, after pointing out these shortcomings the Monitoring Team concluded on 14 May 2008 that much progress had been 'made in

[352] Case T-256/07, *OMPI II* (n 174 above), para 136.

[353] Williams, 'Warning indicators and Terrorist Finances' (n 10 above), p 74.

[354] Sixth report of the Analytical Support and Sanctions Monitoring Team, UN S/2007/132 (8 March 2007), para 23, emphasis added.

[355] Eighth Report of the Analytical Support and Sanctions Monitoring Team (n 46 above), para 24, p 12.

improving the information on the list in recent month with contributions from 19 Member States leading to 44 proposed amendments in the six months since the Team last reported at the end of September 2007'.[356]

Enormous practical difficulties are attached to implementing individual sanctions.[357] This results partly from the fact that implementation mechanisms for state sanctions are used for individual sanctions.[358] Competent authorities are under-funded and badly equipped for their tasks.[359] The effectiveness of regulatory programmes depends largely on voluntary compliance, since the competent authorities do not have the resources or the power to enforce them. Sometimes there are long delays between the announcement and the promulgation,[360] and the lists are incomplete and already outdated at the time of official publication.[361] Further, it is enormously difficult to identify individuals unambiguously.[362] Enforcement measures remain secret and there are cases where actions were taken against people that are not on the list.[363] Particularly harsh critics judge individual sanctions an ineffective tool in the fight against terrorism.[364]

Implementation in practice is crucial for the overall effectiveness of individual sanctions – not only, but also because the perception of effectiveness contributes to compliance and hence to effectiveness, particularly in international law.[365] Yet an assessment of the practical functioning of UN sanctions regimes alone remains myopic; it does not answer the basic question of whether individual sanctions are the right policy choice.

[356] Eighth Report of the Analytical Support and Sanctions Monitoring Team, ibid, para 27, p 13.

[357] Peter Fitzgerald, 'Compliance Issues Associated with Targeted Economic Sanctions' (n 39 above) pp 149–58; for the US: Peter Fitzgerald, 'Managing "Smart Sanctions" against Terrorism Wisely' New England Law Review, 36 (2002), pp 957–83.

[358] Fitzgerald, 'Compliance Issues Associated with Targeted Economic Sanctions' (n 39 above), p 150.

[359] Fitzgerald, 'Managing "Smart Sanctions" against Terrorism Wisely' (n 357 above), p 962.

[360] ibid, p 966.

[361] ibid, p 971.

[362] ibid, p 974; Fitzgerald, 'Compliance Issues Associated with Targeted Economic Sanctions' (n 39 above), p 151; see on the difficulties of identifying individuals at the UN level: Dewulf and Pacquée (n 39 above), p 616 et seq.

[363] Fitzgerald, 'Managing "Smart Sanctions" against Terrorism Wisely' (n 357 above), p 976.

[364] Andrea Bianchi, 'Assessing the Effectiveness of the UN Security Council's Anti-terrorism Measures: The Quest for Legitimacy and Cohesion', *European Journal of International Law*, 17 (2007) pointing out the lack of political support.

[365] Meinhard Hilf and Saskia Hörmann, in Pierre-Marie Dupuy (ed), *Völkerrecht als Wertordnung: Festschrift für Christian Tomuschat: essays in honour of Christian Tomuschat* (NP Engel Verlag 2006).

By way of conclusion, the effectiveness of individual sanctions depends primarily on whether they contribute significantly to reducing the financial funds available to terrorists. Yet, this is extremely difficult to judge. From the available studies this contribution appears to be limited. Part of the effectiveness of individual sanctions depends on effective perception and implementation. The error rate and inefficiencies of the UN sanctions regime, as well as the considerable restrictions (or violations) of human rights might be easier to assess. Their impact on the effectiveness of individual sanctions should not be underestimated. Moreover, *even if* a measure is an effective means to attain a legitimate policy goal the respect for fundamental rights may impose limits on its use. Fundamental rights concerns will be the focus of the rest of this book.

Conclusions

Acts of terrorism gravely violate human rights. This is the common ground for global counter-terrorist measures.[366] However, terrorism has an additional dimension. It threatens the core values of societal existence.[367] This is the case, not only because it denies the existence of those values, such as human life and dignity, but also because it has triggered counter-terrorist policies that depart from these values. This book takes the traditional perspective on human rights violations that focuses on the exercise of public power. It is argued that finding a way to fight terrorism without negating the most basic values of our societies is the greatest challenge. This goes above and beyond balancing the rights of victims (and potential victims) of terrorism against the rights of those subject to counter-terrorist measures.

International terrorism is a problem that needs to be addressed, at the international as well as at the domestic level. This overall assessment, however, cannot replace the assessment of the proportionality of each counter-terrorist policy and its implementation at the different levels. Individual sanctions form part of a general counter-terrorist strategy. The following assessment of these particular measures does not allow for an overall judgment on the necessity to fight terrorism or the financing of

[366] Implementation of the UN Global Counterterrorism Strategy (n 1 above), p 3.

[367] Christian Tomuschat 'Internationale Terrorismusbekämpfung als Herausforderung für das Völkerrecht', Vortrag anlässlich der Eröffnung des Wintersemesters 2005/2006, Speyer, 15. November 2005, Speyer, Deutsche Hochschule für Verwaltungswissenschaften 2006, p 6.

terrorism. However, it allows for conclusions on the necessity to fight terrorism in compliance with human rights.

Individual sanctions are unique in how they concern individuals. It is true that there are a number of examples where international law directly impacts on the legal position of individuals.[368] However, individual sanctions are different in that they create a direct link between international legal instruments and ordinary private individuals, without involving a judge. Private individuals are listed as terrorist suspects both by the UN and by the EU in procedures that were previously only used to adopt measures of general application. These mechanisms do not provide for the necessary procedural rights. Further, the UN level does not provide any judicial remedy, while Union lists of terrorist suspects are subject to preliminary rulings only. In this way, UN Security Council resolutions and CFSP common positions have an unprecedented direct impact on the rights of individual persons.

Two types of European sanctions against individuals can be distinguished depending on whether the identification of those suspected to support terrorism takes place at the UN level or at the EU level. The main difference between sanctions giving effect to UN lists and those giving effect to European lists is that in the latter case the European institutions exercise discretion. They decide autonomously who is targeted by restrictive measures under European law.

Individual sanctions have raised many human rights concerns. These concerns continue to exist irrespective of the improvements that have been made in the adoption procedures both at the UN level and at the EU level, such as the delisting procedure and the possibility to apply for humanitarian exemptions. Apart from competence issues the most pressing concern is the lack of effective judicial protection at both levels. This will be the focus of the following six chapters.

[368] Cassese, *International Law* (n 238 above), p 234 et seq; Thomas Franck, 'Individuals and Groups of Individuals as Subjects in International Law', p 97 et seq and Stephan Hobe (1998), 'Individuals and Groups as Global Actors', both in: Rainer Hofmann and Nils Geissler (ed), *Non-State Actors as New Subjects of International Law* (Berlin: Duncker & Humblot, 1999), p 115 et seq; Anne-Marie Slaughter, 'Rogue Regimes and the Individualization of International Law', *New England Law Review*, 36 (2002), p 815, at 818; Theodor Meron, *The Humanization of International Law* (Leiden: Brill Publishers, 2006), p 353.

2

The Legal Basis of Community Sanctions: Moving Competences from One Pillar to Another?

Introduction

Since the introduction of Articles 301 and 60 EC in the Treaty of Maastricht, it is generally accepted that the European Community (EC; Community) is competent to adopt sanctions against states.[1] Sanctions against private individuals by contrast are not covered by a literal reading of Article 301 EC. Even after the courts of the European Union (EU courts) have repeatedly confirmed that the Community is competent to adopt individual sanctions,[2] this competence remains contentious in academic debate.[3] Moreover, the original reason why the Community started

[1] Torsten Stein, 'Außerpolitisch motivierte (Wirtschafts-)Sanktionen der Europäischen Union: Nach wie vor eine rechtliche Grauzone' in Ulrich Beyerlin, Michael Bothe, Rainer Hofmann and Ernst-Ulrich Petersmann (eds), *Recht zwischen Umbruch und Bewahrung. Festschrift für R Bernhardt* (Berlin: Springer 1995), p 1129 et seq; Kathrin Osteneck, *Die Umsetzung von UN-Wirtschaftssanktionen durch die Europäische Gemeinschaft* (Berlin: Springer-Verlag, 2004).

[2] Cases C-402/05 P and C-415/05 P, *Kadi and al Barakaat*, judgment of 3 September 2008, not yet reported, para 121 et seq; Case T-306/01, *Ahmed Ali Yusuf and al Barakaat International Foundation v Council and Commission* [2005] ECR II-3533, para 107 et seq; Case T-315/01, *Yassin Abdullah Kadi v Council and Commission* [2005] ECR II-3649, para 87 et seq.

[3] See eg: Sandra Bartelt and Helge Elisabeth Zeitler, 'Intelligente Sanktionen' zur Terrorismusbekämpfung in der EU', *Europäische Zeitschrift für Wirtschaftsrecht* (2003), p 715; Martin Nettesheim, 'UN Sanctions Against Individuals: A Challenge to the Architecture of European Union Governance', *Common Market Law Review*, 44 (2007), p 567 et seq; Takis Tridimas and Gutierrez-Fons, 'EU Law, International Law and Economic Sanctions Against Terrorism: The Judiciary in Distress?', *Fordham International Law Journal* (2009); Gráinne de Búrca, 'The European Court of Justice and the International Legal Order after Kadi Europe's Judicial

adopting sanctions against states, namely because they are intrinsically related to external trade, for which the Community has exclusive competence, does not appear to apply to individual sanctions.

The present chapter analyses the competences of the Community and the European Union (EU) to adopt sanctions against individuals. It will be argued that, *de lege lata*, neither the EU nor the Community have the competence to adopt sanctions against private individuals. If, however, such measures were to be adopted within the EU certain parts of the procedure, such as identifying those that will be targeted with sanctions, would have to take place under the first pillar (Community law). Section One focuses on the competences of the *Community* to adopt individual sanctions. It pays particular attention to the rulings of the Court of First Instance (CFI) in the cases of *Yusuf* and *Kadi*[4] and of the European Court of Justice (ECJ) in the appeal decision in *Kadi and al Barakaat*.[5] Both courts, as well as Advocate-General Maduro, ruled that the Community is competent to adopt restrictive measures against individuals. Yet, all three offered very different legal constructions for that competence. In particular, the CFI and the ECJ departed in different ways from the existing case-law and redefined the relationship between the pillars. First, the sanctioning practice of the European institutions is outlined. Secondly, it is argued that Articles 301 and 60 EC do not cover sanctions against

Resolution and the UN Security Council', *Jean Monnet Working Paper January 2009*; very critical: Amadine Garde, 'Is it Really for the European Community to Implement Anti-Terrorism UN Security Council Resolutions?', *Cambridge Law Journal*, 65/2 (2006), p 281 et seq; Christina Eckes, 'Judicial Review of European Anti-Terrorism Measures: The Yusuf and Kadi Judgments of the Court of First Instance', *European Law Journal* (2008) forthcoming; Torbjöm Andersson, Iain Cameron and Kenneth Nordback, 'EU Listing: The Renaissance of Imperial Power, but on a Global Scale', *European Business Law Review* (2003), pp 120–2 (they concede that the wording of Art 301 EC appears to exclude the adoption of individual sanctions, but give a number of substantive reasons which could support a dynamic interpretation); Christian Tietje and Sandy Hamelmann, 'Gezielte Finanzsanktionen der Vereinten Nationen im Spannungsverhältnis zum Gemeinschaftsrecht und zu Menschenrechten', *JuS* (2006), p 299; on the contrary, arguing that the recourse to Articles 301, 60 and 308 EC is entirely persuasive: Christian Tomuschat, 'Case law: Case T-306/01, *Ahmed Ali Yusuf and Al Barakaat International Foundation v Council and Commission*, judgment of the Court of First Instance of 21 September 2005; Case T-315/01, *Yassin Abdullah Kadi v Council and Commission*, judgment of the Court of First Instance of 21 September 2005, nyr', *Common Market Law Review*, 43 (2006), p 540; Markus Kotzur, 'Eine Bewährungsprobe für die Europäische Grundrechtsgemeinschaft: Zur Entscheidung des EuG in der Rs Yusuf ua gegen Rat', *Europäische Grundrechte Zeitschrift*, 33 (2006), p 21; Nikolaos Lavranos, 'UN Sanctions and Judicial Review', *Nordic Journal of International Law*, 76 (2007) p 12; Panos Koutrakos, *EU International Relation Law* (Oxford: Hart Publishing, 2005), p 196.

[4] Case T-306/01, *Yusuf* and Case T-315/01, *Kadi* (both n 2 above).

[5] Cases C-402/05 P and C-415/05 P, *Kadi and al Barakaat* (n 2 above).

individuals. They provide neither a full nor a partial legal basis and cannot be applied by analogy to individual sanctions either. Thirdly, Articles 301, 60, and 308 EC are examined as to whether they could jointly serve as a legal basis for the adoption of individual sanctions. This is equally rejected. It is concluded that the Community lacks *de lege lata* the competence to adopt individual sanctions.

Section 2 focuses on the two Union pillars (Common Foreign and Security Policy (CFSP) and Police and Judicial Cooperation in Criminal Matters (PJCC)). It is difficult to attribute the legal instruments used in the adoption of individual sanctions to one of the two Union pillars. Article 301 EC sets out a two-tier procedure that first requires a CFSP instrument authorizing the Council to then adopt Community sanctions. Hence, in practice the Council draws up lists of terrorist suspects in CFSP common positions who are then targeted by Community sanctions. Some of the common positions are adopted in the second pillar only and some are based on a dual legal basis, namely Article 15 (CFSP, second pillar) and Article 34 TEU (PJCC, third pillar). Additionally, in the case of *Segi* the CFI found the applicants who were listed in a common position based on Articles 15 and 34 TEU to be affected by the third pillar part of that measure only.[6] Allocation is even more difficult, because *substantially* it could be argued that individual sanctions are rather a matter of PJCC than of foreign policy. However, it is submitted that neither of the Union pillars provides safeguards strong enough to adopt measures as intrusive as listing individual persons as terrorists. Such lists could legitimately only be adopted in a legal environment that offers the protection required by the rule of law. At the moment this is the case only in the Community pillar, notwithstanding the argument made in Chapter 6 that the EU courts have the mandate to review Union lists of terrorist suspects.

Section 3 analyses how the current way of adopting individual sanctions threatens the competence distribution between the three pillars of the EU (horizontal division), while Section 4 looks into the power balance between the EU and its Member States (vertical division).[7] It is argued that

[6] Case T-338/02, *Segi and others* [2004] ECR II-01647, para 33.

[7] See the distinction at: Case C-301/06, *Ireland v Parliament and Council (Data Retention Directive)*, judgment of 10 February 2009, not yet reported, para 56:

> ...the question of the areas of competence of the European Union presents itself differently depending on whether the competence in issue has already been accorded to the European Union in the broad sense or has not yet been accorded to it. In the first hypothesis, it is a question of ruling on the division of areas of competence within the Union and, more

the adoption of individual sanctions without an appropriate legal basis and in violation of fundamental rights might lead national constitutional courts to challenge the supremacy of European law.

Section 5 addresses the changes under the Lisbon Treaty and discusses to what extent the existing problems are resolved by the new provisions. The discussion is based on the assumption that if individual sanctions should be adopted in the EU at all it would be desirable to create a Community competence subject to clearly defined rules, according to which both the actual asset freezes and the listings are subject to judicial control. Finally, a conclusion picks up the main arguments and closes the discussion.

1. The Legal Basis of Community Measures

1.1 Listing Practice under the European Treaties

At present, Community sanctions against individuals are adopted as regulations on the joint basis of Articles 301, 60, and 308 EC.[8] The adoption procedure is determined by Article 301 EC. It requires the adoption of a common position (or a joint action) in the second pillar (CFSP) enabling the Community to adopt a measure–in practice always a regulation–containing the actual operative measures. Only the latter (first pillar) instrument was contested in *Yusuf* and *Kadi* (CFI) and *Kadi* and *al Barakaat* (ECJ) respectively. The choice of Articles 301, 60, and 308 EC as a joint legal basis for Community sanctions against individuals was expressly and repeatedly confirmed by both courts.[9] Here however, it is submitted that neither the chosen provisions nor any other provision of the EC Treaty confer upon the Community the powers to adopt sanctions against individuals in their current form.[10]

particularly, on whether it is appropriate to proceed by way of a directive based on the EC Treaty or by way of a framework decision based on the EU Treaty. By contrast, in the second hypothesis, it is a question of ruling on the division of areas of competence between the Union and the Member States and, more particularly, on whether the Union has encroached on the latters' areas of competence....

[8] Since EC Council Regulation 881/2002, of 27 May 2002, [2002] OJ L 139/9.

[9] Case T-306/01, *Yusuf* (n 2 above), para 170; Case T-315/01, *Kadi* (n 2 above), para 135; Case T-253/02, *Chafiq Ayadi v Council* [2006] ECR II-2139, paras 87–90; Cases C-402/05 P and C-415/05 P, *Kadi and al Barakaat* (n 2 above), para 158 et seq.

[10] For post-Lisbon see Section 5 below.

Originally, sanctions against individuals were adopted on the basis of Articles 301 and 60 EC only.[11] The addition of Article 308 EC started with Regulations 2580/2001[12] and 881/2002.[13] The change in the choice of the legal basis could be interpreted as an acknowledgement of the Council, possibly as a reaction to the criticism in the literature, that Articles 301 and 60 EC do not suffice.[14] Article 301 EC confers on the Council the power to take the necessary urgent measures where action by the Community to interrupt or reduce economic relations with third countries is provided for in a common position or in a joint action adopted according to the Treaty on European Union (TEU). From the beginning, Article 301 EC was used both to adopt regulations giving effect to the UN sanctions regimes and to adopt autonomous European sanctions.[15] Introduced by the Treaty of Maastricht, Article 301 EC codified the existing practice of first coordinating economic sanctions within the European Political Co-Operation (EPC)[16] and then adopting them on the basis of Article 133 EC (ex-Article 113). For economic sanctions against states Article 301 EC is now *lex specialis* to Article 133 EC. Article 60 EC by contrast is *lex specialis* to Article 301 EC for measures relating to financial transactions. It refers to the procedure in Article 301 EC and has never been used alone.[17] Article 308 EC is designed to fill the gap where no specific provision of the EC Treaty confers on the Community institutions express or implied powers to act, if such powers appear nonetheless to be necessary to enable the Community to carry out its functions with a view to attaining one of the objectives laid down by that Treaty.[18]

1.2 Articles 301 and 60 EC as the Legal Basis for Individual Sanctions

Articles 301 and 60 EC cannot be stretched to provide a legal basis for restrictive measures against individuals. The clear wording of a provision

[11] EC Regulations 337/2000, of 14 February 2000, OJ 2000 L 43/1; 467/2001, of 6 March 2001, OJ 2001 L 67/1.

[12] Governing the autonomous European sanctions regime; EC Council Regulation 2580/2001, OJ 2002, L 116/33.

[13] Governing the European sanctions regime giving effect to UN terrorist lists (n 12 above).

[14] Andersson, Cameron and Nordback, 'EU Listing: The Renaissance of Imperial Power, but on a Global Scale' (n 3 above), p 122.

[15] See for an overview of the early sanctioning practice of the EU: Margaret P Doxey, *International Sanctions in Contemporary Perspective* (London: Macmillan, 1996), pp 36–46.

[16] Prior to the TEU the EPC was organized on the basis of Title III of the SEA.

[17] Monika Gudrun Zagel, 'Article 301 TEC (Economic Sanctions)' in Hans Smit and Peter E Herzog, '*Law of the European Union – a Commentary*' (New York: LexisNexis, 2006), § 402.05.

[18] Opinion 2/94, ECHR [1996] ECR I-1759, paras 29–30.

must constitute the ultimate limit of interpretation,[19] and Article 301 EC speaks a clear language that does not encompass individual sanctions. Neither a literal nor a teleological interpretation can extend 'third countries' to cover private individuals, including EU citizens and including persons who participate to a very limited extent in economic life – regardless of their place of residence.[20]

The wording of Article 301 EC was also the main reason for all parties,[21] the CFI,[22] and the ECJ[23] to agree that Articles 301 and 60 EC did not constitute a sufficient legal basis for sanctions targeting those associated with Al-Qaida. Only Advocate-General Maduro argued that Articles 301 and 60 EC suffice as a legal basis for restrictive measures against private individuals.[24] He suggested a wide and dynamic interpretation of Articles 301 and 60 EC that reflects the 'economic realities' of our times, in which trade with third countries is in fact a multitude of economic exchanges between individuals.[25] Both the CFI[26] and the ECJ[27] found Articles 301 and 60 EC – even though they do not suffice on their own – do not exclude the adoption of sanctions against individuals either.

Beyond the obvious textual difficulties resulting from the reference to 'third countries', there are also substantive reasons why even a dynamic

[19] Vlad Constantinesco, 'The ECJ as a Law-maker: Praetor Aut Contra Legem?' in David O'Keeffe and Antonio Bavasso, *Judicial Review in European Union Law: Liber Amicorum in Honour of Lord Slynn of Hadley* (The Hague: Kluwer Law International, 2000), Vol I, p 78. However, European law poses specific difficulties, because all different language versions are equally authentic (Art 53 TEU, Art 314 EC), but not necessarily identical in their meaning; the Court has in the past disregarded some of the Community languages when interpreting the law, see for instance: Case 150/80, *Elefanten Schuh GmbH v Jacqmain* [1981] ECR 1671 and also: Case 283/81, *CILFIT* [1982] ECR 3415.

[20] See the examples of Mr Yusuf, a Swedish national in Case T-306/01, *Yusuf* (n 2 above).

[21] Including the Council and the Commission.

[22] The CFI based its reasoning why Art 301 EC could *not* justify the adoption of the contested regulation on the wording, which refers to 'economic relations with [...] *third countries*' (Case T-315/01, *Kadi* (n 2 above), para 95).

[23] Cases C-402/05 P and C-415/05 P, *Kadi and al Barakaat* (n 2 above), para 168.

[24] This is also the position of: Tridimas and Gutierrez-Fons, *EU Law, International Law and Economic Sanctions Against Terrorism: The Judiciary in Distress?* (n 3 above); see also the Commission's submission, at: Cases C-402/05 P and C-415/05 P, *Kadi and al Barakaat* (n 2 above), para 135 et seq.

[25] AG Maduro argued that the contested measures 'are targeted *predominantly* at individuals and groups within third countries' (AG Maduro in Case C-402/05 P, *Kadi v Council and Commission*, 16 January 2008, para 13 emphasis added).

[26] Case T-315/01, *Kadi* (n 2 above), paras 90–1 and 121 et seq.

[27] Cases C-402/05 P and C-415/05 P, *Kadi and al Barakaat* (n 2 above), paras 166–7.

interpretation[28] or a legal analogy cannot justify an adoption of individual sanctions based on Articles 301 and 60 EC, either alone or in part. Legal analogy is a common way of constructing the law, including public law.[29] It extends a norm to fill a gap in the regulation system where the existing law is silent as to how a factual situation should be dealt with.[30] Yet, legal analogy has its literal as well as normative limits.[31]

Dynamic interpretation and analogy must be used restrictively in a system based on the principle of conferred powers, such as Community law. Article 5(1) EC stipulates that the Community has competence only within the limited areas in which it has been given powers. As a consequence, when identifying the necessary gap it has to be taken into account that European law differs in its nature from national law precisely in that it does *not* purport to be a complete system of regulation. The Community legal order is not 'self-authenticating':[32] new powers cannot be generated within the Community order itself. On the contrary, the European Treaties deliberately leave certain areas to national law. Furthermore, the principle of subsidiarity[33] contains a general presumption that competence should be exercised at the lowest adequate level. As a consequence, the creation of Community powers by means of legal analogy is possible only where it complies with these principles, namely where a gap can be identified in an interpretation of European law that respects the distribution of competences between the Member States and the Community. The European Treaties, while setting out a Community competence for state sanctions, do not speak of individual sanctions. This is explicable by the fact that in 1992 when Article 301 EC was introduced the UN had not yet adopted international sanctions against private persons. Thus, the Treaties' silence can be assumed to be an unintentional gap in the regulation system and not a conscious choice to leave the competence for individual sanctions to the

[28] The Court applies a dynamic interpretation to European law; good examples are: Case 283/81 *CILFIT* and Case 59 /85, *Reed*.

[29] Katja Hemke, *Methodik der Analogiebildung im öffentlichen Recht* (Berlin: Duncker & Humblot, 2006).

[30] Wolfgang Fikentscher, *Methoden des Rechts in vergleichender Darstellung* (Tübingen: Mohr, 1977), Chapter 32, in particular pp 283–312; see also: Stig Strömholm, *Rätt, rättskällor och rättstillämpning* (Stockholm: Norstedts Juridik, 1996), p 459.

[31] Fikentscher, *Methoden des Rechts in vergleichender Darstellung* (n 30 above), Chapter 32, in particular p 288 et seq.

[32] Anthony Arnull (et al), *The European Union and its Court of Justice* (Oxford: Oxford University Press, 2006), p 85.

[33] Article 5(2) EC and the Protocol on the application of the principles of subsidiarity and proportionality annexed to the Treaty of Amsterdam.

Member States. This first requirement for constructing an analogy is hence satisfied.

The boundaries imposed by the normative sense of the existing law are what distinguish an analogy from creating new law;[34] and the *normative sense* of Article 301 EC imposes an obstacle extending it to individual sanctions. An analogy is only possible if it can be assumed that the legislator would have regulated the situation in question in the same manner as the situation regulated by law, ie if the provision's aims cover the situation at hand.[35] Because of the fundamental differences between state sanctions and individuals sanctions, in particular with regard to the identification procedure, the necessary procedural safeguards, and the consequences of the sanctions both for the sanctioning state and the target, this assumption would be difficult to defend for individual sanctions. The same is true for implied powers in the narrow sense.

Article 301 EC was introduced to allow the Community to adopt measures of external trade in order to enforce foreign policy decisions. Article 301 EC has hence a political and an economic dimension. Freezing the financial assets of private individuals because of their alleged involvement in terrorism has an obvious political dimension. However, there are great differences in the politics involved in state sanctions and in individual sanctions. Multilateral state sanctions must strike a balance between the interests of the states adopting them. On the one hand, state sanctions have the intended effects on the *targeted* state but on the other, there are great unintended effects on the economy and political relations of the *targeting* state, as well as the population of the targeted state. Sanctions against terrorists are a shared strategic interest of all states. They do not raise the same foreign policy concerns. And, above all, they increase the powers of the executives over their subjects.[36] As a consequence, an inter-governmental decision is easier reached to target an alleged terrorist than to target a third country.[37]

[34] ibid, p 301.

[35] Hemke, *Methodik der Analogiebildung im öffentlichen Recht* (n 29 above), p 29.

[36] Concluding that this is the reason why despite all human rights concerns the listing procedure has been changed so little since its introduction: Spiegel (Spiegel-Verlag, Hamburg), issue No 14/2006, p 43.

[37] With regard to foreign policy in a broad sense it has been argued that 'there is no European Union' (Sara Dillon, 'Looking for the Progressive Empire: Where is the European Union Foreign Policy?', *Connecticut Journal of International Law*, 19 (2003), p 280) and the European

Moreover, reliance on Article 301 EC cannot be justified by the fact that the majority of both state sanctions and individual sanctions intend to implement UN Security Council resolutions. It is true that Article 301 EC is predominantly used to implement sanctions adopted under the auspices of the UN. However, it does not speak of the UN and does not blindly entitle the Community to adopt all measures necessary to render UN Security Council resolutions effective, irrespective of their content. Community sanctions adopted pursuant to Article 301 EC are based on a CFSP decision and one objective of the CFSP is 'to preserve peace and strengthen international security' (Article 11 TEU). However, the fact that Article 301 EC requires a CFSP decision is not a general incorporation of all CFSP objectives. On the contrary, the location of Article 301 EC in the Treaty Establishing the European Community separates it from the CFSP. The EC Treaty refers (apart from the Preamble) only in Article 297 EC to Chapter VII activities of the Security Council. Article 297 EC stipulates that Member States shall consult each other when taking *unilateral* action 'in order to carry out obligations [they have] accepted for the purpose of maintaining peace and international security'. Thus, Article 301 EC cannot be said to confer on the Community the competence to adopt 'all measures' required by UN Security Council resolutions,[38] neither in isolation nor when read in the wider context of the other provisions of the EC Treaty. Any other interpretation would allow the Security Council to directly determine the competences of the Community.[39]

UN sanctions against individuals without any link to a territory or state were adopted as part of the wider sanctions regime that first targeted the Taliban who at the time controlled the Afghan territory. The Taliban then lost this control and the sanctions were extended – as part of the broader

Union's failures to act in a unified manner in the face of various foreign policy crises in the 1990s have been extensively discussed (Sergio Baches Opi and Ryan Floyd, 'A shaky Pillar of Global Stability: The Evolution of the European Union's Common Foreign and Security Policy', *Columbian Journal of European Law*, 9 (2003), p 300). By contrast, changing the list of individuals threatened under a specific resolution passes usually painless. The individual name is not even discussed.

[38] The Commission argued that: 'the fact that similar words are used in Article 41 of the Charter of the United Nations and in Article 301 EC shows that the authors of that latter provision clearly intended to provide a platform for the implementation by the Community of all measures adopted by the Security Council that call for action by the Community' (Cases C-402/05 P and C-415/05 P, *Kadi and al Barakaat* (n 2 above), para 136).

[39] Andersson, Cameron and Nordback, 'EU Listing: The Renaissance of Imperial Power, but on a Global Scale' (n 3 above), p 121.

international counter-terrorism strategy – to target every person and entity associated with Al-Qaida. Since Al-Qaida, however, is a 'franchise network' based on a shared ideology rather than structural connections that would be capable of proof, the nature of the sanctions regime as a whole changed fundamentally. The CFI argued that so long as the Taliban were still in control of the Afghan territory, the territorial link was still sufficiently strong to consider sanctions against them as sanctions against 'third countries'.[40] This opened the door to adopting individual sanctions in the Community pillar. The CFI then explained that Article 308 EC was added to reflect 'the developments of the international situation' after 'the collapse of the Taliban regime'.[41]

The distinction between targeting third country regimes and targeting private individuals as such is convincing. For the Taliban sanctions this would mean that even though the sanctions against the Taliban regime could at the outset be adopted on the basis of Article 301 EC, this is now no longer the case even if some of the persons and entities on the lists remained the same. This change might prima facie appear to be arbitrary. However, there are many good reasons why private individuals should have more judicial safeguards at their disposal than states or their leaders.[42] Hence as a matter of principle there is a distinction to be made between states and individuals, even if in certain grey areas this distinction is less intuitive and requires careful consideration, ie where sanctions target not only those holding official positions in a regime of a third country but also their supporters and families, or for the exceptional case of Taliban leaders who lost control of the Afghan territory after they were listed.

Along the same lines it might be arguable that sanctions against government officials and those officially cooperating with them still fall within the external politics dimension of Article 301 EC. It might be persuasive that the link between private individuals and a political regime can be so strong that the distinction between an official and a private person is only a formality. However, this argument finds less and less support the more remote the cooperation is. It is definitely no longer tenable where private persons in other countries, including EU Member States, are targeted who have allegedly given financial support to groups, which do not have a connection to a specific regime themselves.

[40] ibid, para 90: these sanctions constituted 'genuine sanctions on the targeted regime and those in charge of it'.

[41] Case T-315/01, *Kadi* (n 2 above), para 87–97.

[42] See for the difference between state sanctions and individual sanctions below, but also Chapter 1, Section 1.

The trade dimension of Article 301 EC does not apply to individual sanctions either. Article 301 EC was introduced to allow the Community to take a uniform approach to trade with certain third states. One of its objectives was to avoid distortion of competition and disturbances of the common market through national differences in the implementation of trade embargoes. This could still justify a common approach to groups of individuals categorized based on their participation in the market. However, the Common Commercial Policy is not influenced by targeted sanctions against a few hundred individuals due to their alleged political beliefs rather than (the extent of) their economic activity.[43] Intrinsically political decisions without evident impact on trade, such as visa and entry restrictions, have been implemented by the Member States all along.[44]

Additionally, state sanctions and individual sanctions differ with regard to their impact on human rights. State sanctions can have devastating effects on the human rights of the entire population of the targeted state.[45] Individual sanctions, by contrast, directly affect singularized private individuals with far-reaching fundamental rights restrictions. They are adopted in legislative instruments that have a direct impact on the well-being of those targeted who therefore have rights both under the European Convention on Human Rights (ECHR)[46] and under the general principles of European law.[47] The use of mechanisms drawn up to impose trade embargoes made it possible to target individuals without offering any of the necessary procedural safeguards. This in itself illustrates that these mechanisms are not intended, and indeed ill-suited, to adopt sanctions against individuals. Since the ECJ's ruling in *Kadi* and *al Barakaat* judicial protection is offered at the European level, but the discrepancy between the effects that international law has on individuals' rights and their possibilities of defence has raised many questions that continue to deserve attention. After all, the applicants were placed in a *Kafkaesque* situation for

[43] Different: Cases C-402/05 P and C-415/05 P, *Kadi and al Barakaat* (n 2 above), para 229 et seq, see below for a further discussion.

[44] Zagel, 'Article 301 TEC (Economic Sanctions)' (n 17 above), § 402.02.

[45] See Chapter 1, Section 1 with further references.

[46] Above all fair trial rights, see Chapter 3 and for an overview of the ECtHR's case-law on Art 6: Clare Ovey and Robin CA White, *Jacobs and White: The European Convention on Human Rights* (Oxford: Oxford University Press, 2002).

[47] Article 6 ECHR forms part of the general principles of EU law; see in particular the ECJ's early case-law on access to justice: Case 222/84, *Johnston* [1986] ECR 1651, para 18 and Case 222/86, *UNECTEF v Heylens and Others* [1987] ECR 4097, para 11.

the past seven years and despite the ECJ's ruling in their favour the sanctions remain in place for the time being. [48]

Finally, the rule of law prohibits an analogous application of provisions where this would result in a burden for the individual. This is undisputed with regard to penal sanctions, but covers arguably also administrative measures where they amount to a similar burden. The exclusion of analogies to the detriment of the individual and the understanding of fundamental rights as being universal are also the reason why a suggested distinction between EU citizens and non-EU citizens[49] is untenable. True, sanctions against EU citizens appear even more remote to the term 'third countries' than sanctions against non-EU citizens, but Article 301 EC cannot be 'stretched' to cover the latter either. The adoption of individual sanctions pursuant to the procedure in Article 301 EC is alien to the value choices of the European legal system. The European legal system considers individuals as legal subjects with their own rights that pertain to them on the one hand by virtue of their status as human beings[50] and on the other as citizens of the EU.[51] Under European law individuals are protagonists in their own right; they are not objects at the will of the state, as was traditionally the case under international law. Adopting sanctions against individuals based on a mechanism tailored to target political entities, which does not give them any right of participation, degrades them from rights holders to objects. In the decision-making procedure the rights of individuals are not taken into account; on the contrary, they are reduced to a factor in the equation of what is politically desirable in the fight against terrorism.

[48] Commission Regulation (EC) No 1190/2008 of 6 November 2008, L 229/23 (8.11.2008) and Commission Regulation (EC) No 1190/2008 of 28 November, L 322/25 (2.12.2008); see also Chapter Five, Section Five and Chapter Seven, Section Two.

[49] The applicants in Case T-306/01, *Yusuf* (n 2 above), para 84; see also: Iain Cameron, 'European Union Anti-Terrorist Blacklisting', *Human Rights Law Review*, 4 (2004), p.233.

[50] See Chapter Three, Section 1 and 2 for the EU's commitment to human rights.

[51] See the fast developing body of case-law on EU citizenship as an example of the rights holders approach of the ECJ: C-274/96, *Bickel and Franz* [1998] ECR I-7637; C-378/97, *Wijsenbeek* [1999] ECR I-6207; C-85/96, *Martinez Sala* [1998] ECR I-2691; C-184/99, *Rudy Grzelczyk* [2001] ECR I-6193; C-224/98, *d'Hoop* [2002] I-6191; C-413/99, *Baumbast* [2002] ECR I-7091; C-138/02, *Collins* [2004] I-2703; C-456/02, *Trojani* [2004] ECR I-7573; C-200/02, *Kunqian Catherine Zhu Chen* [2004] ECR I-9925; C-209/03, *Dany Bidar* [2005] ECR I-2119; but also Directive 2004/38/EC (OJ 2004 L 158/77–123); see further for the exalted role of the individual in regional and local democracies in Europe: John P Loughlin and Eliseo Aja (eds), *Subnational Democracy in the European Union: Challenges and Opportunities* (Oxford: Oxford University Press, 2001).

In conclusion, Articles 301 and 60 EC do not enable the Community to legally adopt sanctions against individuals, either directly or in an analogous application. In *Yusuf* and *Kadi* the CFI pointed out that the change from sanctions against government officials to private persons[52] cut the last possible link to the wording of Article 301 EC, while at the same time failing to acknowledge that the Community–at least in the current state of the law–is not competent to adopt such sanctions.[53] Unfortunately, the ECJ confirmed the CFI's finding of competence on appeal, albeit based on a different construction.

1.3 Articles 301, 60, and 308 EC as a Joint Legal Basis: the Healing Power of Article 308 EC

Articles 301 and 60 EC do not constitute a legal basis for individual sanctions. Recourse to Article 308 EC has the advantage that individual sanctions are not entirely adopted behind closed doors: the European Parliament is at least consulted. Article 308 EC also requires a unanimous decision by the Council. Yet, the question remains whether it can heal the shortcomings of Articles 301 and 60 EC as a legal basis for adopting individual sanctions.[54]

The use of the joint legal basis of Articles 301, 60, and 308 EC results in a peculiar combination of the Community's sweeping residual competence under Article 308 EC and the highly exceptional connection between the powers of the Community and the Union pillars in Article 301 EC. The use of Article 308 EC as part of a joint legal basis in order to complement powers conferred on the Community by other provisions is not new.[55] And even though such past practice of the institutions is of course not as such determinative of its validity[56] it is useful to point at the *differences* between the past practices and the construction of a joint legal basis for individual sanctions. Needless to say that rejecting Articles 301, 60, and 308 EC as a

[52] A change which occurred almost unnoticed, see: Nicola Vennemann, 'Country Report on the EU' in Christian Walter, Silja Vöneky, Volker Röben and F Schorkopf (eds), *Terrorism as a challenge for national and international law: security versus liberty?* Beiträge zum ausländischen öffentlichen Recht und Völkerrecht, vol 169 (Berlin: Springer, 2004), p 28.

[53] Case T-306/01, *Yusuf* (n 2 above), para 130 et seq.

[54] See n 3 above for the different opinions in the literature.

[55] See eg: Case 242/87, *Commission v Council (Erasmus)* [1989] ECR I-1425.

[56] Case T-315/01, *Kadi* (n 2 above), para 115, with reference to Case 114/88, *Delbar* [1989] ECR 4067, para 72.

legal basis for individual sanctions does not have implications for the combined use of several provisions of the EC Treaty in general.

1.3.1 Articles 301 and 60 EC as a Partial Legal Basis

First, in the past the Treaty provisions used in combination with Article 308 EC have always provided a *partial* (albeit not sufficient) legal basis for the instruments in question. One of the examples given in *Kadi* was Council Regulation (EEC) 3599/85, establishing generalized tariff preferences. It was adopted on the basis of ex-Articles 235[57] and 113[58] EC. Article 235 was added because the instrument in question had, besides commercial policy aims, which were covered by Article 113 EC, development policy aims.[59] However, there is not and was never any doubt that Article 113 EC constituted at least a *partial* legal basis for the regulation in question (as opposed to individual sanctions for which Articles 301 and 60 EC do not even provide partial competence). Later the ECJ even ruled that Article 113 EC was sufficient on its own.[60] Another example mentioned in *Kadi* was EC Council Regulation 1035/97 establishing a European Monitoring Centre on Racism and Xenophobia; it was adopted on the basis of Articles 213[61] and 235[62] EC. Here, Article 235 EC was needed as an additional basis because, while Article 213 EC permitted the Commission to collect data, only the addition of Article 235 EC could cover the establishment of an autonomous body for this purpose.[63]

The use of Article 308 EC in combination with other provisions of the EC Treaty may be justified where the other provisions are not alone sufficient to adopt the measure in question, but where they partially cover the subject matter.[64] The adoption of individual sanctions on the basis of Articles 301, 60, and 308 EC is very different from the described practice.

[57] Now Art 308 EC.

[58] Now Art 133 EC.

[59] Case 45/86, *Commission v Council* [1987] ECR 1493, para 10.

[60] ibid, paras 13–21.

[61] Now Art 284 EC.

[62] Now Art 308 EC.

[63] See in that regard the 26th recital:

> Whereas the powers provided for in Article 213 of the Treaty to collect and analyze information on several of the Community's areas of activity do not permit such information to be collected through a specialized, autonomous body with its own legal personality; whereas Article 235 must therefore also be used as the legal basis for the establishment of such a body and to enable the information to be transmitted to Community institutions and bodies and to the Member States.

[64] This was the case mentioned by the Council in Case T-306/01, *Yusuf* (n 2 above), para 97.

Articles 301 and 60 EC are concerned with sanctions against third countries. They are inadequate to support *any part* of the restrictive measures adopted against individuals. The latter are of a distinctive nature and belong to a different category of measures than state sanctions. They do not only include an aspect additional to the subject matter for which the Community was authorized to take action in Article 301 EC but are inherently different.[65] This does not as such exclude the use of Article 308 EC alone; yet, the use of Article 308 EC as a single legal basis will be rejected below for other reasons.

1.3.2 Article 301 EC as a Bridge to the TEU

Secondly, all practice of using Article 308 EC as a joint legal basis[66] has so far been *limited to the first pillar*, while the addition of Article 308 EC in the present scenario results in a considerable extension of the highly exceptional procedure in which the Community necessitates a CFSP decision to take action. The CFI conferred on Article 301 EC the function of a 'bridge' to the TEU. It concluded in *Kadi*[67] that Articles 301 and 60 EC are:

> wholly special provisions of the EC Treaty, in that they expressly contemplate action by the Community [...] in order to achieve [...] one of the objectives specifically assigned to the Union by Article 2 TEU, namely, the implementation of a common foreign and security policy.

It is true that Article 301 EC has the specific task of enabling the Community to take action following a CFSP decision.[68] However, because this linkage is an exception to the general division of the pillars, as apparent in Article 47 TEU,[69] it must be construed narrowly and cannot be extended to allow for any measure outside of the scope of the wording of Article 301 EC.[70] This article confers on the Community the delimited power to implement CFSP common positions or joint actions concerning economic

[65] See Section 1.2 above.

[66] The ECJ had not yet resolved the question of whether a joint legal basis is admissible and institutional practice alone cannot change the rules of the Treaty (Case T-315/01, *Kadi* (n 2 above), para 115); as was claimed to have been the case in Case 114/88, *Delbar* (n 56 above).

[67] Case T-315/01, *Kadi* (n 2 above), para 124.

[68] Case T-306/01, *Yusuf* (n 2 above), para 161; Case T-315/01, *Kadi* (n 2 above), para 124 et seq.

[69] See also: Case C-176/03, *Commission v Council (Environmental Crime case)* [2005] ECR I-787; Case C-440/05, *Commission v Council (Ship Source Pollution)* [2007] ECR I-9097; Case C-91/05, *Commission v Council (ECOWAS)* [2008] ECR I-3651.

[70] The exceptional character of a norm can exclude analogies (Hemke, *Methodik der Analogiebildung im öffentlichen Recht* (n 29 above), p 36).

relations with third countries; it is not a power to implement *any* CFSP decision and even less a general power to take action to achieve the Union objectives. The combined use of Articles 301, 60, and 308 EC as it was advocated by the CFI blurs the distinction between action by the Community and action by the Union and levels the way for a general use of first pillar instruments for Union purposes.[71] The ECJ correctly rejected the CFI's construction in its appeal decision in *Kadi* and *al Barakaat* holding that the link between the Community pillar and the Union pillars is strictly limited to Articles 301 and 60 EC and cannot be extended to other provisions of the EC Treaty, including Article 308 EC.[72] The CFI's construction would allow what the ECJ has always – at least in argument – carefully rejected: the extension of Community powers beyond the EC Treaty. Neither sanctions against individuals, nor the fight against terrorism, nor international peace and security fall within the primary objectives of the EC Treaty.[73] The Common Commercial Policy and the common market have been identified as other EC objectives that could require the adoption of individual sanctions.[74] Yet, individual sanctions do not have an impact on the functioning of the common market that is sufficiently significant to require adoption by the Community.[75] Union objectives by contrast, although taken into account by the Community when acting in the sphere of its own competence, cannot create a new competence.[76]

1.3.3 Article 308 EC in Opinion 2/94

Community competences have been gradually extended with recourse to 'the textual ambiguity and institutional connivance' of Article 308 EC.[77] Yet, the use of Article 308 EC is not unlimited. In *Opinion 2/94*, the leading authority on the scope of Article 308 EC[78] the ECJ held explicitly that Article 308 EC 'cannot serve as a basis for widening the scope of

[71] Eckes, 'Judicial Review of European Anti-Terrorism Measures: The Yusuf and Kadi Judgments of the Court of First Instance' (n 3 above), p 79 et seq.

[72] Cases C-402/05 P and C-415/05 P, *Kadi and al Barakaat* (n 2 above), para 197.

[73] Articles 2 and 3 EC; this was conceded by the CFI in Case T-306/01, *Yusuf* (n 2 above), para 139.

[74] See eg the Commission's argument at: Case T-315/01, *Kadi* (n 2 above), para 74.

[75] See the CFI's findings at: Case T-315/01, *Kadi* (n 2 above), para 111 confirmed by the ECJ, Cases C-402/05 P and C-415/05 P, *Kadi and al Barakaat* (n 2 above), paras 180–1 (the ECJ acknowledged a link to the common market, para 229 et seq), but also text accompanying n 44–5 above.

[76] Case T-306/01, *Yusuf* (n 2 above), paras 153–6.

[77] Arnull (et al), *The European Union and its Court of Justice* (n 32 above), p 89; examples are the Community's regional, environmental and development co-operation policies.

[78] The CFI referred to this case in its argument: Case T-315/01, *Kadi* (n 2 above), para 64.

Community powers beyond the general framework created by the provisions of the EC Treaty as a whole'.[79] Despite the specific reference to the ECHR in Article 6(2) TEU[80] the ECJ held that the Community did not have a general legislative competence for human rights. The Court considered Article 6(2) TEU to be insufficient to allow for action of the Community under Article 308 EC:[81] a provision of the TEU could *not* supply the necessary *objective of the Community*. As a consequence, action based on Article 308 EC, which goes beyond the scope of the EC's objectives, activities and tasks referred to in Articles 2, 3 and 4 EC, appears to be excluded.[82]

Equally with a reference to *Opinion 2/94*[83] the ECJ tore down the CFI's extension of the 'Article 301 EC bridge' as linking Article 308 EC to the Union objectives in the second pillar.[84] Instead, the Court found an interpretation of Article 301 EC that provided the possibility to adopt sanctions against individuals exclusively under the first pillar. It identified Article 301 EC to have the objective 'of making it possible to adopt [economic] measures [in order to implement CFSP decisions] through the efficient use of a Community instrument'.[85]

'Efficient use of a Community instrument' recalls the ECJ's *effet utile* approach, ensuring the maximum effectiveness of Community law.[86] However, the ECJ used the argument differently in *Kadi* and *al Barakaat* than it usually does. The Court applied it here to justify Community competence,[87] while usually the *effet utile* argument is used to justify a specific interpretation of national law.[88] In *Kadi* and *al Barakaat*, the ECJ

[79] Opinion 2/94 (n 18 above), para 30.

[80] Ex-Art F(2) TEU.

[81] The question was whether the Community could accede to the ECHR; Opinion 2/94 (n 18 above), para 32.

[82] Arnull (et al), *The European Union and its Court of Justice* (n 32 above), p 90.

[83] Cases C-402/05 P and C-415/05 P, *Kadi and al Barakaat* (n 2 above), para 203.

[84] ibid, paras 195–7.

[85] ibid, para 226.

[86] See for an illustrative example of an effet utile reasoning: Case C-437/97, *Evangelischer Krankenhausverein Wien v Abgarenberufungskommission Wien and Wein &; Co HandelsgesmbH v Oberösterreichische Landesregierung* [2000] ECR I-1157.

[87] In effectiveness was used to establish Community competence for criminal measures: see critical: Ester Herlin-Karnell, 'Commission *v* Council: Some Reflections on Criminal Law in the First Pillar', *European Public Law*, Vol 13(1) (2007), at p 73.

[88] See most prominently: Case C-213/89, *R v Secretary of State for Transport ex parte Factortame Ltd* [1990] ECR I-2433 and Joint Cases C-6 and 9/90, *Francovich and Bonifaci v Italy* [1991] ECR I-5357; but also, exploring the use of the effectiveness argument for European criminal law: Herlin-Karnell, *Commission v Council: Some Reflections on Criminal Law in the First Pillar* (n 87 above).

found 'efficient use of Community law' as an 'instrumental objective' in Article 301 EC. This interpretation might surprise given the Court's preceding remarks that Article 301 EC does *not* give the Community the *competence* to sanction individuals. How can this article then have the *objective* to do so?

There are further reasons why *Opinion 2/94* does not support constructing a Community competence for individual sanctions. The ECJ ruled that the Community had no competence to accede to the ECHR, because it did not have any general human rights competence. The Court's main argument was that accession to the ECHR would constitute a Treaty amendment, which could only be agreed to by the Member States pursuant to Article 48 TEU. It is worth questioning whether the 'effect [of the Community's accession to the ECHR] could, in substance, be to amend the Treaty'.[89] However, this is what the ECJ claimed and this is not the place to question this claim further. In the present context it is important to notice that the ECJ held in *Opinion 2/94*[90] that the institutional implications of the Community's accession to the ECHR were of constitutional significance and could hence only be brought about by a Treaty amendment. As became clear in the Court's considerations, part of the motivation for the ruling in *Opinion 2/94* was to avoid having its own decisions submitted to the judgment of an organ external to the Community legal order.[91] Adopting individual sanctions under European law does not prima facie appear to imply such a fundamental change that it could be considered an amendment of the European Treaties. Nonetheless, the *changes* that individual sanctions bring to the *institutional balance* of the EU are significant. The current adoption procedure gives the Union an unprecedented immediate power to govern the legal sphere of individuals.[92] It creates a general competence of the Community to adopt all measures necessary to implement Security Council resolutions, as well as autonomous European sanctions. And, it extends the Union's powers to use

[89] *Opinion 2/94* (n 18 above), para 30. It could be argued that the ECJ had largely integrated the substantive rules of the ECHR already and that it would therefore not have been an actual fundamental change of the protection of fundamental rights in the Community legal order (see Piet Eeckhout, *External Relations of the European Union: Legal and Constitutional Foundations* (Oxford: Oxford University Press, 2004), p 86 et seq).

[90] Arnull (et al), *The European Union and its Court of Justice* (n 32 above), p 90.

[91] See Eeckhout, *External Relations* (n 89 above), p 87.

[92] See Chapter Three, Sections 3.2.2 and 3.2.3. So far only the Community (first pillar) had adopted measures with direct and intense effect on individuals' rights, eg competition fines.

Community law at its will.[93] This is not only an extension of Community powers into a new substantive area beyond the boundaries of the EC Treaty, but constitutes considerable qualitative change. In conclusion, applying the ECJ's reasoning in *Opinion 2/94* to individual sanctions should have led the CFI (and in the end also the ECJ) to *reject* Community competence for such measures.

1.3.4 The Missing Boundaries of Community Competence

The CFI's construction of a bridge between the pillars is a dangerous undertaking. Even though the CFI emphasized that the bridge was established for, and hence assumingly limited to, Community actions imposing economic sanctions,[94] it argued at the same time that precisely the combination of Articles 301 and 308 EC extends Community competences beyond the wording of the former to comprise sanctions against individuals. Hence, the wording of Article 301 EC ceases to establish clear boundaries for permissible action. Sanctions against private individuals adopted in the general fight against terrorism have little in common with traditional state sanctions: they no longer compare to trade regulations, but instead possess characteristics of criminal law.[95] Arguably, criminal law is as such no longer a taboo area for Community law-making.[96] However, if a substantive shift from trade embargoes to measures with a strong criminal dimension is possible, few actions seem to be fundamentally excluded under Article 301 EC.[97] The combined use of Articles 301, 60, and 308 EC as it is advocated by the CFI blurs the distinction between action by the Community and action by the Union and levels the way for a general use of first pillar instruments for Union purposes.[98]

The use of first pillar instruments in order to attain Union law objectives is particularly dangerous, because Union law has less clearly defined boundaries. The language of the EC Treaty, including the objectives, is much more specific in terms of limiting the scope of Community activity,

[93] See below in Section 3.

[94] Case T-306/01, *Yusuf* (n 2 above), para 159.

[95] See Chapter 1, Section 1 and Chapter 3, Section 3.2.2.

[96] Case C-176/03, *Environmental Crime* (n 69 above); Herlin-Karnell, *Commission v Council: Some Reflections on Criminal Law in the First Pillar* (n 87 above).

[97] Eg sanctions against an EU Member State appear to remain excluded.

[98] Case T-306/01, *Yusuf* (n 2 above), para 161; Case T-315/01, *Kadi* (n 2 above), para 125: '[u] nder Articles 60 EC and 301 EC, action by the Community is [...] in actual fact action by the Union, the implementation of which finds its footing on the Community pillar [...]'.'

whereas the TEU does not provide any clear boundaries to the actions that the Union can take under Title V of the TEU.[99] On the contrary, the Treaty language taken in isolation is not specific enough to lend itself as a tool of delimitation.[100] Article 11(1) TEU sets out that '[t]he Union shall define and implement a common foreign and security policy covering *all* areas of foreign and security policy'.[101] Title V of the TEU is based on a sort of 'catch all' approach supplementing the EC Treaty. In other words, if not only the Treaty objectives, but also the objectives pursued by the Member States under the CFSP were covered by Article 308 EC, it would become boundless. The substantive limits of what the Community is entitled to do would be lifted with regard to the CFSP. Through the bridge of Article 301 EC the Community would become competent to take action in all those areas where today CFSP common positions are adopted, including trade in arms, travel bans, participation in international organizations, the conclusion of international conventions on toxin weapons, and the implementation of decisions of international tribunals.[102] The list would be almost open-ended.

Additionally, because the CFSP falls in principle outside the jurisdiction of the Court, there is no body of case-law interpreting the boundaries. Due to the Court's limited competences under Articles 46 and 47 TEU the only existing case-law has to take a negative approach ensuring that nothing in the TEU affects the EC Treaty. This does not contribute to a comprehensive definition of Union competences, but merely protects the *acquis communautaire*. Except for a possible limiting impact that the practice under Title V of the TEU[103] might have, the substantive scope for CFSP

[99] Compare Arts 2 and 3 EC to Arts 11 and 12 TEU.

[100] Eeckhout, *External Relations* (n 89 above), p 141 et seq; see particularly for the nevertheless compulsory language of the TEU, p 144.

[101] Article 11(1) TEU, emphasis added.

[102] Some examples of the diversity and scope of CFSP common positions are: restrictions of the trade in arms with Somalia: Council Common Position 2007/391/CFSP of 7 June 2007 amending Common Position 2002/960/CFSP concerning restrictive measures against Somalia, OJ 2007 L 146/23; travel bans on specific persons from Uzbekistan: Council Common Position 2007/338/CFSP of 14 May 2007 renewing certain restrictive measures against Uzbekistan, OJ 2007 L 128/50; Council Common Position 2007/150/CFSP of 5 March 2007 renewing measures in support of the effective implementation of the mandate of the International Criminal Tribunal for the former Yugoslavia (ICTY), OJ 2007 L 66/21; Council Common Position 2006/244/CFSP of 20 March 2006 on participation by the European Union in the Korean Peninsula Energy Development Organisation (KEDO), OJ 2006 L 88/73; Council Common Position 2006/242/CFSP of 20 March 2006 relating to the 2006 Review Conference of the Biological and Toxin Weapons Convention (BTWC), OJ 2006 L 88/65.

[103] Eeckhout, *External Relations* (n 89 above), p 143.

measures is virtually unlimited and unpatrolled by the Court. This makes the extension of Article 301 EC to pursue the objectives of the Union unacceptable.

Admittedly, the ECJ's construction of Articles 301, 60 and 308 EC as a joint legal basis does not blur the distinction between the pillars: where the means in Article 301 EC become the objectives for the use of Article 308 EC the scope of the combined legal basis corresponds to the scope of Article 301 EC. Based on this reasoning it will not be possible to justify the adoption of a measure in order to attain just any objective defined by the Union under the second pillar. Yet, the ECJ's construction has other perils. Objectives determine for which purpose means can be used. They express a value choice, set a framework, and outline a direction. Means as such are devoid of such value choices. They are empty tools and can be used for any purpose. By setting the precedent of using the means in Article 301 EC as objectives within the meaning of Article 308 EC the ECJ stripped the latter article of an important inherent limitation that gave this article direction. Article 308 EC is itself a means and as such devoid of a value choice. Article 308 EC provides for 'action to attain [...] one of the objectives of the Community'. This fills its use with the spirit of the EC Treaty and ensures that it is used within the framework of the Community legal order. Using Article 308 EC in combination with another 'empty' enabling provision frees the Community legislator (entirely) from the value choices expressed in the Community Treaty, which are–because of their fundamental nature–phrased in such a broad and open manner that in any event they leave room for a wide range of actions.

The ECJ tried to avoid the criticism that it over-stretched the boundaries of Article 308 EC, by giving the common market element unprecedented importance.[104] The wording of Article 308 EC imposes the requirement that it is used 'in the course of the common market'. However, so far the ECJ has not given this condition a strict interpretation.[105] Indeed, the absence of any link to the common market has so far never convinced the ECJ to annul a measure adopted on the basis of Article 308 EC. It is also noteworthy that the Treaty of Lisbon abandons the reference to the common market entirely in the new flexibility clause in Article 352 TFEU.[106] In line with the

[104] Cases C-402/05 P and C-415/05 P, *Kadi and al Barakaat* (n 2 above), para 229.

[105] See the leading case of the early period of interpretation of Art 308 EC: Case 8/73, *Hauptzollamt Bremerhaven v Massey Ferguson* [1973] ECR 897.

[106] Article 352(1) TFEU: If action by the Union should prove necessary, within the framework of the policies defined by the Treaties, to attain one of the objectives set out in the Treaties, and

relevance for the common market and in contrast to the CFI[107] the ECJ ruled that individual sanctions could amount to a 'distortion of competition.'[108] If they were adopted by a multitude of national measures they would create without economic reasons advantages or disadvantages for certain economic operators. However, whether individual sanctions could have a considerable impact on the common market appears doubtful.[109] In the words of the CFI:[110]

> if a mere finding of a risk of disparities between the various national rules and a theoretical risk of obstacles to the free movement of capital or payments or of distortions of competition liable to result therefrom were sufficient to justify the choice of Article 308 EC as a legal basis for a regulation together with Article 3(1)(c) and (g) EC, not only would the provisions of Chapter 3 of Title VI of the EC Treaty be rendered ineffective, but also review by the Court of the correctness of the choice of the proper legal basis might be rendered wholly ineffective.

While the ECJ's new focus on the common market element finds full support in the wording of Article 308 EC, the substantive argument that the adoption of individual sanctions at Community level is necessary in the course of the common market, or even to avoid the distortion of competition, as such appears artificial. Moreover, all 27 EU Member States are also members of the UN. They would have to comply with the obligations flowing from the UN sanctions regime in any event. This would further eliminate any risk of distortions, at least where UN sanctions do not leave any margin of discretion to the implementing member states.[111]

the Treaties have not provided the necessary powers, the Council, acting unanimously on a proposal from the Commission and after obtaining the consent of the European Parliament, shall adopt the appropriate measures. Where the measures in question are adopted by the Council in accordance with a special legislative procedure, it shall also act unanimously on a proposal from the Commission and after obtaining the consent of the European Parliament.

[107] Case T-315/01, *Kadi* (n 2 above), para 111–12, citing C-376/98, *Germany v Parliament and Council* [2000] ECR I-8419.

[108] Cases C-402/05 P and C-415/05 P, *Kadi and al Barakaat* (n 2 above), para 229.

[109] See p 88 above.

[110] Case T-315/01, *Kadi* (n 2 above), para 111: Chapter 3 of Title VI governs the approximation of laws; see however also the ECJ's recent ruling in the Data Retention Case where the Court found that a directive with the principal objective of the investigation, detection and prosecution of crime met the Art 95 EC criterion of having the 'object the establishment and functioning of the internal market' (which is even higher than the threshold in Art 308 EC), Case C-301/06, *Data Retention Directive* (n 7 above), paras 71–2.

[111] This is the case under the first sanctions regime, which is based on UN lists of terrorist suspects (as opposed to general call to fight the financing of terrorism under the second sanctions regime), see Chapter One for a more detailed distinction.

In conclusion, the Community does not have the competence to adopt sanctions against private individuals, irrespective of whether they are EU citizens or non-EU citizens. A combination of three insufficient legal bases cannot create adequate competences either. The CFI's interpretation would extend the competences conferred on the Community by the Treaties to an unpredictable scope. Or, even more far-reaching, the Union would be vested with the power to adopt Community instruments.[112] The ECJ's construction has the advantage of keeping the pillars apart, but it is in argument equally unconvincing. The objective 'of making it possible to adopt [economic] measures [in order to implement CFSP decisions] through the efficient use of a Community instrument'[113] is an empty shell that could potentially be used for a wide range of measures, departing even further from the strict wording of Article 301 EC.

2. CFSP versus PJCC

Pursuant to Article 301 EC Community sanctions have to be preceded by a CFSP decision. In practice, this has always been a common position adopted on the basis of Article 15 TEU. Unlike Article 301 EC, Article 15 TEU does not set out any of the substantive limits discussed above. Neither does Article 11 TEU, which stipulates that the 'Union shall define and implement a common foreign and security policy covering *all areas* of foreign and security policy'. Consequently, while the Community sanctions against private individuals were additionally based on Article 308 EC to extend Articles 301 and 60 EC beyond their wording, the legal basis of the underlying common positions remained the same irrespective of the absence of any territorial link.[114]

Nonetheless, the case for Union competences is not incontrovertible either. It is true that the Council can in principle take any action in line with the objectives of the TEU. However, the choice of CFSP common

[112] See in this regard Case T-306/01, *Yusuf* (n 2 above), para 161; Case T-315/01, *Kadi* (n 2 above), para 125.

[113] Cases C-402/05 P and C-415/05 P, *Kadi and al Barakaat* (n 2 above), para 226.

[114] However, today some CFSP Common Positions are additionally based on Art 34 TEU, since they require Member States to take measures in the third pillar relating to police and judicial cooperation in criminal matters (PJCC) (eg: CP 2001/931/CFSP, of 27 December 2001, [2001] OJ L 344 /93–6).

positions to adopt European lists of terrorist suspects within the Union pillar structure is still not obvious. Indeed, it is submitted, first, that as long as no fundamental structural changes are introduced, only the Community pillar could provide the necessary legal safeguards to list individuals as terrorist suspects in compliance with the principles of European law. This would, of course, require a Treaty amendment creating the necessary Community competences. Secondly, it is argued that in the present division of the EU according to the subject matters dealt with, individual sanctions would rather fall in the third than in the second pillar.

There are a number of reasons why lists of terrorist suspects are adopted in the form of CFSP common positions. First, Articles 301 and – by reference – 60 EC require a CFSP decision preceding the adoption of Community sanctions. Hence, Community asset freezes, or potentially any other first pillar measure, based on Article 301 EC depend on the prior adoption of a CFSP decision. Secondly, European sanctions against individuals are adopted in the course of the global effort to fight terrorism. They often implement UN Security Council resolutions[115] and have an undisputable international law element. Moreover, apart from the existing practice there are arguments in favour of a coordinated international approach to fighting terrorism. Unilateral sanctions seem to be much less effective, since the listed individuals could easily evade the consequences by moving their financial assets from the state that adopts sanctions to one that does not–facilitated by the free movement rights within the Community. Short time lapses in the adoption of asset freezes suffice to give those targeted the time to move their financial assets.

At the same time, the fact that individual sanctions call for some form of international cooperation alone is not sufficient to draw them into the area of CFSP. Nor is the requirement of a CFSP decision in Article 301 EC, since this article does not, in fact, provide for the adoption of individual sanctions. By their nature, individual sanctions are more similar to the subject matters dealt with in the third pillar than those dealt with in the second pillar. They concern individuals rather than third countries and they are not foreign policy decisions, but have considerable criminal law implications.[116] This argument applies not exclusively, but even more strongly where European citizens are concerned.

[115] See Chapter 1, Sections 2 to 3.

[116] Discussed in detail in Chapter 3.

Undeniably, there is a third pillar dimension to individual sanctions. Common Position 2001/931/CFSP, for instance, was adopted on a dual legal basis consisting of Articles 15 and 34 TEU. It is a hybrid measure comprising both PJCC and CFSP elements. Advocate-General Mengozzi distinguished in his opinion in *Segi* between the objectives that come 'within the framework of the common foreign and security policy' and some of the 'operational instruments' that come 'within the scope of police and judicial cooperation in criminal matters'.[117] It is correct that some of the provisions of the *operational part* of Common Position 2001/931/CFSP provide for third pillar cooperation.[118] With regard to the objectives the matter is less clear. Article 29 TEU lists the fight against terrorism as one of the primary objectives of PJCC, and the European Council has dealt with terrorism primarily as a third pillar issue,[119] while terrorism as such is not mentioned in Title V of the TEU at all. Thus on the one hand, on substance the argument could be made that sanctions against private individuals fall rather in the third pillar than in the second pillar (in any event they would continue to require implementation under the first pillar).

On the other, it remains doubtful whether European lists could be legitimately adopted in the third pillar. The PJCC is characterized by a specific reserve of state sovereignty. Article 34(2) b and c TEU, for instance, explicitly provide that framework decisions and decisions cannot have direct effect. Article 33 TEU sets out that Title VI 'shall not affect' Member States' responsibility to maintain 'law and order' and to safeguard 'internal security'. Even though enforcement (direct effect) and the choice of the most appropriate legal basis are two different issues, the explicit exclusion of direct effect indicates for which types of measures framework decisions and decisions are intended. This makes it doubtful whether lists of terrorist suspects could be adopted in the third pillar. Because of Article 34 TEU, at least framework decisions and decisions are incapable of containing measures that directly affect individual persons. Clearly, Union lists

[117] AG Mengozzi in: C-354/04 P, *Gestoras Pro Amnistia* and Case C-355/04 P, *Segi v Council* [2007] ECR I-1657, para 55.

[118] Even if this does not allow the conclusion that those to whom the application of CP 2001/931/CFSP was limited to certain operational measures providing for PJCC, were affected by third pillar measures only; see Chapter 1, Section 4.2 and Chapter 3, Section 3.2.2.

[119] In the plan of action of the extraordinary European Council meeting on 21 September 2001 the European Council called upon the Justice and Home Affairs Council to undertake identification of presumed terrorists in Europe and of organisations supporting them.

of terrorist suspects create an immediate link between the legal instrument they are contained in and those listed: individuals are affected even before any operational measures are adopted against them simply by being listed. Whether these lists entail direct effect *de stricto sensu* has not been established yet. However, national authorities are obliged to interpret national law in conformity with European law.[120] This allows third parties to rely on framework decisions in national courts against those listed, albeit within certain limits. Firstly, they can only be relied on indirectly as a prescription of how to interpret national law (excluding a *contra legem* interpretation of the latter). Secondly, substantive national criminal law cannot be interpreted consistently to the detriment of the individual.[121] Identifying specific individuals as terrorist suspects and giving this identification a de facto enforceability in national courts could be seen as contrary to the value choice of Article 34 TEU. The EU Treaty explicitly states that they may not entail direct effect. Adopting lists of terrorist suspects in framework decisions would go beyond the scope that the EU Treaty sets out for this type of instrument.

Admittedly, adopting individual sanctions in the third pillar would increase their democratic legitimacy–but only marginally. Framework decisions–as opposed to conventions, which are the traditional form of cooperation in the third pillar–do not require approval by national parliaments. National parliaments are merely informed six weeks before a decision is taken[122] and the European Parliament is consulted.[123] This would be an improvement compared to the second pillar, where the participation of the European Parliament is limited to being informed and having budgetary powers,[124] while national parliaments are not even informed.[125] An additional advantagc of adopting individual sanctions in the third, instead of in the second pillar, is the fact that the ECJ's limited jurisdiction for

[120] Case C-105/03, *Pupino* [2005] ECR I-5285.

[121] ibid, paras 44–6.

[122] Protocol on the Role of National Parliaments in the European Union, adopted under the Treaty of Amsterdam.

[123] Article 39(1) TEU. However, the consultation procedure of the TEU is different from the consultation procedure of the EC Treaty. The Council can impose a time-limit of not less than three month for the delivery of the EP's opinion, after which it may act in any event.

[124] In the second pillar the participation of the European Parliament is limited to budgetary powers: Daniel Thym, 'Beyond Parliament's Reach? The Role of the European Parliament in the CFSP', *European Foreign Affairs Review*, 11 (2006), p 113 et seq.

[125] Article 21 TEU applies to the European Parliament only and the information duties under the Protocol on the Role of National Parliaments are limited to Title VI TEU.

preliminary rulings is explicitly codified in the former.[126] With regard to the second pillar the ECJ's ruling in the *Segi* case allows for the conclusion that preliminary rulings are possible for Union lists; yet, this possibility is not codified and has not yet been used in practice.[127] However, the improvement would be far from sufficient for measures having such a grave impact on human rights as individual sanctions do.

De lege lata it appears difficult to draw sufficient additional legitimacy from the European institutional structures to adopt lists of terrorist suspects in the Union pillars at all. Relying on national law and national channels of control could here be a possible solution. This is what Advocate-General Mengozzi suggested for Union lists in the case of *Segi*, when he wanted to submit the European law instrument to scrutiny by national courts.[128] The European legislator has also made attempts to draw legitimacy from national law. The PJCC instrument[129] supplementing Common Position 2001/931/CFSP, for instance, explicitly requires that all action should be taken in conformity with national law.[130] Additionally, *national implementation measures* can of course be challenged in national courts irrespective of whether they implement second or third pillar measures.[131] However, Advocate-General Mengozzi's suggestion was (at least indirectly) dismissed by the ECJ.[132] National courts cannot offer adequate

[126] Article 35 TEU.

[127] Case C-355/04 P, *Segi* (n 117 above).

[128] Opinion of AG Mengozzi in Case C-355/04 P, *Segi* (n 117 above).

[129] Council Decision 2003/48/JHA of 19 December 2002 on the implementation of specific measures for police and judicial cooperation to combat terrorism in accordance with Article 4 of Common Position 2001/931/CFSP, OJ 2003, L 16/68–70; see Chapter 1, Section 4.2.

[130] Recital 7 calls on the 'Council [...] [to] draw the necessary consequences from any final finding and enforceable interim orders to the contrary by a court of the Member States'. Recital 8 states that the decision is not to interfere with 'fundamental rights and [that it] observes the principles recognised by Article 6' TEU. It even goes one step further in providing that '[n] othing in this Decision may be interpreted as allowing infringement of the legal protection afforded under national law to the persons, groups and entities listed in the Annex to Common Position 2001/931/CFSP'. Articles 2 para 2 (communicating information to Europol), Arts 3 para 2 (communicating information to Eurojust) and 7 (communicating information to other Member States) reiterate this with regard to each of these actions.

[131] As it was the case in: German Constitutional Court, Decision of 18 July 2005, decision on the EAW Act: The applicant appealed a court decision to extradite him (see the commentary of Parga, 2006); see also the pending challenge of the national implementation of the Data Retention Directive (Directive 2006/24/EC, OJ 2006 L105/54) before the German Constitutional Court; see also the interim decision at: 1 BvR 256/08.

[132] By accepting a preliminary ruling request from national courts which question the validity or interpretation of common positions (Case C-355/04 P, *Segi* (n 117 above), para 54), the ECJ

judicial protection from European law. Further, the reference in Council Decision 2003/48/JHA applies to the national implementation measures only. In conclusion, the third pillar does not offer the kind of control mechanisms required to legitimately adopt terrorist lists either.

Assuming that there is a need to adopt sanctions against private individuals at the EU level, the best way of increasing the democratic legitimacy of individual sanctions would be to amend the EC Treaty. The EC Treaty would have to provide for a Community competence for individual sanctions, subject to clear listing criteria,[133] outlined in an instrument of secondary law that requires approval by the European Parliament under the co-decision procedure. These criteria would further have to be subject to full judicial control by the EU courts. This appears at the moment to be the only way to sufficiently increase both democratic and judicial control. The two Union pillars, as they are organized so far, are not capable of providing for the necessary control mechanisms to adopt lists of terrorist suspects; and it is highly questionable whether a possible introduction of the necessary control mechanisms in the second pillar would even be desirable.[134] Should and could the CFSP be subject to control by the European Parliament to the extent that would be necessary to endorse lists with the necessary democratic legitimacy? The traditional high politics of the CFSP might be better placed under the control of national parliaments.[135]

3. Uneven Partners, Each Striving for Dominance: the Binding Force of Union Law on the Community

Despite the continuing approximation of the three pillars of the EU,[136] they still confer different legal powers to the European institutions and to

indirectly rejected that national courts come to their own conclusion on that question. Review of Union law by national courts will equally be rejected in Chapter 6, Section 4.2.1.

[133] See Chapter 7, Section 1.3.

[134] Thym, 'Beyond Parliament's Reach? The Role of the European Parliament in the CFSP' (n 124 above), p 121 et seq.

[135] Eileen Denza, *The Intergovernmental Pillars of the European Union* (Oxford: Oxford University Press, 2002), p 325.

[136] Armin von Bogdandy, 'The Legal Case for Unity: The European Union as a Single Legal System', *Common Market Law Review*, 36 (1999), pp 887–910.

the Member States.[137] Neither the general objective of consistency between the different pillars, set out in Article 3 TEU, nor the other provisions assuring a harmonious co-existence of the three pillars change this distribution of powers. The CFI considered the recourse under Article 308 EC to Union objectives necessary 'for the sake of the requirement of consistency laid down in Article 3 TEU'.[138] By doing so, it appears to overlook that Article 3 TEU requires the institutions to ensure consistency 'each *in accordance with its respective powers*'. Article 3 TEU does not contain a qualification of the otherwise strict separation of the pillars.[139]

A process of approximation between the three pillars can be identified.[140] This could be seen as weighing in favour of the CFI's interpretation that Community power under Article 308 EC could (in the limited field of sanctions) also be used to attain Union objectives. First, the Treaties do not provide an exact distinction between the second and first pillar.[141] Secondly, European law is governed by its own autonomous principles distinct from the law of the Member States and from general international law.[142] Thirdly, the EU has a single institutional framework with an accountability that is linked to the institutions, not to their competences in the different pillars.[143] The same persons at the same meeting take decisions in the

[137] Bruno de Witte, 'The Pillar Structure and the Nature of the European Union: Greek Temple or French Gothic Cathedral?' in Ton Heukels, Niels Blokker and Marcel Brus (eds), *The European Union after Amsterdam* (The Hague: Kluwer Law International, 1998), p 66:

> The essence of the Pillar structure is the variation in the allocation of powers among the institutions. The Member States consider that primary responsibility for certain matters should remain in the hands of the national executives meeting in the Council.

[138] Case T-315/01, *Kadi* (n 2 above), para 128.

[139] This was suggested to be the CFI's position in *Yusuf* and *Kadi*: Tietje and Hamelmann, 'Gezielte Finanzsanktionen der Vereinten Nationen im Spannungsverhältnis zum Gemeinschaftsrecht und zu Menschenrechten' (n 3 above), p 300.

[140] von Bogdandy, 'The Legal Case for Unity: The European Union as a Single Legal System' (n 136 above); arguing that the Amsterdam Treaty added velocity to the process of unification: de Witte, 'The Pillar Structure and the Nature of the European Union: Greek Temple or French Gothic Cathedral?' (n 137 above).

[141] Roberto Baratta, 'Overlaps between European Community Competence and European Union Foreign Policy Activity' in Enzo Cannizzaro (ed), *The European Union as an Actor in International Relations* (The Hague: Kluwer Law International 2002), pp 70–1.

[142] Heribert Franz Köck, 'On the Unity of European Law: European Law as a Separate Body of Law and as an Independent Subject of Legal Doctrine' in Jost Delbrück (ed), *New Trends in International Lawmaking: International 'Legislation' in the Public Interest* (Berlin: Duncker & Humblot, 1997).

[143] von Bogdandy, 'The Legal Case for Unity: The European Union as a Single Legal System' (n 136 above).

Council for all three different pillars.[144] At the officials' level there is no division at all: the Committee of Permanent Representatives prepares all Council meetings and decisions, including those related to the General Affairs Council and the CFSP; the Secretariat of the Council serves the institution exercising its different tasks. Broadly speaking the mode of operation is the same across all three pillars.[145] Fourthly, the decision-making methods are overlapping.[146] The CFSP has some 'supranational' features[147] and in the Community some areas remain 'intergovernmental'.[148] CFSP decisions are, as a rule, charged to the Community budget[149] over which the European Parliament has considerable control.[150]

Moreover, the ECJ has passed a number of judgments supporting an approximation of the pillars. In this regard, it could be argued that the CFI's bridge construction[151] is in fact in line with the development of EU law.[152] In the case of *Pupino*[153] for instance, the ECJ applied the principle of interpretation in conformity, which it developed for directives in the first pillar, to framework decisions in the third. The Court observed that the

[144] Eg: Council Decision 2001/927/EC of 27 December 2001 establishing the list provided for in Art 2(3) of Council Regulation (EC) No 2580/2001 on specific restrictive measures directed against certain persons and entities with a view to combating terrorism, OJ 2001 L 344/83; Council Regulation (EC) No 2580/2001 of 27 December 2001 on specific restrictive measures directed against certain persons and entities with a view to combating terrorism, OJ 2001 L 344/70; Council Common Position 2001/931/CFSP of 27 December 2001 on the application of specific measures to combat terrorism, OJ 2001 L 344/93; Council Common Position 2001/930/CFSP of 27 December 2001 on combating terrorism, OJ 2001 L 344/90.

[145] Arnull (et al), *The European Union and its Court of Justice* (n 32 above), p 338.

[146] Deirdre Curtin and Inge Dekker, 'The EU as a "Layered" International Organisation: Institutional Unity in Disguise' in Paul Craig and Gráinne de Búrca (eds), *The Evolution of EU Law* (Oxford: Oxford University Press, 1999), p 83.

[147] Eg: the Commission is fully associated, may propose legislation, the Parliament must be informed, may ask questions, Art 23(2) TEU allows for a qualified majority vote when the Council takes decisions on the basis of a common strategy.

[148] An intergovernmental element in the first pillar is in particular the important role of the European Council.

[149] Horst G Krenzler and Henning G Schneider, 'Die Gemeinsame Außen- und Sicherheitspolitik der Europäischen Union', *EuR* (1994), p 154.

[150] On the EP's success in exercising 'democratic blackmail' to increase its powers in the second pillar: Thym, *Beyond Parliament's Reach? The Role of the European Parliament in the CFSP* (n 124 above), p 113 et seq.

[151] Case T-306/01, *Yusuf* (n 2 above); Case T-315/01, *Kadi* (n 2 above).

[152] Tietje and Hamelmann, 'Gezielte Finanzsanktionen der Vereinten Nationen im Spannungsverhältnis zum Gemeinschaftsrecht und zu Menschenrechten' (n 3 above), p 300.

[153] Case C-105/03, *Pupino* (n 120 above), para 43.

TEU's objective to create an 'ever closer union among the peoples of Europe', as it is set out in Article 1(2) and (3) TEU, would be difficult to attain if the principle of loyal cooperation was not applicable in the third pillar.[154] After *Pupino*, this principle requires Member States, including national courts, to ensure the effectiveness of European law under all three pillars.

Despite the fact that scholars point out the gradual approximation and the increasing number of similarities between the pillars, in the majority they agree that the EU is *not (yet) one unitary structure*,[155] but continues to consist of a separate and autonomous pillar structure in which all three pillars keep their formal autonomy.[156] This point is equally supported by the ECJ's case-law. For instance, in the case of *Commission v Council*[157] the Court confirmed EC competence for criminal law and established a relationship between the pillars that is far from unity. It looked at the collision rules enshrined in Articles 47 and 29 TEU according to which the supranational track enjoys primacy[158] and emphasized its own role as the guardian of the Community powers against encroachments by Union measures.[159] Even though it can be argued that the judgment transfers more and more competences into the Community pillar[160] it is an acknowledgement of the differences between the Community and the intergovernmental pillars,[161] and an attempt to keep them separate. In conclusion, it would be difficult to maintain that the approximation between the three pillars was sufficiently developed to justify Community action to attain Union objectives.

Because of the continuing differences between the pillars, in particular the different allocation of powers between the European institutions and the Member States, it remains relevant under which pillar an act is adopted.

[154] ibid, paras 41–2.

[155] Curtin and Dekker, 'The EU as a "Layered" International Organisation: Institutional Unity in Disguise' (n 146 above), p 84, fn 143; Koutrakos (2001), pp 131–63; Denza, *The Intergovernmental Pillars of the European Union* (n 135 above).

[156] Ricardo Gosalbo Bono, 'Some Reflections on the CFSP Legal Order', *Common Market Law Review*, 43 (2006), p 351.

[157] Case C-176/03, *Environmental Crime* (n 69 above); see also: Case C-440/05, *Ship Source Pollution* (n 69 above); Case C-91/05, *ECOWAS* (n 69 above).

[158] ibid, paras 38–9.

[159] ibid, para 16.

[160] Herlin-Karnell, *Commission v Council: Some Reflections on Criminal Law in the First Pillar* (n 87 above).

[161] The ECJ's ruling in Cases C-402/05 P and C-415/05 P, *Kadi and al Barakaat* (n 2 above) did also emphasize the difference between the first and the second pillar.

While state sanctions are based on a general policy decision under the CFSP,[162] which is then implemented in the first pillar, individual sanctions are adopted by CFSP common positions that meticulously predetermine the content of the Community measure. Here, the two instruments can no longer be divided into a general policy decision to take action on the one hand and an operational instrument putting this decision into practice on the other. The identification of those sanctioned takes place in the second (and third) pillar and deprives the institutions of all discretion in the first pillar. The implementation by the Community no longer requires any meaningful decision; it is only an administrative action of copying the names listed in the CFSP instrument. This shifts the power to determine the details of the measure from the Community to the Union and hereby changes the traditional allocation of powers between the CFSP and the Community in the field of sanctions.

Already before the adoption of individual sanctions scholars pointed at the risk that hybrid measures requiring actions under both the first and the second pillar would reduce the Community institutions' discretion[163] to the point of making them the subordinates of the Member States.[164] Individual sanctions are in this regard a new form of cross-pillar measures, that allow the Union more control over the Community than ever. The combined use of a CFSP decision and a Community regulation for the adoption of sanctions pursuant to Article 301 EC codified the existing practice of adopting the general political decision to take action against a country under the EPC and then adopting the actual sanctions measures in the Community pillar. The intention behind this mechanism has never been to allow the Union to make use of Community law. It is a reflection of

[162] Eg: 93/614/CFSP: Council Decision of 22 November 1993 on the Common Position defined on the basis of Art J.2 of the Treaty on European Union with regard to the reduction of economic relations with Libya, OJ 1993 L 295/7; 94/779/CFSP: Common Position of 28 November 1994 defined by the Council on the basis of Art J.2 of the Treaty on European Union on the objectives and priorities of the European Union towards Ukraine, OJ 1994 L 313/1; 95/91/CFSP: Common Position of 24 March 1995 defined by the Council on the basis of Art J.2 of the Treaty on the European Union, with regard to Burundi, OJ 1995 L 072/1; more recently however state sanctions have also become more detailed: eg Council Common Position 2003/495/CFSP of 7 July 2003 on Iraq and repealing Common Positions 96/741/CFSP and 2002/599/CFSP, OJ 2003 L 169/72; Council Common Position 2007/140/CFSP of 27 February 2007 concerning restrictive measures against Iran, OJ 2007 L 61/49.

[163] Osteneck, *Die Umsetzung von UN-Wirtschaftssanktionen durch die Europäische Gemeinschaft* (n 1 above), p 190.

[164] Reinhardt Rummel and Jörg Wiedemann, 'Identifying Institutional Paradoxes of CFSP', *EUI Working Paper RSC*, No 97/67 (1997), p 55.

the separation of foreign policy and external trade in the EU. Still, the present way of adopting individual sanctions deprives the Community of its autonomy, which is an essential element of the Community's *sui generis* nature. Individual sanctions as presently adopted allow the Union to determine the actions of the Community. Community law, however, benefits from special characteristics, such as supremacy and direct enforceability in national law, which make it not only more effective than Union law, but give it a particular power to impact on the rights of individuals.

When individual sanctions are adopted pursuant to the procedure in Article 301 EC CFSP decisions are transposed one to one into directly applicable legislative measures under Community law. This gives Member States gathering in the framework of the second pillar (Union action) tools of unknown effects and allows them to exclude public debate and democratic control by the European Parliament. The extent of the Member States' control over Community action depends on whether the CFSP decision is considered to be binding for the Community institutions.

While the CFI found that the European institutions were not authorized to set up any mechanism of examination or re-examination when adopting sanctions based on UN lists,[165] it found that the Community takes discretionary decisions when adopting autonomous European sanctions pursuant to Article 301 EC.[166] On the one hand, the CFI ruled that:[167]

> the Community does not act under the powers circumscribed by the will of the Union or by that of its Member States as it may be expressed in a common position adopted in the sphere of the CFSP.

The CFI considered the adoption of sanctions 'the exercise of the Community's own powers, entailing a discretionary assessment by the Community.'[168] On the other, the CFI had considered the contested regulation to be in fact action by the Union, not by the Community.[169] The latter consideration appears to imply a great influence of the Union over the precise content of the Community measure.

Until *Kadi* and *al Barakaat* the furthest the ECJ had gone in acknowledging that CFSP instruments could pose obligations on the Community

[165] Case T-315/01, *Kadi* (n 2 above), para 258.

[166] Case T-47/03, *Jose Maria Sison v Council and Commission* [2007] ECR II-73 (sum pub), para 153

[167] ibid.

[168] Case T-47/03, *Sison* (n 166 above), para 154.

[169] Case T-306/01, *Yusuf* (n 2 above), para 161; Case T-315/01, *Kadi* (n 2 above), para 125.

institutions, was a reference in the *ECOWAS* judgment[170] to the contested CFSP joint action, which itself referred 'to the obligation of the Council and the Commission to ensure the consistency of the Union's activities'.[171] At the same time, in *ECOWAS*, the ECJ strengthened the Community pillar by emphasizing that if a measure pursues objectives both of the first and of the second pillar and the Community objective is not incidental[172] this measure should be adopted under the first pillar. Moreover, the Court pointed out that 'Article 47 EU aims, in accordance with the fifth indent of Article 2 EU and the first paragraph of Article 3 EU, to maintain and build on the *acquis communautaire*'.[173] In *Kadi and al Barakaat*, by contrast, the ECJ went beyond ECOWAS by ruling without further qualification that Article 301 EC obliges the Community to take action if so required in a CFSP common position, albeit within the strict parameters of that article.[174] After *Kadi and al Barakaat* even an action for failure to act under Article 232 EC appears imaginable.[175]

Even if CFSP instruments are in strict legal terms binding on the Member States only,[176] in the adoption procedure pursuant to Article 301 EC CFSP decisions are not without legal effects on the European institutions. Article 301 EC restricts the Commission's independence and general right to initiate action[177] in that it may only propose if and to the extent that it is provided for in a CFSP decision.[178] Article 301 EC further reads: 'the Council *shall* take the necessary urgent measures'. Hence, possible action by the Community institutions is confined by the content of the CFSP decision. The stricter these constraints are phrased the less discretion is left to them.

Moreover, in the *Pupino* case the ECJ acknowledged that the principle of sincere cooperation referred to in Article 10 EC is applicable to Union law.[179]

[170] Case C-91/05, *ECOWAS* (n 69 above), para 107; Cited by the ECJ at Cases C-402/05 P and C-415/05 P, *Kadi and al Barakaat* (n 2 above), para 292.

[171] See Arts 8 and 9 of Council Joint Action 1999/34/CFSP of 17 December 1998, OJ 1999 L9/1.

[172] Hence, if both objectives are equally prevalent.

[173] Case C-91/05, *ECOWAS* (n 69 above), para 59.

[174] Cases C-402/05 P and C-415/05 P, *Kadi and al Barakaat* (n 2 above), para 296: '[...] because of the adoption of such an act [the CFSP decision] the Community is bound to take, under the EC Treaty, the measures necessitated by that act'.

[175] See also Chapter 6 on judicial review of the CFSP common position.

[176] Eeckhout, *External Relations* (n 89 above), p 396 et seq.

[177] Articles 211 and 213 EC.

[178] Zagel, *Article 301 TEC (Economic Sanctions)* (n 17 above), Art 301, § 402.04 [4].

[179] Case C-105/03, *Pupino* (n 120 above), para 42.

It was even considered 'a constitutional principle within EC external relations law'[180] applying across the pillars as it applies in relation to shared competences.[181] The ECJ has further read into Article 10 EC a general obligation of cooperation, which is not only addressed to the Member States but also to the European institutions.[182] As a consequence, even if CFSP instruments are not directly binding on the European institutions in strict legal terms, they entail certain legal effects when they are used as part of the Article 301 EC adoption mechanism. The Community is obliged to cooperate loyally and not to obstruct the effects of the common position. Even if not directly legally bound, the Community would infringe the principle of loyal cooperation if it set up its own review mechanism controlling the decision of the Council to list a specific person taken within the second pillar.

This is confirmed by the obligation to ensure the consistency of European law enshrined in Article 3 TEU. This obligation of inter-institutional cooperation tries to address the danger of inconsistency resulting from the pillar structure of the EU.[183] It is true that the Treaty does not outline the exact consequences of the requirement of consistency.[184] Article 3 TEU alone does not allow the conclusion that the institutions have to comply in the Community pillar with the will of the Member States in the second pillar. In fact, other provisions of the Treaty, such as Article 47 TEU, exclude such an interpretation. However, the adoption mechanism pursuant to Article 301 EC in combination with the obligation to ensure consistency appears to exclude that the Community starts questioning the listing decisions taken by the Council in the second pillar. On the contrary, it places on the institutions a burden of justification. If they want to depart from the request to take action in the Community pillar adopted in a CFSP common position, they will have to legally justify this. The burden of justification in itself is an indirect legal consequence of the adoption of the CFSP common position.

The applicants and then appellants in the case of *Segi* were criticized for failing to cite a legal basis in the EC Treaty that had been disregarded by

[180] Marise Cremona, 'External Relations of the EU and the Member States: Competence, Mixed Agreements, International Responsibility, and Effects of International Law', *EUI Law working papers* 22 (2006), p 6.

[181] ibid, p 15.

[182] Case 2/88, *Zwartveld* [1990] ECR I-3365; Peter E Herzog, in Hans Smit and Peter E Herzog, *Law of the European Union – a Commentary* (New York: LexisNexis, 2006), para 86–12.

[183] Eeckhout, *External Relations* (n 89 above), p 152 et seq.

[184] ibid, p 153.

the Council when adopting lists of terrorist suspects in the Union pillars.[185] This is only logical since there is no provision of the EC Treaty conferring upon the Community the competence to adopt individual sanctions; they do not therefore impinge on substantive powers reserved to the Community. Yet, this does not exclude an encroachment upon the Community's freedom of decision and action.

In practice it must be conceded that CFSP lists of terrorist suspects and EC lists of terrorist suspects are usually drawn up by the same people at the same meeting.[186] The Commission's standing invitation to take part in the Council meetings applies irrespective of the legal basis of the subject matter; and the Commission's representative can make active contributions to the debate.[187] This does not change the distinction between the Council acting as a Community institution and the Council acting under the Union pillar. The Council has different powers and must follow different rules depending on its role. The CFSP decision is adopted by unanimity, while the Community regulation pursuant to Article 301 EC is in principle adopted by qualified majority. The list of terrorist suspects is currently drawn up in a CFSP common position and therefore requires unanimous support. The same is true for a potential delisting[188] and for the adoption of the Council decision pursuant to Article 2(3) of 2580/2001/EC in combination with Common Position 2001/931/CFSP. Further, determining the content of a Community measure by a legal instrument adopted by the Union would be an easy way to exclude the Commission and at least potentially the European Parliament from influencing the Community measure. The Commission must initiate Council action in the first pillar and the European Parliament, while it does not have a say in the adoption of sanctions under Article 301 EC, is at least consulted where measures are adopted pursuant to Article 308 EC. However, since Article 308 EC was added a unanimous decision of the Council is also required for the adoption of the EC regulation in the first pillar.

Article 301 EC requires a two-tier adoption process. Any adoption without the underlying CFSP decision, even if it would not infringe CFSP competences, would directly infringe the EC Treaty. Yet, there is no reason, why, *if* individual sanctions could be adopted as Community

[185] Case C-355/04 P, *Segi* (n 117 above), para 159.
[186] See for example the measures adopted on 27 December 2001, at n 144 above.
[187] Article 5(2) of the Council Rules of Procedure [2004] OJ L106/22.
[188] See Chapter 1, Section 4 on the adoption procedure.

measures,[189] it should not also be for the Community to identify those sanctioned. The general political decision to fight terrorism could be taken in a CFSP common position and the list of persons suspected of financing terrorism could be drawn up in the Community pillar. This would reflect the division of competences in the Union reserving foreign policy decisions to the CFSP, while allowing only the Community to immediately change the legal position of individuals.

In conclusion, CFSP decisions pursuant to Article 301 EC have shifted from general decisions to take action to detailed prescriptions of whom to sanction and which measures to take. Irrespective of whether the CFSP decisions are directly binding on the Community (this appears to be the position of the ECJ), they place far-reaching restrictions on the Community's freedom of action. This obliges the Community to act as 'the Union's servant' for the latter's purposes and is an encroachment upon Community competences, which also justifies jurisdiction of the EU courts based on Article 46 and 47 TEU.[190]

4. Power Balance between the EU and its Member States

In *Yusuf* and *Kadi*[191] the CFI missed the opportunity to reject the Council's extensive interpretation of its powers to take action on the basis of Articles 301, 60, and 308 EC. This practice of adopting individual sanctions on an improper legal basis endangers the power balance between the EU and the Member States and thereby risks a reaction by the national constitutional courts of the Member States, which in the past have threatened to ensure that neither the EU, nor the Community step outside their defined boundaries.[192] As a consequence, the supremacy of European law, and with it the entire functioning of the European legal order, could in fact be challenged.

[189] *De lege lata* there is no Community competence to adopt individual sanctions; yet, it could be established, see Section Five on the Treaty of Lisbon below.

[190] See for more detail Chapter Six, Section 3.1.

[191] Case T-306/01, *Yusuf* (n 2 above); Case T-315/01, *Kadi* (n 2 above).

[192] See eg: the *Maastricht* judgments of the German and Danish courts: GCC, *Maastricht* decision of 12 October 1993, BVerfGE 89, 155; for a translation of the Maastricht decision see: *Brunner v European Union Treaty*, 57 *CMLRev* 1994 (see also Chapter 5, n 193); Danish Supreme Court, Case I 361/1997 *Carlsen v Rasmussen*. See also most recently: GCC judgment of the Second Senate of 30 June 2009 (*Treaty of Lisbon*), 2 BvE 2/08; 2 BvE 5/08, 2 BvR 1010/08; 2 BvR 1022/08; 2 BvR 1259/08; 2 BvR 182/09.

4.1 Community Law

For Community law the German Constitutional Court (GCC) famously preserved a final authority of review, and although the Court routinely rejects reviewing Community law until today it has not waived this right to have the ultimate say.[193] In the *Maastricht* decision,[194] the Court only accepted the supremacy of Community law so long as the Community stayed within the confined powers transferred to it pursuant to the rules in the German Constitution. Besides compliance with fundamental rights[195] one requirement was compliance with the principle of certainty. The Court saw the latter requirement satisfied because the Maastricht Treaty determined the future course of action of the Community in a predictable manner.[196] At the same time, the GCC clearly warned against the Community claiming powers beyond those specified in the Treaties. After the *Maastricht* decision, it was clear that any possible ultra vires actions of the Community could be challenged before the GCC, which explicitly retained an authority to ensure that the Community did not assume powers beyond what was transferred to it in the EC Treaty. Consequently, if the Community continues to adopt measures like individual sanctions despite the fact that the Treaties do *not* establish the necessary competences, the GCC could–and should–step in to protect the power balance between the Community and the Member States–even though this challenges not only the ECJ's ruling in *Foto-Frost*.[197]

[193] See for the more recent signs that the GCC might challenge the ECJ's authority: Roman Herzog and Lüder Gerken, 'Comment: Stop the European Court of Justice', *10.9.2008, available at: euobserver.com*; see also the pending case challenging the national implementation of the Data Retention Directive and the interim decision of 11 March 2008, 1 BvR 256/08 and GCC (n 192 above).

[194] As the GCC stated in its *Maastricht* decision (n 192 above), para 99: 'Whereas a dynamic extension of the existing Treaties has so far been supported on the basis of an open-handed treatment of Article 235 of the EEC Treaty as a 'competence to round-off the Treaty' as a whole, ... in future it will have to be noted in regard to interpretation of enabling provisions by Community institutions and agencies that the Union Treaty as a matter of principle distinguishes between the exercise of a sovereign power conferred for limited purposes and the amending of the Treaty, so that its interpretation may not have effects that are equivalent to an extension of the Treaty. Such an interpretation of enabling rules would not produce any binding effects for Germany.'

[195] See Chapter Five, Section 4.1 for more details.

[196] GCC, *Maastricht* decision (n 192 above), para 59; GCC, Treaty of Lisbon (n 192 above), paras 236 et seq.

[197] Case 314/85, *Foto-Frost* [1987] ECR 4199: the ECJ held that the EU courts are the sole arbitrator upon the validity of Community law.

In the section on the requirement of legal certainty the GCC specifically considered Article 308 EC (ex-Article 235) and distanced itself from the use of this article before the adoption of the Maastricht Treaty. It argued that because of the distinction between the circumscribed powers of the Community and the possibility of amending the Treaty pursuant to Article 48 TEU, any interpretation of Article 308 EC could 'not have effects that are equivalent to an extension of the Treaty'.[198] The Court became even more specific in stating that '[s]uch an interpretation of enabling rules would not produce any binding effects for Germany'.[199] Thus, the GCC left no doubt that it would declare (secondary) European law non-binding in the German legal order where the Community stepped outside its circumscribed powers and, in particular, where Article 308 EC was used to achieve a Treaty amendment through the backdoor.

There was even a direct mention of Article 301 EC (ex-Article 228a) in which the GCC confirmed that it would offer adequate protection of constitutional rights if they were threatened to be infringed by Community measures implementing decisions of the Council taken under the TEU.[200] The *Maastricht* judgment demonstrates that the GCC considered the adoption of hybrid measures based on Article 301 EC a potential threat to fundamental rights.

The Danish Supreme Court was also asked to rule on the legality of the conclusion of the Maastricht Treaty[201] and gave a ruling of rare importance for the distribution of competences between the Member States and the European institutions.[202] The central question was whether from the perspective of Danish constitutional law the transfer of powers in the Treaty of Maastricht was too wide and unspecified. The relevant section of the Danish Constitution provided that powers may be transferred 'to such extent as shall be provided by statute'.[203] The Court found that the transfer of powers in the Maastricht Treaty conformed to the Danish Constitution and rejected the plaintiff's submission that the ECJ's activism in the past

198 ibid, para 99.
199 ibid, para 99.
200 ibid, para 23.
201 Danish Supreme Court, Case I 361/1997, *Carlsen v Rasmussen*.
202 Per Lachmann, 'The Treaty of Maastricht vs the Danish Constitution', *Nordic Journal of International Law*, 67 (1998), p 365.
203 Section 20, available at: http://www.um.dk; see Lachmann, 'The Treaty of Maastricht' (n 202 above), p 366.

made the future interpretation of the EC Treaty unpredictable. Examining the confinement of powers in the Maastricht Treaty the Danish Supreme Court equally looked to ex-Article 235 (now Article 308) EC. In this regard, the Danish Supreme Court pointed out that decisions adopted pursuant to this article required a unanimous decision by the Member States and that the Danish Government could not legally assist in the adoption of an act going beyond the scope of the EC Treaty. If the Danish Government nonetheless voted in favour of an ultra vires act its vote in the Council could be challenged in national courts. The legal action could either be directed to damages and/or to a declaration that the EC measure is inapplicable in the Danish legal order. It would even be perceivable that the Danish Supreme Court required the Danish Government to take action at the EC level to reverse the decision. The Danish Supreme Court acknowledged that the compatibility of the act with the EC Treaty has to be tried by the EU courts.[204] In other words, the national courts would have to refer a preliminary ruling to the ECJ. However, in the last instance–and the Danish Supreme Court was very clear about this part–it is for the Danish courts to ultimately decide whether the Community exceeded the limits of the sovereign rights transferred to it pursuant to the Danish Constitution.[205] If the Community has gone beyond its competences, the measure would be inapplicable in Denmark.

In conclusion, there is clear evidence that some national courts will not turn a blind eye towards an excessive use of Community competences and in particular of Article 308 EC. They have demonstrated their willingness to declare EC law inapplicable in their national legal order if it goes beyond the sovereign powers conferred on the Community in conformity with national constitutional law.

4.2 Union Law

Individual sanctions consist both of Community and of Union law instruments. National courts are ready to restrain the Community within the boundaries of the EC Treaty. Yet, national courts would be even more likely to rule–at least incidentally–on the conformity of *Union* law with national constitutional law. Despite the fact that CFSP lists of terrorist suspects are adopted by unanimity and hence are approved by the

[204] Danish Supreme Court, Case I 361/1997, *Carlsen v Rasmussen*, p 861, para 29.

[205] Section 20 of the Danish Constitution; ibid, para 32.

representatives of all EU Member States, national courts could declare Union law unconstitutional. National Courts might take a different view than the political representatives of their country on the compatibility of the decision with the competences of the Union. Interesting in this regard are the challenges of the implementation of the controversial[206] framework decision on the European Arrest Warrant (EAW)[207] into national law in the Czech Republic, Cyprus, Germany and Poland. The judgments of the highest national courts of these countries[208] triggered 'a far-reaching debate concerning the risk of incompatibility between the constitutions of the Member States and European Union law'.[209] The GCC declared the national implementation act void for breaching national constitutional rules, including the prohibition to extradite nationals and fair trial guarantees.[210] Similarly, the Polish Constitutional Court and the Supreme Court of Cyprus declared the respective national implementation unconstitutional for breaching the prohibition to extradite nationals. The Czech Constitutional Court, by contrast, confirmed the validity of the implementation of the EAW framework decision in the Czech Republic.

In particular the GCC was harshly criticized for taking a national perspective and ignoring the wider context of 'European Constitutionalism'.[211] The Court was even accused of a 'misuse of institutional choice' by not attempting to solve the conflict by interpreting the German law consistently with European law but by forcing the national legislator to take action.[212]

[206] See above all: Rob Blekxtoon and Wouter FW van Ballegooij (eds), *Handbook on the European Arrest Warrant* (Hague: TMC Asser Press, 2004), calling the EAW 'collateral, perhaps unavoidable damage from 9/11'.

[207] Council Framework Decision of 13 June 2002 (2002/584/JHA–OJ 2002, L 190/1).

[208] Supreme Court of Cyprus, Judgment of 7 November 2005 (Case 294/2005); Polish Constitutional Court, Judgment of 27 April 2005, No P 1/05; see also: Czech Constitutional Court, Judgment of 3 May 2006 (Case 66/04).

[209] AG Colomer, Case C-303/05, *Advocaten voor de Wereld* [2007] ECR I-3633, para 8.

[210] On 24 November 2004 the GCC first granted an injunction against the extradition of the applicant to the United Kingdom; eight month later the Court declared the German European Arrest Warrant Act 2004 (Gesetz zur Umsetzung des Rahmenbeschlusses über den Europäischen Haftbefehl und die Übergabeverfahren zwischen den Mitgliedstaaten der Europäischen Union, Europäisches Haftbefehlgesetz of 21 July 2004, Bundesgesetzblatt I-1748) void on the grounds that it violated Art 2(1) in conjunction with Arts 20(3), 16(2), and 19(4) of the German Constitution (Grundgesetz), EAW Decision of 18 July 2005 (2 BvR 2236/04).

[211] Jan Komárek, 'European Constitutionalism and the European Arrest Warrant: In Search of the Limits of 'Contrapunctual Principles', *Common Market Law Review*, 44 (2007), 9–40.

[212] ibid, pp 38–9.

It is true, the GCC applied national constitutional rules to the national instrument of implementation[213] and came to the conclusion that the 'legislature could have chosen an implementation that shows a higher consideration in respect of the fundamental right concerned without infringing the binding objectives of the framework decision'.[214] The decision does not consider the wider European context. This is demonstrated, inter alia, in that the GCC did *not* refer to the ECJ's judgment in *Pupino*[215] and in that the Court considered third pillar instruments from a different angle than Community law. Even though the majority did *not* mention the *Maastricht* decision[216] it became perfectly clear that the Court does not show the same deference to the Luxembourg courts in the Union pillars. In its decision on the *EAW* the GCC defended the *full standard* of protection provided by the German Constitution. Without directly addressing the constitutionality of the framework decision, it stated that the German legislator did not exhaust 'the margins afforded by the framework legislation when incorporating it into national law'.[217] Thus, it indicated that the framework decision could be incorporated in conformity with the German Constitution. However, the GCC discussed the possibility of national bodies breaching EU law obligations where compliance is irreconcilable

[213] See for a more detailed analysis of the GCC's EAW decision: Christian Tomuschat, 'Inconsistencies–The German Federal Constitutional Court on the European Arrest Warrant', *European Constitutional Law Review*, 2 (2006), pp 209–26; see also: Christian Tomuschat, 'Ungereimtes–Zum Urteil des Bundesverfassungsgerichts vom 18. Juli 2005 über den Europäischen Haftbefehl', *Europäische Zeitschrift für Grundrechte* (2005), p 456.

[214] ibid, para 94; this is appears a difficult argument to make given the wording of Art 5(3) of the EAW Framework Decision (n 207 above):

> where a person who is the subject of a European arrest warrant for the purposes of prosecution [different for the execution of a custodial sentence or detention order, see Art 4(6)] is a national or resident of the executing Member State, surrender [must take place but] may be subject to the condition that the person, after being heard, is returned to the executing Member State in order to serve there the custodial sentence or detention order passed against him in the issuing Member State.

[215] Case C-105/03, *Pupino* (n 120 above); the majority did not mention the judgment, only Judge Gerhardt mentioned it in his dissenting opinion. AG Colomer in C-303/05, considered *Pupino* to be 'the suitable starting point' of the procedural validity of the EAW framework decision [para 4]. See for more details on this judgment: Eleanor Spaventa, 'Opening Pandora's Box: Some Reflections on the Constitutional Effects of the Decision in Pupino', *European Constitutional Law Review*, 3: 5–24 (2007).

[216] In this decision the GCC ruled that the Community had a system of protection comparable to the German Constitution and announced that it would refrain from reviewing secondary Community law, although the Court also asserted its residual competence to step in if the level of protection at the Community level dropped below the minimum guarantees of the German Constitution.

[217] ibid, para 97.

with the German Constitution.[218] This implies that the Court places national constitutional standards for the political bodies above obligations arising from Union law and that it is willing to hold the political organs responsible for adopting acts that go beyond the Union's competences.[219] Advocate-General Colomer critically suspected that the GCC's ruling was 'inspired by that old mistrust and is a reaction to the restrictions on judicial control in the third pillar...' However, he also agreed[220] with the Court to the extent that:

> [i]t is rather paradoxical that, in an area where the Union has an increased influence on the fundamental rights of individuals, the powers of the Court have been somewhat [sic] restricted.

Both the Polish and German Constitutional Courts sent clear warning signals to Luxembourg. They demonstrated that obligations under Union law will not keep them from fully scrutinizing all national law as to its compatibility with their constitutions. However, neither court ruled on the validity of the European framework decision. In a reference from Belgium, by contrast, the question of the validity of the framework decision was brought to the ECJ,[221] and following Advocate-General Colomer who considered the rulings of the courts in Cyprus, Czech Republic, Germany, and Poland,[222] the ECJ confirmed the lawfulness of the framework decision on 3 May 2007.[223]

The EAW decision was not the first time that the GCC dealt with Union law. Already in the *Maastricht* decision, the applicant argued that the limitations of the jurisdiction of the ECJ in Article 46 TEU (ex-Article L) created an unconstitutional *lacuna*.[224] In its reply[225] the GCC specifically stated that jurisdiction of the EU courts is only excluded:

[218] Judge Lübbe-Wolf critically remarked that the freedom to infringe the law could not legitimately be an endorsement of democracy in the EU (ibid, para 177).

[219] See Chapter 6, Section 3.

[220] AG Colomer in Case C-303/05, *Advocaten voor de Wereld* (n 209 above), endnote 81.

[221] Case C-303/05, *Advocaten voor de Wereld* [2007] ECR I-3633.

[222] AG Colomer in Case C-303/05 (n 209 above), para 7.

[223] See also: ECtHR, *Kafkaris v Cyprus*, Application No 21906/04; in their joint partly dissenting opinion, Judges Tulkens, Cabral Barreto, Fura-Sandström, Spielmann and Jebens recently referred to Art 5 of the EAW framework decision as reflecting common trends of clemency in criminal justice by requiring review of life-time detention after 20 years. Admittedly, this does not directly concern the extradition procedures.

[224] GCC, *Maastricht* decision (n 192 above), para 14.

[225] English translation from: Lachmann, 'The Treaty of Maastricht' (n 202 above), p 57 et seq.

in respect of provisions of the Union Treaty which do not confer powers on the Union to take measures which have direct effect on holders of constitutional rights within the territory of member-States.

This view of Union law appears no longer adequate in view of the Union lists of terrorist suspects, which – even if they are neither directly applicable nor directly binding on individuals–have a direct impact on the constitutional rights of those listed in them.[226]

The GCC further required that:

[i]f at some future date measures of constitutional relevance are envisaged in the course of co-operation under Articles J and K [Titles V and VI of the TEU], a further assenting Act will be needed for those purposes which can then be scrutinised in its turn to see if there are any gaps in the legal protection.'[227]

The Court referred here to an act of ratification, transposing a Treaty amendment into the national legal order. Hence, the Court required a new transfer of powers for the Union to be competent to adopt measures which directly impact the legal position of its subjects.

In conclusion, in the light of the GCC's case-law there is a considerable likelihood that the GCC would consider the adoption of Union lists of terrorist suspects beyond the powers transferred to the Union in the TEU and that it would not hesitate to intervene.

5. Treaty of Lisbon

The Treaty of Lisbon acknowledges the need for action by the Union to fight terrorism in numerous provisions.[228] The Lisbon Treaty will introduce two possible legal bases for restrictive measures against individuals: Articles 75 and 215 of the Treaty on the Functioning of the European Union (TFEU). This is an improvement as such. Further, the Lisbon Treaty addresses the criticism that individual sanctions infringe procedural

[226] See Chapter 3, Sections 3.2.2 and 3.2.3.

[227] GCC, *Maastricht* decision (n 192 above), para 15.

[228] See the new Art 43 (common security and defence policy) TEU; and the new Arts 75 (area of freedom, security and justice), 83 (minimum rules for serious crimes), 88 (Europol), and 222 (solidarity clause) TFEU–*all references to the new Articles of the Treaties after the Lisbon Treaty enters into force*. At present the only references to terrorism are in Arts 29 and 31 TEU (Police and Judicial Cooperation in Criminal Matters).

rights: both Article 75 and Article 215 TFEU contain a clause stipulating that '[t]he acts referred to in this Article shall include necessary provisions on legal safeguards'[229] and Article 275 TFEU explicitly confers on the EU courts jurisdiction to review restrictive measures against natural and legal persons.

The sanctioning procedure in Article 215 TFEU is the same as in Article 301 EC; only, that it contains an explicit competence for sanctions 'against natural or legal persons and groups or non-State entities'.[230] Despite the involvement of the High Representative of the Union for Foreign Affairs and Security Policy the Union's competences to adopt individual sanctions are *not* limited to EU-external terrorist suspects. Article 215 TFEU abandons the reference to 'third countries' entirely. This would appear to address the unease of those who argue that the wording of Article 301 EC does not allow the adoption of sanctions against EU-internal terrorists.[231]

Under Article 215 TFEU the European Parliament has the right to be informed. This is an improvement in comparison to the procedure in Article 301 EC, which does not foresee any role for the European Parliament. In practice, however, since Article 308 EC has been added to form part of the joint legal basis for individual sanctions the European Parliament is consulted.

Article 75 TFEU, by contrast, differs considerably from Article 60 EC. While the former allowed for the adoption of 'necessary urgent measures on the movement of capital and on payments as regards the third countries concerned' pursuant to the procedure set out in Article 301 EC, Article 75 TFEU is a legal basis in its own right. Its objective is to ensure that the Union constitutes an area of freedom, security and justice.

Since Articles 75 and 215 TFEU set out very different procedures, the choice of the legal basis is crucial for the involvement of the different institutions of the Union and the Member States respectively. Pursuant to Article 75 TFEU a 'framework for administrative measures with regard to capital movements and payments' is established under the ordinary legislative procedure, which the Council then implements by qualified

[229] Article 215(3) and Art 75(3) TFEU respectively.

[230] Article 215(2) TFEU.

[231] See Recital 14 of Regulation 2580/2001/EC: 'The list referred to in Article 2(3) of this Regulation may include persons and entities linked or related to third countries as well as those who otherwise are the focus of the CFSP aspects of Common Position 2001/931/CFSP. For the adoption of provisions in this Regulation concerning the latter, the Treaty does not provide powers other than those under Article 308.'

majority[232] following a proposal of the Commission. Article 215 TFEU, by contrast, requires a unanimous CFSP decision pursuant to Article 25 TEU that provides for further action by the Union. The CFSP decision is then implemented by the Council acting with qualified majority; the European Parliament is informed only. Hence the two main differences are the voting requirements in the Council[233] and the involvement of the European Parliament.[234]

The choice of the legal basis appears to depend on the origins of the list of the terrorist suspects: while Article 75 TFEU appears to serve as the basis for sanctions against terrorist suspects adopted in the autonomous sanctioning procedure, Article 215 TFEU appears to constitute *lex specialis* for financial sanctions against individuals based on UN lists, irrespective of whether the measures target EU-internal or EU-external terrorists. Hence, the Lisbon Treaty provides separate legal bases for the two different sanctions regimes of the EU: on the one hand the EU-mandated autonomous sanctions regime and on the other the one based on UN lists of terrorist suspects.

As a consequence, Article 75 TFEU would establish an entirely new competence of the Union for *autonomous* financial sanctions against *EU-internal terrorists*, such as asset freezes against *Segi*. At present these measures are adopted by the Member States because they are thought to fall outside the scope of Article 301 EC. Hence, if Articles 75 and 215 TFEU are interpreted in the way here proposed, cases where those listed in a CFSP instrument are not subject to further operational measures at the European level will no longer occur. This would also preclude the creation of a new jurisdictional vacuum based on a reading of Article 275 TFEU that limits judicial review to CFSP decisions effectively 'providing for restrictive measures.' Listings of EU-internal terrorists would be based on Article 75 TFEU, which is in any event subject to the jurisdiction of the EU courts.

If it enters into force, the Lisbon Treaty will improve the situation of those listed and sanctioned by the Union. It introduces two explicit legal bases for restrictive measures against natural and legal persons, both including specific references to legal safeguards, and establishes jurisdiction

232 Qualified majority is the default voting requirement in the Council if the Treaty does not state otherwise (Art 16(3) TEU).

233 Qualified majority under Art 75 TFEU and unanimity under Art 215 TFEU.

234 Ordinary legislative procedure under Art 75 TFEU, while under Art 215 TFEU the EP is merely informed.

of the EU courts for these measures. However, with the introduction of the two new legal bases for individual sanctions in the Lisbon Treaty, the distinction between internal and external European terrorist suspects could have been abandoned. It is best understood in the light of Article 301 EC's reference to third countries. Yet, a link to foreign policy exists both with regard to external European terrorist suspects and with regard to sanctions imposed as a consequence of a listing at the UN level. A distinction between restrictive measures giving effect to UN lists of terrorist suspects and those based on EU-managed lists of terrorist suspects could be seen as more intuitive. Further, sanctions against private individuals are used as counter-terrorist measures and terrorism is correctly perceived as both an internal and an external threat in the EU.[235] This makes the distinction between internal and external terrorist suspects even more difficult to justify in practice.

Conclusions

Articles 301, 60, and 308 EC do not confer upon the Community the competence to adopt sanctions against individuals, either independently or jointly.[236] Hence, under current law such measures cannot lawfully be adopted in the first pillar. This conclusion is drawn from the wording, but also from an examination of the normative meaning of Article 301 EC.

Article 301 EC vests the Community with the power to interrupt economic relations as a form of political pressure on third states. This is significantly different from adopting restrictive measures against individuals that amount, at least in their effect, to criminal measures. State sanctions and individual sanctions follow distinct political and economic rationales. The identification of the target in particular plays a very different role. And most importantly, the adoption procedure would have to be changed in order to provide for the necessary procedural safeguards.

[235] Jörg Monar, 'Common Threat and Common Response? The European Union's Counter-Terrorism Strategy and its Problems', *Government and Opposition*, Vol 42, No 3 (2007), pp 292–313; Ariane Chebel d'Appollonia and Simon Reich (eds), *Immigration, Integration, and Security, America and Europe in Comparative Perspective* (Pittsburgh: University of Pittsburgh Press, 2008).

[236] This conclusion differs from the ECJ's ruling in Cases C-402/05 P and C-415/05 P, *Kadi and al Barakaat* (n 2 above).

The fact that individual sanctions do not fall within the competences of the Community under Article 301 EC cannot be healed by adding Article 308 EC. Finding the Community competent to adopt individual sanctions might be desirable from an effectiveness perspective, but it is not supported by a compelling legal argument. A comparison of the three (very) different ways in which the ECJ, the CFI, and Advocate-General Maduro construed a Community competence for individual sanctions reveals that all three struggled to reach the 'right result', by stretching the scope of Articles 301 and/or 308 EC beyond the clear wording of these articles and beyond their past application.

The EU courts' pragmatism in finding a Community competence for individual sanctions avoided much tension. It allows the political institutions (Council and Commission, while the European Parliament is only consulted) to comply with the necessities of the international cooperation in the fight against terrorism. It also avoided turbulences in the inter-institutional balance, not only with the Community institutions but also with the Council acting unanimously under the second pillar. Another pragmatic consideration of the EU courts might have been that the human rights situation of those sanctioned would have been unlikely to improve after a ruling that Community sanctions against individuals are ultra vires. This would have relocated competence to the Member States. However, how many national courts would dare to annul individual sanctions for breaching fundamental procedural rights is uncertain.[237]

Notwithstanding the particular situation under European law, there are two main reasons why individual sanctions should not be adopted on a general legal basis for state sanctions. The first is that these provisions do not consider the procedural rights of individual as active participants. The second main reason is that adopting measures as specific as individual sanctions on a legal basis for general measures such as state sanctions changes the constitutional division of competences. Both problems are likely to persist if sanctions are adopted by the Member States.[238]

Effectively, individual sanctions are an example of an area where the Member States, the Council, the Commission, and the EU courts (including the Advocate-General) agree that the Community (following a decision of the Council under the second pillar) can adopt measure that fall outside

[237] See the discussion in Chapter 5, Section 5.2.2.

[238] See also Chapter 1, Section 5 on the national adoption procedures.

the EC Treaty. It demonstrates that in this particular area there is a political consensus to emancipate the Community from the Treaty constraints. Yet, it is necessary to acknowledge that it is a victory of pragmatism over legality that results in a self-authorization.

The cross-pillar nature of the European sanctioning procedure added to the complexity. It entails the particular danger that the Community institutions are reduced to a purely executive role. By ruling that the Community institutions are bound to implement the CFSP common position the ECJ has effectively allowed the Council acting under the second pillar to determine Community action. Further, despite the undisputed commitment to the rule of law the Union pillars provide only for strictly limited judicial review. Therefore, they are not suitable to adopt measures that directly impinge on the rights of individuals, such as lists of terrorist suspects. This is the case both for the second and for the third pillar. Yet by their substance, individual sanctions would rather belong to the third pillar than to the second pillar.

The Treaty of Lisbon creates two new legal bases for the adoption of sanctions against private individuals. If it enters into force it will improve legal certainty and reduce the likelihood of disturbances of the institutional balance and the power division between the EU and its Member States, caused by the current way of taking ultra vires actions. Further, the provision of legal safeguards is made an express requirement of adopting individual sanctions. Besides these general rules an instrument of secondary law should set out criteria for the listing and sanctioning of individuals. This would restrict the margin of discretion of the European institutions in the individual case and thereby increase predictability for those sanctioned.

3

The Right of Access to Justice

Introduction

The right of access to justice is well-established within the European Union (EU). The European Convention on Human Rights (ECHR, the Convention), European Union law (EU law), the legal orders of all the EU Member States,[1] as well as international human rights instruments[2] acknowledge the importance of judicial protection. Hence, as a matter of principle it is undisputed that individuals must have at their disposal remedies to challenge the legality of measures adversely affecting their legal position. This includes measures taken in the fight against terrorism, such as sanctions against private individuals. However, a number of judgments of the European Court of Human Rights (ECtHR),[3] the Court of

[1] Eg: Art 19(4) of the German Constitution: 'Should any person's rights be violated by state acts, recourse to the courts shall be open to him. [...]'.

[2] See also: Art 14(1) of the International Covenant on Civil and Political Rights:

> All persons shall be equal before the courts and tribunals. In the determination of any criminal charge against him, or of his rights and obligations in a suit at law, everyone shall be entitled to a fair and public hearing by a competent, independent and impartial tribunal established by law. The press and the public may be excluded from all or part of a trial for reasons of morals, public order (*ordre public*) or national security in a democratic society, or when the interest of the private lives of the parties so requires, or to the extent strictly necessary in the opinion of the court in special circumstances where publicity would prejudice the interests of justice; but any judgment rendered in a criminal case or in a suit at law shall be made public except where the interest of juvenile persons otherwise requires or the proceedings concern matrimonial disputes or the guardianship of children.'

and Art 8 of the Universal Declaration of Human Rights:

> 'Everyone has the right to an effective remedy by the competent national tribunals for acts violating the fundamental rights granted him by the constitution or by law.

[3] ECtHR, *Segi and others v all 15 MS*, Application No 6422/02, judgment of 23 May 2002; ECtHR, *Bosphorus Hava Yollari Turizm veTicaret AS v Ireland* (45036/98) (2006) 42 EHRR 1.

First Instance (CFI),[4] and of national courts[5] have recently given reason for concern. In particular the CFI introduced a new, lower level of protection for sanctions giving effect to UN lists[6] and denied access to court altogether for Union lists of terrorist suspects.[7] The CFI's rulings on sanctions giving effect to UN lists were followed by some national courts,[8] but have later been repealed by the ECJ.[9] The CFI's rulings on Union lists of terrorist suspects have been mitigated: the ECJ opened the preliminary ruling procedure to common positions containing terrorist lists.[10]

Nonetheless, the judiciary's attitude towards individual sanctions has demonstrated that the right of access to justice is not so well-established that it is inalienable. Additionally, the ECtHR has introduced a new threshold for judicial review of measures adopted by the Community[11] and denied those labelled as terrorists under Union law the status of a victim, because it requires implementation.[12] The overwhelming objective of fighting terrorism has made it possible to think and argue that individuals can be stripped of their well-established procedural rights in the EU. Union lists of terrorist suspects continue to remain not directly challengeable.

[4] Eg: Case T-306/01, *Ahmed Ali Yusuf and Al Barakaat International Foundation v Council and Commission* [2005] ECR II-3533; Case T-315/01, *Yassin Abdullah Kadi v Council and Commission* [2005] ECR II-3649, repealed: Cases C-402/05 P and C-415/05 P, *Kadi and al Barakaat*, judgment of 3 September 2008, not yet reported; Case T-49/04, *Hassan v Council and Commission* [2006] ECR II-52; appealed: C-399/06 P, *Hassan v Council and Commission*, OJ 2006 C 294/30; Case T-253/02, *Chafiq Ayadi v Council* [2006] ECR II-2139; appealed: C-403/06 P, *Ayadi v Council*, OJ 2006 C 294/32; Case T-338/02, *Segi and others* [2004] ECR II-01647; but also Case T-228/02, *Organisation des Modjahedines du peuple d'Iran v Council and UK (OMPI I)* [2006] ECR II-4665; Case T-256/07, *People's Mojahidin Organization of Iran v Council (OMPI II)*, judgment of 23 October 2008, not yet reported; appeal pending: Case C-576/08 P, *People's Mojahedin Organization of Iran* and Case T-284/08, *People's Mojahedin Organization of Iran v Council (OMPI III)*, judgment of 4 December 2008, not yet reported.

[5] Most prominently: Swiss Supreme Court (Schweizer Bundesgericht), *Youssef Mustapha Nada v SECO*, Staatssekretariat für Wirtschaft, judgment of 14 November 2007, 1A.45/2007/daa.

[6] Case T-306/01, *Yusuf* (n 4 above); Case T-315/01, *Kadi* (n 4 above); Case T-49/04, *Hassan* (n 4 above); Case T-253/02, *Ayadi* (n 4 above).

[7] Case T-338/02, *Segi* (n 4 above); Case T-228/02, *OMPI I* (n 4 above); see however: Case C-355/04 P, *Segi v Council* [2007] ECR I-1657.

[8] Swiss Supreme Court, Nada (n 5 above); also some lower courts, see eg in: Germany VG Ansbach, 1st Chamber, judgment of 14 December 2006, AN 1 K 06.30883; See however also: GCC, judgment of 30 June 2009 (*Treaty of Lisbon*), 2 BvE 2/08, 2 BvE 5/08; 2 BvR 1010/08; 2 BvR 1022/08; 2 BvR 1259/08; 2 BvR 182/09.

[9] Cases C-402/05 P and C-415/05 P, *Kadi* and *al Barakaat* (n 4 above), see Chapter 5, in particular Section 1.

[10] Case C-355/04 P, *Segi* (n 7 above), see Chapter 6, Section 2.

[11] ECtHR, *Bosphorus* (n 3 above).

[12] ECtHR, *Segi* (n 3 above).

Chapter 3 examines the right of access to justice of those sanctioned as a matter of principle. An important objective is to identify the effects both of Union listings and of Community asset freezes on the legally protected interests of those listed and sanctioned. The potential restrictions for reasons of security will be analysed in Chapter 4.

Chapter 3 examines the ways in which European sanctions against private individuals clash with the well-established right of access to justice, both under the ECHR and under EU law. Particular attention is paid to the criminal implications of individual sanctions. Throughout, Union lists of terrorist suspects and Community asset freezes are distinguished.[13] This is necessary because the two measures differ in their effect on the legal position of individuals. Further where justified, the differences are pointed out between sanctions giving effect to UN lists of terrorist suspects and those giving effect to Union lists.[14] Sections 1 and 2 set the scene. While Section 1 outlines the commitment of the EU to the rule of law, Section 2 emphasizes the importance of the ECHR for EU law and points out the difference of fundamental rights protection under the ECHR and under EU law. Section 3 conducts a detailed analysis of whether and to what extent those listed as terrorist suspects under Union law and those sanctioned by the Community can rely on Article 6 ECHR in light of the case-law of the ECtHR. It shows that both the CFI and the ECtHR departed from established standards of fundamental rights in cases concerning individual sanctions. It is submitted that those targeted by European sanctions against individuals have a right to judicial review according to Article 6 ECHR and, even if only applied subsidiarily, a right to an effective remedy under Article 13 ECHR. It is further argued that the criminal characteristics of individual sanctions require a strict application of Article 6 ECHR.

1. A Union of Law

The EU is committed to the rule of law.[15] The ECJ has repeatedly confirmed this commitment, including by extending its own jurisdiction

[13] See Chapter 1, Section 4 for the adoption procedure of individual sanctions and the different instruments involved.

[14] See Chapter 1, Section 2 on the distinction between the two different types of sanctions.

[15] Case 294/83, *Parti Ecologiste 'Les Verts' v Parliament* [1986] ECR 1339, para 23; Case 314/85, *Foto-Frost* [1987] ECR 4199, para 16; Case C-314/91, *Weber v Parliament* [1993] ECR I-1093, para 8; Joined Cases T-222/99, T-327/99 and T-329/99, *Martinez*, para 48; see also Opinion 1/91, para 21 and AG Mengozzi in: C-354/04 P, *Gestoras Pro Amnistia* and Case C-355/04 P, *Segi* (n 7 above), para 73 et seq.

beyond the limits defined by the wording of individual provisions of the European Treaties.[16] The commitment to the rule of law is undisputed, notwithstanding the extensively criticized absence of a catalogue of fundamental rights in the Treaties, which is only insufficiently compensated by a cryptic reference to the ECHR. Under the current Treaties, the rule of law is explicitly recognized as one of the foundations of the EU in Article 6(1) TEU. It is further confirmed by the evolving constitutionalization of European law.[17]

The rule of law, however, is not a clearly delimited concept.[18] Some consider it to be comprised of substantive values. Others understand it as purely formal concept. A substantive definition of the rule of law includes a choice of values, such as fundamental rights. Albert Venn Dicey, the well-known nineteenth-century legal theorist, proposed that the rule of law consists of three elements: first, it means supremacy of law as opposed to the influence of arbitrary power; secondly, it signifies equality before the law; and, thirdly, it expresses that the law is not the source, but the consequence, of the rights of individuals.[19] This definition can be contrasted with more positivist views, taken for example by Joseph Raz. According to the latter the rule of law is a purely formal concept stipulating that first 'people should be ruled by the law and obey it' and secondly that 'the law should be such that people will be able to be guided by it'.[20] This more formal definition (only) requires laws to 'be expressed in the clearest and most precise way possible', 'interpreted objectively' and 'obeyed and enforced'.[21] However, all definitions of the rule of law share certain core elements. Even the more formal positivist conception of the rule of law includes certain 'substantive elements'. As a minimum, they

[16] See above all: Case 294/83, *Les Verts*, ibid, para 23 et seq; Case 2/88, *Zwartveld* [1990] ECR I-3365, paras 15–24.

[17] Jo Shaw, 'Postnational Constitutionalism in the European Union', *Journal of European Public Policy*, 6 (1999), pp 579–97.

[18] For the rule of law under international law see Chapter 5, Section 4.2.1; for the Member States and in the EU: Erik Wennerström, *The Rule of Law and the European Union* (Uppsala: Iustus, 2007), p 19 et seq and p 84 et seq.

[19] Albert Dicey, *Introduction to the Study of the Law of the Constitution* (London: MacMillan, 1885), p 202 et seq.

[20] Joseph Raz, 'The Rule of Law and its Virtue', in *The Authority of Law: Essays on Law and Morality* (Oxford: Oxford University Press, 1979), p 212.

[21] Raz, 'The Rule of Law', ibid; see also: Trevor Hartley, *Constitutional Problems of the European Union* (Oxford: Hart Publishing, 1999), p 23.

require that everybody's rights are set out in law and that observance of the law is controlled by judges whose judgments are subject to enforcement.[22] Law can only guide people if it is prospective and stable, and if its making is subject to open, stable, clear, and general rules. Further, the rule of law requires the subjection of more particular laws to more generalized ones and a certain separation of powers. Finally, compliance with (the different elements of) the rule of law is never absolute but a matter of degree.[23]

European law is a unique combination of features of international and national law. It shows characteristics of common and civil law systems, but, in the end, it is different from both of them.[24] Under European law, despite the absence of a clear hierarchy of legal instruments, the Treaties are 'the constitutional charter'[25] of the EU. The ECJ interprets the Treaties and forms, through its interpretation, constitutional principles. The right of access to justice, even though not expressly stated in the Treaties, is a fundamental procedural right and an important element of the rule of law in the EU. In the words of Advocate-General Mengozzi:

> [t]he rule of law is based not so much on rules and the proclamation of rights as on mechanisms that make it possible to ensure respect for rules and rights (*ubi ius ibi remedium*). The 'right to challenge a measure before the courts is inherent in the rule of law', it is the 'corollary' to it, and both 'a victory over and an instrument' of it.[26]

The right of access to justice is guaranteed under Articles 6 and 13 ECHR, which forms by way of Article 6(2) TEU part of the *aquis communitaire*. The right of access to justice is also part of the general principles

[22] Rafael A Benitez, 'Administrative Justice in a World in Transition: Pan-European Values in Administrative Justice', *Common Law World Review*, 30 (2001), p 437, setting out the common values in the handbook of the European Council, 1996; critical to the inexistence of a written bill of rights in binding European law: Matej Avbelj, 'European Court of Justice and the Question of Value Choices: Fundamental Human Rights as an Exception to the Freedom of Movement of Goods', Jean Monnet Working Papers, 6/04 (2004), http://www.jeanmonnetprogram.org/papers/04/040601.html.

[23] Raz, 'The Rule of Law' (n 20 above), p 211.

[24] Vlad Constantinesco, 'The ECJ as a Law-maker: Praetor Aut Contra Legem?' in David O'Keeffe and Antonio Bavasso, *Judicial Review in European Union Law: Liber Amicorum in Honour of Lord Slynn of Hadley* (The Hague: Kluwer Law International, 2000), pp 73–9.

[25] Case 294/83, *Les Verts* (n 15 above).

[26] AG Mengozzi, in: Case C-355/04 P, *Segi* (n 7 above), para 101; referring to AG Darmon in Case 222/84, *Johnston* [1986] ECR 1651, para 3 and AG Léger in Case C-224/01, *Köbler* [2003] ECR I-10239, para 86.

of EU law as they result from the constitutional traditions common to the Member States (Article 6(2) TEU) .[27]

Article 6(2) TEU refers to the 'general principles of *Community* law'. It does not, by its wording, include the second and third pillar, even though it is located in general provisions at the beginning of the TEU and not in the TEC. Yet, the wording 'principles of *Community* law' is not meant to limit the application of the general principles to the first pillar. It must be understood in the context of European integration. When the TEU, which created the EU, was drafted it referred to the existing 'general principles of the Community' in order to submit the EU as a whole to the rule of law and to those principles.[28] The same ambition is present in the Charter of Fundamental Rights (Charter), which takes a unitary approach to the EU and is largely understood as reaffirming already existing rights.[29] It does not newly extend fundamental rights to the Union pillars, but follows the existing understanding that the Union as a whole is bound by fundamental rights, including the right of access to court (Article 47 of the Charter). Hence, the European institutions are bound by the rule of law and by fundamental rights when they act as Community institutions, but also when they act under the second or third pillar.[30]

Indeed, long before the EU was founded the ECJ specified[31] for the European Economic Community that:

> [a]n action for annulment must [...] be available in the case of all measures adopted by the institutions, whatever their nature or form, which are intended to have legal effects.'

[27] See in particular: Case 222/84, *Johnston* (n 26 above), para 18 and Case 222/86, *UNECTEF v Heylens and Others* [1987] ECR 4097, para 11, but also: Case 70/88, *Chernobyl I* [1990] ECR I-2041; Case C-97/91, *Oleificio Borelli v Commission* [1992] ECR I-6313, para 14, Case C-1/99, *Kofisa Italia* [2001] ECR I-207, para 46; Case C-424/99, *Commission v Austria* [2001] ECR I-9285, para 45–47, and Case C-50/00 P, *Unión de Pequeños Agricultores v Council (UPA)* [2002] ECR I-6677, para 39.

[28] Despite the limited jurisdiction of the EU courts, the respect for fundamental rights in the Union influences the outcome of the Council's debates: Anthony Arnull, *The European Union and its Court of Justice* (Oxford: Oxford University Press, 2006), p 342.

[29] Piet Eeckhout, 'The EU Charter of Fundamental Rights and the Federal Question', *Common Market Law Review*, 39 (2002), pp 947–8, referring to a number of AG opinions (footnote 10); the Charter was recently cited by the ECJ: Case C-540/03, *EP v Council* [2006] ECR I-5769, paras 31, 32, 34 and 58.

[30] Ricardo Gosalbo Bono, 'Some Reflections on the CFSP Legal Order', *CML Rev*, 43 (2006), p 337 et seq, at 347; Case C-355/04 P, *Segi* (n 7 above), para 53.

[31] Case 22/70, *Commission v Council (ERTA)* [1971] ECR 263, para 42; Case 294/83, *Les Verts* (n 15 above), para 24.

In the *Les Verts* case the ECJ left no doubt about the commitment of the Court to deliver justice to anyone whose rights are potentially violated by an action of a European institution.[32] The Court was asked to review an act of the European Parliament despite the fact that the Treaty, at that time, did not provide for a specific review mechanism for acts of the European Parliament. The ECJ explicitly recognized[33] that:

> the Community [is] based on the rule of law, inasmuch as neither its Member States nor its institutions can avoid a review of the question whether the measures adopted by them are in conformity with the basic constitutional charter, the Treaty.

The Court went in *Les Verts* beyond the strict limits of individual Treaty provisions in order to comply with the Treaty's general scheme based on the rule of law.[34] This is based on an understanding of the rule of law as going beyond a purely formalistic hierarchy of law and containing also substantive elements. The right of access to justice looms large in the ECJ's understanding of the rule of law.

The arrival of individual sanctions within the European legal order has brought a new challenge to the EU courts. They must reconcile international efforts to fight terrorism with the rule of law as it is understood in the European legal order. Respect for the rule of law is purported to be part of EU counter-terrorist policies.[35]

2. The Relevance of the ECHR for EU Law

The ECHR is the single most important international agreement compelling the EU Member States to respect fundamental rights. All Member States are without exception Contracting Parties to the Convention. Article 1 ECHR stipulates that the Convention governs all actions within the jurisdiction of the Contracting Parties. National (implementation) measures fall straightforwardly under the Convention. Consequently, those legally affected by national measures enjoy, as a matter of principle, a right

[32] The parties in the appeal in *Segi* still rely on this landmark case: Opinion of AG Mengozzi in Case C-354/04 P, *Segi* (n 7 above), paras 166 and 168 et seq.

[33] Case 294/83, *Les Verts* (n 15 above), para 23. [34] ibid.

[35] Eg: EU Council Secretariat, 'The European Union and the Fight against Terrorism', Brussels, 9 March 2007; available: http://www.eurunion.org.

to an effective remedy and a right of access to justice under the ECHR. This includes all national measures adopted in order to implement European legal instruments containing lists of terrorist suspects,[36] such as the exchange of information.[37] It also includes the transmission of relevant information by the competent national authorities to the EU, which leads to the listing of a particular person.[38]

The Convention's relevance for actions of the European institutions is less straightforward. It is well-known that the EU is not a signatory to the ECHR and therefore not directly bound by it. However, the Strasbourg Court has decided that, notwithstanding the EU's qualification as a legal person in international law, EU Member States remain responsible for actions of the institutions that they have created and take part in.[39]

In this regard, Community law and Union law must be distinguished. In the case of *Bosphorus*[40] the ECtHR established a general presumption that the protection of fundamental rights under Community law is equivalent to the protection under the Convention. At the same time the ECtHR assured that this presumption can be rebutted in the individual case: Community law can become directly subject to review in Strasbourg where the protection offered by the Community is shown to be manifestly deficient. Hence, Community law enjoys a special status that makes full review by the Strasbourg Court less likely, but does not rule it out as a matter of principle.[41]

The situation is different for Union law. Union law is subject to full review in Strasbourg, where it is regarded to violate Convention rights. In *Bosphorus* the ECtHR emphasized that the judgment only concerned Community law,[42] but formulated the presumption of equivalent protection in an open manner referring to 'international organisations'.[43] Yet, it

[36] See Chapter 5, Section 5.1.2 for a discussion of whether the ECtHR could consider that the UN origin of a national measure excludes the protection under the Convention.

[37] See Art 4 of Common Position 2001/931/CFSP, OJ 2001 L 344/93, of 21 December 2001.

[38] See Art 1(4) of Common Position 2001/931/CFSP, ibid.

[39] It is settled case-law that the Contracting Parties cannot escape responsibility by cooperating under international law; see in particular: ECtHR, *Bosphorus* (n 3 above).

[40] ibid.

[41] See: Christina Eckes, 'Does the European Court of Human Rights Provide Protection from the European Community? The Case of Bosphorus Airways', *European Public Law*, 13 (2007), p 47 et seq.

[42] ECtHR, *Bosphorus* (n 3 above), para 72.

[43] ibid.

is unlikely that the ECtHR would apply that presumption to the second and third pillar (Union law).[44] The ECtHR focussed in its analysis in *Bosphorus* predominantly on judicial protection.[45] Under the current system however, the ECJ's jurisdiction is severely limited under the third pillar (Police and Judicial Cooperation in Criminal Matters (PJCC)) and nearly excluded under the second pillar (Common Foreign and Security Policy (CFSP)). Judicial review is limited or absent in fields that potentially have a great impact on fundamental rights, such as PJCC. The listing of individuals as terrorist suspects in cross-pillar Union instruments is only one example.[46] Prominent voices have expressed severe doubts whether the existing limitations to the protection of fundamental rights under the Union pillars are compatible with the ECHR.[47] Judge Ress in his concurring opinion in *Bosphorus* even used Union law as an example of where the protection was manifestly deficient in procedural terms.[48] Thus, the EU does not fulfil the decisive criterion for equivalent protection and the ECtHR can be expected to exercise full jurisdiction over Union activities where they infringe Convention rights. Hence, the exclusion of jurisdiction of the EU courts under the Union pillars would, as a direct consequence, lead to full judicial review by the ECtHR.

In the case of *Segi*[49] the applicants alleged an infringement of their rights under Article 6 ECHR by a Union list of terrorist suspects.[50] The ECtHR found that the applicants did not satisfy the standing requirements of Article 34 ECHR and advised them to seek judicial protection from potential measures of implementation.[51] Thus, Union lists of terrorist suspects were found to lack sufficient direct impact on the legal situation of

[44] Likewise, AG Mengozzi in Case C-355/04 P, *Segi* (n 7 above), para 86 for the third pillar.

[45] ECtHR, *Bosphorus* (n 3 above), para 150 et seq.

[46] See also eg: Council Framework Decision of 13 June 2002 on the European Arrest Warrant (EAW) (2002/584/JHA, OJ 2002 L190/1-20); see also the discussion of challenges against national measures implementing the EAW framework decision in Chapter Two, Section 4.2 and 6, Section 4.2.2.

[47] See above all Advocate-General Jacobs at: Francis Geoffrey Jacobs, 'The question of effective judicial remedies and access of individuals to the European Court of Justice', Working Group II, Working Document 21, (2002), http://european-convention.eu.int/docs/wd2/3299.pdf and 'Necessary Changes to the System of Judicial Remedies', Working Group II, Working Document 20 (2002), http://european-convention.eu.int/docs/wd2/3222.pdf.

[48] ECtHR, *Bosphorus* (n 3 above), Concurring Opinion of Judge Ress, p 54, para 3 referring to ECtHR, *Segi* (n 3 above).

[49] ECtHR, *Segi* (n 3 above).

[50] See on the adoption procedure Chapter 1, Section 4 and on judicial protection from Union lists of terrorist suspects Chapter 6, Section 2 and 3.

[51] No implementation measures had been adopted against Segi.

individuals. However, because the Court held that the applicants failed to satisfy the requirements of admissibility, it did not directly rule on the question of whether Union law could be subject to full review.

Irrespective of whether individuals can bring a case against Community or Union law in Strasbourg, the Convention is highly relevant for their rights under European law. The ECJ has taken much inspiration from the Convention. Long before a reference to the ECHR was incorporated into the Treaties, the Court had acknowledged the special significance of the Convention.[52] Advocates-General have extensively cited the ECHR and the ECtHR's case-law. They have also commented on the value of these legal sources and, hence, indirectly on the relationship between the two courts from the perspective of the EU. While they have shown hesitation to regard the ECtHR's case-law as directly binding,[53] they considered the Convention itself 'as part of Community law' and accepted that it 'can be invoked as such'.[54] In many cases the ECJ used both general principles of EU law and the ECHR to support its argument.[55] More recently the Court has even dropped its earlier 'general principles' or 'source of inspiration' approach. It has started to refer directly to the rights guaranteed in the ECHR.[56] Hence, even if one does not agree that the ECHR and the case-law of the ECtHR have been brought within the orbit of Community law,[57] it is uncontested that both are highly relevant to the determination of rights in the Luxembourg courts.

At the same time the context and ambition of the European legal order differs from those of the Convention. Although judicial protection within

[52] Case 222/84, *Johnston* (n 26 above), para 18.

[53] Opinion of AG Darmon, in Case 374/87, *Orkem* [1989] ECR 3283.

[54] Opinion of AG Jacobs, in Case C-84/95, *Bosphorus* [1996] ECR I-3953, at para 53.

[55] Case 4/73 *Nold* [1974] ECR 491; Case 222/84, *Johnston* (n 26 above), para 18; see also on the right to judicial review Case C-424/99, *Commission v Austria* (n 27 above), paras 45–7; Case C-13/94, *P v S* [1996] ECR I-2143, para 18; Case C-185/97, *Coote v Granada Hospitality* [1998] ECR I-5199, paras 21–3; Case 44/79, *Hauer* [1979] ECR 3727; Case 63/83, *Kirk* [1984] ECR 2689; Case C-60/00, *Carpenter* [2002] ECR I-6279; Case C-112/00, *Schmidberger* [2003] ECR I-5659.

[56] Case C-413/99, *Baumbast* [2002] ECR I-7091, para 72; Case C-60/00, *Carpenter* (n 55 above), paras 41–2; Case C-200/02, *Kunqian Catherine Zhu Chen* [2004] ECR I-9925, para 16.

[57] Nikolaos Lavranos, 'Concurrence of Jurisdiction between the ECJ and other International Courts and Tribunals', EUSA Ninth Biennial International Conference, 31 March–2 April 2005, Austin, Texas, 30, http://aei.pitt.edu/3016/01/EUSA_paper_LAVRANOS_FINAL-1.txt, p 30.

the European legal order is frequently criticized[58] the European legal order purports to offer fundamental rights protection equivalent to the protection in the legal orders of its Member States. Indeed, this was a condition for the GCC to recognize the supremacy of European law.[59]

The Convention, by contrast, ensures a minimum standard of human rights protection through an external review mechanism. The ECHR is 'a [...] mix of constitutional and international elements of law',[60] which was designed to provide a system of protection of fundamental rights subsidiary to the domestic ones and which remained incomplete in many ways.[61] It cannot and does not purport to replace the protection of fundamental rights in the domestic legal orders of the Contracting Parties. In accordance with this general nature of the ECHR, Articles 6 and 13 ECHR require a minimum standard of judicial and procedural protection.

The final report of working group II of the Convention on the Future of Europe pointed out that the Union legislation and the Charter of Fundamental Rights 'although based on the ECHR, go beyond the ECHR because Union law *acquis* had already reached a higher level of protection;' it specifically referred to the right of access to justice in this context and

[58] Albertina Albors-Llorens, *Private Parties in European Community Law: Challenging Community Measures* (Oxford: Clarendon Press, 1996); Henry Schermers and Denis Waelbroeck, *Judicial Protection in the European Union* (The Hague: Kluwer Law International, 2001); see in particular the criticism of the strict limitation of *locus standi* in the EU courts: Francis Geoffrey Jacobs, The question of effective judicial remedies and access of individuals to the European Court of Justice', Working Group II, Working Document 21, (2002), http://european-convention.eu.int/docs/wd2/3299.pdf; and to mention some of the more recent academic studies: Anthony Arnull, 'Private Applicants and the Action for Annulment since Codorníu', *Common Market Law Review*, 38 (2001), p 7; Filip Ragolle, 'Access to Justice for Private Applicants in the Community Legal Order: Recent (R)Evolutions', *ELR*, 29 (2003), p 90; John Temple Lang, 'Actions for Declarations that Community Regulations are Invalid: The Duties of National Courts under Article 10 EC', *ELR*, 28 (2003), p 102; John Usher, 'Direct and Individual Concern: An Effective Remedy or a Conventional Solution?', *ELR*, 28 (2003), p 575; Denis Waelbroeck, 'Editorial: Le droit au recours juridictionnel effectif du particulier. Trois pas en avant, deux pas en arrière', *Cahiers de Droit Européen*, 38 (2002), p 3; further: Paul Craig, *EU Administrative Law* (Oxford: Oxford University Press, 2006), pp 331–47; Arnull, *The European Union and its Court of Justice* (n 28 above), p 69 et seq; Angela Ward, *Judicial Review and the Rights of Private Parties in EC Law* (Oxford: Oxford University Press, 2000).

[59] See *Solange* case-law (Chapter 5, nn 215, 216 below).

[60] Iain Cameron, *National Security and the European Convention on Human Rights* (The Hague: Kluwer Law International, 2000), p 3.

[61] ibid, p 5 (with reference to the Preamble: '... to take the first steps for the collective enforcement of certain of the rights stated in the Universal Declaration' – emphasis added).

concluded that 'the guaranteed rights in the Charter reflect higher levels of protection in existing Union law'.[62] Along the same lines, Advocate-General Mengozzi argued in his opinion in the appeal case of *Segi* that simply because the ECtHR had *not* found a violation, this does not exclude 'the possibility of a breach of the appellants' right to effective judicial remedy in this case from the point of view of Union law'.[63] The standard of fundamental rights protection within the European legal order goes in many ways beyond the minimum protection of the ECHR.

By way of conclusion, the ECHR directly determines the rights of those targeted by national implementation measures, both in actions in the national courts and before the ECtHR. With regard to the acts of the European institutions the Convention is on the one hand an important source of persuasive law for review in Luxembourg, on the other, where the EU courts fail to protect fundamental rights it remains possible to challenge EU law directly before the ECtHR.[64] The Convention organs have ruled in settled case-law that the Contracting Parties remain responsible under the Convention, where they transfer sovereignty to an international organization.[65] They must ensure that the organization provides equivalent fundamental rights protection. For measures adopted under the first pillar the applicants would have to rebut the presumption of equivalent protection; for those adopted under the Union pillars the ECtHR would presumably ensure the full protection offered by the Convention.

3. The Right of Access to Justice under the Convention

3.1 Scope of the Convention Rights – Distinction Between Articles 6 and 13 ECHR

The ECHR protects the right to a fair trial in Article 6 ECHR and subsidiarily the right to an effective remedy in Article 13 ECHR. While the former article confers the right to judicial review, the latter does not require review by a judicial authority. The requirements of Article 13

[62] Final report of working group II of 22 October 2002, CONV 354/02, p 7.

[63] AG Mengozzi in: Case C-355/04 P, *Segi* (n 7 above), para 88.

[64] Needless to say, the respondent would not be the EU but the 27 EU Member States.

[65] European Commission of Human Rights, *M & Co v Germany*, Application No 13258/87, Commission decision of 9 February 1990, Decisions and Reports (DR) 64, p 145; and recently: ECtHR, *Bosphorus* (n 3 above), para 155.

ECHR can be satisfied by alternative administrative remedies, or even an ombudsman as long as these means are 'effective'. Article 6 ECHR constitutes *lex specialis* in respect of the procedural guarantees attached to judicial proceedings.[66] Where the Court finds a violation of Article 6 ECHR, there is no legal interest in re-examining the same substantive complaints under the less stringent requirements of Article 13 ECHR.[67] It will be argued that Article 6 ECHR applies to Union lists of terrorist suspects, as well as to Community asset freezes. Nonetheless, Article 13 ECHR will be briefly examined, first because the ECtHR ruled that where there is no overlap between different measures a separate examination of Article 13 ECHR is possible in the same case[68] and, secondly, because the application of Article 6 ECHR to Union lists might be contested, Article 13 ECHR could become relevant subsidiarily.

3.2 Article 6 ECHR

The ECtHR regards Article 6 ECHR to hold such a prominent place in democratic societies that a restrictive interpretation would be contrary to the aim and purpose of that provision.[69] Beyond the wording of Article 6(1) ECHR that requires a fair trial the ECtHR has interpreted this article to require access to court in the first place.[70] A fair trial is ensured where the prosecution has presented evidence capable of fulfilling the burden of proof and the defence has had an opportunity to influence the court's view at least to the same extent.[71] Article 6 ECHR is applicable when 'civil rights or obligations' (*droit et obligations de caractère civil*) or a 'criminal charge' (*bien-fondé de toute accusation en matière pénale*) are determined. Article 6(2) and (3) ECHR set out specific rights for those who are subject to criminal proceedings.

[66] ECtHR, *EH v Finland (dec)*, Application No 60966/00, judgment of 16 March 2004.

[67] ECtHR, *Kudla v Poland*, Application No 30210/96, judgment of 26 October 2000; ECtHR, *Kadlec and Others v Czech Republic*, Application No 49478/99, judgment of 25 May 2004.

[68] In ECtHR, *Kudla* (n 67 above). Article 13 was applied only to the length of the proceedings; in ECtHR, *Dostál v Czech Republic*, Application No 52859/99, judgment of 25 May 2004, different sets of proceedings were examined.

[69] ECtHR, *Delcourt*, 17 January 1970, A.11, para 15.

[70] ECtHR, *Golder v UK*, of 21 February 1975, Series A No 18, para 27, 1 EHRR 524, paras 28–36.

[71] Colin Warbrick, 'The Principles of the European Convention on Human Rights and the Response of States to Terrorism', *European Human Rights Law Review* (2002), pp 301–5.

3.2.1 Excluded by Nature

Article 6(1) s 1 ECHR applies to cases governed by civil and criminal law only. Thus, as a first step it must be determined whether the listings and asset freezes qualify as either criminal or civil in nature. The application of Article 6 ECHR could be excluded if individual sanctions are administrative measures only, constitute foreign policy decisions, or because they are adopted in international cooperation.

Administrative Measures. The argument was made that individual sanctions are 'mere administrative measures and not [...] any form of penalty or confiscation [...] capable of extending [...] the protection of Article 6 ECHR'.[72] Indeed, an indication of the purely administrative nature of Community sanctions could be the fact that the Council does not take discretionary decisions. It does not verify the identification of the individual or judge the substance of the allegation. The Council simply adopts sanctions against those identified as terrorist suspects either by the UN Sanctions Committee or by the Council itself acting under the Union pillars.

However, with regard to administrative measures the ECtHR ruled that[73]

> [t]he character of the legislation which governs [...] the matter' is 'of little consequence';[74] that any dispute falls under Article 6(1) ECHR, as long as the public authority's 'decision was to be decisive for the relations in civil law.

Despite the term 'civil' rights, the first paragraph of Article 6 ECHR is applicable to many proceedings which in themselves have a public character, but which determine a civil law right.[75] Hence, the fact that sanctions

[72] Argument of the Council in Case T-315/01, *Kadi* (n 4 above), paras 149 and 167; see for UN sanctions: Larissa van der Herik and Nico Schrijver, 'Section Two: Human Rights Concerns in Current Targeted Sanctions Regimes from the Perspective of International and European Law' in Thomas J Biersteker and Sue E Eckert, *Strengthening Targeted Sanctions Through Fair and Clear Procedures*, White Paper prepared by the Watson Institute Targeted Sanctions Project, Brown University, 30 March 2006, 26, p 12; third report of the 1526 Analytical Support and Sanctions Monitoring Team, UN Doc S/2005/572, 9 September 2005, para 41.

[73] ibid.

[74] ECtHR, *Ringeisen*, ECHR A 13, of 16 July 1971.

[75] Pieter van Dijk and Godefridus JA van Hoof, *Theory and Practice of the European Convention on Human Rights* (The Hague: Kluwer Law International, 1998), p 403 et seq; the authors themselves argue (p 406) that:

> the most satisfactory way to end legal uncertainty and maximalise effective legal protection is to recognise that [...][Art 6(1) ECHR] is applicable to all cases in which a determination by a public authority of the legal position of a private party is at stake, regardless of whether the rights and obligations involved are of a private character.

are governed by public law does not exclude that they concern 'civil rights or obligations' within the meaning of Article 6(1) ECHR. In the past, the ECtHR has considered the expropriation of property[76] and certain forms of social security[77] to fall within the realm of Article 6(1) ECHR, whereas disputes relating to tax liability have so far been viewed as issues of public law only and consequently as excluded from the application of Article 6(1) ECHR. In sum, the matter is not whether individual sanctions are of an administrative nature, but whether they (equally) qualify as a criminal charge or a determination of civil rights.

Political Question Doctrine. Union lists of terrorist suspects are adopted in CFSP common positions. As a consequence they could be considered 'political decisions' that are not subject to judicial control,[78] but fall under a 'European political question doctrine'.[79]

In this regard, the Council, the Commission, and the United Kingdom contended that European sanctions giving effect to UN lists of terrorist suspects do not lend themselves to judicial review.[80] Advocate-General Maduro discussed the matter in his opinion in the joint cases of *Kadi and al Barakaat*. He did not categorically reject the idea of a political question doctrine but opined that it is 'untenable' that 'even the most humble degree of judicial interference would be inappropriate.'[81] Advocate-General Maduro argued that despite the high importance of maintaining international peace and security, it is 'the duty of the courts to assess the lawfulness of measures that may conflict with other interests that are equally important' (such as human rights).[82] He cited the case of *Korematsu* of the US Supreme Court, [83] in which Justice Murphy argued that 'the allowable

[76] ECtHR, *Sporrong and Lönnroth v Sweden*, Judgment, 23 September 1982, A/52, paras 80–3.

[77] ECtHR, *Feldbrugge v The Netherlands*, Judgment 29 May 1986, paras 26–40 (sickness insurance); ECtHR, *Deumeland*, paras 60–74 (industrial-accident insurance), and ECtHR, *Schuler-Zgraggen*, paras 44–6 (invalidity pension).

[78] Benitez, *Administrative Justice in a World in Transition: Pan-European Values in Administrative Justice* (n 22 above), p 449.

[79] See on the political question doctrine in the US: US Supreme Court, *Luther v Borden*, 48 US 1 (1849), per Chief Justice Taney.

[80] See AG Maduro, Opinion in Cases C-402/05 P and C-415/05 P, *Kadi and al Barakaat* (n 4 above), para 33.

[81] ibid, para 34.

[82] ibid.

[83] US Supreme Court, *Korematsu v United States*, 323 US 214, 233–4 (1944), Murphy J, dissenting.

limits of [discretion], and whether or not they have been overstepped in a particular case, are judicial questions'.[84]

Fundamentally criticizing judicial abdication based on the political question doctrine Thomas Franck distinguishes two different forms of 'constitutionally mandated limits.'[85] The narrower reading of these limits restricts courts from replacing the judgment of the political branch with their own preferences if in *their opinion* the latter has acted within its constitutionally allotted ambit of political discretion. The more expansive reading of constitutionally mandated limits states that:[86]

> [i]f *in the opinion of one of the political branches* that branch is authorized by the Constitution to take an action, the Court will not substitute its view of whether such action is constitutionally authorized for that of the political branch.

While the first reading has not been seriously disputed and is a logical consequence of the separation of powers, the second exonerates the political branch from the control of law.[87] The wide interpretation gives the political branches carte blanche which is contrary to the rule of law. Judicial control of the *limits* of the powers of the political branches cannot be entirely abdicated.

Besides constitutional grounds, judicial abdication is frequently advocated based on prudential reasons. Four different but overlapping categories of prudential reasons are brought forward by judges to justify abdication where foreign policy is concerned: that courts are unsuited to obtain or assess the factual evidence; that legal standards are inapplicable or unascertainable; that the question concerns the survival of the nation and must be determined by foreign policy experts; and that the political branches might ignore the judges' decision.[88]

Some of these might appear applicable to individual sanctions. In particular, factual evidence that substantiates a UN listing appears extremely difficult to obtain. Moreover, the Council has demonstrated in the *OMPI* cases that it will defend every inch and attempt to adapt the listing procedure as little as possible to reach the minimum of procedural protection

[84] See AG Maduro, Opinion in Cases C-402/05 P and C-415/05 P, *Kadi and al Barakaat* (n 4 above), para 34.

[85] Thomas M Franck, *Political Questions/Judicial Answers* (Princeton, NJ: Princeton University Press, 1992), p 31 et seq.

[86] ibid (emphasis added).

[87] ibid, p 32.

[88] ibid, p 45 and Chapter 4.

required by the EU courts.[89] However, individual sanctions are not policy decisions, and as a consequence the prudential arguments cannot be applied to individual sanctions. The decision to impose sanctions on another state is a matter of foreign policy and national security. It weighs general political interests. As long as the political actor is competent to take this type of decision, the *political necessity* to impose state sanctions falls within the discretion of the political institutions and should remain outside of judicial control.[90] Despite the fundamental differences between state sanctions and sanctions against individuals,[91] the latter are unfortunately often also treated as a policy tool.[92] However, individual sanctions constitute the concrete application of a policy decision to a specific set of information.

The sanctioning of terrorist suspects including groups like Segi[93] or the PKK[94] is *motivated* by politics. Yet, listing an individual person or organization is *not a matter of policy*. The decision to list someone can only be taken if there is sufficient evidence (or clues (sic!)) that the particular person supports terrorism. Despite potential complexity, it is not the judgment of an abstract political situation, but–just like any decision taken by a criminal court–a weighing of evidence and the application of a general standard to a particular person in a specific situation. Legal standards are perfectly applicable. Further, irrespective of whether state sanctions can have the same severe impact on fundamental rights of individual persons, the immediateness of the infringement distinguishes individual sanctions from state sanctions. It makes the damage to fundamental rights foreseeable to the institutions and gives those listed a right that their interests are taken into account when the legal instrument is adopted. The application of a policy to the specific case is a matter of human rights and it is the role and responsibility of courts to contribute to the human rights discourse.[95]

[89] See Chapter 7, Section 1.1.

[90] See for the US: Peter Fitzgerald, 'Managing "Smart Sanctions" against Terrorism Wisely' *New England Law Review*, 36 (2002), pp 957–83.

[91] Case T-228/02, *OMPI I*; Case T-256/07, *OMPI II*; Case T-284/08, *OMPI III* (all n 4 above); see also Chapter 1.

[92] The Stanley Foundation, 'The United Nations and Multilateral Sanctions: New Options of US Policy?', Report of the 33rd Strategy for Peace, US Foreign Policy Conference, 22–24 October 1992, p 6.

[93] Case T-338/02, *Segi* (n 4 above).

[94] Case T-229/02, *Kurdistan Workers' Party, Kurdistan National Congress v Council (PKK)* [2005] ECR II-539.

[95] See Chapter 7, Section 3.1 on the role of the judiciary.

The approach of the EU courts[96] and the judicial traditions in the Member States[97] do not reflect a consistent position as regards cases with foreign policy implications which immediately concern individuals in their constitutionally guaranteed rights. The Italian courts, for instance, have repeatedly rejected jurisdiction for 'political acts'.[98] The German Federal Constitutional Court (GCC) does not apply a political question doctrine either. The GCC was much criticized for not adjudicating on the deportation of seven Sudanese from Frankfurt Airport in 1995.[99] In 2005 in the *European Arrest Warrant* case[100] the GCC held:[101] that the examination of the severity of the potential punishment after extradition

> is not a question of freedom of assessment under foreign-policy aspects but one that very significantly affects the protection of the prosecuted person's fundamental rights and even the guarantee of his or her human dignity.

The GCC found the courts competent to answer the question of whether or not the fundamental rights of an individual were infringed. This question was not considered a matter of foreign policy.

Moreover, the ECtHR ruled that, where the conditions of Article 6 ECHR are met otherwise, judicial review cannot be fully excluded–not even because of considerations of national security.[102] After applying Article 6 ECHR to extraterritorial acts that give rise to an action under national law, the ECtHR accepted however in the recent case of *Malkovic* that the jurisdiction of national courts can be limited in scope because the contested act is 'a manifestation of political decisions'.[103] Judicial review

[96] '[T]he EU judicial text which comes closest to establishing some kind of political question doctrine in the framework of EU constitutional law' is the Opinion of AG Jacobs in the FYROM case (Piet Eeckhout, *External Relations of the European Union: Legal and Constitutional Foundations* (Oxford: Oxford University Press, 2004), p 452 et seq). The case was withdrawn after the AG gave his opinion; the ECJ never ruled on the question. See above AG Maduro in *Kadi* and *al Barakaat*; the ECJ did not directly address the political question doctrine in its ruling.

[97] The German Constitutional Court does not apply a 'political-question-doctrine'; however, it shows considerable judicial restraint in cases concerning foreign policy (Ernst Benda, 'Deutsche Außenpolitik vor Gericht-Bundesverfassungsgericht und auswärtige Gerwalt', *Internationale Politik*, 12 (1995), pp 39–46).

[98] ECtHR, *Markovic and others v Italy*, Application No 1398/03, judgment of 14 December 2006, para 26; see also the exception made for the royal prerogative concerning acts of war in UK Courts (ECtHR, *Council of Civil Service Unions v Minister of Civil Service* [1985] AC 374, p 398).

[99] *Frankfurter Allgemeine Zeitung*, 9.10.1995, p 10.

[100] See Chapters 2, Section 4.2 and Chapter 6, Section 4.2.2.

[101] German Constitutional Court, *EAW Decision* of 18 July 2005, 2 BvR 2236/04, para 114, see also Chapter 2, Section 4.2.

[102] ECtHR, *Tinnelly and McElduff v UK* (1998) 27 EHRR 249, para 72; see below at 3.4.

[103] ECtHR, *Markovic* (n 98 above), para 106.

can be limited including where the applicant is not enabled to secure a decision on the merits so long as the limitation 'does not amount to recognition of an immunity but is merely indicative of the extent of the courts' powers of review of acts of foreign policy such as acts of war'. The ECtHR came to the conclusion that such an inability to bring an action against the state can be 'the result [...] of the principles governing the substantive right of action in domestic law'.[104]

The latter statement appears to indicate that limitations imposed on the national judiciary because of the political nature of the decision do not exclude the *application* of Article 6 ECHR. The limitations are a matter of national substantive law. They must be determined in the review of the merits, since they do not constitute an *absence*, but a *restriction* of the rights under Article 6 ECHR. According to this reading limitations have to be justified and comply with the principle of proportionality.[105] Thus, the political question doctrine cannot exclude rights under Article 6 ECHR, but only justify restrictions within the framework of this article.

By way of conclusion, the different national legal systems as well as the European legal order take different approaches to political decisions, but as a matter of principle the exercise of public power is considered legitimate only in so far as it is demonstrably within the pre-existing law, rational, principled, and proportionate.[106] The application of Article 6 ECHR is hence not excluded by the possible political nature of individual sanctions.

International Cooperation. Difficulties in applying Article 6 ECHR could further arise because sanctions against individuals are adopted in international cooperation. This is first because the ECHR is tailored to serve as a yardstick for fundamental rights protection in the national context[107] and Contracting Parties are responsible within their 'jurisdiction' only. Secondly,

[104] ibid, para 114.

[105] With regard to the *Markovic* case (n 98 above): Sangeeta Shah, 'Seeking Remedies for Violations of International Humanitarian Law: Markovic v Italy', *Human Rights Law Review*, 7 (2007), p 417.

[106] Ian Leigh, 'National Legal Dimension of the Democratic Control of the Security Sector: Values and Standards in Developed Democracies', 2006, http://www.dcaf.ch/, p 10.

[107] Christine van den Wyngaert, 'Rethinking the Law of International Criminal Cooperation: Restrictive Function of International Human Rights Through Individual-Oriented Bars' in Albin Eser and Otto Lagony (eds), *Principles and Procedures for a New Transnational Criminal Law: Documentation of an International Workshop in Freiburg* (Freiburg i Br: Max-Planck-Institut für Ausländisches und Internationales Strafrecht, 1992), p 491.

individuals were traditionally treated as objects without standing rights in international cooperation.[108]

The ECtHR holds in settled case-law that the ECHR must be interpreted in compliance with international law.[109] However, the Convention does not provide for a general derogation from Convention rights for acts adopted in international cooperation. In the past the ECtHR has accepted international cooperation to be a legitimate objective when examining the proportionality of a limitation of Convention rights. In the *Bosphorus* case, for instance, Judge Ress mentioned in his concurring opinion the 'importance of international cooperation'.[110] However, he did not make the argument that international cooperation added legitimacy. And, more importantly, the Court indirectly rejected the view that the existence of a binding UN Security Council resolution could free the Contracting Parties from their obligations under the Convention.[111]

Further, a dynamic interpretation of the ECHR must take into consideration the evolution of the objectives of international cooperation. The promotion of fundamental rights was traditionally one reason for expanding and intensifying international cooperation.[112] The aim of fundamental rights protection led indeed to the abolishment of traditional and 'time-honoured' obstacles to international cooperation, resulting from the doctrines of state sovereignty and domestic jurisdiction that focussed on the interests of individual states.[113] In the fight against terrorism, however, the interests of states partially merge into a common interest. International cooperation in the fight against terrorism does not promote a higher standard of fundamental rights protection. On the contrary, it has been subject to manifold criticism for illegitimately infringing fundamental rights.[114] At the same time we can witness an increasing overall importance

[108] Bert Swart, 'Human Rights and the Abolition of Traditional Principles' in Albin Eser and Otto Lagony (eds), *Principles and Procedures for a New Transnational Criminal Law: Documentation of an International Workshop in Freiburg* (Freiburg i Br: Max-Planck-Institut für Ausländisches und Internationales Strafrecht, 1992), p 505 et seq.

[109] ECtHR, Grand Chamber decision as to the admissibility of *Bankovic* (ECtHR, *Bankovic* case, Application No 52207/99, judgment of 12 December 2001).

[110] ECtHR, *Bosphorus* (n 3 above), p 56, para 5.

[111] See Chapter 5, Section 5.1.

[112] Albin Eser and Otto Lagony (eds), *Principles and Procedures for a New Transnational Criminal Law: Documentation of an International Workshop in Freiburg* (Freiburg i Br: Max-Planck-Institut für Ausländisches und Internationales Strafrecht, 1992), p 506.

[113] See Malcolm Shaw, *International Law* (Cambridge: Cambridge University Press, 5th ed, 2003), p 252 et seq.

[114] See Chapter 1.

given to fundamental rights in the last six decades. This has led to the conviction that the protection of fundamental rights must also not only be ensured through international cooperation within the national sphere but also when states cooperate under international law.

In the case of *Soering*[115] for instance the ECtHR ruled that fair trial rights may become an obstacle to international criminal cooperation. In this case the ECtHR was asked to consider whether the extradition of a person from the United Kingdom to the United States should be refused because, if extradition was granted, the person was likely to spend several years on 'death row' awaiting execution. It was argued, that this would be inhuman and degrading treatment in the sense of Article 3 ECHR. The ECHR first conceded that:[116]

> Article 1 *cannot* be read as justifying a general principle to the effect that [...] a Contracting State may not surrender an individual unless satisfied that the conditions awaiting him in the country of destination are in full accord with each of the safeguards of the Convention.

It then, however, ruled that the decision to extradite a fugitive can nonetheless engage the responsibility of a Contracting Party under the Convention, where substantial grounds have been shown for believing that the person concerned, if extradited, faces a real risk of being subjected to such grave fundamental rights violations as torture or inhumane treatment. With regard to the fair trial requirements in Article 6 ECHR the ECtHR explicitly stated[117] that it does

> not exclude that an issue might exceptionally be raised under Article 6 [ECHR] by an extradition decision in circumstances where the fugitive has suffered or risks suffering a flagrant denial of a fair trial in the requesting country.

In the *Soering* case itself however, the Court held that if the applicant were to be extradited this would be a violation of Article 3 ECHR, while it did not find a violation of Article 6 ECHR.

In sum, not every safeguard of the Convention is applicable in the international context, but a flagrant denial of fair trial is an obstacle to international cooperation. Extradition is a way of giving effect to international agreements. A direct causal link exists between the extradition of a person and any treatment which this person is subject to in the receiving state. However, the treatment of the extradited person in a foreign legal

[115] ECtHR, *Soering v UK*, Application No 14038/88, judgment of 7 July 1989.

[116] ibid, para 86. [117] ibid, para 113.

order is not an act of the extraditing state and for obvious reasons that state has limited influence on this treatment.[118] Consequently, the extraditing state does not directly induce the fundamental rights violation.

Individual sanctions are different. UN sanctions against individuals are given effect by domestic implementation measures. This is the classic situation of implementation. EU law must in this context be regarded as 'domestic law'.[119] European sanctions form part of the domestic legal sphere. For the domestic exercise of public power, even if it is based on international agreements, deference is not justified to the same extent. In principle measures within the 'jurisdiction' of the Contracting Parties[120] must satisfy the full Convention standards irrespective of whether they were adopted out of the necessity to comply with international legal obligations.[121]

Community regulations are binding legal instruments that directly change the position of those targeted. They are directly applicable and bind their addressees without requiring a national measure of implementation.[122] Regulations adopting sanctions against individuals are implemented by Council or Commission decisions containing the lists of persons to whom the regulation is applied. In combination the two instruments directly oblige the financial institutions, as well as all other persons, to check whether they hold any financial assets or other economic resources belonging to those listed. If so, they are required to freeze the respective accounts or other funds and report their findings to the competent national authority. Both the Community regulations and the Council or Commission decisions adopted under the first pillar are directly part of the jurisdiction of the EU Member States, which are all Contracting Parties of the ECHR.

Common positions, by contrast, do not directly address private actors. They are addressed to the Member States and it is highly contested

[118] See the reasoning in: ECtHR, *Soering* (n 115 above), para 86.

[119] This term is used both by the CFI in Case T-315/01, *Kadi* (n 4 above); Case T-306/01, *Yusuf* (n 4 above); the ECJ however does not directly use this term in Cases C-402/05 P and C-415/05 P, *Kadi and al Barakaat* (n 4 above).

[120] Compare Art 1 ECHR .

[121] ECommHR, *M & Co v Germany*, Application No 13258/87, Commission decision of 9 February 1990, Decisions and Reports (DR) 64, p 145; ECtHR, *United Communist Party of Turkey and Others v Turkey*, judgment of 30 January 1998, Reports, 1998-I, para 29; ECtHR, *Waite and Kennedy v Germany*, ECHR 1999-I, para 67; ECtHR, *Matthews v UK*, Application No 24833/94, judgment of 18 February 1999, paras 29 and 32–4; ECtHR, *Prince Hans Adam II of Liechtenstein v Germany [GC]*, Application No 42527/98, ECHR 2001 VIII, para 47.

[122] See: Art 249(2) EC.

whether they can have direct effect.[123] Further, Article 15 TEU is not clear on whether Member States can be obliged by a common position to take a *specific* action. It stipulates only that Member States are required to ensure that their policies conform to common positions.[124] However, Member States are legally bound[125] even if common positions do not usually impose detailed obligations but rather give more general policy guidelines. Moreover, lists of terrorist suspects adopted in common positions directly impact on the legal positions of individuals.[126]

In conclusion, both Community regulations and common positions are domestic European law instruments, which are either directly applicable in the jurisdictions of the Member States (regulations), or which have a direct impact on the rights of individuals (common positions). There is no reason why domestic measures, including both national implementation measures and European law, should not have to comply with the full Convention standard, irrespective of whether they are adopted in order to comply with international agreements. The ECtHR's ruling in *Bosphorus*[127] does not depart from that principle, although it makes the finding of a breach of the Convention more difficult when a EU Member State/Contracting Party takes action at the national level in order to comply with Community law obligations.[128]

By way of conclusion, the application of Article 6 ECHR cannot be excluded because of the *legal nature* of the measures in question. All measures that determine a civil right or constitute a criminal charge fall within the application of Article 6 ECHR. Security implications and the fact that they are adopted in order to comply with measures of international cooperation can justify a restriction; they do not lead to exclusion of Article 6 ECHR.

[123] See below Section 3.2.3.

[124] It is highly disputed whether the Treaty of Maastricht binds the Member States more or in a different way than international treaties usually do. For the third pillar see: Francis Snyder, 'Institutional Development in the European Union: Some implications of the Third Pillar', in Joerg Monar and Roger Morgan (eds), *The Third Pillar of the European Union* (Brussels: European Interuniversity Press, 1995), p 89. Further, the principle of interpretation in conformity, already extended to framework decisions (Case C-105/03, *Pupino* [2005] ECR I-5285), could potentially be applied to second pillar measures.

[125] By their wording they 'impose a strong discipline as regards respect for, implementation of, and participation in, the CFSP by the Member States' (Eeckhout, *External Relations of the European Union: Legal and Constitutional Foundations* (n 96 above).

[126] See below Section 3.2.3.

[127] ECtHR, *Bosphorus* (n 3 above).

[128] Eckes, *Does the European Court of Human Rights Provide Protection from the European Community? The Case of Bosphorus Airways* (n 41 above).

3.2.2 Criminal Charge

European sanctions against private individuals could amount to a criminal charge.[129] The classification as a criminal charge is important because stronger procedural safeguards are required in criminal proceedings. While Article 6(1) ECHR is applicable both to disputes determining civil rights and obligations and to criminal charges, Articles 6(2) and (3) ECHR are only applicable to the latter. The presumption of innocence for instance applies to proceedings of a criminal character only.

Community asset freezes and Union lists of terrorist suspects must be considered separately. This distinction is necessary because, despite the fact that both have a considerable impact on fundamental rights, Community asset freezes and Union lists might give rise to different fair trial guarantees. While Community measures directly change the legal position of the targeted persons the direct effect of Union measures is disputed.

The focus here is on *European* listings and sanctions. It is inductive to look at the discussion at the UN level though. Scholars differ in their evaluations of the Strasbourg case-law as to whether the Court would consider individual sanctions a criminal charge.[130] The UN Monitoring Team does *not* consider the inclusion on the UN lists of terrorist suspects to be a criminal charge.[131] Consequently, it considers that the standard of procedural protection may be lower than that required under criminal law. The Special Rapporteur explicitly rejects this view. He argued that the determination of whether a measure amounts to a criminal charge depends essentially on the severity of the punishment and where individuals remain permanently listed the measures fall within the scope of criminal law for

[129] Eg: Joined Cases T-110/03, T-150/03, and T-405/03, *José Maria Sison v Council* [2005] ECR II-1429, para 48.

[130] See with regard to UN sanctions: Iain Cameron, 'Report to the Swedish Foreign Office on Legal Safeguards and Targeted Sanctions (2002), http://resources.jur.uu.se/repository/5/PDF/staff/sanctions.pdf, p 30; Göran Lysén, 'Targeted UN Sanctions: On the Issue of Legal Sources and their Application and also some Procedural Matters', Swedish Institute of International Law, Uppsala University, 2003, http://www-hotel.uu.se/webbtjanster/hotell.php; Gernot Biehler, 'Individuelle Sanktionen der Vereinten Nationen und Grundrechte', *Archiv des Völkerrechtes*, 41 2003, pp 169–81; for European sanctions: Sandra Bartelt and Helge Elisabeth Zeitler, '"Intelligente Sanktionen" zur Terrorismusbekämpfung in der EU', *EuZW* (2003), p 712 et seq; Torbjöm Andersson, Iain Cameron and Kenneth Nordback, 'EU Listing: The Renaissance of Imperial Power, but on a Global Scale', *European Business Law Review* (2003), pp 111–41; van der Herik and Schrijver, *Section Two: Human Rights Concerns in Current Targeted Sanctions Regimes from the Perspective of International and European Law* (n 72 above), p 13 seem to reject that UN sanctions would be classified as a criminal charge.

[131] See S/2005/572, paras 40–3.

the purposes of international human rights law.[132] In view to all the consequences that such a listing entails the latter view is convincing.

In its settled case-law the ECtHR sets out three criteria[133] to determine whether proceedings involve the determination of a criminal charge: the classification, the nature of the conduct in question and the severity of any possible penalty.[134] In the following paragraphs these criteria will be examined with regard to European sanctions against individuals. However, it must be kept in mind that formal classification of a measure as a criminal charge is only a tool of application. In the end fairness is the central element governing Article 6 ECHR,[135] and the same general principles apply to both civil and criminal proceedings.

Classification of the Proceedings in Domestic Law. The first criterion is the classification of the proceedings in domestic law. Usually a criminal charge relates to an unlawful action. The textbook example is an infringement of the national criminal code. The case for individual sanctions is less clear. The adoption of sanctions does not follow the process of an ordinary conviction. It does not distinguish between a general rule prohibiting a certain action or omission on the one hand and an application of that general norm to the concrete action of the individual person on the other.

A formal comparison between usual criminal convictions and individual sanctions is very difficult, due to the great differences in the process. This does not however change the fact that individual sanctions have certain criminal characteristics. The listed persons are officially labelled to be

[132] Robert K Goldman, Report of the Independent Expert on the Protection of Human Rights and Fundamental Freedoms while Countering Terrorism, E/CN.4/2005/103, para 35.

[133] Keir Starmer, *European Human Rights Law: The Human Rights Act 1998 and the European Convention of Human Rights* (London: Legal Action Group, 1999), p 119; first laid down in: ECtHR, *Engel and Others*, judgment of 8 June 1976, Series A No 22, para 82; see also: ECtHR, *Öztuürk*, Series A No 73, judgment of 21 February 1984, and ECtHR, *Campbell and Fell*, judgment of 28 June 1984, Series A No 80; ECtHR, *Demicoli*, Application No 13057/87 [1991] ECHR 37, judgment of 27 August 1991, para 31.

[134] The criteria can be applied alternatively, not cumulatively: ECtHR, *Lauko v Slovakia*, Application No 4/1998/907/1119, para 56 et seq; critical: Iain Cameron, 'UN Targeted Sanctions, Legal Safeguards and the European Convention on Human Rights', *Nordic Journal of International Law*, 72 (2003), p 166 et seq, at 192.

[135] ECtHR, *Kamasinski v Austria*, Application No 9783/82, Series A 168, judgment of 19 December 1989, para 62; ECtHR, *Hadjianastassiou v Greece*, Series A, No 252-A, 16 EHRR 219, judgment of 16 December 1992, para 31; ECtHR, *Hamer v France*, of 7 August 1996, RJD 1996-III, No 13.

involved in a 'terrorist act'[136] and the European definition of a terrorist act requires necessarily that the action is incriminated under national law.[137] The listing itself is consequently an allegation by the public authorities that the subjects have at least 'attempted', 'participated in', or 'facilitated' a criminal activity.[138] No personal guilt is alleged. Yet, the listing has effects similar to a quasi-conviction of the designated person, only without due process.[139]

National courts have begun to take account of a listing in reaching their decisions in criminal cases involving terrorism. For instance, the Swedish and the Italian authorities reported that their national courts consider the listing on the UN list of terrorist suspects as a relevant fact when they determine in the course of criminal proceeding whether the accused is connected with terrorism.[140] This is another argument that those listed should have the opportunity to defend themselves like they would in criminal proceedings, since even if the listings and sanctions are not directly considered to be of a criminal nature they entail additional adverse consequences, including under criminal law.

Considering the UN listings as relevant facts in national criminal procedures is a circular argument. This practice must be strongly criticized. The listings are based on requests by executives of the UN member states. The governments are not obliged to substantiate their requests with transparent evidence. Hence, the listings are based on allegations only. In

[136] For instance Common Position 2001/931/CFSP stipulates to apply to persons 'involved in terrorist acts' (Common Position 2001/931/CFSP, OJ L 344 of 28 December 2001, p 93).

[137] See Chapter 7 on Art 1(3) of Common Position 2001/931/CFSP (n 37 above); see also: Art 4 of the Framework Decision of 13 June 2002 on combating terrorism (FD 2002/475/JHA, OJ 2002 L 164/3), for more detail: Eugenia Dumitriu 'The EU's Definition of Terrorism: The Council Framework Decision on Combating Terrorism', *German Law Journal*, 5 (2004), p 592. See also SC Res 1373, which in intention and wording requires penal action against those alleged to be involved in terrorism, see in particular at 1(b), 2(e), and (f); yet, the guidelines of the Sanctions Committee state in para 6(c): 'A criminal charge or conviction is not necessary for inclusion on the List as the sanctions are intended to be preventive in nature'.

[138] See Chapter 7 on Art 1(2) of Common Position 2001/931/CFSP; see however also for UN sanctions: 1526 Analytical Support and Sanctions Monitoring Team (n 37 above), third report, UN Doc. S/2005/572, 9 September 2005, para 39: 'The List is not a criminal list.' It contains names of individuals 'regardless of whether any authority has formally charged them with a criminal offence.'

[139] Compare to the case of the tree Somali-Swedes: Elin Miller, 'The Use of Targeted Sanctions in the Fight Against International Terrorism: What about Human Rights?' in American Society of International Law, *An Imperial Security Council? Implementing Security Council Resolutions 1373 and 1390. Proceedings of the Annual Meeting* (Washington DC: American Society of International Law, 2003), vol 97, 41, p 48.

[140] See Sixth report of the Analytical Support and Sanctions Monitoring Team, UN S/2007/132 (8 March 2007), box 1, p 14.

later court proceedings the executive of the same state can then use the same listing as 'relevant fact' to prove exactly the alleged affiliation with terrorism. At the international level, it would not surprise if the fact that a national court endorsed the allegation could then be used again in support of the listing. As the Special Rapporteur pointed out the placement on the lists should not be considered as evidence for legal proceedings.[141] The state has to resort to normal rules and standards of proof.[142]

It must be conceded though, that the ECtHR did not appear to consider the listing in a CFSP common position to possess sufficient similarities with a conviction in the case of *Segi*.[143] Indeed, the Court held that '[t]he reference in question [...] does not amount to the indictment of the "groups or entities" listed and still less to establishment of their guilt.'[144]

Moreover, European sanctions against individuals are not formally classified as a criminal charge. European lists are a result of an 'instigation of an investigation or prosecution' in a Member State.[145] Consequently, the listing takes place at the investigative stage; before a criminal charge in the national proceedings has been formally determined. However, the adoption of 'criminal law' by the Community[146] that directly changes the potential criminal liability of the individual can no longer be excluded as a matter of principle.[147] After the *Environmental Crime Case*[148] it is perceivable that the Community imposes criminal charges in form of so-called secondary sanctions.[149] In *Environmental Crime*, the Commission challenged a framework decision on the protection of the environment through criminal law.[150] The contested third pillar instrument had been adopted against the

[141] Robert K Goldman, Report of the Independent Expert on the Protection of Human Rights and Fundamental Freedoms while Countering Terrorism, E/CN.4/2005/103, para 36.

[142] ibid.

[143] ECtHR, *Segi* (n 3 above); as stated above the *Segi* case was rejected for lack of standing the ECtHR did not rule on the merits.

[144] ECtHR, *Segi* (n 3 above), p 9.

[145] Art 1(4) of Common Position 2001/931/CFSP (n 37 above).

[146] See eg: Case 56&58/64, *Grundig* [1966] ECR 299; Case 45/69, *Boehringer* [1970] ECR 769; Case 155/79, *AM&S* [1982] ECR 1575; and Arts 135, 280 EC stipulation that the application of national criminal law remains unaffected by Community law; see for the EU: Arts 29–42 TEU are limited to coordinating measures. They do not confer a competence to adopt directly effective criminal law (Art 34(2)(b) TEU explicitly for framework decisions).

[147] Ester Herlin-Karnell, 'Commission v Council: Some Reflections on Criminal Law in the First Pillar', *European Public Law*, Vol 13(1) (2007), pp 69–84.

[148] Case C-176/03, *Commission v Council (Environmental Crime Case)* [2005 ECR I-7879; see also: Christa Tobler, 'Case C-176/03, *Commission v. Council*, Judgment of the Grand Chamber of 13 September 2005, nyr, Commentary', *CML Rev*, 43 (2006), p 840.

[149] See on secondary sanctions: Chapter 1, Section 4.

[150] Council Framework Decision 2003/80/JHA, OJ 2003, L 29/55.

objections of both the Commission and the European Parliament, disregarding a proposal for a Community directive on the same matter presented by the Commission in 2001. Advocate-General Colomer argued that:[151]

> the case-law does not explicitly recognize any power on the part of the Community to require the Member States to classify as criminal offences conduct which hinders achievement of the objectives laid down in the Treaties.

At the same time, he considered criminal penalties imperative because they are 'the only sanction which fulfils the requirements [...] of being effective, proportionate and dissuasive'.[152] The Advocate-General concluded that the Community must be in the position to effectively exercise its competences. The ECJ took Article 47 TEU as the starting point of its analysis and followed in essence Advocate-General Colomer's opinion.[153] The ECJ's ruling in *Environmental Crime* is convincing, at least in relation to the primacy of Community law over EU law under Article 47 TEU.[154]

The CFI did not specify whether it considered Community asset freezes to be criminal charges, nor did it refer to any specific part of Article 6 ECHR. It simply stated that:[155]

> the right to such protection is part of the general legal principles deriving from the constitutional traditions common to the Member States and has been enshrined in Articles 6 and 13 of the ECHR.

In any event, the ECtHR does not consider itself bound by any national or international classification[156] but defines 'criminal charge' autonomously. The domestic classification, being a mere indication, does not constitute an obstacle to the finding of a criminal charge. However, *if* a matter is classed as criminal under national law, this will be enough to bring it within the scope of Article 6 ECHR.[157]

Both Community and Union lists publicly state that individuals placed on them have attempted, participate in, or facilitated criminal acts–or, worse, a terrorist act. The public stigma of being involved in terrorism compares to having committed a serious crime. Hence, despite having the

[151] AG Colomer, Opinion in Case C-176/03, *Environmental Crime* (n 148 above), para 38.
[152] AG Colomer, ibid, para 43. [153] See for the differences: Tobler, 2006, 840.
[154] ibid, p 850. [155] Case T-228/02, *OMPI I* (n 4 above), para 110.
[156] Compare: ECtHR, *Weber*, Series A No 177, judgment of 22 May 1990, p 17, para 30 and the other judgments referred to therein; ECtHR, *Demicoli* (n 133 above), para 31.
[157] Clare Ovey and Robin CA White, *Jacobs and White: The European Convention on Human Rights* (Oxford: Oxford University Press, 2002), p 141.

same stigmatizing effect as a criminal conviction individual sanctions are not formally classified as such.

Nature of the Offence or Conduct in Question. The second criterion is the nature of the offence or conduct in question. It depends on the circle of potential addressees and the intention of the law. A small and closely defined group of potential offenders is suggestive of a disciplinary or administrative rather than a mainstream criminal offence.[158]

Individual sanctions could potentially be targeted at anybody. They are potentially applicable to the world population, including European citizens. UN sanctions against individuals are not limited to those who have committed a crime. They are not based on general laws and it is one of their particularities that the listing criteria are not publicly available.[159] The UN lists are adopted in connection with Security Council resolutions and are largely thought to share the general compelling force of these resolutions.[160] Similarly, EU lists of terrorist suspects are adopted in legislative instruments (CFSP common positions and EC Council or Commission decisions) setting out a definite circle of targets. Nonetheless, this does not change the fact that before the adoption of the list the potential circle of persons that could be sanctioned is indeterminate.

In principle individual sanctions are not intended to be a punitive charge, but to limit the financial means available to terrorists.[161] Their main aim is not to penalize the individual person; in fact, they do not even require a subjective wrongdoing and those listed for supporting a terrorist organization do not have to know about the terrorist activities of that organization.[162] Notwithstanding the fact that there is no *de minimis* rule and that therefore even a minimal form of – usually financial – support appears to be sufficient for a listing, individuals are targeted because of their contribution to the threat to international peace and security.[163] This is decisively different from criminal law, which – subject to exceptions – requires a

[158] ibid.

[159] See both Chapter 1, Section 3.1.1 and Chapter 7, Section 1.3 on UN and EU listing criteria.

[160] See Chapter 1, Sections 2, 3, and 4 on the adoption procedure and Chapter 5, Sections 1 and 3 on the binding force of UN terrorist lists.

[161] Case T-256/07, *OMPI II* (n 4 above), para 107 et seq; see also: Chapter 1, Section 7 on effectiveness and Chapter 7, Section 1.3 on the listing criteria.

[162] Miller, *The Use of Targeted Sanctions in the Fight Against International Terrorism: What about Human Rights?* (n 139 above), p 48.

[163] Cameron, *UN Targeted Sanctions, Legal Safeguards and the European Convention on Human Rights* (n 134 above), p 202.

personal wrongdoing. Yet, as was discussed in Chapter 1, individual sanctions might also have additional ancillary objectives, such as general prevention, which is a typical intention of criminal law.

In short, the main purpose of the listing is not the conviction of those targeted. The listing as such is not reflected in the target's criminal record. International sanctions against individuals do not deal with individuals as legal subjects with rights and obligations. On the contrary, individual sanctions take a functional objective approach to those listed: individuals are thought of in terms of their contribution to a threat that must be disarmed. In many ways this can be considered the traditional view on individuals in international law. It is the view before fundamental rights were acknowledged to be the 'third dimension' of international criminal law forcing the cooperating states to take individuals in their quality as rights owners into account.[164] However, even if the main objective of individual sanctions is the prevention of 'terrorism' and even if individual sanctions do not primarily serve a punitive intention, their effects on the legal position of the listed individual cannot be ignored. Stigmatization as a terrorist and impairment of property rights can give individual sanctions a punitive character irrespective of their main objective. The general commitment to fundamental rights no longer allows states to reduce individuals to pure objects of cooperation between states, irrespective of the primary purpose of the cooperation.

Further, while the publication of Community sanctions is necessary because they require third party compliance, the publication of Union lists of terrorist suspects does not serve an additional purpose except for publically labelling those listed as terrorists. This could support the conclusion that there is a certain punitive intention behind their *publication*. Where individuals are only listed on Union lists but not sanctioned by the Community, there is no obvious reason for publishing the listed names. For instance in the case of *Segi*[165] the only 'legal consequence' aimed at is the cooperation between Member State law enforcement authorities. The public announcement that Segi is a terrorist organization appears to be unnecessary for that aim. The Member States could have cooperated on the basis of non-public communication.[166] In any event, publication *results* in stigmatizing the listed persons.

[164] Van den Wyngaert, *Rethinking the Law of International Criminal Cooperation: Restrictive Function of International Human Rights Through Individual-Oriented Bars* (n 107 above), p 491.

[165] Case T-338/02, *Segi* (n 4 above).

[166] Secret measures also have human rights implications. See: Cameron, *National Security and the European Convention on Human Rights* (n 60 above).

In conclusion, the nature of individual sanctions is hybrid. Despite the lack of a clear punitive intention, individual sanctions publicly label those listed as terrorists and the circle of potential targets comprises the entire population.

Severity of Any Possible Penalty. The third and most important criterion[167] in determining whether a measure amounts to a criminal charge is the severity of the potential penalty. The severity is determined by the length and intensity of the interference with the rights of the charged person.

Union lists of terrorist suspects and Community asset freezes, once they are adopted, remain in force for an unlimited period of time.[168] In the *PKK* case the Council and the Commission acknowledged that the renewed list was *not* based on a re-examination of the individual case.[169] However, the CFI assumed in the same case that 'the Council, in each new act, reviews the disputed list'. It even ruled[170] that:

> such a review cannot be limited to the inclusion of new persons or entities or the removal of certain persons or entities since, in a community governed by the rule of law it cannot be accepted that an act establishing continuing restrictive measures in respect of persons or entities could be applicable without limitation unless the institution which has promulgated them re-adopts them regularly following a review.

In view of the statement of the Council and the Commission, the Court's statement appears contrary to reality.

Although some sanctions instruments provide for a 'constant review',[171] it can be assumed that this is only a routine confirmation mechanism.[172]

[167] ECtHR, *Malige v France*, 28 September 1998; critical of the exclusive focus on severity: Iain Cameron, *UN Targeted Sanctions, Legal Safeguards and the European Convention on Human Rights* (n 134 above), p 192.

[168] SC Res 1333 (see para 23) is limited to a period of 12 month, after which the decision must be taken to extend the measures for them to continue. This logically limits EC Regulation 467/2001 implementing SC Res 1333. By contrast, SC Res 1390 (see para 3) is adopted for an open ended period of time, subject to a 12 months review aiming at improvement of the adopted measures. EC Regulation 881/2002 implementing SC Res 1390 reflects this change.

[169] Case T-229/02, *PKK* (n 94 above), para 18.

[170] ibid, para 44. [171] Eg: Art 6 of Common Position 2001/931/CFSP (n 37 above).

[172] In the *PKK* case (Case T-229/02, *PKK* (n 94 above), para 19) the Council claimed that the summary report of the Coreper proceedings of 4 December 2002 (15 191/02 EXT 1 CRS/CRP 51) did not contain any information relevant to the applicant's listing in the new decision (EC Council Dec 2002/974, OJ 2002 L 337/85–6); see also Chapter 1 on the voting practices within the Council.

Such a review mechanism cannot be understood as a temporal limitation of the individual's charge. Hence, autonomous European sanctions are in principle adopted for an unlimited period of time. Similarly, European sanctions giving effect to UN lists of terrorist suspects depend entirely on the listing or delisting decisions of the UN Sanctions Committee. As was outlined in Chapter 1, UN lists are also adopted for an unlimited period of time: the delisting of a particular person is subject to a unanimous decision by the Sanctions Committee. As a consequence, European sanctions based on UN lists should also be considered to apply by default for an unlimited period of time.

The final and decisive element of a criminal charge is the *intensity* of the interference with fundamental rights. The scope is very large. Even petty crimes fall within the scope of Article 6 ECHR.[173] Relevant is the penalty that the violator of the norm is threatened with,[174] not the actual sentence. The usual starting point of the examination is thus the legal basis of the conviction (criminal code) and not the sentence the particular person was given (judgment).

For individual sanctions the situation differs from the textbook example. For those listed the law is at the same time the conviction. There is no separation between the legislator adopting the general norm setting out the conduct that justifies the sanction and the actor applying the concrete measure. Yet, this does not exclude the conclusion that those listed are subject to a criminal charge. Indeed, the contrary could be argued: the lack of separation could prove to infringe Convention rights, *if* individual sanctions were found to be criminal charges. The decisive criterion is the potential substantive charge.

The ECtHR ruled in the case of *Demicoli*[175] that parliamentary criminal justice is in principle inadmissible. In this case the Court reviewed whether the proceedings, which led to the finding of a breach of privilege by a satirical journalist, ie a private person, not a member of parliament, gave rise to a violation of Article 6(1) ECHR. Mr Demicoli satirically reported the parliamentary debates in a political periodical. In the particular case he ridiculed the speeches of two members of the Maltese House of

[173] See for examples: Andreas Kley-Struller, *Artikel 6 EMRK als Rechtsschutzgarantie gegen die öffentliche Gewalt: Die aktuelle Praxis der Konventionsorgane zur Anwendung des Artikel 6 EMRK in der Verwaltungsrechtspflege* (Zürich: Schulthess, 1993), p 10.

[174] Dijk and Hoof, *Theory and Practice of the European Convention on Human Rights* (n 75 above), p 412.

[175] ECtHR, *Demicoli* (n 133 above), paras 36–42.

Representatives. The House, following the prima facie opinion of its speaker, passed a resolution holding the article to be in breach of parliamentary privilege. A few weeks later the House passed a motion summoning the applicant to appear before the House and to declare 'why he should not be found guilty of breach of privilege'.[176] The applicant did not follow the summons, and the House found him guilty. In the following proceedings the Constitutional Court upheld the House's decision, fined Mr Demicoli and ordered him to publish the House's resolution in his periodical. The Constitutional Court did not find it relevant whether 'the act constituting the contempt or breach of privilege amounts to a criminal act or not'.[177] The government argued that the final decision had been taken by the judgment of the Constitutional Court, which found the parliament competent to enact laws establishing its privileges, immunities, and power,[178] and that the aim of parliamentary privilege differs from the one of criminal law.[179]

The ECtHR did not accept either argument. It concentrated exclusively on the predetermination of the applicant's guilt by the parliamentary summons and on the severity of the charge. In *Demicoli* the imposed penalty was 250 Maltese lira and the possible maximum penalty of 60 days' imprisonment or 500 Maltese lira (ca €1,170). Despite the fact that until the proceedings in Strasbourg the penalty had neither been paid, nor had any measures been taken to enforce it,[180] the imposition as such sufficed to characterize the charge as criminal. The ECtHR,[181] as well as the Strasbourg Commission,[182] considered the determination by parliament to be a criminal charge within the meaning of Article 6(1) ECHR.

For those listed on an autonomous European list of terrorist suspects the 'penalty' would be the destruction of their reputation, the more concrete impact this stigmatization has on their private and professional lives, and the threat that Community asset freezes might follow. Those (additionally) targeted by Community sanctions further find all their financial assets frozen for an unlimited period of time. The factual and legal consequences here are the same both for Community measures giving effect to UN lists and those giving effect to Union lists.

176 ibid, para 12. 177 ibid, para 32.
178 ibid, para 26. 179 ibid, para 33.
180 ibid, para 46. 181 ibid, paras 31–5. 182 ibid, para 30.

Demicoli is of particular relevance to the Union listings. Common positions publicly declare those listed to support terrorist acts as defined in European law.[183] The European definition of a terrorist act in turn requires a punishable criminal offence in national jurisdictions.[184] However, common positions do not impose immediate enforcement measures, but provide the legal basis for Member State action under the third pillar and Community asset freezes in the first. Some of the persons listed are not targeted by Community asset freezes, but–at least potentially–by national measures. The distinction between those subject to national measures (both Member States cooperation under the third pillar and potentially national asset freezes) and those subject to Community sanctions depends on the person's country of nationality/residence, or–where legal persons are concerned–the country of their main seat.[185] EU-internal terrorists were considered to fall within national rather than Community competence.

Those listed by the Union but not subject to Community sanctions are in a position similar to that of the applicant in *Demicoli.* It is argued that listing and sanctioning constitutes a criminal charge. Yet, the case of *Segi* should be recalled in this regard.[186] In *Segi* the ECtHR found that the applicants (who brought a case in the name of an organization that was only listed on a Union list but not targeted by Community asset freezes) had not made a credible claim to be victims within the meaning of Article 34 ECHR. The ECtHR did not rule on the merits of the case. The Court held that the two applicable common positions[187] could not even potentially violate the applicants' Convention rights because they required further implementation. Finally, the Court pointed out that *if* the applicants were affected by any measures of implementation, such implementation would be subject to judicial review in either the national courts or the EU courts.[188] It appears

[183] See in: Jan Wouters and Frederik Naert, 'Of Arrest Warrants, Terrorist Offences and Extradition Deals: An Appraisal of the EU's Main Criminal Law Measures against Terrorism after 11 September', *Common Market Law Review*, 41 (2001), pp 909–35.

[184] Common Position 2001/931/CFSP (n 37 above), as well as the Framework Decision of 13 June 2002 on Combating Terrorism, 2002/475/JHA, OJ 2002 (L 164)/3–7, apply a cross-sector approach and constitute the basis for all EU anti-terrorism action. In both the notion of a terrorist act depends on the classification of a punishable offence under national law. A concept common to many international legal instruments: Kirsten Schmalenbach, 'Der internationale Terrorismus: Ein Definitionsversuch', *Neue Zeitschrift für Wehrrecht*, 42 (2000), p 19. See also Chapter 7.

[185] See Chapter 2.

[186] ECtHR, *Segi* (n 3 above).

[187] Common Position 2001/930/CFSP, OJ 2001 L 344/90–2 and Common Position 2001/931/CFSP (n 37 above).

[188] ECtHR, *Segi* (n 3 above), p 10.

that the ECtHR was blinded by the formal appearance of common positions. Formally, they are measures of general application. However, Common Position 2001/931, containing a list of persons, including their names, date and place of birth, and address, is, in fact, not of general application. It is argued that the ECtHR in *Segi* limited its examination to technical observations and disregarded thereby the special nature of individual sanctions. In particular, the Court's statement that:[189]

> [t]he *mere fact* that the names of two of the applicants [...] appear in the list referred to in that provision as 'groups or entities involved in terrorist acts' may be *embarrassing*, but the link is much too tenuous to justify application of the Convention

amounts to an ironic comment in the light of the potential repercussions that the listing has on the applicants.

Compared for instance with the decision in the *Demicoli* case, the rejection of the applicants' application because they were not sufficiently affected to be victims was also surprising. This assessment finds confirmation in other case-law on Article 34 ECHR, which bears similarities to lists of terrorist suspects. In the *Rotaru* case,[190] for example, which admittedly concerned the determination of a civil right, the ECtHR ruled on the impairment of the recording of information on a supposed legionnaire service in a secret intelligence file, which was, however, (at least partially) publicly revealed during judicial proceedings. As regards the concept of victim in Article 34 ECHR the Court maintained[191] that 'under certain conditions' a person may

> be the victim of a violation occasioned by the mere existence of secret measures or of legislation permitting secret measures, without having to allege that such measures were in fact applied to him.

The ECtHR held the applicant to be a victim in the sense of Article 34 ECHR and then found a violation of the applicant's rights.[192] This case bears much resemblance to the CFSP listings. In both scenarios, some of the measures that may apply to those affected are not clear yet, but the potential basis for further human rights interferences has been adopted. In the case of the CFSP listings further national measures – inter alia under

[189] ibid, p 9, emphasis added.

[190] ECtHR, *Rotaru v Rumania*, Application No 28341/95, 4 May 2000.

[191] ECtHR, *Rotaru*, ibid, para 35; see also: ECtHR, *Klass v Germany*, Application No 5029/71 [1978] ECHR 4 (6 September 1978), para 34–the case is further discussed below.

[192] Art 8 ECHR, Art 13 ECHR and even Art 6 ECHR albeit for not considering the applicant's claim for non-pecuniary damages.

the third pillar – and Community measures may follow. In particular a possible exchange of information under the third pillar would also remain secret.

In any event, the indicative value of *Segi* is limited first by the fact that the ECtHR did not rule on the merits and, secondly, at least in the explicit reading of the ECJ,[193] by the fact that the ruling concerned a case in which the applicants were not themselves listed as terrorist suspects, but brought an application as third parties claiming to be negatively affected by *Segi's* listing.

A further indication of the ECtHR's position on what constitutes a criminal charge is the *Phillips* case.[194] In this case the Court was asked whether the procedure according to which national courts assess the amount of a confiscation order on the basis of assumed, but unproven, prior drug crimes constituted a criminal charge that would lead to the application of the presumption of innocence in Article 6(2) ECHR. The Court ruled that:[195]

> the right to be presumed innocent under Article 6(2) ECHR arises only in connection with the particular offence 'charged'. Once an accused has properly been proved guilty of that offence, Article 6(2) can have no application in relation to allegations made about the accused's character and conduct as part of the sentencing process, unless such accusations are of such a nature and degree as to amount to the bringing of a new 'charge' within the autonomous Convention meaning.

Phillips was considered to indicate that the presumption of innocence does not apply to individual sanctions.[196] It is true the Court did not consider the official assumption that the accused had obtained property through unproven drug crimes a new charge within the meaning of Article 6 ECHR. Further, the statement in *Phillips* bears similarities with the listings in European counter-terrorist instruments. However, after denying the applicability of Article 6(2) ECHR, the Court continued in *Phillips* by stating that 'in addition to being specifically mentioned in Article 6(2), a person's right in a criminal case to be presumed innocent and to require the prosecution to bear the onus of proving the allegations against him or her forms part of the general notion of a fair hearing under Article 6(1).'[197]

[193] Case C-229/05 P, *PKK and KNK v Council* [2007] ECR I-439, paras 77–84.

[194] ECtHR, *Phillips v UK*, Application No 41087/98, judgment of 5 July 2001.

[195] ibid, para 35.

[196] Cameron, *Report to the Swedish Foreign Office on Legal Safeguards and Targeted Sanctions* (n 130 above), p 30.

[197] ECtHR, *Phillips* (n 194 above), para 40 with a reference to: ECtHR, *Saunders v United Kingdom*, Reports 1996-VI, p 2064, judgment of 17 December 1996, para 68.

In its examination of Article 6(1) ECHR the Court then pointed out[198] that the determination

> system was not without safeguards. In *Phillips*, the assessment was carried out by a court with a judicial procedure including a public hearing, advance disclosure of the prosecution case and the opportunity for the applicant to adduce documentary and oral evidence.

Additionally, the ECtHR stressed that:[199]

> [t]he principal safeguard [...] was that the assumption [...] could have been rebutted if the applicant had shown, again on the balance of probabilities, that he had acquired the property other than through drug trafficking.

All of this is not the case in the European sanctioning procedure. At the UN level the decision to list someone is taken by the Sanctions Committee. At the European level it is taken by the Council. In neither case is there intervention by an independent judicial organ, nor have those listed been granted any procedural participation. In fact, those listed do not have access to the relevant information that led to the listing.[200] They do not even have the opportunity to address directly the organ taking the decision.[201]

Moreover, the ECtHR does not take a formalistic approach to Article 6 ECHR but uses it primarily to ensure fairness. In *Phillips*, even though the Court rejected applying Article 6(2) ECHR to the allegation that the applicant had committed a particular crime, overall there were a number of procedural safeguards in place that the Court took into account in its judgment and which find no parallel in the European listing procedure. The *Phillips* case is therefore only of a limited predictive value for the qualification of Union lists of terrorist suspects.

Further, Article 6(2) ECHR not only applies to judges but also to other public authorities.[202] In the case of *Ribemont*, for instance, a simple and unqualified reference by senior officials to the accused as an 'accomplice to murder' was considered to amount to a declaration of guilt in breach of

[198] ECtHR, *Phillips* (n 194 above), para 43.

[199] ibid, para 43.

[200] See Chapter 6, Section 1.1.2 and Chapter 7, Sections 1.4 and 2.

[201] See Chapter 1 for the changes at the UN level after the introduction of the so-called focal point in SC Res 1730.

[202] Ovey and White, *Jacobs and White: The European Convention on Human Rights* (n 157 above), p 181.

Article 6(2) ECHR.[203] This case could be used in support of the argument that lists of terrorist suspects can be classified as criminal allegations and that Article 6(2) ECHR could find application.

As regards Community sanctions measures, they directly freeze the entire financial belongings that the person holds in the EU and thereby directly interfere with the property rights of those sanctioned. However, the Community regulations containing individual sanctions are adopted following a CFSP list that already sets out each individual person targeted.[204] Consequently, the Community instruments do not involve any additional naming and shaming. They cannot be considered to have elements of condemnation. Yet, together with the public allegation in the Union list, the Community asset freezes contribute to the severity of the charge. Since the Community cannot take action pursuant to Article 301 EC without a preceding CFSP instrument, everybody sanctioned by the Community is also declared to be a terrorist suspect in a CFSP instrument. Both the CFSP and the Community instrument are published in the Official Journal even if the latter does not impose an additional social stigma.

Conclusion – a Criminal Charge?. Autonomous European listings are attached to a common position entitled 'on the application of specific measures to combat terrorism'.[205] Those listed have attempted, participated in, or facilitated the commission of a terrorist act.[206] A terrorist act is necessarily a criminal offence under national law.[207] Hence, even though their conduct does not necessarily meet the conditions of a criminal offence, they are involved in the commission of a crime. Moreover, the terms 'terrorist' and 'terrorism' entail an additional negative stigma that goes beyond a common criminal conviction.[208] It could even be argued that the publication of Union lists has a certain pillorying function. Furthermore, the consequences of a listing are akin to a criminal conviction, which is publicly known but not immediately followed by a punishment. Finally, national courts have wrongly started to attach meaning to the

[203] ECtHR, *Allenet de Ribemont v France*, Judgment of 10 February 1995, Series A, No 308 (1996) 22 EHRR 582.

[204] See Chapter 1, Section 4 on the adoption procedure pursuant to Art 301 EC.

[205] Common Position 2001/931/CFSP.

[206] Article 1(4) of Common Position 2001/931/CFSP (n 37 above).

[207] Article 1(3) of Common Position 2001/931/CFSP (n 37 above).

[208] Henner Hess, 'Like Zealots and Romans: Terrorism and Empire in the 21st Century', *Crime, Law and Social Change*, 39 (2003), pp 339–57.

listings in national criminal proceedings. In sum, it is submitted that the identification of an individual on a European list has *criminal implications.*

Whether this amounts to a criminal charge in the meaning of Article 6 ECHR is admittedly a more difficult question. The administrative preventive character of individual sanctions[209] makes it hard to judge them in repressive penal categories. Yet, this does not change their severe effects. The listing criteria do not require a subjective element. Those listed do not have to be aware that their actions might contribute to financing terrorism. However, the fact that sanctions are *categorized* as preventive administrative measures and do not require the kind of evidence necessary to bring a criminal charge cannot, in itself, lead to the conclusion that they are not criminal. On the contrary, the low evidentiary burden necessary to publicly stigmatize someone as a terrorist suspect is an additional argument why the need for judicial review is so pressing.

As regards Community asset freezes they are not the initial declaration in the EU that someone is a terrorist suspect. Thus, it could be argued that they do not entail the same stigmatizing effect as Union lists of terrorist suspects. Nonetheless, Community asset freezes deprive individuals of all their financial assets for an indefinite period of time because these persons are suspected of supporting terrorism. The immediate economic consequences of an asset freeze are more severe than the listing. In any event, the combination of the two measures reinforces their criminal nature. Someone listed on a Union list of terrorist suspects is not only stigmatized as a terrorist, but also a potential target of freezing measures. Those whose assets are frozen by the Community were targeted because they are terrorist suspects. Hence, in combination with the label of terrorism the deprivation of property takes even more the character of a punishment.

In conclusion, even if individual sanctions do not fit in the traditional pattern of criminal law and even if they do not satisfy all criteria in a straightforward application, they do possess clear characteristics of criminal law, which must be taken into account in the application of Article 6 ECHR.[210] This is true both for Union lists and Community asset freezes.

[209] Miller, 'The Use of Targeted Sanctions in the Fight Against International Terrorism: What about Human Rights?' (n 139 above), p 48; see also the interpretation of the CFI at: Case T-228/02, *OMPI I* (n 4 above) para 130 and Case T-47/03, *Sison* (n 129 above), para 177.

[210] See below Section 3.2.4.

3.2.3 The Determination of Civil Rights and Obligations

Case-law of the ECtHR on Civil Rights. Community sanctions as well as Union lists are further decisive to the determination of a civil right.[211] As with the term 'criminal charge,' the ECtHR applies its own autonomous definition of what are 'civil rights and obligations'.[212] However, while 'civil' is an autonomous notion, 'rights and obligations' depend in principle on the substantive law of the Contracting Party.[213] There must be an arguable basis for the right in domestic law.[214]

The right to property is acknowledged in the European legal order,[215] as well as in the national legal orders of all the Member States. European law will here be considered an expression of the common core of the national law of the 27 Member States, since this is not the place to conduct a comparative survey of civil rights and obligations in the national legal orders of the Member States. Further, although the ECtHR does not usually create a substantive right, which has no basis under national law,[216] it is likely to find a right where proceedings concern serious interferences with other fundamental rights guaranteed by the Convention.[217]

Although procedural protection is a separate issue, the availability of judicial remedies and administrative appeals has great influence on the justifiability of an interference with substantive Convention rights. In the *Sporrong* and *Lönnroth* case[218] for instance the applicants succeeded because there was no procedure by which they could challenge the long-continued application of the expropriation permits[219] blighting their property, nor were they entitled to any compensation for the loss that this situation had

[211] Eg: ECtHR, *Ringeisen* (n 74 above).

[212] Kley-Struller, *Artikel 6 EMRK als Rechtsschutzgarantie gegen die öffentliche Gewalt: Die aktuelle Praxis der Konventionsorgane zur Anwendung des Artikel 6 EMRK in der Verwaltungs-rechtspflege* (n 173 above), p 19

[213] Karen Reid, *A Practitioners Guide to the ECHR* (London: Thomson/Sweet & Maxwell, 2004), p 70.

[214] ECtHR, *Markovic* (n 98 above), para 26.

[215] On the right to property, e.g.: Case 44/79, *Hauer* (n 55 above), para 4; further, on the right to exercise an economic activity: Case 4/73, *Nold* (n 55 above), para 14; Case 25/70, *Köster* [1970] ECR 1162; Case 230/78, *Eridania* [1979] ECR 2749, para 20; Joint Cases C-143/88 and C-92/89, *Zuckerfabrik Süderdithmarschen und Zuckerfabrik Soest* [1991] ECR I-415, para 72; see also: Arts 16 and 17 of the Charter of Fundamental Rights.

[216] ECtHR, *Z and Others v UK*, Application No 29392/95, ECHR 2001-V; ECtHR, *Markovic* (n 98 above), para 93 with further references.

[217] Reid, *A Practitioners Guide to the ECHR* (n 213 above), p 70; referring to: ECtHR, *Price v UK*, Application No 12402/86, 14 July 1988, 55 DR 224.

[218] ECtHR, *Sporrong and Lönnroth* (n 76 above).

[219] 23 years in *Sporrong*'s case and eight in *Lönnroth*'s case, ibid.

brought about.[220] Despite the so-called 'margin of appreciation' doctrine, which will restrain the Court from intervening with domestic decisions

> an absence of procedural protection will lend credence to a claim that the interference is not justified–or at least, the respondent government will find it difficult to show that the various interests were indeed carefully balanced.[221]

Thus, procedural rights and substantive rights are so closely interrelated that they cannot be examined separately.

In principle, Community freezing measures, irrespective of whether they could qualify as administrative measures, directly interfere with the property rights of those listed.[222] The right to property is protected in Article 1 of Protocol 1 to the Convention. This provision allows the Contracting parties to 'control the use of property', but prohibits the deprivation of property 'except in the public interest and subject to the conditions provided for by law'. In a number of cases the ECtHR has declared that the confiscation of property used in crime is in principle classified as a way to 'control the use of property' within the meaning of Article 1 of Protocol 1 to the Convention.[223] The duration is relevant for this classification. Even if it is not seen as a deprivation from the start, the longer the freezing goes on, the more likely it is that the Court would view the measure as a deprivation of property.[224] In any event, for the initial application of Article 6(1) ECHR it does not matter whether the asset freezes are classified as 'deprivation of possessions' or 'control of property'. Both are a determination of civil rights within the meaning of Article 6 ECHR.

More problematic are European lists of terrorist suspects. With regard to natural persons they cause prima facie non-material damage only, and the Convention does not explicitly recognize a right to reputation. It could be questionable whether this is sufficient to rely on Article 6 ECHR. The Strasbourg Court found that reputation is part of the 'civil rights and obligations' of a person in terms of Article 6(1) ECHR, which the person

[220] Harris O'Boyle and Colin Warbrick, *Law of the European Convention on Human Rights* (London: Butterworths, 1995), p 526.

[221] Bill Bowring, 'Terrorist Designation with Regard to European and International Law: The Case of the PMOI', paper presented at the International Conference of Jurists in Paris on Wednesday, 10 November 2004, p 20.

[222] See the discussion on the scope of the interference: Case C-117/06, *Möllendorf and Möllendorf v Niehuus* [2007] ECR I-8361; see also the opinion of AG Mengozzi in this case.

[223] ECtHR, *AGOSI v UK*, 24 October 1986, A/108.

[224] ECtHR, *Sporrong* (n 76 above).

must have a right to defend in court.[225] As with other rights and obligations, the right to reputation for the purpose of Article 6(1) ECHR is (in principle) guaranteed within the limits of domestic law.[226] Additionally, however, the ECtHR has more recently recognized a human right to reputation under the right to privacy.[227]

In the national legal orders of the EU Member States the right to an unharmed reputation is protected either directly[228] or as a result of the protection of economic[229] or family rights depending on the reputation of a person. In the European legal order it is protected beyond the direct economic interest in good reputation. This is sensible. Anything else would make the right to good reputation depending on the wealth of a person.

A forceful example within the European legal order for the recognition of the right to judicial protection from public acts harming one's reputation is the case of *Pergan Hilfsstoffe*.[230] In this case the applicant challenged the decision of the Commission to reject his application for removal of all reference to him in a decision concerning proceedings under Article 81 EC. The decision was addressed to a third party and published in the public domain. The CFI found in favour of the applicant. It pointed out that because the applicant did not have standing to bring an action against the published decision–because it was not the addressee–the publication was contrary to the principle of the presumption of innocence and infringed the protection of professional secrecy. The Court ruled that the latter requires that respect for the reputation and dignity of the applicant be ensured.[231] In particular the CFI observed[232] that the presumption of innocence

[225] ECtHR, *Golder* (n 70 above), para 27; ECtHR, *Helmers v Sweden*, Series A, No 212, 15 EHRR 285, judgment of 29 October 1991, para 27; ECtHR, *Miloslavsky*, Application No 18139/91, para 58.

[226] In ECtHR *F v UK*, Application No 11862/85, of 18 July 1986, the European Commission of Human Rights accepted that national law may exclude actions for group defamation.

[227] Concurring opinion of Justice Loucaides in ECtHR, *Lindon*, Application Nos 21279 & 36448/02, and the references there.

[228] In Germany for instance the GCC has developed, in settled case-law, a personal right based on Arts 2(1) and 1(1) of the German Constitution, which includes the protection of good reputation (*allgemeines Persönlichkeitsrecht*).

[229] This is the case in the UK.

[230] Case T-474/04, *Pergan Hilfsstoffe für industrielle Prozesse v Commission* [2007] ECR II-4225,

[231] ibid, para 80.

[232] ibid, para 76 referring to: Joined Cases T-22/02 and T-23/02, *Sumitomo Chemical and Sumika Fine Chemicals v Commission* [2005] ECR II 4065, para 106.

precludes any formal finding and even any allusion to the liability of an accused person for a particular infringement in a final decision unless that person has enjoyed all the usual guarantees accorded for the exercise of the rights of defence in the normal course of proceedings resulting in a decision on the merits of the case.

The Court continued in pointing out that 'the guilt of a person accused of an infringement is established definitively only where the decision finding that infringement has acquired the force of *res judicata* [...]'.[233]

Before the case of *Segi* the ECtHR had not been consulted on the specific matter of public lists. There are, however, other judgments on similar issues that shed light on the Court's general position on non-material damages resulting from wrong allegations. Generally, the ECtHR has accepted the existence and the civil character of the right to good reputation both of private persons[234] and of public officials.[235] In the case of *Golder*,[236] for instance, the applicant was a prison inmate who wanted to bring an action against his warden for having alleged that he had been assaulted by Golder. Although the charges had been dropped the entries about the alleged assault together with a note that no charges were pursued remained in the applicant's prison record. The applicant admitted that 'the libel' had 'not materially harmed' him.[237] Nonetheless, the ECtHR accepted that 'the right which Golder wished, rightly or wrongly, to invoke against [the prison officer] [...] was a civil right within the meaning of Article 6(1) [ECHR]',[238] that the allegation and the entry could violate the rights guaranteed in the Convention and that it is 'for an independent and impartial court to rule on any claim that might be brought.'[239] The Court found a violation of Article 6 ECHR.

Moreover, in the case of *Helmers*[240] the applicant was not selected for appointment to an academic post. He introduced private prosecutions and a claim for damages against the alleged initiators because he considered that the decision was discriminatory and based on a defamation campaign led against him. Both proceedings were considered decisive for the 'civil right'

[233] Case T-474/04, *Pergan Hilfsstoffe* (n 230 above), para 76.

[234] See further: ECtHR, *ISOP v Austria*, Application No 808/60, Yearbook V (1962), p 108, p 122; ECommHR, *Al Fayed and Others*, Commission report of 7 April 1993, A.294-B, p 6; ECommHR, Tolstoy Miloslavsky, Commission report of 17 January 1994, A.316-B, p 8. With regard to statements made in Parliament and parliamentary immunity: ECtHR, *Agee v UK*, Application No 7729/76, D&R 7 (1977), p 164 (175), p 175.

[235] ECtHR, *Golder* (n 70 above)

[236] ibid. [237] ibid, para 16. [238] ibid, para 27.

[239] ibid, para 40.

[240] ECtHR, *Helmers* (n 225 above), in particular para 29.

at issue. The symbolic nature of the claim for damages–the applicant claimed one Swedish krona–did not affect this assessment. The existence of a dispute does not necessarily depend on whether or not monetary damages are claimed. In both cases, proceedings against alleged defamation were considered a contestation of a civil right within the meaning of Article 6(1) ECHR. Hence, with regard to the Union lists it is not necessary to prove direct financial loss as a result of the listing. Depending on domestic law, the right to an unharmed reputation is affected even if no financial damage can be proven. *To be labelled as a terrorist suspect* (for an unlimited period of time) is in itself serious enough to interfere with the right to good reputation irrespective of whether this has an impact on the person's economic activities. It entails a total loss of social standing.

In the *Fayed* case,[241] by contrast, the ECtHR ruled that the publication of a provisional report did not determine the applicant's civil right to a good reputation, notwithstanding that the report contained largely unfavourable conclusions about the applicant's business practices. A different understanding would unduly hamper the effective regulation of the public interest in complex financial and commercial activities.[242] However, the report in *Fayed* stated that it was not dispositive of anything. It mainly recorded facts that were intended as the basis for action by other authorities. Individual sanctions do not record facts but purport merely that those listed are involved in terrorism without setting out any information in support of this allegation. They are a definite judgment in the sense that they are not necessarily followed by any further analysis or determination of the individual's position.[243] No further investigation into these allegations is required. Sanction lists do not posses the preliminary nature of the report in *Fayed*, which led to the denial of the right of access to court. Consequently, this case is not conclusive for individual sanctions.

Practical Consequences of being Listed and Sanctioned. With regard to organizations, such as Segi, individual sanctions have effects equal to prohibiting the organization.[244] In the Netherlands for instance, all legal persons listed by the EU pursuant to Common Position 2001/931/CFSP

[241] ECtHR, *Fayed v United Kingdom* (1994) 18 EHRR 393.

[242] ibid, para 61–61.

[243] See the discussion of the criteria for subsequent listings in autonomous European terrorist lists in Chapter 6, Section 1.1.1 and Chapter 7, Section 1.2

[244] See on the consequences: Iain Cameron, 'The European Convention on Human Rights: Due Process and United Nations Security Council Counter-Terrorism Sanctions', Report to the Council of Europe, of 6 February 2006, http://www.coe.int/., p 8

are prohibited *ipso jure* and cannot take legal acts.[245] Further, if the organization is targeted by Community sanctions it will necessarily lose all support. The threat of potential secondary sanctions[246] will keep its members from exercising their membership. This interferes both with the rights of the members and with the rights of the organization. However, the declaration that an organization is suspected to support terrorism alone is relevant for the determination of civil rights. To choose freely to join a legal organization is the exercise of a civil right. Corresponding to this right is the right of the organization not to be prohibited or otherwise deprived of members. The declaration that the particular organization supports terrorism deters potential members from participating in, or otherwise supporting, the organization. They would have to fear that their participation is registered and that, as a result, they could be targeted by sanctions themselves. This is a realistic threat of negative consequences, which is sufficient to constitute a limitation of the protected freedom. A large part of the population will refrain from supporting this organization as a consequence of the listing.[247] This necessarily impairs the organization's right to act and potentially even to exist. Moreover, the possibilities for legal persons to qualify for an exemption remain entirely unclear.[248]

For natural persons the situation is not much different. Natural persons listed and sanctioned as terrorist suspects will be unable to access their financial assets or receive any payment. They will have to apply for exemptions for the most basic needs.[249] Moreover, Community sanctions entail secondary sanctions against those who do not comply with the imposed rules and do business with those listed. Third parties should hence have a right to withdraw from agreed business with those listed. An aggravating factor in this regard is that the standard of what constitutes

[245] 'Van rechtswege verboden', Art 2:20 Section 3 of the civil code (*Burgerlijk Wetboek*).

[246] See Chapter 1, Section 4.

[247] Individual sanctions do not require a subjective wrong; a good example for the listing of individuals purely because of their work for an alleged terrorist organization is the *Yusuf* case (Case T-306/01, *Yusuf* (n 4 above)). See also Chapter 7, Section 1.3 on 'guilt by association'.

[248] Van der Herik and Schrijver, *Section Two: Human Rights Concerns in Current Targeted Sanctions Regimes from the Perspective of International and European Law* (n 72 above), p 31.

[249] See Chapter 1, Section 3.1.3 and on the scope of Community sanctions: Case C-117/06, *Möllendorf and Möllendorf* (n 222 above); High Court, *M, A, MM v HM Treasury* [2006] EWHC 2328 (Admin), para 64; Court of Appeal *M, A, MM v HM Treasury* [2007] EWCA Civ 173, para 17; application in Case C-340/08, *M (FC) and Others*, OJ [2008] C 260/8; see also Chapter 5, Section 5.3 and Chapter 7, Section 4.

non-compliance is criticized for being very uncertain.[250] Hence, even where exemptions are granted the only sure way to avoid violation of sanctions rules is not to engage in economic activity with those listed at all. Thus, those sanctioned by the Community find themselves in total economic isolation.[251]

Direct Impact on the Rights of Those Listed. Union lists of terrorist suspects have a direct impact on the rights of those listed, even if they are devoid of direct applicability. Generally, CFSP decisions do not confer rights or obligations on individuals.[252] They are usually held not to be self-executing.[253] However, this does not exclude that individuals are affected by Union measures.

In light of the ECJ's ruling in *Segi*[254] an authoritative interpretation by the EU courts regarding the status of CFSP measures has become more likely. Thus far, the matter has not been of great importance either to the EU or the national judiciary, since CFSP decisions usually deal with the external relations of the Union and are therefore not 'unconditional and sufficiently precise' for individuals to rely on before the national courts.[255] However, the ECJ held in its appeal decision in *Segi* that Union lists of terrorist suspects do have legal effects on the position of those listed[256] and that they go beyond what is possible to adopt in the form of a common position.[257] Further, the Court acknowledged the new form of immediate connection between the Union instrument and the individual, resulting from the identification of the latter by the former, and opened up the

[250] Peter Fitzgerald, 'Compliance Issues Associated with Targeted Economic Sanctions' in House of Lords, Select Committee on Economic Affairs, 2nd Report of Session 2006–07, 'The Impact of Economic Sanctions', Vol II: Evidence (2007), p 152 et seq.

[251] Compare the excessively generous reading: T-253/02, *Ayadi* (n 4 above), para 129 et seq. The Court argued that it is not the economic activity itself or the acquiring of economic resources which are prohibited, but that these funds are simply frozen and not available to those sanctioned.

[252] Eileen Denza, *The Intergovernmental Pillars of the European Union* (Oxford: Oxford University Press, 2002), p 261 gives the absence of any mention of direct effect for common positions short shrift by stating that this reflects 'the fact that they will not create legal rights or obligations'. This statement appeared contentious before, but now, in the light of individual sanctions, this analysis appears to require a second thought.

[253] Ramses Wessel, 'Good Governance and EU Foreign Security and Defence Policy', *CES Working Paper No* 2/04, p 20 referring to: Deirde Curtin and Ronald H van Ooik, 'Revamping the European Union's Enforcement Systems with a View to Eastern Enlargement', *Working Document W 110, Scientific Council for Government Policy, The Hague, October 2000*, pp 30–1.

[254] Case C-355/04 P, *Segi* (n 7 above), Chapter 6.

[255] Curtin and van Ooik, 'Revamping the European Union's Enforcement Systems with a View to Eastern Enlargement' (n 253 above), para 14.1.

[256] Case C-355/04 P, *Segi* (n 7 above), para 53.

[257] ibid, para 54.

possibility of bringing a preliminary reference, irrespective of the form of the measure.

Moreover, in the case of *Pupino*[258] the ECJ applied the principle of conform interpretation under the third pillar. This entails an implicit acknowledgement that third pillar instruments enjoy supremacy. The *Pupino* reasoning is indicative of the quality of Union law both under the third pillar and under the second pillar. Additionally, in the third pillar Article 34(2)(b) TEU restrained the Court from giving framework decisions direct effect, while there is no parallel provision in the second pillar. Hence, for the time being one must assume that CFSP instruments could in principle be directly effective.[259] It is not impossible to imagine a private party trying to rely on a CFSP instrument in national courts if it is sufficiently clear and precise.[260] This potential direct effect of CFSP provisions is a strong argument for their decisiveness for the civil rights of those sanctioned.

Two scenarios are imaginable in which individual sanctions can be of relevance before national courts. First, an individual could sue her bank in a civil law action for release of her funds. Secondly, the state could prosecute an individual in a criminal law action for having breached sanctions by making money available to a terrorist suspect (imposition of secondary sanctions).

Determination. Some European lists of terrorist suspects are identical copies of UN lists. In those cases the first allegation is contained in a Security Council resolution and the European institutions merely rubber-stamp the UN allegation. Hence, it could be argued that the European lists are not decisive for the disreputable allegations. However, the transposition of UN lists into EU law vests those lists with additional effects. First, both Community and Union law instruments are 'harder' law than UN resolutions with regard to their effects on the legal position of the

[258] Case C-105/03, *Pupino* (n 124 above), para 43.

[259] Deirdre Curtin and Inge Dekker, 'The Constitutional Structure of the European Union: Some Reflections on Vertical Unity-in-Diversity' in Paul Beaumont; Carole Lyons and Neil Walker (eds), *Convergence and Divergence in European Public Law* (Oxford: Hart Publishing, 2002), p 68 arguing that the explicit exclusion of direct effect of some third pillar instruments in European law (Art 34(2)(b) and (c) TEU) reflects the Member States' understanding that the status of Union law is no longer to be decided by their domestic law; a bit more reluctant, but not excluding direct effect: Wessel, 'Good Governance and EU Foreign Security and Defence Policy' (n 253 above), p 20.

[260] Wessel, 'Good Governance and EU Foreign Security and Defence Policy' (n 253 above), p 20.

individual. The necessity to interpret national law in conformity with Union law, supremacy and direct enforceability were mentioned above. Security Council resolutions, by contrast, are not considered to be directly applicable within the domestic legal order.[261] Secondly, European law attaches additional legitimacy to the terrorist lists. EU Member States are exclusively law-abiding democracies, which signed up to the ECHR, and the EU itself is committed to fundamental rights and the rule of law. Hence, the simple fact that a UN list is reproduced in a European law instrument gives extra-support to the allegation that those listed are terrorists and contributes to destroying the reputation of those listed.[262]

A further problem could be the classification as 'temporary precautionary measure[s]'.[263] Interim measures do not usually qualify[264] as decisive for the determination of a civil right or obligation[265] because they are subject to further investigation. Nonetheless, despite the fact that individual sanctions are adopted under the label of emergency measures, their application is not temporarily limited.[266] Moreover, even if one accepts that individual sanctions qualify as emergency measures, some form of access to court must be granted if they are caught by Article 6 ECHR.[267]

The ECJ further limits judicial review to *final* measures. Preparatory, provisional, and preliminary acts 'intended to pave the way for the final decision'[268] are–except for when they can be separately enforced[269]–excluded from judicial review.[270] Individual sanctions are an 'act or decision adopted by a procedure involving several stages'.[271] Pursuant to Article 301 EC they require a CFSP decision, followed by an EC

[261] See Chapter 1, Section 5.

[262] The ECJ explicitly referred to the negative impact of the listing on the reputation of those listed: C-229/05 P, *PKK* (n 193 above), para 110.

[263] Eg: Case T-315/01, *Kadi* (n 4 above), para 248.

[264] ECtHR, *Markass Care Hire ltd v Cyprus*, Application No 51591, judgment of 23 October 2001.

[265] ECtHR, *Fayed* (n 241 above).

[266] See Section 3.2.2 above.

[267] See Chapter 4 on the case law of the ECtHR and selected national courts.

[268] See eg Case 60/81, *IBM v Commission* [1981] ECR 2639, para 10 et seq Case 53/85, *AKZO Chemie v Commission* [1986] ECR 1965, para 16 et seq; see also Case C-47/91, *Italy v Commission* [1992] ECR I-4145, para 30 – in the last case the challenged letter prohibited the Italian government from paying a proposed aid before the procedure had resulted in a final decision. The Court considered the underlying decision to be more than a preparatory step, to have legal effect and, consequently, to be susceptible to be challenged based on Art 230 EC.

[269] Case 46/87, *Hoechst v Commission* [1989] ECR 2869.

[270] Case T-212/95, *Officimen v Commission* [1997] ECR II-1161; Case 60/81, *IBM* (n 268 above), para 10.

[271] As the letter of the Commission in Case 60/81, *IBM* (n 268 above).

regulation. It could be argued that the CFSP lists therefore do not constitute the final measure but are rather a necessary stage in the process of adopting sanctions. This would also be in line with the ECtHR's position in *Segi* that CFSP listings do not already affect the applicants sufficiently to be a victim, but still have to be implemented to impact their rights.[272] Based on a similar argument the ECJ ruled in the *IBM* case[273] that the Commission's communication of the statement of objections was not enough to change the applicant's legal position, since it only indicated that a fine might follow.[274] However, in the same case the Court stated[275] that:

> any measure the legal effects of which are binding on, and capable of affecting the legal interests of, the applicant by bringing a distinct change in his legal position is an act or decision which may be the subject of an action under Article 173 [now 230 EC] for a declaration that it is void.

CFSP listings change the legal position of those listed; they are not a provisional, but a final decision of the CFSP Council to sanction a specific person. They are 'the culmination of a special procedure distinct from'[276] the decision to adopt Community sanctions, and they cannot be regarded as a purely internal measure[277] because they are formally published.[278] Moreover, contrary to the situation where the European institutions only reproduce UN lists, autonomous EU lists of terrorist suspects consist of a bundle of discretionary decisions by the Council to list a particular person.[279] These listing decisions are taken in a specific procedure based on the information produced by the Member States: the information is actually revealed to the Council[280] and the latter takes an informed decision. Finally, even if common positions are usually the first stage to the adoption

[272] ECtHR, *Segi* (n 3 above); however, the Court's view was rejected above.

[273] Case 60/81, *IBM* (n 268 above).

[274] See also more recently: Joined Cases T-377/00, T-379/00, T-380/00, T-260/01 and T-272/01, *Philip Morris International and Others v Commission* [2003] ECR II-1, para 79; confirmed by: C-131/03 P, *RJ Reynolds Tobacco Holdings Inc v Commission* [2007] ECR I-7795, paras 56–8.

[275] Case 60/81, *IBM* (n 268 above), para 9.

[276] ibid, para 11.

[277] See Wolfram Cremer, 'Artikel 230' in Christian Callies and Matthias Ruffert (eds), *Kommentar zum EU-/EG-Vertrag* (Neuwied: Luchterhand, 2002), para 18 for examples.

[278] Despite the fact that the TEU does not contain a parallel provision to Art 254(2) EC, all CFSP common positions are published in the Official Journal of the European Communities; see also Section 3.2.1(c) of the inter-institutional style guide of the publication office.

[279] AG Mengozzi in: Case C-355/04 P, *Segi* (n 7 above), para 57.

[280] ibid, para 16.

of Community sanctions, the *Segi* case[281] demonstrates that this is not always so.[282] Here, the listing in the common position was the final, and only, reason for grievance. Consequently, it is not tenable that CFSP lists are only preparatory acts and do not need to be subject to judicial review.

By way of conclusion, European lists of terrorist suspects as well as Community asset freezes determine the civil rights and obligations of those listed and sanctioned.[283] Thus, those listed can rely on Article 6 ECHR. The extent to which this right can be made subject to limitations will be discussed in Chapter 4.

3.2.4 Application of Article 6 ECHR

Whether a particular situation falls within the scope of Article 6 ECHR requires a 'yes' or 'no' answer. The substantive requirements of Article 6 ECHR, by contrast, allow for a certain degree of flexibility. In principle Article 6 ECHR sets high standards,[284] but due process is not a static right. The intrinsic aim of the individual requirements is to ensure, or contribute to ensuring, the fairness of the proceedings as a whole. Consequently, the safeguards are necessary to a greater or lesser degree depending on the nature of the proceedings and the possible compensation measures taken by the state to make up for the reduction of protection in one area. This dynamic is reflected in the structure of Article 6 ECHR, as well as in the case-law of the ECtHR. The Strasbourg Court tends to take a pragmatic view and assess the fairness of the proceedings looked at as a whole rather than setting out rigid procedural rules.[285]

In the case of *Helmers*[286] for instance, the ECtHR applied a reasoning that it usually applies in criminal cases (concerning the right of the applicant to be present at the proceedings) to the determination of a civil right. The Court did this because of the importance of what was at stake, namely the professional reputation and career of the applicant. *Helmers* is a good

[281] Case T-338/02, *Segi* (n 4 above).

[282] All European citizens and organizations with their seat within the EU listed in CP 2001/931/CFSP (n 37 above) were in the same position.

[283] Van der Herik and Schrijver, *Section Two: Human Rights Concerns in Current Targeted Sanctions Regimes from the Perspective of International and European Law* (n 72 above), p 14 conclude: 'it is not certain that the ECtHR would consider the sanctions as civil obligations'.

[284] Article 6 ECHR requires 'within a reasonable time' a 'fair and public hearing' by an 'independent tribunal established by law.'

[285] Ovey and White, *Jacobs and White: The European Convention on Human Rights* (n 157 above), p 177; Reid, *A Practitioners Guide to the ECHR* (n 213 above), p 57.

[286] ECtHR, *Helmers* (n 225 above), in particular p 38.

example of the flexible application of Article 6(1) ECHR aiming above all to ensure a *fair* trial.

The criminal nature of the listings is highly contested.[287] It is not clear that the ECtHR would take the position here argued and consider those listings a criminal charge. However, it is undisputed that both Union lists and Community sanctions restrict Convention rights to a considerable degree, not only but also because they have characteristics of a criminal charge. The intensity of the interference with Convention rights determines the necessary judicial safeguards. As a consequence, the high degree of interference and, in particular, the criminal implications must be reflected in the quality of the judicial safeguards provided in the listing procedure.

Based on the hypothesis that international sanctions – even if they do not fully classify as criminal law in the traditional sense–have many similarities with the latter, they must also be treated in a similar manner. This means, for instance, that the rule of law requires some form of a presumption of innocence that protects the individual from wrongful convictions irrespective of the good reasons that the state might have for pursuing this conviction. Moreover, the Commission has explicitly emphasised the importance of the presumption of innocence in the European law context.[288] Thus, even if Article 6(2) ECHR does not apply, it can serve as an indication of which safeguards are necessary in criminal proceedings. At the same time, it is clear that certain presumptions of fact must operate in a sanctioning system.

3.2.5 Independent and Impartial Tribunal

It is submitted that Article 6(1) ECHR is applicable to individual sanctions and that those listed have the right to be heard by an independent and impartial tribunal. In *Demicoli*[289] the ECtHR considered it a breach of Article 6 ECHR that the applicant had not been heard before the speaker of the House established a prima facie judgment. The Court first stipulated that the House of Representatives 'undoubtedly exercised a judicial function in determining the applicant's guilt'.[290] It then examined whether the

[287] See Section 3.2.2 above.

[288] See in particular on the presumption of innocence: the European Commission Green Paper on the Presumption of Innocence, COM(2006) 174 final.

[289] ECtHR, *Demicoli* (n 133 above), see also Section 3.2.2 above.

[290] ibid, para 40.

House of Representatives could constitute a tribunal within the meaning of this article. The Court decided that:[291]

> [a] 'tribunal' is characterised in the substantive sense of the term by its judicial function, that is to say determining matters within its competence on the basis of *rules of law* and after *proceedings conducted in a prescribed manner*...

The conclusion was *not* that a parliament *cannot* exercise a judicial function, but rather that the impartiality of the House of Representatives was open to doubt. This conclusion was based on the participation of the members of parliament whose actions were criticized in Mr Demicoli's article. They were defending their own honour and hence acting as judges in their own cause. The adoption process of individual sanctions differs considerably. Nonetheless, *Demicoli* is indicative for the Court's understanding of what is a 'tribunal'.

First, it is argued that already the first listing is equivalent to a conviction with regard to the harmful effects on the reputation of those listed. The House of Representatives in *Demicoli* passed its resolution on the basis of existing law. Sanctions against individuals, by contrast, are adopted as an 'all in one' instrument. The listing procedure remains obscure.[292] No formal or material requirements are set out in a general legal instrument.[293] Clearly, the listing procedure does not guarantee *proceedings conducted in a prescribed manner*. Secondly, although the measures might not serve any immediate personal interest of those adopting them, parallels can be drawn between the *delisting procedure* and *Demicoli*. The same body/institution first draws up the list and then examines the delisting requests. The same body/institution that adopted the measures cannot offer an 'independent' review. Depending on the type of sanctions, the decision to include an individual on a European list is taken either by the UN Sanctions Committee or by the Council after an EU Member State has suggested that the person should be listed. Any delisting is equally dependent on those two institutions. They cannot qualify as independent in the meaning of Article 6 ECHR. Hence, any administrative recourse to the authorities in charge of the initial listing cannot satisfy the requirements under Article 6 ECHR.

[291] ibid, para 39 (emphasis added).

[292] See the discussion of the voting practice in the Council in Case T-284/08, *OMPI III* (n 4 above), para 27 et seq.

[293] See however the guidelines adopted by the Council: doc 15579/03 of 8 December 2003, updated by doc 6749/05 and doc 15114/05; see also Chapter 7, Section 1.1.

It should be added, that national security was not an issue in the *Demicoli* case. However, possible national security considerations, while they can limit the substantive scope of the judicial safeguards required by Article 6 ECHR, cannot lead to the conclusion that either the Sanctions Committee or the European institutions are 'an independent and impartial tribunal'.

In a different case the ECtHR was asked whether or not other tribunals (as opposed to courts of law) are 'independent and impartial', in particular whether the members of the tribunal cannot be susceptible to executive influence. It ruled that the presence of one military officer as one out of three judges was enough to presume that the tribunal was not independent.[294] In a trial on terrorist charges where the defendant was prevented from attending, the ECtHR held that the defendant must be allowed to be present notwithstanding security concerns.[295] The CFI's argument[296] that:

> the Security Council intended to take account, so far as possible, of the fundamental rights of the persons entered in the Sanctions Committee's list and in particular their right to be heard

can be considered under Article 13 ECHR. It does not influence a finding that the listed persons have *not* received a 'fair and public hearing… by an independent and impartial tribunal' as required by Article 6 ECHR at the UN level.

Originally, both for UN lists and European lists it was not known to those listed who had requested the listing and who held the information on which the listing decision was based. This remains true for UN lists and, consequently, for European sanctions giving effect to UN lists. For listings taking place within the EU, the CFI held in the case of *OMPI I* that the institutions have to issue a personalized statement of reasons setting out inter alia which Member State requested the listing.[297] Thus, it is now possible to bring an action before the national courts of the state that requested the listing. The courts of the Member States qualify as independent tribunals within the meaning of Article 6 ECHR. The same is true for the EU courts. Hence, where recourse either to national courts or to the EU courts is possible, the requirement of an independent tribunal within the meaning of Article 6 ECHR is satisfied. Any substantive

[294] ECtHR, *Incal v Turkey* (1998-IV), 1547.
[295] ECtHR, *Zana v Turkey* (1999) 27 EHRR 667.
[296] Case T-306/01, *Yusuf* (n 4 above), para 312.
[297] Case T-228/02, *OMPI I* (n 4 above), para 143; Chapter 6, Section 1.2.

limitation would have to be proportionate in order to comply with the Convention.[298]

3.3 Article 13 ECHR

Article 6 ECHR applies both to CFSP listings and to Community sanctions. If the ECtHR agrees with this evaluation Article 13 ECHR would no longer be applicable.[299] If, however, for one of the two measures Article 6 ECHR were found not to apply, Article 13 ECHR would still offer some degree of protection. Article 13 ECHR requires neither a traditional judicial remedy nor a bi-polar decision of whether individual sanctions are of a criminal nature or not. In this regard, it offers more flexibility to reconcile effective counter-terrorist policies with effective protection of the rights of individuals.

Article 13 ECHR applies whenever an arguable claim can be made that a substantive right has been violated.[300] As demonstrated above, those listed on a European list of terrorist suspects, be it a copy of a UN list or one drawn up autonomously by the European institutions, as well as those targeted by Community sanctions, have an arguable claim that their Convention rights were breached. Article 13 ECHR also applies to a possible violation of the right to an unharmed reputation.[301]

Article 13 ECHR offers a lower level of protection than Article 6 ECHR. Indeed, the ECtHR's case-law on Article 13 ECHR could make the finding of a violation difficult. In the case of *Klass* the Court accepted, for instance, that 'the aggregate of [a number of] remedies', which, taken alone, were not considered to be effective, could satisfy Article 13 ECHR.[302] In this examination the ECtHR took into account rather ineffective remedies such as a complaint to the Commission in charge of supervising the application of the law allowing for secret surveillance and a subsequent constitutional complaint to the GCC.[303] Nonetheless, the

[298] See for the limitations Chapter 6, Sections 1.3 and 2; for their proportionality Chapter 7, Section 4.

[299] See above Section 3.1 for the relationship between Arts 6 and 13 ECHR.

[300] ECtHR, *Klass* (n 191 above), para 64.

[301] See for instance: European Commission For Democracy Through Law (Venice Commission), Opinion on a possible solution to the issue of decertification of police officers in Bosnia and Herzegovina, of Strasbourg, 24 October 2005, Opinion No 326/2004, CDL-AD (2005)024.

[302] ECtHR, Klass (n 191 above), para 72; see also: ECtHR, *Leander v Sweden* (1987) 9 EHRR 433, ECtHR, *Esbester v UK*, Application No 18601/91, judgment of 2 April 1993.

[303] ECtHR, *Klass* (n 191 above), para 70.

Court examined 'whether these remedies are effective in the circumstances' of the particular case.[304] Further, in *Klass* the applicant had a whole range of legal actions at his disposal after the surveillance measures were discontinued.[305] Thus, the Court's generous acceptance of quantity instead of quality of protection mechanisms must be read in a purposive manner. Only where the aggregation of stand-alone ineffective remedies has an added value, and renders them in a complementing way effective, is the purpose of Article 13 ECHR satisfied.

With regard to European sanctions based on UN lists, the CFI took various non-judicial remedies into account.[306] However, it took a rather incoherent approach to the safeguards at the UN level. Indirectly, the Court acknowledged that its jurisdiction did not extend to the procedures at the UN level and refused to look more closely at the compliance with the right to a fair hearing at the UN level.[307] With regard to the right to a judicial remedy, by contrast, the CFI took the opposite position: it argued that it had to review 'indirectly the lawfulness of the resolutions of the Security Council at issue, in the light of the higher rules of international law falling within the ambit of *jus cogens*'.[308] The CFI came to the conclusion that *jus cogens* was not breached. Those sanctioned by the UN now have the possibility to address their claims to the so-called focal point and to petition their governments to file a delisting request.[309] Taking into account these improvements, the ECJ came to the conclusion that 'clearly that re-examination procedure [at the UN level] does not offer the guarantees of judicial protection'.[310] The ECJ did not comment on procedural rights other than judicial protection. The UN Human Rights Committee,[311] by contrast, argued that Belgian law offered an effective remedy against sanctions giving effect to UN lists, because those listed were able to take the Belgian government to the national courts and to obtain 'an order requiring it to submit a delisting request to the Sanctions Committee'.[312] The latter appears surprising since the possibility to compel a national

[304] ibid, para 65. [305] ibid, para 71.

[306] Case T-306/01 *Yusuf* (n 4 above), para 311 et seq, 345.

[307] Case T-315/01, *Kadi* (n 4 above), para 272. [308] ibid, para 282.

[309] Chapter 1, Section 3.1.2.

[310] Cases C-402/05 P and C-415/05 P, *Kadi and al Barakaat* (n 4 above), para 322.

[311] UN Human Rights Committee 'Views of the Committee Concerning the Communication Submitted by Sayadi and Vinck' (29 December 2008) CCPR/C/94/D/1472/2006.

[312] ibid, 4.7.

government to submit a delisting request is only as effective in terms of fundamental rights protection as the delisting procedure that might then follow. If the latter falls short of protecting the rights of those listed the former is only window-dressing.

The safeguards provided at the UN level are outside the scope of European law and therefore are not directly decisive for the legality of legal measures taken by the European institutions. This distinction between the UN level and the EU level allows the EU courts to review domestic implementation measures without challenging the external legal instrument that led to their adoption. However, where UN lists are directly copied into European law, without any further investigation, the procedures at the UN level are critical for the legitimacy of the European implementation measures. In principle, it is not the role of domestic courts to judge the legality of measures adopted outside of their judicial system.[313] Yet, external safeguards can substitute (to a certain extent) for the absence of safeguards in the internal system.[314] International cooperation requires in many ways the reliance on external value choices and assessments. The total absence of effective remedies in the external sphere makes the provision of effective remedies in the domestic legal order even more pressing.

Article 13 ECHR does not require a court of law. However, the authority must be clearly 'identified and composed of members who are impartial and who enjoy safeguards of independence'.[315] Hence, a delisting request that is brought to the same authority that took the listing decision in the first place cannot alone satisfy Article 13 ECHR. Within the European legal system, those listed have the general administrative safeguards at their disposal. They have a right to a hearing (on limited issues) at the national and at the Community level.[316] They can further petition the

[313] See the position of the ECJ in Chapter 5, Section 1.

[314] GCC, *Solange II* BVerfGE 73, 339, decision of 22 October 1986, 2 BvR 197/83 and the discussion of the *Solange* approach in Chapter 5, Section 4; see also: GCC, *Maastricht* decision, BVerfGE 89, 155, of 12 October 1993; GCC, *Alcan* decision, of 17 February 2000, EuZW 2000, 445; Banana decision, of 7 June 2000, EuZW 2000, 702, BvL 1/97; see also ECtHR, *Matthews* (n 121 above).

[315] Committee of Ministers of the Council of Europe, Recommendation R (98) 13, adopted during the 641st meeting, 18 September 1998; this recommendation concerns the right of rejected asylum seekers to an effective remedy against decisions on expulsion in the context of Art 3 ECHR; however it has been considered a guideline as to what constitutes an effective remedy in the context of Art 13 ECHR (van der Herik and Schrijver, *Section Two: Human Rights Concerns in Current Targeted Sanctions Regimes from the Perspective of International and European Law*' (n 72 above), p 15).

[316] See Chapter 6, Section 1.1.

European Ombudsman and the Commission. Finally, they can bring their case to the EU courts.[317] In principle, the institutional mechanisms within the European legal order are in place. Problems arise rather with regard to the substantive scope and effectiveness in light of the practical difficulties, such as access to the relevant information.

Conclusions

The right of access to justice–as it is recognized by the ECHR, the general principles of EU law, the Charter of Fundamental Rights, and the national legal orders–requires access to an independent judge both for Community sanctions against private individuals and for Union lists of terrorist suspects. The former constitute a considerable interference with property rights. The latter mainly interfere with the right to an unharmed reputation. There is no need to point out that the right to judicial review exists irrespective of whether the allegations are correct. Yet, it should be noted that identical or similar names, translation difficulties, and widespread hesitation to share confidential information, make the identification procedure unreliable.[318] This is an additional argument why the need for judicial review is so pressing.

The right of access to justice is guaranteed by Article 6(1) ECHR. As has been demonstrated, Union lists and Community sanctions both fall within the scope of this article. Its application cannot be excluded based on the argument that individual sanctions are either administrative in nature or foreign policy decisions; nor can international cooperation justify a lowering of the Convention standard. On the contrary, it is submitted that sanctions against individuals possess many similarities with criminal law. As a consequence, fairness requires a strict application of the safeguards guaranteed by Article 6 ECHR, even if it were held that individual sanctions do not qualify as a criminal charge within the strict meaning of Article 6(1) ECHR.[319]

[317] See for a discussion of the details: Chapters 5, Section 1, Chapter 6, Sections 1.3 and 2, and Chapter 7, Section 1.2 on further necessary changes.

[318] Chapter 1, Section 7.

[319] Van der Herik and Schrijver, *Section Two: Human Rights Concerns in Current Targeted Sanctions Regimes from the Perspective of International and European Law* (n 72 above), p 13 argue with regard to UN sanctions that the admitted criminal connotations cannot justify the assumption of a criminal charge.

Moreover, the general principles of EU law recognize an even higher standard of judicial protection. Those sanctioned by the Community, as well as those listed by the Union, also enjoy the right of access to justice as it is protected in European law. Additionally, as mentioned above, all EU Member States must comply with the ECHR, otherwise the country would have to fear being taken to the ECtHR.

The EU courts have introduced different degrees of judicial review for the different European sanctions measures and instruments. Community instruments are in principle subject to full judicial review, irrespective of whether they give effect to UN lists or Union lists.[320] Yet the CFI has introduced substantive limitations of its jurisdiction in the case of *OMPI I*.[321] Limitations could potentially be justified on security grounds.[322] For Union lists the situation is more complicated and will be explored in more detail in Chapter 6.

[320] See for autonomous sanctions: Case T-228/02, *OMPI I* (n 4 above), Chapter 6, Section 3.1; for sanctions giving effect to UN lists: Cases C-402/05 P and C-415/05 P, *Kadi and al Barakaat* (n 4 above), Chapter 5, Section 1.

[321] See in particular Case T-228/02, *OMPI I* (n 4 above), paras 133 et seq (fair hearing), 148 et seq (statement of reasons) and 156 et seq (access to justice).

[322] See more broadly Chapter 4.

4

Limits of Fundamental Rights in the Face of Terrorism

Introduction

The rule of law is most needed in times when well-established values and principles are challenged. Security considerations are not a magic spell[1] that let all legal restrictions disappear. Increasingly, courts have been asked to reconcile rights and interests that play a role in the fight against terrorism. This includes both rights violated by terrorist activities, but also rights affected to their core by counter-terrorist measures. The European Court of Human Rights (ECtHR), the House of Lords, courts in the United States of America (US), as well as the Supreme Court of Israel have given rulings on a wide range of counter-terrorist measures. Some of these measures differ fundamentally from individual sanctions adopted against terrorist suspects, which are the focus of this book. Nonetheless, the courts' considerations in these cases can give some guidance on how fundamental rights and the public interests of fighting terrorism can be lawfully reconciled. This is an objective that needs still to be achieved in the area of individual sanctions.

Following the principled discussion of the right to fair trial in Chapter 3, Chapter 4 considers to what extent terrorism could justify exceptional restrictions on ordinary principles and rights. It seeks to identify how the ECtHR and a selection of national courts assess whether restrictions on fundamental rights can be justified in the fight against terrorism. Particular

[1] Aharon Barak, 'Introduction: The Supreme Court and the Problem of Terrorism' in: Israel Supreme Court (ed), *Judgments of the Israel Supreme Court: Fighting Terrorism within the Law* (2005), p 19.

attention will be paid to the non-disclosure of information to those affected by counter-terrorist measures.[2]

The objective of the present examination must be modest. Inspiration and guidance is drawn for the in-depth analysis of individual sanctions in the following chapters. A systematic study of the terrorism jurisprudence would have to pay greater attention to the political and historical context in which these cases arose,[3] as well as to the meaning that the courts give to the term 'terrorism'. This cannot be achieved in the present context.

The structure of Chapter 4 is as follows. Section 1 addresses the duty of the state to protect its citizens from terrorist attacks. Section 2 examines to what extent terrorism is an emergency situation justifying a derogation from well-established human rights standards. This examination is based on Article 15 ECHR but allows broader conclusions for other human rights instruments. Section 3 examines the case-law of the ECtHR in which the Court considered whether and to what extent security considerations can justify restricting Convention rights. A particular focus will be on the non-disclosure of evidence. Section 4 turns to the UK House of Lords. In the UK, counter-terrorist measures, such as the indefinite detention of foreigners, control orders, and the admissibility of third party torture evidence have been challenged as to their compatibility with the 1998 Human Rights Act and the ECHR. The House of Lords has given several principled rulings on what cannot be compromised even under the threat of terrible atrocities. Section 5 analyses the case-law of the US courts and of the Supreme Court of Israel. The US courts, including the Supreme Court, have ruled in a series of cases on whether the detainees at Guantanamo Bay can rely on the right of *habeas corpus*. Finally, the US Supreme Court of Israel has more often been asked to rule on the legality of counter-terrorist measures. In a ruling on 'preventive strikes' or 'targeted killings', the Court considered whether the political question doctrine might apply to counter-terrorist policies.

[2] Non-disclosure of relevant information has proven to be a great obstacle to effective judicial protection from individual sanctions, see Chapter 6, Section 1.1.2 and Chapter 7, Section 1.4 and 2.

[3] Eg the House of Lords gave its ruling in the *Belmarsh detainees* case (*A (FC) and others; X (FC) and others v Secretary of State for the Home Department*, judgment of 16 December 2004, [2004] UKHL 56, [2005] 2 AC 68, [2005] 2 WLR 87, [2005] HRLR 1 (see below Section 4) before the terrorist attacks on London on 7 July 2005 (and the attempt on 21 July 2005).

1. Duty to Protect

Terrorist acts aim at the destruction of human rights, democracy and the rule of law.[4] States have therefore not only the legitimate right, but also a duty, to ensure national security and protect the rights of those under its jurisdiction. This has been recognized by courts in different contexts.

The Israeli Supreme Court has recognized a duty to protect society from terrorism.[5] When ruling on the Government's policy of 'targeted killings' or 'preventive strikes',[6] the Court argued:

> The question is not whether it is possible to defend ourselves against terrorism. Of course it is possible to do so, and at times it is even a duty to do so. The question is how we respond.[7]

Similarly the ECtHR has acknowledged that due weight must be accorded to the duty to defend society from terrorism.[8] The Strasbourg Court has granted states a considerable margin of appreciation in determining what is necessary in this regard. In the case of *Kiliç*,[9] the ECtHR held that states are under a positive duty to protect their citizens from interference of third parties; they must criminalize particularly serious abuses and set up an effective judicial system.[10] In particular, the ECtHR stated[11] that Article 2(1) s 1 ECHR

> enjoins the State not only to refrain from the intentional and unlawful taking of life, but also to take appropriate steps to safeguard the lives of those within its jurisdiction. ... This involves a primary duty on the State to secure the right to life by putting in place effective criminal law provisions to deter the commission of offences against the person, backed up by law-enforcement machinery for the prevention, suppression and punishment of breaches of such provisions. It also

[4] See Chapter 1, Introduction, Sections 6 and 7, and Conclusions; but also Chapter 7, on the definition of a 'terrorist act' under EU law.

[5] Supreme Court of Israel, HCJ 769/02 [2006] HCJ 769/02, *Public Committee against Torture in Israel et al v Government of Israel et al*, 13 December 2006; available in English at: http://elyon1.court.gov.il/Files_ENG/02/690/007/a34/02007690.a34.pdf, at para 63.

[6] See below at Section 5.2 for more detail.

[7] Supreme Court of Israel, HCJ 769/02 [2006] HCJ 769/02, *Public Committee against Torture* (n 5 above), para 63.

[8] ECtHR, *Erdem v Germany* (2001) 35 EHRR 383, see in particular paras 64 and 69; see below Section 3.2 on this case.

[9] ECtHR, *Kiliç v Turkey* (2001) 33 EHRR 58.

[10] See also the decision of the Inter-American Court of Human Rights: *Velásquez Rodríguez Case*, Inter-Am Ct HR, Ser C, No 4, para 166 (1988); holding that state parties must investigate and punish any violation of the rights recognized by the American Convention on Human Rights.

[11] ECtHR, *Kiliç v Turkey* (n 9 above), para 62; see also: ECtHR, *Osman v UK*, judgment of 28 October 1998, Reports of Judgments and Decisions 1998-VIII, para 115.

extends in appropriate circumstances to a positive obligation on the authorities to take preventive operational measures to protect an individual or individuals whose life is at risk from the criminal acts of another individual. …

In a judgment on the constitutionality of a legislative authorisation to shoot down aircraft abducted by terrorists, the German Constitutional Court (GCC) outlined the ultimate limits of the state duty to protect individuals from terrorism.[12] The GCC declared that if innocent passengers are on board such an authorization is incompatible with human dignity as protected under Article 1(1) of the German Constitution.[13]

In this judgment the GCC ruled that the state was not permitted to violate human dignity in order to protect the right to life. Where uninvolved passengers of an aircraft were killed as a result of the state's decision to shoot down the aircraft, 'the state treats them as mere objects of its rescue operation for the protection of others'.[14] One life would be taken for the benefit of other lives.

The Court did acknowledge that the state had a duty to protect the life of every individual from unlawful attacks and interference by third parties.[15] The GCC found the basis of this duty equally in the guarantee of human dignity. Balancing these obligations, the Court found that while the exact content of the state's duty to respect human dignity could not be determined once and for all,

the obligation to respect and protect human dignity generally precludes making a human being a mere object of the state. What is thus absolutely prohibited is any treatment of a human being by public authority which fundamentally calls into question his or her quality of a subject … by its lack of the respect of the value which is due to every human being for his or her own sake, by virtue of his or her being a person.[16]

A state duty to protect those under its jurisdiction from terrorism has hence been recognized by a number of courts, including the ECtHR. However, as the Supreme Court of Israel pointed out, the question is less whether there

[12] GCC, judgment of 15 February 2006 (*Aviation Security Act*), 1 BvR 357/05, 115 BVerfGE 118; Nina Naske and Georg Nolte, 'Aerial Security Law.' Case No 1 BvR 357/05. 115 BVerfGE 118, *American Journal of International Law*, Vol 101, No 2 (Apr 2007), pp 466–71.

[13] Article 1(1) GG: 'Die Würde des Menschen ist unantastbar. Sie zu achten und zu schützen ist Verpflichtung aller staatlichen Gewalt.' ('Human dignity shall be inviolable. To respect and protect it shall be the duty of all state authority.')

[14] GCC, *Aviation Security Act* (n 12 above), para 124 (122 in the English translation).

[15] GCC, *Aviation Security Act*, ibid, para 120 (118 in the English translation).

[16] GCC, *Aviation Security Act*, ibid, para 121 (119 in the English translation).

is such a duty, but more how far this duty reaches and how it influences the necessary and legally possible response to the threat of terrorism. States must take measures to contain the threat of terrorism, as they must take measures to protect those under their jurisdiction from other forms of crime. This duty alone does not justify any particular measure. It does not answer the question of whether a specific human rights restriction is proportionate–in the words of Lord Hofmann in the *Belmarsh detainees case*:

> Of course the government has a duty to protect the lives and property of its citizens. But that is a duty which it owes all the time and which it must discharge without destroying our constitutional freedoms...[17]

2. Terrorism as Exceptional Circumstances

Terrorism may lead to a state of emergency.[18] This is not contested. Yet, it is argued that this is the case only under very specific circumstances. The fact that a terrorist attack could happen at any place and at any time does not justify a 'global emergency'.

National courts contrast fundamental principles as 'the norm' of how a legal order should function with rules that govern under the exceptional circumstances of a society threatened by terrorism.[19] Under which circumstances does international terrorism amount to a threat of such magnitude that it cannot be dealt with pursuant to the general rules of international, European, and national constitutional law? When can departure from fundamental principles be justified?

The procedural rights under the Convention are not absolute. Article 15 ECHR[20] allows the Contracting Parties to curtail temporarily some human rights. The state can hence adopt measures that would otherwise violate

[17] House of Lords, *Belmarsh detainees case* (n 3 above), para 95 per Lord Hoffmann; see also below.

[18] This was accepted for Northern Ireland in: ECtHR, *Lawless v Ireland (No 3)*, Application No 332/57, judgment of 1 July 1961; ECtHR, *Ireland v United Kingdom* (1978) 2 EHRR 25.

[19] See below Section 4 and 5.

[20] Article 15 ECHR:

'Derogation in time of emergency

(1) In time of war or other public emergency threatening the life of the nation any High Contracting Party may take measures derogating from its obligations under this Convention to the extent strictly required by the exigencies of the situation, provided that such measures are not inconsistent with its other obligations under international law.'

the Convention. Certain rights of the Convention are excluded.[21] They are non-derogable.

Article 6 ECHR does not belong to this group of non-derogable rights. It does not even set out a core minimum of fair trial rights that are non-derogable. The same is true for Article 14 of the International Covenant on Civil and Political Rights (ICCPR), the fair trial provision under the Covenant. The present book argues that individual sanctions are unlawful, predominantly because they infringe the most basic procedural rights of those affected.[22] The central question in the present context is hence whether international terrorism allows states to derogate (lawfully) from the very core of fair trial guarantees.

Three criteria have to be met to derogate lawfully from the Convention under Article 15 ECHR: (1) there has to be an emergency situation (designation), (2) the derogation has to be necessary, and (3) the derogation is not inconsistent with other obligations of the derogating state under international law.[23] The same criteria are required under Article 4 ICCPR.

As to the question of designation (first criterion), both the ECHR and the ICCPR lack a definition of what constitutes a 'public emergency'. The

See also: Art 4 International Covenant on Civil and Political Rights (ICCPR):

(1) In time of public emergency which threatens the life of the nation and the existence of which is officially proclaimed, the States Parties to the present Covenant may take measures derogating from their obligations under the present Covenant to the extent strictly required by the exigencies of the situation, provided that such measures are not inconsistent with their other obligations under international law and do not involve discrimination solely on the ground of race, colour, sex, language, religion or social origin.

(2) No derogation from articles 6, 7, 8 (paragraphs 1 and 2), 11, 15, 16 and 18 may be made under this provision.

(3) Any State Party to the present Covenant availing itself of the right of derogation shall immediately inform the other States Parties to the present Covenant, through the intermediary of the Secretary-General of the United Nations, of the provisions from which it has derogated and of the reasons by which it was actuated. A further communication shall be made, through the same intermediary, on the date on which it terminates such derogation.

[21] See Art 15(2) ECHR referring to Arts 2, 3, 4(1) and 7 ECHR.

[22] This was held repeatedly by the CFI for individual sanctions under the autonomous European sanctions regime, eg: Case T-228/02, *Organisation des Modjahedines du peuple d'Iran v Council and UK (OMPI I)* [2006] ECR II-4665; Case T-256/07, *People's Mojahidin Organization of Iran v Council (OMPI II)*, judgment of 23 October 2008, not yet reported; appeal pending: Case C-576/08 P, *People's Mojahedin Organization of Iran*; Case T-284/08, *People's Mojahedin Organization of Iran v Council (OMPI III)*, judgment of 4 December 2008; see also Chapter 6.

[23] See also: Matthias Maslaton, *Notstandsklauseln im regionalen Menschenrechtsschutz. Eine vergleichende Untersuchung der Artikel 15 EMRK and 27 AMRK* (Frankfurt am Main: Peter Lang, 2002).

determination of the Security Council that international terrorism is a threat to international peace and security weighs in favour of the assumption of an emergency; yet, it does not automatically justify the application of emergency derogations. Neither the ECHR nor the ICCPR allow for a general derogation 'to maintain or restore international peace and security',[24] nor do they determine the relevance of actions taken under a collective security system in any other way. Further, according to legal methodology derogations have to be construed narrowly. An emergency cannot be established at a general abstract level, it can only allow for derogation with regard to a specific situation and with regard to a particular rights holder.

The International Court of Justice (ICJ) has had several times the occasion to rule on the application of human rights law in armed conflict. It found international humanitarian law and human rights law simultaneously applicable.[25] The ICJ also held that the existence of an emergency alone does not lead to a disapplication of human rights regimes, but that the acting state first has to derogate validly from a provision.[26]

Temporariness is not an explicit requirement of either Article 15 ECHR or Article 4 ICCPR. However, the exceptional and temporary nature is implied in the term 'emergency'. The UN Human Rights Committee observed with regard to Article 4 ICCPR that '[m]easures derogating from provisions of the Covenant must be of an exceptional and temporary nature'.[27] The textual and contextual similarities between the two derogation provisions justifies using the UN Human Rights Committee's comments as persuasive authority for the interpretation of Article 15 ECHR.[28] Similarly, comments of the UN Human Rights Committee in state reports and individual cases can give some guidance. The Committee has frequently emphasized its concern with regard to duration of emergency derogations.[29]

[24] Article 39 UN Charter.

[25] ICJ, *Case Concerning Armed Activities on the Territory of the Congo (Democratic Republic of the Congo v Uganda)*, Jurisdiction of the Court, Judgment, ICJ Report 2005, 1–104, 71 (para 220).

[26] ICJ, *Legality of the Threat or Use of Nuclear Weapons*, Advisory Opinion, ICJ Reports 1996, 226–67, 240 (para 25); *Legal Consequences of the Construction of a Wall in the Occupied Palestinian Territory*, Advisory Opinion, ICJ Reports 2004, 134–203, 178 (para 106).

[27] UN Human Rights Committee, General Comment No 29 (24 July 2001) on Art 4 of the International Covenant on Civil and Political Rights, para 2.

[28] This is what Lord Bingham did: House of Lords, *Belmarsh detainees case* (n 3 above), para 22.

[29] See eg: CCPR/CO/76/EGY, para 6 (2002); CCPR/CO/71/SYR, para 6 (2001); CCPR/C/79/Add.93, para 11 (1998); CCPR/C/79/Add. 81, para 19 (1997), all available at: http://www2.ohchr.org/english/bodies/hrc/index.htm.

Further, it can be argued that if a derogation is not possible in an armed conflict, which is arguably a serious and concentrated form of an emergency, it cannot be established in an on-going, open-ended legal fight against terrorism.[30]

In November 2001, the UK Government declared that 'a public emergency threatening the life of the nation' exists in the UK, which justifies derogating from Article 5(1) of the Convention.[31] The order referred in its explanatory paragraphs to the terrorist attacks in New York, Washington DC and Pennsylvania on 11 September 2001 and to Security Council Resolutions 1368 (2001) and 1373 (2001), declaring terrorism a threat to international peace and security.[32] At this time (before July 2005), there had been no terrorist attacks on UK territory that were linked to 'international terrorism'.[33]

In the *Belmarsh detainees* case the House of Lords evaluated the Government's declaration of emergency.[34] They did so in the light of the first two criteria in Article 15 ECHR (designation and necessity).[35] Lord Bingham argued that '[g]reat weight' should be given to the judgment of the political branches on this question, because declaring a state of emergency is 'a pre-eminently political judgment'.[36] Yet, he also emphasized that 'it is the proper function of the judiciary to subject the government's reasoning on these matters to very close analysis'.[37] A majority of eight (with the exception of Lord Hoffmann) held that there could be said to exist a 'public emergency threatening the life of the nation'. However, seven of these eight found that the detention provision was disproportionate. Only Lord Walker considered that not only was there a public emergency but the detention provision was also proportionate.[38]

[30] See also: Evelyne Schmid, 'The Right to a Fair Trial in Times of Terrorism: A Method to Identify the Non-Derogable Aspects of Article 14 of the International Covenant on Civil and Political Rights', *Göttingen Journal of International Law* 1 (2009), p 38 et seq.

[31] Human Rights Act 1998 (Designated Derogation) Order 2001, SI 2001 No 3644.

[32] See Chapter 1, Section 3.

[33] As is well-known, 'terrorist acts' had been committed in the Northern Irish context.

[34] House of Lords, *Belmarsh detainees case* (n 3 above).

[35] Only Lord Scott questioned how the domestic courts could enforce Art 15 ECHR since it does not form part of the Convention rights incorporated into domestic law by the Human Rights Act 1998 (House of Lords, *Belmarsh detainees case* (n 3 above), para 152).

[36] House of Lords, *Belmarsh detainees case* (n 3 above), para 29 per Lord Bingham of Cornhill.

[37] House of Lords, *Belmarsh detainees case* (n 3 above), para 116 per Lord Hope of Craighead.

[38] House of Lords, *Belmarsh detainees case* (n 3 above), para 191 et seq, per Lord Walker of Gestingthorpe.

The House of Lords' position is not surprising given the large margin of appreciation that the Strasbourg Court gives Contracting Parties in determining what constitutes an emergency. In *Lawless v Ireland*,[39] the ECtHR defined

> other public emergency threatening the life of the nation' as 'an exceptional situation of crisis or emergency which afflicts the whole population and constitutes a threat to the organised life of the community of which the State is composed.

The emergency must further be either 'actual' or 'imminent'.[40] In practice however, the ECtHR appears to accept that an emergency within the meaning of Article 15 ECHR exists when the Contracting Party declares that one exists.[41]

At the same time Lord Bingham concluded from the case-law of the ECtHR that the longer the state of emergency is thought to continue, the more rigorously its existence has to be scrutinized.[42] With regard to international terrorism this should lead to the strictest judicial review of whether such an emergency exists in the particular country and at the particular time when it is declared.

The threat of terrorism is not limited either in time or space.[43] This abstraction (as opposed to a concrete attack) entails a danger that the exception becomes normality and the most fundamental rules are permanently suspended, until it appears to the collective memory as if they were abolished. Considering terrorism a state of emergency is only sensible so long as the exception does not become the norm.[44] Increasingly trends are identified that risk becomes the organizing principle of today's society.[45]

[39] ECtHR, *Lawless* (n 18 above), para 28.

[40] ECtHR, *The Greek case* (1969) 12 Yearbook ECHR 1, para 153.

[41] See eg: 'By reason of their direct and continuous contact with the pressing needs of the moment, the national authorities are in principle in a better position than the international judge to decide both on the presence of such an emergency and on the nature and scope of derogations necessary to avert it.' (ECtHR, *Ireland v UK* (1978) (n 18 above), para 207).

[42] House of Lords, *Belmarsh detainees case* (n 3 above), para 17–18, referring to: ECtHR, Lawless (n 18 above); ECtHR, *The Greek case* (1969) (n 40 above); ECtHR, *Ireland v UK* (1978) (n 18 above); ECtHR, *Brannigan and McBride v UK* (1993) 17 EHRR 539; ECtHR, *Aksoy v Turkey* (1996) 23 EHRR 553; ECtHR, *Marshall v UK* (Application No 41571/98) (unreported) 10 July 2001.

[43] See also: Louise Richardson, *What Terrorists Want: Understanding the Enemy, Containing the Threat* (London: Random House, 2006), Chapter Seven 'Why the War on Terror Can Never Be Won'.

[44] Explaining how exceptional circumstances threaten to become the norm: Ulrich Beck, *Weltrisikogesellschaft* (Frankfurt am Main: Suhrkamp Verlag, 2007), p 24 et seq.

[45] Ulrich Beck, *Weltrisikogesellschaft*, ibid.

Moreover, the threat of terrorism is typically not sufficiently clear so as to justify a general derogation from human rights commitment. Lord Hope argued that 'it has to be recognized that, as the attacks are likely to come without warning, it may not be possible to identify a stage when they can be said to be imminent.'[46] In view of the boundlessness of the threat of international terrorism it appears questionable whether an emergency exists without evidence that this threat has become more concrete for a particular country. It is argued that general references to terrorist attacks in other countries cannot substantiate the existence of an emergency under the Convention.

In the *Belmarsh detainees* case, several of their Lordships raised strong concerns regarding the derogation sought by the Government. Baroness Hale, for example, pointed out that '[u]nwarranted declaration of emergency are a familiar tool of tyranny.'[47] Lord Hoffmann (the only one of their Lordships who did not agree that there was a state of emergency) remarked on the state of national emergency:

> The Home Secretary has adduced evidence, both open and secret, to show the existence of a threat of serious terrorist outrages.[48]
>
> But the question is whether such a threat is a threat to the life of the nation. The Attorney General's submissions...treated a threat of serious physical damage and loss of life as necessarily involving a threat to the life of the nation. But in my opinion this shows a misunderstanding of what is meant by 'threatening the life of the nation'. Of course the government has a duty to protect the lives and property of its citizens. But that is a duty which it owes all the time and which it must discharge without destroying our constitutional freedoms. ...[49]
>
> ... Terrorist violence, serious as it is, does not threaten our institutions of government or our existence as a civil community. ...[50]
>
> ... The real threat to the life of the nation, in the sense of a people living in accordance with its traditional laws and political values, comes not from terrorism but from laws such as these. That is the true measure of what terrorism may achieve. It is for Parliament to decide whether to give the terrorists such a victory.[51]

By way of conclusion, the above discussion raised fundamental questions of whether terrorism qualifies as an emergency that justifies derogating from well-established human rights standards. International terrorism appears to

[46] House of Lords, *Belmarsh detainees case* (n 3 above), para 119 per Lord Hope of Craighead.
[47] House of Lords, *Belmarsh detainees case* (n 3 above), para 226 per Baroness Hale.
[48] ibid, para 94 per Lord Hoffmann.
[49] ibid, para 95 per Lord Hoffmann.
[50] ibid, para 96 per Lord Hoffmann.
[51] ibid, para 97 per Lord Hoffmann.

be a phenomenon different from the situation envisaged in Article 15 ECHR. It remains a threat at an abstract level that will most likely exist for an unlimited period of time.

Courts are placed in a difficult position when applying the existing derogation provisions. An additional problem is created by lack of information. In the *Belmarsh detainees* case for instance, their Lordships decided on the existence of an emergency and the proportionality of the derogation without seeing the 'closed material'.[52] This placed the House of Lords in a similar position as the EU courts in the cases on individual sanctions.[53] Only, the EU courts have not so far ruled on the merits in any of the sanctions cases; they annulled the contested measures for breach of procedural rights.[54]

The second criterion ('necessity') requires that any derogation from the Convention or the Covenant must be 'strictly required by the exigencies of the situation'. 'Strictly required' implies a more vigorous examination than 'proportionate'. Hence, even if terrorism constitutes an emergency sufficient to derogate from well-established human rights standards, any such derogation will have to be strictly required.

The third criterion (consistence with other obligations under international law) is particularly helpful in establishing the non-derogable minimum of the Convention (and Covenant) rights, including the core of the fair trial guarantees in Article 6 ECHR and Article 14 ICCPR.[55] The principle of consistency that is expressed both in Article 15 ECHR and Article 4(1) ICCPR excludes derogations that are inconsistent with their other obligations under international law, in particular the fair trial articles in the two 1977 Additional Protocols to the Geneva Conventions.[56] This allows the conclusion that even in a state of emergency minimum judicial protection cannot be abolished for an indefinite period of time.[57]

[52] See also on this point: Colin Turpin and Adam Tomkins *British Government and the Constitution*, (New York: Cambridge University Press, 6th ed, 2007), p 766.

[53] Compare also Chapter 6, Section 1.1.2 and Chapter 7, Section 1.4.

[54] Chapter 5, Section 1; Chapter 6, Section 1.

[55] Evelyne Schmid, 'The Right to a Fair Trial in Times of Terrorism' (n 30 above), p 37 et seq.

[56] Protocol Additional to the Geneva Conventions of 12 August 1949, and Relating to the Protection of Victims of International Armed Conflicts, 8 June 1977, art 75, 1125 UNTS 3 and Protocol Additional to the Geneva Conventions of 12 August 1949, and Relating to the Protection of Victims of Non-International Armed Conflicts, 8 June 1977, art 6, 1125 UNTS 609.

[57] The ECtHR ruled that adjudication could not be excluded automatically: ECtHR, *Osman* (n 11 above), paras 150–1

3. Case-law of the European Court of Human Rights

Many times the ECtHR has been asked to rule whether human rights restrictions could be justified for reasons of public security.[58] The ECtHR allows the Contracting Parties a margin of appreciation when restricting Convention rights.[59] This margin is particularly wide for matters of national security,[60] even without invoking Article 15 ECHR. The Convention organs have been reluctant to give an abstract definition of 'national security,'[61] but the fight against terrorism can safely be considered a matter of national security.[62]

A group of cases dealing with the specific question of the compatibility of non-disclosure of evidence with Article 6 ECHR is particularly interesting in the context of judicial protection from individual sanctions.[63] The EU courts have lacked the necessary information to rule on the merits of any of the challenges of individual sanctions before them.[64] This is true both for the cases concerning sanctions giving effect to UN lists of terrorist suspects and those concerning autonomous European sanctions.[65] The inability or unwillingness of the Council and the Commission to share the relevant

[58] See generally: Iain Cameron, *National Security and the European Convention on Human Rights* (The Hague: Kluwer Law International, 2000); see also: Stefan Sottiaux, *Review of Terrorism and the Limitation of Rights: The ECHR and the US Constitution* (Oxford: Hart Publishing, 2008).

[59] ECtHR, *Waite and Kennedy v Germany* (2000) 30 EHRR 261, para 59.

[60] See, by way of example, ECtHR, *Chahal v United Kingdom* (1996) 23 EHRR 413, judgment of 15 November 1996, para 131, and ECtHR, *Jasper v United Kingdom* (2000) 30 EHRR 441, paras 51–3; ECtHR, *Tinnelly and McElduff v United Kingdom* (1998) 27 EHRR 249, judgment of 10 July 1998, para 76, all with further references.

[61] Cameron, *National Security* (n 58 above), p 55 with a reference to: ECtHR, *Esbester v UK*, Application No 18601/91, judgment of 2 April 1993.

[62] ECtHR, *Klass v Germany* (1978) 2 EHRR 214, Series A No 28, para 48; ECtHR, *Zana v Turkey* (1999) 27 EHRR 667, paras 48–50; see also Art IX.3 of the Guidelines on Human Rights and the Fight against Terrorism, adopted by the Committee of Ministers of the Council of Europe on 11 July 2002.

[63] ECtHR, *Rowe v UK* (2000) 30 EHRR 1, paras 60–3; *Atlan v UK* (2002) 34 EHRR 33; ECtHR, *Dowsett v UK* (2004) 38 EHRR 41; ECtHR, *Fitt v UK* (2000) 30 EHRR 480; ECtHR, *Jasper* (n 60 above); ECtHR, *Edwards v UK* (1993) 15 EHRR 417; ECtHR, *Botmeh and Alami v UK*, Application No 15187/03, 7 June 2007, (2008) 46 EHRR 31.

[64] Autonomous sanctions: Case T-47/03, *Jose Maria Sison v Council and Commission* [2007] ECR II-73 (sum pub), para 225, see also: Case T-228/02, *OMPI I* (n 22 above), para 172; sanctions giving effect to UN lists: Cases C-402/05 P and C-415/05 P, *Kadi and al Barakaat*, judgment of 3 September 2008, not yet reported, para 350 et seq. See also most recently the first case in which the CFI followed the ECJ's ruling in the *Kadi* appeal: Case T-318/01, *Omar Mohammed Othman v Council and Commission*, judgment of 11 June 2009, not yet reported.

[65] See Chapter 1, Section 2 for the two sanction regimes.

information is one of the greatest obstacles to a fair trial. They do not only fail to inform the parties of the case against them but also fail to place the EU courts in the position that they are capable of giving judgment on the merits.[66]

3.1 Non-Disclosure of Evidence

The entitlement to disclosure of relevant evidence is not an absolute right. Competing interests, either of another individual or of the public, might make it necessary to withhold certain evidence from the defence. Yet, the Court reiterated on a number of occasions that only those measures that were strictly necessary could be permissible in the light of Article 6(1) ECHR and – this is central in the present context–only a national court with full access to the evidence in the light of all the facts can take a decision on this.

In a series of British cases, *Rowe*, *Atlan*, *Dowsett*, *Fitt*, *Jasper*, *Edwards*, and *Botmeh*,[67] the ECtHR established rules on how the non-disclosure of evidence to the defence could be counter-balanced by additional procedural safeguards. All of these cases concerned criminal offences; and in all of them, the prosecution decided to withhold relevant information from the defence.

Both in *Rowe* and in *Atlan*[68] the ECtHR found a violation of Article 6(1) ECHR. The Strasbourg Court held that the prosecution could not, without the knowledge and approval of the trial judge, decide that the evidence in question should not be disclosed. Hence, it was not the actual withholding as such, but the absence of any scrutiny of the withheld information by the trial judge that was relevant. This could not be remedied by revealing the information to the Court of Appeal. Similarly, in *Dowsett*[69] the Court found a violation because the prosecution withheld evidence on its own initiative and without placing it before the court in an *ex parte* procedure.

By contrast in *Fitt*[70] and *Jasper*,[71] all the evidence that the prosecution intended to withhold was placed before the trial judge, *ex parte*, for his ruling on disclosure. In these cases, the ECtHR found the procedure to

[66] See Chapter 7, Sections 1.4 and 2.
[67] All cases n 63 above.
[68] ECtHR, *Atlan* (n 63 above).
[69] ECtHR, *Dowsett* (n 63 above).
[70] ECtHR, *Fitt* (n 63 above).
[71] ECtHR, *Jasper* (n 63 above).

meet the requirements of Article 6 ECHR. Hence, the ECtHR was satisfied that where the trial judge was in the position to consider the well-foundedness of the prosecution's decision not to reveal evidence to the defence, no violation of Article 6 ECHR occurred.

Slightly differently, both in *Edwards*[72] and in *Botmeh*[73] the Court accepted that evidence was withheld from the trial judge but placed before the Court of Appeal. In contrast with the cases of *Rowe* and *Atlan* the appeal judges in *Edwards* and *Botmeh* were able to assess the evidence in the light of full and informed defence submissions.

These cases demonstrate that the ECtHR does not assess the necessity of the withholding of evidence itself. Instead, it carries out the task to

> ascertain whether the decision-making procedure applied in each case complied, as far as possible, with the requirements of adversarial proceedings and equality of arms and incorporated adequate safeguards to protect the interests of the accused.[74]

Hence, the limitation of the defendants' rights must be counterbalanced by procedural guarantees in order to ensure an overall fair trial. The national judge must be in the position to verify the well-foundedness of the non-disclosure.

The significant difference between *Rowe*, *Atlan*, and *Dowsett* on the one hand and *Fitt*, *Jasper*, *Edwards*, and *Botmeh* on the other, was not that in some cases the trial judge and in others the appeal judge took the decision, but that in the latter group of cases procedural fairness was guaranteed because the national judge who ruled on the necessity of withholding the evidence had full factual assessment powers and full access to all the evidence relevant to the case. In the attempt to strike a fair balance the ECtHR relies heavily on the judgment of a fully informed national judge.

This appears to be in line with the CFI's rulings in the cases concerning the autonomous sanction regime.[75] The CFI held that while information can be withheld from those listed the Council cannot rely on information that is not shared with the EU courts.[76]

In the case of *Fox, Campbell and Hartley*, the ECtHR elaborated that even in an emergency situation a 'proper balance between the *defence of institutions of democracy* in the common interest and the protection of individual

[72] ECtHR, *Edwards* (n 63 above). [73] ECtHR, *Botmeh and Alami* (n 63 above).

[74] ECtHR, *Atlan* (n 63 above), para 37 et seq, at 41 with reference to the leading case ECtHR, *Rowe* (n 63 above), paras 60–3. [75] Case T-228/02, *OMPI I* (n 22 above).

[76] Case T-284/08, *OMPI III* (n 22 above), para 73.

rights' must be struck.[77] This case concerned arrests made by UK authorities under the Northern Ireland (Emergency Powers) Act 1978.[78] In particular, two questions arose: first, whether the level of suspicion required for arrest could be lower where terrorist offences are concerned and, secondly, whether and what information the authorities have to disclose to the courts in order to have the lawfulness of the arrest tested where this arrest was based on confidential intelligence.[79]

The ECtHR accepted that 'reasonable suspicion'[80] may depend on the type of crime and that 'terrorist crimes' fall 'into a special category' that 'cannot always be judged according to the same standards as are applied in dealing with conventional crime'.[81] However, the Court also added:

> [n]evertheless, the exigencies of dealing with terrorist crime cannot justify stretching the notion of "reasonableness" to the point where the essence of the safeguard secured by Article 5(1)(c) is impaired (…).[82]

> [T]he Court must be enabled to ascertain whether the essence for the safeguard afforded by Article 5(1)(c) has been secured. Consequently, the respondent Government has to furnish at least some facts or information capable of satisfying the Court that the arrested person was reasonably suspected of having committed the alleged offence. This is all the more necessary where, as in the present case, the domestic law does not require reasonable suspicion, but sets a lower threshold by merely requiring honest suspicion.[83]

The ECtHR's observations concerning 'reasonable suspicion' and the amount of information that must be shared with the courts are informative in the present context. They demonstrate the Court's willingness to accept terrorism as justifying exceptional measures, but they also show that the

[77] ECtHR, *Fox, Campbell and Hartley v UK*, A 182 (1990); (1991) 13 EHRR 157, para 28 (emphasis added); see also: ECtHR, *Klass* (n 62 above), para 59 and ECtHR, *Brogan and Others*, judgment of 29 November 1988, Series A No 145-B, para 48.

[78] See Wilson Finnie, 'Anti-Terrorist Legislation and the European Convention on Human Rights', *Modern Law Review* 54.2 (1991), pp 288–93.

[79] John A E Vervaele, 'Terrorism and information sharing between the intelligence and law enforcement communities in the US and the Netherlands: emergency criminal law?', *Utrecht Law Review*, Vol 1.1 (2005), p. 1 et seq. available at: http://www.utrechtlawreview.org/.

[80] Article 5(1)(c) ECHR:

> the lawful arrest or detention of a person effected for the purpose of bringing him before the competent legal authority on reasonable suspicion of having committed an offence or when it is reasonably considered necessary to prevent his committing an offence or fleeing after having done so.

[81] ECtHR, *Fox, Campbell and Hartley* (n 77 above), para 32.

[82] ibid.

[83] ECtHR, *Fox, Campbell and Hartley* (n 77 above), para 34.

Court insists that the executive must be subject to judicial control. Finally, the ECtHR made clear that these two aspects are related. The greater the executive's powers are (eg, in *Fox, Campbell and Hartley*, the lower level of suspicion), the higher is the need for judicial control by a judge who is able to consider all the factual evidence.

3.2 Terrorism

The perspective of the ECtHR on terrorism is shaped by its role as the protector of human rights from acts of states.[84] It usually considers the limitations of rights as a result of counter-terrorist measures and how far these limitations can be justified in the light of the Convention. At the same time, the ECtHR also recognized a duty of the state to defend society from the threat posed by terrorism[85] 'in all its forms'.[86]

In the case of *Erdem*, the applicant was arrested on suspicion of being a member of a terrorist organization and of forging documents. While he was in detention pending trial, his correspondence with his lawyer was intercepted and monitored. The Strasbourg Court examined whether the monitoring was a breach of Article 8 ECHR. After identifying that 'adequate and sufficient safeguards against abuse' were in place and that the exception to the privilege attached to correspondence with legal counsel applied to precisely circumscribed situations,[87] the Court found the limitation of the applicant's rights under Article 8 ECHR proportionate. The ECHR also considered the specific traumatic effects that the attacks by the Red Army Faction (RAF) had on German society,[88] because the legislation on the basis of which Mr Erdem's communication was monitored had been adopted in the time of the proceedings against the RAF.

In another case, *Segerstedt-Wiberg*, the EctHR was equally asked to address the justification of restrictions of the right to respect for private life (Article 8(1) ECHR).[89] The case concerned the collection and storage of information on the secret police register. Restrictions of Article 8(1)

[84] See also Chapters 3, Sections 2 and 3.

[85] ECtHR, *Erdem* (n 8 above), see in particular paras 64; ECtHR, *Klass* (n 62 above), para 48.

[86] ECtHR, *Erdem* (n 8 above), para 69, see also above Section 1.

[87] ibid, paras 65–7. [88] ibid, para 63.

[89] ECtHR, *Segerstedt-Wiberg v Sweden* (2006) 44 EHRR 14; the Court referred repeatedly to ECtHR, *Leander v Sweden* (1987) 9 EHRR 433; see also: ECtHR, *Al-Nashif v Bulgaria* (2003) 36 EHRR 655; ECtHR, *Murray v UK* (1995) 19 EHRR 193; ECtHR, *Brinks v The Netherlands* (2005) 41 EHRR SE 76.

ECHR must be 'in accordance with the law'. The ECtHR requires in settled case-law that this

> law must be compatible with the rule of law, which means that it must provide a measure of legal protection against arbitrary interference by public authorities with the rights safeguarded by paragraph 1 of Article 8.[90]

In *Segerstedt-Wiberg* the Court stated further:[91]

> [e]specially where ... a power of the executive is exercised in secret, the risks of arbitrariness are evident. Since the implementation in practice of measures of secret surveillance is not open to scrutiny by the individuals concerned or the public at large, it would be contrary to the rule of law for the legal discretion granted to the executive to be expressed in terms of an unfettered power. Consequently, the law must indicate the scope of any such discretion conferred on the competent authorities and the manner of its exercise with sufficient clarity, having regard to the legitimate aim of the measure in question, to give the individual adequate protection against arbitrary interference.

The Court found that the Swedish law on collection and storage of information satisfied these requirements, and concluded that there was no violation of Article 8(1) ECHR.[92]

By way of conclusion, while the ECtHR recognized the threat of terrorism and the need to restrict Convention rights to contain this threat it attributes particular importance to the legal limits of discretion, the procedural rights of those concerned, and the role of domestic courts in ensuring that the executive remains within the limits of its discretion. The ECtHR further takes the circumstances of the exercise of executive powers into account: where the executive exercises great discretion and where it takes its decisions based on confidential information strict judicial review is all the more required. As will be discussed in Chapters 6 and 7, both factors play a role in the adoption of individual sanctions.

4. The House of Lords on Terrorism

The House of Lords has commented several times on the role courts should play in controlling the exercise of executive powers in the fight

[90] ECtHR, *Segerstedt-Wiberg*, (n 89 above), para 71.

[91] ibid, citing ECtHR, *Malone v the United Kingdom*, judgment of 2 August 1984, Series A No 82, pp 32–3, paras 67–8.

[92] ECtHR, *Segerstedt-Wiberg* (n 89 above), para 104.

against terrorism. Particularly informative are the *Belmarsh detainees* case[93] and three cases concerning 'control orders'.[94]

Several of the control orders have been subject to challenges in UK courts. Three cases ended before the House of Lords in 2007.[95] Besides the question of whether control orders constituted a deprivation of liberty within the meaning of Article 5 ECHR, the House was asked to decide whether they constitute a criminal charge within the meaning of Article 6 ECHR; and whether the non-disclosure of evidence was compatible with Article 6 ECHR.[96]

The joint cases of *MB* and *AF*[97] are the most interesting control order cases in the present context. *MB* and *AF* concerned the application of the criminal law safeguards of Article 6 ECHR and the non-disclosure of evidence to a person subject to a control order.

As to the first point, their Lordships unanimously concluded that control orders did not constitute a criminal charge within the meaning of Article 6 ECHR.[98] Control orders are imposed to address a risk that a criminal

[93] House of Lords, *Belmarsh detainees case* (n 3 above), on this case: Sangeeta Shah, 'The UK's Anti-Terror Legislation and the House of Lords: The First Skirmish' (2005) 5 *Human Rights Law Review* 403; David Feldman, 'Terrorism, Human Rights and their Constitutional Implications, Case Note on *A and others v Secretary of State for the Home Department*, judgment of 16 December 2004', *European Constitutional Law Review* 2005, 1: 531–52; see also: Thomas Poole, 'Harnessing the Power of the Past? Lord Hoffmann and the Belmarsh Detainees Case', *Journal of Law and Society*, Vol 32.4 2005, p 537; Stefan Sottiaux, *Review of Terrorism and the Limitation of Rights: The ECHR and the US Constitution* (Oxford: Hart Publishing, 2008), Chapter 5.

[94] House of Lords, *Secretary of State for the Home Department v MB; Same v AF*, decisions of 31 October 2007, [2007] UKHL 46; House of Lords, *Secretary of State for the Home Department v JJ* [2007] 3 WLR 642, HL; House of Lords, *Secretary of State for the Home Department v E* [2007] 3 WLR 720, HL.

[95] House of Lords, *JJ* (n 96 above); House of Lords, *MB* and *AF* (n 94 above); House of Lords, *E* (n 94 above); see Christopher Forsyth, 'Control Orders, Conditions Precedent and Compliance with Article 6(1)', *Cambridge Law Journal* 67(1), pp 1–4; David Feldman, 'Deprivation of Liberty' in: 'Anti-Terrorism Law', *Cambridge Law Journal*, 67:1 (2008), pp 4–8; Ed Bates, 'Anti-terrorism control orders: liberty and security still in the balance', *Legal Studies* 29.1 (2009), pp 99–126; Meg Russell and Maria Sciara, 'The Policy Impact of Defeats in the House of Lords', *BJPIR* 10 (2008), 571–89; Dora Kostakopoulou, 'How to do Things with Security Post 9/11', *Oxford Journal of Legal Studies* 28.2 (2008), pp 317–42; Derek McGhee, 'Deportation, Detention & Torture by Proxy: Foreign National Terror Suspects in the UK', *Liverpool Law Journal* 29 (2008), pp 99–115.

[96] See on the first issue (Art 5 ECHR): Feldman, 'Deprivation of Liberty' (n 95 above), pp 4–8; on the latter two issues (Art 6 ECHR) in particular: Bates, 'Anti-terrorism control orders', (n 95 above), p 107 et seq.

[97] House of Lords, *MB* and *AF* (n 94 above).

[98] House of Lords, *MB* and *AF* (n 94 above), paras 13–34 per Lord Bingham; expressing agreement: Lord Hoffmann (paras 48–9), Lord Carswell (79), Brown (90) and Baroness Hale (56).

offence is committed, in a situation where the state is either unwilling or unable to bring a charge. The Court acknowledged that they can be 'devastating for individuals and their families'.[99] Yet, Lord Bingham attested the UK Parliament had 'gone to some length to avoid a procedure which crossed the criminal boundary.'[100]

The House of Lords' ruling in *MB* and *AF* must be seen in the light of the judgment in *E*.[101] This case was decided on the same day and also concerned a control order. In *E*, the House of Lords pointed out[102] that

> the control order regime is not intended to be an alternative to the ordinary processes of criminal justice, with all the safeguards they provide for those accused, in cases where it is feasible to prosecute with a reasonable prospect of success.

Hence, the House of Lords not only held that control orders do not constitute a criminal charge, but also made an attempt to limit the use of control orders to the preventative, pre-trial sphere. The executive is not free to choose control orders where it is able to bring a charge with a reasonable prospect of success.

As regards the non-disclosure of evidence, the Terrorism Act 2005 (under which the control orders are imposed) provides for special procedures in which the Home Secretary may apply to court not to disclose 'all relevant material'. The court must allow the application if disclosure 'would be contrary to the public interest'.[103] The application is made in absence of those controlled or their representatives.[104] Instead, a special advocate is appointed who represents those controlled in court.[105] The operation of these provisions had in the cases of *MB* and *AF* virtually excluded disclosure of any evidence to the appellants.[106]

Their Lordships made a principled statement in support of the importance of the right to fair trial. Lord Brown for instance[107] could

> not accept that a suspect's entitlement to an essentially fair hearing is merely a qualified right capable of being outweighed by the public interest in protecting the

[99] ibid, 23 per Lord Bingham of Cornhill.

[100] House of Lords, *MB* and *AF* (n 94 above), para 24; however, the effects of a preventative measure may be so adverse that it is considered a criminal charge irrespective of the intention of Parliament, see Chapter 3, Section 3.2.2.

[101] House of Lords, *E* (n 94 above).

[102] ibid, para 14.

[103] Schedule to the 2005 Act, para 4(3)(b) and (d).

[104] ibid, para 4(3)(c).

[105] ibid, paras 4(2)(c) and 7.

[106] House of Lords, *MB and AF* (n 94 above) para 26–7 and 38 per Lord Bingham of Cornhill.

[107] House of Lords, *MB and AF* (n 94 above) para 91 per Lord Brown.

> state against terrorism. … On the contrary, it seems to [him] not merely an absolute right but one of altogether too great importance to be sacrificed on the altar of terrorism control.

On the balance of things however, the House of Lords held four to one (Lord Hoffmann dissenting) that the provisions of the Terrorism Act 2005 did not necessarily infringe the core of Article 6(1) ECHR. The cases of *MB* and *AF* were referred back for consideration to the first instance judge.[108] In the light of the House of Lords' approach the judge was asked to make 'strenuous efforts' to accord the controlled person 'a substantial measure of procedural justice'.[109] Hence, although *MB* and *AF* demonstrate that the use of a special advocate does not *under all circumstances* lead to a fair trial, the case also shows that as a matter of principle the special advocate system can offer a fair solution. At the same time the House of Lords gave the trial judge the task to ensure that the law is applied in a manner ensuring that the individual enjoys procedural justice.

A common pattern can be identified in the 'terrorist cases' before the House of Lords. After stating the fundamental principles that govern the legitimate exercise of power the court takes a more pragmatic and less principled approach in the concrete balancing exercise in the case at hand.[110] This is visible in *MB*, but also, in particular, in *the Torture Evidence case*.[111]

[108] See for the difficulties of the High courts to interpret the House of Lords' decision: House of Lords, *Secretary of State for the Home Department v AE* [2008] EWHC 132 (Admin); House of Lords, *Secretary of State for the Home Department v AN* [2008] EWHC 372; House of Lords, *Secretary of State for the Home Department v AF* [2008] EWHC 453 (Admin); House of Lords, *Secretary of State for the Home Department v AE (Rev 1)* [2008] EWHC 585 (Admin); House of Lords, *Secretary of State for the Home Department v AF* [2008] EWHC 689 (Admin), [2008] 4 All ER 340 and House of Lords, *Secretary of State for the Home Department v AH* [2008] EWHC 1018 (Admin); for the Court of Appeal: House of Lords, *Secretary of State for the Home Department v AF and Others* [2008] EWCA Civ 1148; see also: Ed Bates, 'Anti-terrorism control orders' (n 97 above), p 114 et seq.

[109] House of Lords, *MB and AF* (n 94 above) para 66 per Baroness Hale of Richmond.

[110] See also: Thomas Poole, 'Courts and conditions of uncertainty in "times of crisis" ', *Public Law* (2008), p 242.

[111] House of Lords, *A and Others v Secretary of State for the Home Department* [2005] UKHL 71 (*Torture Evidence case*), on this case: Sangeeta Shah, 'The UK's Anti-Terror Legislation and the House of Lords: The Battle Continues', *Human Rights Law Review* 6:2 (2006), pp 416–34. Helen Fenwick, 'The Reaction of Great Britain's Legal Order to September 11, 2001' in: Bernd Rill (eds), *Terrorismus und Recht – Der wehrhafte Rechtsstaat* (Hanns Seidel Stiftung, 2003), p 57 et seq; Brice Dickson, 'Law versus Terrorism: Can Law Win?' [2005] 1 EHRLR, p 11 et seq. This case was decided shortly after the attacks on London in July 2005.

The House of Lords held on 8 December 2005[112] that 'evidence which has or may have been procured by torture inflicted, in order to obtain evidence, by officials of a third state without the complicity of the British authorities' was not admissible before the Special Immigration Appeals Commission. Lord Bingham, giving the leading opinion, made a strong statement of principle in that not only was the reliability of evidence obtained through torture questionable,[113] but more importantly the condemnation of torture can be 'categorised as a constitutional principle'[114] and is supported by strong authority under international law.[115] Similarly principled, Lord Hoffmann saw 'the integrity of the administration of justice' threatened if evidence obtained through torture by third parties was admitted.[116] Lord Bingham further emphasized that that no derogation from the prohibition to use torture is permitted[117] and that the exclusion of evidence obtained through torture extends to 'proceedings related to terrorism'.[118]

However, despite these principled remarks the *Torture Evidence* case was a 'bitter-sweet' victory for human rights.[119] Differences arose as regards the standard of proof to demonstrate that evidence had been obtained through torture, for evidence to be excluded from the proceedings. Lord Bingham suggested that '[i]f SIAC is unable to conclude that there is not a real risk that the evidence has been obtained by torture, it should refuse to admit the evidence'.[120] However, the majority of four judges agreed on a lower standard of proof.[121] Lord Hope formulated the test for the majority to be that any statement is excluded that '"is established" to have been made under torture'.[122] The majority relied predominantly on a

[112] House of Lords, *Torture Evidence case*, (n 111 above), para 1 per Lord Bingham of Cornhill. The House held unanimously, in a panel of seven, that torture evidence was not admissible. On the standard of proof the panel was divided four to three.

[113] ibid, para 17 per Lord Bingham of Cornhill.

[114] ibid, para 12 per Lord Bingham of Cornhill.

[115] Lord Bingham referred to the UN Convention Against Torture, the ECHR, Universal Declaration of Human Rights 1948, the ICCPR, decisions of the ECtHR and decisions of the International Criminal Tribunal for the Former Yugoslavia (para 27 et seq).

[116] House of Lords, *Torture Evidence case* (n 111 above), para 91 per Lord Hoffmann.

[117] ibid, para 33 per Lord Bingham of Cornhill.

[118] ibid, para 45 per Lord Bingham of Cornhill.

[119] Shah, 'The Battle Continues' (n 111 above), p 418.

[120] House of Lords, *Torture Evidence case* (n 111 above), para 56 per Lord Bingham of Cornhill, joined by Lord Nicholls and Lord Hoffmann.

[121] Lord Hope of Craighead, Lord Nicholls of Birkenhead, Lord Rodger of Earlsferry, and Lord Brown of Eaton-under-Heywood.

[122] House of Lords, *Torture Evidence case* (n 111 above), paras 120–1.

practicality argument.[123] Lord Hoffmann's remarks were interpreted to display an implicit acknowledgement that the test he advocated 'may not be as fair as' necessary under the European Convention.[124] In any event, the majority was willing to balance rights and interests to the point that, where it could not be established that evidence was obtained by torture, the possibility that this might have been the case should be taken into account in the weight given to the evidence (rather than exclude that evidence categorically from the proceedings). This affects the very essence of the right to fair trial. Where, as part of practicality considerations, evidence that might have been obtained through torture is considered in judicial proceedings (albeit with limited weight), the very core of the right to fair trial is no longer inalienable but subject to a trade-off with other interests.

By way of conclusion, despite the principled language, in the *Torture Evidence* case the House of Lords made the core of fair proceedings subject to practicality considerations and trade-offs.

5. Terrorism Jurisprudence in Non-EU Member States

5.1 US Courts

National courts outside of Europe are equally faced with cases concerning counter-terrorist measures. Particularly in the US and in Israel, national courts had to rule on measures that were considered by many to go beyond what can be justified even in the face of terrorism. The cases challenging the long-term internment of aliens designated as enemy combatants at Guantanamo Bay are perhaps the most well-known example.[125]

In January 2002, the first prisoners were brought from Afghanistan to Guantanamo Bay.[126] They had no access to courts or to the relevant

[123] House of Lords, *Torture Evidence Case* para 121 per Lord Hoffmann.

[124] Shah, 'The Battle Continues' (n 111 above), p 430.

[125] See for more background information: Congressional Research Service, The Supreme Court and Detainees in the War on Terrorism: Summary and Analysis, CRS Report RS21884, of 12 July 2004 and *Boumediene v Busch*: Guantanamo Detainees' Right to *Habeas Corpus*, CRS Report RL34536, of 16 June 2008; see also: Johan Steyn, 'Guantanamo Bay: The Legal Hole', *ICLQ* 53 (2004), 1–15.

[126] Eg Yaser Esam Hamdi, see US Supreme Court, *Yaser Esam Hamdi and Esam Fouad Hamdi as next friend of Yaser Esam Hamdi, Petitioners v Donald H Rumsfeld, Secretary of Defense, et al*, 542 US 507; 124 S Ct 2633; 159 L ed 2d 578; 2004 US LEXIS 4761; 72 USLW 4607; 2004 Fla L Weekly Fed S 486.

information supporting the cases against them. The lower US courts made the attempt to avoid the hard questions by relying on the assumption that Guantanamo Bay was Cuban territory (and therefore does not fall within their jurisdiction) – notwithstanding that Cuba has no control over Guantanamo.[127]

In 2004 however, in the case of *Rasul* v *Bush*, the Supreme Court brought the discussion back by ruling that *habeas corpus* is applicable even outside the sovereign territory of the US if the affected person is held in detention by American authorities.[128] Yet, the Supreme Court did not address in *Rasul* whether people can be lawfully tried by military bodies without access to independent judicial review.[129]

On 7 July 2004, nine days after the Supreme Court's decision in *Rasul*, the US Government issued an order creating military tribunals competent to review the detainees' status as 'enemy combatants' ('Combatant Status Review Tribunals'). This order appears to be the first formal document officially defining the term 'enemy combatant'.[130]

After *Rasul* was referred back to the Court of Appeal for further fact finding,[131] US District Judge Joyce Hens Green held on 31 January 2005 that the detainees had a right to fair process and that the Combatant Status Review Tribunals did not meet that standard.[132] Her enquiry is enlightening on how far the fight against terrorism justifies restrictions on fundamental rights. Judge Green conducted a detailed balancing test assessing what due process means in the light of the significant interest of safeguarding security.

[127] US Supreme Court, *Odah v US*, 11 March 2003, ILM 42 (2003), p 408.

[128] US Supreme Court, *Rasul v Bush*, 28 June 2004, 124 S Ct 2686 (2004); see also the criticism of Tomuschat, at: Christian Tomuschat, 'Internationale Terrorismusbekämpfung als Herausforderung für das Völkerrecht', *Vortrag anlässlich der Eröffnung des Wintersemesters* 2005/2006, Speyer, 15. November 2005, Speyer, *Deutsche Hochschule für Verwaltungswissenschaften* (2006), p 21, acknowledging that after a long discussion of the case-law on extraterritoriality the Court does briefly mention the actual issue of 'whether the federal courts have jurisdiction to determine the legality of the Executive's potentially indefinite detention of individuals who claim to be wholly innocent of wrongdoing' at the end.

[129] Tomuschat, ibid: 'fully exposed to the discretion of military bodies'.

[130] US District Court for the District of Columbia, *Re Guantanamo Detainee Cases*, judgment of 31 January 2005, 355 F Supp 2d 443 (DDC 2005), p 450.

[131] See Congressional Research Service, Report for Congress, Order Code RS 22173, updated 20 July 2005.

[132] US District Court for the District of Columbia, *Re Guantanamo Detainee Cases* (n 130); Point B, Specific Requirements of the Fifth Amendment's Due Process Clause, starting on p 465; compare however: US District Court for the District of Columbia, *Khalid v Bush* 355 F Supp 2d 311 (Richard J Leon J).

Judge Green identified three factors that need consideration in defining the exact contours of the right to due process: first, 'the private interest of the person asserting the lack of due process; [secondly], the risk of erroneous deprivation of that interest ... and the probable value of additional or substitute procedural safeguards; and [thirdly] the competing interests of the government'[133] in safeguarding national security.

Moreover, Judge Green pointed out[134] that the Government's allegations that those imprisoned were affiliated with terrorist organizations cannot impact on the detainees' right to fair trial, since

> [t]he purpose of imposing a due process requirement is to prevent mistaken characterizations and erroneous detentions, and the government is not entitled to short circuit this inquiry by claiming *ab initio* that the individuals are alleged to have committed bad acts.

This is a clear statement in favour of independent judicial review. It distinguishes between fundamental rights restrictions that might be justified because a person is a terrorist (eg detention) and restrictions of procedural rights (eg non-disclosure) that might be justified because of security considerations.

Judge Green cited the Supreme Court's ruling in the case of *Hamdi* verbatim to express the highly significant interest on the other side: '[T]he law of war and the realities of combat may render ... detentions both necessary and appropriate, and due process need not blink at those realities.'[135] She pointed out that the Supreme Court had confirmed the Executive's authority to seize and detain Taliban fighters as long as the conflict in Afghanistan continues.

The case of *Hamdi*, of 28 June 2004, had been decided before the creation of the Combatant Status Review Tribunals.[136] In this case, the Supreme Court dismissed an *habeas corpus* petition brought on behalf of Yaser Esam Hamdi, a US citizen being detained indefinitely as an 'illegal enemy combatant'. The Court recognized the power of the government to detain unlawful combatants,[137] but ruled that detainees who are US citizens must be able to challenge their detention before an impartial judge.[138]

[133] US District Court for the District of Columbia, *Re Guantanamo Detainee Cases* (n 130 above) at 465, citing US Supreme Court, *Mathews v Eldridge*, 424 US 319, 335; 96 S Ct 893.

[134] ibid, at 466, citing US Supreme Court, *Hamdi v Rumsfeld*, 124 S Ct 2633, at 2647.

[135] ibid, at 466, citing US Supreme Court, *Hamdi v Rumsfeld*, 124 S Ct 2633, at 2647.

[136] ibid, at 466, citing US Supreme Court, *Hamdi*, 124 S Ct 2633, at 2647.

[137] ibid.

[138] ibid, at 2643 et seq.

The Supreme Court stated that the detainee 'must receive notice of the factual basis for his classification, and a fair opportunity to rebut the Government's factual assertions before a neutral decision maker'.[139] However, the Court also addressed ways in which the right to fair trial could be limited having regard to the specific circumstances. It specifically considered the possibility of 'appropriately authorized and properly constituted military tribunals'.[140] Acknowledging that meeting the evidential standard could potentially be very difficult under the given circumstances, the Court accepted that it would not violate due process if the decision-maker considered hearsay as the most reliable evidence.[141] It affirmed, however, that the detainee 'unquestionably [had] the right to access to counsel in connection wit the proceedings on remand'.[142]

The US Supreme Court did not avoid pointing out uncomfortable aspects of the fight against terrorism in *Hamdi*. It explicitly asked:[143]

> [i]f the Government does not consider this unconventional war [on terror] won for generations, and if it maintains during that time that Hamdi might, if released, rejoin forces fighting against the United States, then the position it has taken throughout the litigation of this case suggests that Hamdi's detention could last for the rest of his life.

In *Rasul*, Judge Green found that the Combatant Status Review Tribunals fail to satisfy constitutional due process requirements in several respects. She grouped her criticism in two categories. The first category consists of criticism that applies to all cases, while the criticism in the second category might not cause problems in all cases.

First, the Combatant Status Review Tribunals did not provide the detainees with access to the evidence on which they based their decision whether a person was an 'enemy combatant', and no assistance of counsel was permitted to compensate the lack of access to evidence.[144] Judge Green

[139] ibid, at 2648.
[140] ibid, at 2651.
[141] ibid, at 2649.
[142] ibid, at 2652.
[143] ibid, at 2641 – as is well known, the Bush administration coined the term 'war on terror' for the fight against terrorism to justify the means deployed based on a war analogy; see also the ruling of the US District Court Judge Richard Leon in US District Court for the District of Columbia, *Khalid v Bush* (n 132 above), granting the US President the authority to detain foreign enemy combatants outside the territory of the US for 'the duration of the war', irrespective of where they were arrested.
[144] US District Court for the District of Columbia, *Re Guantanamo Detainee Cases*, (n 132 above), at 468 et seq.

concluded that the detainees were deprived of any meaningful opportunity to challenge the evidence against them. The oral hearing of the detainee becomes no more than a farce if the evidence he is asked to respond to is not revealed to him.[145] In her analysis of the unfairness not to disclose relevant evidence, Judge Green did not ignore the strong interest in not disclosing classified evidence to individuals believed to be terrorists. She pointed out that the same US District Court (District of Columbia) had even prohibited 'the disclosure of any classified information to any of the prisoners in these *habeas* cases'.[146] Judge Green found interests 'fairly balanced' in requiring the 'disclosure of all relevant classified information to the petitioners' counsel who have the appropriate security clearances', citing in her support the rules regulating the military commission proceedings for aliens.[147]

Secondly, acknowledging that this might not be relevant to all cases, Judge Green opposed the reliance on statements possibly obtained through coercion and the overly broad definition of 'enemy combatant' that in fact included every person who has ever been in contact with individuals or organizations tied to terrorism, even without knowing about this link.[148]

In the context of individual sanctions[149] Judge Green's remarks on the 'overly broad definition of enemy combatant' are of particular interest. She pointed out that although the Government had detained 'enemy

[145] To illustrate her point Judge Green cited US Supreme Court, *Boumediene v Bush*, 04-CV-1166 (RJL): It was alleged that the detainee associated with a known Al-Qaida operative while living in Bosnia. In response, the following exchange occurred:

> Detainee: Give me his name. Tribunal President: I do not know. Detainee: How can I respond to this? Tribunal President: Did you know of anybody that was a member of Al-Qaida? Detainee: No, No Tribunal President: I'm sorry, what was your response? Detainee: No Tribunal President: No? Detainee: No This is something the interrogators told me a long while ago. I asked the interrogators to tell me who this person was. Then I could tell you if I might have known this person, but not if this person is a terrorist. Maybe I knew this person as a friend. Maybe it was a person that worked with me. Maybe it was a person that was on my team. But I do not know if this person is Bosnian, Indian or whatever. If you tell me the name, then I can respond and defend myself against this accusation. Tribunal President: We are asking you the questions and we need you to respond to what is on the unclassified summary.

[146] As p 208 at 471, citing para 30 of the Amended Protective Order and Procedures for Counsel Access to Detainees at the United States Naval Base in Guantanamo Bay, Cuba, 344 F Supp 2d 174, 180 (DDC 2004).

[147] US District Court for the District of Columbia, *Re Guantanamo Detainee Cases*, (n 130 above) at 471 citing Procedures for Trials by Military Commissions of Certain Non-United States Citizens in the War Against Terrorism, 32 CFR § 9.6(b)(3).

[148] US District Court for the District of Columbia, *Re Guantanamo Detainee Cases*, (n 130 above) at 472 et seq.

[149] See in Chapter 7 the discussion on the listing criteria and on 'guilt by association'.

combatants' since 2001 'it apparently did not define the term until the July 7, 2004 Order creating the [Combatant Status Review Tribunals]'.[150] Further, the Government's definition in this Order was significantly broader than what had been considered to be the definition given by the Government by the plurality of judges in *Hamdi*.[151] The Government's definition in *Hamdi* was thought to imply that 'enemy combatants' had engaged in an armed conflict against the US in Afghanistan, while the definition in the Order creating the Combatant Status Review Tribunals turned out to apply to persons solely because they had 'contacts with individuals or organizations tied to terrorism and not because of any terrorist activities that [they] aided, abetted, or undertook [themselves]'.[152] Judge Green made a clear statement[153] that:

> at least with regard to some detainees, the expansive definition of 'enemy combatants' currently in use in the [Combatant Status Review Tribunals] proceedings violates long standing principles of due process by permitting the detention of individuals based solely on their membership in anti-American organizations rather than on actual activities supporting the use of violence or harm against the United States.

However, Judge Green also drew clear limits to the interpretation of her ruling,[154] by indicating that it should not be

> interpreted to require the immediate release of any detainee, nor should the conclusions reached be considered to have fully resolved whether or not sufficient evidence exists to support the continued detention of any petitioner.

A year and a half after Judge Green's ruling in *Rasul*, on 29 June 2006, the US Supreme Court decided the case of *Hamdan*.[155] The Supreme Court agreed with Judge Green's decision in *Rasul*. It held that the military commissions set up by the Bush administration to try detainees at Guantanamo Bay lack 'the power to proceed because its structures and procedures violate both the Uniform Code of Military Justice and the four Geneva Conventions signed in 1949'. More specifically, the Court ruled

[150] US District Court for the District of Columbia, *Re Guantanamo Detainee Cases*, (n 130 above) at 474.

[151] US Supreme Court, *Hamdi* 124 S Ct 2633, at 2639, see above.

[152] US District Court for the District of Columbia, *Re Guantanamo Detainee Cases*, (n 130 above) at 476.

[153] US District Court for the District of Columbia, *Re Guantanamo Detainee Cases*, ibid, at 475.

[154] US District Court for the District of Columbia, *Re Guantanamo Detainee Cases*, ibid at 477.

[155] US Supreme Court, *Hamdan v Rumsfeld* 548 US 557 (2006).

that Common Article 3 of the Third Geneva Convention[156] was violated. Judge Breyer in his concurring opinion[157] remarked that:

> judicial insistence upon that consultation does not weaken our Nation's ability to deal with danger. To the contrary, that insistence strengthens the Nation's ability to determine–through democratic means–how best to do so.

Two years later, on 12 June 2008, the US Supreme Court decided the case of *Boumediene*.[158] In *Boumediene*, the Court held that aliens detained as enemy combatants at Guantanamo Bay were entitled to the privilege of *habeas corpus* to challenge the legality of their detention;[159] the Detainees Treatment Act of 2005 (DTA)[160] review procedures are an inadequate substitute;[161] and the detainees do not need to exhaust the review procedures in the Court of Appeals before bringing their *habeas corpus* actions.[162] The Supreme Court emphasized that in view of the length of the detainees' detention further delays could not be justified.[163]

Boumediene did not provide a comprehensive examination of the requisites for an adequate substitute for *habeas corpus*, but it outlined certain factors on which the scope of the *habeas* review depends and certain minimum elements that must be present in the review. First, the intensity of the review depends upon the rigor of any earlier proceedings;[164] secondly, the detainee must have a meaningful opportunity to demonstrate that he is being held unlawfully; and, thirdly, the court must have the power to order the release of the petitioner. As to the second point, this includes that the court is competent to engage with a review of the facts, including all

[156] Common Art 3, which appears in all four Conventions, provides that, in a 'conflict not of an international character occurring in the territory of one of the High Contracting Parties (ie, signatories), each Party to the conflict shall be bound to apply, as a minimum,' certain provisions protecting

> [p]ersons ... placed hors de combat by ... detention,' including a prohibition on 'the passing of sentences ... without previous judgment ... by a regularly constituted court affording all the judicial guarantees ... recognized as indispensable by civilized peoples. (*Hamdan*, ibid).

[157] ibid, at 636.

[158] US Supreme Court, *Boumediene v Bush* (2008), 128 S Ct 2229; see: Ernesto Hernández-López, '*Boumediene v Bush* and Gantánamo, Cuba: Does the "Empire Strike Back"?', 61 *SMU Law Rev* 2009, pp 117–200.

[159] US Supreme Court, *Boumediene*, 128 S Ct 2229, at 2240–62.

[160] PL 109–148,Title X (2005).

[161] US Supreme Court, *Boumediene*, 128 S Ct 2229, at 2271–4.

[162] US Supreme Court, *Boumediene*, ibid, at 2274–6.

[163] US Supreme Court, *Boumediene*, ibid, at 2275–6, see even stronger: Justice Souter at 2278–9.

[164] US Supreme Court, *Boumediene*, 128 S Ct 2229, at 2268.

relevant exculpatory evidence, including evidence that was not introduced during the earlier proceedings.

The Supreme Court stood by the fundamental constitutional principle of *habeas corpus*. It stated the principles that govern normality, but it did not then turn around to reach the conclusion that they should be suspended or displaced in the face of the exceptional threat emanating from terrorism. It acknowledged that besides being of 'vital instrument for the protection of individual liberty',[165] *habeas corpus* is also a time-tested device to maintain the 'delicate balance of governance'.[166]

At the same time, the Court carefully outlined the limits of its ruling. On the one hand, the Court pointed out that it did not mean to imply that DTA review would be a constitutionally sufficient replacement for *habeas corpus* 'but for [the] limitations on the detainee's ability to present exculpatory evidence'.[167] On the other hand, the Court made clear that any substitute for *habeas corpus* proceedings must not necessarily duplicate that writ in all respects, and that the ruling does not imply that a *habeas* court should intervene 'the moment an enemy steps foot in a territory where the writ runs'.[168] The Court's intention to strike a fair and practically viable balance is evident not only in the clearly defined limits of the ruling but also in the statements of principle. The Court stated that its 'opinion does not undermine the Executive's powers as Commander in Chief' and that '[t]he law must accord the Executive substantial authority to apprehend detain those who pose a real danger to...security'.[169]

The Supreme Court's ruling in *Boumediene* is a delicate jurisprudential manoeuvre, aiming to protect society, both from the threat of terrorism and from undermining its own foundations under the flag of self-protection. Essentially, the Supreme Court tried to identify the line where self-protection results in self-destruction because the exception becomes normality and the most fundamental rules are permanently suspended, until it appears to the collective memory as if they were abolished. The Supreme Court appreciated this danger. This is visible in several passages, ie where Judge Kennedy commented on the particular difficulty

[165] US Supreme Court, *Boumediene*, ibid, at 2246.

[166] US Supreme Court, *Boumediene*, ibid, at 2247, citing US Supreme Court, *Hamdi*, 124 S Ct 2633.

[167] US Supreme Court, *Boumediene*, ibid, at 2274.

[168] US Supreme Court, *Boumediene*, ibid, at 2276.

[169] US Supreme Court, *Boumediene*, ibid, at 2277.

faced because of the indeterminable duration of the fight on terrorism.[170] Even more to the point, he stated that:

[t]he laws and Constitution are designed to survive, and remain in force, in extraordinary times. Liberty and security can be reconciled; and in our system they are reconciled within the framework of the law.

The Supreme Court held that '[t]he writ of *habeas corpus* is itself an indispensable mechanism for monitoring the separation of powers'.[171] *Habeas corpus* forms part of the existing legal framework and its self-defence mechanism, which allows the reconciliation of its most fundamental values. This is true for the US Constitution in particular, but also for constitutional structures built on the rule of law more generally:[172]

To hold that the political branches may switch the Constitution on or off at will would lead to a regime in which they, not this Court, say 'what the law is'.

US courts were faced with an extreme situation when ruling on the position of the Guantanamo Bay detainees. This should be kept in mind when drawing conclusions for individual sanctions. Individual sanctions stigmatize individuals as terrorists.[173] They deprive individuals of their economic existence.[174] Yet, they do not immediately endanger the life[175] or the physical well-being of those listed.[176] However, the considerations on the constitutional value of judicial review in particular are transferable.

[170] US Supreme Court, *Boumediene*, ibid, at 2277: 'Because our Nation's past military conflicts have been of limited duration, it has been possible to leave the outer boundaries of war powers undefined. If, as some fear, terrorism continues to pose dangerous threats to us for years to come, the Court might not have this luxury.'

[171] US Supreme Court, *Boumediene*, ibid, at 2259.

[172] US Supreme Court, *Boumediene v Bush*, ibid, at 2236 citing: *Marbury v Madison*, 1 Cranch 137, 177, 2 L Ed 60.

[173] See Chapter 3, Section 3.2.2.

[174] ibid.

[175] The contrary argument was made for UN sanctions (Larissa van den Herik and Nico Schrijver, 'Section Two: Human Rights Concerns in Current Targeted Sanctions Regimes from the Perspective of International and European Law', in: Thomas J Biersteker and Sue E Eckert, *Strengthening Targeted Sanctions Through Fair and Clear Procedures*, White Paper prepared by the Watson Institute Targeted Sanctions Project, Brown University, 30 March 2006, 26, available at: http://watsoninstitute.org/pub/Strengthening_Targeted_Sanctions.pdf, p 10) before the humanitarian exemptions were introduced (see Chapter One, Section 3.1.3), but irrespective of the value of this argument at that point, it does no longer apply.

[176] This can be contrasted with the situation and in particular with the suicide cases in Guantanamo: http://www.reprieve.org.uk/.

5.2 Supreme Court of Israel

The existence of the State of Israel has been threatened ever since its creation. This has confronted Israeli courts with challenges of difficult decisions made under extreme circumstances.[177] One may agree or disagree with the individual decisions; nonetheless, the case-law of the Supreme Court of Israel presents us with sophisticated analyses of real life issues surrounding the hard choices of how to fight threats to the foundations of a legal system within the framework of that legal system.

In a ruling on the legality of Israel's official policy of 'targeted killings' or 'preventative strikes'[178] the Israeli Supreme Court elaborated on the application of the principle of proportionality in an international armed conflict,[179] on the justiciability of the Government's policy of 'preventative strikes',[180] and on the scope of judicial review that can apply in these circumstances.[181] In his opinion in *Kadi* and *al Barakaat* (concerning European sanctions giving effect to UN lists of terrorist suspects) Advocate-General Maduro refers to a passage of this judgment.[182] In this passage, Aharon Barak, the former President on the Supreme Court of Israel, explained the fundamental role of the law in the fight against terrorism:[183]

It is when the cannons roar that we especially need the laws ... Every struggle of the state–against terrorism or any other enemy–is conducted according to rules and

[177] Israel Supreme Court (ed), *Judgments of the Israel Supreme Court: Fighting Terrorism within the Law* (2005).

[178] For a legal assessment of this policy see: Helen Keller and Magdalena Forowicz, 'A tightrope walk between legality and legitimacy: an analysis of the Israeli Supreme Court's judgment on targeted killing', Case Comment, *Leiden Journal of International Law* (2008); S Schondorf, 'The Targeted Killings Judgment: A Preliminary Assessment' (2007) 5 (2) *Journal of International Criminal Justice* 301; A Cohen and Y Shany, 'A Development of Modest Proportions: The Application of the Principle of Proportionality in Targeted Killings Case' (2007) 5 (2) *Journal of International Criminal Justice* 310; O Ben-Naftali, 'A Judgment in the Shadow of International Law' (2007) 5 (2) *Journal of International Criminal Justice* 322; W J Fenrick, 'The Targeted Killings Judgment and the Scope of Direct Participation in Hostilities' (2007) 5 (2) *Journal of International Criminal Justice* 332; A Cassese, 'On Some Merits of the Israeli Judgment on Targeted Killings' (2007) 5 (2) *Journal of International Criminal Justice* 339; O Ben-Naftali and K Michaeli, 'Public Committee Against Torture in Israel et al v Government of Israel' (2007) 101 (2) *AJIL* 459.

[179] Supreme Court of Israel, *Public Committee against Torture* (n 5 above), point 7, paras 41–6, see on proportionality: Chapter 7, Section 4.

[180] ibid, point 8, paras 47–54.

[181] ibid, point 9, paras 55–9.

[182] AG Maduro, Cases C-402/05 P and C-415/05 P, *Kadi and al Barakaat* (n 64 above), Opinion of 16 January 2008; see Chapter 5, in particular Section 1.

[183] Supreme Court of Israel, *Public Committee against Torture* (n 5 above), paras 61 and 62 (internal quotation marks omitted).

law. There is always law which the state must comply with. There are no 'black holes'. ...The reason at the foundation of this approach is not only the pragmatic consequence of the political and normative reality. Its roots lie much deeper. It is an expression of the difference between a democratic state fighting for its life and the fighting of terrorists rising up against it. The state fights in the name of the law and in the name of upholding the law. The terrorists fight against the law, while violating it. The war against terrorism is also law's war against those who rise up against it.

In the context of access to justice against individual sanctions the Israeli Supreme Court's considerations on the justiciability of counter-terrorism measures are particularly informative. The Government of Israel had argued that 'the dominant character of the issue is not legal and the attribute of judicial restraint requires that the Court refrain from stepping down into the combat zone'.[184] Therefore, the choice of means fell within the exclusive remit of the executive power. President Barak, who wrote the majority opinion, distinguished between normative non-justiciability (there is no legal standards for the issue in question) and institutional non-justiciability (the issue in question should not be decided by a court because it is undesirable).[185] He rejected the doctrine of normative non-justiciability and declared boldly that:[186]

there is always a legal norm according to which the dispute can be solved, and the existence of a legal norm provides the basis for the existence of legal standards for such decision. It may be easy to identify the norm and the standards behind it; it may be difficult to do so. However, at the end of the day, a legal norm will always be found, and legal standards will always be found. That norm can be general, eg 'a person is permitted to do everything except that which has been forbidden, and the government is permitted to do only what it has been permitted to do'.

President Barak then acknowledged that Israeli law recognizes institutional non-justiciability within very limited boundaries,[187] but identified four reasons why it does not apply to the policy of 'targeted killings' or 'preventative strikes'. First, there is no application of the institutional non-justiciability doctrine where recognition of it might prevent the examination of impingement upon human rights and the questions before the court impinged upon the right of life.[188] Secondly, the dominant character of the disputed question

[184] ibid, para 47.
[185] ibid, para 48, recalling earlier decisions of the Israeli Supreme Court.
[186] ibid.
[187] ibid, para 49 et seq.
[188] ibid, para 50.

was legal: it addressed whether the policy was permitted by law. Thirdly, similar questions had already been dealt with by the judiciary. Fourthly, it is indeed desirable that military conduct is subjected to an *ex-post* examination by an independent court applying objective judicial standards.

In particular, the first criterion for a dispute to be judiciable is convincing: international and domestic human rights law depend in their effectiveness on judicial scrutiny. *Ubi jus ibi remedium* – there is no right without a remedy. Human rights law can only serve their purpose when backed by judicial protection. Human rights instruments are formulated in a wide and open manner. They require interpretation and application by the judiciary to amount to meaningful guidelines.

Individual sanctions impinge on the rights of those listed and sanctioned.[189] Indeed, where specific counter-terrorist measures are challenged there will almost always be scope (and need) for a human rights argument, and hence for judicial review. As a matter of principle, courts are competent to determine the lawfulness of acts of states regulating a particular situation and changing the rights of a specific person, including where these measures form part of a broader counter-terrorist policy.

The question remains however: how far does this judicial scrutiny reach? What is the scope of judicial review in these cases? President Barak approached the scope of judicial review in the judgment on 'preventative strikes' or 'targeted killings' by identifying the two ends of the spectrum:[190]

> on the one hand the determination of the applicable law, on the other the decision of the executive branch to perform a preventative act, made on the basis of its knowledge at the time. The former is a determination that should be made by the court. With regard to the latter, however, the court should be careful not to substitute the decision of the executive for its own decision.

Conclusions

The examination of a selection of decisions of the ECtHR, the House of Lords, the US Supreme Court, and the Supreme Court of Israel, as well as the considerations on derogation in time of emergency allow the conclusion that judicial review of specific counter-terrorist measures is

[189] See Chapter 3, Section 3.2.2 and 3.2.3.

[190] Antonio Cassese, 'On Some Merits of the Israeli Judgment on Targeted Killings' (2007) 5 (2) *Journal of International Criminal Justice* p 344, referring to para 56 of the judgment.

appropriate and desirable in a state of law. In challenges concerning a broad range of counter-terrorist measures, courts of different jurisdictions have repeatedly demonstrated that they will set limits on counter-terrorist measures by invoking fundamental rights and the principle of proportionality.[191] In cases concerning the restriction of fundamental rights for reasons of public security the requirement that these restrictions must be strictly necessary is recurring.

One of the core questions is whether and to what extent international terrorism can justify a departure from the rule of law and in particular the ordinary rules of judicial protection. This question cannot be answered in the abstract. Each case is different and the particularities of each case require consideration. However, it is for the courts to draw absolute lines that the executive cannot cross in its attempt to fight even the greatest threat. The rule of law has an inherent logic. Breaking with this logic would mean the state loses its moral high ground.

At the same time, the approaches of the different courts to 'terrorism' demonstrate considerable discrepancies. For instance, the implications of the guarantee of 'human dignity' were interpreted very differently by the GCC and by the Supreme Court of Israel. The GCC applied a rigid Kantian formula,[192] prohibiting all balancing of innocent lives. The Israeli Supreme Court, by contrast, applied the guarantee of human dignity, including in armed conflict, but found it to impose stringent limits without ruling out the weighing of lives as a matter of principle.

Principled statements are made more easily than a decision in the specific case that counter-terrorist measures have crossed the line of what is constitutionally permissible. The latter is an unpopular position when the majority under the abstract fear of terrorist attacks calls for stricter laws. While the courts took different positions on what the very essence of the right to fair trial is, they all agreed that this very essence cannot be subject to a trade-off. Long-term measures with criminal characteristics must be subject to review by an independent and impartial judge.

In the context of European sanctions against individuals, it will be argued in Chapters Five, Six and Seven that the limitations placed on the judicial review cannot be justified on grounds of public security. Thus far, for instance, the ECJ has only confirmed that Union lists of terrorist

[191] See Chapter 7, Section 3.1 on the role of courts and Section 4 on the proportionality of individual sanctions.

[192] Naske and Nolte, 'Aerial Security Law' (n 12 above).

suspects can be made subject to preliminary ruling requests.[193] The preliminary ruling procedure, however, entails that access to justice is limited to those who can bring an action in national courts and whose request to start a preliminary ruling procedure before the ECJ is followed up by the national judges. The preliminary ruling procedure alone does not satisfy the requirements of Article 6 ECHR.[194] Limiting judicial review to preliminary rulings is consequently a restriction that requires justification. With regard to national security issues, however, it does not seem to make any difference whether the measure is reviewed in the course of the preliminary ruling procedure or whether it is challenged by a direct action.[195]

The same is true for limited review of Community sanctions based on UN lists, as suggested by the CFI (but repealed by the ECJ).[196] Judicial review reduced to the standard of *jus cogens* could not be justified on national security grounds. Lowering the threshold of what is considered a violation of fundamental rights does not serve security interests, even if it increases the discretion of the political branch by simply exonerating it from the Convention standards.

Other restrictions, by contrast, could as a matter of principle be justified on grounds of security. In *OMPI I*,[197] the CFI pointed out that the procedural rights, such as the right to a fair hearing and the right to effective judicial protection, could be considerably limited because of security

[193] Case C-355/04 P, *Segi v Council* [2007] ECR I-1657; see Chapter 6, Section 2.

[194] See: AG Jacobs in: Case C-50/00, *UPA* (Chapter 6, n 224 above); Case T-177/01, *Jégo-Quéré* [2002] ECR II-2365, appealed in: Case C-263/02 P, *Jégo-Quéré & Cie SA* [2004] ECR I-3425; but also: Case C-188/92, *Textilwerke Deggendorf v Germany* [1994] ECR I-833, confirming that Art 234 and 230 EC are seen as alternative and not as parallel procedures to challenge a Community act; in the literature: Frédérique Berrod and Flavien Mariatte, 'Le pourvoi dans l'affaire Unión de Pequeños Agricultores c/Conseil: le retour de la procession d'Echternach', *Europe, Editions du Juris-Classeur*, 12/10 (2002); Albertina Albors-Llorens, *Private Parties in European Community Law: Challenging Community Measures* (Oxford: Clarendon Press, 1996); Henry Schermers and Denis Waelbroeck, *Judicial Protection in the European Union* (The Hague: Kluwer Law International, 2001); see also: Francis Geoffrey Jacobs, 'Necessary Changes to the System of Judicial Remedies', Working Group II, Working Document 20 (2002), http://european-convention.eu.int/docs/wd2/3222.pdf and 'The question of effective judicial remedies and access of individuals to the European Court of Justice', Working Group II, Working Document 21 (2002), http://european-convention.eu.int/docs/wd2/3299.pdf; see also discussion in Chapter 6, Section 3.3

[195] See on the limitations of the review of Union lists of terrorist suspects Chapter 6, Sections 2 and 3.

[196] Case T-315/01, *Yassin Abdullah Kadi v Council and Commission* [2005] ECR II-3649; Cases C-402/05 P and C-415/05 P, *Kadi and al Barakaat* (n 64 above); see Chapter 5, Section 1.

[197] Case T-228/02, *OMPI I* (n 22 above); see Chapter 6.

implications. In fact, with regard to access to the relevant information, which is essential for the rights of the defence, the Court went as far as saying[198] that it

> is also conceivable that the restrictions on access may concern the specific content or the particular grounds for that decision, or even the identity of the authority that took it. It is even possible that, in certain, very specific circumstances, the identification of the Member State or third states in which a competent authority has taken a decision in respect of a person may be liable to jeopardise public security, by providing the party concerned with sensitive information which it could misuse

and can therefore be kept secret from the parties.

These limitations were considered too restrictive by some.[199] However, as a matter of principle they contribute to protecting confidential information and could qualify as acceptable restrictions of the right of access to justice if they satisfied the test of proportionality in the individual case. Further, these considerations would of course come equally into play for judicial review of CFSP lists of terrorist suspects and Community measures based on UN lists.

[198] Case T-228/02, *OMPI I* (n 22 above), para 136.

[199] Critical: Frank Meyer, 'Lost in Complexity: Rechtsschutz gegen Smart Sanctions in der EU', *ZEuS* (2007).

5

Judicial Review of European Sanctions Giving Effect to UN Lists of Terrorist Suspects

Introduction

European sanctions against private individuals giving effect to UN Security Council resolutions have raised fundamental constitutional questions and it is fair to say that the Court of First Instance (CFI) and the European Court of Justice (ECJ) approached these questions from diametrically opposed positions. The issue with the most far-reaching implications not only for the protection of fundamental rights but also for the existence and functioning of the European Union (EU) concerns the relationship between the 'Community legal order' and the 'international legal order under the United Nations'.[1] This is also where the CFI and the ECJ disagreed most basically and essentially. The CFI found that Community acts implementing obligations under the United Nations (UN) Charter fell as a matter of principle outside of the scope of its jurisdiction. It essentially conferred on Security Council resolutions a supra-constitutional status within the European legal order, capable of justifying departure from primary European law, including the general principles. With this understanding the CFI departed from the

[1] Cases C-402/05 P and C-415/05 P, *Kadi and al Barakaat*, judgment of 3 September 2008, not yet reported, para 249 et seq; Case T-306/01, *Ahmed Ali Yusuf and al Barakaat International Foundation v Council and Commission* [2005] ECR II-3533, para 231 et seq and Case T-315/01, *Yassin Abdullah Kadi v Council and Commission* [2005] ECR II-3649, para 181 et seq; see also the new application in Case T-45/09 *al Barakaat v Commission* and Case T-85/09, *Kadi v Commission*, action brought on 26 February 2009, OJ 2009 C 90/37; see also the first case in which the CFI followed the ECJ's ruling in the *Kadi* appeal: Case T-318/01, *Omar Mohammed Othman v Council and Commission*, judgment of 11 June 2009, not yet reported.

ECJ's settled case-law on the autonomy of the European legal order and of the relationship between European law and international law so far. The ECJ, by contrast, ruled that a violation of internal fundamental rights standards could not be justified only because the contested measures were adopted within the context of the wider international security framework. It applied settled case-law and ensured that those targeted by European sanctions enjoy full legal protection.

While the most pressing questions after the CFI's ruling concerned the consequences of its deference to the Security Council for the European legal order, the most pressing questions after the ECJ's ruling concern the consequences of the EU's 'disobedience' for the UN system.

Chapters 3 and 4 have set the scene by discussing the *right of access to justice* and how far the fight against terrorism can justify imposing *limits* on this right. Chapter 5 turns to judicial protection from European sanctions based on UN lists of terrorist suspects more in particular. As was demonstrated in the cases before the CFI and the ECJ, much depends on the status given to UN Security Council resolutions within the European legal order. This is therefore the focus of Chapter 5.

Both types of sanctions, those based on UN lists and those based on autonomous European lists[2] require a Common Foreign and Security Policy (CFSP) decision for their adoption. However, the legal instruments adopted in the second and/or third pillar (Union pillars) impinge even further on the fundamental rights of those listed when they contain *autonomous* European lists of terrorist suspects than when they copy UN lists. Judicial review of Union instruments will therefore be dealt with in the context of the analysis of judicial protection from *autonomous European sanctions* in Chapter 6. It suffices to point out that, as a matter of principle, the problems resulting from the limited jurisdiction of the EU courts in the Union pillars are the same for both types of sanctions.

The structure of Chapter 5 is as follows. Section 1 sets out the (potential) friction that the multi-layered adoption procedure of sanctions giving effect to UN lists creates between the European legal order and international law. Section 2 turns to the perspective of international law on the binding force and on the status of Security Council resolutions. The third Section examines the perspective of European law. It demonstrates that neither the European Treaties nor the case-law of the ECJ justify the Community itself being bound by decisions of the Security Council. The

[2] See Chapter 1, Section 2 for the exact distinction.

CFI's reasoning in *Yusuf, Kadi, Hassan,* and *Ayadi*[3] is examined and challenged. Contrary to the CFI's understanding, the reasoning of *International Fruit Company*[4] is not transferable to the UN. In a second step, Section 3 analyses whether Security Council resolutions could claim primacy over European primary law if they were found to be binding. It concludes that, *even if* the Community was bound by the obligations under the UN Charter, this would not allow the assumption that Security Council resolutions prevail over European primary law, including general principles of EU law. Section 4 discusses alternatives to the positions of the CFI and the ECJ. In particular, it rejects a *Solange* approach similar to the one of the German Constitutional Court to European law. Section 5 places the EU courts' decisions in context. It analyses the case-law of the European Court of Human Rights (ECtHR) and of a selection of national Supreme Courts concerning the review of domestic acts implementing Security Council resolutions. The Strasbourg Court has not been directly consulted on the judicial protection from Community sanctions against individuals. However, in the cases of *Bosphorus*[5] and *Behrami* and *Saramati*[6] the ECtHR was asked to review acts of the Contracting Parties that gave effect to Security Council resolutions. Also, some national courts have reviewed national measures implementing Security Council resolutions.[7] The last part of this section takes a brief look at the interplay between the different courts in Europe and how their decisions influence each other. In a conclusion, the discussion is wrapped up and the main points are restated.

1. Individual Rights Lost in Hierarchy

To begin the discussion on judicial protection in the EU courts several preliminary remarks are in order. First, no judicial protection is available at

[3] Case T-306/01, *Yusuf* (n 1 above); Case T-315/01, *Kadi* (n 1 above); confirmed in: Case T-49/04, *Hassan v Council and Commission* [2006] ECR II-52; Case T-253/02, *Chafiq Ayadi v Council* [2006] ECR II-2139. [4] Cases 21-24/72, *International Fruit Company* [1972] ECR 1219.

[5] ECtHR, *Bosphorus Hava Yollari Turizm veTicaret AS v Ireland* (45036/98) (2006) 42 EHRR 1.

[6] ECtHR, *Behrami v France; Saramati v France, Germany and Norway* (2007) 45 EHRR 10, Application Nos 71412/01 and 78166/01.

[7] House of Lords, *R (Al-Jedda) v Secretary of State for Defence (Justice and another intervening)* [2007] UKHL 58; [2008] 1 AC 332; more specifically on individual sanctions: Swiss Supreme Court (Schweizer Bundesgericht), *Youssef Mustapha Nada v SECO, Staatssekretariat für Wirtschaft*, judgment of 14 November 2007, 1A.45/2007/daa, see also more generally on actions were filed in national courts on behalf of persons and entities listed by the UN Sanctions Committee: S/2006/750, annex III; S/2006/154, annex; S/2005/572, annex II; S/2005/83, annex II.

the UN level to those listed as terrorist suspects.[8] Secondly, national courts will not easily offer protection since in principle they all accept the supremacy of European law. Thirdly, after the ECtHR has introduced the presumption of equivalent protection in *Bosphorus*, applicants would have to demonstrate that the protection in Luxemburg has fallen below a level comparable to the protection under the Convention in order to have their case reviewed in Strasbourg.

European sanctions against individuals that give effect to UN lists of terrorist suspects exemplify how individuals could lose established fundamental rights protection from domestic measures because these measures implemented 'supreme' international law. The single most important case on individual sanctions giving effect to UN lists in the EU is the case of *Kadi* (jointly with the cases of *Yusuf* in the first instance and with *al Barakaat* on appeal).[9] On 21 September 2005 the CFI delivered its (in)famous rulings in the cases of *Yusuf* and *Kadi*. Before the CFI had only dealt with individual sanctions originating at the UN level in interim proceedings.[10] Seven months later the CFI confirmed the main points of *Yusuf* and *Kadi* in the cases of *Ayadi* and *Hassan*.[11]

In *Yusuf* and *Kadi* the CFI was asked to annul an EC regulation that listed in an annex the applicants' names.[12] The annex was an identical copy of the UN lists of terrorist suspects drawn up pursuant to Resolutions 1267, 1333, and 1390.[13] Before turning to the alleged fundamental rights violations,[14] the CFI examined as a preliminary issue the scope of its own jurisdiction. Based on a combination of Article 27 of the Vienna Convention on the Law of Treaties (VCLT) and Article 103 of the UN Charter

[8] See Chapter 1, Section 3 but also: Iain Cameron, 'Report to the Swedish Foreign Office on Legal Safeguards and Targeted Sanctions' (2002), http://resources.jur.uu.se/repository/5/PDF/staff/sanctions.pdf, and Iain Cameron, 'The European Convention on Human Rights: Due Process and United Nations Security Council Counter-Terrorism Sanctions', Report to the Council of Europe, of 6 February 2006, http://www.coe.int/; Gernot Biehler, 'Individuelle Sanktionen der Vereinten Nationen und Grundrechte', *Archiv des Völkerrechtes*, 41 (2003), p 169 et seq.

[9] Case T-315/01, *Kadi* (n 1 above); Case T-306/01, *Yusuf* (n 1 above); Cases C-402/05 P and C-415/05 P, *Kadi and al Barakaat* (n 1 above).

[10] Case T-306/01 R, *Aden and others v Council and Commission* [2002] ECR II-2387; Case T-229/02, *Kurdistan Workers' Party, Kurdistan National Congress v Council (PKK)* [2005] ECR II-539.

[11] Case T-49/04, *Hassan* (n 3 above); Case T-253/02, *Ayadi* (n 3 above).

[12] Regulation 467/2001 (OJ 2001 L 67/1–23), the predecessor of Regulation 881/2002 (OJ 2002 L 139/9) relied on the Commission for the drafting of the list of individuals.

[13] Recitals 1, 2 and 7 of Reg 881/2002, ibid.

[14] See for the discussion on Competence Chapter 2.

(UNC) the CFI found Security Council resolutions to prevail over any other form of law, both international and domestic. The CFI then found the Community 'bound by the obligations under the Charter of the United Nations in the same way as its Member States, by virtue of the Treaty establishing it'[15] Finally, the CFI reasoned that where the European institutions gave effect to Security Council resolutions without exercising any discretion the review of the domestic instrument of implementation would amount to an indirect review of these Security Council resolutions. And, because the EU courts are not competent to exercise such indirect review the CFI found its own jurisdiction to review European implementation measures directly limited by the prevailing Security Council resolutions. In the end, however, the CFI did not abandon judicial review entirely, but saw itself under a duty to scrutinize the contested EC regulation, including the underlying UN resolutions, in the light of *jus cogens*.[16]

Much has already been written on the *Yusuf* and *Kadi* judgments. The critiques cover the whole scope from agreement[17] to (partially harsh) criticism.[18] The CFI displayed a mixture of deference to the Security Council in refusing to review Community law measures taken in order to comply

[15] Case T-315/01, *Kadi* (n 1 above), para 193; Case T-306/01, *Yusuf* (n 1 above), para 243.

[16] The CFI introduced its own definition of '*jus cogens*', which appears to differ from Arts 53 of the Vienna Convention on the Law of Treaties, without citing further authority for it, see: Mielle Bulterman, 'Fundamental Rights and the United Nations Financial Sanction Regime: The Kadi and Yusuf Judgments of the Court of First Instance of the European Communities', *Leiden Journal of International Law*, 19 (2006), pp 753–72, at 767 et seq.

[17] Christian Tomuschat, 'Case law: Case T-306/01, Ahmed Ali Yusuf and Al Barakaat International Foundation v Council and Commission, Judgment of the Court of First Instance of 21 September 2005; Case T-315/01, Yassin Abdullah Kadi v Council and Commission, judgment of the Court of First Instance of 21 September 2005, not yet reported', *CML Rev*, 43 (2006), p 537; Christoph Möllers, 'Das EuG konstitutionalisiert die Vereinten Nationen', *Europarecht*, 3 (2006), p 426; Mehrdad Payandeh, 'Rechtskontrolle des UN-Sicherheitsrates durch staatliche und überstaatliche Gerichte', *Zeitschrift für Ausländisches Öffentliches Recht und Völkerrecht*, 66 (2006), p 41; Fredrik Stenhammar, 'Swedish State Practice 2004-05: United Nations Targeted Sanctions', *Nordic Journal of International Law*, 75 (2006), p 319, interprets the CFI's rulings as a warning to the Security Council.

[18] Piet Eeckhout, 'EC Law and UN Security Council Resolutions: In Search of the Right Fit', *European Constitutional Law Review*, 3 (2007), p 183; Iain Cameron, 'Skyddet för Mänskliga Rättigheter inom EU: Någon Annans Problem?', *Europarättslig tidskrift* (2005), pp 631–44; Saskia Hörmann, 'Völkerrecht bricht Rechtsgemeinschaft? Zu den rechtlichen Folgen einer Umsetzung von Resolutionen des UN-Sicherheitsrates durch die EG', *AVR*, 44 (2006), p 267; Christina Eckes, 'Judicial Review of European Anti-Terrorism Measures: The Yusuf and Kadi Judgments of the Court of First Instance', *European Law Journal* (2008), pp 74–92; Nikolaus Graf Vitzthum, 'Les compétences législatives et juridictionnelles de la Communauté européenne dans la lutte contre le terrorisme–l'affaire « Kadi »', *ZEuS* (2008), pp 375–429.

with Security Council resolutions, and presumptuousness in reviewing Security Council resolutions in the light of *jus cogens*. The CFI focused on systemic considerations of how to reconcile the obligations of the Member States under the UN Charter with Community competence in that area. The Court did not put the rights of individuals at the centre of its considerations. It saw the formal or systemic hierarchy based on the authorship of the measure limited only by a (very) basic core of substantial rights and principles identified as *jus cogens*. As a result, the fundamental rights protection in the European legal order was considerably reduced in the attempt to place the Community harmoniously within the international legal order.

In the *Kadi and al Barakaat*[19] appeal, Advocate-General Maduro principally disagreed with the CFI and wrote a strong opinion defending European law as an autonomous legal order able and ready to defend both the rights of its citizens and its constitutional framework. He took a purely domestic outlook. In his view, the central question in the *Kadi and al Barakaat* appeal was: 'is there any basis in the Treaty for holding that the contested regulation exempt from the constitutional constraints normally imposed by Community law, since it implements a sanctions regime imposed by Security Council resolutions?'[20] Advocate-General Maduro answered this question unambiguously in the negative, examined the contested measures in the light of European fundamental rights standards and came to the conclusion that the appellants' rights were violated. At the end of his opinion, however, Advocate-General Maduro hinted at the possibility that he might reconsider his present view that the European legal order is impermeable to obligations under the UN Charter. He opined[21] that:

> [h]ad there been a genuine and effective mechanism of judicial control by an independent tribunal at the level of the United Nations, then this might have released the Community from the obligation to provide for judicial control of implementing measures that apply within the Community legal order.

[19] See n 1 above. On the side of Al Barakaat the very first application for interim measures were filed by Al Barakaat and three other applicants – Ahmed Yusuf, Abdirisak Aden and Abdi Abdulaziz Ali–all of whom were delisted in the meantime both at the UN and at the EU level. Mr Yusuf, the first applicant at first instance, had his assets frozen for nearly five years without ever having an effective remedy at his disposal to challenge these measures.

[20] Opinion of AG Maduro, in Cases C-402/05 P and C-415/05 P, *Kadi and al Barakaat* (n 1 above), para 25.

[21] ibid, para 54, see also para 44: 'Respect for other institutions is meaningful only if it can be built on a shared understanding of these values and on a mutual commitment to protect them.'

The ECJ merged the appellants' claims into the core question of whether the CFI was right in holding that because the contested regulation gave effect to a Security Council resolution, it remained outside the scope of jurisdiction save with regard to its compatibility with *jus cogens*.[22] Just as Advocate-General Maduro had, the ECJ took the standpoint of European law. First, the ECJ explained explicitly that it was neither qualified nor did it attempt to rule on the *validity* of the UN listings. Secondly, it stated that declaring the internal implementation measure contrary to constitutional principles of European law did 'not entail any challenge to the primacy' of the underlying Security Council resolution.[23] In contrast to the CFI, the ECJ made a clear distinction between the validity of the Security Council resolutions and its effects within the European legal order.[24] Emphasizing the Community's autonomy, both at the institutional and at the substantive level, the ECJ could limit its observations to the legal effect within the internal European sphere; it did not enter into a discussion of whether the Community is bound by obligations under the UN Charter at all.[25] Giving final judgment in *Kadi* and *al Barakaat*, the ECJ ruled that the appellants' rights of defence were 'patently not respected'.[26] Yet, although this does not influence the legal analysis below, it should be noted that Mr Kadi and al Barakaat remain listed and their assets remain frozen in the EU even after the ECJ's rulings.[27]

A central question is how the different layers of law relate to each other. As a matter of principle both the CFI and Advocate-General Maduro could envisage a formal or systemic hierarchical relationship, albeit limited by certain substantive considerations. The latter, however, considered it only as a (remote) theoretical scenario in the event that the review mechanisms at the UN level changed dramatically. The ECJ, by contrast, rejected the idea of a possible 'substantive and systemic continuum'[28] between

[22] Cases C-402/05 P and C-415/05 P, *Kadi and al Barakaat* (n 1 above), para 280; see a summary of the CFI's approach at para 105.

[23] ibid, para 288.

[24] Compare Case T-315/01, *Kadi* (n 1 above), para 224 and the analysis above.

[25] See ibid, paras 295–6.

[26] ibid, paras 333–53.

[27] Commission Regulation (EC) No 1190/2008 of 6 November 2008, L 229/23 (8.11.2008) and Commission Regulation (EC) No 1190/2008 of 28 November 2008, L 322/25 (2.12.2008); see Chapter 7 for a discussion of the effects of the EU courts' annulments and the power balance between the Court and the Council.

[28] Jean d'Aspremont and Frédéric Dopagne, 'Two Constitutionalisms in Europe: Pursuing an Articulation of the European and International Legal Orders', *ZaöRV (Heidelberg Journal of International Law)* (2009), pp 1–39, at 31 and 37.

European law and international law. The following sections will shed light on this question first from the perspective of international law and then from the perspective of European law.

2. From the Standpoint of International Law

The relationship between the European legal order and the UN Charter presents itself differently depending on whether one takes the perspective of international law or the perspective of European law. Yet, any examination of this relationship has to consider both standpoints and even though the present analysis takes the perspective of European law, international law cannot be entirely disregarded. It has also played an important role in the proceedings in EU courts concerning European sanctions giving effect to UN Security Council resolutions.

The EU was founded pursuant to the rules of international law and continues to pay particular respect to its rules. Indeed, international law was even considered to be supplementary constitutional law for the EU[29] and after the Treaty of Lisbon has entered into force European Treaties will emphasize the EU's commitment to international law even more strongly than at present.[30] Whether international law obliges the EU or the Community to give effect to Chapter VII resolutions and whether these resolutions prevail over European law is hence also relevant for the European law perspective.

As a general rule, international legal actors are bound by obligations to which they have consented[31] and customary international law.[32] Needless to say, neither the EU, nor the Community is a member of the UN.[33] Hence, under the law of international treaties they are not formally bound by obligations under the UN Charter.[34] There are two ways by which UN

[29] Markus Krajewski, 'Foreign Policy and the European Constitution', *YEL*, 23 (2004), p 436.

[30] Articles 3(5) and 21 TEU and Art 214(2) TFEU

[31] JS Watson, 'State Consent and the Sources of International Obligation', *Proceedings of the American Society of International Law* (1992), p 108.

[32] Malcolm Shaw, *International Law* (Cambridge: Cambridge University Press, 5th ed, 2003), p 6.

[33] Pursuant to Art 4 UNC, only states can be members of the UN. The EU and the EC are not considered de facto members either. See: Kathrin Osteneck, *Die Umsetzung von UN-Wirtschaftssanktionen durch die Europäische Gemeinschaft* (Berlin; Springer-Verlag, 2004), p 236 et seq.

[34] See Art 34 VCLT; see also: Art 34 of the 1986 Vienna Convention on the Law of Treaties between States and International Organizations or between International Organizations (not in force–VCLT 1986).

Charter obligations could nevertheless be directly binding on the EU or the EC as a matter of international law: First, the UN system could be in the position to impose obligations on non-contracting third parties. Secondly, the EU or the EC could be considered to replace the EU Member States in a de facto succession.

Whether the UN system can impose obligations on third parties that have not consented to the UN Charter (non-members) is contested. In this regard it must be conceded that there is an extraordinary authority attached to decisions taken at the UN level. UN membership extends to nearly all countries in the world.[35] And, prima facie Security Council resolutions benefit from a presumption of legality.[36] The Security Council can do what member states cannot when acting alone: it determines what constitutes a 'threat to the peace'.[37] Yet, despite this high authoritative power, the sole involvement of more–and powerful–international actors cannot justify considering an obligation to be of a hierarchically higher rank. The UN is created under an international treaty. As a matter of principle, it creates obligations for those who are contracting parties. Anything else requires additional legal justification.

The UN Charter partially codifies customary international law[38] and is to that extent universally binding. Yet, these parts are binding *because* they satisfy the requirements of customary international law, not because they form part of the UN Charter. Further, this partial

[35] With Montenegro joining in 2006, there are 192 UN member states.

[36] ICJ, *Certain Expenses of the United Nations*, ICJ Reports 1962 p 168; Derek Bowett, 'The Impact of Security Council Decisions on Dispute Settlement Procedures', *EJIL*, 5 (1994), p 93; evident breaches of fundamental principles of international law are rare: Alexander Orakhelashvili, 'The Impact of Peremptory Norms on the Interpretation and Application of United Nations Security Council Resolutions', *EJIL*, 16 (2005), p 86; even if individual sanctions, in particular in the form they were first adopted (without any possibilities for delisting or exemptions, see Chapter 1) could be considered an evident breach of fundamental rights.

[37] Compare the discussion at: José Alvarez, 'The Security Council's War on Terrorism: Problems and Policy Options', in Erika de Wet and André Nollkaemper, *Review of the Security Council by Member States* (Antwerp: Intersentia, 2003), p 124.

[38] Customary international law exists where an actual practice and *opinio iuris* of states can be identified (ICJ, *Continental Shelf* (Libyan Arab Jamahinya/Malta), ICJ Reports 1985, 29). In fact, evidence of a conviction that the practice concerned was rendered obligatory by the existence of a rule of law, the so-called *opinio iuris sive necesitatis* rule must be provided (ICJ, *North Sea Continental Shelf Cases*, ICJ Reports 1969, 4, 77; ICJ, *Legality of the Threat or Use of Nuclear Weapons Case*, ICJ Reports 1996, 68). Eg: states are bound by customary international law not to violate the sovereignty of other states; this principle is codified in Art 2(4) UNC which dictates that: 'All Members shall refrain in their international relations from the threat or use of force against the territorial integrity or political independence of any state.'

codification of customary law does not make the UN Charter unique; and above all Chapter VII of the UN Charter cannot be said to be customary law.

However, in Resolution 1333 the Security Council – as it does routinely[39] – did not address the UN member states but 'calls on ... all States and all international and regional organisations ... to act strictly in accordance with the provisions of this resolution'[40] Hence, from the strict wording it appears that the Security Council can bind non-members, or at least that it assumes to have this power.

Beyond this, Article 103 UNC and Article 2(6) UNC are partially interpreted to stipulate that UN Charter obligations can also bind non-contracting third parties (states and international organizations).[41] Article 103 UNC reflects the special status of the UN in the international legal order. It establishes a unique claim of primacy of UN Charter obligations over all other international treaty obligations. However, both the precise effect and scope of Article 103 UNC are contested.[42] Some read Article 103 UNC to have (quasi-) constitutional force, expressing the will of the UN member states to declare the UN Charter *lex superior* to which other treaty regimes must conform.[43] Others interpret Article 103 UNC to require only suspension of conflicting norms for the time of validity of the Security Council resolution.[44] Regarding the scope, a strong body of academic opinion agrees that Article 103 UNC extends to any conflict arising from obligations under the Charter, not only to intrinsic inconsistencies

[39] Compare ie: SC Res 1160 (1998), 1593 (2005), and 1850 (2008).

[40] SC Res 1333, para 17.

[41] Bardo Fassbender, *UN Security Council Reform and the Right of Veto: A Constitutional Perspective* (The Hague: Kluwer Law International, 1998), p 108 et seq; Wolfgang Graf Vitzthum, in Bruno Simma (ed), *The Charter of the United Nations: A Commentary* (Oxford: Oxford University Press, 2002), Art 2(6), at 22.

[42] Rain Liivoja, 'The Scope of the Supremacy Clause of the United Nations Charter', *ICLQ*, 57 (2008), pp 583–612, discussing whether art 103 deals only with treaties or with other obligations of international law.

[43] Dinah Shelton, 'International Law and "Relative Normativity"', in Malcolm Evans (ed), *International Law* (Oxford: Oxford University Press, 2nd ed, 2006); Bardo Fassbender, 'The United Nations Charter as Constitution of the International Community', *Columbia Journal of Transnational Law*, 36 (1997), pp 529–619, at 577–8 and 594; Rudolf Bernhardt, 'Article 103', in Bruno Simma (ed), *The Charter of the United Nations: A Commentary* (Oxford: Oxford University Press, 2002), at 11; see also: ICJ judgment of 26 November 1984, *Nicaragua* v *United States of America*, ICJ Reports (1984), p 392, para 107 (case concerning military and paramilitary activities in and against Nicaragua).

[44] Hörmann, 'Völkerrecht bricht Rechtsgemeinschaft?' (n 18 above), p 274 et seq.

between the Charter and obligations under other international treaties.[45] Article 2(6) UNC stipulates that:

> [t]he Organization shall ensure that states which are not Members of the United Nations act in accordance with these Principles [those of the UN in the preceding articles] so far as may be necessary for the maintenance of international peace and security.

Reading Articles 103 and 2(6) UNC as an expression of the comprehensive authority of the principles laid down in the UN Charter that vests the Charter with constitutional force[46] and binds third parties would indeed be 'revolutionary' given the principle of *pacta tertiis non nocent*.[47] However, such a universal force cannot simply be created by the will of the member states.

Further, *even if* Articles 2(6) and 103 UNC could in isolation be read as indicating that the UN member states had the intention to create a 'world constitution' and bind third parties, other provisions of the Charter make a clear distinction between members and non-members.[48] Further, Article 48 UNC specifically governs the situation where UN member states make use of an international organization in order to implement their obligations under the UN Charter. It does not assume that the international organization itself is bound in this event.[49]

Finally, the European Union's practice of adopting sanctions intended to give effect to Security Council resolutions could be considered as a

[45] Leland M Goodrich, Edvard Hambro and Anne Patricia Simons (eds), *Charter of the United Nations: Commentary and Documents* (3rd ed, 1969), pp 615–16; *Yearbook of the International Law Commission* (1979), Vol II, Part One, para 14; Danesh Sarooshi, *The United Nations and the Development of Collective Security: The Delegation by the UN Security Council of its Chapter VII Powers* (Oxford: Oxford University Press, 1999), pp 150–1. The most recent and perhaps clearest opinion on the subject is that of Nico Krisch and Jochen Frowein, 'Chapter VII: Action with respect to the Peace, Breaches of the Peace and Acts of Aggression. Introduction', in Bruno Simma (ed), *The Charter of the United Nations: A Commentary* (Oxford: Oxford University Press, 2002), p 729; for dissenting voices: Eric Stein, 'Collective Enforcement of International Organisations', *Zeitschrift für ausländisches öffentliches Recht und Völkerrecht*, 47 (1987), p 60.

[46] In particular Fassbender, 'The United Nations Charter as Constitution of the International Community' (n 43 above) assumes such a constitutional character. However, he does not argue that the universally binding force results from the Charter's constitutional character, but that this universal force leads to the Charter's constitutional status.

[47] See Graf Vitzthum, 'Article 2(6)' (n 41 above), with references to Kelsen's view that art 2(6) UNC indirectly obliges non-members; the author himself does not consider Art 2(6) UNC capable of obliging a third state.

[48] Not only Art 2(6) UNC itself, but also: Arts 4, 11(2), 32, 35(2), 50 and 93(2) UNC.

[49] See also further below in this section.

unilateral act of submission that creates an international commitment.[50] However, the particular adoption procedure of sanctions and the particular set up of the EU that preserve significant powers in the area of national security to the EU Member States, does not appear to reflect such an intention. Member States act in a coordinated manner in the UN framework, but they have not surrendered their autonomous representation.

Consequently, only the EU Member States (as members of the UN) are directly bound by UN Security Council resolutions, not the EU or the EC. Yet, the EU could still be bound because it was founded as an international organization and all the EU Member States are members of the UN. From the standpoint of European law the European legal order constitutes 'a new legal order', albeit 'of international law';[51] it has constitutional treaties,[52] and possesses specific characteristics that distinguish it from international law.[53] However, international law does not set out any special rules for 'the special kind of international organization that is the EU'.[54] Moreover, the membership of most international organizations, including the UN, is open to states only.[55] Article 48(2) UNC stipulates that the UN member states can exercise their duties *through their action* in an international organization. The domestic arrangement of competences does not alter the addressees of the UN Charter obligations. Sanctions adopted by the Community are, from the point of view of the UN Charter, actions taken by the UN member states through an international organization. The transfer of competences from the EU Member States to the EU or the EC might be relevant for the obligations within the domestic European law context;[56] it does not change the international law obligations of the UN member states. This reasoning is precisely based on the good faith argument, that the EU Member States cannot use the EU or the EC as a shield

[50] Aspremont and Dopagne, 'Two Constitutionalisms in Europe' (n 28 above), p 21; see also Erik Suy, Unilateral Acts of States as a Source of International Law: some New Thoughts and Frustrations, in: Olivier Corten (ed), *Droit du pouvoir, pouvoir du droit: mélanges offerts à Jean Salmon* (2007), pp 631–42 and ICJ, *Nuclear Tests Case*, of 20 December 1974, ICJ Reports, 1974, p 253.

[51] Case 26/62, *van Gend* [1963] ECR 1; at the time it was still the European Economic Community.

[52] Case 294/83, *Parti Ecologiste 'Les Verts' v Parliament* [1986] ECR 1339.

[53] General direct applicability of regulations, direct effect, supremacy.

[54] Inge Govaere, Jeroen Capiau and An Vermeersch, 'In-Between Seats: The Participation of the European Union in International Organisations', *European Foreign Affairs Review*, 9 (2004), p 155.

[55] Article 4 UNC.

[56] See below for the discussion of the succession argument under European law.

against their own UN Charter obligations:[57] only the UN member states are bound, but they remain responsible under the UN Charter, irrespective of whether they join another international organization in order to carry out their obligations. Consequently, the EU and the EC are not directly bound by the UN Charter as subjects of international law.

The CFI found the Community in *Yusuf* and *Kadi* bound by virtue of the European Treaties and not directly by international law,[58] while the ECJ did not examine in the appeal whether the Community could be bound by obligations under the UN Charter *as a matter of international law*. Taking a purely domestic outlook the ECJ did not address this question.[59] Yet, it considered that 'due account' must be taken of the underlying Security Council resolutions.[60] This indicates that the ECJ did not consider the Community directly bound by obligations under the UN Charter.

As regards the status of Security Council resolutions, Article 103 UNC gives UN Charter obligations primacy over all other international treaty obligations. According to the International Court of Justice (ICJ), all international agreements, whether regional, bilateral, and even multilateral, that the parties have entered into must always be subject to the provisions of Article 103 UNC.[61] The CFI read Article 103 UNC in combination with Article 27 VCLT to extend the primacy of UN Charter obligations directly to domestic law.[62] Article 27 VCLT excludes internal law as justification for a state's failure to perform its duties under an international agreement and complements the principle of *pacta sunt servanda* in Article 26 VCLT. Neither Article 27 VCLT nor Article 103 UNC[63] are concerned with domestic law. While under international law Charter obligations prevail and states cannot rely on domestic law to justify non-compliance with international obligations international law does not actually address its own status within domestic law. This is left to the

[57] Based on the same reasoning as ECtHR, *Matthews v UK*, Application No 24833/94, ECtHR, *Bosphorus* (n 5 above).

[58] Case T-315/01, *Kadi* (n 1 above), para 192, arguing that the Community is neither a member of the UN, nor the successor if the rights and obligations of the Member States for the purposes of public international law.

[59] Cases C-402/05 P and C-415/05 P, *Kadi* and *al Barakaat* (n 1 above), para 295–6.

[60] ibid, paras 296–7, with reference to Case C-117/06, *Möllendorf and Möllendorf-Niehuus* [2007] ECR I 8361, para 54.

[61] ICJ judgment of 26 November 1984, *Nicaragua v United States of America*, ICJ Reports 1984, p 392, para 107 (case concerning military and paramilitary activities in and against Nicaragua).

[62] Case T-306/01, *Yusuf* (n 1 above), para 232.

[63] Bernhardt, 'Article 103' (n 43 above), at 22.

domestic legal order in question. The CFI's approach of blurring the dividing line between external-international and internal-European law and giving precedence to UN Charter obligations over any other legal obligation of both domestic law and other international law[64] might be desirable from the standpoint of international law and it might avoid international liability, but it is not required.

3. From the Standpoint of European Law

3.1 The Binding Force of Security Council Resolutions

Even though the Community is not directly bound by Security Council resolutions as a matter of international law, European law itself could vest them with binding force within the European legal order.

The UN is mentioned three times in the EC Treaty,[65] but there is no special provision dealing with *Security Council resolutions*. Article 301 EC codified the existing practice that the Community implemented UN Sanctions when the Member States decided that this was necessary.[66] It confers upon the Community the *competence* to take action; yet, it does not speak of the UN and does not compel the latter to implement Security Council resolutions. Any Community act adopted on the basis of Article 301 EC requires prior authorization by a CFSP decision.[67]

The TEU defines the objectives of the CFSP to be inter alia to promote democracy and human rights and 'to preserve peace and strengthen international security, in accordance with the principles of the United Nations Charter' (Article 11(1) TEU). The TEU also explicitly deals with the representation of the Member States in the Security Council. It requires the permanent members of the Security Council to 'ensure the defence of

[64] Case T-315/01, *Kadi* (n 1 above), para 181; Case T-306/01, *Yusuf* (n 1 above), para 231.

[65] In the Preamble of the EC Treaty: '... desiring to ensure the development of their prosperity, in accordance with the principles of the Charter of the United Nations;' in Art 177(3) EC (concerning development policy): 'The Community and the Member States shall comply with the commitments and take account of the objectives they have approved in the context of the United Nations and other competent international organisations;' and in Art 302(1) EC (following Art 300 EC on the adoption of international agreements and Art 301 EC on the adoption of sanctions): 'It shall be for the Commission to ensure the maintenance of all appropriate relations with the organs of the United Nations and of its specialised agencies.'

[66] See Chapter 2, Section 1.1.

[67] The same is true for Art 60 EC.

the positions and the interests of the Union, without prejudice to their responsibilities under the provisions of the United Nations Charter'[68] Article 19(2) TEU explicitly speaks of the responsibilities *of the EU Member States* under the provisions of the UN Charter; it does not define the status of Security Council resolutions within the European legal order either.

However, in a 'declaration' made in the context of adopting the Lisbon Treaty the Member States agreed that 'the European Union and its Member States will remain bound by the provisions of the Charter of the United Nations and, in particular, by the primary responsibility of the Security Council and of its Members for the maintenance of international peace and security.'[69] This expresses the political intention that both the EU and its Member States are bound by the UN Charter.

3.1.1 International Fruit Company

In the case of *International Fruit Company*, the ECJ found the Community bound by international law obligations of the Member States where it de facto succeeded them. This is where the Community is vested with competence in a specific area of law, in which all EU Member States were bound by an international agreement before they created, respectively joined the Community, and where such a de facto succession is covered by the will of the Member States. In *Yusuf* and *Kadi* the CFI argued along these lines. In the appeal, the ECJ did not consider whether *International Fruit Company* could be applied.

The CFI ruled that even if the Community is not directly bound by the UN Charter,[70] it is bound by virtue of the Treaty establishing it,[71] essentially because all Member States were members of the UN when the Community was created. The Court referred to the case of *International Fruit Company* as a primary precedent.[72] In this case the ECJ dealt with the question of whether a Community regulation was invalid for breaching the General Agreement on Tariffs and Trade (GATT); and what is most relevant for present discussion is that the ECJ found that the GATT was binding on the Community.

In *International Fruit Company* the ECJ was invited first to rule on whether the term 'validity' in (now) Article 234 EC also refers to the validity of

[68] Article 19(2) TEU.

[69] Declaration No 13, OJ, 17 December 2007, C 306/255.

[70] Case T-306/01, *Yusuf* (n 1 above), para 242 with reference to its own case-law in Case T-184/95, *Dorsch Consult* [1998] ECR II-667, para 74.

[71] Case T-306/01, *Yusuf* (n 1 above), para 243.

[72] Cases 21-24/72, *International Fruit Company* (n 4 above).

Community law under international law, namely the GATT, and secondly whether measures adopted by the European institutions could be reviewed in the light of and possibly be declared invalid for breaching the latter. The ECJ ruled that its jurisdiction could not be limited by the grounds on which the validity of a measure was contested, and that the EU courts are in fact obliged to examine whether the validity of Community law may be affected by reason of the fact that it is contrary to a rule of international law.[73] Further, the Court considered whether the Community was bound by the GATT and came to an affirmative answer.[74] Finally, the ECJ analysed whether in the European legal order private parties could rely on the GATT; that is, whether the latter is directly effective.[75] This last question the Court answered in the negative.[76]

The Court identified a number of important arguments why the Community was bound by the GATT, despite the fact that it was not itself a Contracting Party. First, the Court pointed out that the Member States could not withdraw from their obligations towards third states by setting up the Community.[77] Secondly, the ECJ turned to the will of the Member States. Here, it identified a desire of the Member States to observe the undertakings of the GATT which followed as much from the very provisions of the (now) EC Treaty, as from the declarations made by Member States on the presentation of the EEC Treaty[78] to the Contracting Parties of the GATT in accordance with the obligation under Article XXIV[79] thereof.[80] The Court looked in particular at ex-Articles 111 to 113 EEC Treaty[81] and ruled that by conferring the powers under these articles on the Community, the Member States demonstrated their will to bind it by the obligations entered into under the GATT. Further, the Court found confirmation in Article 234 EEC Treaty (now Article 307 EC), which provides that the rights and obligations arising from multilateral agreements concluded with the participation of the Member States before the

[73] ibid, paras 5–6.
[74] ibid, paras 10–18.
[75] ibid, para 19 et seq.
[76] ibid, para 27.
[77] ibid, para 11.
[78] Treaty on the European Economic Community.
[79] Article XXIV of the GATT provides an important exception to the most favourite nation clause in Art I GATT by permitting states to enter into a customs union or a free-trade area.
[80] Cases 21–24/72, *International Fruit Company* (n 4 above), para 12.
[81] Now Arts 132 and 133 EC Treaty; Art 111 EEC was repealed.

entry into force of the E(E)C Treaty are not affected by its provisions.[82] Thirdly, the Court pointed out that the Community had actually exercised the powers previously held by the Member States in the area governed by the GATT and that this exercise had been recognized by third states in trade agreements concluded on behalf of the Community.[83]

It must be conceded that there are certain parallels between the GATT and the UN and that some of the ECJ's conclusions in *International Fruit Company* are transferable to the cases concerning individual sanctions. First and most importantly, all the Member States of the Community were Contracting Parties to the GATT by the time the Community came into existence, just like they were members of the UN.[84] Further, it is true that Article 307 EC is a general recognition of the Member States' obligations under international law existing prior to the conclusion of the E(E)C Treaty, which applies both to the GATT and to the UN Charter.

However, despite these similarities, the differences prevail.[85] *International Fruit Company* was decided in 1972. At that time the Community was still the European Economic Community (EEC) and, despite its political ambitions, the heart of the EEC was precisely what the GATT aimed at: the establishment of an economic space.[86] International security, by contrast, which is the main objective of the UN, remains a competence of the Member States.[87] Even if today the Member States have set up the CFSP as a framework for cooperation, they remain the main actors. When the Community adopts sanctions pursuant to Article 301 EC it is dependent on a prior CFSP decision that these sanctions are 'necessary'.[88] This is reflected in the nature of the competences: Article 133 EC gives the

[82] Cases 21–24/72, *International Fruit Company* (n 4 above), para 13.

[83] ibid, paras 16–18.

[84] Germany was not formally admitted until 18 September 1973, but it was nevertheless bound by the obligation of the UN Charter (Final Act of the Conference of the Nine Powers and the Paris Agreements singed on 23 October 1954).

[85] Agreeing that the analogy to *International Fruit Company* is wrong because there is no functional succession: Christoph Ohler, 'Die Verhängung von smart sanctions durch den UN-Sicherheitsrat: Eine Herausforderung für das Gemeinschaftsrecht', *EuR* (2006).

[86] It must be conceded that, while both aimed at the establishment of an economic space, the GATT 1947 pursued this through liberalisation, while the EEC did so through integration (see the comparison: Federico *Ortino*, *Basic Legal Instruments for the Liberalisation of Trade* (Oxford: Hart Publishing, 2004), p 2 et seq).

[87] Articles 297 and 307 EC.

[88] See Chapter 2, Section 1.

Community exclusive competences for the Common Commercial Policy (CCP),[89] while the nature of the Community competences pursuant to Article 301 EC is by no means certain.[90] Arguably, comprehensive trade embargos could be covered by exclusive competence of the Community under Articles 133 and 301 EC;[91] this cannot be said about individual sanctions.[92] Member States are hence precluded from taking (unilateral) action within the area of the GATT as far as the Community's exclusive competence reaches,[93] while they continue to be able to adopt sanctions.[94] Admittedly, the ECJ did not refer to exclusive competence in *International Fruit Company*;[95] however, the difference is not only the exclusivity of the Community competence, but the different practical effects of unilateral actions of the Member States in the area of external trade and in the area of (individual) sanctions.[96]

Turning to the arguments used by the ECJ to establish the binding force of the GATT for the Community, it is difficult to defend the position that the Member States had *the will* to let the Community take their place in the UN. First, the general subject-matters dealt with by the UN go far beyond the competences of the Community. Here, it is useful to distinguish between the Community and the Union: The Community, whose legal

[89] See: Opinion 1/75, *Understanding on a Local Cost Standard* [1975] ECR 1355, at 1364; on the substantive limits of Art 133: Opinion 1/94, *WTO Agreement* [1994] ECR I-5267; for a critical comment: Pierre Pescatore, 'Opinion 1/94 on 'Conclusion' of the WTO Agreement: Is there an Escape from a Programmed Disaster?', *CML Rev*, 36 (1999), pp 387–405.

[90] Case C-124/95, *Centro-Com* [1997] ECR I-81, para 56; Kirsten Schmalenbach, 'Terrorismus: Der Vorrang des UN-Rechts vor EU-Recht', *Juristenzeitung* (2006), p 352; but: Gudrun Monika Zagel, 'Article 301 TEC (Economic Sanctions)', in Hans Smit and Peter E Herzog, *Law of the European Union – a Commentary* (New York: LexisNexis, 2006).

[91] Christian Callies, 'Article 297', in Christian Callies and Matthias Ruffert (eds), *Kommentar zum EU-/EG-Vertrag* (Neuwied: Luchterhand, 2002), Art 297, at 10.

[92] Case T-253/02, *Ayadi* (n 3 above), para 108 et seq, with reference to Art 60(2) EC; see Chapter 2.

[93] Piet Eeckhout, *External Relations of the European Union: Legal and Constitutional Foundations* (Oxford: Oxford University Press, 2004), on mixed agreements in general: Chapter 7 and on the GATT in particular: p 197 et seq.

[94] Four cases brought before the CFI in 2006 (T-135/06, *al-Faqih v Council, pending* [application of 15 July 2006, OJ [2006] C 165/29]; T-136/06, *Sanabel Relief Agency v Council, pending* [application of 15 July 2006, OJ [2006] C 165/30]; T-137/06, *Abdrabbah v. Council, pending* [application of 15 July 2006, OJ [2006] C 165/30]; T-138/06, *Nasuf v. Council, pending* [application of 15 July 2006, OJ [2006] C 165/30]) challenged Community sanctions based on UN lists for breaching the principle of subsidiarity and for not stating why the measures considered necessary cannot be determined by individual Member States.

[95] Eeckhout, *External Relations of the European Union* (n 93 above), p 438, who points out that the Court had not yet decided on the exclusivity of the CCP.

[96] See below at the very end of this section.

personality (Article 281 EC) is limited by the principle of conferred powers (Article 5 EC), is not competent for the full range of matters covered by the UN Charter and dealt with by the General Assembly. Further, those competences held by the Community are largely exercised together with the Member States, eg humanitarian and cultural development. However, even if the discussion is limited to the subject-matters dealt with by the Security Council under Chapter VII UNC, the Community's competence to adopt sanctions pursuant to Article 301 EC can only be exercised after a CFSP decision has declared Community action necessary, and even the ECJ's concept of implied powers does not justify Community powers for security issues beyond Article 301 EC.[97] The EC Treaty does not seem to reflect a will of the Member States to confer on the Community the powers necessary to carry out all actions required by the Member States under the UN Charter. On the contrary, pursuant to Article 297 EC it remains a prerogative of the Member States to adopt national security measures.

The Union, by contrast, could take all actions covered by the UN Charter,[98] including the matters of international security dealt with by the Security Council, provided a common position can be reached. Article 24 TEU gives the EU a general competence to conclude international agreements 'when it is necessary in implementation' of the CFSP, and nowadays the EU also possesses the necessary legal personality.[99] However, by nature the CFSP competences cannot be exclusive. The Union can only act if a common position is reached. Member States remain competent to take action where no common position can be adopted,[100]

[97] See on implied powers: Case 22/70, *Commission v Council (ERTA)* [1971] ECR 263, paras 12-19; Opinion 1/76, *Draft Agreement on the establishment of European Laying-up Fund for Inland Waterway Vessels* [1977] ECR 741; see also Chapter 2, Section 1.2.

[98] See on the broad range of issues that could be dealt with under the CFSP: Chapter 2, Section 1.3.4.

[99] Different: Koen Lenaerts and Eddy de Smijter, 'The EU as an Actor under International Law', *YEL*, 19 (1999–2000), 97, p 121; but see further on this matter: Dominic McGoldrick, *International Relations Law of the European Union* (London: Longman, 1997), pp 26–8 and 37; Mary Eaton, 'Common Foreign and Security Policy', in David O'Keeffe and Patrick Twomey (eds), *Legal Issues of the Maastricht Treaty* (London: Chancery Law Publishing, 1994), p 224; Eeckhout, *External Relations of the European Union* (n 93 above), p 160; Govaere, Capiau and Vermeersch, 'In-Between Seats' (n 54 above), p 158; more in general on the capacity of the EU as a foreign actor: Jan Klabbers, 'Presumptive Personality: The European Union in International Law', in Martti Koskenniemi (ed), *International Law Aspects of the European Union* (The Hague: Kluwer Law International, 1998), pp 231–53.

[100] See also on the EU's competences and the UN, in particular for examples of non-compliance with an existing common position: Govaere, Capiau and Vermeersch, 'In-Between Seats' (n 54 above), p 176 et seq.

irrespective of whether the Union has exercised these powers at an earlier occasion. This is different from the first pillar: here, Member State action is excluded where the Community has exclusive competence or has exercised a shared competence.

This is different for action in the framework of the UN Charter. Some of the EU Member States are permanent members of the Security Council and continue to enjoy–as a state rather than as a member of the EU–special rights under the UN Charter. These rights find explicit recognition in Article 19(2) TEU, and there is no sign either in the UN Charter or in the European Treaties that those states wanted to confer on the Community the power to take over their rights and obligations under the UN Charter. Article 48 UNC only allows member states to fulfil (part of) their obligations *through the medium of* an international organization; it does not transfer the obligations to the international organization.

The ECJ pointed out in *International Fruit Company* that the Community had actually taken over the position of the Member States as the Contracting Parties of the GATT. The Community took part in the negotiations and was a partner to the agreements under the GATT, while in the Security Council it is still excluded from the decision-making process.[101] The GATT sets a framework, which imposes in principle only negative obligations; this is mainly the obligation not to create barriers to trade. The more detailed rules of the GATT are actually agreements that governments have negotiated. There is no legally binding agreement that sets out by what percentage the tariffs are to be cut. Instead, individual countries listed their commitments in 'schedules of concessions' annexed to the GATT. Already in 1972, before the Community officially became a member of the WTO,[102] it negotiated the schedules of concessions in the areas of its competence. In the UN, on the other hand, neither the Community nor the EU are represented or have any say. Further, there are obvious practical advantages for letting the Community negotiate trade agreements in place of the Member States: it benefits in these negotiations from its much stronger economic power.

Looking at the *underlying rationale* of the ECJ's reasoning, in *International Fruit Company* the Court attempted to avoid the situation that

[101] See below why *International Fruit Company* cannot serve as an authority for the primacy of Security Council resolutions.

[102] Article IX(1) of the WTO Agreement.

Community action breaches the international law obligations of the Member States. However, if the Community does not comply with the GATT when adopting general internal trade regulations, or when entering into international agreements, the Member States end up in a position where they have to choose either to comply with their international obligations and derogate from Community law based on Article 307 EC, or to comply with Community law, but breach their international obligations. The former choice would render Community law ineffective (in particular in the event that all Member States derogate from it),[103] while the latter choice would usually make the Member States liable for damages under international law. For state sanctions it could still be argued that this rationale applies to a certain extent. However, the situation is different because the most likely conflict situation does not involve an *active breach* of UN Charter obligations by the Community, but rather a failure by the Community to implement a Security Council resolution. The most probable scenario is that the Community does not adopt sanction measures. Here, Member States remain competent to take action. If they were to adopt state sanctions in order to comply with their UN Charter obligations, this would of course undermine to some extent the regulation of the internal market; however, it is different from adopting measures and allowing for trade in clear breach of a Community regulation or of an international trade agreement concluded by the Community. The damage done to the credibility and effectiveness of Community law is much greater in the latter scenario. In the case of individual sanctions the situation is again different. As was demonstrated in Chapter 2, the internal market does not require a uniform approach to individual sanctions. Unilateral sanctions against individuals would not undermine the effectiveness of Community law in any considerable way. Thus, the underlying rationale of *International Fruit Company* does not require the assumption of a de facto succession either.

In conclusion, the argument made by the ECJ in *International Fruit Company* is not only based on the fact that all the EU Member States were bound by the GATT prior to the conclusion of the EC Treaty, but it draws on the will of the Member States and the third countries involved, as it is expressed in the EC Treaty, in the GATT and in the recognition of the Community as a trade partner under the GATT. Such an intention cannot be demonstrated with regard to the UN. Hence, at face value the reasoning

[103] Unilateral action of the Member States would distort competition and disturb the internal market.

of *International Fruit Company* cannot be transferred to cases concerning individual sanctions.

3.1.2 Articles 297 and 307 EC

Besides *International Fruit Company*, the CFI[104] used Articles 297 and 307 EC and the *Centro-Com* case[105] for its reasoning on the relationship between the UN Charter and European law. First, the CFI correctly concluded that the Community cannot impede the EU Member States from complying with their obligations under the UN Charter. More surprisingly, the CFI then found Member States bound, *in their capacity as EU Member States*, to take all measures to ensure that Security Council resolutions are put into effect and if necessary to disregard their Community law obligations.[106] The Court finally interpreted Article 307 EC, as well as Article 297 EC, to support its understanding that the European Treaties bind the Community to comply with Security Council resolutions and justify the limitation of its jurisdiction.[107]

The latter two conclusions are remarkable. Articles 297 and 307 EC, particularly as they are interpreted by the ECJ in *Centro-Com*, actually appear to support an argument to the contrary. In this case the ECJ ruled in essence that the Member States retain powers in the field of foreign and security policy, but that they must exercise these powers in a manner consistent with Community law. The Court then analysed conceptually[108] whether Member States can rely on Article 307 EC to justify measures contrary to the CCP.

Articles 297 and 307 EC stipulate the right of the EU Member States to derogate from Community law where this is justified either by national security considerations or by prior international law obligations. Yet, even though Articles 307 and 297 EC explicitly only govern obligations of the Member States towards the Community, in combination with Article 10 EC they establish a negative obligation of the Community not to hinder

[104] Case T-315/01, *Kadi* (n 1 above), para 185 et seq.

[105] Case C-124/95, *Centro-Com* (n 90 above); the CFI referred to: para 54 et seq.

[106] Case T-315/01, *Kadi* (n 1 above), para 188 et seq.

[107] ibid, para 223: '[...] such jurisdiction would be contrary to provisions both of the EC Treaty, especially Arts 5 EC, 10 EC, 297 EC and the first paragraph of Art 307 EC, and of the Treaty on European Union, in particular Art 5 EU, in accordance with which the Community judicature is to exercise its powers on the conditions and for the purposes provided for by the provisions of the EC Treaty and the Treaty on European Union'.

[108] It left the decision of whether the conditions of Art 307 EC were fulfilled to the national courts.

Member States to comply their obligations under the UN Charter. However, these provisions can hardly be interpreted to set out a *Community law obligation* to comply with UN Charter obligations, either for the Member States or for the Community.[109] The Member States might be required to derogate from Community law by their obligations under the UN Charter, but there is no general Community law obligation compelling Member States *not* to comply with EU law where compliance could result in a breach of UN Charter obligations. It is for the Member States first to reconcile their different obligations, and only where this is not possible Article 307 EC gives them an exceptional right to derogate from Community law.

Further and most importantly, why would there be a need for a provision like Article 307 EC if the Community itself was bound by Security Council resolutions? If the Community was directly bound, all Community law should be susceptible of being interpreted in conformity with them. Consequently, a conflict between obligations of the Member States under Community law and those under the UN Charter should not occur, and the Member States would not ever need to derogate from Community law in order to comply with UN Charter obligations. Otherwise, any declaration of the EU courts that a Member State lawfully derogated from Community law would automatically amount to a statement that the Community breached its own UN Charter obligations, since such a declaration would indirectly confirm that European law could not be reconciled with the UN Charter.

Finally, the CFI's reasoning that Security Council resolutions are a binding obligation for the EU Member States under *European law* could possibly place the EU courts in a position where they have to enforce Security Council resolutions against the Member States. If an EU Member State failed to adopt freezing measures against an individual listed by the Community, the EU courts would have to enforce European secondary law

[109] Arts 297 and 307 in combination with Art 10 EC impose passive obligations on the Community only: Karl M Meessen, 'The Application of Rules of Public International Law within Community Law', *CML Rev*, 13 (1976), p 491; Pierre Pescatore, 'External Relations in the Case-Law of the Court of Justice of the European Communities', *CML Rev*, 16 (1979), p 636 et seq; see also: Case 812/79, *Burgoa*, [1980] ECR 2787, referred to by the CFI in support of its argument (Case T-306/01, *Yusuf* (n 1 above), para 247 and Case T-315/01, *Kadi* (n 1 above), para 197). However, in this case the ECJ explicitly emphasized that the 'duty of the Community institutions is directed only to permitting the member state concerned to perform its obligations under the prior agreement and does not bind the Community as regards the non-member country in question' (para 9).

predetermined by Security Council resolutions directly against this EU Member State.

3.1.3 National Measures

Mr Kadi was targeted by national *and* Community measures; and he challenged the sanctions both before UK courts and in Luxembourg. In the national proceedings the UK Government argued that any annulment of national measures would be futile because it would not affect the EC regulation and as long as the EC regulation remained in place the situation of the applicant would not change. This is true. EC regulations are directly applicable and hence are directly binding on all financial institutions of the UK without need for implementation under national law. In national courts, Mr Kadi would only be able to stop national measures from taking effect, such as the exchange of information in the third pillar and secondary (criminal) sanctions.[110]

Conversely, a declaration that the Community regulation is invalid for breaching general principles of European law does not oblige the Member States to annul national measures. The Member States are not automatically obliged to de-freeze the applicant's accounts. Further, if the EU courts declare an EC regulation imposing individual sanctions invalid, there is no longer binding European law on that specific matter. Based on the assumption that individual sanctions do not have a relevant impact on the common market or competition policy, the Member States would not even have to derogate from European law when imposing sanctions on those individuals who were listed in the original European law instrument that was declared void.[111] The practicability of this option is a different matter. It is difficult to imagine that national (constitutional) courts would accept a measure as lawful under national law, after the identical European version of that measure was struck down by the EU courts for breaching fundamental rights. After all, the standard of fundamental rights protection under European law is based on the constitutional principles 'common to the Member States'[112] and the European institutions and national authorities

[110] See on secondary sanctions Chapter 1, Section 4 and on the possibility of adopting criminal sanctions under Community law Chapter 3, Section 3.2.2.

[111] AG Maduro argued that Member States would have to comply with Community rules 'to the extent that their actions come within the scope of the Community Treaty' (Opinion of AG Maduro, in Cases C-402/05 P and C-415/05 P, *Kadi and al Barakaat* (n 1 above), para 30). This is true, but it is here argued that would not be the case if Member States reinstated sanctions against particular individuals.

[112] Article 6(1) TEU.

are in a similar position when they adopt sanctions based on UN lists: the evidence that led to the listing at the UN level remains obscure.[113]

The present section has demonstrated that no binding force of UN Security Council resolutions on the Community can be established by virtue of European law. The rationale of *International Fruit* cannot be transferred to the UN and Articles 297 and 307 EC do not support the assumption of a European law obligation to implement UN Security Council resolutions either.

3.2 The Prevailing Force of Security Council Resolutions

Irrespective of whether the Community could be bound by Security Council resolutions by virtue of the EC Treaty, within the European legal order they do not rank above primary European law. The CFI considered obligations under the UN Charter to prevail over the European Treaties, including general principles of European law.[114] In the appeal, the ECJ took a very different view.

3.2.1 International Fruit Company

The CFI referred to *International Fruit Company* not only as an authority for the binding force of Security Council resolutions[115] but also for their *primacy*.[116] However, the significance of *International Fruit Company* for the sanctions discussion is equally limited with regard to primacy as it was with regard to the binding force of UN Charter obligations on the Community: besides the fundamental differences between the relationship between the EEC and the GATT on the one hand, and between the EC and the UN on the other, in *International Fruit Company* the ECJ did not allow the GATT to prevail over European primary law and has never done so for any form of international law, including the GATT/WTO law[117] and the UN Charter.[118]

International Fruit Company could rather be used for an argument to the contrary: the ECJ indeed ruled that 'the jurisdiction of the court cannot

[113] See Chapter 1, Section 5.

[114] Case T-315/01, *Kadi* (n 1 above), para 181; Case T-49/04, *Hassan* (n 3 above), para 116; T-253/02, *Ayadi* (n 3 above), paras 116 and 146.

[115] See Section 3.1.1 above.

[116] Cases 21-24/72, *International Fruit Company* (n 4 above).

[117] Quite to the contrary, it took a position of deference to the political institutions, see only: Case C-149/96, *Portugal v Council* [1999] ECR I-8395, paras 34–52 and also more recently: Case C-377/02, *Van Parys* [2005] ECR I-1465; Case T-19/01, *Chiquita* [2005] ECR II-315.

[118] See below.

be limited by the grounds on which the validity of those measures may be contested'[119] On the contrary, it found[120] that its

> jurisdiction extends to all grounds capable of invalidating those measures, the Court is obliged to examine whether their validity may be affected by reason of the fact that they are contrary to a rule of international law.

Hence, *International Fruit Company* confirms that international law *cannot* determine the scope of jurisdiction of the EU courts to review European law.

Further, and with the concession that direct effect and primacy are two separate concepts, it must be noticed that by denying GATT/WTO law direct effect, the ECJ has in practice avoided submitting the Community to the dictate of international law. In *Germany v Council*[121] the ECJ decided that the GATT was binding on the Community but that the contested regulation could not be controlled as to its compatibility with the GATT. The Court did not make a distinction between direct effect and possible review. As with the concept of implied powers,[122] one intention behind *not* conferring direct effect on the GATT was to safeguard the *effet utile*, the effectiveness of Community law. Despite the binding force of the GATT, the ECJ did not annul the Community regulations at stake. It held that individuals could not rely on the GATT in Luxembourg, because the GATT did not have direct effect. The ECJ's willingness to accept judicial review of secondary legislation *except* in the light of WTO law is explicable by the Court's aim to protect the autonomy of European law.

3.2.2 State Sanctions under Review

The UN Charter usually affects EU law only indirectly.[123] Yet, UN sanctions are exceptional in this regard. It is accepted practice that the EU and the Community in joint action adopt state sanctions giving effect to Security Council resolutions.[124] Today, as a matter of fact, the EU and the Community adopt individual sanctions following the same procedure. Hence, in the area of sanctions the EU and the Community have for a long

[119] Cases 21–24/72, *International Fruit Company* (n 4 above), para 5.

[120] ibid, para 6.

[121] Case C-280/93, *Germany v Council* [1994] ECR I-4973.

[122] See Chapter 2, Section 1.2.

[123] Robert Uerpmann, 'International Law as an Element of European Constitutional Law: International Supplementary Constitutions', *Jean Monnet Working Papers* 9/03 (2003), http://www.jeanmonnetprogram.org/papers/03/030901-02.html, p 6.

[124] Arts 301 and 60 EC.

time adopted the necessary measures to ensure compliance with the Member States' obligations under the UN Charter. Because UN sanctions against individuals do not leave any margin of discretion to the implementing entity they increase the direct influence of the Security Council on acts adopted by the EU. However, the relationship between UN Security Council resolutions and European law is in principle the same.

Before its rulings on the validity of sanctions against individuals in *Kadi* and *al Barakaat* the ECJ had on several occasions adjudicated upon disputes concerning the implementation of UN trade embargoes (state sanctions).[125] In all of these cases the ECJ reviewed the validity and interpretation of Community measures in the light of European law and referred to the underlying UN sanctions resolution as a means of interpretation only.[126] The Court has not, at any point, indicated an absolute deference to the Security Council.

In the *Bosphorus* case[127] Ireland had impounded an airplane in order to comply with an EC Council regulation that implemented a number of Security Council resolutions. The Irish Supreme Court asked the ECJ in the preliminary ruling procedure whether the EC regulation applied to the seized aircraft. The ECJ held that in interpreting the EC regulation 'account must [...] be taken of the text and the aim of those [Security Council] resolutions'.[128] It interpreted the wording of the EC regulation with reference to the wording of the Security Council resolutions; yet, it did not deny jurisdiction because of the existence of the latter. The Court invoked its earlier case-law, in which it accepted that the exercise of fundamental rights can be 'subject to restrictions justified by objectives of general interest pursued by the Community'.[129] By referring to 'objectives pursued by the Community' the ECJ did not accept the Security Council resolutions as an absolute justification to limit fundamental rights. One could of course argue that cooperation within the UN itself is an objective of the Community.[130] However, restricting the exercise of fundamental rights because of *a Community objective*–the objective of complying with

[125] Case C-124/95, *Centro-Com* (n 90 above); Case C-177/95, *Ebony Maritime* [1997] ECR I-1111; Case C-84/95, *Bosphorus Airways* [1996] ECR I-3953.

[126] See eg: the reference to Resolution 820 (1993) in Case C-84/95, *Bosphorus Airways* (n 125 above), para 12.

[127] Case C-84/95, *Bosphorus Airways* (n 125 above).

[128] ibid, para 14.

[129] ibid, para 21.

[130] On the basis of the Preamble and Arts 177(3), 302 and arguably 297 EC, as well as Art 11(1) TEU.

Security Council resolutions–is not the same as granting them absolute primacy. On the contrary, *only* because the ECJ does not consider Security Council resolutions supreme is it necessary to take compliance with them into account as an objective of *Community law*.

It must be conceded though that the ECJ demonstrated in practical terms a considerable restraint in reviewing the merits in the *Bosphorus* case. The Court chose a textual approach aiming for consistent interpretation, instead of its regular teleological method of interpretation.[131] This allowed the Court to interpret the EC regulation literally in the meaning of the Security Council resolution. Further, the ECJ conducted only a limited test of proportionality. It pointed out 'the importance of the aims pursued by the regulation'[132] and argued that this importance could 'justify negative consequences, even of a substantial nature'[133] concluding that in the light of 'an objective of general interest so fundamental for the international community, which consists in putting an end to the state of war…' the interference with the applicant's fundamental rights cannot be regarded as disproportionate.[134]

A further example of the ECJ's approach to Security Council resolutions is the above discussed *Centro-Com* case.[135] Here, the Court examined[136] whether and how Member States could rely on Article 307 EC to justify derogation from Community law. It did not rule that Security Council resolutions enjoy general primacy over Community law, but accepted derogation from the latter based on *Community rules* only. This allows a similar conclusion to be drawn as in *Bosphorus*. If the ECJ had conferred primacy on Security Council resolutions, it would not have had to rely on Community law to allow Member States to derogate from the latter in order to comply with the former. The mere existence of a Security Council resolution would have sufficed to justify the non-compliance of Member States with Community law.

The ECJ's approach to international law has been received with mixed feelings. On the one hand, the ECJ has been extensively criticized for not conferring sufficient force first on the GATT,[137] then on WTO law,[138]

[131] Iris Canor, '"Can Two Walk Together, Except They be Agreed?": The Relationship Between International Law and European Law. The Incorporation of United Nations Sanctions Against Yugoslavia Into European Community Law Through the Perspective of the European Court of Justice', *CML Rev*, 35 (1998), pp 172–3.

[132] Case C-84/95, *Bosphorus Airways* (n 125 above), paras 22–3.

[133] ibid, paras 22–3.

[134] ibid, para 26.

[135] Case C-124/95, *Centro-Com* (n 90 above), para 54 et seq.

[136] It left the decision of whether the conditions of Art 307 EC were fulfilled to the national courts.

[137] Cases 21–24/72, *International Fruit Company* (n 4 above), para 27.

[138] Case C-149/96, *Portugal v Council* (n 117 above); Case C-93/02 P, *Biret International v Council* [2003] ECR I-10497, para 52; Case C-377/02, *Van Parys* (n 117 above), para 39.

and finally on the decisions of the Appellate Body.[139] On the other hand, the ECJ has been criticized for granting the executive more room for manoeuvre by choosing a textual approach (and not its usual teleological method) to the interpretation of measures giving effect to Security Council resolutions.[140] It has been argued that the ECJ confronts Security Council resolutions with a 'minimalistic approach' in order to achieve a 'maximalistic objective'.[141] The ECJ did not expound on the problem of ruling on such a highly political measure like sanctions. Neither did it discuss the question of whether reviewing the proportionality of a particular implementation measure could undermine the Security Council's monopoly to define and deal with threats to international peace and security. It could, however, be argued that the Court's self-restraint was a practical choice, which helped to ensure that Member States accepted the Community's legislation and the Court's jurisdiction in areas where the Community's competence was at the beginning very controversial.[142] Today, however, it must be acknowledged that the Member States have expressed their political will to move the adoption of Security Council sanctions within the jurisdiction of the Court by creating an original Community competence by introducing Article 301 EC.[143] Nonetheless, sanctions are still adopted as hybrid measures based on both the first and the second pillar; and at least when based on international cooperation in the UN, they touch upon core competences of the Member States in the area of national security.

In any event, the ECJ agreed to review European law even where it implements UN resolutions without applying any structural limitations. Moreover, it is difficult to argue that the Member States wanted to introduce the cross-pillar procedure in Article 301 EC as a way to circumvent domestic constitutional rules usually applicable when they implement UN resolutions. There is no evidence that the Member States wanted to establish a mechanism that funnels UN obligations directly into the domestic legal order and excludes judicial scrutiny.

[139] Case C-351/04, *Ikea Wholesale Ltd v Commissioners of Custom & Excise* [2007] ECR I-7723, para 35; see also: Anne Thies, 'Biret and beyond: The status of WTO rulings in EC Law', *CML Rev*, 41 (2004), pp 1661–82; Anne Thies, 'Case annotation on the judgments of 14 December 2005, Court of First Instance in Cases T-69/00, T-151/00, T-301/00, T-320/00, T-383/00 and T-135/01 FIAMM et al.', *CML Rev*, 43 (2006), pp 1145–68.

[140] Canor, 'Can Two Walk Together, Except They be Agreed?' (n 131 above).

[141] See: Panos Koutrakos, *Trade, Foreign Policy and Defence in EU Constitutional Law* (Oxford: Hart Publishing, 2001), p 149.

[142] Before Art 301 EC was introduced sanctions were adopted on the basis of the Common Commercial Policy in Art 133 EC, see Chapter 2, Section 1.2.

[143] ibid.

3.2.3 Review of Individual Sanctions

The CFI argued that reviewing Community sanctions against individuals in the light of the principles of European law would amount to an indirect review of the UN sanctions they intend to implement.[144] The Court feared that this would severely undermine the authority of the Security Council. The rationale is similar to the one in *Dorsch Consult*.[145] In this case the applicant claimed damages for harm allegedly suffered as a result of the adoption of a Community regulation preventing trade with Iraq and Kuwait, without providing for possible economic reprisals by the Iraqi authorities. The CFI held that the alleged damage could not be attributed to the adoption of the Community sanctions regulation but only to the Security Council resolution that the former intended to implement[146] and dismissed the applicant's application. In *Yusuf* and *Kadi* however, the CFI went a considerable step further: it not only rejected liability for damages but denied full judicial review of secondary Community law because of an existing UN Charter obligation.

In the academic debate it was claimed that the real measure of the dispute in *Yusuf* and *Kadi* was not so much the EC regulation but the Security Council resolution,[147] and that review by the EU courts of the European implementation of individual sanctions would amount to making the Security Council 'accountable for any possible legal flaws of its actions.'[148] Parallels were drawn[149] with the *Tadic* case[150] of the Appeals Chamber of the International Criminal Tribunal for the former Yugoslavia (ICTY) and the *Kanyabashi* of the International Criminal Tribunal for Rwanda

[144] Case T-306/01, *Yusuf* (n 1 above), para 268.

[145] Case T-184/95, *Dorsch Consult* (n 70 above); see: Marise Cremona, 'External Relations of the EU and the Member States: Competence, Mixed Agreements, International Responsibility, and Effects of International Law', *EUI Law working papers*, 22 (2006), p 33.

[146] Case T-184/95, *Dorsch Consult* (n 70 above), para 74.

[147] Enzo Cannizzaro, 'Machiavelli, the UN Security Council and the Rule of Law', Hauser Global Law School Program, *Global Law Working Paper* 11/05, http://www1.law.nyu.edu/nyulawglobal/workingpapers/glwp_0106.htm, p 16.

[148] Tomuschat, 'Case law: Case T-306/01, Ahmed Ali Yusuf and Al Barakaat International Foundation v Council and Commission' (n 17 above), p 538.

[149] Tomuschat, 'Case law: Case T-306/01, Ahmed Ali Yusuf and Al Barakaat International Foundation v Council and Commission' (n 17 above), p 545 (Tadic); Larissa van der Herik and Nico Schrijver, 'Section 2: Human Rights Concerns in Current Targeted Sanctions Regimes from the Perspective of International and European Law', in Thomas J Biersteker and Sue E Eckert, *Strengthening Targeted Sanctions Through Fair and Clear Procedures*, White Paper prepared by the Watson Institute Targeted Sanctions Project, Brown University, 30 March 2006, p 19.

[150] ICTY, *The Prosecutor v Tadic*, Appeal Decision, Judgment of 2 October 1995, ILM 35 (1996), paras 14–22.

(ICTR).[151] In the former case the ICTY scrutinized whether the Security Council possessed the powers to establish an international judicial body for the prosecution of war crimes, such as the ICTY itself, and eventually found that the Security Council had not acted ultra vires. In the latter case the ICTR, referring repeatedly to the *Tadic* case, did the same with regard to its own establishment.

The desire for some form of judicial control of Security Council resolutions is entirely comprehensible. However, the usefulness of the decisions of the ICTY and the ICTR as a parallel to the review of European sanctions based on UN lists of terrorist suspects is contested. UN sanctions were not and cannot be directly challenged in the EU courts. Hence, the comparison with *Tadic* and *Kanyabashi* is misleading, since the Luxembourg Courts were never asked to rule on the competences of the Security Council to adopt individual sanctions. The issue at stake before the EU courts was the legality of a European legal instrument.[152] Any review by a European Court is only a judgment of the legal situation under European law. As the ECJ correctly pointed out in *Kadi and al Barakaat*,[153] it does not imply a legal judgment on the legality of the activity of the Security Council under international law. Whatever the limits to the actions of the Security Council are, the validity of the decisions of the Security Council does not depend on their compliance with European law.

Having said this, reviewing individual sanctions for their compliance with substantive fundamental rights is not without political implications for international law. A distinction should be made between reviewing compliance with procedural rules and reviewing compliance with substantive rights. The adoption procedure of individual sanctions within the EU is governed by the Treaties. An evaluation of the procedural aspects of the adoption of the European sanctions in principle has no substantive link to the UN resolution lying at its origin. Reviewing whether the Community was competent,[154] whether the Council followed the correct procedure, or

[151] ICTR, *The Prosecutor v Kanyabashi*, Decision, 8 June 1997.

[152] While on the one hand arguing that a review of the EC regulation would amount an indirect review of the SC resolution the CFI also conceded (Case T-315/01, *Kadi* (n 1 above), para 272) that 'the sole subject-matter of [this dispute] [...] is the lawfulness of the contested regulation'.

[153] Cases C-402/05 P and C-415/05 P, *Kadi and al Barakaat* (n 1 above), para 288.

[154] The Court examined the Community's competence in Case T-306/01, *Yusuf* (n 1 above) and Case T-315/01, *Kadi* (n 1 above).

whether those sanctioned were granted a right to a fair hearing[155] does not as such contain any implicit appraisal of the underlying UN sanctions.

With regard to substance, ie the listing of a particular individual, judicial review has more far reaching political implications for the underlying Security Council resolutions. The ECJ could not easily transfer its approach of literal interpretation to the underlying Security Council resolution.[156] Implementing state sanctions entails the exercise of discretion. This allows distinguishing between the UN sanctions regime and the general legislative instrument of implementation on the one hand and the individual decision applying sanctions to the particular case on the other. In the case of individual sanctions no such substantive distinction can be made. UN sanctions lists are copied name by name without any further examination into European law.[157] European institutions have no discretion in the matter. They simply give effect to the UN lists. This is indeed the very defect that vitiates European sanctions against individuals.[158]

By declaring the measures challenged in *Kadi* and *al Barakaat* contrary to *principles of European law* the ECJ did not rule on the validity of the underlying UN resolution. Any examination of domestic implementation measures in the light of European law can only determine that the former do not comply with the latter. *Even if* one agrees that the implementation of sanctions against individuals cannot be separated from the UN lists, because the former are identical copies of the latter, the yardstick of the EU courts is still European law. Therefore, *even if* the Security Council adopts resolutions contrary to European law standards, this has *no implications for the legality of those resolutions under international law*.

The ECJ's clear separation between the legal effects of its ruling within the European legal order and those under international law is legally correct and extends both to Security Council resolutions and to the lists of terrorist suspects drawn up by the UN Sanctions Committee. However, this cannot disguise the fact that the ECJ passed a de facto judgment about the listing procedure at the UN level by declaring these identical implementation measures contrary to principles that are by no means peculiar to the EU but roughly identical to human rights standards promoted by the UN. Additionally, the ECJ did not refrain from (and arguably could not

155 Case T-306/01, *Yusuf* (n 1 above), paras 304–31.
156 Case C-84/95, *Bosphorus Airways* (n 125 above).
157 Case T-315/01, *Kadi* (n 1 above), para 258.
158 Argument of the applicant, ibid, para 150.

avoid) embarking on an assessment of the UN sanctioning regime[159] that ended in the explicit statement that fundamental rights are not adequately protected at the UN level.[160] This is an open challenge to the legitimacy of the UN sanctions regime.

The EU courts have a comprehensive mandate to 'ensure that in the interpretation and application of this Treaty the law is observed' (Article 220 EC). 'The law' here refers in principle to all legal obligations created within and according to the rules of the European legal order, including the rule of law.[161] If every obligation originating outside the domestic legal order excluded judicial review of internal implementation measures judicial scrutiny could be easily avoided by signing up to international cooperation and thereby entering into external obligations.[162] The limitation is not that measures giving effect to obligations originating outside of the internal legal order cannot be reviewed. The substantive limitation is that they are only reviewed in the light of the principles of the internal order. This does not entail a judgment about the legality of the external obligation.

Indeed, it is the CFI's decision to apply *jus cogens*[163] instead of European Law that could give the impression that the Court reviewed the legality of UN resolutions. On the one hand, the CFI argued that it cannot review *European law* in the light of the principles of *European law* because this would amount to a review of the underlying Security Council resolution. On the other it examined the contested legal measures in the light of *jus cogens*. However, it is precisely the choice of *jus cogens* as the basis of review that results in an implicit scrutiny of Security Council resolutions.

3.2.4 Autonomy of the European Legal Order

The ECJ followed in *Kadi* and *al Barakaat* Advocate-General Maduro in his domestic outlook. Advocate-General Maduro had considered 'the landmark ruling in *Van Gend en Loos*'[164] as the 'logical starting point' of the

[159] ibid, para 321 et seq.

[160] ibid, see in particular para 323: 'submitting a request to be removed from the summary list at what is called the 'focal' point, the fact remains that the procedure before that Committee is still in essence diplomatic and intergovernmental'.

[161] See also Chapter 6, Section 3.2 on the principle of wider jurisdiction.

[162] Compare also the settled case law of the ECtHR, that Contracting Parties cannot escape their Convention obligations through international cooperation: ECtHR, *Bosphorus Airways* (n 5 above), para 153; but also earlier the Commission on Human Rights: ECtHR, *M & Co v Germany*, Application no 13258/87, Commission decision of 9 February 1990, Decisions and Reports (DR) 64.

[163] Case T-315/01, *Kadi* (n 1 above), para 226.

[164] Opinion of AG Maduro, in: Cases C-402/05 P and C-415/05 P, *Kadi and al Barakaat* (n 1 above), para 21.

discussion and emphasized that the role and function of the Court was '... first and foremost, to preserve the constitutional framework created by the Treaty'[165] The ECJ defended the Community's autonomy, both at the institutional and at the substantive level, by stating that obligations under international agreements can neither 'affect the allocation of powers fixed by the Treaties',[166] nor can they 'have the effect of prejudicing the constitutional principles of the EC Treaty'.[167] For support the Court cited its previous case-law in the *Mox Plant* case[168] (institutional autonomy) and in *Germany v Council*[169] concerning a framework agreement on bananas (substantive autonomy). After these general defensive statements, the Court turned[170] more specifically to the question

> whether, as the Court of First Instance held, as a result of the principles governing the relationship between the international legal order under the United Nations and the Community legal order any judicial review of the internal lawfulness of the contested regulation in the light of fundamental freedoms is in principle excluded.

The ECJ answered this question unambiguously in the negative.[171]

However, the ECJ's reasoning made clear, that by contrast with the CFI, it considered these 'governing principles' to be exclusively principles of *European law*. The Court briefly recalled the Community's track record of respecting international law.[172] It then left no doubt that:[173]

> [t]he question of the Court's jurisdiction arises in the context of the internal and autonomous legal order of the Community, within whose ambit the contested regulation falls and in which the Court has jurisdiction to review the validity of Community measures in the light of fundamental rights.

Hence, the ECJ saw no reason for denying judicial review *in the EC Treaty*.[174]

The ECJ's ruling in *Kadi and al Barakaat* is well in line with its prior case-law. The Court has always been very strict in protecting the integrity

[165] ibid, para 24.
[166] ibid, para 282.
[167] ibid, para 285.
[168] ECJ, C-459/03, *Commission v Ireland* [2006] ECR I 4635, para 123 and Opinion 1/91 [1991] ECR I 6079, paras 35 and 71. [169] Case C-122/95, *Germany v Council* [1998] ECR I-973.
[170] Cases C-402/05 P and C-415/05 P, *Kadi and al Barakaat* (n 1 above), para 290.
[171] ibid, para 299. [172] ibid, para 291. [173] ibid, para 317. [174] ibid, para 300.

of the domestic European legal order.[175] When called upon to enforce rules of international law, it has done so, yet firmly rooted in European primary law. Pursuant to Article 300(7) EC international agreements are binding Community law if they are validly concluded. The ECJ has ruled that:[176]

an agreement concluded by the Council with a non-member country in accordance with the provisions of the EC Treaty is an act of a Community institution, and the provisions of such an agreement form an integral part of Community law.

Thus, international agreements can become an integral part of Community law, but *only if* they have been properly concluded according to Community rules.[177] This was already implied as early as 1974 in the *Haegeman* case,[178] but the ECJ has made this point even clearer in later case-law, in which it declared (internal) acts of conclusion of international agreements void.[179] From the standpoint of Community law, the binding force of international agreements does not depend on whether they have been validly concluded according to the rules of *international law*, but on whether they have been entered into in compliance with the rules of *primary Community law*. In any event, neither the EU nor the Community have acceded to the UN Charter and Article 300(7) EC is not directly applicable. Yet, in *Kadi and al Barakaat*, the ECJ considered the hypothetical place that obligations under the UN Charter '*would* occupy'[180] within the hierarchy of Community norms, '*supposing*' Article 300(7) EC to be applicable to the Charter.[181] The ECJ found that if the Community was bound by the UN Charter, just as any other international agreement, the Charter would rank between primary and secondary EC law.[182]

[175] For Community law: Lenaerts and De Smijter, 'The EU as an Actor under International Law' (n 99 above), p 137.

[176] Case 12/86, *Demirel v Stadt Schwäbisch Gmünd* [1987] ECR 3719, para 7; Art 300 EC sets out the conditions which must be satisfied for international agreements to be validly concluded, and their valid conclusion is the requirement for their binding force within the European legal order.

[177] Iain MacLeod, Ian Hendry and Stephen Hyett, *The External Relations of the European Communities* (Oxford: Clarendon Press, 1996), p 132.

[178] Case 181/73, *Haegeman v Belgium* [1974] ECR 449, para 5.

[179] Case C-122/95, *Germany v Council* (n 169 above), para 42; Case C-360/93, *Parliament v Council* [1996] ECR 1145; Case C-327/91, *France v Commission* [1994] ECR 3641, para 45.

[180] Cases C-402/05 P and C-415/05 P, *Kadi and al Barakaat* (n 1 above), para 305.

[181] ibid, para 307.

[182] The Court herewith took an approach similarly defensive of domestic constitutionalism as the German Constitutional Court, see for instance the ruling on the status of the ECHR.

In Opinion 1/91[183] and arguably in Opinion 2/94[184] the ECJ precisely rejected the view that institutions outside the legal order of the Community could determine the content of domestic Community law. In the former, the ECJ did not hide its concern to subject the Community to other institutional structures, such as the European Economic Area (EEA). The ECJ in fact protected the autonomy of the EC legal order against external institutional structures by applying a double test: it checked first whether the competence of the Community remains unaltered and, secondly, whether the decisions of legal supervision within that external system do not have the effect of binding the Community and its institutions in the exercise of their internal powers.[185] Any other conclusion would allow the Community to alter its own powers by entering into international treaty obligations. Both these criteria would fail if we imagined for a moment that the Community wanted to join an international organization producing binding obligations to sanction listed individuals and whose decisions not only prevail over Community law but are further immune to judicial review. The Community could not 'set up' an institutional structure like the one of the UN seen through the eyes of the CFI.

Indeed, in *MOX Plant* the ECJ referred to its view in Opinion 1/91, the only case up to that point in which the ECJ touched upon exclusive jurisdiction in Article 292 EC,[186] and confirmed that:[187]

> an international agreement cannot affect the allocation of responsibilities defined in the Treaties and, consequently, the autonomy of the Community legal system, compliance with which the Court ensures under Article 220 EC.

MOX Plant clearly demonstrated that the ECJ considers itself to hold the competence to determine whether, and if so to what extent, provisions of the international agreement in question fall outside its jurisdiction. Further, the conclusion of *MOX Plant* can only be that the autonomy of the Community legal order must be considered immune from interferences that result from the external activities of the Community and of the

[183] Opinion 1/91 [1991] ECR I 6079, paras 30–46; see also: Opinion 1/92, *EEA Agreement*, [1992] ECR I-2821, in which the ECJ approved of the EEA.

[184] Opinion 2/94, *ECHR*, [1996] ECR I-1759; see Chapter 2, Section 1.3.3.

[185] Govaere, Capiau and Vermeersch, 'In-Between Seats' (n 54 above), p 170 (with regard to setting up institutional structures).

[186] Nikolaos Lavranos, 'The Scope of the Exclusive Jurisdiction of the Court of Justice', *ELR*, 32(1) (2007), p 84

[187] Case C-459/03, *Commission v Ireland (MOX)* [2006] ECR I-4635, para 123.

Member States.[188] This is a necessary condition for the constitutional integrity of the European legal order. In a sense it is the 'external dimension of European constitutionalism'.[189]

This position finds additional support in the ECJ's position on the status of the ECHR within the European legal order. Despite the fact that all EU Member States were Contracting Parties to the ECHR, just like they were members of the UN, when they concluded the EEC, the ECJ has never ruled that the Community is bound by the ECHR as a matter of European law. On the contrary, the Court uses the ECHR as a source of persuasive law.[190] Yet in *Kadi* and *al Barakaat*, not only did both the Advocate-General and the ECJ take a more antagonist approach towards the UN regime,[191] also neither of them engaged in a discussion of the standard of protection under international human rights law. International law does not consist exclusively of the UN Charter. There is a large body of international human rights law, in particular the International Covenant of Civil and Political Rights (ICCPR) and the European Convention on Human Rights (ECHR), but also the Universal Declaration of Human Rights and human rights as part of customary international law.[192] The potential of finding inspiration in these international sources of human rights law would have been great.

The general principles of European Law, which the CFI set aside, are based on the constitutional traditions common to the Member States; and as a consequence of the supremacy of European law the CFI's interpretation sets aside not only the common traditions of the Member States at the European level, but also their constitutional law at the national level. The former were–at least partially–introduced as a response to the concerns of national constitutional courts. Member States' courts accepted the supremacy of European law based on the premise that the EU courts provided

[188] Lavranos, 'The Scope of the Exclusive Jurisdiction of the Court of Justice' (n 186 above), p 90.

[189] Daniel Halberstam and Eric Stein, 'The United Nations, the European Union, and the King of Sweden: Economic Sanctions and Individual Rights in a Plural World Order', *CML Rev*, 46 (2009), p 62.

[190] *Rechtserkenntnisquelle* as opposed to *Rechtsquelle*; see Chapter 3, Section 2 on the status of the ECHR in European law.

[191] Guy Harpaz, 'The European Court of Justice and its Relations with the European Court of Human Rights: The Quest for Enhanced Reliance, Coherence and Legitimacy', *CML Rev*, 46 (2009), p 127.

[192] Eckhart Klein (ed), *Menschenrechtsschutz als Gewohnheitsrecht* (Berlin: Berliner Wissenschafts-Verlag, 2003).

protection of fundamental rights.[193] Arguably, the CFI suggested departing from this tacit agreement. By contrast, the ECJ's ruling in *Kadi* and *al Barakaat* does not have immediate consequences for the functioning of the European legal order. By defending the autonomy of the Community legal order, it defended the status quo in practice. Conferring primacy on Security Council resolutions is not a constitutional tradition common to the Member States. On the contrary, most countries do not confer a special status on Security Council resolutions.[194] In most of the EU Member States Security Council resolutions require some form of implementation in order to take effect within the domestic legal order, but even where Security Council resolutions become directly binding within the legal order of a Member State they are usually not considered superior to national constitutional law.[195]

Compliance with the UN sanction regime against individuals does not indicate that states consider obligations under the UN Charter as directly binding and supreme within the domestic legal order either. Many states do not fully comply with the reporting obligations,[196] and only a few states report the names of those they sanction.[197] The Chairman of the Sanctions Committee explicitly criticized the implementation practice of those UN member states, which relied on criminal law for the implementation of

[193] GCC, *Solange II-decision*, BVerfGE 73, 339; *Maastricht decision* of 12 October 1993, BVerfGE 89, 155; *Alcan decision* of 17 February 2000, EuZW 2000, 445; *Banana decision* of 7 June 2000, EuZW 2000, p 702 et seq; for a translation of the Maastricht decision see: *Brunner v European Union Treaty*, 57 *CMLRev* 1994, for annotations: Ulrich Everling, 'The Maastricht Judgment of the German Federal Constitutional Court and its Significance for the Development of the European Union', *YEL*, 14 (1994), p 1 et seq; Kay Hailbronner, 'The European Union from the Perspective of the German Constitutional Court', *GYIL*, 37 (1994), p 93 et seq; Matthias Herdegen, 'Maastricht and the Constitutional Court: Constitutional Restraints for an Ever Closer Union', *CML Rev*, 31 (1994), p 235 et seq; Stephan Hobe, 'The German State in Europe after the Maastricht Decision of the German Constitutional Court', *GYIL*, 37 (1994), p 113 et seq; Joachim Wieland, 'Germany in the European Union: The Maastricht Decision of the Bundesverfassungsgericht', *EJIL*, 5 (1994), p 259 et seq; Juliane Kokott, 'German Constitutional Jurisprudence and European Integration II', *EPL*, 2 (1996), p 428 et seq. For a broader discussion see: Armin von Bogdandy, 'The European Union as a Human Rights Organization? Human Rights and the Core of the European Union', *CML Rev*, 37 (2000), p 1322 et seq.

[194] Antonio Cassese, *International Law* (Oxford: Oxford University Press, 2005), p 232 et seq.

[195] The Netherlands, Greece, Spain, and France (see: Cassese, *International Law*, ibid).

[196] By March 2008 153 reports were submitted and 39 states did not report at all. None of these non-reporting states was in Europe though (S/2008/324, para 108, p 34). See a more detailed assessment of the reporting practices of member states under Resolution 1455 (2003) at: S/2006/1046, December 2006.

[197] Fifth Report of the 1267 Committee, 31 December 2004, S/2004/1039, para 24.

sanctions against those listed. He pointed out that this is not in conformity with member states' obligations under Chapter VII UNC,[198] because it does not automatically give effect to the UN lists. Implementation then depends on national evidentiary standards and requires compliance with national procedural rules. The UN Monitoring Team[199] has repeatedly pointed out the lack of information on implementation,[200] which raises doubts regarding the actual implementation. Hence, there is some evidence that UN member states, irrespective of their UN Charter obligations, apply national rules to the adoption of sanctions against those listed by the UN; this includes certain procedural guarantees. This is a choice that the EU Member States are deprived of if Security Council resolutions are considered to prevail over European law.

Therefore, even if one accepted on the basis of *International Fruit Company* that EU Member States could not transfer to the Community rights they do not have under international law, this does not translate into the primacy of Security Council resolutions within the *domestic* legal order. Even if the EU as a creation of international law cannot take actions breaching the Member States' obligations under the UN Charter, a limitation of the powers transferred to the Community does not justify an encroachment on the Member States' rights, which they did *not* transfer to the Community. Member States have not surrendered their sovereignty over national security measures within their territory to the Community.

3.2.5 Amending the European Treaties?

Since neither the EU nor the Community are bound by the UN Charter as a matter of international law, they cannot directly breach obligations under the UN Charter. The annulment of an EC regulation on the grounds that it was contrary to Community standards could, however, even for the EU, amount to a breach of *European law*. Needless to say that irrespective of what the Community does, the Member States would continue to be bound by Security Council resolutions under international law. This position is

[198] Letter dated 1 December 2005 from the Chairman of the Security Council Committee established pursuant to resolution 1267 (1999) concerning Al-Qaida and the Taliban and associated individuals and entities addressed to the President of the Security Council, 6 December 2005, S/2005/760, at II.

[199] See Chapter 1, Section 3 on the establishment and role of the Monitoring Team.

[200] See eg: Sixth report of the Analytical Support and Sanctions Monitoring Team, UN S/2007/132 (8 March 2007), para 39.

based on the understanding that, from the standpoint of international law, member states cannot oppose their domestic law, or the setting up of a regional organization in compliance with their domestic law, to their international law obligations (Article 27 VCLT).

The CFI's position could be considered a breach of Article 48 TEU. The EU courts have the mandate to ensure the compliance of acts of the European institutions with the European Treaties, they cannot alter the latter. To establish primacy of Security Council resolutions within the European legal order goes beyond the competences of the EU courts. They cannot disapply Treaty provisions by finding them to be inconsistent with international law.[201] Vesting Security Council resolutions with absolute primacy is not simply a misinterpretation of a specific Treaty position. It (potentially) allows the Security Council to change the constitutional foundations of the European Union.

Article 307 EC does not recognize the primacy of UN Security Council resolutions. It does not free the Community institutions from their obligations of European primary law, but allows *Member States* to derogate from *their Community law obligations*. What is a sensible way of reconciling international legal obligations of the Member States with their obligations under Community law, all under the roof of their own constitutions, would otherwise turn out to free the Community from all guarantees of fundamental rights where it implements Security Council resolutions. Vesting Security Council resolutions with primacy over European law is also qualitatively different from an acknowledgement that international legal obligations could be self-executing and hence entail direct effect in the Community legal order. It is an institutional primacy that confers the power to directly determine the content of domestic Community law on institutions outside the legal order of the Community. There is no textual evidence for such an interpretation, which therefore constitutes an illegitimate alteration of the Treaties and is a breach of Article 48 TEU according to which Member States alone can change the Treaty.

By way of conclusion the ECJ decision to set aside the CFI's ruling on individual sanctions giving effect to UN Security Council resolutions was the correct choice from a European law perspective. The ECJ's interpretation is well supported by the European Treaties and a consistent

[201] Along similar lines: Lenaerts and De Smijter, 'The EU as an Actor under International Law' (n 99 above), p 106.

continuation of its settled case-law confirming the autonomy of the European legal order.

4. Between a Rock and a Hard Place: Determining the Status of Security Council Resolutions

From the standpoint of the European legal order the ECJ had little choice in *Kadi* and *al Barakaat* but to take a defensive stand. It could not have followed the CFI without putting into peril the delicate balance between the institutions and the Member States. It appears unlikely that national courts would accept that the 'check point' on the bridge between European law and national law continues to be abolished (as it is currently the case with the acceptance of the primacy of European law), if there is no mechanism to check actions of institutions that do not form part of the domestic European legal order and that directly impact on the legal position of individuals. Not only in the light of the past *Solange* rulings of the German Constitutional Court (GCC), but also given the more recent signs that the GCC might challenge the ECJ's authority,[202] the ECJ could not allow the Security Council to determine directly the content of European law without so much as a filter of the most fundamental European law principles. Anything else would have been a test of how far national courts would turn a blind eye to the hollowing out of the rights of individuals for the sake of saving the European legal order.[203]

[202] Roman Herzog and Lüder Gerken, 'Comment: Stop the European Court of Justice', of 10.9.2008, http://euobserver.com; and in particular: GCC, 1 BvR 256/08; EAW Decision of 18 July 2005 (2 BvR 2236/04).

[203] Admittedly, some national courts followed the CFI's ruling in *Kadi* (see eg: *M v HM Treasury* [2006] EWHC 2328 (UK) and *VG Ansbach*, 1st Chamber, judgment of 14 December 2006, AN 1 K 06.30883 (Germany)). See also the position of the Swiss Supreme Court: it found that the national law giving effect to UN sanctions affected the applicant's fundamental rights but argued that taking influence through political channels is the only option for Switzerland since anything else would put Switzerland in breach of its UN Charter obligations (Swiss Supreme Court (Schweizer Bundesgericht), *Youssef Mustapha Nada v SECO, Staatssekretariat für Wirtschaft*, judgment of 14 November 2007, 1A.45/2007/daa). However, it is difficult to see how the GCC would have accepted the listing of individuals as terrorist suspects without giving them any form of remedy (see in support of this argument the GCC's case-law on public warnings against youth sects and poisoned wine in the national context (finding them reviewable but justifiable): BvR 670/91 and BvR 558/91 and 1428/91, decisions of 26 June 2000).

The CFI attempted to offer a compromise solution. Choosing neither to defend fully the values of European law nor to bow unconditionally to the Security Council it offered a review on the basis of *jus cogens*. However, the CFI's *jus cogens* review combined 'the worst of both worlds'.[204] On the one hand, the CFI left the sanctions in place and the applicants without effective protection.[205] Rubber-stamping individual sanctions that fail to provide the most basic procedural rights[206] undermines the credibility of the European legal order even more than no judicial review at all. On the other hand, the CFI took on the role of judging whether Security Council resolutions comply with *jus cogens*.[207] This puts the CFI in the position of an interpreter of generally accepted legal norms, applying them to an act of an institution outside its judicial reach. An assessment of EC regulations in the light of European principles would have been in this respect a more humble approach. By reviewing Security Council resolutions on the basis of peremptory norms of international law the CFI accepted a task that the ICJ has rejected up to this point.[208] Indeed, the ICJ pointed out explicitly that the peremptory nature of norms does not as such confer on tribunals powers that they do not otherwise have.[209] The Luxembourg Court accepted being the judge of whether the Security Council complied with *jus cogens*–rules that are strongly suggested to be the limits of its competences.[210] If the CFI had reached the conclusion that the UN sanctions were incompatible with *jus cogens*, in the eyes of a considerable proportion

[204] Eeckhout, 'EC Law and UN Security Council Resolutions' (n 18 above).

[205] See for a harsh critique of UN sanctions against individuals: Dick Marty, Report of the Committee on Legal Affairs and Human Rights to the Council of Europe, Document 11454, of 16 November 2007, which was endorsed by the parliamentary assembly on 23 January 2008 in Recommendation 1824 (2008) and Resolution 1597 (2008).

[206] See Cases C-402/05 P and C-415/05 P, *Kadi and al Barakaat* (n 1 above), para 331 et seq.

[207] Case T-315/01, *Kadi* (n 1 above), para 226.

[208] The ICJ considered in the *South West Africa* case, p 3 (45), that 'the court does not possess powers of judicial review or appeal in respect to the decisions taken by the United Nations organs concerned'; see further the *Lockerbie* case; on the role of the ICJ as a Judge of the Security Council: José Alvarez, 'Judging the Security Council', *AJIL*, 90 (1996), pp 1-39; Mohammed Bedjaoui, *Nouvel ordre mondial et contrôle de la légalité des actes du Conseil de Sécurité* (Brussels: Bruylant, 1994), p 131 et seq.

[209] ICJ, Case concerning Armed Activities on the Territory of the Congo (*Democratic Republic of the Congo v Rwanda*), judgment of 3 February 2006, ICJ Reports (2006), at para 64.

[210] See above.

of scholars, this would have been a declaration that the Security Council acted ultra vires.[211]

4.1 A European Solange-*Approach*

The *Solange* approach is an alternative approach that has repeatedly been suggested to the EU courts as a way of showing deference to the Security Council while defending the human rights standards of the EU.[212] Before the ECJ the well-known 'so-long-as' argument was raised both by the appellants[213] and by the Commission;[214] only the appellants argued along the lines of *Solange I*[215] and the Commission along the lines of *Solange II*.[216] While in the former dictum the GCC essentially agreed to review every case 'so long as' the European judiciary does not provide a sufficient level of fundamental rights protection, in the latter the GCC established that 'so long as' the ECJ provided sufficient protection it would leave the review of every single case to the ECJ and maintain only a residual competence to ensure that the general standard of protection does not drop.

[211] See above all: Karl Doehring, 'Unlawful Resolutions of the Security Council and their Legal Consequences', in Jochen A Frowein and Rüdiger Wolfrum (eds), *Max Planck Yearbook of United Nations Law*, vol 1 (The Hague: Kluwer Law International, 1997), pp 104–8 and even further going: Erika de Wet and André Nollkaemper, 'Review of Security Council Decisions by National Courts', *GYIL*, 45 (2002), p 166 et seq; Jan Klabbers, *An Introduction to International Institutional Law* (Cambridge: Cambridge University Press, 2002), p 249; further on the 'constitutional limitations' of the Security Council through the purposes and principles and through the end of the measure itself: Terry Douglas Gill, 'Legal and Some Political Limitations of the Power of the UN Security Council to Exercise its Enforcement Powers under Chapter VII of the Charter', *Netherlands Yearbook of International Law*, 33 (1995), pp 73–106; Separate Opinion Lauterpacht to the ICJ in *Application of the Convention on the Prevention and Punishment of the Crime of Genocide*, p 440, para 100; Bedjaoui, *Nouvel ordre mondial* (n 208 above), p 46; Christian Tomuschat, 'Peace Enforcement and Law Enforcement: Two Separate Chapters of International Law?', in *Studi di diritto internazionale in onore di Gaetano Arangio-Ruiz* (Napoli: Editoriale Scientifica, 2004), p 1767; yet, *jus cogens* is not the only criteria which can render the exercise of power by the Security Council ultra vires, see: Hörmann, 'Völkerrecht bricht Rechtsgemeinschaft? (n 18 above), p 286 et seq.

[212] Opinion of AG Maduro, in Cases C-402/05 P and C-415/05 P, *Kadi and al Barakaat* (n 1 above), para 56; see also: Eeckhout, 'EC Law and UN Security Council Resolutions' (n 18 above), p 183 et seq.

[213] Cases C-402/05 P and C-415/05 P, *Kadi and al Barakaat* (n 1 above), para 256.

[214] ibid, para 319.

[215] GCC, *Solange I*, BVerfGE 37, 271, of 29 May 1974

[216] GCC, *Solange II*, see also: GCC, *Maastricht* decision, *Alcan* decision, *Banana* decision, available at: www.bundesverfassungsgericht.de.

Advocate-General Maduro's consideration[217] that

> [h]ad there been a genuine and effective mechanism of judicial control by an independent tribunal at the level of the United Nations, then this might have released the Community from the obligation to provide for judicial control of implementing measures that apply within the Community legal order

suggests a *Solange I* reasoning in all but terminology. It hints at the possibility of greater deference in the future if the Security Council provides for the necessary procedural protection at the UN level.

The ECJ, by contrast, did not go any further than stating:[218]

> the Community judicature must, in accordance with the powers conferred on it by the EC Treaty, ensure the review, *in principle the full review*, of the lawfulness of all Community acts in the light of the fundamental rights forming an integral part of the general principles of Community law, including review of Community measures which, like the contested regulation, are designed to give effect to the resolutions adopted by the Security Council under Chapter VII of the Charter of the United Nations.

Even if it is presumed that 'in principle' indicates the possibility of exceptions, this is the only hint of a *Solange* consideration in the ECJ's ruling. It does not however give the slightest indication when this exception from full review might come into play. In this it is very different from the elaborations of the GCC in its *Solange* rulings,[219] which did not close the door but opened a dialogue with the ECJ. Similarly the ECJ held that the examination mechanism at the UN level '*cannot* give rise to generalized immunity[220] from jurisdiction with the internal legal order'[221] This was interpreted as a categorical statement rejecting even the theoretical possibility of *Solange*.[222]

It is here argued that *not* applying *Solange* to the present situation is consistent with the *Solange rationale*. A *Solange* reasoning by the ECJ would

[217] Opinion of AG Maduro, in Cases C-402/05 P and C-415/05 P, *Kadi and al Barakaat* (n 1 above), para 54.

[218] Cases C-402/05 P and C-415/05 P, *Kadi and al Barakaat* (n 1 above), para 326 (emphasis added).

[219] GCC, *Solange II*-decision, but see also: GCC, *Maastricht* decision, and GCC, *Banana* decision (all n 193 above).

[220] The term 'immunity from jurisdiction' was also used by the Case T-315/01, *Kadi*, (n 1 above), para 288 – 'l'immunité de juridiction'. It is otherwise not used in this book because it might be misleading: commonly 'immunity' is applied to legal subjects rather than legal acts.

[221] Cases C-402/05 P and C-415/05 P, *Kadi and al Barakaat* (n 1 above), para 321 (emphasis added).

[222] Halberstam and Stein, 'The United Nations, the European Union, and the King of Sweden' (n 189 above), p 60.

have been mere window-dressing in the present context. First, the UN is far away from meeting the necessary requirements to justify a judicial deference similar to the hands-off approach of the GCC. Secondly, the UN is not built on the same political vision of the centrality of the individual. While the UN is committed to respect and promote some of the core values of the European legal order, such as human rights, it does not share the ideology that constitutes the very identity of the European legal order. Hence, the ECJ's uncompromising stand on its own judicial competence and responsibility is no more than an acknowledgement of reality.

The *Solange* criteria that the GCC applied are to some degree determined by the particularities of German constitutional law. However, looking at the original criteria can give some orientation of what is considered indispensable for a *Rechtsstaat*[223] to open its legal order to external governance without exercising full judicial control. The GCC identified the unalienable *essentialia* that form the fundaments of the German Constitution. These are the guarantee of human dignity, democracy, the rule of law, and the fact that Germany remains a Federal Republic.[224] In the later *Maastricht* decision the GCC examined more specifically whether the national law of ratification violated the complainant's right to elect members of the German Parliament (*Bundestag*) by reducing the Parliament's power below the minimum required by the principle of democracy.[225] *Solange I* was criticized for threatening the uniformity and the functioning of the European legal order, while *Solange II* was welcomed for paying more respect to the European courts. However, neither did any (lasting) harm to the process of European integration; and the underlying *rationale* of the two rulings is the same. The GCC demonstrated willingness to open the national legal order towards European law but not at the price of selling out the very core of the constitutional principles of the German

[223] See on the different concepts and elements of the rule of law in the EU Member States: Erik Wennerström, *The Rule of Law and the European Union* (Uppsala: Iustus, 2007); see also below.

[224] Art 79(3) in combination with Art 1 and 20 of the Basic Law can give some guidance on these *essentialia*. However, whether the 'unaufgebbaren, zur Verfassungsstruktur des Grundgesetzes gehörenden Essentialia' are identical to the principles protected in Art 79(3) GG has been extensively discussed (see for more details: 'Art. 24, 32 GG', in Horst Dreier (ed), *Grundgesetz Kommentar* (Commentary on the German Basic Law), vol II (Tübingen: Mohr Siebeck, 2004)).

[225] The principle of democracy is guaranteed Art 20(1) and (2) GG, enjoying special protection through Art 79(3) GG.

Basic Law. In fact, the GCC pressured the EU to a stronger commitment to these core values shared by all Member States.

The 'very foundations'[226] of the European legal order are expressed in Article 6(1) TEU. These are the values on which the Union rests and which provide a substantive constitutional foundation for the European legal order.[227] Accession to the Union is conditional on respect for these foundations (Article 49 EU) and they enjoy particular protection through Article 7 TEU. These are the principles of liberty, democracy, respect for human rights and fundamental freedoms, as well as the rule of law. These very foundations lie at the heart of the European Union's identity. Advocate-General Maduro turned to these foundations in Article 6(1) TEU when addressing the argument that Article 307 EC on rights and obligations of the EU Member States that predate the entering into force of the European Treaties could allow for derogation from European law in its entirety. However, he saw 'no basis' for an interpretation of Article 307 EC as a source of a possible derogation from the very foundations of the European Union in Article 6(1) EU. This alludes to a relationship between predating treaty obligations protected by Article 307 TEC and the foundations in Article 6(1) EU, in which the latter takes a hierarchically higher rank in the 'constitutional framework of the Community'[228] This constitutional framework appears to go beyond the framework established by the black letter law of the provisions of the European Treaties.

The ECJ picked up this thought and developed it further. In the true spirit of defending the constitutional framework of the EU the ECJ elevated these 'foundations of the Community legal order' expressed in Article 6(1) EU to a new layer of law that is hierarchically superior to the rules expressed in the Treaties.[229] These 'foundations' appear to be what forms the core of the long-established general (or fundamental) principles of Community law, but in *Kadi* and *al Barakaat* the ECJ has vested this core with a new elevated status. The Court acknowledged that Article 307 EC

[226] In *Kadi* the ECJ referred to Art 6(1) TEU in this precise way (Cases C-402/05 P and C-415/05 P, *Kadi and al Barakaat* (n 1 above), paras 303–4).

[227] See eg: Lorna Woods, 'The European Union and Human Rights, in: Raija Hanski and Markku Suksi (eds), *An Introduction to the International Protection of Human Rights: A Textbook* (Turku/Åbo: Åbo Akademi University, Institute for Human Rights, 1999), pp 283–300; Nanette Neuwahl and Allan Rosas (eds), *The European Union and Human Rights* (The Hague: Martinus Nijhoff Publishers, 1995), Antonio Cassese, Andrew Clapham, Joseph Weiler (eds), *European Union: The Human Rights Challenge*, vol I–III (Baden-Baden: Nomos, 1991).

[228] AG Maduro, in: Cases C-402/05 P and C-415/05 P, *Kadi and al Barakaat* (n 1 above), para 31.

[229] Cases C-402/05 P and C-415/05 P, *Kadi and al Barakaat* (n 1 above), para 304.

allows for a derogation from *primary law*[230] but pointed out that it 'may in no circumstances permit any challenge to the principles that form part of the very foundations of the Community legal order.'[231] Article 307 EC gives rights and obligations predating the European Treaties a special status. Their effect goes beyond the effect of international agreements in general (those concluded after the entering into force of the European Treaties). Member States are–under certain circumstances–allowed to derogate from the European Treaties in order to comply with pre-existing agreements. Hence, if these pre-existing international agreements can justify derogation from (all) Treaty provisions but not from the 'foundations of the Community legal order' these foundations appear to be hierarchically higher not only than pre-existing agreements, but also than (all the ordinary) provisions of the European Treaty.

The 'very foundations' or 'inalienable *essentialia*' of the European legal order and the legal orders of its Member States require an independent (judicial) control mechanism (which appears to have been the requirement of the *Solange* approach suggested by Advocate-General Maduro[232]) as a central element;[233] yet, judicial control is not the only one. Judicial review does not work in isolation. It is an important part of a system of checks and balances representing the rule of law; however, this system also requires other elements that have a more preventative function in eliminating the abuse of power, such as democracy and transparency. Traditional judicial review is reactive. As we have seen in the cases of *Yusuf*[234] and *Kadi*,[235] it takes a very long time until a court reaches the conclusion to annul a measure. It contributes to responsible

[230] ibid, para 301.

[231] ibid, para 304.

[232] Opinion of AG Maduro, in Cases C-402/05 P and C-415/05 P, *Kadi and al Barakaat* (n 1 above), para 54.

[233] See also: Angela Ward, 'National and EC Remedies under the EU Treaty', in: Catherine Barnard and Okeoghene Odudu (eds), *The Outer Limits of European Union Law* (Oxford: Hart Publishing, 2009), pp 329–61, at 332: 'the rights of "individuals" to effective judicial review to enforce their rights has, from the outset, formed a foundation of the constitutional matrix, justifying the enforcement of EC law over conflicting national member State laws...'.

[234] Mr Yusuf had his assets frozen for nearly five years without ever having an effective remedy at his disposal to challenge these measures. He was delisted before the ECJ reached a decision at the appellate stage (see: Case T-315/01, *Yusuf* (n 1 above)).

[235] On 3 September 2008 when the ECJ found that these freezing measures infringed the Mr Kadi's rights to fair trial and to property, his assets had been frozen for nearly seven years; and for the moment they will remain frozen (see on this latter point the discussion above) (Case T-315/01, *Kadi* (n 1 above); Cases C-402/05 P and C-415/05 P, *Kadi and al Barakaat* (n 1 above)); see also the time frame for the 'administrative review' by the Sanctions Committee until 30 June 2010 (the Committee established pursuant to Resolution 1267 (1999)) in SC Res 1822, para 25.

governance but it does not provide responsible governors at the outset. Providing judicial protection to individuals is an indispensable element of the foundations of the European Union, but it is not the only one. Today, the EU exercises in many ways the same function as a state, but it also purports to meet the same human rights standards as a state. The European legal order is founded on the assertion that 'the individual is paramount. His dignity is inviolable. His rights are inalienable'.[236]

The differences between the European legal order and the UN Charter justify the ECJ's choice *not* to take a *Solange* approach. While the EU offers a political and legal framework that can ensure the necessary legitimacy and confers on the individual a sufficiently active role to counterbalance direct interferences with the rights of individuals, the UN is set up in an entirely different manner. Traditionally, the ECJ has emphasized the direct link between the European legal order and its citizens to ensure its own normative authority.[237] Within the European legal order the ECJ has strengthened (some would argue established) this direct link by *granting* individuals rights under European law. It did not allow the Security Council to establish a similar link (and the necessary primacy) by *restricting* the rights of individuals.

In the EU the assumption of independent normative authority has required the adoption of constitutional doctrines to constrain and legitimate that authority. European constitutionalism was thus instrumental to and limited by the claim of normative authority.[238] In adopting measures that directly affect individuals the UN tried to beat the EU at its own game. However, while defending the EU's autonomy as a necessary precondition for its independent normative authority, the ECJ's position entailed a rejection of the UN's claim to such an independent normative authority.

4.2 The Constitutionalization of the UN – Work in Progress?

On a more principled level, it is questionable whether international law and in particular the UN system could and should satisfy a standard of

[236] Berlin Declaration of the European Council Summit held in Berlin on 24/25 March 2007 in celebration of the 50th anniversary of the signature of the Treaties of Rome.

[237] Most prominently in the familiar cases of Case 26/62, *van Gend* (n 51 above); Case 6/64, *Costa v ENEL* [1964] ECR 585.

[238] See also Neil Walker, 'EU Constitutionalism in the State Constitutional Tradition', *EUI Working Papers LAW*, No 2006/21, p 17 et seq, and Miguel Poiares Maduro, 'The Importance of Being Called a Constitution: Constitutional Authority and the Authority of Constitutionalism', *International Journal of Constitutional Law*, 3 (2005), pp 332–5.

protection of fundamental rights and the rule of law equivalent to the standard protected in the EU.

4.2.1 Rechtsstaatsprinzip

One element considered to be indispensable to the legitimate exercise of public power is a certain degree of compliance with the rule of law. It forms part of the constitutional foundations both of the European legal order and of the Member States. A number of definitions of 'the rule of law' exist both in international and in national law.[239] The abundance of definitions of the rule of law and the *Rechtsstaatsprinzip*[240] in national law all describe how the exercise of power must be restrained. This is not to any comparable degree part of the rule of law in international law. Even if the rule of law in international law theoretically required the same possibilities of judicial review,[241] international law does not provide them. The relationship between states and individuals is not necessarily an element of the rule of law in international law at all. Some interpret the latter to require that international law subjects act within the rules of international law that apply to all *international actors* and are the *same* for all.[242] Others introduce substantive requirements.[243] The rule of law in international law – this is accepted despite all differences – does not impose the same strict requirements as the rule of law in national law.[244] Any other understanding challenges the very existence of the rule of law in international law–even the possibility of its existence.

[239] See for a comparison: Wennerström, *The Rule of Law and the EU* (n 223 above), p 19 et seq and p 84 et seq; see also: Chapter 3, Section 1.

[240] On the different understandings of the rule of law in the EU Member States: Wennerström, *The Rule of Law and the EU* (n 223 above); for a clear legal-technical concept of the principle of legality: Jürgen Schwarze, *European Administrative Law* (London: Sweet & Maxwell, 1992), p 212; conceptually: Friedrich von Hayek, *The Road to Serfdom* (London: Routledge, 1944), p 72; see Chapter 3.

[241] Questionable: Dissenting Opinion of Judge Sir Robert Jennings, *Lockerbie* (Preliminary Objections), p 8 et seq.

[242] Arthur Watts, 'The International Rule of Law', *GYIL*, 36 (1993), p 16; Ian Brownlie, *The Rule of Law in International Affairs* (The Hague: Nijhoff, 1998), p 1.

[243] Watts, 'The International Rule of Law' (n 242 above), p 23; Martti Koskenniemi, 'The Place of Law in Collective Security', *Michigan Journal of International Law*, 17 (1995–96), p 477; Ian Brownlie, *Principles of Public International Law* (Oxford: Oxford University Press, 2003).

[244] Under national law the accepted minimum requirements appear to be: (1) a fair degree of predictability; (2) legislation which is general applicable, published, and largely prospective; (3) a basic separation of powers between the legislative, the judicial and the executive functions of government; and (4) the submission of all to the law, Richard Fallon, '"The Rule of Law" as a Concept in Constitutional Discourse', *Columbia Law Review*, 97 (1997), p 1 et seq.

The UN recognizes the value of the rule of law,[245] not only as a formal concept[246] but also as containing material elements.[247] The UN Charter makes references to substantive criteria, such as democracy and fundamental rights, and it recognizes that they are interconnected with the rule of law.[248] Human rights, democracy, and the rule of law are considered as 'interlinked and mutually reinforcing' and as belonging to 'universal and indivisible core values and principles' of the UN.[249]

Regularly, the UN calls upon its member states to strengthen the respect for the rule of law.[250] However, the UN rule of law is focused on setting standards for the legal system of states.[251] States are seen as the most important actors that are able to protect individuals through the rule of law.[252] Within the international legal system the rule of law is seen as the existence of a legal system of rules.[253] Elements of these rules are the

[245] See eg: Strengthening the rule of law, report of the Secretary-General, 5 August 2002, A/57/275; UN Secretary General (2005). In larger freedom: towards development, security and human rights for all, United Nations.; UN Secretary General (2004). The rule of law and transitional justice in conflict and post-conflict societies. S/2004/616; UN Secretary General (2002). Strengthening the rule of law, report of the secretary general. A/57/275; Strengthening the rule of law, General Assembly Resolution 51/96, 12 December 1996.

[246] 'The "Rule of Law" ... refers to a principle of government in which all persons, institutions and entities, public and private, including the state itself, are accountable to laws that are publicly promulgated, equally enforced and independently adjudicated, ... It requires as well, measures to ensure adherence to the principles of supremacy of law, equality before the law, ..., legal certainty, avoidance of arbitrariness and procedural and legal transparency.' UN Secretary General (2004), The rule of law and transitional justice in conflict and post-conflict societies. S/2004/616; 'The key elements of the Rule of Law include an independent judiciary, ... governing the conduct of the police and other security forces that are consistent with international standards.' UN Secretary General (2002), Strengthening the rule of law, report of the secretary general. A/57/275, p 3.

[247] UNGA (2005). In larger freedom: towards development, security and human rights for all: Report of the Secretary-General. A/59/2005.

[248] 2005 Resolution of the UN Human Rights Commission on democracy and the rule of law, HR Res 2005/32.

[249] UNGA (2005). World Summit Outcome. A/RES/60/1; UN Secretary General (2002). Strengthening the rule of law, report of the secretary general. A/57/275. p 9; UN General Assembly (2000). United Nations Millennium Declaration. A/RES/55/2, p 6.

[250] By way of example: para 2 of the Preamble of the Universal Declaration of Human Rights (UDHR); Millennium Declaration of 2000, A/RES/55/2.

[251] UNGA (2005). In larger freedom: towards development, security and human rights for all: Report of the Secretary-General. A/59/2005, 19.

[252] UNGA (2001). Road map towards the implementation of the United Nations Millennium Declaration: Report of the Secretary-General. A/56/326, 15.

[253] UNGA (1970). Declaration on the occasion of the 25th anniversary of the United Nations. A/RES/2627(XXV), 3.

participation of states in international fora, the existence and application of international treaties[254] and the administration of justice through the ICJ and other international courts including the ICC.[255] The UN *member states* are to respect the rule of law, while 'the rule of law among nations'[256] addressed to the UN bodies is not clearly defined. The rule of law is not applied to the UN itself. For instance, it is not named as a demand for institutional change. Further and more importantly, there is no conditionality; there are no sanctions attached to its requirements at the UN level.[257] In a constitutional system the rule of law must be applicable between those exercising power and those subject to their decisions. Imposing a hierarchy as a result of which decisions of the UN bodies directly shape the legal position of individuals requires a form of rule of law that acknowledges individuals at the UN level.

Also, the UN lacks other – albeit very controversial – elements that are thought to make a constitution.[258] Irrespective of whether we look for formal properties or for substantive properties, the UN has difficulties meeting these criteria to a sufficient degree. The former are codification, supremacy, and *pouvoir constituant.* The latter require, depending on whether we take a functionalist or a legitimist approach, the basic rules and principles that organize and limit the exercise of public power, but also offer guidelines for value choices. Formally, international law has only embryonic hierarchical elements, and *jus cogens* is thought to constitute a

[254] UNGA (2001). Road map towards the implementation of the United Nations Millennium Declaration: Report of the Secretary-General. A/56/326, 14; See also: UNGA (2003). Report of the Secretary-General on the work of the Organisation. A/58/1, 191–2; UNGA (2005). In larger freedom: towards development, security and human rights for all: Report of the Secretary-General. A/59/2005, 136.

[255] UNGA (2000). United Nations Millennium Declaration. A/RES/55/2, p 8; UNGA (2005). In larger freedom: towards development, security and human rights for all: Report of the Secretary-General. A/59/2005, 138-9; UNGA (2005). World Summit Outcome. A/RES/60/1, 134.

[256] 4th recital of the Preamble of the Declaration on Principles of International Law concerning Friendly Relations and Co-operation among States, 1970, A/RES/25/2625, 1970.

[257] Wennerström, *The Rule of Law and the EU* (n 223 above), p 23 et seq.

[258] Anne Peters, 'Global Constitutionalism in a Nutshell', in: Klaus Dicke, Stephan Hobe, Karl-Ulrich Meyn, Anne Peters, Eibe Riedel, Hans-Joachim Schütz, Christian Tietje (eds), *Weltinnenrecht, Liber amicorum Jost Delbrück* (Berlin: Duncker & Humblot, 2005). See in particular with regard to the CFI's ruling in *Kadi*: Hörmann, 'Völkerrecht bricht Rechtsgemeinschaft? (n 18 above); Tomuschat, 'Case law: Case T-306/01, Ahmed Ali Yusuf and Al Barakaat International Foundation v Council and Commission' (n 17 above), p 537.

body of norms superior to the UN Charter.[259] More importantly, on substance, the UN Charter does not codify enough of what is important and basic in international law.[260] A more detailed analysis of the UN Charter's constitutional character would go beyond the scope of this discussion. It suffices to say that a lot of what would have to be covered is missing and there is a lot of constitutional substance outside of the Charter. And, the UN hardly satisfies the basic values of democracy, the rule of law, and the separation of powers.[261] On a more practical note, individual sanctions exemplify the difficulty of regarding the Security Council's authority under the UN Charter as absolute. It allows an international political body to declare individual persons lawless in disregard of well-established legal principles.

4.2.2 Limits of Actions by the Security Council

One objective of the rule of law is defining and imposing limits on the exercise of public power. A detailed discussion of whether the Security Council acted ultra vires in adopting sanctions against individuals is not the aim of this book. It suffices to say that there are no undisputed or even widely agreed substantive limits restraining the Security Council to do whatever it considers necessary or opportune. Having the power to determine what constitutes a threat to peace, the Security Council can certainly do what member states cannot when acting alone.[262] It is not *directly* bound by the large number of widely ratified human rights treaties, irrespective of whether those treaties are ratified by (all) permanent members of the Security Council and independently from the reservations made. They are not imported into the Charter by Article 1(3) UNC[263] or Articles 55 and 56 UNC.[264] It remains contested whether the Security Council is actually bound by international human rights law at all.[265]

[259] Robert Uerpmann, 'Internationales Verfassungsrecht', *Juristen-Zeitung*, 56 (2001), 565 (571–2); see also: ICJ, *Application of the Convention on the Prevention and Punishment of the Crime of Genocide, Separate Opinion Lauterpacht*, ICJ Reports (1993), 4, pp 325, 440, para 100; 95 ILR, pp 43, 158 stating that Art 103 UN Charter ranks below *jus cogens* and would have to give way in the event of conflict. [260] Peters, 'Global Constitutionalism in a Nutshell' (n 258 above).

[261] See also below the discussion of on the *Rechtsstaatsprinzip*.

[262] Compare the discussion at: Alvarez, 'The Security Council's War on Terrorism' (n 37 above), p 124.

[263] Agreeing: Alvarez, 'The Security Council's War on Terrorism' (n 37 above), p 125.

[264] Robert Jennings and Arthur Watts (eds), *Oppenheim's International Law*, vol I: *Peace: Introduction and Part 1* (London: Longman, 1992), p 989.

[265] Irene Couzigou, 'La lutte du Conseil de Sécurité contre le terrorisme international et les droits de l'homme', *Revue Générale de Droit International Public* (2008), pp 49–84.

Having said that, a consensus in doctrine appears to have emerged that the Security Council does not have absolute powers.[266] Many possible restraints have been identified. Within the legal framework of the Charter, Articles 24(2) jointly with 1(1)[267] and 1(3)[268] UNC have been used as a basis to argue that the Security Council is indeed bound by principles of justice and international law and by human rights and fundamental freedoms. Additionally, more open legal principles,[269] such as good faith[270] and proportionality,[271] have been identified as restraining the Security Council. Finally, beyond the framework of the Charter, a number of restrictions under general international law have figured in the discussion, ie general customary law or *jus cogens*.[272] In this regard, it has been pointed out that 'the hierarchy of norms that has emerged within the international legal order in the form of peremptory norms or *jus cogens*, predominantly concerns human rights norms'.[273] The difficulty with any of these limits is

[266] David Schweigmann, *The Authority of the Security Council under Chapter VII of the UN Charter: Legal Limits and the Role of the International Court of Justice* (Berlin: Springer, 2001), p 163 et seq; Doehring, 'Unlawful Resolutions of the Security Council' (n 211 above), p 92; Cannizzaro, 'Machiavelli, the UN Security Council and the Rule of Law' (n 147 above); Bernhardt, 'Article 103' (n 43 above), at 23; Krisch and Frowein, 'Chapter VII' (n 45 above), p 705 et seq, speak of humanitarian law and human rights norms as forming 'guidelines,' rather than 'precise limits'; see also: Dissenting Opinion of President Schwebel, *Lockerbie* (Preliminary Objections), p 8.

[267] Geoffrey R Watson, 'Constitutionalism, Judicial Review, and the World Court', *Harvard International Law Journal*, 34 (1993), pp 1–45 (4).

[268] De Wet and Nollkaemper, 'Review of Security Council Decisions by National Courts' (n 211 above), p 166 et seq.

[269] Problems persist in that particularly the open legal concepts would require judicial interpretation to be able to play a meaningful power-limiting role in practice, and that some of the identified limits set a standard that is too low to provide a yardstick for effective protection; Cannizzaro, 'Machiavelli, the UN Security Council and the Rule of Law' (n 147 above), defending a decentralized system of control in domestic courts.

[270] ibid.

[271] Michael Bothe, 'Les limites des pouvoirs du Conseil de Sécurité' in: Rene-Jean Dupuy (ed), *Le Dévelopement de la rôle du Conseil de Sécurité* (Dordrecht: Martin Nijhoff Publishers, 1993), p 67 et seq, on p 78; doubtful that the principle of proportionality amounts to a general principle of public international law: Rosalyn Higgins, *Problems & Process: International Law and How we Use it* (Oxford: Clarendon Press, 1994), p 236 et seq.

[272] Case T-315/01, *Kadi* (n 1 above); set aside by Case C-402/05 P and C-415/05 P, *Kadi and al Barakaat* (n 1 above).

[273] Erika de Wet, 'The International Constitutional Order', *International and Comparative Law Quarterly*, 55 (2006), p 58.

that the lack of any effective remedy against the Security Council does not allow anyone to enforce these constraints at the UN level.[274]

Furthermore, the UN Charter does not provide for other mechanisms of checks and balances; the UN was set up as a practical forum to control the use of armed forces outside of all judicial scrutiny.[275] The only form of control mechanism is the veto in the hands of the victorious states,[276] and it remains controversial whether 'unlawful' UN resolutions–this is resolutions that are contrary to the UN Charter–have binding force on the member states.[277] Hence, even though the Security Council does not have absolute powers, in practice limits are nearly impossible to define and enforce.

4.2.3 Effectiveness[278]

Giving Security Council resolutions primacy over domestic law is, however, well in line with the recent developments of international law, in the same way as supremacy and direct effect complement each other. International law becomes more like national law in that it directly governs the legal sphere of individuals.[279] Individuals increasingly derive rights and

[274] Even the question of whether the ICJ, as the principal judicial organ of the United Nations, can review the legality of Security Council resolutions is highly contentious: separate Opinion of Judge Rezek, the Dissenting Opinion of Judge Schwebel, and the Dissenting Opinion of Judge Jennings in *Lockerbie* (Preliminary Objections). The same question was also addressed, albeit in less detail, in Dissenting Opinion of Judge Weeramantry, at p 155, and the Dissenting Opinion of Judge Skubiszewski, at p 251, two dissenting opinions to the Judgment of 30 June 1995 in the case concerning East Timor; Bernd Martenczuk, 'The Security Council, the International Court and Judicial Review: What Lessons to Learn from Lockerbie?', *EJIL*, 10 (1999), pp 517–47; Cannizzaro, 'Machiavelli, the UN Security Council and the Rule of Law' (n 147 above), p 12. Some considered such a prospect even straight-away harmful: Michael Reisman, 'The Constitutional Crisis in the United Nations', *AJIL*, 87 (1993), p 94.

[275] Cannizzaro, 'Machiavelli, the UN Security Council and the Rule of Law' (n 147 above), p 10.

[276] Reisman, 'The Constitutional Crisis in the United Nations' (n 274 above), p 95; ibid, p 10.

[277] Barbara Lorinser, *Bindende Resolutionen des Sicherheitsrates* (Baden-Baden: Nomos, 1996), p 126 et seq; Theodor Schilling, 'Die 'neue Weltordnung' und die Souveränität der Mitglieder der Vereinten Nationen', *AVR* (1995), p 101.

[278] See Chapter 1, Section 7 on the effectiveness of individual sanctions as a counter-terrorist policy.

[279] See for the growing importance of individuals as addressees in international law already before the adoption of individual sanctions: Thomas Franck, *The Empowered Self: Law and Society in the Age of Individualism* (New York: Oxford University Press, 1999); Thomas Franck, 'Individuals and Groups of Individuals as Subjects in International Law', p 97 et seq. and Stephan Hobe, 'Individuals and Groups as Global Actors', p 115 et seq, both in: Rainer Hofmann and Nils Geissler (eds), *Non-State Actors as New Subjects of International Law* (Berlin: Duncker & Humblot, 1999); Anne-Marie Slaughter, 'Rogue Regimes and the Individualization of International Law', *New England Law Review*, 36 (2002), p 818; Theodor Meron, *The Humanization of International Law* (Leiden: Brill Publishers, 2006), p 353.

obligations directly from international law without need for national implementation.[280] Correspondingly, national law becomes more porous. National courts recognize international rules as part of the national legal order[281] and allow individuals to directly rely on them. At the same time, the CFI's reasoning in *Yusuf* and *Kadi* is based on the recognition that international law making has a growing significance for matters of security.

To confer primacy on UN lists of terrorist suspects, which are an example of international law creating direct links to individuals, strengthens the impact of Security Council resolutions within the internal European legal sphere, just as supremacy of European law vests direct effect with force. As a result, UN sanctions are placed at a hierarchically superior place, excluding all forms of judicial review. By the medium of unreviewable European law, UN sanctions are indirectly vested with the specific features of European law, such as direct applicability and supremacy over national law.[282] They become directly binding within the legal orders of the Member States.[283] Prima facie this strengthens international law since, as the law stands, most states do not accord primacy to international rules in their national legal system.[284] The

[280] Examples for this development in the UN are the establishment of two International Criminal Tribunals for the Former Yugoslavia and Rwanda (SC Res 827 of 25 May 1993), allowing for the prosecution of individuals directly under international law, as well as individual sanctions themselves. Further, the creation of the International Criminal Court (ICC) shows such a trend in international law in general. Further: Elisabeth van Sliedregt, *The International Responsibility of Individuals for Violations of International Humanitarian Law* (The Hague: TMC Asser Press, 2003); Cassese, *International Law* (n 194 above), p 234 et seq.

[281] See eg House of Lords, *Al-Jedda* (n 7 above).

[282] Security Council resolutions are normally considered neither self-executing nor directly applicable: Eric Stein, 'Application and Enforcement of International Organization Law by National Authorities and Courts', in Stephen Schwebel (ed), *The Effectiveness of International Decisions* (Leyden: Sijthoff, 1971), p 68; Vera Gowlland-Debbas, 'Comments', in Harry Post (ed), *International Economic Law and Armed Conflict* (Dordrecht: Nijhoff, 1994), p 165; Riccardo Pavoni, 'UN Sanctions in EU and National Law: The Centro Com Case', *ICLQ*, 48 (1999), pp 582–612.

[283] See already the decision of a German administrative court (*VG Ansbach*, n 203 above, para 83 et seq) on the repeal of the applicant's status as asylum seeker because he was supporting the PKK, which was also listed on an autonomous European terrorist list. The German court referred the CFI's judgment in Case T-301/01, *Yusuf* (n 1 above), declared the interpretation of the UNHCR of Art 1 F (c) of the Geneva Convention on the Status of Refugees as incompatible with this decision (para 86) and indirectly extended the overriding force of Security Council resolutions to the listing decisions of the Council taken in order to implement Resolutions 1373. This is particularly interesting given the reference in Art 63(1) TEU.

[284] The Monitoring Team asks the UN member states to implement sanctions automatically in administrative procedures: Third report of the Monitoring Team, of 9 September 2005, S/2005/572, pp 15–16; see also: Steven Dewulf and Didier Pacquée, 'Protecting Human Rights in the War on Terror: Challenging the Sanctions Regime Originating from Res 1267 (1999)', *Netherlands Quarterly of Human Rights*, 24/4 (2006), p 613 et seq.

conferral of primacy on Security Council resolutions is not 'common to the constitutional traditions' of the Member States.[285]

It is true that an(y other) interpretation, which denies Security Council resolutions primacy over other forms of law, could amount to a threat to its effective implementation. The purposive interpretation based on an argument of effectiveness of European Law in *van Gend and Loos*[286] and *Costa v ENEL*[287] could be transferred to Security Council resolutions. On a theoretical level this is true for all international agreements: primacy and direct effect render them prima facie more effective. However, even the argument of increased effectiveness stretches only so far.[288] The effectiveness of the cooperation at the UN level depends on the goodwill of the parties involved.[289]Security Council resolutions lose their legitimacy if they oblige Member States to continuously infringe fundamental rights guarantees. This is reflected in the ruling of the ECJ in *Kadi* and *al Barakaat*, in few national proceedings in which courts have annulled national measures implementing UN sanctions for infringing national law,[290] but also to some extent in the lack of compliance with the UN sanctions regime against individuals.[291]

Admittedly, international law is not only complied with because of its moral value, but also because of utilitarian aspects[292] in that compliance

[285] See the discussion on judicial protection in national courts Section 5.2 below.

[286] Case 26/62, *van Gend* (n 51 above).

[287] Case 6/64, *Costa* (n 237 above).

[288] The ECJ was well aware of its dependency of member state support; the Court introduced both direct effect and supremacy in a gradual manner. See below the conditional acceptance of supremacy of European law by the Member States' courts.

[289] Security Council resolutions depend on their high legitimacy in the UN member states' view: Hilding Eek, Ove Bring and Lars Hjerners, *Folkrätten* (Stockholm: Norstedts, 1987), p 120; advocating a managerial model of compliance: Abram Chayes and Antonia Handler Chayes, *The New Sovereignty: Compliance with International Regulatory Agreements* (Cambridge, MA: Harvard University Press, 1996); Thomas Franck, *The Power of Legitimacy Among Nations*, (New York: Oxford University Press, 1990) and Thomas Franck, *Fairness in International Law and Institutions* (Oxford: Clarendon Press, 1995), see in particular the theoretical analysis on pp 7–46; Andrea Bianchi, 'Assessing the Effectiveness of the UN Security Council's Anti-terrorism Measures: The Quest for Legitimacy and Cohesion', *EJIL*, 17 (2007), pointing out the lack of political support.

[290] See below; ie: Luxembourg released funds after a court challenge of its freezing measures, because of insufficient intelligence information provided to justify the freeze (Second Report of the Monitoring Group established pursuant to Security Council resolution 1363 (2001) and 1390 (2002), UN Doc S/2002/1050 (2002), para 39)

[291] Reports of the 1267 Monitoring Team, S/2005/572, para 37; see also Chapter 1, Section 3.

[292] Franck, *Fairness in International Law* (n 289 above); Franck, *The Power of Legitimacy* (n 289 above).

serves the interest of the states.[293] This is in principle also the case for individual sanctions. Much weaker political and economic deterrents keep states from adopting individual sanctions than from adopting state sanctions. At the same time, the actual impact of individual sanctions on the financing of terrorism is highly disputed.[294] What is in the interest of the adopting state is the political symbolic value of individual sanctions;[295] this however depends not only on the trustworthiness of the adoption procedure,[296] but also their political acceptance at home. Where measures routinely infringe domestic fundamental rights standards, political opposition can be expected.

Further, the implications of the CFI's understanding of the relationship between the European legal order and the UN Charter excludes judicial review of implementation measures on the basis of domestic standards, but that at the same time each and every court could declare Security Council resolutions contrary to *jus cogens.* The undermining effect for the UN system could definitely not be greater if a domestic court declared the national implementation measures contrary to national constitutional standards. The latter would only oblige the national authorities to find a way to comply with the Security Council resolutions without breaching national fundamental rights guarantees. It would not free the state from complying with its UN Charter obligations; this however could arguably be the case if a Security Council resolution was found to be contrary to *jus cogens.*

[293] This is admittedly a 'realist argument', see eg: Jack Goldsmith and Eric Posner, *The Limits of International Law* (New York: Oxford University Press, 2005), p 10 et seq.

[294] See in particular: House of Lords, Select Committee on Economic Affairs, 2nd Report of Session 2006–07, 'The Impact of Economic Sanctions', Vol I: Report, published 9 May 2007: '"Targeted" financial sanctions have been relatively ineffective. They have often been imposed on people and entities selected on non-transparent or dubious grounds.' Iain Cameron, 'The European Convention on Human Rights: Due Process and United Nations Security Council Counter-Terrorism Sanctions', Report to the Council of Europe, of 6 February 2006, http://www.coe.int/, p 11, with reference to the: National Commission on Terrorist Attacks on the United States, 'The 9/11 Commission Report', http://www.9-11commission.gov/report/911Report.pdf, p 382 and the report of the Sanction Committee in 2004, S/2004/1039, and the reports of the Monitoring Team, S/2005/572 and S/2005/761; contrary to this: Dewulf and Pacquée, 'Protecting Human Rights in the War on Terror' (n 284 above), p 608, generally speak of 'the great value this list has proven to be'. Obviously, the effectiveness depends on the definition of the objective of individual sanctions; see Chapter 3.

[295] Peter Fitzgerald, 'Compliance Issues Associated with Targeted Economic Sanctions', in House of Lords, Select Committee on Economic Affairs, 2nd Report of Session 2006–07, 'The Impact of Economic Sanctions', Vol II: Evidence (2007), p 149.

[296] See Chapter 1, Section 1 for the difficulties attached to identifying terrorist suspects.

4.2.4 Primacy

The CFI referred to the status of Security Council resolutions in terms of traditional European law concepts[297] by purporting that they take 'primacy' over any other form of law.[298] The references[299] to *Internationale Handelsgesellschaft*,[300] *Keller*,[301] and *Dow Chemical Ibérica*[302] demonstrate that the CFI thought within the parameters of European law. In all these cases the ECJ dealt with the issue of whether acts of the *EC institutions* could be evaluated in the light of *national constitutions*. The ECJ answered that question in the negative, stating that 'the validity of measures adopted by the institutions of the Community can only be judged in the light of Community law'[303] This concept of primacy is an exceptionally strong constitutional term of European law. Besides direct effect, primacy is what distinguishes European law from international law, and already the transfer of the concept of primacy to the Union pillars is controversial because their nature seems closer to international law.[304]

However, it must be conceded that some arguments that led the ECJ to find European law supreme to national law can be transferred to the UN. In the well-known decision of *Costa* the ECJ established[305] the supremacy of Community law because the Community was created for an

> unlimited duration, having its own institutions, its own personality, its own legal capacity and capacity of representation on the international plane and, more particularly, real powers stemming from a limitation of sovereignty or a transfer of powers from the States to the Community.

All these points are also true for the UN.[306]

At the same time, there are even stronger arguments against the primacy of Security Council resolutions and in particular against the CFI's competence to introduce it. First, at a substantive level, *Costa* built on the

[297] Damian Chalmers, Christos Hadjiemmanuil, Giorgio Monti and Adam Tomkins, *European Union Law* (Cambridge: Cambridge University Press, 2006), pp 46–7 and 196–209.

[298] Case T-306/01, *Yusuf* (n 1 above), paras 131–4.

[299] Case T-315/01, *Kadi* (n 1 above), para 224 and Case T-306/01, *Yusuf* (n 1 above), para 275.

[300] Case 11/70, *Internationale Handelsgesellschaft* [1970] ECR 1125, para 3

[301] Case 234/85, *Keller* [1986] ECR 2897, para 7.

[302] Joined Cases 97/87 to 99/87, *Dow Chemical Ibérica and Others v Commission* [1989] ECR 3165, para 38.

[303] Case 11/70, *Internationale Handelsgesellschaft* (n 300 above), para 3.

[304] Christiaan Timmermans, *The Constitutionalization of the European Union*, 31 Yearbook of European Law (2001–02), pp 9–11.

[305] Case 6/64, *Costa* (n 237 above).

[306] See for a comparative introduction to both UN and EU law: Göran Lysén, *Att Studera Folkrätt och EG/EU* (Uppsala: Iustus, 2005).

reasoning in *van Gend*,[307] in which the ECJ emphasized that Community law is not like conventional international law in that it recognizes private parties as subjects, who have rights and can enforce them. Even if the view can be held that the rights of individuals and their capacity to enforce them depend less on the text of the Treaties, but on the interpretation of the ECJ,[308] these rights were part of the Community legal order (as interpreted by the ECJ) at the time its supremacy was 'found'.[309] In the institutional structure of the UN, on the other hand, individuals are objects only;[310] they have no say and no mechanism of judicial recourse. Secondly, the EU courts are not in the position to control the exercise of power within the UN system. Some national courts arguably accepted the ECJ's view of European Law as a new and supreme legal order only because the ECJ accommodated their queries for fundamental rights protection.[311] However, the EU courts have effective means at their disposal to regiment the EU Member States, including their courts. Today, it is prima facie even accepted within the European legal order that the CFI has the power to vest Security Council resolutions with primacy.[312] At the UN level, EU courts do not possess any power to assure respect for fundamental rights; they could only use their influence on the EU Member States to urge them to take a specific action within the UN system.

4.3 A Compromise on Substance rather than Forum

A *Solange* approach implies the quest for a hierarchy, asking essentially who has the last word. It is submitted that this is not the right question with regard to the relationship between the UN and the EU. The two organizations serve very different purposes. Additionally, the Security Council has a particular function within the UN. Placing European law and Security Council resolutions in a formal or systemic hierarchical relationship with each other means disregarding these differences and the particular role of the Security Council. It appears helpful to distinguish between

[307] Case 26/62, *van Gend* (n 51 above).

[308] Chalmers et al, *European Union Law* (n 297 above), p 50.

[309] See under the title of 'What makes the European Union different', ibid, p 45 et seq.

[310] This is the traditional position of international law: Georg Schwarzenberger, *International Law as Applied by International Courts and Tribunals*, vol II, *The Law of Armed Conflict* (London: Stevens, 1968), p 62.

[311] Most famously the GCC, see the *Solange* case-law (nn 215, 216 above).

[312] See the reception of the CFI's ruling in *Kadi* in the UK courts and in Germany: *M v HM Treasury* and VG Ansbach (both n 203 above).

a formal or systemic hierarchy of institutions, and a hierarchy of substantive values.

In contrast to the CFI, the ECJ did not establish in *Kadi* and *al Barakaat* a formal hierarchical order, in which authorship of a norm determines its status. The fact that the Security Council has endorsed certain obligations does not give them automatically a higher rank than the European Treaties agreed by the Member States. On the contrary, the ECJ granted a special status to the foundations of the Community legal order based on their content and not on the status of their author. The ECJ demonstrated that it has a fundamentally different vision of the European legal order and the 'international legal order'.[313] If we accept this difference, the ECJ could be seen as contributing to rather than undermining the emergence of a shared value system under international law, enforced by decentralized institutions competing on the basis of legal argument rather than formal status.

With regard to standards that could be required from the UN, it should be recalled that it was possible to set up a sanctions regime at the UN level that does not offer any effective protection to those listed as terrorist suspects.[314] This allows for conclusions not only about the sanctions regime in particular but also about the functioning of the UN more in general. However, it is acknowledged that different functions can justify different standards. The required standard of human rights protection and compliance with the rule of law is directly interlinked with the type of normative authority exercised. Normative acts that directly impact on the rights of individuals–without involving any intermediate action or with compulsory and meticulously predetermined implementation, as is the case for sanctions against individuals–require that the affected individuals are given an active role. The limited normative authority traditionally exercised by international organizations is one of the moral justifications underpinning the acknowledgement that it would be an 'unrealistic view' to require from international organizations the

[313] A term used by AG Maduro, in: Cases C-402/05 P and C-415/05 P, *Kadi and al Barakaat* (n 1 above), creating an image of international law as being tidy and organized – similar to domestic legal orders.

[314] Similarly, the EU adopted sanctions against individuals without offering the necessary legal safeguards; however, cases like Cases C-402/05 P and C-415/05 P, *Kadi and al Barakaat* (n 1 above) and the *OMPI* cases (Case T-228/02, *Organisation des Modjahedines du peuple d'Iran v Council and UK (OMPI I)* [2006] ECR II-4665; Case T-256/07, *People's Mojahidin Organization of Iran v Council (OMPI II)*, judgment of 23 October 2008, not yet reported; appeal pending: Case C-576/08 P, *People's Mojahedin Organization of Iran* and Case T-284/08, *People's Mojahedin Organization of Iran v Council (OMPI III)*, judgment of 4 December 2008) demonstrate that at the EU level there are mechanisms of protection in place.

same standards of fundamental rights protection and democracy that are applied to states.[315] Inspirational for the standard required from international organizations is the 'complex standard of legitimacy' developed by Allen Buchanan and Robert Keohane.[316] They start from the presumption that compliance with human rights is an inherent factor of legitimacy. One of the three substantive requirements of the legitimacy of 'global governance institutions'[317] is not to violate persistently the least controversial human rights. However, in view of the CFI's decision in *Kadi* it should be noted that these 'least controversial human rights' cannot be *jus cogens*, which by its historical development and content does not serve this function.

There is a convincing argument that the Security Council does not have to meet the same standards that are required from states committed to the rule of law. Yet on this basis, it remains questionable (to say the least) whether the UN could then claim the necessary normative authority to list individuals as terrorist suspects in instruments that are supreme to domestic law as European law is to national law. This means to adopt acts that impose measures and set norms that apply for an indefinite period of time (and hence normality as opposed to emergency situations), and which directly impact on the rights of individuals.

On the contrary, it is argued that the Security Council takes a specific function within the UN and that this function is not to pass normative acts that directly determine the rights of individuals for an indefinite period of time. The two main bodies within the UN system are the General Assembly and the Security Council. While the former places all member states on an equal footing the power division in the Security Council is intended to reflect power rather than (democratic) representation. It serves the very important but limited function of maintaining international peace and security. The Security Council is meant to react to crisis and has therefore a form of emergency powers. Emergency situations however are characterized by the fact that human rights can be restricted further than under ordinary circumstances for a limited period of time and that decisions can be taken without the time delays of democratic decision-making. Measures like the sanctions imposed on Mr Kadi, which stand in blatant

[315] Allen Buchanan and Robert O Keohane, 'The Legitimacy of Global Governance Institutions', *Ethics and International Affairs*, 20/4 (2006), p 406. [316] ibid.

[317] The criterion itself is 'minimal moral acceptability'; the other two are 'comparative benefit' (performance of the functions invoked to justify the institution's existence) and 'institutional integrity' (coherence between the actual performance and major goals of the institution), ibid, p 419 et seq.

contrast to the human rights promoted by the UN, seem to demonstrate that the Security Council is ill-equipped to determine directly the legal position of individuals and that adopting these measures is a claim of normative authority that goes in many ways beyond the role and function of the Security Council. This cannot be healed by introducing a review mechanism alone.

By way of conclusion, the ECJ was right in rejecting a *Solange* approach to UN sanctions lists. The UN system, even though it has improved the rights of individuals within the listing procedure and granted them a more active role, is far from providing a framework that would justify the EU courts refraining from exercising their review powers. More importantly, it has a different objective and is based on a different conceptual understanding of what the position of the individual should be. The ECJ indicated that it is willing to take the role of finding a balance on substance.

Hence, while there is no room for a *Solange* dialogue with the UN, the ECJ was obliged to provide for judicial control of implementing measures that apply within its own legal order because of the absence of a constitutionalized international legal order.

5. The European Legal Order in Context

5.1 The Strasbourg Court

Even though the case-law of the ECtHR is not binding on the EU courts it is an influential source of inspiration for the EU courts.[318] The protection available to the individual in the ECtHR from European sanctions giving effect to UN lists of terrorist suspects depends on the Court's view of the relationship between the Convention and Community law on the one hand and the Convention and the UN Charter on the other. While the ECtHR has demonstrated great deference to the EU courts, it has largely avoided taking a clear stand on the UN Charter.

5.1.1 Protection from Community Law

In the case of *Bosphorus*[319] the ECtHR seized the occasion to clarify whether and under which conditions it would provide protection from fundamental rights violations by Community law. However, *Bosphorus* did not concern individual sanctions, but a national measure implementing Community

[318] See Chapter 3, Section 3.

[319] ECtHR, *Bosphorus* (n 5 above).

sanctions against the Federal Republic of Yugoslavia (FRY), which in turn were adopted in order to comply with a UN sanctions regime.

The Strasbourg Court was asked to declare that the seizure by Ireland of an airplane leased by the Turkish applicant from a Yugoslavian company breached the applicant's right to property;[320] however, the Court held unanimously that there was no violation of the ECHR.[321] The national measure was adopted in order to comply with an EC regulation,[322] which in turn implemented the UN sanctions regime[323] against the FRY. Earlier, the European law obligation had been confirmed by an ECJ decision,[324] which was consequently also subject to the ECtHR's review. The Strasbourg Court accepted that European law compelled the Irish authorities to impound the applicant's aircraft and that the national authorities did not exercise any discretion.

The ECtHR introduced a strict line of deference to the EU courts in the area of Community law.[325] First it established a presumption that fundamental rights in the Community are protected at a standard equivalent to the one in the ECHR. It then concluded that any act taken in order to comply with obligations from a membership of an international organization, which benefited from such a general presumption of equivalent protection, was presumed *not* to have violated the Convention. Here, the Court would not exercise full jurisdiction, but limit its examination to the question of whether the general presumption can be rebutted in the case at hand. In essence, the applicant would have to show either that a systemic procedural dysfunction within the legal system of the international organization occurred,[326] or that the protection was 'manifestly deficient' in the particular case.[327] The latter

[320] Article 1 of Protocol No 1 to the Convention.

[321] Ten of the 17 judges sitting in the Grand Chamber signed on to the majority opinion and seven submitted concurring opinions.

[322] EC Council Regulation 990/93, *OJ* 1993 L102/4.

[323] Set up by SC Res 820 (1993).

[324] ECtHR, *Bosphorus* (n 5 above).

[325] ECtHR, *Bosphorus* (n 5 above), in particular: para 159 et seq.

[326] The Court establishes its presumption on the basis of a long examination of the judicial system of the Community (ECtHR, *Bosphorus*, ibid, paras 72–101). In spite of the fact that the discussion of a possible rebuttal focuses on the individual case, it must be possible to prove the entire presumption as no longer correct. The ECtHR even conceded that 'any such finding of equivalence could not be final and would be susceptible to review in the light of any relevant change in fundamental rights' protection' (ECtHR, *Bosphorus*, ibid, para 155).

[327] The ECtHR explained that 'any such presumption can be rebutted if, in the circumstances of *a particular case*, it is considered that the protection of Convention rights was *manifestly deficient*.' (ECtHR, *Bosphorus*, ibid, para 156, emphasis added).

question would be answered in the positive only if the organization failed to provide the remedies that are obviously required by the Convention. In cases where the applicant can demonstrate that one of the two conditions is satisfied the ECtHR will exercise full review. Hence, the Court introduced a high threshold for full examination of alleged violations induced by Community law. In *Bosphorus* itself the ECtHR refrained from conducting any convincing review on the merits. By means of the described presumption it accepted compliance with Community obligations as an overriding interest, which justified comprehensively any measures taken by the Contracting Parties. Prima facie, this is the case irrespective of the impact of these implementation measures on the applicant's fundamental rights.

Even though *Bosphorus* did not concern *individual* sanctions, it is relevant for the judicial protection for those targeted by individual sanctions. The presumption of equivalent protection applies to all Community law, including restrictive measures against individuals. After *Bosphorus* the protection of individuals from Community measures in Strasbourg is reduced to an examination of whether the general presumption of equivalent protection can be rebutted in the specific case. This offers a far lower protection than the usual examination of whether the Convention rights of the applicant are breached. Consequently, protection offered by the ECtHR from Community law is reduced to grave violations; it does not cover all infringements of Convention rights.[328] The ECtHR, in the words of Advocate-General Mengozzi, provides a 'marginal' review from Community law only.[329]

5.1.2 *Primacy of Security Council Resolutions*

Up to this point the ECtHR has not taken an explicit position on the hierarchy between Security Council resolutions and the ECHR. However, the Court came particularly close to pronouncing its view on the status of Security Council decisions in 2005 in the case of *Bosphorus*[330] and in 2007 in the joined cases of *Behrami* and *Saramati*.[331]

[328] See for more detail: Christina Eckes, 'Does the European Court of Human Rights Provide Protection from the European Community? The Case of Bosphorus Airways', *European Public Law*, 13 (2007), p 47 et seq.

[329] AG Mengozzi, in C-355/04 P, *Segi v Council* [2007] ECR I-1657, para 86.

[330] ECtHR, *Bosphorus* (n 5 above).

[331] ECtHR, *Behrami* and *Saramati*, (n 6 above). For a discussion on the cases see, Aurel Sari, 'Jurisdiction and International Responsibility in Peace Support Operations: The *Behrami* and *Saramati* Cases', *Human Rights Law Review*, 8(1) 2008, 151–70.

In the latter cases the ECtHR was asked to rule on alleged violations of the Convention resulting from acts and omissions under a UN Security Council mandate. This case has stirred up a great deal of controversy on the Court's understanding of the relationship between the European Convention and Security Council resolutions. *Behrami* and *Saramati* concerned events that arose from the UN peace-keeping mission in Kosovo. In these cases the ECtHR attributed to the UN both the omission by UNMIK[332] to clear a cluster bomb that led to the death and injury of two children (*Behrami*) and the detention of Mr Saramati by the Kosovo Force (KFOR).

In *Behrami* and *Saramati* the ECtHR ruled with regard to the military operations in Kosovo that:[333]

> the Convention cannot be interpreted in a manner which would subject the acts and omissions of Contracting Parties which are covered by UNSC Resolutions and occur prior to or in the course of such missions, to the scrutiny of the Court…It would also be tantamount to imposing conditions on the implementation of a UNSC Resolution which were not provided for in the text of the Resolution itself.

In isolation this passage of *Behrami* and *Saramati* reads as if the ECtHR sweepingly accepted that any acts of the Contracting Parties implementing Security Council resolutions adopted under Chapter VII will be exempted from judicial control in Strasbourg.[334] However, for two reasons it would be wrong to read *Behrami* and *Saramati* as establishing that Security Council resolutions simply absolve Member States from their obligations under the Convention.

First, in *Behrami* the ECtHR did not rule on the relationship between the Charter and the Convention, but found itself incompetent *ratio personae* because the acts and omissions were attributable to the UN.[335] It did not actually address the submissions of the third parties that Article 103 UN Charter vests the Security Council with the authority to make binding decisions that prevail over other international obligations including the Convention.[336] This limits the authority of *Behrami* considerably on this matter.

[332] UN interim administration for Kosovo.

[333] ECtHR, *Behrami* and *Saramati* (n 6 above), para 149.

[334] Indeed, this appears to have been Lord Bingham's reading when he cited this passage in *Al-Jedda* (n 7 above), para 36.

[335] Critical on this point: Sari 'Jurisdiction and International Responsiblity' (n 331 above), pp 151–70.

[336] ECtHR, *Behrami* and *Saramati* (n 6 above), paras 97 (Denmark), 102 (Estonia), 106 (Germany), 113 (UK). The Court mentioned Art 103 UNC only once and in passing, para 147.

Secondly, the Court's position in *Behrami* should be – and was[337] – contrasted with the case of *Bosphorus.*[338] *Bosphorus* also concerned the implementation of a Security Council resolution.[339] Here however, the ECtHR avoided all discussion of the Security Council resolution[340] by hiding behind the existence of a Community regulation that had been adopted to implement the Security Council resolution and that had been interpreted by the ECJ to apply to the contested act.[341] As a consequence, the ECtHR did not mention Article 103 UNC in *Bosphorus* at all. According to the parameters of the UN Charter, Security Council resolutions claim primacy over all other international treaty obligations, including the ECHR. On the basis of this reading the ECtHR could not have examined Ireland's actions in *Bosphorus* any further. The underlying Security Council resolution would have worked as a 'joker' justifying all measures of implementation, notwithstanding opposed Convention rights. However, by reviewing Ireland's non-discretionary implementation of a Community regulation putting into effect UN sanctions the ECtHR indirectly took a stance on the hierarchy of norms. It made clear that it will scrutinize the actions of the Contracting Parties as to their compatibility with the Convention, notwithstanding the fact that they were non-discretionary measures implementing UN Charter obligations. Here, it is useful to point out that in *Bosphorus* Ireland did not have any margin of discretion in the implementation of the Community regulation, which in turn implemented a Security Council resolution. In fact the competent UN Sanctions Committee had specifically decided that the airplane of the applicant fell within the scope of the UN sanctions regime. In this regard, the situation compares very closely to individual sanctions. This implies that, at least from the point of view of the Strasbourg Court, a binding Security Council resolution is not the end of discussion. The finding that a Member State has violated the Convention by complying with a UN resolution remains possible.[342]

[337] ECtHR, *Behrami* and *Saramati* (n 6 above), para 151 et seq.

[338] ECtHR, *Bosphorus* (n 5 above).

[339] See for more details: Eckes, 'Does the ECtHR provide protection from the EC?' (n 328 above), p 47 et seq.

[340] Fabienne Kauff-Gazin, 'L'arrêt Bosphorus de la CEDH: quand le juge de Strasbourg décerne au système communautaire un label de protection satisfaisante des droits fondamentaux', *Les Petites Affiches* No 234 (2005), p 13.

[341] Case C-84/95, *Bosphorus* (n 125 above).

[342] See Chapter 3 on the position of the ECtHR to international cooperation.

In conclusion, from the fact that the ECtHR ruled on the merits in *Bosphorus* it appears that the Strasbourg Court does not simply accept the existence of a Security Council resolution as sufficient to suspend Convention rights. Hence, *Bosphorus* appears to suggest a different reading of *Behrami*. Advocate-General Maduro argued to the same effect that:[343]

> when the authorities of a contracting State have taken procedural steps to implement a Security Council resolution in the domestic legal order, the measures thus taken are attributable to that State and therefore amenable to judicial review under the Convention.

Moreover, in *Bosphorus* the ECtHR, when examining whether the Community offered a protection of fundamental rights equivalent to the protection of the Convention, focused on the judicial remedies available to individuals in the EU. Hence, in view of the fact that at the UN level there are no judicial remedies available, it appears clear that the ECtHR would not find the protection at the UN level 'comparable'[344] to the ECHR. No presumption of equivalent protection would apply, and the ECtHR would exercise full jurisdiction over domestic measures implementing Security Council resolutions.

By establishing the presumption of equivalent protection the ECtHR has considerably reduced the protection of individuals: where they are affected in their Convention rights by *Community* law as opposed to national measures, individuals have a much more difficult case to argue. Those listed under Community law would have to demonstrate that the protection of fundamental rights in the Community has systematically dropped below the Convention standards, or that the protection they were offered was 'manifestly deficient'. At the same time the existence of a UN Charter obligation does not exempt the acts of the Contracting Parties from scrutiny. The ECtHR has not made the Convention rights conditional to the will of the Security Council. However, after the ECJ's ruling in *Kadi* and *al Barakaat*, individuals targeted by Community sanctions enjoy in the Luxembourg Courts full judicial protection in the light of European law. There is hence no need for the ECtHR to decide whether the review the light of *jus cogens* offered by the CFI in *Yusuf* and *Kadi* is 'manifestly deficient' within the meaning of *Bosphorus*.

[343] Opinion of AG Maduro, in Cases C-402/05 P and C-415/05 P, *Kadi and al Barakaat* (n 1 above), n 42 with a reference to ECtHR, *Beric an Others* v *Bosnia and Herzegovina*, admissibility decision of 16 October 2007, paras 27–9.

[344] ECtHR, *Bosphorus* (n 5 above).

5.2 National Courts

5.2.1 Primacy of Security Council Resolutions in National Law

Most national systems do not accord UN resolutions absolute primacy over domestic law.[345] Security Council resolutions normally are not seen as self-executing or directly applicable,[346] but require transposition to take force. And, even if the Security Council can create nearly unlimited and unconditional obligations under international law, this does not mean that national actors have equally unfettered competences to give effect to these obligations under domestic law.[347]

In the UK, the House of Lords was recently asked to consider the application of obligations under the ECHR to acts of the UK forces adopted in the context of the invasion in Iraq.[348] In the case of *Al-Jedda* the appellant claimed that, by detaining him without trial in a military prison in Iraq, the UK had breached his rights under Article 5(1) ECHR.[349] After attributing the appellant's internment to the UK, the House of Lords ruled in agreement with the lower courts that the relevant UN Security Council resolution[350] qualified the UK's obligations under the ECHR 'by reason of the operation of articles 25 and 103 of the United Nations Charter'[351] It dismissed the appeal. The House of Lords' judgment in *Al-Jedda*

[345] Cassese, *International Law* (n 194 above), p 232 et seq; with regard to individual sanctions: Third report of the Monitoring Team, of 9 September 2005, S/2005/572, pp 15–16; Dewulf and Pacquée, 'Protecting Human Rights in the War on Terror; (n 284 above), p 613 et seq; Hörmann, 'Völkerrecht bricht Rechtsgemeinschaft? (n 18 above), p 289 et seq. Criticising the national implementation: Fifth report of the Analytical Support and Sanctions Monitoring Team appointed pursuant to resolutions 1526 (2004) and 1617 (2005) concerning Al-Qaida and the Taliban and associated individuals and entities (S/2006/750), para 30 et seq.

[346] Stein, 'Application and Enforcement' (n 282 above), p 68; Gowlland-Debbas, 'Comments' (n 282 above), pp 163–73, at 165; Pavoni, 'UN Sanctions in EU and National Law (n 282 above), pp 582–612.

[347] See on this point: Hörmann, 'Völkerrecht bricht Rechtsgemeinschaft? (n 18 above), p 289.

[348] House of Lords, *Al-Jedda* (n 7 above); see also: Christina Eckes, 'UN Mandated Military Operations: Orientations of State Responsibility and the Hierarchy of International Law', *EuConst* (2009, forthcoming); see also: House of Lords, *R (Al-Skeini) v Secretary of State for Defence (The Redress Trust Intervening)* [2007] UKHL 26; [2008] 1 AC 153.

[349] The ECHR is incorporated into domestic law by the Human Rights Act 1998; however because of the 'mirror rule' (see *R (Quark Fishing Ltd) v Secretary of State for Foreign and Commonwealth Affairs* [2006] 1 AC 529, paras 33–4) the House of Lords dealt exclusively with the question of whether the appellant would have any rights in Strasbourg.

[350] UN SC Res 1542 (2004).

[351] House of Lords, *Al-Jedda* (n 7 above), para 3; see also Baroness Hale for a critic of the lack of precision in the use of the terms 'displacing' and 'qualifying', at para 126.

confirmed that the Security Council can qualify rights to the extent necessary to ensure international peace and security. However, the House of Lords stated at several occasions that further proceedings were required to determine the necessity of the specific measures giving effect to the Security Council resolution.[352] In *Al-Jedda*, in contrast to the discussion on individual sanctions, the Security Council resolution did not impose a specific obligation to detain the appellant. Therefore, a central question in *Al-Jedda* was how far the authorization of the Security Council stretched. The House of Lords specifically considered judicial assessment of the limits of the Security Council's authorization, potentially also limits imposed by considerations of human rights protection and proportionality.

In Germany, the internal validity and the internal status of international treaties, including the UN Charter, is determined by Article 59(2) GG.[353] This provision confers on the UN Charter the status of normal federal legislation, irrespective of its status under public international law.[354] The national implementation of Security Council resolutions could be subject to review even in ordinary courts.[355] Additionally, the compliance of any public measure with the German Constitution can be challenged in a constitutional complaint to the German Constitutional Court (GCC).[356] Pursuant to Article 1(3) GG, all exercise of public power in Germany is bound to respect fundamental rights as they are set out in the Constitution.[357] No exception is provided for measures taken in order to comply with international law obligations.[358] Where the implementation of international obligations would infringe the domestic constitution, national

[352] See in particular: House of Lords, *Al-Jedda* (n 7 above), paras 39 (Lord Bingham stating that the Security Council's authorisation covered only 'necessary' measures), para 127–9 (Baroness Hale referring specifically to further proceedings).

[353] Jochen Frowein, 'Implementation of Security Council Resolutions taken under Chapter VII in Germany', in Eibe Riedel (ed), *German Reports on Public Law* (Baden-Baden: Nomos, 2002), p 9; GG refers to the German Constitution (*Grundgesetz*).

[354] Rudolf Geiger, *Grundgesetz und Völkerrecht* (München: Beck, 2002), p 187.

[355] Ie a third party is prosecuted in national courts for breaching s 34 of the Foreign Trade Act (Aussenwirtschaftsgesetz); see also Chapter 1, Section 5 on secondary sanctions. If the defendant also challenged the underlying European sanctions instrument as being unlawful, the national court would have to request a preliminary ruling form the ECJ.

[356] Under very particular circumstances this extends to European law; see Chapter 2, Section 4 and Chapter 6, Section 4.2.2.

[357] Biehler, 'Individuelle Sanktionen der VN und Grundrechte' (n 8 above), p 170.

[358] For a very critical analysis of anti-terrorism measures: Heinz Düx, 'Globale Sicherheitsgesetze und weltweite Erosion von Grundrechten: Statt „Feindstrafrecht" globaler Ausbau demokratischer Rechte', *ZRP* (2003).

actors lack the competence to transpose it into national law.[359] However, the constitutional complaint is not an ordinary remedy. It cannot alone provide effective judicial protection. The GCC recognizes international cooperation as a public interest competing in a balancing test with other interests, including fundamental rights.[360] Hence, the fact that a national measure was adopted in order to comply with international law is one factor weighing against fundamental rights.[361] However, analogous to the above argument concerning the *Bosphorus* case before the ECJ, the balancing of interests itself demonstrates that the GCC is not ready to surrender its control powers to the UN.

5.2.2 Reviewing Individual Sanctions

In the academic debate it was suggested that those targeted by individual sanctions might find protection in the national judiciaries.[362] As of May 2008 the UN Monitoring Team reports 26 past and present legal challenges to UN sanctions against individuals. Besides the challenges in the EU courts,[363] the Monitoring Team reported challenges in Belgium, Italy, Pakistan, Switzerland, Turkey, UK, and the US.[364]

[359] See for Germany: GCC BVerfGE 6, p 295 et seq; BVerfGE 16, p 227 et seq; BVerfGE 22, p 293 et seq; BVerfGE 29, p 198 et seq; BVerfGE 30, 272 et seq; BVerfGE 37, p 271 et seq; BVerfGE 36, p 14 et seq; BVerfGE 38, p 49 et seq; BVerfGE 45, p 83 et seq.

[360] The GCC applies a particular balancing exercise called 'Praktische Konkordanz', which intends to give the rights on both sides the optimal effectiveness.

[361] Udo Di Fabio, 'Das Bundesverfassungsgericht und die internationale Gerichtsbarkeit', in Andreas Zimmermann (ed), *Deutschland und die internationale Gerichtsbarkeit* (Berlin: Duncker & Humblot, 2004), p 111.

[362] Imelda Tappeiner, 'The Fight against Terrorism: The Lists and the Gaps', *Utrecht Law Review*, 1 (2005), p 97 et seq.

[363] Case before the CFI: Case T-306/01, *Yusuf* (n 1 above); Case T-315/01, *Kadi* (n 1 above); Case T-253/02, *Ayadi* (n 3 above); Case T-49/04, *Hassan* (n 3 above); Case T-318/01, *Othman v Council and Commission*, judgment of 11 June 2009, nyr; Case T-135/06, *Al-Faqih v Council, pending* [application of 15 July 2006, OJ 2006 C 165/29]; Case T-136/06, *Sanabel Relief Agency v Council, pending* [application of 15 July 2006, OJ 2006 C 165/30]; Case T-137/06, *Abdrabbah v Council, pending* [application of 15 July 2006, OJ 2006 C 165/30]; Case T-138/06, *Nasuf v Council, pending* [application of 15 July 2006, OJ 2006 C 165/30]; Cases before the ECJ: Case C-402/05 P and C-415/05 P, *Kadi and al Barakaat* (n 1 above); pending: Case C-399/06 P, *Faraj Hassan v Council and Commission* (application of 25 September 2006, OJ [2006] C 294/30); Case C-403/06 P, *Chafiq Ayadi v Council* (application of 27 September 2006 OJ [2006] C 294/32).

[364] See for an account of individual sanctions cases decided or pending in national courts the reports of (what is now called) the 'Analytical Support and Sanctions Monitoring Team': S/2008/324, annex I; S/2007/677, annex I; S/2007/132, annex I; S/2006/750, annex III; S/2006/154, annex; S/2005/572, annex II; S/2005/83, annex II.

The most successful challenge thus far was an action brought by Mr Kadi[365] in the Turkish courts. On 4 July 2006 the Turkish State Council annulled the freezing[366] of his assets in Turkey.[367] It ruled that it could not uphold the asset freeze, if the documents and information that led to the allegation that Mr Kadi was associated with Al-Qaida were not presented to the judiciary in Turkey, because a judicial examination of the allegations would not be possible under these circumstances.

In the Netherlands, the Dutch Public Prosecution Service requested the national courts to ban and dissolve the national branch of the al-Haramain Foundation known as Stichting al-Haramain Humanitarian Aid,[368] as well as to release any credit balance of its bank account to the state. In January 2006, an appeals court upheld a district court decision against the Dutch Government, ruling that prosecutors had not proven that the Dutch branch of al-Haramain, separate and apart from the international organization, had supported terrorism.[369] The appeals court also found that dissolving the organization required expropriating its assets, which goes further than the freezing required by UN sanctions. The Government chose not to appeal the higher court's ruling. The organization's assets however remain frozen.

Generally speaking, however, national courts have been reluctant to challenge the authority of UN resolutions; they have tried to avoid open conflict. In the case of *Nada* the Swiss Supreme Court rejected on 14 November 2007 the applicant's request to be deleted from the Swiss list implementing the lists of the 1267 Sanctions Committee.[370] The Swiss Supreme Court found the applicant's complaint admissible because the national law freezing his assets directly affected his fundamental rights.[371] The Court ruled that because of the duration of the measure (the applicant's assets were already frozen for more than five years, and an end was not foreseeable) Article 6(1) ECHR was applicable. The Court did not, however, discuss a possible criminal nature of the asset freeze. After acknowledging the primacy of obligations under the UN Charter, including Security Council resolutions,[372] the Court stated clearly that it considered the Security Council obliged to act according to the

[365] Despite the partially different spelling ('al-Qadi') this is the same applicant as in: Case T-315/01, *Kadi* and Case C-402/05 P, *Kadi* (n 1 above).

[366] The relevant sections of the Cabinet decision of 22 December 2001.

[367] See: S/2006/750, annex III; S/2006/154, annex; S/2005/572, annex II; S/2005/83, annex II.

[368] See case: LJN: AT2894, Rechtbank Amsterdam, 301437/HA RK 04–948 of 31 March 2005.

[369] NJF 2006/281, Hof Amsterdam (Handelskamer), 5 january 2006, nr 987/05.

[370] Swiss Supreme Court (Schweizer Bundesgericht), *Youssef Mustapha Nada* v *SECO*, Staatssekretariat für Wirtschaft, judgment of 14 November 2007, 1A.45/2007/daa.

[371] ibid, at 2.1. [372] ibid, at 5.1 and 5.2.

objectives and principles of the Charter and that these include in Article 1(3) respect for human rights.[373] Citing the CFI's decision in *Kadi* the Swiss Supreme Court elaborated that as a matter of principle the UN member states cannot however avoid the binding force of Security Council resolutions based on the argument that they are contrary to the Charter.[374] The Court developed a narrower definition of *jus cogens* than the CFI did in *Kadi*, which does not include the right to fair trial (except for certain procedural guarantees against arbitrary detention which do not apply to Nada's case).[375] After concluding that the UN sanctions regime does not leave any margin of discretion to the member states, the Court concluded that Switzerland would breach its obligations under the UN Charter if it deleted the applicant's name from the list and that it cannot therefore take the unilateral decision to do so.[376] The Swiss Supreme Court stated further that effective protection can only be offered at the UN level. It questioned whether an annulment of the national implementing measures would actually grant the applicant relief since he would in any event remain on the UN list[377] and consequently all other UN member states would remain obliged to adopt sanctions against him. This reasoning shows the Swiss Supreme Court's consideration for the larger whole of international law. The Court also emphasized that Switzerland and a number of other countries take active steps to work towards the introduction of an effective control mechanism.[378] Finally, the Court stated explicitly that the Member States are obliged by the ECHR to ensure that the UN sanctioning practice is in conformity with the Convention and that they can be held responsible under the Convention for failing to do so.[379]

In the UK courts were called several times to rule on issues relating not only to terrorism[380] but also to individual sanctions more particularly. In the case of *A, K, M, Q & G v HM Treasury*[381] the UK courts were called

[373] ibid, at 5.3.
[374] ibid, at 5.3 and 5.4.
[375] ibid, at 7.3.
[376] ibid, at 8.1 and 8.3.
[377] ibid, at 8.2.
[378] ibid, at 8.3.
[379] ibid, at 5.5.
[380] See Chapter 4.
[381] Court of Appeal, *G v HM Treasury*; *A and others v Same* [2008] EWCA Civ 1187, [2008] WLR (D) 339 (CA: Sir Anthony Clarke MR, Sedley and Wilson LJJ; 30 October 2008); High Court, *A, K, M, Q & G v HM Treasury* [2008] EWHC 869 (Admin); funnily enough in the UK courts cases against terrorist listings are anonymized while the names of the applicants are readily available on the UN website

upon to rule on whether domestic freezing orders implementing UN lists of terrorist suspects were valid. The case concerned both the Al-Qaida and Taliban (United Nations Measures) Order 2006 ('the AQO') and the Terrorism (United Nations Measures) Order 2006 ('the TO'). The former implements the Security Council's own managed scheme for designating persons as being members or 'associates' of Al-Qaida, whereas the latter implements the UN sanctions regime under Resolution 1373, which leaves the designation of terrorist suspects to the UN member states. After the High Court had struck down both domestic orders as being ultra vires, the case reached the Court of Appeal. The Court of Appeal held that the order was lawful and validly made provided certain words were severed.[382] Essentially putting into practice the House of Lords' guidelines in *Al Jedda*,[383] the Court of Appeal examined with regard to the TO whether the national measures go further than what is required under the relevant Security Council resolutions. While Resolution 1373 required the UN member states to freeze the assets of any individual 'who is' a terrorist supporter, in implementing the UK had gone further by allowing asset freezes to be imposed on any individual 'who is or may be' a terrorist supporter. The Court of Appeal found that this implementation went beyond what was required by Resolution 1373 and deemed that the words 'or may be' would have to be excised in order to correct the defect. *A, K, M, Q & G v HM Treasury* demonstrates that UK courts do not easily accept that domestic implementation measures go further than what is necessary under the UK's obligations under the UN Charter. Yet, it would be wrong to conclude that the opposite is true. *A, K, M, Q & G v HM Treasury* does not indicate that UK courts accept any implementation measure, irrespective of whether it violates human rights, as long as it does not go beyond what is required under the relevant Security Council resolutions.

With regard to the AQO the Court of Appeal also examined due process.[384] The applicant had been listed by the UN Sanctions Committee. He had never had any contact with the Committee and had no idea who precisely made the decision or upon what evidence it was based. Only at the actual proceedings did he become aware that it was the UK Government that requested that he be listed.[385] The Court of Appeal accepted[386]

[382] Article 4(2) Terrorism (United Nations Measures) Order 2006.

[383] See above and Chapter 4.

[384] Court of Appeal, *G v HM Treasury; A and others v Same* [2008] EWCA Civ 1187, [2008] WLR (D) 339, paras 107–21.

[385] ibid, para 108.

[386] ibid, para 119.

the submission that the court has power to consider an application for judicial review by a person to whom the AQO applies as a result of designation by the Committee and, on such an application, to ask the court, so far as it can, to consider what the basis of the listing was.

The Court further considered that '[t]his will not be a challenge to the AQO itself'.[387] More specifically on access to the information that led to the listing, the Court of Appeal ruled that '[t]here must be procedures to enable [the applicant], again so far as possible, to discover the case against him, so that he may have an opportunity to meet it'.[388] In the particular case the UK was in the possession of all the relevant evidence, because the UK had requested the listing of the applicant. Hence, the Court did not have to address the question of what happens where the UK is not in possession of the information that led to the listing because it had been requested by another state that does not share the relevant information. The Court of Appeal could avoid the hard question of whether the domestic implementation measure is justified where it is required by the Security Council resolution but infringes nonetheless the procedural rights of the applicant, eg because the UK cannot place the applicant in the position to effectively exercise his rights because it simply has no information on the listing decision. The UN lists identifying individual persons as terrorist suspects are drawn up by the Sanctions Committee and not by the Security Council itself. Yet, the lists would probably have to be understood as an authoritative interpretation of whose assets the member states are required to freeze under the relevant Security Council resolutions. This would not leave any 'wiggle room' to the domestic courts.

The interpretation of what is 'necessary' under the UN sanctions regime to fight terrorism will remain a central question in disputes against individual sanctions giving effect to UN lists of terrorists. This concerns not only the question of the procedural rights but also the substantive scope of these sanctions, ie which resources are covered. In the earlier case of *M*,[389] the UK High Court ruled on the HM Treasury's interpretation of the EC regulation[390] implementing the UN sanctions regime under Resolutions 1267 and 1390. The Treasury had taken the view that the payment of social security benefits to spouses of those listed falls within the meaning of

[387] ibid.

[388] ibid, para 120.

[389] High Court, *M, A, MM v HM Treasury* [2006] EWHC 2328 (Admin); Court of Appeal, *M, A, MM v HM Treasury* [2007] EWCA Civ 173; see also Chapter 7.

[390] See Art 2(2) of Regulation 881/2002/EC (n 12 above).

'economic resources' 'made available' 'for the benefit of' the listed person. The High Court shared the Treasury's interpretation that the social security benefits to spouses is covered by the EC regulation and that consequently those payments need to be licensed.[391] The High Court also held[392] that the strict interpretation was necessary to give full effect to the underlying Security Council resolution and

> the intention of the Security Council [...] to remove [...] all economic support from listed persons, with a view to achieving public policy objectives of the highest importance, namely, combating international terrorism and promoting peace, security and safety.

On appeal, the Appellate Committee of the House of Lords took a different view.[393] It advised the House to refer a preliminary ruling to the ECJ because it considered that 'this intrusive regime' is required neither by the EC Regulation, nor by the Security Council resolution.[394] The case is currently pending before the ECJ.[395]

5.3 Interplay between the Different Courts

The different courts in Europe complement each other. Because there is a potential overlap of jurisdiction they also act as watchdogs of what the others do. An exchange of warning signs has taken place, which could in the end strengthen judicial review of individual sanctions in Europe.

The ECJ's attitude towards the ECHR has developed much throughout its case-law. After refusing in the beginning to rule on compliance with fundamental rights at all, the ECJ developed its own system of protection by relying on general principles of EU law, which it derived from the constitutional traditions common to the Member States and from the ECHR. In its current jurisprudence the Court relies on the ECHR in an extended manner, even if it continues to take 'inspiration' from the

[391] See Chapter 1, Section 3.1.3 on humanitarian exemptions.

[392] High Court, *M, A, MM v HM Treasury* [2006] EWHC 2328 (Admin), para 64; Court of Appeal, *M, A, MM v HM Treasury* [2007] EWCA Civ 173, para 17.

[393] See the report from the Appellate Committee of 30 April 2008, at: House of Lords, *R (on the application of M) v HM Treasury* [2008] UKHL 26.

[394] ibid, para 12.

[395] Case C-340/08, *M (FC) and Others*, OJ [2008] C 260/8; see also: Case C-117/06, *Möllendorf* (n 60 above).

Convention rather than to directly apply it.[396] Going beyond the ECHR the ECJ has established fundamental rights as part of the general principles of European law. It offers a protection that goes beyond the minimum protection of the ECHR.[397] Continuing down this road, the ECJ set aside the CFI's judgments on individual sanctions giving effect to UN lists of terrorist suspects.

The ECtHR recognized the ECJ's willingness and capability to protect fundamental rights in its *Bosphorus* judgment.[398] The ECJ has the privilege of ensuring compliance with fundamental rights in the area of Community law. According to its settled case-law, this does also entail a review of national measures implementing EC law.[399] It could be argued that a potential, unconfirmed review of Community law by the ECtHR might have done better to discipline European and national courts, as well as legislators. Instead, *Bosphorus* established an explicitly declared 'marginal' review of Community law by the ECtHR. On the other hand, the ECtHR took the stricter approach than the European Commission of Human Rights in its earlier case-law.[400] The latter did not provide for the possibility of a rebuttal in the individual case. In that regard *Bosphorus* could even be interpreted as a warning to the European institutions, including the ECJ.[401]

In *Bosphorus*, the ECtHR asserted that the EU courts protect fundamental rights under Community law at a level equivalent to the Convention. Aside from an explicit rebuttal of the presumption of equivalent protection one should not expect the Strasbourg Court to step in and protect the rights of individuals against infringements by Community law. However, the finding of a violation sufficiently grave to rebut the general presumption of equivalent protection is tenable. There is another glimpse of hope in the *Bosphorus* judgment of the ECtHR. The Strasbourg Court

[396] Case C-413/99, *Baumbast* [2002] ECR I-7091; Case C-60/00, *Carpenter* [2002] ECR I-6279; Case C-200/02, *Kunqian Catherine Zhu Chen* [2004] ECR I-9925; but see also: Case T-315/01, *Kadi* (n 1 above), paras 210, 234 and 287; AG Maduro Opinion in Joined Cases C-402/05 P & C-415/05 P, *Kadi and Al Barakaat* (n 1 above), especially paras 36–37; Chapter 3, Section 2.

[397] See Chapter 3, Section 2.

[398] See above Section 5.1.1.

[399] Case 5/88, *Wachauf v Bundesamt für Ernährung und Forstwirtschaft* [1989] ECR 2609, para 19 (regulations); Joined Cases C-20 and C-64/00, *Booker Aquaculture Ltd and Hydro Seafood GSP Ltd v The Scottish Minister* [2003] ECR I-7411 (directives).

[400] ECommHR, *M v Germany* Application No 13258/87.

[401] Iain Cameron, 'Rapports: European Court of Human Rights. January 2005–March 2006', *European Public Law*, 13 (2007), p 7.

did not accept the existence of a Security Council resolution as an absolute reason for justification. Contrary to the CFI it did not exclude scrutinizing legislative acts of the Contracting Parties giving effect to UN resolutions.

At the same time, where the protection of fundamental rights in the EU courts obviously drops below the standard of the protection in the Member States, albeit only in a certain area, such as individual sanctions, there is the lingering threat that the GCC or possibly another national court exercise their residual control and declare Community law contrary to the core principles of their national constitutions. If the ECJ had confirmed the CFI's position it would have risked a domino effect in national law. From the standpoint of European law national courts are not competent to review the legality of Community law.[402] With very limited–but well-known–exceptions[403] national courts have accepted this view. The primacy of Community law requires national authorities, including courts,[404] to comply as a matter of principle with the (unreviewed) European legal instrument. Under these conditions, the rulings of the CFI in *Yusuf* and *Kadi* would have created a chain of prevailing legal obligations, which in principle also excludes judicial review by the national courts. Yet, after the ECJ's decision in *Kadi and al Barakaat* such a chain does no longer exist.

It is interesting to note that the ECJ's appeal decision in *Kadi and al Barakaat* was given between the ruling of the Swiss Supreme Court in *Nada* and the UK Court of Appeal's ruling in *A, K, M, Q & G v HM Treasury*. While the Swiss Court took a hands-off-approach, the Court of Appeal took a consistent line to that of the ECJ. Without wanting to make a *post hoc ergo propter hoc* argument, the ECJ's appeal decision will not have escaped the notice of national courts called upon to rule on the validity of individual sanctions giving effect to UN lists of terrorist suspects. It might encourage them to take a firmer stand on human rights.

By way of conclusion, heightened attention to each other's rulings enhance the authority, influence and effectiveness of the EU courts and the ECtHR,[405] but also the national courts. That is not to advocate absolute reliance. Differences in composition, jurisdiction *ratione personae*, *locus standi* rules, the identity of the litigants, their objectives and the political

[402] Case 314/85, *Foto-Frost* [1987] ECR 4199.

[403] See the *Solange* case-law of the GCC (n 193 above).

[404] Ordinary courts are generally not in the position to review European legal instruments and Supreme or Constitutional Courts have limited their residual control to very exceptional situations.

[405] Harpaz, 'The ECJ and its Relations with the ECHR' (n 191 above), p 120.

context also justify a critical distance to their respective judgments.[406] In the area of individual sanctions the courts appear to have engaged in a constructive dialogue.[407]

Conclusions

UN sanctions against private individuals are an example of the increasing and closer interaction between different layers of law that confront courts with fundamental questions about the autonomy and identity of their domestic legal orders. They raise the classical conflict between the rights and freedoms of individuals and the public interest in (the functioning of the state-based system that maintains) peace and security. Only, this conflict no longer arises exclusively within the domestic legal order; it entails further questions of a formal or systemic hierarchy between different legal regimes.

In *Kadi and al Barakaat* in particular, the ECJ had to address the relationship between the European legal order and the UN Charter. The Court confirmed that the European legal order is more resistant to intrusions by the UN than the CFI held in its decisions on Community law giving effect to UN sanctions lists. The ECJ's firm stand in favour of the autonomy of the Community legal order was the right choice not only from an *effet utile* perspective of European law, but it is also justifiable in a normative dimension. The most laudable outcome of the ECJ's ruling in *Kadi* and *al Barakaat* is that it ensures that Member States cannot use European legal instruments in order to circumvent national constitutional guarantees.[408]

The ECJ rejected unambiguously the CFI's proposition that obligations under the UN Charter could affect the institutional and substantive framework in which the Community institutions operate. The ECJ did not even pretend to pay deference to the Security Council based on a *Solange* approach. This is an honest confirmation of reality: there is no scope for *Solange* in the relationship between the EU and the UN. The UN does not benefit from state-like legitimacy; it should hence not be treated as a world

[406] ibid, p 125.

[407] See for a critical analysis: Bjørn Kunoy and Anthony Dawes, 'Plate Tectonics In Luxembourg: The Ménage À Trois Between EC Law, International Law and the European Convention On Human Rights following the UN Sanctions Cases, *CMLaw Rev*, 46 (2009), pp 73–104.

[408] See in this regard also: Case C-355/04 P, *Segi* (n 329 above).

government. International and domestic norms form a transnational constitutional network, in which they cannot be aligned in a linear hierarchy. Therefore, conflicts between different fundamental norms require a balancing of interests, rather than a formalistic hierarchical approach resulting in the surrender of domestic constitutional principles. Domestic courts have a role to play in reconciling international cooperation with fundamental rights. By conferring on Security Council resolutions internal primacy balanced only by *jus cogens* control, the CFI had taken a formal or systemic approach, introducing Security Council resolutions as a supreme level of law within the European order because of the authority of their author reviewing them in the light of very basic principles only. This view provides much form with little substance. Review on the basis of *jus cogens* is little more than a symbolic gesture. As a matter of principle, the desire for a formal hierarchy under international law is understandable; in practice, however, it allows actors unfettered by constitutional constraints to set aside the existing constraints at 'lower levels' of this hierarchical construction. Ultimately this hollows out the existing constitutional foundations from above; it does not reinforce shared values in international law. Or, to put it differently, 'disregard of the UN is inevitable when the UN entrenches upon core principles that legitimize the use of coercive public power'[409] In contrast to the CFI, the ECJ held that it is not for the EU courts to review Security Council resolutions at all. In this regard it could be argued that the CFI's position contributed to the constitutionalization[410] by imposing limits on the actions of the Security Council that could be controlled by all national courts; however, it has been widely acknowledged that *jus cogens* does not offer enough substance to impose meaningful constraints.[411] The ECJ's approach by contrast might, at least in the long run, contribute to the legitimacy of the UN. Instead of allowing the Security Council to set aside fundamental principles of European law within the European legal order the Court increased the pressure on the Security Council to reconsider its course. This could lead to further

[409] Halberstam and Stein, 'The United Nations, the European Union, and the King of Sweden' (n 189 above), p 62.

[410] See on the contribution of the Kadi case to the constitutionalization of international law: d'Aspremont and Frédéric Dopagne, 'Two Constitutionalisms in Europe' (n 28 above).

[411] Tomuschat, 'Case law: Case T-306/01, Ahmed Ali Yusuf and Al Barakaat International Foundation v Council and Commission' (n 17 above), p 537, who was otherwise in favour of the CFI's ruling in *Kadi*; Thomas Meerpohl, *Individualsanktionen des Sicherheitsrates der Vereinten Nationen: Das Sanktionsregime gegen die Taliban und Al-Qaida vor dem Hintergrund des Rechts der VN und der Menschenrechte* (München: Herbert Utz Verlag, 2008), p 132 et seq.

reaching procedural rights within the UN listing procedure, or ultimately to the finding that the UN cannot actually meet the necessary standards. The aim can only be a dialogue on substance not blind submission to global governance. Admittedly there is some scope within the judgment where the ECJ could have demonstrated more willingness to open a dialogue with the Security Council. Whether a dialogue similar to the one between the ECJ and national constitutional courts could evolve between the ECJ and the Security Council is doubtful. Because of their different function it might not be appropriate to extend this judicial dialogue paradigm to political institutions.

Defending both the autonomy of the European legal order and the rights of individuals is the ECJ's traditional role. Moreover, taking the individual as the starting point is consistent with the more general legal developments both under European and under public international law.[412] From the standpoint of the individual, *Kadi and al Barakaat* created a conflict between different layers of law that can be pictured closer (European law) of further away (the UN Charter) depending on how immediate their impact is on the legal position of individuals This creates, in addition to the delicate task of balancing the involved interests, the need to relate these different layers of law. The ECJ's usual soft way of showing respect to the Security Council by interpreting EC law literally in the light of Security Council resolutions could not be transferred to individual sanctions. Since those sanctions do not leave any margin of discretion to the European institutions but require a verbatim transposition, it is hardly possible to interpret the identical copy of a list of names based on a literal interpretation of the original UN list. Instead the ECJ stood up to the Security Council. It opted for a stand firmly rooted in the domestic European order. This was its starting point and consequently the norms setting the legal framework in which everything else is judged.

As in any other multi-layered legal system there can be no doubt that the absolute primacy of the 'higher layers' will contribute to the effectiveness of the system. This is true also for Security Council resolutions. If we confer absolute primacy on them, this will prima facie increase the effectiveness of the UN system. Any other interpretation, on the other hand, could endanger the effective implementation of Security Council resolutions. Even if one disagrees with the CFI's position that review of European sanctions would result in an indirect review of Security Council resolutions,

[412] Cf Franck, *The Empowered Self* (n 279 above).

such a review is not without implications in the international sphere. The finding that a European list, which is an identical copy of the lists adopted at the UN level, violates fundamental rights protected under EU law, challenges the political credibility of UN sanctions.

Moreover, even though the ECJ's position of defending the autonomy of the European legal order does no more than keep the status quo, it creates other internal tensions. First, the European institutions are placed in a position where they have to provide the person listed the opportunity to know the case against them and to respond. However, in the existing sanctioning practice it appears doubtful that the European institutions actually have the information on which the listing decisions were made. They can, however, only share information that they actually have. Secondly, based on a technical legal view the Member States could still adopt national measures to comply with Security Council resolutions; however, they would have to justify why they take measures that were found to breach fundamental rights as guaranteed by the ECHR and, as they result from the constitutional traditions common to the Member States,[413] this appears nearly untenable. Yet, they will have to come to grips with potentially opposing obligations under the UN Charter and European law.[414] By contrast, conferring primacy on Security Council resolutions under European law would endanger the relationship of cooperation between the European institutions and the Member States even more strongly. The supremacy rules under European law subordinate national law to European law, including to the unreviewed European copies of UN sanctions against individuals. Hence, the CFI's approach of wiping out the line between international and European law would allow international law to shape directly the rights of those sanctioned both under European law and under national law, without allowing for any further mechanism of control.

The Security Council directly lists individuals as terrorist suspects and imposes in principle an absolute obligation on the UN member states to adopt measures against these individuals with far-reaching adverse effects on their fundamental rights. No effective remedy is available at the UN level; and international law does not accept that states justify non-

[413] See Art 6 TEU.

[414] See for a discussion of 'What's next?': Andrea Gattini, 'Joined Cases C-402/05 P & 415/05 P, Yassin Abdullah Kadi, Al Barakaat International Foundation v Council and Commission, judgment of the Grand Chamber of 3 September 2008, not yet reported.', *CML Rev* 46 (2009), p 235 et seq.

compliance with an annulment of the implementation measures by a domestic court. These UN sanctions against individuals challenge the core understanding that has led to the development of the European legal order to its current state. This is that where a legal system builds direct links with individuals, affords them rights and directly governs their 'legal heritage'[415] it must also grant them the opportunity to actively participate in that legal system. Despite the increasing reliance by individuals on international law in domestic courts and consequently its increasing importance for the rights and obligations of individuals, individual sanctions are a very particular instrument. Usually international bodies in non-judicial functions do not directly interfere with the rights of individuals without further discretionary application measures that could be challenged. The ECJ's decision in *Kadi and al Barakaat* is consequently an exceptional case. It is not a sign of a general disregard for international law.

[415] Case 26/62, *van Gend* (n 51 above).

6

Protection from Autonomous European Sanctions: Community Law and Union Lists

Introduction

Individual sanctions giving effect to European Union lists of terrorist suspects have repeatedly been annulled for breaching the most basic rights of the defence. However, this does not allow for the conclusion that the successful applicants were either removed from the terrorist lists or could access their financial assets. Further, these challenges have not led the Council to reconsider the use of individual sanctions as a counter-terrorist policy in principle. The Council continues to identify individuals as terrorist suspects and to freeze their financial assets, albeit under a reformed procedure.[1] Finally, the Court of First Instance (CFI) has only annulled EC Council decisions listing individuals for the application of operational measures in the Community pillar. The underlying lists of terrorist suspects adopted in the Union pillars remain outside of the reach of the judicial remedies available to individuals at the European level.

From the start the CFI took a fundamentally different view on autonomous sanctions than on sanctions giving effect to UN lists of terrorist suspects (see Chapter 5). As was explained in Chapter 5 the two types of European sanctions reflect the two sanctions regimes at the UN level. On the one hand, the European Union (EU) adopts sanctions against those listed by the UN Sanctions Committee (first UN sanctions regime under Resolutions 1267, 1333, and 1390). On the other, the EU also adopts its own autonomous sanctions based on terrorist lists the Council draws up

[1] See: Council doc 11309/07, 29 June 2007 and Council doc 10826/07, 21 June 2007; see also: Chapter 7.

under the Union pillars in order to comply with Security Council Resolution 1373 (second UN sanctions regime). The present chapter will examine protection from autonomous European sanctions.

In the cases of *Yusuf* and *Kadi* the CFI denied the applicants full judicial review of European sanctions giving effect to UN lists of terrorist suspects.[2] By contrast the Court agreed from the start to exercise full judicial review in the light of the standards of European law over autonomous sanctions. The CFI justified the difference in its approach with the lack of discretion of the EU institutions when adopting sanctions against those identified by the UN. The UN lists of terrorist suspects determine exactly against whom the institutions should take action. This, in combination with the assumption that obligations under the UN Charter prevail over European law, led the CFI to the conclusion that any examination of the lawfulness of a European law instrument would automatically contain an unauthorized incidental evaluation of the underlying UN lists.[3] As a consequence, the CFI rejected full judicial review.

By contrast, the CFI did not consider the similarly specific listing requests of Member States[4] in the autonomous sanctions procedure to create a binding obligation. Here, the CFI held that the Council takes a discretionary decision both when listing someone initially and when keeping someone listed (subsequent decision).[5] The adoption procedure and the legal basis of European sanctions against private individuals were discussed in Chapters 1 and 2. It suffices to recall that Article 301 EC requires first the adoption of a CFSP decision (in practice a common position), on which basis the Community then adopts sanctions under the first pillar. The CFSP common position contains a list of terrorist suspects (Union list). In the adoption procedure of autonomous sanctions the common positions are cross-pillar instruments (second and third pillar). The Council draws up the Union list based on proposals of the Member States.[6] Member States

[2] Case T-306/01, *Ahmed Ali Yusuf and al Barakaat International Foundation v Council and Commission* [2005] ECR II-3533; Case T-315/01, *Yassin Abdullah Kadi v Council and Commission* [2005] ECR II-3649; confirmed in: Case T-49/04, *Hassan v Council and Commission* [2006] ECR II-52; Case T-253/02, *Chafiq Ayadi v Council* [2006] ECR II-2139; this position was repealed in: Cases C-402/05 P and C-415/05 P, *Kadi and al Barakaat*, judgment of 3 September 2008, not yet reported; see Chapter 5 on the European sanctions regime giving effect to UN terrorist lists.

[3] Case T-306/01, *Yusuf* (n 2 above), para 267.

[4] On proposals of third states, see Council doc 10826/07, 21 June 2007, para 7.

[5] Article 1(4) and (6) of Common Position 2001/931/CFSP; see eg: Case T-47/03, *Jose Maria Sison v Council and Commission* [2007] ECR II-73 (sum pub), para 161 et seq.

[6] Working methods of the Working Party, Council doc 10826/07, 21 June 2007, Annex II, para 6.

propose listings based on decisions of their competent national authority within the meaning of Article 1(4) of Common Position 2001/931/CFSP. The initial listing decision and the subsequent listing decisions must be distinguished. The former refers to the first decision of the Council to list a person as a terrorist suspect. The latter refers to the Council's decision in the review procedure that the listing should be maintained. Union lists of terrorist suspects are reviewed every six month (Article 1(6) of Common Position 2001/931/CFSP).

Since the European Court of Justice (ECJ)'s appeal decision in the cases of *Kadi* and *al Barakaat* both sanctions giving effect to UN lists and sanctions giving effect to Union lists are subject to full judicial review. However, distinguishing between the two types of sanctions remains useful. First, the practical implications of annulling sanctioning measures are different depending on whether they give effect to UN or Union lists. An annulment of European sanctions giving effect to UN lists will leave unaffected both the existence of the UN lists (and the formal public allegation that those listed are terrorists) and the international obligation of the EU Member States to give effect to decisions of the Security Council. Secondly, ensuring that courts have access to the relevant information appears considerably more difficult where Community measures implement decisions taken at the UN level; and meaningful judicial review depends on access to that information.

The Council adopts lists of individuals who have allegedly supported terrorism in the second and third pillar (Common Foreign and Security Policy (CFSP) and Police and Judicial Cooperation in Criminal Matters (PJCC)).[7] With few exceptions those listed in the Union pillars are then targeted by sanctions in the Community pillar, where individuals can bring direct challenges against European legal instruments. An EC Council decision copies the Union list of terrorist suspects, excluding those who are not subject to Community asset freezes.[8] The CFI's rulings that Community sanctions breach the general principles of European law and in particular the defence rights of those listed is transferable to the underlying Union lists.

The aim of Chapter 6 is twofold: first, to examine the quality of procedural and judicial protection from Community regulations and secondly, to demonstrate that judicial review of Union lists is not only necessary from the

[7] Common Position 2001/931; see Chapter 1 for more details on the Art 301 EC adoption procedure.

[8] See below and Case T-338/02, *Segi and others* [2004] ECR II-1647 and Case C-355/04 P, *Segi v Council* [2007] ECR I-1657.

perspective of the individual, but that such a review is also required by European law. The structure of this chapter is as follows. Section 1 examines the protection offered to those targeted by European sanctions giving effect to Union lists of terrorist suspects. This includes both protection from Community and Union law. The discussion pays close attention to the case-law of both the CFI and the ECJ.

Section 2 discusses different avenues that lead to judicial review of Union law. This includes the preliminary ruling in Article 35 TEU, procedural guarantees under Union law that are subject to judicial review, and the possibility of reviewing Union law incidentally in a challenge directed at Community law. This section also examines the principle of wider jurisdiction[9] as a justification for judicial review of Union lists of terrorist suspects. It seeks to demonstrate that the fundamental rights guarantees in Article 6(2) TEU and the ECJ's case-law on Union law allow and even require the EU courts to review Union lists.

In Section 3 the protection from Union listings before the European Court of Human Rights (ECtHR) is briefly analysed, while Section 4 examines the possibility of judicial review of Union law in national courts. The starting point for the latter examination is the Opinion of Advocate-General Mengozzi in the case of *Segi*. Section 5 analyses the interplay between the different courts in Europe. It attempts to point out how the decisions of the ECtHR and the national courts influence the rulings in the EU courts. A conclusion wraps up the discussion.

1. Protection from Community Acts Giving Effect to Union Lists

The single most important case on Community sanctions based on Union lists of terrorist suspects is the case of *Organisation des Modjahedines du peuple d'Iran (OMPI)*.[10] In this case the CFI annulled for the first time a Community regulation freezing the assets of terrorist suspects designated by the EU. Indeed, after this initial annulment on 16 December 2006

[9] This principle requires judicial review of acts that adversely affect the legal rights of individuals even where the strict wording of the Treaty does not provide for a competence, see most prominently: Case 294/83, *Parti Ecologiste 'Les Verts' v Parliament* [1986] ECR 1339.

[10] Case T-228/02, *Organisation des Modjahedines du peuple d'Iran v Council and UK (OMPI I)* [2006] ECR II-4665; see also Chapter 7.

(*OMPI I*), the CFI annulled the listing of the same organization two more times on 23 October 2008 (*OMPI II*)[11] and on 3 December 2008 (*OMPI III*).[12]

In *OMPI I*, the applicant organization sought to have its name deleted from *all* European lists of terrorist suspects; hence, it sought annulment of both the Union list contained in a common position[13] and the Community list contained in an EC Council decision.[14] The CFI declined jurisdiction for the common position. It referred to Article 46 TEU and pointed out that this article does not foresee review of second pillar instruments. With regard to the *EC Council decision*[15] the Court held that it infringed the applicant's procedural rights and annulled the measure in so far as it concerned the applicant.[16] The CFI found the rights of the defence, the duty to state reasons in Article 253 EC, and the right to a fair trial, *fully applicable* to sanctions against individuals adopted by the EU.[17] The CFI held that the listing procedure failed to comply with all three.[18] The CFI expressly stated that it did not feel, 'even at this stage of the procedure, in a position to review the lawfulness of [...] [the contested] decision'[19] The Court could hardly have expressed its criticism more clearly: the secretive procedure pursuant to which the listing decisions are taken does not allow the EU courts to take an informed decision.[20] Since *OMPI I* the CFI has confirmed its position on autonomous sanctions in a series of rulings.[21] The ECJ had the occasion to rule on autonomous sanctions in the appeal decision in the

[11] Case T-256/07, *People's Mojahidin Organization of Iran v Council (OMPI II)*, judgment of 23 October 2008, not yet reported; appeal pending: Case C-576/08. P, *People's Mojahedin Organization of Iran*.

[12] Case T-284/08, *People's Mojahedin Organization of Iran v Council* (*OMPI III*), judgment of 4 December 2008, not yet reported; see for more detail Chapter 7, Section 3.

[13] Common Position 2005/936/CFSP, OJ 2005 L 340/80.

[14] Council Decision 2005/930/EC, OJ 2005 L 340/64.

[15] The applicant was first listed in Council Decision 2002/334/EC, OJ 2002, L 116/33 and from then on in every updated list; last in the contested decision: Council Decision 2005/930/EC, OJ 2005, L 340/64.

[16] Case T-228/02, *OMPI I* (n 10 above), para 174.

[17] ibid, paras 108–13; see also: Case T-47/03, *Sison* (n 5 above), para 138–60 surprisingly the CFI did not in this section directly refer to its judgment in *OMPI I* in which it had already made a similar argument, but repeatedly referred to Case T-306/01, *Yusuf* (n 2 above).

[18] ibid, para 218 (duty to state reasons); para 214 (rights of the defence); and para 225 (right to a fair trial).

[19] ibid, para 173.

[20] ibid, para 155 et seq.

[21] Case T-47/03, *Sison* (n 5 above), Case T-327/03, *al-Aqsa v Council* [2007] ECR II-79 (sum pub); see also: Case T-333/02, *Gestoras pro Amnistia*, Case T-229/02, *Kurdistan Workers' Party, Kurdistan National Congress v Council (PKK)* [2005] ECR II-539, set aside and referred back in: Case C-229/05 P, *PKK and KNK* v *Council* [2007] ECR I-439; Case T-253/04, *Kongra-Gel*.

PKK case. After reiterating the Community's commitment to judicial protection in general, the ECJ stated[22] unambiguously:

It is particularly important for that judicial protection to be effective because the restrictive measures ... have serious consequences. Not only are all financial transactions and financial services thereby prevented in the case of a person, group or entity covered by the regulation, but also their reputation and political activity are damaged by the fact that they are classified as terrorists.

... [A] person, group or entity can be included in the disputed list only if there is certain reliable information, and the persons, groups or entities covered must be precisely identified. In addition, it is made clear that the name of persons, groups or entities can be kept on the list only if the Council reviews their situation periodically. All these matters must be open to judicial review.

Rights of defence, the obligation to state reasons, and the right to effective judicial protection are inseparably interlinked. The CFI has repeatedly acknowledged these links in the context of individual sanctions based on Union lists of terrorist suspects.[23]

1.1 Rights of Defence

1.1.1 Right to a Fair Hearing

The right to a fair hearing is a central right of defence. It is categorized as 'fundamental' under European law[24] and must be guaranteed 'even in the absence of any rules' in 'all proceedings initiated against a person which are liable to culminate in a measure adversely affecting that person'.[25] In principle,

[22] Case C-229/05 P, *PKK and KNK v Council* [2007] ECR I-439, paras 110–11, appeal against the order in Case T-229/02, *PKK and KNK v Council* [2005] ECR II-539; the appeal concernid the admissibility of the applications only and the ECJ referred the case back to the CFI.

[23] Eg: Case T-47/03, *Sison* (n 5 above), para 137 and para 187; Case T-284/08, *OMPI III* (n 12 above), para 75.

[24] Case T-228/02, *OMPI I* (n 10 above), para 91. Article 41 of the Charter of Fundamental Rights of the European Union, OJ C 364/1, 18.12.2000; on the status of the right to be heard: Deirdre Curtin, 'The Right to Fair Procedures in Administrative Law' in James O'Reilly (ed), *Human Rights and Constitutional Law: essays in honour of Brian Walsh* (Dublin: The Round Hall Press, 1992), pp 293, 299 and 309; Takis Tridimas, *The General Principles of EU Law* (Oxford: Oxford University Press, 2nd ed, 2006), pp 34–42; see also: Klara Kanska, 'Towards Administrative Human Rights in the EU. Impact of the Charter of Fundamental Rights', *European Law Journal*, 10 (2004), p 296 (309); and: Case C-49/88, *Al-Jubail Fertilizer Company (Samad) and Saudi Arabian Fertilizer Company (Safco) v Council* [1991] ECR I-3187, para 15; Case C-28/05, *Dokter and others* [2006] ECR I-5431, paras 73–5.

[25] Case T-260/94, *Air Inter v Commission* [1997] ECR II-997, para 59; Case C-135/92, *Fiskano v Commission* [1994] ECR I-2885, para 39; Case 234/84, *Belgium v Commission* [1986] ECR 2263; see also Case T-228/02, *OMPI I* (n 10 above), para 91.

the adverse effect of the measure is the decisive criterion for the right to a fair hearing in the procedure leading up to that measure.[26] Individuals should be in the position to seek anticipated procedural protection of their adversely affected interests as a complement to judicial review. The EU courts have taken a pragmatic approach to the right to a fair hearing.[27] This leaves the EU courts room to accommodate the specific situation, but in want of a clear conceptual approach it is difficult to predict the outcome in less clear-cut cases.

The European institutions and national authorities cooperate for the adoption of individual sanctions in a so-called double-staged procedure:[28] competent national authorities take a decision in respect of a specific person on the basis of which the Community determines whether it lists and sanctions that person. The rights of defence at the Community level depend in these procedures on the division of tasks between the national authorities and the European institutions. The standard of protection both at the European and at the national level should be at least the standard of European law.[29] It is

[26] Hanns Peter Nehl, *Principles of Administrative Procedure in EC Law* (Oxford: Hart Publishing, 1999), pp 71 and 84; see however: Case T-277/97, *Ismeri Europa v Court of Auditors* [1999] ECR II-1825; Case C-315/99 P, *Ismeri Europa v Court of Auditors* [2001] ECR I-5281, where the fact that procedures were initiated appears to have been the criterion: Itai Rabinowitz, *The Fundamental Right to Be Heard in the Administrative Procedures of the European Union*, unpublished PhD at King's College London awarded on 1 August 2008.

[27] Critical: ibid, pp 95 and 98; more positive: Eric Babier de La Serre, 'Procedural Justice in the European Community Case-Law Concerning the Rights of the Defence: Essentialist and Instrumentalist Trends', *European Public Law*, 12(2) (2006), p 225 et seq, at 248–50.

[28] Also called 'mixed' or 'cooperative procedure'. See above and: Nehl, *Principles of Administrative Procedure* (n 26 above), pp 88–90; Sabino Cassese, 'European Administrative Proceedings', *Law And Contemporary Problems*, Vol 68:21 (2004), p 24 et seq; Giacinto della Cananea, 'The European Union's Mixed Administrative Proceedings', *Law and Contemporary Problems*, 68 (2004), p 197 et seq, at 211 et seq; see also Chapter 1 for more details on the listing procedure.

[29] See the ECJ's criticism of the procedural guarantees at the European level in Case C-49/88, *Al-Jubail* (n 24 above), para 16:

> It should be added that, with regard to the right to a fair hearing, any action taken by the Community institutions must be all the more scrupulous in view of the fact that, as they stand at present, the rules in question do not provide all the procedural guarantees for the protection of the individual which may exist in certain national legal systems.

Case C-269/90, *Technische Universität München v Hauptzollamt München-Mitte* [1991] ECR I 5469, para 14; see also: Joseph Weiler, 'Fundamental Rights and Fundamental Boundaries: On Standards and Values in the Protection of Human Rights', in Nannette A Neuwahl and Allan Rosas (eds), *The European Union and Human Rights* (Martinus Nijhoff, 1995), pp 72–3; Tridimas, *General Principles of EU Law* (n 24 above), p 323, referring to Joined Cases C-20 and C-64/00, *Booker Aquaculture Ltd and Hydro Seafood GSP Ltd v The Scottish Minister* [2003] ECR I-7411; Claudio Franchini, 'European Principles Governing National Administrative Proceedings', *Law And Contemporary Problems*, Vol 68:21 (2004), p 183 et seq, at 190 et seq argues that the principles are substantially the same in Community law and in the law of the Member States.

settled case-law that the Member States have to comply with fundamental rights when adopting national measures in order to implement EU law;[30] this includes both substantive and procedural rights. Relevant for individual sanctions is that the rights of defence are not limited to decisions addressed to the applicant. It is sufficient that the act expressly refers to the applicant.[31]

The EU courts have taken the position that the right to be heard must be realized 'where the actual decision is taken'. An important purpose of the right to be heard is to influence the decision-making; this is best realized where the decision is taken.[32] In double-staged procedures where 'the actual decision' is taken at the national level this leads to a limitation of the rights of defence at the Community level. Where the decision-taking is split between the national and the Community level, a hearing can be required for parts of the decision leading to the adoption of the measure at both levels. This splitting up of the hearing has some perils:[33] for instance that relevant information is lost[34] or that the person affected cannot make their views known on all relevant aspects of the decision that adversely affect them. This is highly relevant for the double-staged procedure leading to the adoption of individual sanctions.

The CFI developed the specific content of the rights to defence in the context of individual sanctions in its rulings in the *OMPI* saga and in the case of *Sison*.[35] The division of competences in the autonomous European listing procedure differs depending on whether an *initial* decision is taken

[30] The Member States must comply with fundamental rights protected in the form of general principles of EU law where they implement Community rules: Case 5/88, *Wachauf v Bundesamt für Ernährung und Forstwirtschaft* [1989] ECR 2609, para 19 (regulations); Joined Cases C-20 and C-64/00, *Booker Aquaculture Ltd and Hydro Seafood GSP Ltd v The Scottish Minister* [2003] ECR I-7411 (directives).

[31] Case C-32/95, *Commission v Lisrestal* [1996] ECR I-5373 recognized the defence rights of the beneficiary of the European Social Fund because the regulation in question established a direct link between the beneficiaries and the Commission; see also for individual sanctions: Case T-228/02, *OMPI I* (n 10 above); Case T-257/07, *OMPI II* (n 11 above); Case T-284/08, *OMPI III* (n 12 above); Case T-47/03, *Sison* (n 5 above).

[32] See eg: Case T-346/94, *France Aviation v Commission* [1995] ECR II-2841, paras 26–38; Case T-198/01, *Technische Glaswerke Ilmenau v Commission* [2004] ECR II-2717, paras 152–60; in the context of individual sanctions: Case T-47/03, *Sison* (n 5 above), para 165 referring to Case T-189/00 R, *'Invest' Import und Export and Invest Commerce v Commission* [2000] ECR II-2993, paras 40–1; Case C-32/95 P, *Commission v Lisrestal and others* (n 32 above), paras 21–43 and Case C-462/98 P, *Mediocurso v Commission* [2000] ECR I-7183, paras 36–44.

[33] Nehl, *Principles of Administrative Procedure* (n 20 above).

[34] Case T-346/94, *France Aviation v Commission* (n 32 above).

[35] Case T-228/02, *OMPI I* (n 10 above); Case T-257/07, *OMPI II* (n 11 above); Case T-284/08, *OMPI III* (n 12 above); Case T-47/03, *Sison* (n 5 above).

to list someone and freeze his funds or whether a *subsequent* decision is taken to maintain the person on the list and to keep his funds frozen (Article 2(3) of EC Regulation 2580/2001 read in conjunction with Article 1(4) and Article 1(6) of Common Position 2001/931/CFSP respectively).[36]

In the course of the initial listing the CFI found that the Council is only competent to verify '*that there exists a decision* of a national authority meeting the definition' in Article 1(4) of Common Position 2001/931/CFSP.[37] At the same time, the CFI held that the listing decision is a discretionary decision of the Council.[38] Hence, even if a decision of a national authority exists (and the Member State proposes listing) the Council is not obliged to list the person.

The principle of loyal cooperation[39] 'entails, for the Council, the obligation to defer as far as possible to the assessment conducted by the national authority, at least where it is a judicial authority.'[40] Typically, the national act would be a decision to instigate investigations. The CFI stated that usually the competent national authority is a judicial authority, not an administrative one.[41] However, as the *OMPI* cases demonstrate, the competent authority can also be part of the executive.[42] When the initial decision is taken '[t]he rights of the defence of the person concerned must be effectively safeguarded in the first place as part of the national procedure'[43] At the Community level, the hearing extends only to the narrow legal question whether a decision existed that meets the definition of the Community regulation.[44] It does not usually extend to the substance of that decision: the appropriateness or well-foundedness of the decision

[36] Case T-47/03, *Sison* (n 5 above), para 161; this becomes obvious in the word 'whereas' in para 164.

[37] Case T-228/02, *OMPI I* (n 10 above), para 117 (emphasis added); Case T-47/03, *Sison* (n 5 above), para 164.

[38] Case T-228/02, *OMPI I* (n 10 above), para 159.

[39] Article 10 EC, relations between the Member States and the Community institutions are governed by reciprocal duties to cooperate in good faith (see Case C-339/00, *Ireland v Commission* [2003] ECR I-11757, paras 71 and 72.

[40] Case T-257/07, *OMPI II* (n 11 above), para 133; see also: Case T-228/02, *OMPI I* (n 10 above), para 122.

[41] Article 1(4) of Common Position 931/2001/CFSP: ... For the purposes of this paragraph 'competent authority' shall mean a judicial authority, or, where judicial authorities have no competence in the area covered by this paragraph, an equivalent competent authority in that area.
Case T-228/02, *OMPI I* (n 10 above), para 116.

[42] In the case of OMPI the listing was based on an order of the UK Home Secretary under the Terrorism Act 2000, see in particular: Case T-256/07, *OMPI II* (n 11 above), paras 2 and 144.

[43] Case T-228/02, *OMPI I* (n 10 above), para 119; nearly identical: Case T-47/03, *Sison* (n 5 above), para 166.

[44] Case T-228/02, *OMPI I* (n 10 above), para 120.

cannot be questioned at the European level.[45] The strict limitation of the hearing appears to contrast with the fact that the Council exercises discretion.

Since it is not for the Council to examine whether the fundamental rights of the party concerned were respected by the national authorities, the hearing does not cover the fairness of the procedure at the national level either.[46] However, where the Member State submits to the Council evidence that has not been assessed by the competent national authority, this newly-adduced evidence must be subject of the hearing before the Council.[47] Finally, the CFI acknowledged that a hearing *before* the initial decision 'would be liable to jeopardise the effectiveness of the listing'.[48]

With regard to the subsequent decisions the CFI considered it necessary that the Council verified '*the consequences of that decision* at the national level'[49] Here, those listed have more extensive rights at the Community level to make their views known. The CFI explicitly stated that '[a]ny subsequent decision to freeze funds must accordingly be preceded by the possibility of a further hearing and, where appropriate, notification of any new incriminating evidence'[50] In *OMPI II* and *OMPI III* the CFI examined in detail the rights of defence at the Community level where the Council takes a subsequent listing decision to continue sanctions against a specific person. The right to be heard extends to all the information that the Council is obliged to consider in the subsequent decision. This includes appeal decisions at the national level and, if applicable, the Member State's omission to take further measures, ie to carry out further investigations, after the first decision.[51]

The CFI's position on hearing rights in the autonomous listing procedure can be contrasted with its position on hearing rights where sanctions giving effect to UN lists of terrorist suspects are concerned. In the cases of *Yusuf* and *Kadi*[52] the CFI denied the applicants a right to be heard by the Council, since the Council was bound by UN law to adopt the contested

[45] ibid, para 121.
[46] ibid.
[47] Case T-228/02, *OMPI I* (n 10 above), para 125.
[48] Case T-47/03, *Sison* (n 5 above), para 175, see also: Case T-228/02, *OMPI I* (n 10 above), para 128; restricting hearing right in 'emergency situations' is well accepted, see also: Case T-372/00 *Campolargo v Commission* [2002] ECR II-223, para 32.
[49] Case T-47/03, *Sison* (n 5 above), para 164.
[50] ibid, para 178.
[51] See Chapter 7 on the criteria for a subsequent listing.
[52] Case T-306/01, *Yusuf* (n 2 above); Case T-315/01, *Kadi* (n 2 above); see Chapter 5.

measure and therefore lacked the discretion that would activate the right to be heard.[53] The CFI ruled that, although persons did not have the opportunity to be heard by the Sanctions Committee, they had 'a right to present a request for review of their case to [their] government' of nationality or residence guaranteed not only by the Guidelines of the Sanctions Committee but also by Community law.[54] The CFI further stated that Member States would not be justified in refusing a petition 'solely because the persons concerned could not provide precise and relevant information'.[55] The fact that a request cannot be refused because the individual cannot provide relevant information implies not only that the person does not know the allegations that led to the listing, but also appears to amount in practice to a *right* that a request for removal is presented to the UN Sanctions Committee. Additionally, the CFI noted that those listed could bring an action against a wrongful refusal under domestic law.[56]

The CFI referred to an earlier case on state sanctions against the then Federal Republic of Yugoslavia (the *'Invest' Import und Export* case)[57] and explained that 'Community law itself recognizes the lawfulness of such procedural adaptations in the context of economic sanctions against individuals'[58] With 'procedural adaptations' the CFI meant the possibility that procedural rights at one level substitute for the rights at another level. In *'Invest' Import und Export* the CFI had found justified certain limitations imposed on the right to a fair hearing at the European level, because 'the right ... to be heard must actually be secured *in the first place* in the relations between that undertaking and the competent national administrative authority'.[59]

The Council had adopted a regulation ordering the freezing of all assets of Yugoslav companies in the EU. The Commission drew up the updated list of companies to whom the regulation applied. The applicant company was listed by the Commission on application by the competent national

[53] Case T-315/01, *Kadi*, ibid, paras 258–9; Case T-306/01 *Yusuf*, ibid, paras 328–9.

[54] See Case T-253/02, *Ayadi* (n 2 above), para 145; see also Chapter 7, Section 3.3 on the right to diplomatic protection.

[55] Case T-253/02, *Ayadi* (n 2 above), para 148.

[56] Case T-315/01, *Kadi* (n 2 above), paras 268–70; Case T-306/01, *Yusuf* (n 2 above), paras 315–17.

[57] Case T-189/00 R, *'Invest' Import und Export* (n 32 above); see below.

[58] Case T-315/01, *Kadi* (n 2 above), para 269.

[59] Case T-189/00 R, *'Invest' Import und Export* (n 32 above), para 40, emphasis added. The order was approved on appeal with no reference to the question of the right to be heard, see: Case C-317/00 P(R), *'Invest' Import und Export and Invest Commerce v Commission* [2000] ECR I-9541.

authorities of Germany and France. Hence, the procedure consisted of two stages (national and Community stage). The regulation contained a cursory reference to rights of defence, stipulating that persons could request through the competent national authorities to be delisted.[60]

The Commission had listed the applicants without giving them the opportunity to be heard. The applicants brought an action for breach of their hearing rights arguing that 'in the end it is the Commission which is responsible for ensuring that the undertakings concerned receive a lawful hearing'[61] The CFI found the applicant's allegation unsubstantiated. Not denying that the Commission had not given the applicants the opportunity to be heard, the Court turned to the national level where in the present procedure the right to be heard must be guaranteed in the first place. The CFI pointed out that the applicants had made no submissions as to any breach by the national authorities of their right to be heard, but that, on the contrary, they had been heard at the national level.'[62]

Two important conclusions can be drawn from the *'Invest' Import und Export* case. First, even though in this case the Commission was not obliged to grant the opportunity for a hearing, such an obligation is not excluded in principle (the CFI found that the right has to be guaranteed 'in the first place' at the national level). This is confirmed by the earlier case of *France Aviation*.[63] In this case, concerning a double-staged procedure for the remission of customs duties, the CFI had ruled that the Commission was under the obligation to hear the applicant, even though 'in the first place' this was the obligation of the national authorities.[64] Secondly, the CFI was not as a matter of principle unwilling to review that the applicants had the opportunity to be heard in the national procedure. The Court discussed the fact that the applicants had been heard by the national authorities, even though this had not directly been raised as an issue by either of the parties.

'Invest' Import und Export can further be contrasted with the cases of *Yusuf* and *Kadi*.[65] In *Yusuf* and *Kadi* the CFI relied on the rationale of *'Invest' Import and Export*. However, while as a matter of principle

[60] Article 8(4) of Council Regulation (EC) No 1059/2000 of 18 May 2000 amending Regulation No 723/2000, OJ 2000 L 119/1.

[61] Case T-189/00 R, *'Invest' Import und Export* (n 32 above), para 26.

[62] ibid, para 40–1.

[63] See also: Case T-346/94, *France Aviation* (n 32 above); Case T-42/96, *Eyckeler&Malt AG v Commission* [1998] ECR II-401.

[64] See below; see also on both cases: Itai Rabinowitz, *The Fundamental Right to Be Heard* (n 26 above).

[65] Case T-306/01, *Yusuf* (n 2 above); Case T-315/01, *Kadi* (n 2 above), see above around n 52.

'procedural adaptations' are justifiable in procedures involving the European institutions and the national authorities, this cannot be transferred to the UN. The CFI's ruling in *Yusuf* and *Kadi* is not convincing. The UN is external to the European legal system. A division of the obligation to provide the opportunity to be heard might be justifiable between the national level and the European level, where the EU courts maintain the ultimate power of control. They can review Member States' compliance with procedural rights in double-staged administrative procedures.[66] This is not the case for UN procedures.[67] Here, the European institutions have to take full responsibility for the procedural rights of those sanctioned.

Discretion is a central element in the CFI's assessment of the individual's right to a fair hearing at a particular stage of the procedure. The CFI appears to limit the right to a fair hearing to discretionary decisions. This could be concluded not only from the comparison between sanctions giving effect to UN lists[68] but also to the scope of the hearing at the European level for autonomous sanctions. However, this is not fully in line with the case-law of the ECJ. For instance in the case of *Technische Universität München*[69] (concerning the refusal of an exemption from customs duties), the ECJ pointed out that where the EU institutions have wide powers of appraisal the respect for procedural rights is of even more fundamental importance. Yet, the ECJ did not rule that the right to be heard is *limited* to discretionary decisions. Because discretionary decisions are not fully reviewable, courts attach particular importance to compliance with procedural rules. In *Technische Universität München*, even though the national authorities recommended a refusal and the Commission followed this recommendation, the ECJ held that not only the national authorities but also the Commission had to provide a right to a fair hearing on the documents considered by it in its decision.

In the discussion on the right to be heard in the sanctioning procedure, it is important to note that the Council's decision to list and sanction someone has far-reaching additional consequences for the concerned individuals. The EU does not only attach its name to the allegation that

[66] See also Section 1.3 below.

[67] Chapter 5, Section 4.

[68] See the CFI's reasoning in Case T-306/01, *Yusuf* (n 2 above); Case T-315/01, *Kadi* (n 2 above), but also in Case T-346/94, *France Aviation* (n 32 above).

[69] Case C-269/90, *Technische Universität München* (n 29 above), para 14. However, the need for a hearing was based on the duty of care (it was necessary for a well-founded decision on a highly technical question) and not on the party's right to the defence.

someone is a terrorist suspect and vests this allegation thereby with additional force, it also makes a difference whether the assets of a person are frozen in one country or in all 27 EU Member States. Further, Member States, after having suggested a listing at the EU level, can request a delisting; however, they no longer have the power to take the unilateral decision to delist a person. Even if a Member State publically renounces its original assessment that the person was a terrorist, the word of the Member State will stand against the continuous listing at the European level.[70]

Limiting the hearing to discretionary decisions can raise problems in double-staged procedures. In the listing procedure the power-sharing unfolds in an ascending way: it is not the Member States that implement EU law (agency situation),[71] but the Community that takes an action based on the decision of the national authorities. However, this does not justify a departure from the general rule that the EU institutions bear ultimate responsibility.[72] The listing and freezing of assets serves a different purpose than the national procedures. This also explains the Council's discretion to continue measures even after a successful appeal against the national decision. In *OMPI II* the Council explicitly made the argument that even if the POAC's findings were giving an accurate picture the listing and freezing of the applicant's funds at the EU level could still be justified.[73] Also the considerations of the CFI on newly adduced evidence that has not been assessed by the competent national authority implies that the proposal or request of the Member States that leads to the listing at the Community level is a separate act from the procedures that culminate in the 'decision of the competent national authority'. The purpose of this proposal appears to lie exclusively in initiating a listing and freezing of funds at the European level. However, this proposal is an internal preliminary act and cannot as such be contested in the national system.

Despite the separate proceedings, leading to different measures (eg, investigation and proscription at the national level; listing and freezing of funds at the Community level), the quality and accuracy of the Community decision depends on the quality and accuracy of the national decision.

[70] See also Chapter 1, Section 4.2.

[71] This might be the case where secondary sanctions are adopted later in the sanctioning procedure, but this is not the subject of the present discussion.

[72] Cassese, *European Administrative Proceedings* (n 28 above).

[73] Case T-256/07, *OMPI II* (n 11 above), para 163. The British Proscribed Organisations Appeal Commission (POAC) had ordered the removal of OMPI from the list stating that it would be 'perverse' to maintain a terrorist designation for OMPI. See also Chapter 7, pp 378, 402.

Because of the particular division of responsibility a defect of the national procedure is not easily healed at the Community level. The listing at the European level would be tainted with the same breach of procedural rights occurring at the national level. And, such a defect is only subject to limited review by the EU courts. This can be seen in the case of *OMPI II*.[74] On appeal before a quasi-judicial authority the decision of the competent national authority was found to be unreasonable and perverse. The competet national authority had failed to take the more recent information on the activity of OMPI into account. Yet, the Council had listed and sanctioned OMPI exclusively based on this national decision and consequently attached additional adverse effect to a flawed decision.

The Council attaches additional adverse effects to the decision of a national authority, but exercises (according to the CFI) only very limited discretion. The CFI explicitly held that the Council exercises discretion, but cannot verify the factual decision that someone is a terrorist suspect. It can only verify that a decision of a competent national authority exists.

If, however, the Council cannot engage in an examination of the factual basis, it is difficult to see the Council's substantive considerations when it takes the 'discretionary decision' to list someone. Moreover, the mandate of the permanent Working Party (CP 931 WP), which was set up by the Council in response to the CFI's annulments of Community sanctions under the autonomous sanctions regime,[75] appears to confirm that the Council does consider the content of the terrorist allegation.

Irrespective of whether the Council does in practice examine the factual bases of the terrorist allegation or the likelihood that funds are used to finance terrorist activities if not frozen,[76] the hearing has to extend to the well-foundedness of the listing decision. This includes beyond the existence of the national decision the reasons why in addition to the national proceedings a listing is justified. This will by definition include a factual assessment of the situation.

[74] Case T-256/07, *OMPI II* (n 11 above); see also: Case T-346/94, *France Aviation* (n 32 above) and Case T-198/01, *Technische Glaswerke Ilmenau* (n 32 above), paras 145, 153–60 and 183. In this case, the receiver of a state aid complained that confusion between the Commission and the responsible Member State denied it the opportunity to comment on important documents. This problem would have been avoided had the applicant had direct access to the Commission's file.

[75] Council Document 10826/07 on the fight against the financing of terrorism – implementation of Common Position 2001/931/CFSP, of 21 June 2007; see also: Chapter 7, Section 1.1.

[76] See the purpose of asset freezes both in Chapter 1, Section 7 and in Chapter 7, Section 4.

From the perspective of the public interest the exercise of the right to a fair hearing at the stage where the actual decision is formed may be sufficient. This is the stage where a hearing contributes most to the accuracy of the decision. From the perspective of the individual, this is also where the decision-making can be best influenced. However, the interest of the individual goes beyond influencing the decision. The individual has an even greater interest to seek protection from adverse effects. Hence, the procedural protection must match the intensity of the interference with the person's legal sphere.[77] If the bulk of the decision is formed at the national level it is reasonable that the responsibility to hear those listed lies in the first place with the national authorities, as the CFI held already in *'Invest' Import und Export*. Besides striking a balance between the rights of the affected individual and interests of security, the principle of subsidiarity and the sovereignty of the Member States must be taken into account when the right level for a hearing is determined. The European institutions can only offer the opportunity of a fair hearing to the extent that they do not interfere with the rights of the Member States to conduct their own procedures of criminal investigations. However, it is here argued the European institutions have a responsibility grounded in the additional adverse affect that they attach to the national decision.

It is submitted that the European institutions must ensure certain conditions of procedural fairness. Some of these conditions have been confirmed or at least implied by the EU courts. Some are a consequence of the fact that procedural adaptations are possible only to the extent that they do not erode the rights of defence.

First, in agreement with the CFI's ruling in the CFI in the *OMPI* cases,[78] it is submitted that the European institutions must provide a hearing for new information. This applies to all situations where the European institutions take into account information that has not been considered in a hearing at the national level.

Secondly, it is submitted that the decision of the competent national authority must be subject to effective judicial review in the national system.[79]

[77] Joana Mendes, 'Participation an participation right in EU law and governance', in Herwig Hofmann and Alexander Türk (eds), *The Move to an Integrated Administration – Legal Challenges in EU Administrative Law* (Cheltenham: Edward Elgar, 2008) makes a distinction between the different rationales of participation right and argues in favour of the the 'dignitarian rationale', the 'stronger' meaning of participation.

[78] See Section 1 above.

[79] This should be clearly indicated in the standardised form for the listing request, see Chapter 7, Section 1.2

This is the case irrespective of whether the original decision was taken by a (quasi-)judicial authority. This condition has not explicitly been formulated by the EU courts. However, the CFI did emphasize the importance of judicial review by the national courts or, as the case may be, by the ECtHR.[80]

Thirdly, it is argued that the Council must attend in a hearing to credible information that is brought to its attention indicating that a Member State acted unreasonably in requesting the listing of a specific person. This was in essence the situation in *OMPI II*.[81] This includes where the information indicates that a Member State has not – after initiating a listing at the European level – taken any follow-up measures to investigate the initial suspicion that the person is a terrorist supporter. The CFI explicitly required consideration of the 'consequences' of a listing decision at the national level.[82] Yet, the Court also found that the Council does not have to discuss the argument of substance save where an appeal body has quashed the original decision of the national authorities.[83] Hence, the interpretation suggested here goes beyond what the CFI considered necessary.

Fourthly, while the Council cannot in principle control compliance with procedural rights at the national level because this would go against the principle of loyal cooperation,[84] it is submitted that the EU courts must do so. The competence to review compliance with fundamental procedural rights in independent criminal proceedings conducted by the national authorities might appear contrary to the spirit of Article 35(5) TEU,[85] even though this provision is not directly applicable. If Member States do not provide for the necessary safeguards, the European institutions cannot legitimately attach adverse effects to their decisions. This does not question the validity of the national decision as such. Full judicial scrutiny includes ensuring that procedural rights are only restricted where this is necessary given imperative considerations of security or international cooperation.[86]

[80] Case T-228/02, *OMPI I* (n 10 above), para 121.

[81] Case T-256/07, *OMPI II* (n 11 above).

[82] Case T-47/03, *Sison* (n 5 above), para 164.

[83] Compare the CFI's remarks on Council Decision 2007/445/EC (appeal before the POAC pending) and Council Decision 2007/868/EC (the POAC had ruled in favour of the applicant) both in: Case T-256/07, *OMPI II* (n 11 above).

[84] This was the CFI's view, see: Case T-257/07, *OMPI II* (n 11 above), para 133; Case T-228/02, *OMPI I* (n 10 above), para 122.

[85] Article 35(5) TEU: The Court of Justice shall have no jurisdiction to review the validity or proportionality of operations carried out by the police or other law enforcement services of a Member State or the exercise of the responsibilities incumbent upon Member States with regard to the maintenance of law and order and the safeguarding of internal security.

[86] The CFI appears to do this, see: Case T-284/08, *OMPI III* (n 12 above).

Indeed, the EU courts must even offset any alleged restrictions on the right to a fair hearing at the national level with a strict judicial review.[87] The CFI appeared to be willing to ensure compliance with procedural rights at the national level in *'Invest' Import und Export*.[88] Yet, in *OMPI III* the CFI mentioned only review by the national courts and the ECtHR and not by the EU courts.[89]

1.1.2 Access to Information

Access to the incriminating information is essential for the rights of defence. The fact that individuals are listed as terrorists and sanctioned without knowing why (or who is making the allegation) is one of the fundamental deficiencies of the listing procedure.[90] The rights of defence, including the right to a fair hearing, cannot be exercised effectively if those affected cannot oppose the allegations against them, because they (or possibly a special advocate in their place[91]) do not know what these allegations are. In the case of *Sison*, the CFI considered that 'the parties concerned can make genuine use of their right to a judicial remedy only if they have precise knowledge of the content of and the reasons for the act in question'.[92]

However, both in *Sison* (and also in *OMPI*) the CFI found that at no time before the judicial proceedings was the evidence notified to the applicant.[93] Mr Sison did not know on which national decisions the listing was based. In fact, not even in the judicial proceedings could the CFI establish with certainty whether the listing was exclusively based on the decisions mentioned by the Council,[94] which also were not taken by the 'competent national authority'.[95]

[87] Case T-284/08, *OMPI III* (n 12 above), para 75, with a reference to Case C-341/04, *Eurofood IFSC* [2006] ECR I-3813.

[88] The CFI appears to be willing to examine the national procedure, see remarks at: Case T-189/00 R, *Invest-Import and Export* (n 32 above), para 41–2.

[89] Case T-284/08, *OMPI III* (n 12 above), para 75.

[90] See eg the harsh criticism at: Iain Cameron, 'European Union Anti-Terrorist Blacklisting', *Human Rights Law Review*, 4 (2004); see also: Dick Marty, Report of the Committee on Legal Affairs and Human Rights to the Council of Europe, Document 11454, of 16 November 2007.

[91] Chapter 7, Section 1.4.

[92] Case T-47/03, *Sison* (n 5 above), para 137; the court here referred to ECJ 19 February 1998, Case C-309/95, *Commission v Council*, para 18 and CFI 29 May 1997, Case T-89/96, *British Steel v Commission*, para 33.

[93] Case T-228/02, *OMPI I* (n 10 above), para 161; Case T-47/03, *Sison* (n 5 above), para 208.

[94] Case T-47/03, *Sison* (n 5 above), para 222.

[95] ibid, para 224.

In the case of *Sison* the applicant brought additional proceedings against the Council's refusal to grant him access to documents containing information that led to his listing as a terrorist suspects.[96] However, the applicant based his application for access to these documents on the public right of access to documents set out in Regulation 1049/2001.[97] Even though it has been argued that the public and the personal right of access to documents gradually merge,[98] a right based on personal interests cannot be exercised by having recourse to Regulation No 1049/2001.[99] The general public right of access to documents is derived from the democratic principle serving to bring about open government and accountability, while the 'right of access to one's file' is a procedural right having the specific purpose to ensure the 'equality of arms' in administrative procedure.[100] This latter personal right to information is based on different considerations. First, individuals have a general right to know what the state knows about them and, secondly, they have a particular interest to answer to the allegations made against them.

Those listed and sanctioned have a personal right of access to information based on the great impact on their legal position. While the CFI acknowledged that security considerations can justify restricting access to information, it also made clear that these restrictions have to be considered and justified with regard to the individual case and document.[101] So far the information shared with the applicants and even with the EU courts has been so limited that the courts have not been in the position to review the merits of the sanction cases.[102] As a matter of principle, this is contrary to the personal right of access to information of those listed and sanctioned. This is not to say that relevant information cannot be concealed from the parties for reasons of security. However, whether information can be concealed would have to be subject to judicial control.[103] Further, substantive restrictions would have to be counterbalanced by the automatic appointment of a special advocate to ensure an overall fair procedure. The

[96] Joined Cases T-110/03, T-150/03 and T-405/03, *Jose Maria Sison v Council* [2005] ECR II-1429.

[97] Regulation 1049/2001, OJ 2001 L 145/43.

[98] Nehl, *Principles of Administrative Procedure in EC Law* (n 26 above), p 60.

[99] Case C-266/05 P, *Sison v Council* [2007] ECR I-1233, para 48.

[100] ibid, p 51.

[101] See also Section 1.2 below on the duty to state reasons.

[102] Case T-228/02, *OMPI I* (n 10 above), paras 162, 165, and 166; for sanctions giving effect to UN lists see: Cases C-402/05 P and C-415/05 P, *Kadi and al Barakaat* (n 2 above), paras 348 and 351.

[103] See also the ECtHR's case-law on non-disclosure in Chapter 4, Section 3.1.

continuing restrictions[104] are likely to be subject to further litigation in Luxembourg.

In *OMPI II* and *OMPI III* the CFI demonstrated that it will defend its ground. In particular, *OMPI III* makes clear that the Court will annul a listing if the Council does not or cannot demonstrate the specific reasons why a person was listed. Confirming its earlier position that considerations of security or international relations cannot justify concealing information from the EU Court, the CFI ruled that the Council is not entitled to base decisions on information that is not communicated to the Court.[105] In particular the OMPI saga demonstrates the difficulties that individuals face when seeking protection from terrorist listings. However, OMPI's problems in finding justice were largely due to the reactive role of the judiciary and not to the level of review proposed by the CFI.[106]

1.2 Obligation to State Reasons

The requirement to state reasons has the objective to protect the individual from arbitrary measures, to encourage the institutions to self-restraint, to allow the applicant in practice to defend its rights, and to enable the court to review the decisions fully from the legal point of view.[107] The requirements imposed on the statement of reasons in the double-staged listing procedure also depend on the division of tasks between the Community and the Member States. For the initial decision the statement must refer 'to the reasons why the Council considers, in the exercise of its discretion, that such measures must be adopted in respect of the party concerned'.[108] Since the existence of the national decision is enough 'reason' for a listing, this means that those listed must in principle be informed of the decision which was found to satisfy the criteria in Article 1(4) of Common Position 2001/931/CFSP, the (national) author of this decision, and–only where applicable–of any new incriminating evidence that had not been scrutinized by the national authorities. The more specific the measure is the more specific the statement of reasons must be.[109] Hence, since individual sanctions

[104] Chapter 7, Section 1.4.

[105] Case T-284/08, *OMPI III* (n 12 above), para 73.

[106] See Chapter 7, Section 3.2.

[107] Eg: Case 18/57, *Nold* [1958] ECR 41, p 51; Case 294/81, *Control Data* [1983] ECR 911, para 14 et seq; Case C-269/90, *Technische Universität München* (n 29 above).

[108] Case T-228/02, *OMPI I* (n 10 above), para 146–51.

[109] ibid, para 141.

identify specific persons the reasons stating why this person is listed cannot remain at a general stereotypical level.[110]

For the subsequent decision the CFI ruled that the statement must set out 'the actual and specific reasons why the freezing of the funds remains justified'[111] In *OMPI II*[112] the CFI found the statement of reasons issued to the applicant insufficient in that it did not mention the appeal decision of the POAC. In this decision the POAC had drastically criticized the decisions of the UK Home Secretary by stating that the only conclusion a reasonable decision-maker could have reached was to delist OMPI. Also, this was the first decision of a national quasi-judicial body on the matter, because the competent national authority was the UK Home Secretary.[113]

On 3 December 2008 (*OMPI III*) the CFI annulled for the first time the listing of OMPI that was still in force on the day of the oral hearing[114] on the grounds that the Council failed to substantiate the claim that it could not follow acceptable procedures that would have protected the procedural rights of the applicant when taking the subsequent decision to keep OMPI listed. The statement of reasons issued to OMPI with regard to this last Council decision pointed out that the original national decision was no longer in force, but that the Council had been provided with 'new information'.[115] The new information related to a judicial inquiry opened by the anti-terrorist prosecutor's office of the court of first instance of Paris in April 2001 and to supplementary charges brought by the Paris anti-terrorist prosecutor's office on 19 March and 13 November 2007. The Council had information on the substance of these charges but did not communicate that information to the applicant.[116]

The identification of the possible restrictions defines the true content of the rights to defence in practice. The initial statement of reason does not have to be issued *before* the measures are enacted and 'it is also conceivable that restrictions on access may concern the specific content of or the particular reasoning of that decision, or even the identity of the authority that took it. It is even possible that, in certain, very specific circumstances, the identification of the Member State or third country in which a competent

[110] ibid, para 143.
[111] ibid, para
[112] Case T-256/07, *OMPI II* (n 11 above), para 157 et seq; see also n 73 above.
[113] See Section 1.1 above for the rights of defence
[114] See also Chapter 7, Section 3.2.
[115] Case T-284/08, *OMPI III* (n 12 above), para 9–10.
[116] Case T-284/08, *OMPI III* (n 12 above), para 41.

authority has taken a decision in respect of a person may be liable to jeopardize public security, by providing the party concerned with sensitive information that it could misuse.'[117] 'Overriding considerations concerning the security of the Community and its Member States, or the conduct of their international relations' may exceptionally trump the Council and Commission's obligation to state reasons to the extent that evidence adduced against the parties is not communicated to them during the administrative procedure.[118] However, the CFI's ruling in *OMPI III* demonstrates that the Council is not free to raise general security concerns to justify disregarding the rights of those sanctioned. On the contrary, the Council has to substantiate with specific reasons why a restriction of procedural rights was necessary in the particular case. In principle, the Council has to substantiate restrictions at the administrative stage; the failure to issue a statement of reasons cannot be remedied in judicial proceedings.[119]

The rights of those listed and sanctioned continue to be infringed. However, the Council could not entirely disregard the CFI's rulings. Changes have been introduced that have made the listing procedure more transparent and that have given individuals some information why they were targeted.[120] Since *OMPI I* the European institutions issue statements of motivation for each person listed.[121] However, the quality of information remains questionable in the light of *OMPI II* and *OMPI III*.

1.3 *Judicial Review*

Despite the fact that the CFI annulled the Community listing of OMPI three times, it is still controversial whether the level of judicial review outlined by the CFI in *OMPI I* offers effective protection.[122] The CFI agreed to review that fundamental procedural rules and the obligation to

[117] Case T-228/02, *OMPI I* (n 10 above), para 136. see also: Case T-47/03, *Sison* (n 5 above), para 183.

[118] Case T-228/02, *OMPI I* (n 10 above), para 148; see above for the restrictions on access to information.

[119] Case T-228/02, *OMPI I* (n 10 above), para 139; Case T-257/07, *OMPI II* (n 11 above), para 182.

[120] See Chapter 7, Section 1.1.

[121] *EU backing down on terror list secrecy*, EU observer of 16 January 2007.

[122] Critical with regard to the level of protection in Case T-228/02, *OMPI I* (n 10 above): Frank Meyer, 'Lost in Complexity: Rechtsschutz gegen Smart Sanctions in der EU', *Zeitschrift für Europarechtliche Studien*, (2007); critical with regard to the review in all three cases: Iain Cameron, 'Sökandet efter en rättvis lösning pa FN:s riktade sanctioner: ett sisyfosarbete', *Svensk Juristtidning* (2009), pp 64–83.

state reasons are complied with, that the facts are substantially correct, and that no manifest error of assessment or an ultra vires action has occurred.[123] On the one hand, the Court was acting cautiously in pointing out that considerable restrictions can be imposed on the right of access to justice in order to protect public security and international relations in an area as sensitive as counter-terrorist measures.[124] Limitations of the right of access to justice in order to safeguard security interests are well accepted by the case-law of the ECtHR, to which the CFI made reference.[125] On the other, the Court was equally clear that the EU courts themselves must have access to the relevant information to be able to judge the lawfulness of the decision to place a particular person on the list.[126]

More specifically, the CFI stated that

> it is for the Court to ensure, *inter alia*, that the legal conditions for applying Regulation No 2580/2001 to a particular scenario, as laid down in Article 2(3) of that regulation and, by reference, either Article 1(4) or Article 1(6) of Common Position 2001/931, depending on whether it is an initial decision or a subsequent decision to freeze funds, are fulfilled. That implies that the judicial review of the lawfulness of the decision in question extends to the assessment of the facts and circumstances relied on as justifying it, and to the evidence and information on which that assessment is based.[127]

The Court further conceded that

> [t]he question whether the applicant and/or its lawyers may be provided with the evidence and information alleged to be confidential, or whether they may be provided only to the Court, in accordance with a procedure which remains to be defined so as to safeguard the public interests at issue whilst affording the party concerned a sufficient degree of judicial protection, is a separate issue on which it is not necessary for the Court to rule in the present action.[128]

In *OMPI I* the CFI did not address the consequences of the fact that the Union listings gave effect to Security Council resolutions, nor the legality of the EC Council Resolution, which was the basis for the adopted list of

[123] Case T-228/02, *OMPI I* (n 10 above), para 159.

[124] ibid, para 127 et seq for the right to fair hearing; para 147 et seq for the obligation to state reasons; para 156 et seq for the right to effective judicial protection.

[125] ECtHR, *Chahal v United Kingdom* (1996) 23 EHRR 413, judgment of 15 November 1996 and ECtHR, *Jasper v United Kingdom*, judgment of 16 February 2000, No 27052/95, not published in Reports of Judgments and Decisions.

[126] Case T-228/02, *OMPI I* (n 10 above), para 172 et seq.

[127] ibid, para 154. [128] ibid, para 158.

terrorist suspects. It did not respond to the reservation expressed by the Council that:[129]

> the Court has no jurisdiction to review the internal lawfulness of the relevant provisions of [the EC Council regulation] [...], because they were adopted by virtue of powers circumscribed by Security Council Resolution 1373 (2001) and therefore benefit from the principle of primacy.

Indeed, the Court left explicitly open whether the EC regulation could benefit from primacy effects.[130] It limited its review to the lawfulness of the contested Council decision, which listed the applicant and which none of the parties contested fell within the Court's competence. The more principled question of whether the adoption of a regime of individual sanctions in the form of EC Council Regulation 2580/2001 was in compliance with the general principles of EU law was not considered by the Court. This limits the implications of *OMPI* to the adoption of lists of terrorist suspects, without allowing for more fundamental conclusions on European sanctions against individuals as a counter-terrorist policy.

The judiciary is confronted with several practical problems when reviewing individual sanctions. First, the core competence of the EU courts does not lie in the field of criminal law. Secondly, the evidentiary standard to justify a listing pursuant to Article 1(4) of Common Position 931/2001/CFSP is rather imprecise. This provision stipulates that the decision by the competent national authority should be 'based on serious and credible evidence or clues, or condemnation for such deeds'. Hence, the evidentiary standard necessary to list someone requires as a minimum the existence of 'clues'. And, while the CFI appears to use the terms 'information', 'evidence' and 'clues' interchangeably,[131] these terms carry a different meaning and have different weight in criminal law. 'Evidence' is an accepted term under international criminal law[132] and under national criminal law. 'Clues' by contrast is exclusively used at the investigatory stage. This might confront the judiciary with practical problems to verify the well-foundedness of a national decision based on 'clues'. However, where the existence of clues is sufficient to take far-reaching measures against an

[129] ibid, para 112.

[130] ibid, para 113.

[131] Case T-228/02, *OMPI I* (n 10 above); Case T-257/07, *OMPI II* (n 11 above); Case T-284/08, *OMPI III* (n 12 above).

[132] See eg: International Criminal Court, Rules of Procedure and Evidence, UN Doc PCNICC/2000/1/Add.1 (2000); see also: William A Schabas, *Introduction to the International Criminal Court* (Cambridge: Cambridge University Press, 2007).

individual the review should be stricter rather than leaving greater room for discretion to the political institutions.

Despite the limitations that the CFI outlined in *OMPI I* the Court established for the first time that EC Council decisions containing terrorist lists are subject to judicial review in the light of European standards of fundamental rights protection. The Court also annulled the contested measure as far as the applicant was concerned. Not only the result, but also the CFI's clear criticism, the requirements it imposed on the European institutions as regards the sharing of information, and the consequences of the judgment demonstrate that the limitations imposed by the CFI did not exclude a meaningful control of the Council's decisions. A central point is that the CFI made clear that the EU courts must be given all the relevant information on which the particular listing decision is based.

2. Protection from Union Lists: the Status Quo

The strict limitation of the jurisdiction of the EU courts in the Union pillars (second and third pillar) makes it possible for the Council to adopt lists publicly alleging that certain persons are supporting terrorism without giving them the opportunity to challenge this allegation effectively. Individuals who are identified as terrorist suspects by the EU itself and whose assets are frozen by the Community do have the chance in the EU courts to challenge the Community instrument, but not the CFSP list.

While both types of sanctions, those based on Union lists and those based on UN lists, require a CFSP decision, the lack of judicial review of CFSP instruments is for two reasons even more relevant in the context of autonomous sanctions. First, where action by the European institutions is based on UN lists of terrorist suspects, the listing in the CFSP instrument is not the *first* public allegation that the person is involved in terrorism. It is an additional, but not the initial, stigmatization. Secondly, where the EU takes action against those identified by the UN Sanctions Committee, they are all first listed in the CFSP common position and then targeted by the Council regulation. The list of names is *always identical.* By contrast, not every person listed on an autonomous European list is also targeted by Community sanctions.

In the autonomous European sanctions regime the Council distinguishes EU-internal terrorist suspects and EU-external terrorist suspects. Segi and all those who have close links with the EU fall within the former group. While the Union lists them as alleged terrorist supporters in CFSP common positions, their assets are not frozen by the *Community* but by the *Member States.*[133] This is due to the fact that with regard to EU-internal terrorist suspects there is no consensus whether the EU is in fact competent to adopt sanctions against them. This is a further difference between autonomous sanctions and UN-based sanctions. As was demonstrated by the case of *Yusuf*, the EU institutions and the EU courts consider it possible to adopt individual sanctions against EU citizens based on the joint legal basis of Articles 301, 60, and 308 EC where these sanctions give effect to UN lists. Autonomous sanctions against EU-internal terrorists, by contrast, are considered to be outside the realm of Article 301 EC.[134]

Where an individual is listed in a CFSP common position only, there is no Community regulation that the person could challenge to dispute the public stigmatization as a terrorist suspect. The allegation remains at the European level in a judicial vacuum. Individuals can only attempt either to challenge the Union instrument directly in national courts (if national courts prove willing to review Union law directly) or to ask the national court to refer a preliminary question (in those Member States that have made a declaration under Article 35 TEU). This is particularly concerning since Union lists of terrorist suspects are subject to the same procedural flaws that led the CFI to annul the Community listings.[135] Declaring a Community list contrary to the general principles of EU law implies that the second pillar instrument that was adopted in the same procedure also breaches principles of EU law, as far as the two instruments contain the same names.

The case of *Segi*[136] is of particular importance in the discussion on judicial review of Union lists of terrorist suspects. It differs from the *OMPI* cases, *Sison*, and *al Aqsa* because Segi was listed in a Union instrument *without* being targeted by Community sanctions. Segi was exclusively listed in Common Position 2001/931/CFSP, which remained the initial and only

[133] Statens Öffentliga Utredninga, *Internatinalla Sanktioner*, *Betänkande av Sanktionslagutredningen* (SOU 2006:41) (Stockholm 2006), pp 22–3.

[134] ibid.

[135] The ECJ correctly held that judicial review of Community regulation that give effect to UN lists of terrorist suspects does not amount to an incidental review of the underlying UN list (Cases C-402/05 P and C-415/05 P, *Kadi and al Barakaat* (n 2 above), para 288; see Chapter 5, Section 1). In contrast to CFSP common positions, Security Council resolutions do not have to comply with European law. Hence, they are not illegal if they breach the general principles of EU law.

[136] Case T-338/02, *Segi* (n 8 above), para 33.

public allegation that Segi is associated with terrorism and hence the only possible cause of a fundamental rights violation. In *Segi* the applicants asked the CFI to grant damages for Segi's allegedly illegitimate inclusion in the list annexed to Common Position 2001/931/CFSP 'on the application of specific measures to combat terrorism'. A footnote at the bottom of the list clarifies that Segi and a number of other persons, all of which are apparently European citizens or legal persons constituted within the EU,[137] 'shall be the subject of Article 4 only'. Article 4 of Common Position 2001/931/CFSP is addressed to the Member States and calls upon them to assist each other through police and judicial cooperation (third pillar measures). According to the CFI, the provision did not have any CFSP or Community implications. This led the Court to the conclusion that the applicants could claim damages for an illegal third pillar measure only, but that its own jurisdiction was indeed limited in the third pillar, so that it could not rule on the applicants' action.[138] Consequently, the Court declared itself manifestly incompetent to give a ruling on the claim for damages resulting from Common Position 2004/931/CFSP.[139]

In substance, the CFI limited its examination to two points: First, it investigated whether the Council acting in its capacities under the Union pillars had illegally assumed Community competences and encroached upon the first pillar. Secondly, the Court examined whether the alleged infringement could entitle the applicants to damages under Articles 235, 288(2) EC. Limited by a strict interpretation of its own competences, the CFI conducted a purely technical examination. In other words, the actual grievance of the applicants was not the subject of the Court's examination, but only the institutional question of whether the third pillar measure transgressed into Community competences.

The applicants in *Segi* claimed that the listing infringed their fundamental rights and thus gave rise to an action for damages. They pointed out that the lack of any judicial remedy itself must give them a course of action. The CFI did not follow the latter argument. It rejected the claim that the rule of law and fundamental rights, in particular the right of access to justice, could require the EU courts to exercise jurisdiction. The Court considered a possible competence resulting from Article 6(2) TEU,[140] and rejected it with reference to Article 46(d) TEU, since the latter does not

[137] Torbjörn Andersson, Iain Cameron and Kenneth Nordback, 'EU Listing: The Renaissance of Imperial Power, but on a Global Scale', *European Business Law Review* (2003), p 118.

[138] Case T-338/02, *Segi* (n 8 above), para 35.

[139] ibid, para 40.

[140] ibid, para 37.

establish any additional judicial competences for fundamental rights. The Court did not avoid expressly stating the result of its own reasoning: it conceded that it is likely that the European legal system does not provide the applicants with an effective remedy. However, as much as it considered this result to be unsatisfactory, it concluded that in a system of conferred competences as it is set out by Article 5 TEU, the lack of a judicial remedy itself cannot establish a Community competence beyond those attributed to it by the European Treaties.[141]

In the appeal both Advocate-General Mengozzi[142] and the ECJ explicitly rejected the CFI's finding that those listed in a Union instrument *only* do not dispose of an effective judicial remedy. The Advocate-General agreed with the CFI that the EU courts are not competent to rule on an action for damages in the Union pillars. He suggested that *national courts* should fill this gap. Arguing that the *Foto-Frost* rule[143] does not apply in the Union pillars the Advocate-General found a competence – or even obligation – of the national courts to review Union law based on the principle of loyal cooperation in Article 10 EC. He considered that the current state of integration, and in particular the limited jurisdiction of the EU courts in the Union pillars, justify a competence of the national courts to rule on the lawfulness of Union law in the light of the general principles of EU law.[144]

The ECJ went down a different path. It relied on review by the national courts of 'any decision or other *national* measure relating to the drawing up of an act of the European Union or to its application' supplemented by the possibility of seeking a preliminary ruling.[145] Yet, the Court remained vague on how the right to judicial protection could be effectively exercised at the national level.

[141] ibid, para 38:

(...) it must be noted that indeed probably no effective judicial remedy is available to them, whether before the Community Courts or national courts, with regard to the inclusion of Segi on the list of persons, groups or entities involved in terrorist acts. (...) the absence of a judicial remedy cannot in itself give rise to Community jurisdiction in a legal system based on the principle of conferred powers, as follows from Article 5 EU (...).

[142] AG Mengozzi 26 October 2006, Opinion in C-354/04 P, *Gestoras Pro Amnistia and others v Council* and Case C-355/04 P, *Segi* (both n 8 above).

[143] In *Foto-Frost*, the ECJ held that the EU courts are the sole arbitrator upon the validity of Community law (Case 314/85, *Foto-Frost* [1987] ECR 4199).

[144] The so-called 'general principles of Community law' apply to all three pillars, see Art 6 TEU. In the following they are therefore called 'general principles of EU law'. See in this regard also: Tridimas, *General Principles of EU Law* (n 24 above); *General Principles of EC Law* (2nd ed, 2006).

[145] Case C-355/04 P, *Segi* (n 8 above), para 56, emphasis added.

Most importantly, the ECJ extended Article 35(1) TEU to allow for preliminary rulings on the validity of common positions. The Court held that:

> [a]s is clear from Article 6 TEU, the Union is founded on the principle of the rule of law and it respects fundamental rights as general principles of EU law. It follows that the institutions are subject to review of the conformity of their acts with the treaties and the general principles of law, just like the Member States when they implement the law of the Union.[146]

> Article 35(1) TEU, in that it does not enable national courts to refer a question to the Court for a preliminary ruling on a common position but only a question concerning the acts listed in that provision, treats as acts capable of being the subject of such a reference for a preliminary ruling all measures adopted by the Council and intended to produce legal effects in relation to third parties. Given that the procedure enabling the Court to give preliminary rulings is designed to guarantee observance of the law in the interpretation and application of the Treaty, it would run counter to that objective to interpret Article 35(1) TEU narrowly. The right to make a reference to the Court of Justice for *a preliminary ruling must therefore exist in respect of all measures adopted by the Council, whatever their nature or form, which are intended to have legal effects in relation to third parties* (...).

> As a result, it has to be possible to make subject to review by the Court a common position which, because of its content, has a scope going beyond that assigned by the EU Treaty to that kind of act. (...).[147]

Being listed as a terrorist suspect in a Union instrument affects the legal position of individuals. This was clearly confirmed by the ECJ in the case of *Segi*. By contrast to the CFI, the ECJ did not address the question of whether the applicants were affected by a third pillar or a second pillar instrument.

Article 4 is the only operational provision of Common Position 2001/931/CFSP that applied to Segi. This led the CFI to the conclusion that the effects of the listing are for the applicants limited to the third pillar. This however is not justified.[148] The legal effects of the stigmatization are not limited to the third pillar irrespective of the scope of the operational provisions of that instrument.

Common Position 2001/931/CFSP applies to a clearly defined group of persons (those listed in the annex). Yet, it is not legally complete but

[146] ibid, para 51.

[147] ibid, paras 53–4.

[148] See also: Christina Eckes, 'How not Being Sanctioned by a Community Instrument Infringes a Person's Fundamental Rights: The Case of Segi', *King's College Law Journal* (2006), p 144 et seq.

requires implementing measures by the Member States and by the Community in their respective fields of competence. For European citizens and organizations (internal-European terrorists), such as Segi, the operational scope is limited to the third pillar. The Community does not freeze the assets of these internal-European terrorists. Nonetheless, Union lists of terrorist suspects directly impinge on the fundamental rights of those listed, irrespective of the adoption of further measures of implementation.[149]

The listings have to be read in the context in which they are adopted. They are part of a cross-pillar measure entitled: 'on the application of specific measures to combat *terrorism*'. All provisions of the common position, including the annex, fall under that heading. Article 1 literally labels those listed in the annex to be 'persons, groups and entities involved in *terrorist* acts'. The only formal partition is a footnote to the heading of the list, which indicates that the '[p]ersons marked with [an asterisk] shall be subject of Article 4 only'. Segi – like the other European citizens and organizations – is marked with an asterisk. Nevertheless, the partition does not limit the allegation that those listed are terrorists. The stigmatizing effect of Common Position 2001/931/CFSP is the same for all of those listed.

The ECJ phrased its ruling in *Segi* in a very open manner. The Court stated[150] that:

> [t]he right to make a reference to the Court of Justice for a preliminary ruling must therefore exist in respect of all measures adopted by the Council, whatever their nature or form, which are intended to have legal effects in relation to third parties.

This draws on the ECJ's case-law under Article 230 EC[151] and appears to imply that preliminary references are also considered possible with regard to lists adopted under the second pillar. Moreover, in *Segi* the ECJ acknowledged that *being listed* on a Union list of terrorist suspects (alone) has a relevant impact on the legal position of those listed.[152] The ECJ outlined its position on all Union listings irrespective of any measures of implementation or application: judicial protection is necessary as a matter

[149] See Chapter 3, Section 3.2.2 and 3.2.3.

[150] Case C-355/04 P, *Segi* (n 8 above), para 53, emphasis added.

[151] The ECJ ruled that an annulment action is available 'in the case of all measures adopted by the institutions, whatever their nature or form, which are intended to have legal effects.': Case 22/70, *Commission v Council (ERTA)* [1971] ECR 263, para 42; see also C-57/95, *France v Commission (Re Pension Funds Communication)* [1997] ECR I-1627, para 7.

[152] Case C-355/04 P, *Segi* (n 8 above): measures '*intended to have legal effects in relation to third parties*'.

of principle for those listed as terrorist suspects. Any operative measures that potentially follow constitute additional measures subject to a separate examination.

After the ruling of the CFI the applicants in *Segi* appeared to be left without judicial protection at all. The ECJ's ruling however not only showed the applicants a new way of access to the EU courts but must also be seen as a judgment of principled importance with regard to judicial protection from Union law that directly impacts on the rights of individuals. It acknowledged that the nature of Union law has changed and that therefore the exclusion of judicial review by the ECJ is no longer justifiable in the light of the rule of law. The right of access to justice as it is protected by the general principles of EU law depends on the legal effects of the measures on the position of the individual, and even though Union law instruments do not usually directly impact on the rights of individuals, lists, which directly identify individuals as being involved in terrorism,[153] entail legal effects vis-á-vis individuals.[154] This is sufficient to make judicial review necessary.

The conclusions that were drawn from the *Segi* case are not limited to the third pillar. They apply to both Union pillars. The CFI's view that the applicants were affected by a third pillar measure only disregards the stigmatizing effect of the cross-pillar Union listings. On appeal the ECJ was not asked to rule on whether the CFI was correct. The ECJ did not explicitly limit its considerations to the third pillar.

3. Review of Union Law

The second pillar (CFSP) is a compromise solution somewhere in between international and Community law. CFSP instruments are of a hybrid nature: the European institutions are involved in their adoption (the Commission and the European Parliament in a limited way only)[155] but they do not have the same characteristics as Community law, such as direct applicability. Further, the jurisdiction of the EU courts is largely excluded in the second pillar.

[153] Case T-228/02, *OMPI I* (n 10 above).

[154] Case C-355/04 P, *Segi* (n 8 above), para 53.

[155] Deirde Curtin and Inge Dekker, 'The EU as a "Layered" International Organisation: Institutional Unity in Disguise' in Paul Craig and Gráinne de Búrca (eds), *The Evolution of EU Law* (Oxford: Oxford University Press, 1999).

Yet, several lines of reasoning support the granting of judicial review. First, under Article 35 TEU the EU courts are competent to give *preliminary rulings* on the interpretation and validity of third pillar instruments. Secondly, the EU courts control whether certain *procedural principles* were complied with in the Union pillars.[156] Thirdly, they are competent to carry out an *indirect review* of Union law to ensure that it does not encroach upon Community competences.[157] Finally, the EU is 'founded on the principle of the rule of law'; this requires judicial review of legally relevant acts[158] based on the *principle of wider jurisdiction*.

3.1 Indirect Review

Individual sanctions are a distinct form of cross-pillar measures, in the adoption of which the Union determines in CFSP common positions the content of the following EC regulations. This is a particularity of individual sanctions which gives rise to jurisdiction of the EU courts under Articles 46(f) and 47 TEU.

Community law enjoys special protection pursuant to Article 47 TEU. This provision aims to preserve the integrity of the *acquis communautaire*[159] and can potentially cause difficulty with regard to 'inter-pillar mixity'.[160] The European Treaties do not provide an exact distinction between the Union pillars and the first pillar.[161] In practice, it is for the EU courts and

[156] Piet Eeckhout, *External Relations of the European Union: Legal and Constitutional Foundations* (Oxford: Oxford University Press, 2004), p 418 on judicial review of the principles of transparency and access to documents; Ramses Wessel, 'Good Governance and EU Foreign Security and Defence Policy', *CES Working Paper No 2/04*, p 12 et seq.

[157] Ulrich Everling, 'Reflections on the Structure of the European Union', *Common Market Law Review*, 29 (1992), p 1063; Maria-Gisella Garbagnati Ketvel, 'The Jurisdiction of the European Court of Justice in Respect of the Common Foreign and Security Policy', *International and Comparative Law Quarterly*, 55 (2006), p 82 et seq.

[158] Case C-355/04 P, *Segi* (n 8 above), para 51 et seq.

[159] Art 47 TEU protects the entire body of EC law: Case 44/84, *Hurd v Jones (Her Majesty's Inspector of Taxes)* [1986] ECR 29; Cases C-63/90 and C-67/90, *Portugal and Spain v Council* [1992] ECR I-5073; Case C-70/90, *Spain v Council* [1992] ECR I-5159 and Case C-71/90, *Spain v Council* [1992] ECR I-5175.

[160] Marise Cremona, 'External Relations of the EU and the Member States: Competence, Mixed Agreements, International Responsibility, and Effects of International Law', *EUI Law working papers*, 22 (2006), p 14.

[161] See for the second pillar: Roberto Baratta, 'Overlaps between European Community Competence and European Union Foreign Policy Activity' in Enzo Cannizzaro (ed), *The European Union as an Actor in International Relations* (The Hague: Kluwer Law International, 2002), pp 70–1.

the Member States to allocate measures among the pillars. Pursuant to Article 46(f) TEU jointly with Article 47 TEU the ECJ is competent to control Union law as to whether it encroaches upon Community competences.[162] The ECJ has taken a very Community law friendly position on this question. It has found economic measures with strong political implications (third pillar) to be covered by the Common Commercial Policy (CCP–first pillar).[163]

In the *Airport Transit Visas* case the ECJ gave judgment in a challenge to a joint action adopted under the third pillar.[164] The Commission brought an action under Article 230 EC because it considered that the act should have been adopted in the first pillar. The Council claimed that the Court did not have the competence to hear the case since Article 46 TEU excluded jurisdiction. Contrary to the suggestion of Advocate-General Fennelly[165] the ECJ declared the case admissible and accepted the task of ensuring that acts which, according to the Council, fall within the scope of the TEU, do not encroach upon the powers conferred on the Community by the EC Treaty.[166] It pointed out that Article 46(f) TEU confers jurisdiction over Article 47 TEU and that this article is interpreted to comprise the entire *acquis communautaire*. The ECJ even appeared to imply in *Airport Transit Visas* that if a subject-matter can be governed by Community measures, it must be dealt with under the first pillar.[167]

While the ECJ decided against the applicant in *Airport Transit Visas*, in *Environmental Crime* it declared a third pillar measure void because it encroached upon Community law and hence infringed Article 47 TEU.[168] Both cases concerned the demarcation of competences between the Community and the third pillar, but in the *ECOWAS* case the ECJ has recently

[162] Case C-170/96, *Commission v Council* (*Airport Transit Visa* case) [1998] ECR I-2763; but also: Case T-338/02 *Segi* (n 8 above); see in general: Garbagnati Ketvel, 'The Jurisdiction of the European Court of Justice in Respect of the Common Foreign and Security Policy', (n 157 above), p 86 et seq; Everling, *Reflections on the Structure of the European Union* (n 157 above), p 1053 et seq.

[163] C-70/94, *Werner* [1995] ECR 1-3189 and C-83/94, *Leifer* [1995] ECR I-3189.

[164] Case C-170/96, *Airport Transit Visas* case (n 162 above).

[165] Opinion of AG Fennelly in Case C-170/96, *Airport Transit Visa* case (n 162 above).

[166] Case C-170/96, *Airport Transit Visas* case (n 162 above), paras 14–16.

[167] For *Airport Transit Visa*: Garbagnati Ketvel, 'The Jurisdiction of the European Court of Justice in Respect of the Common Foreign and Security Policy' (n 157 above), p 91; Eeckhout, *External Relations of the European Union: Legal and Constitutional Foundations* (n 156 above), p 150.

[168] Case C-176/03, *Commission v Council* (*Environmental Crime case*) [2005] ECR I-07879; see further: Communication from the Commission on the implications of the Court's judgment of 13 September 2005 (Case C-176/03, *Commission v Council*), COM (2005) 583 fin.

ruled that it is equally the task of the Court to ensure that second pillar measures do not encroach upon Community powers.[169] In this case, the ECJ emphasized that if a measure pursues objectives both of the first and of the second pillar and the Community objective is not incidental this measure should be adopted under the first pillar. The ECJ further pointed out that Article 47 TEU aims to maintain and build on the *acquis communautaire*.[170]

In some respect individual sanctions differ from the measures challenged in *Airport Transit Visas*, *Environmental Crime*, and *ECOWAS*. The latter three cases concern third and second pillar measures that should have been adopted in the first pillar. Union lists of terrorist suspects do not encroach upon Community powers in the same way: *there is no Community competence* to adopt individual sanctions – not in combination with a prior CFSP common position and not as an isolated Community measure.[171] Therefore, it is impossible to identify a specific legal basis in the first pillar upon which the CFSP lists encroached. Nevertheless, this does not allow the conclusion that the Union lists do not interfere with Community powers. The encroachment lies in the meticulous predetermination of the Community's action by decisions as specific as terrorists lists adopted in the second pillar.[172] Individual sanctions are hybrid cross-pillar measures adopted pursuant to Article 301 EC: they consist of a CFSP common position and a Community regulation.[173] The CFSP common position determines that action by the Community is necessary. This combined use of second and first pillar instruments gives the Union the factual power to influence the content of Community measures adopted on the basis of Article 301 EC.[174] However, the intention behind this linkage was not that the Union could use Community powers at its will, but to ensure that the Community does not assume foreign policy powers.[175]

The meticulous prescription of the content of the Community measure as it takes place in the adoption of individual sanctions reduces the role of

[169] Case C-91/05, *Commission v Council (ECOWAS)* [2008] ECR I-3651, para 33; see also Chapter 2, Sections 1.3.2 and 3.

[170] Case C-91/05, *ECOWAS* ibid, para 59.

[171] Chapter 2, Section 1.

[172] See for more detail Chapter 2, Section 3.

[173] See Chapter 1, Section 4.

[174] See Chapter 2, Section 3.

[175] Monika Gudrun Zagel, 'Article 301 TEC (Economic Sanctions)' in Hans Smit and Peter E Herzog, *Law of the European Union – a Commentary* (New York: LexisNexis, 2006), para 402.04 [4].

the Community to a subordinate, merely implementing the Member States' will.[176] The Community must copy name by name the lists adopted under the CFSP to freeze the assets of those listed. The Community does not carry out any further scrutiny. This allows CFSP decisions to put the Community under pressure to adopt measures that infringe general principles of EU law, even if it is argued that the CFSP decision is not legally binding on the Commission.[177] The CFSP common position, read in the light of the principle of loyal cooperation and the requirement of consistency enshrined in Article 3 TEU, places the Community institutions not only politically but also legally in a position where they have to justify non-compliance.

This raises the question how much detail common positions can determine in the Article 301 EC procedure. Originally, the CFSP instruments were thought to be strategic decisions to take action. According to the ECJ, they are not supposed to produce by themselves legal effects in relation to third parties.[178] Union lists of terrorist suspects go in this regard beyond what is possible to regulate in common positions. Yet, the jurisdiction of the ECJ to review common positions even incidentally is problematic. It was argued that judicial review of CFSP instruments can only extend to *whether* a decision was taken and not whether it was *adopted lawfully*.[179] This might be convincing where the CFSP decision is a strategic decision to take action; as we have seen in Chapter 3, this must be rejected where CFSP common positions directly shape the legal position of individuals. Here, it is for the ECJ to step in: Articles 46(f) and 47 TEU give the Court the mandate to protect the *acquis communautaire*.

In conclusion, the meticulous predetermination of the content of EC regulations by CFSP common positions as it currently takes place in the area of individual sanctions is contrary to the distribution of competences in the EU. It is further settled case-law that the EU courts are competent to protect Community law by declaring the CFSP decisions

[176] In a different context this risk was pointed out by: Reinhardt Rummel and Jörg Wiedemann, 'Identifying Institutional Paradoxes of CFSP', *EUI Working Paper RSC* No 97/67 (1997), p 55.

[177] See Chapter 2 on the binding effect of the CFSP common position, criticizing: Joint Cases C-402/05 P and C-415/05 P, *Kadi and al Barakaat* (n 2 above), para 296: '[...] because of the adoption of such an act [the CFSP decision] the Community is bound to take, under the EC Treaty, the measures necessitated by that act'.

[178] Case C-355/04 P, *Segi* (n 8 above), para 52.

[179] Wolfram Cremer, 'Artikel 230' in Christian Callies and Matthias Ruffert (eds), *Kommentar zum EU-/EG-Vertrag* (Neuwied: Luchterhand, 2002), para 22.

invalid where they encroach upon the Community pillar. As was argued in Chapter 2, the Community does not currently have the competence to adopt individual sanctions, but *if* such a competence was created (eg if the Treaty of Lisbon enters into force) all terrorist lists would be drawn up in the first pillar.[180]

This would bring the identification procedure unambiguously within the jurisdiction of the EU courts and avoid all allegations that the Council uses the judicial vacuum in the Union pillars to escape control of its acts by the EU courts.[181] The Council decisions taken pursuant to EC Regulation 2580/2001, which contain the list of people whose assets must be frozen, but do not impose operational measures themselves,[182] have in practice been adopted both as CFSP decisions and as EC decisions.[183] This raises the question whether the choice of a CFSP instrument could have led the Court to deny judicial review notwithstanding the fact that these lists implement an EC regulation. This would allow the European institutions under the current legal situation to move the identification of those sanctioned by the Community entirely outside the scope of direct jurisdiction of the Courts.

3.2 The Principle of Wider Jurisdiction

It is uncontested that the EU is committed to act in compliance with fundamental rights and the rule of law.[184] The principle of effective judicial protection is a fundamental part of this commitment; it plays an important role not only from the perspective of the individual but also for the legal system of the Community at large. In the European legal order the rule of

[180] Chapter 2, Section 1 and Conclusions.

[181] See the argument of the applicant in: Case T-338/02, *Segi* (n 8 above), para 24.

[182] See Chapter 1, Section 4 on the adoption procedure of individual sanctions.

[183] On 14 March 2005 Council Decision 2005/221/CFSP was adopted repealing its predecessor Council Decision 2004/306/EC. This was a change from EC Council decisions to CFSP Council decisions as the instruments setting out the persons whose assets are frozen under Regulation 2580/2001. The new CFSP decision was drafted in a manner identical to the prior EC decisions. The 26 persons listed in the CFSP decision were exactly the same as those in the EC decision. On 17 October 2005, after a number of CFSP decisions, the Council returned to use EC decisions; it adopted Decision 2005/722/EC repealing Decision 2005/428/CFSP. The most recent Council decision implementing Art 2(3) of EC Regulation 2580/2001 is Council Decision 2009/62/EC of 27 January 2009, OJ L 23/25–29.

[184] See Chapter 3, Section 1.

law is further an indispensable requirement for the acceptance of supremacy and direct enforceability,[185] as well as the principle of coherent interpretation.[186] Judicial review of legally relevant acts is so central to the European legal order that the EU courts have introduced a principle of interpretation called 'wider jurisdiction'. By virtue of this principle the EU courts have accepted cases outside the express limits of their jurisdiction in the Treaties.[187]

3.2.1 The Mandate of the EU courts and its Limits

According to Article 220 EC, the task of the EU courts is to ensure that 'in the interpretation and the application of this Treaty the law is observed'.[188] The provision not only makes the EU courts the guardian of the EC Treaty, but gives them a broader mandate of being the custodian of the law. The term 'law' in this context has a larger meaning than the black letter law of the EC Treaty. Yet, it is here argued that the judiciary must ensure more widely the coherence of the European legal order and the effectiveness of its general principles. Just as the reference in Article 6(2) TEU to 'the general principles of Community law' the wording of Article 220 EC can be explained historically. It must be read in the light of European integration. The role of the EU courts as the custodians of the rule of law is no longer strictly confined to the Community pillar. It mandates the EU courts to develop a system of legal principles,[189] which the Court did in the 'general principles of EU law',[190] including fundamental rights. Article 6(2) TEU specifically codifies that 'general principles of Community law' must be respected under EU law. The Courts must balance different values and interests, even beyond the black letter law. This includes if necessary an appreciation of values that indirectly establishes a hierarchy between different Treaty provisions.[191] By denying review of Union lists of

[185] As is well-known, some national courts made their acceptance of the supremacy of European law conditional on effective judicial protection at the European level.

[186] Which was extended to the Union pillars in Case C-105/03, *Pupino* [2005] ECR I-5285, para 43.

[187] See arguments of the parties at: Case C-355/04 P, *Segi* (n 8 above), para 28.

[188] Case 294/83, *Les Verts* (n 9 above), para 25 (Art 164 EEC is now Art 220 EC).

[189] Tridimas, *The General Principles of EU Law* (n 24 above), p 19 et seq and Chapter 7, Section 3.

[190] The so-called 'general principles of Community law' apply to all three pillars, they became the 'general principles of EU law'. See also: Tridimas, *General Principles of EC Law* (n 24 above), as compared to *General Principles of EC Law* (2nd ed, 2006).

[191] Vlad Constantinesco, 'The ECJ as a Law-maker: Praetor Aut Contra Legem?', in David O'Keeffe and Antonio Bavasso, *Judicial Review in European Union Law: Liber Amicorum in Honour of Lord Slynn of Hadley* (The Hague: Kluwer Law International, 2000), p 78.

terrorist suspects the CFI placed the limits of its own jurisdiction[192] above the fundamental value of judicial protection. It ruled that the lack of a judicial remedy itself could not create a court competence.[193] It is submitted that this is a misconception of its mandate in Article 220 EC.

As regards the extension of competences based on fundamental rights considerations, it must be conceded that in Opinion 2/94 the ECJ denied 'the Community institutions any general power to enact rules on fundamental rights'[194] In principle, this statement extends to the EU courts: they form part of the EU institutions, and – just as the political institutions – they cannot claim a general competence for the protection of fundamental rights. Yet, in Opinion 2/94 the Court ruled on the accession of the EU to the European Convention on Human Rights (ECHR). The matter at stake was *not* the lawfulness of an internal legal instrument, but whether the EU could enter into an external obligation to protect fundamental rights. While the ECJ rejected that the EU had the competence to accede to the ECHR, it also confirmed its strong stand in favour of the 'constitutionalization' of the EU. The Court recalled that respect for fundamental rights forms 'an integral part of the general principles of [European] law'[195] and is 'a condition of the lawfulness of Community acts'.[196] Further, the right of access to justice holds a special position. It is not only a (subjective) fundamental right, but an (objective) element of the rule of law, which the ECJ has repeatedly confirmed to be the basis of European law.[197] In Opinion 2/94 the Court did not intend to free the European institutions from human rights restraints for actions adopted within the existing Treaty structure. Opinion 2/94 cannot serve as argument against judicial review of acts adopted by the European institutions.

3.2.2 Les Verts

In the landmark judgment of *Les Verts* the ECJ declared actions of the institutions subject to judicial review that could not be challenged according to the strict letter of the Treaties.[198] Advocate-General Mancini

[192] Eg Case T-338/02, *Segi* (n 8 above), and Case T-228/02, *OMPI I* (n 10 above).

[193] Case T-338/02, *Segi* (n 8 above), para 38.

[194] Opinion 2/94, ECHR [1996] ECR I-1759, para 27.

[195] ibid, para 33.

[196] ibid, para 34.

[197] See Chapter 3, Section 1.

[198] Case 294/83, *Les Verts* (n 9 above); see also Chapter 3. See also most recently the extensive interpretation of *Les Verts* by the CFI, allowing for judicial review of agencies with legal personality: Case T-411/06 *Sogelma v EAR*, judgment of 8 October 2008, not yet reported.

acknowledged that 'interpreted literally Article 173 [now Article 230 EC] does not provide for judicial review of the decisions of the Parliament', but he then opined 'that such an interpretation would conflict with the general scheme of the Treaties'.[199] He suggested that the ECJ should take a systematic approach to the interpretation of the Treaties and go beyond their literal wording, arguing that:[200]

> [...] the obligation to observe the law takes precedence over the strict terms of the written law. Whenever required in the interest of judicial protection, the Court is prepared to correct or complete rules which limit its powers in the name of the principle which defines its mission.

The Advocate-General's reasoning demonstrates that he did not ask the Court to do something entirely new. He based his opinion on prior judgments of the Court.

The ECJ followed Advocate-General Mancini and reviewed the decision of the European Parliament despite the lack of a provision establishing formal competence to do so. The Court famously ruled that the European Economic Community was 'a *Community of law* in as much as neither its Member States nor its institutions can avoid a review of the question whether the measures adopted by them are in conformity with the basic constitutional charter, the Treaty' and that 'the general scheme of the Treaty is to make a *direct action* available against all measures adopted by the institutions ... which are intended to have legal effect'.[201] The Court found the Community to be above all a 'Community based on law' in the sense that the relations between its subjects are relations between subjects of law that are to a high degree 'legalized' and under the control of the Court.[202]

The ECJ argued that Article 173 EEC (now Article 230 EC) was in line with the spirit and the general scheme of the Treaty when it was adopted, but that, in the light of the changes of the function and competences of the European Parliament, this was no longer the case at the time the judgment was given. The Court paid particular attention to the powers of the European Parliament to affect third parties, stating that the original version of the EEC Treaty 'merely granted it [the European Parliament] powers of

[199] Opinion of AG Mancini in Case 294/83, *Les Verts* (n 9 above), para 7.

[200] ibid, paraphrasing Case C-44/81, *Germany v Commission* [1982] ECR 1855.

[201] Case 294/83, *Les Verts* (n 9 above), para 24, emphasis added.

[202] Prodromos D Dagtoglou, 'The Legal Nature of the European Community', in Commission of the European Communities, *Thirty Years of Community Law* (Luxembourg: Office for Official Publications of the European Communities, 1982), p 40.

consultation and political control rather than the power to adopt measures intended to have effect vis-à-vis third parties'.[203] The ECJ concluded that a literal interpretation would have excluded judicial review of acts of the European Parliament, even if they were intended to have legal effect on third parties, but that this would go against the spirit and the system of the Treaty. Thus, the Court extended its jurisdiction in accordance with the general scheme of the Treaty.[204]

Admittedly, in some respects the situation in *Les Verts* differs from the adoption of Union lists of terrorist suspects. In *Les Verts* the ECJ looked at the changing role of a particular institution, and not at the development of an area of law. The case concerned the institutional structure of the Community at a time when its democratic nature and the role of the European Parliament were very much in focus. The judgment was delivered in the field of Community law, even before the Union pillars were created. The area of law was not the reason for lack of jurisdiction in *Les Verts*. Lists of terrorist suspects, by contrast, are measures of a new nature adopted under Union law, where the jurisdiction of the Court is in principle inexistent in the second and limited in the third pillar (Article 46 TEU).

Nonetheless, the lack of judicial protection from acts of the institutions impinging on individuals' rights is the central issue in both judgments. The rationale in *Les Verts* was that if the Treaties allowed the European Parliament to adopt acts that affect the legal rights of third parties, they must also allow for judicial review of these acts. Anything else would contradict the fundamental value choices of the European Treaties. The Treaties did not specifically provide the necessary control mechanisms because the enormous increase of the European Parliament's powers was unforeseeable when they were drafted. This rationale is directly transferable to Union lists of terrorist suspects. An approach analogous to the one in *Les Verts* would consequently allow for judicial protection from Union lists.

There are two central elements in the *Les Verts* reasoning: first, the unforeseeable change in the European Parliament's powers, and secondly, the new legal effects of its acts on individuals. For Union lists of terrorist suspects the situation is similar. First, the adoption of lists of terrorist suspects under the Union pillars is a new development. When the Treaty of Maastricht introduced the Union pillars it could not have been predicted that common positions would be used to list individuals as terrorist

[203] Case 294/83, *Les Verts* (n 9 above), para 24. [204] ibid, para 25.

suspects. Even at the UN level sanctions against private individuals are a comparatively recent phenomenon: since the 1990s international sanctions developed first from state sanctions to sanctions against government officials, then to sanctions against quasi-government officials, and finally to sanctions against private individuals.[205] This development and the consequences it had for the measures of implementation under European law were unforeseeable at the time when the Treaty of Maastricht was adopted. Individual sanctions are a phenomenon that appeared years after the decision was taken to exclude CFSP measures from judicial review. Secondly, when listing persons as terrorist suspects Union law has unprecedented effects on the legal position of individuals. Arguably, state sanctions can also have a grave impact on fundamental rights. However, they do not immediately change the legal position of individuals. They remain foreign policy decisions and require implementation in order to affect particular persons. When the Union pillars were introduced they remained 'half way between pure intergovernmental cooperation and the Community "integrationist" model.'[206] The exclusion of jurisdiction in the second pillar was justified in particular by the sensitive nature of CFSP measures and by the fear of the Member States that the ECJ might extend its integrationist doctrines to the CFSP.[207] It was unperceivable at the time that Union law would directly impinge on the rights of individuals without the necessary link of a national implementation measure, since traditionally Union law – and in particular CFSP instruments – provided for measures of cooperation only which then had to be implemented by the Member States. Contrary to this, Union lists of terrorist suspects create a direct link between legal instrument of Union law and the listed individuals; those listed are already affected at the listing stage without any further need for implementation.[208] In view of this the exclusion of judicial review is unjustified.

There is another difference between the increased powers of the European Parliament in *Les Verts* and the use of Union law to list individuals, which, however, strengthens the argument in favour of judicial review. The European Treaties do not actually allow for direct interference with the rights of individuals by CFSP measures.[209] Indeed, in *Segi* the ECJ

[205] See Chapter 1, Section 1.

[206] AG Mengozzi, in: Case C-355/04 P, *Segi* (n 8 above), para 132 with regard to the third pillar.

[207] Eileen Denza, *The Intergovernmental Pillars of the European Union* (Oxford: Oxford University Press, 2002), p 312.

[208] See Chapter 3, Sections 3.2.2 and 3.2.3.

[209] See Chapter 2, Section 2.

correctly pointed out that the Union lists have legal effects on those who are listed and this goes beyond the legal effects attributed to common positions by the Treaty.[210] In *Les Verts*, on the other hand, the powers of the European Parliament were increased by Treaty amendments. It is submitted that where powers are assumed *without* the legitimizing force of a Treaty amendment, judicial review by the EU courts is even more pressing.

Additionally, today the Treaties would make it much easier for the Court to establish a 'general scheme' of commitment to the rule of law and fundamental rights. Even though the ECJ had already recognized fundamental rights within the Community legal order[211] at the time the *Les Verts* judgment was given they did not occupy the same prominent place as today. The importance of fundamental rights as part of Union law is apparent not only in Articles 6, 7, and 49 TEU, but also in the practice of the political institutions[212] and in the case-law of the ECJ, which has developed tremendously since 1984.[213] The same is true for the rule of law, which is expressly recognized in Article 6 TEU and applicable to all three pillars.[214] Hence, today it can be argued even more forcefully that the Union is a 'Union of law'. Article 46(d) TEU does not contradict this conclusion; it does not exclude jurisdiction of the EU courts based on the rule of law. This provision simply makes clear that the EU courts may verify compliance with Article 6(2) TEU where they have jurisdiction *on other grounds*;[215] it does not exclude jurisdiction based on the rule of law as an overarching principle stipulated in the Preamble and Article 6(1) TEU.

By way of conclusion, the EU courts could have relied on the rationale of *Les Verts* to establish jurisdiction over Union lists of terrorist suspects. The central arguments of the reasoning are transferable.

[210] Case C-355/04 P, *Segi* (n 8 above), para 51 et seq.

[211] There are many examples of ECJ judgments giving value to fundamental rights: before 1984: Case C-4/73, *Nold* [1974] ECR 491; Case C-44/79, *Hauer* [1979] ECR 3727; Case C-155/79, *AM&S Europe* [1982] ECR 1575.

[212] Compare the EU annual report on Human Rights 1999–2003; see for the EU's human rights policy in external relations: http://europa.eu.int/comm/external_relations; and the adoption of the Charter on Fundamental Rights in 2000.

[213] Eg: Case C-46/87, *Hoechst v Commission* [1989] ECR 2869; Case C-222/84, *Johnston* [1986] ECR 1651; Case C-5/88, *Wachauf v Bundesamt für Ernährung und Forstwirtschaft* [1989] ECR 2609; Case C-260/89, *Tileorassi* [1991] ECR I-2925; Opinion 2/94, ECHR (n 194 above); Case C-122&125/99 P, *D v Council* [2001] ECR I-4319, Case C-112/00, *Schmidberger* [2003] ECR I-5659.

[214] Ricardo Gosalbo Bono, 'Some Reflections on the CFSP Legal Order', *Common Market Law Review*, 43 (2006), p 347.

[215] AG Mengozzi, in: Case C-355/04 P, *Segi* (n 8 above), para 64.

3.2.3 Attempts to Extend the Powers of the EU courts under the Union Pillars

The principle of wider jurisdiction is based on the insight that the rule of law requires judicial review in situations where the black letter law does not confer powers on the EU courts. The limited powers of the ECJ are particularly unsatisfactory under the Union pillars.[216]

In the *Eurojust* case for instance, Advocate-General Maduro made an attempt to extend the ECJ's jurisdiction based on an argument of wider jurisdiction. He forcefully advocated that the ECJ should admit an action for annulment of calls for application for temporary staff issued by Eurojust.[217] Eurojust was set up as a body of the Union by a Council decision in the third pillar.[218] The Advocate-General interpreted Article 46 TEU to stipulate that 'the provisions of the EC Treaty concerning the powers of the Court of Justice and the exercise of those powers apply to the provisions of the EU Treaty concerning judicial and police cooperation in criminal matters' and maintained that '[i]n a Union governed by the rule of law' the Court must offer review, so long as the measures in question 'are intended to produce legal effects vis-à-vis third parties'[219] The ECJ did not follow his opinion but declared the action inadmissible.[220] However, this should not immediately lead to the conclusion that the ECJ would reject a similar argument with regard to individual sanctions. First, in *Segi* the ECJ applied a rationale similar to the one advocated by Advocate-General Maduro in *Eurojust*: based on a rule of law argument the Court extended judicial review under the preliminary ruling procedure to all acts intended to have legal effects in relation to third parties.[221] Secondly, it can be maintained that lists of terrorist suspects have a more serious impact on fundamental rights than the measures challenged in *Eurojust*.

In *Segi*, Advocate-General Mengozzi made an argument *against* jurisdiction based on the right of access to justice.[222] Yet, he focussed on the possibility of bringing a direct action for damages and did not address extending the preliminary ruling procedure under Article 35 TEU to cover common positions. Advocate-General Mengozzi distinguished *Les Verts* and

[216] Oral presentation by the President of the Court of Justice, Gil Carlos Rodriguez Iglesias, to the 'discussion circle' on the Court of Justice, CONV 572/03, 1–2;

[217] AG Maduro in Case C-160/03, *Spain v Eurojust* [2005] ECR I-2077.

[218] Decision 2002/187/JHA of 28 February 2002, OJ 2002 L 63/1.

[219] AG Maduro, in Case C-160/03, *Eurojust* (n 217 above), para 17.

[220] Case C-160/03, *Eurojust* (n 217 above).

[221] Case C-355/04 P, *Segi* (n 8 above), para 53.

[222] AG Mengozzi, in: Case C-355/04 P, *Segi* (n 8 above), para 159 et seq.

Chernobyl arguing that in these two cases the Court simply defined the scope of an action for annulment based on a systematic teleological interpretation 'without thereby offending against the letter of the Treaty'[223] The Advocate-General considered *Segi* to be more like *UPA*.[224] In the latter case the ECJ was asked to solve an alleged conflict between the right to judicial protection and Articles 7 and 173 EEC (now Articles 12 and 230 EC) in favour of the fundamental right. The Court, however, refused in *UPA* to extend the Treaty provisions beyond their established interpretation.

The Advocate-General in *Segi* reasoned that giving priority to the right of access to justice would imply a hierarchy among primary rules, which would lead to the establishment of 'a kind of "supra-constitutional" value in the respect for fundamental rights.'[225] The ECJ, however, took a different approach: it looked at the right of access to justice as a fundamental element of the rule of law and stretched Article 35(1) TEU beyond its wording to provide for judicial review of all acts intended to have legal effects in relation to third parties.[226] Hence, the ECJ confirmed in *Segi* that lists of terrorist suspects adopted in common positions have legal effects vis-à-vis third parties, which go beyond the effects assigned by the EU Treaty to that kind of act.[227] The case of *Segi* concerned an action for damages and the ECJ was limited by the legal questions brought to it on appeal. It was not asked to declare the Union list in question contrary to European law. However, confirming that the Union is subject to the rule of law the ECJ extended the jurisdiction of the EU courts beyond the strict limits in Articles 46 and 35 TEU.[228]

The ECJ ruled in *Segi* that judicial review of legally relevant acts must be possible. The language of the judgment does not give any indication that the Court only focused on the content rather than the form along the lines of the case-law under Article 230 EC. The ECJ did not only agree to give preliminary rulings on common positions because they are 'decisions in disguise', but stated that in a 'Union of law' all acts that have legal effects vis-à-vis third parties must be subject to judicial control. The ECJ's position deserves endorsement. Additionally, it can be said that judicial review of acts directly affecting the legal position of individuals might be indicated even more strongly by the rule of law in the second pillar than in the first

[223] ibid, para 168.
[224] Case C-50/00, *Unión de Pequeños Agricultores v Council (UPA)* [2002] ECR I-6677.
[225] AG Mengozzi, in: Case C-355/04 P, *Segi* (n 8 above), para 177.
[226] Case C-355/04 P, *Segi* (n 8 above), para 53. [227] ibid, paras 53–4. [228] ibid.

pillar. In the second pillar the executive and legislative functions of the Council merge together, while the Commission and the European Parliament are largely excluded and cannot provide a system of checks and balances. Just as in the first pillar the Council can adopt in the Union pillars at the same time general legal instruments and the necessary acts of implementation.[229] To allow the Council to adopt measures that directly and adversely impact on the legal situation of individuals while excluding these decisions from judicial review creates nearly absolute powers over those individuals.

3.3 Preliminary Ruling Procedure

In the case of *Segi*[230] the ECJ opened up the possibility of a preliminary ruling request concerning the validity of Union lists of terrorist suspects, but it did not depart from the *Foto-Frost* doctrine,[231] as Advocate-General Mengozzi suggested. By implication it confirmed that national courts *cannot* review the validity of European law. It recalled that 'Member States are to take all appropriate measures, whether general or particular, to ensure fulfilment of their obligations under European Union law' and referred in this context to *Pupino*.[232] In this case the ECJ ruled that *national courts* have an obligation to interpret national law to be in conformity with framework decisions under the third pillar.'[233] Hence, by recalling that obligations under European Union law extend to the Member States' courts the ECJ implied that they cannot review that very same law. Further, the ECJ noted that Member States' courts have the obligation to refer a preliminary ruling request when they have doubts concerning the validity of EU acts.

The ECJ's position recalls the reasoning in the case of *UPA*.[234] In this case, the Court justified its restrictive approach on standing of individuals under Article 230(4) EC by reference to what it called a 'complete system of remedies', according to which no Community measure, having legal effect, can escape judicial control either through a direct action, or through

[229] Arts 13, 14, and 34 TEU.

[230] Case C-355/04 P, *Segi* (n 8 above), see in particular para 49 et seq.

[231] Case 314/85, *Foto-Frost* (n 143 above).

[232] Case C-355/04 P, *Segi* (n 8 above), para 52 referring to Case C-105/03, *Pupino* (n 186 above).

[233] The principle of conform or harmonious interpretation was developed by the ECJ as an 'indirect effect' of directives under the first pillar (see eg: Case 14/83 *Von Colson and Kamann v Land Nordrhein-Westfalen* [1984] ECR 1891). In *Pupino* the ECJ applied this principle also under the third pillar.

[234] Case C-50/00 P, *UPA* (n 224 above).

a preliminary ruling requested by the national courts pursuant to Article 234 EC. The Court argued that in the Community pillar the preliminary ruling procedure is an alternative route for private parties to attack allegedly illegal Community acts without having to satisfy the strict standing requirements of Article 230 EC. The ECJ seemed to have this function of the preliminary ruling procedure in mind, when, in *Segi*, it extended Article 35 TEU to allow for preliminary rulings on the validity of common positions in order to have jurisdiction at all.

Thus far, the CFSP decision required by Article 301 EC has always been a common position; hence, all Union lists of terrorist suspects were adopted in common positions. Article 35(1) TEU, however, confers on the ECJ

> jurisdiction, subject to the conditions laid down in this article, to give preliminary rulings on the validity and interpretation of *framework decisions* and *decisions*, on the interpretation of *conventions* established under this title and on the validity and interpretation of the measures implementing them [emphasis added].

Thus, in Article 35(1) TEU there is no mention of common positions. And, since this article is an exception to the general exclusion of jurisdiction of the EU courts in the Union pillars (Article 46 TEU) it would have to be construed narrowly – to the effect that common positions cannot be subject to a preliminary ruling request. In *Segi*, however, the ECJ ruled that the wording of Article 35(1) TEU does not hinder national courts to refer a question on the validity of the Union lists of terrorist suspects.

This stirs up the old discussion of whether the preliminary ruling procedure can provide an effective remedy against illegal acts of the European institutions.[235] It remains controversial whether the preliminary ruling

[235] See: AG Jacobs in: Case C-50/00, *UPA* (n 224 above); Case T-177/01, *Jégo-Quéré* [2002] ECR II-2365, appealed in: Case C-263/02 P, *Jégo-Quéré& Cie SA* [2004] ECR I-3425; but also: Case C-188/92, *Textilwerke Deggendorf*, confirming that Art 234 and 230 EC are seen as alternative and not as parallel procedures to challenge a Community act; in the literature: Frédérique Berrod and Flavien Mariatte, 'Le pourvoi dans l'affaire Unión de Pequeños Agricultores c/ Conseil: le retour de la procession d'Echternach', *Europe, Editions du Juris-Classeur*, 12/10 (2002); Albertina Albors-Llorens, *Private Parties in European Community Law: Challenging Community Measures* (Oxford: Clarendon Press, 1996); Henry Schermers and Denis Waelbroeck, *Judicial Protection in the European Union* (The Hague: Kluwer Law International, 2001); see also: Francis Geoffrey Jacobs, 'Necessary Changes to the System of Judicial Remedies', Working Group II, Working Document 20, (2002), http://european-convention.eu.int/docs/wd2/3222.pdf and 'The question of effective judicial remedies and access of individuals to the European Court of Justice', Working Group II, Working Document 21, (2002), http://european-convention.eu.int/docs/wd2/3299.pdf.

procedure satisfies the requirements of the right of access to justice under Article 6(1) ECHR.[236] Indeed, there are good arguments supporting the view that the preliminary ruling procedure does not offer an equivalent alternative to a direct action before the EU courts. The arguments are well-known and it will suffice to list the most important points: Only the EU courts are in the position to declare EU listings void. The way to the EU courts is very long and unsure if the applicant has to take the detour through national courts. Applicants do not even have a *right* to request a referral. There are not always national implementation measures that can be challenged before the national courts. Preliminary rulings entail additional costs. And, finally, there is the problem of legal certainty.[237]

A strong argument that the preliminary ruling procedure does not offer effective judicial protection is that it is not available where acts of the European institutions do not require any national measures of application or implementation. However, even where Union lists of terrorist suspects do not require further action by the Member States this should not close the way to a preliminary ruling. In *Segi*, the ECJ stated that national courts must review both 'national measures *relating to the drawing up* of' the list and to 'its *application*'.[238] National courts should send a request for a preliminary ruling where the scope of a common position goes 'beyond that assigned by the EU Treaty to that kind of act'[239] Hence, Union listings can be challenged in the ECJ, through a preliminary ruling request, in the course of an action against the decision of the competent national authority within the meaning of Article 1(4) of Common Position 2001/931/CFSP. No additional act of implementation at the national level is necessary. This is the case, provided the Council informs those listed of the identity of the competent national authority.[240]

However, the ECJ's ruling is ambiguous as regards the exact requirements of a preliminary ruling request concerning the legality or interpretation of a Union list of terrorist suspects. The Court stated that such a request would be 'subject to the conditions fixed by Article 35 EU.'[241]

[236] ibid; on the preliminary ruling procedure: Takis Tridimas, 'Knocking on Heaven's Door: Fragmentation, Efficiency and Defiance in the Preliminary Reference Procedure', *Common Market Law Review*, 40 (2003), p 9 et seq.

[237] See above all: AG Jacobs in: C-50/00, *UPA* (n 224 above), para 102.

[238] ibid, para 56, emphasis added.

[239] Case C-355/04 P, *Segi* (n 8 above), para 54.

[240] See above the discussion of the *OMPI* cases.

[241] Case C-355/04 P, *Segi* (n 8 above), para 54.

Apart from the nature of the legal instrument (which was explicitly extended by the ECJ), the most significant condition in Article 35 TEU is that Member States first have to make a declaration under Article 35(2) TEU accepting the jurisdiction of the ECJ, to enable their courts to request a preliminary ruling. Member States can also restrict the right to request a preliminary ruling to the highest courts only (Article 35(3)(a) TEU). Further, under Union law there is no *obligation* to refer a question. However, of the 14 Member States, that have made a declaration under Article 35(2) TEU, nine have informed that their courts of last resort will be under an obligation under national law to refer a question relating to the validity of an act referred to in Article 35(1) TEU.[242] After *Segi*, there appears to be a general obligation *under European law* to refer a question to the ECJ whenever a national court has doubts whether Union law is intended to have legal effect on third parties.[243] However, the Article 35(2) TEU declaration is one of the 'conditions' of Article 35 TEU. Hence, the courts in nearly half of the 27 Member States cannot refer at all. The ECJ did not elaborate what the national courts in these Member States should do. Nonetheless, there are considerable merits in the ECJ's decision in *Segi*. Within the EU access to justice at the national level can substitute to some extent for judicial remedies at the European level. This is common practice in the EU.

The EU courts have been criticized for imposing stricter standards on national authorities, including courts, than on the EU institutions themselves.[244] In view of the right of access to justice this strict approach of the ECJ to procedural standards in national courts improves the position of those seeking justice in the requesting state.[245] In *Borelli* for instance the ECJ stated that 'the requirement of judicial control of any decision of a national authority reflects a general principle of Community law'.[246]

[242] See OJ 1999 L 114/56 for Austria, Belgium, Finland, Germany, Greece, Italy, Luxembourg, the Netherlands, Portugal, Spain, Sweden; for the Czech Republic: see the Final Act to the Treaty of Accession, OJ 2003 L 236/957, at 980; for France and Hungary: OJ 2005 L 327/19.

[243] See below.

[244] Damian Chalmers, Christos Hadjiemmanuil, Giorgio Monti, and Adam Tomkins, *European Union Law* (Cambridge: Cambridge University Press, 2006), p 422.

[245] Examples are the principle of equivalence (Case 45/76, *Comet v Produktschap* [1976] ECR 2043, para 13: '...provided that such rules [to protect rights the individual acquires through Community law] are not less favourable than those governing the same right of action on an internal matter.') and the principle of effectiveness (Case C-78/98, *Shirley Preston and others* [2000] ECR I-3201).

[246] Case C-97/91, *Borelli* [1992] ECR I-6313, paras 12–14; recently in: Case C-424/99, *Commission v Austria* [2001] ECR I-9285, para 45.

Where domestic law excludes judicial control the *Borelli*-principle might help those sanctioned nevertheless to obtain judicial review in national courts based on principles of European law.[247]

Judicial review in the courts of the Member State, whose competent authority took the relevant decision, has a number of advantages. The proceedings take place in the state that possesses the necessary information. The national government would have to cooperate and allow the national judge to see the information that led to the listing. Further, it seems politically more sensible if the courts of the same state declare the national decision illegal than if the EU courts declare the national information on which the request was based unsatisfactory. In preliminary rulings it can be expected that the ECJ confines its remarks to the abstract application of the general principles of EU law and leaves the specific conclusion on the legality of the actions of national authorities to national courts.[248] In this regard, Article 35(5) TEU is no further limitation but merely a codification of the ECJ's practice.

3.4 Direct Actions against Union Lists of Terrorist Suspects

In *Segi*, in contrast to *Les Verts*, the ECJ did not rule that a *direct action* against Union lists of terrorist suspects must be possible. The Court had regard to the existing distinction between the Community pillar and the Union pillars. Starting from Articles 46 and 35 TEU[249] as the basis of its jurisdiction under the Union pillars the ECJ interpreted Article 35 TEU to have the objective to allow *preliminary rulings* for acts intended to produce legal effects in relation to third parties.[250]

As regards direct actions, the ECJ stated that they are possible under Article 35(6) TEU against any Union measure intended to have legal effects on third parties or 'which, because of its content, has a scope going beyond that assigned by the EU Treaty to that kind of act'[251] Article 35(6) TEU gives the ECJ jurisdiction to review the legality of framework

[247] The Borelli principle is seen as an example of the ECJ directing its attention not so much at its own powers and the level of judicial protection which is thereby provided, but rather at the protection available from the national courts: Guiseppe Tesauro, 'The Effectiveness of Judicial Protection and Co-operation between the Court of Justice and the National Courts', *YEL*, (1993), p 1 et seq.

[248] Anthony Arnull (et al), *The European Union and its Court of Justice* (Oxford: Oxford University Press, 2006), p 333.

[249] Case C-355/04 P, *Segi* (n 8 above), para 44 et seq.

[250] ibid, para 53.

[251] ibid, para 54.

decisions and decisions in actions brought by a Member State or the Commission on grounds of lack of competence, infringement of an essential procedural requirement, infringement of the EU Treaty or of any rule of law relating to its application, or misuse of powers. Hence, irrespective of whether the Member State has made a declaration under Article 35(2) TEU, governments can challenge the legality of Union measures before the ECJ. One could even argue that national governments are obliged to bring a case to the ECJ when requested to do so by one of the persons listed on a Union list of terrorist suspects. This goes along the lines of the CFI's creation of a 'European right to diplomatic protection' with regard to *Community* sanctions giving effect to UN lists of terrorist suspects, obliging Member States in practice to request a delisting procedure in the UN Sanctions Committee if petitioned to do.[252] This strict interpretation of the duties of the Member States to provide, as far as they possibly can, remedies against non-justiciable listings of terrorist suspects should not only extend to UN lists, but also to Union lists. Consequently, governments could be at least obliged to initiate an internal review of the listing in the Council, if not to challenge it before the EU courts. Moreover, obligations of the Member States under the European Treaties in principle extend to all national authorities, including courts.[253] Hence, besides an obligation to make a preliminary reference under the national law of some Member States[254] national courts could also be obliged to refer under European law. It might be added that the ECJ has demonstrated in the case of *Köbler* that it will take an obligation to refer a question for a preliminary ruling seriously.[255] This is that the failure to comply with such an obligation might result in state liability.

The limitations of the ruling in *Segi* can be explained in the light of the particular case. The appeal before the ECJ challenged specific points of the CFI's ruling on an action for damages. An action for annulment was not directly the matter. Yet, the Court seized the opportunity to make some more general comments on how Union lists could be challenged pursuant to Article 35(6) TEU, while it did not mention direct actions for private parties. It could be argued that the ECJ intended to respect the pillar structure of the EU. While using all the legal remedies of the Union pillars,

[252] Case T 253/02, *Ayadi* (n 2 above); appealed: Case C-403/06 P, *Ayadi v Council*, OJ 2006 C 294/32, see above and in Chapter 7, Section 3.3.

[253] Settled case-law of the ECJ, eg: Case C-105/03, *Pupino* (n 186 above), para 34 et seq.

[254] See Section 3.3 above.

[255] Case C-224/01, *Köbler* [2003] ECR I-10239.

it did not extend its jurisdiction for direct action in the Community pillar to the Union pillars. By relying on the preliminary ruling procedure the ECJ sought to ensure some form of judicial review without assuming the competence to interfere directly with the Member States' cooperation under the Union pillars. *Segi* alone might not justify the conclusion that the Court would apply the principle of wider jurisdiction to allow direct actions brought by private parties against Union lists, but it does not exclude it either.

3.5 Rights of Defence

The EU courts have not so far discussed the rights of defence of those listed in Union lists of terrorist suspects.[256] Yet, on other occasions the EU courts have acknowledged that a detrimental effect on a person's reputation can trigger procedural rights.[257] It is here argued that Union listings have an impact on the legal position of those listed, which activates the right to judicial review. However, it is useful to point out that procedural rights are arguably triggered even below the threshold of an interference with rights or obligations.[258] Since certain procedural requirements are applicable and justiciable in the Union pillars, this is another avenue for judicial review of Union lists.

Even though only the EC Treaty[259] explicitly sets out a right of access to documents, Article 1 TEU stipulates the principle that decisions in the EU 'are taken as openly as possible and as closely as possible to the citizen' and Article 28(1) EU explicitly refers to Article 255 EC as one of the EC provisions that shall apply to the CFSP. Further, in the *Svenska Journalistförbundet* case[260] and in the *Hautala* case[261] the CFI confirmed that it will review the legality of a decision denying access to documents used in the Union pillars. In the latter case, the CFI held that the Council's political

[256] See below the argument that procedural rights under the Union pillars fall within the jurisdiction of the EU Courts.

[257] Case T-277/97, *Ismeri Europa v Court of Auditors* [1999] ECR II-1825; Case C-315/99 P, *Ismeri Europa v Court of Auditors* [2001] ECR I-5281; see however: Case T-259/03, *Nikolaou*, para 244, in which the CFI distinguished *Ismeri* because the OLAF's findings were not published. In any event, terrorist lists are published.

[258] Itai Rabinowitz, 'The Fundamental Right to Be Heard' (n 26 above).

[259] Pursuant to Art 255(1) EC any citizen of or resident in the Union 'shall have a right of access to European Parliament, Council and Commission documents.'

[260] Case T-174/95, *Svenska Journalistförbundet* [1998] ECR II-2289.

[261] Case T-14/98, *Heidi Hautala MEP* [1999] ECR II-2489.

responsibilities within the CFSP lead to a degree of discretion. The Council must be able to determine the possible consequences of disclosing confidential documents. However, this discretion is not without limits. The Court[262] limited its review

> to verifying whether the procedural rules have been complied with, the contested decision is properly reasoned, and the facts have been accurately stated, and whether there has been a manifest error of assessment of the facts or a misuse of powers.

In the later case of *Kuijer II*, [263] the CFI confirmed that it reviews the denial of access to documents in the Union pillars and extended judicial review beyond purely procedural issues regarding the transparency of decision-making under the Union pillars. In *Kuijer II* the CFI also looked at the content of the documents at issue.[264]

In *Sison* [265]the applicant sought access to Council documents containing information that led to his listing on a *Community list* of terrorist suspects. He filed the application under Regulation 1049/2001, which regulates the *public* right of access to documents only. The *public* right of access to documents extends undisputedly to the Union pillars,[266] yet, it does not allow the consideration of the particular interests of the applicant.[267] However, it appears to be difficult to uphold that the general public has a right of access to documents in the Union pillars, but that those individuals whose legal positions are negatively affected by Union law cannot ask the EU courts to also take *their particular legal position* into account.

3.6 Obligation to State Reasons

The obligation to state reasons is a procedural right ensuring transparency which should be equally justiciable in the Union pillars, not only as regards the decision to grant access to documents but also with regard to the original CFSP decision.[268] The obligation to state reasons goes beyond Article 253 EC. It is a general principle of European law,[269] and it forms

[262] ibid, para 72.

[263] Case T-211/00, *Aldo Kuijer* [2002] ECR II-485.

[264] Wessel, 'Good Governance and EU Foreign Security and Defence Policy' (n 156 above), p 14.

[265] Joined Cases T-110/03, T-150/03 and T-405/03, *Sison* (n 96 above), see also above.

[266] Regulation 1049/2001, OJ 2001 L 145/43.

[267] See Section 1.1.2 above.

[268] As to my knowledge the EU Courts have not yet ruled on the obligation to state reasons with regard to the CFSP decision itself.

[269] Case T-183/97 R, *Micheli and Others v Commission* [2000] ECR II-287, para 56.

also part of the right to good administration in Article 41 of the Charter of Fundamental Rights.[270] It is further recognized by the Council of Europe as a fundamental principle of administrative procedure.[271] In the *OMPI* cases the CFI ruled that the Community lists did not satisfy the obligation to state reasons and that those listed have a right to a personalized statement of reasons.[272] These Community lists were not only identical to the complementary Union list but also drawn up pursuant to the same procedure. Hence, the CFI's findings are transferable to the Union instrument. Beyond this and even more importantly, the obligation to state reasons should be *justiciable* under Union law. *Hautala* confirmed the application of the duty to state reasons for the decision of whether to grant access to CFSP documents.[273] This case also demonstrates that this obligation falls within the–albeit limited–review by the EU courts. Yet, this reasoning is not limited to the decision of whether to grant access but also to the CFSP decision itself. This is even more so because of the great impact of Union lists of terrorist suspects on the personal lives of those listed.[274] The greater the interference with fundamental rights is, the more important become procedural rights to protect the former, irrespective of whether an act is adopted under the Community or under the Union pillar.

Further, the ECJ, in its tendency towards imposing common standards, has extended the obligation to state reasons to the Member States when implementing EU law.[275] In *Segi* the ECJ explicitly obliged Member States to provide judicial protection from the listing requests that result in placing an individual on the CFSP lists of terrorist suspects. The Court's decision demonstrates that what is true for national measures implementing EU law is equally applicable to decisions by the national authorities, which are used

[270] Referred to by the ECJ for the first time in: Case C-540/03, *EP v Council* [2006] ECR I-5769, paras 31, 32, 34 and 58.

[271] Resolution of the Council of Europe (77) 31, of 28 September 1977, on the protection of the individual in the relation to the acts of administrative authorities.

[272] Eg: Case T-228/02, *OMPI I* (n 10 above), para 143; see also Section 1.2 above.

[273] Case T-14/98, *Heidi Hautala MEP* (n 261 above), see also the discussion above.

[274] Arguing this point with regard to the 'Schengen legislation': Deirdre Curtin, 'The Developing Right of Citizen Access to Information on Asylum and Immigration Decision-Making' in Elspeth Guild and Carol Harlow (eds), *Implementing Amsterdam: Immigration and Asylum Rights* (Oxford, Portland: Hart Publishing, 2001), pp 35–63.

[275] Jurgen Schwarze, 'The Procedural Guarantees in the Recent Case-Law of the European Community' in Deirdre Curtin and Ton Heukels (eds), *Institutional Dynamics of European Integration: Essays in Honour of Henry G Schermers* (Dordrecht: Nijhoff, 1994), pp 488–9; See eg: Case 222/86, *Unectef v Heylens* [1987] ECR 4097.

as a basis for adopting Union law. Based on this rationale, the obligation to state reasons under European law should in principle also extend to the listing request by the competent authorities of the Member States. It should further be justiciable not only in a preliminary ruling but in a direct action.

By way of conclusion, procedural rights, such as the right of access to documents and the obligation to state reasons, are applicable in the Union pillars and, as was explicitly confirmed by the EU courts for the right of access to documents, they can be judicially enforced. Union lists of terrorist suspects, notwithstanding in which pillar they are formally adopted, breach the procedural rights of those listed. This was acknowledged for Community lists by the CFI in the *OMPI* cases. Thus, those listed in Union lists of terrorist suspects can directly bring an action before EU Court challenging the breach of their procedural rights.

3.7 Concluding Remarks

Union lists of terrorist suspects should be and could be subject to review in the EU courts. Cases concerning Union lists can be brought to the courts' attention in different ways. First, the meticulous determination of Community action by CFSP decisions unlawfully allows the Union to make use of Community instruments. The EU courts have the jurisdiction over such encroachment upon Community powers under Article 46 (f) TEU in combination with Article 47 TEU. Secondly, the EU courts have the mandate to uphold the rule of law in the EU. They must review Union lists of terrorist suspects because they have effects on the legal position of individuals beyond those attributed to common positions in the European Treaties (principle of wider jurisdiction). Thirdly, since the ECJ's appeal decision in *Segi*, they can be challenged under the preliminary ruling procedure pursuant to Article 35 TEU. Finally, they could be challenged for not complying with procedural rights justiciable in the Union pillars.

The ECJ's position on whether Union lists can be subject to *direct review* remains to be seen. On the one hand, the ECJ has in the past been protective both of the rights of individuals and of Community competences. On the other, the Court did not accept an action for annulment in the *Eurojust* case despite the legal effect vis à vis third parties and in *Segi* the ECJ was cautious to respect the particularities of its jurisdiction under the third pillar.

4. The European Legal Order in Context

4.1 The European Court of Human Rights

The ECtHR has not yet specifically ruled whether the limited jurisdiction of the EU courts is compatible withthe right of access to justice within the meaning of Article 6 ECHR. In *Bosphorus*[276] the ECtHR stated that the protection of fundamental rights in the Community is generally equivalent to the Convention (presumption of equivalent protection).[277] However, in this case the ECtHR explicitly limited its considerations to judicial protection from *Community* law (first pillar).[278] They cannot be transferred to the Union pillars, where the jurisdiction of the EU courts is strictly limited.[279] The ECtHR can be expected to exercise full judicial review of Union measures in the light of the Convention guarantees.

Yet, there are indications that those listed as terrorist suspects will not find justice in Strasbourg either. Before the rulings of the EU courts in *Segi*, [280] the same case was also brought before the ECtHR. The Strasbourg Court was asked to declare the listing of *Segi* contrary to Article 6 ECHR. However, the ECtHR dismissed the application on procedural grounds. It did not rule on the merits. The ECtHR's main line of argument was that the common position still required implementation and that it therefore did not affect the position of the applicants sufficiently directly for them to qualify as victims within the meaning of Article 34 ECHR. *Segi* appears to demonstrate that Union lists will not be subject to judicial scrutiny in the ECtHR because they are not directly operational but require further implementation.

In *Segi* the ECtHR took a very narrow view of the concept of 'victim' within the meaning of Article 34 ECHR. This is (hopefully) no guarantee that the ECtHR could not rule differently in another case concerning Union lists. Indeed, there are good arguments to limit the significance of *Segi*: first, the ECtHR did not give a ruling on the merits; secondly, the applicants were not themselves listed in the common position (they

[276] ECtHR, *Bosphorus Hava Yollari Turizm veTicaret AS v Ireland* (45036/98) (2006) 42 EHRR *1*; see Chapter 3, Section 2 and Chapter 5, Section 5.1.

[277] See: Christina Eckes, 'Does the European Court of Human Rights Provide Protection from the European Community? The Case of Bosphorus Airways', *European Public Law*, 13, (2007), p 47 et seq.

[278] ECtHR, *Bosphorus* (n 276 above), para 72.

[279] This opinion was shared by AG Mengozzi, in: Case C-355/04 P, *Segi* (n 8 above); Chapter 3, Section 2.

[280] ECtHR, *Segi and others vs all 15 MS*, application no. 6422/02, judgment of 23 May 2002.

claimed to be spokespersons of Segi); and, thirdly, the ECtHR's finding in *Segi* appears to differ from the Court's assessment in earlier cases regarding public measures harming the reputation of the applicant.[281]

The right of access to justice in Article 6 ECHR depends on the legal effects of the measures on the position of the individual. Usually, Union law does not entail direct enforceability. This statement continues to be true. However, it requires a more differentiated analysis after the application of the principle of conform interpretation under the third pillar[282] and after the adoption of lists, which directly identify individuals as being involved in terrorism.[283] Hence, irrespective of whether Union law is directly enforceable, it can entail legal effects vis-à-vis individuals.[284] This is sufficient to make judicial review necessary, not only by the ECJ[285] but also by the ECtHR.

4.2 National Courts

4.2.1 Advocate-General Mengozzi's Opinion in Segi

Advocate-General Mengozzi concluded from the lack of judicial protection in the EU courts that it is for national courts to step in and review third pillar instruments in the light of Union law.[286] He based this argument predominantly on the *state of integration* of the Union pillars, pointing out that the European Treaties do not give the EU courts 'exclusive power to assess the legality of the acts by which the Union performs its activities'[287] The Advocate-General argued that the principle of conferred powers in the Union pillars reserved jurisdiction to the Member States if and to the extent to which it has not been conferred on the Union. He referred to Article 6(1) and (2) TEU and the right of loyal cooperation[288] as the legal basis for jurisdiction of national courts to review the legality of Union acts.[289]

[281] See Chapter 3, Sections 3.2.2 and 3.2.3.
[282] Case C-105/03, *Pupino* (n 186 above), para 43.
[283] Case T-228/02, *OMPI I* (n 10 above).
[284] Case C-355/04 P, *Segi* (n 8 above), para 53.
[285] See Section 3.2 above.
[286] AG Mengozzi, in Case C-355/04 P, *Segi* (n 8 above), para 98 et seq and 138.
[287] AG Mengozzi, in: Case C-355/04 P, *Segi* (n 8 above), para 104.
[288] Found to apply in the third pillar: Case C-105/03, *Pupino* (n 186 above), para 43.
[289] ibid, paras 105–6.

Article 46 TEU governs the jurisdiction of the EU courts under the Union pillars. It does not *exclude* review by national courts. However, it remains doubtful whether judicial review of Union law by national courts could offer adequate protection. And, the ECJ did not follow the suggestions of Advocate-General Mengozzi in *Segi*.[290] The Court did not mention *Foto-Frost*, but it (implicitly) defended the monopoly of the EU courts to determine the legality of European law. The ECJ (only) mandated national courts to review the decisions of competent national authorities leading to a listing at the European level and to refer a preliminary question under Article 35(1) TEU with regard to all acts having legal effect.[291] Nonetheless, it is useful to take Advocate-General Mengozzi's opinion in *Segi* as the starting point for considering the consequences of review of Union law in the courts of the Member States.

The Advocate-General argued that the *Foto-Frost* rule does not apply in the third pillar,[292] because the two main assumptions on which this rule is based are not transferable. First, while the Community system offers a complete system of remedies, judicial protection in the third pillar is strictly limited. Secondly, the main purpose of the preliminary ruling procedure under Article 234 EC is to ensure that Community law is applied uniformly by national courts, and Article 35 TEU cannot accomplish this task to the same extent.

The third pillar does not offer the same judicial protection as the Community pillar. This is because the JHA pillar remained 'half way between pure intergovernmental cooperation and the Community "integrationist" model'.[293] Because of the limited degree of integration and the reduced number of supranational elements it was considered sufficient to provide judicial review of third pillar law only incidentally, as part of actions against national implementation measures. At the time the third pillar was created, it was unforeseeable to what degree particular persons are today affected by Union law, without any need for further implementation.[294] The limitation of the jurisdiction of the EU courts was not

[290] Case C-355/04 P, *Segi* (n 8 above).

[291] ibid, para 53.

[292] AG Mengozzi, in: Case C-355/04 P, *Segi* (n 8 above), para 121 et seq; equally against an application of *Foto-Frost* in the context of Art 35 TEU: Anthony Arnull 'The Treaty of Amsterdam and the Court of Justice', in David O'Keeffe and Patrick Twomey (eds), *Legal issues of the Amsterdam Treaty* (Oxford: Hart Publishing, 1999), p 119; in favour: Roland Bieber, Astrid Epiney, and Marcel Haag, *Die Europäische Union: Europarecht und Politik* (Baden-Baden: Nomos, 2005), pp 290–1.

[293] AG Mengozzi, in: Case C-355/04 P, *Segi* (n 8 above), para 132.

[294] Compare Section 3.2.2 above.

based on a principled decision that the review of *Union law* should be reserved to national courts.

The Advocate-General further asserted that Article 35 TEU confirms that third pillar instruments are not exempted from judicial control as a matter of principle.[295] This is, of course, true, but it does not establish review of Union law by *national courts*. Article 35 TEU merely sets out the competences of the ECJ and an *option* for Member States to oblige their own courts under national law to refer questions to the ECJ. Moreover, the Advocate-General purported that national courts act as courts of the Union just 'as with respect to the first pillar'.[296] However, this does not indicate that they are competent to review the validity of Union law. On the contrary, if they have a similar role as in the first pillar judicial review of third pillar instruments should be excluded,[297] since this is the situation in the first pillar. And, even if Article 35 TEU cannot accomplish the same uniformity as Article 234 EC, the two provisions are drafted in a parallel manner and serve the same objective.

The fact that Union law usually requires Member States to adopt acts of implementation does not in itself justify a departure from the Community approach. First of all, Community measures can indeed also require further measures of implementation by the Member States. Secondly, disparities between Member States[298] cannot be avoided by conferring upon national courts jurisdiction to review Union law. Even if national courts assume the power to review the legality of Union law instruments any declaration of invalidity at the national level could take force only *inter partes*.[299] Therefore, in want of the power to declare an illegal instrument of Union law void, national courts can only declare it inapplicable in the particular case. This would actually increase disparities.[300]

In order to bring the application of a Union list to an end in the entire EU those listed would have to bring an action in all 27 Member States.[301] Still, this would not challenge the *validity* of the Union law instrument

[295] AG Mengozzi, in: Case C-355/04 P, *Segi* (n 8 above), para 108 et seq.

[296] ibid, para 110.

[297] Compare Case 314/85, *Foto-Frost* (n 143 above).

[298] AG Mengozzi, in: Case C-355/04 P, *Segi* (n 8 above), para 114.

[299] See also: ibid, para 120.

[300] The danger of inconsistency was pointed out by AG Mengozzi, in: Case C-355/04 P, *Segi* (n 8 above), para 130.

[301] In *Segi* the CFI was correct in its assessment that an action for damages in the national courts against all 27 Member States for their involvement in the adoption of the Union list 'of little effect' (Case T-338/02, *Segi* (n 8 above), para 38).

containing the list: in principle the instrument would continue to remain in force with all its stigmatizing effects. Hence, review by national courts would not resolve the problem of Union lists, since, as the Advocate-General correctly observed, '[t]he harm of which [...] [the appellants] complain [...] arises irrespective of whether national measures implementing [...] [the common position] are actually adopted'[302] An action in the national courts does not provide relief to those listed in a Union instrument. Hence, national courts cannot provide judicial protection within the meaning of Article 6 ECHR.[303] Review of Union law by national courts is further systematically flawed and endangers the uniform application of European law.

The Advocate-General further referred to the principle of loyal cooperation as a basis for the competence of national courts to review Union law.[304] However, the obligation to cooperate loyally is usually invoked in two situations. First, it limits the exercise of powers of the political bodies of a Member State and, secondly, it renders national law inapplicable where it obstructs the effective exercise of rights that individuals have under European law. The principle of loyal cooperation has not so far been invoked to establish jurisdiction for national courts in order to provide *protection from European law*. Advocate-General Mengozzi refers 'by analogy' to the judgment in *UPA*,[305] where the ECJ stated that 'it is for the Member States to establish a system of legal remedies and procedures which ensure respect for the right to effective judicial protection'[306] However, in *UPA* the ECJ referred to the preliminary ruling procedure; at no point did it envisage that national courts should *directly* review European law. Therefore, *UPA* cannot support the argument that national courts are competent to rule on the compliance of a particular European law instrument with general principles of EU law. Essentially, the idea behind the principle of loyal cooperation is to ensure the effectiveness of European law. It alters national law in a way that allows individuals to benefit the most from their rights under European law. Allowing national courts to review European law leads to the contrary: it endangers the functioning of the European legal order because it challenges the supremacy of European law and the monopoly of the EU courts to review EU law.

302 AG Mengozzi, in: Case C-355/04 P, *Segi* (n 8 above), para 92.

303 ECtHR, *Sporrong and Lönnroth v Sweden*, Judgment, 23 September 1982, A/52.

304 AG Mengozzi, in: Case C-355/04 P, *Segi* (n 8 above), para 105.

305 ibid, fn 55.

306 Case C-50/00 P, *UPA* (n 224 above), para 41.

Indeed, Advocate-General Mengozzi's suggestion that national courts should review Union law was based on a peculiar mixture of arguments. On the one hand, he referred to *Pupino* in which the ECJ introduced the principle of conform interpretation to the third pillar. This implies supremacy of Union law. On the other, a competence of the national courts to directly review Union law appears to rule out that Union law is supreme.

4.2.2 The European Arrest Warrant Judgments

Advocate-General Mengozzi argued that 'in the present state of Union law' national courts are entrusted with ensuring judicial protection from Union measures[307] in the light of the fundamental rights as recognized *by the Union.*[308] From the perspective of national governments review of Union law in national courts, albeit in the light of general principles of EU law, is much easier to accept than full judicial review of Union law by the ECJ. Advocate-General Mengozzi's opinion could hence be seen in the same light as the case of *CILFIT*,[309] namely as a pragmatic attempt to allow for some judicial rebellion in order to strengthen compliance with the rules in general.[310] Review by national courts in the light of Union standards might ensure a minimum of uniformity but avoid review of Union law in national courts on the basis of national law.

The Advocate-General might have seen a need for appeasement after a series of judgments on the implementation of the framework decision on the European Arrest Warrant (EAW).[311] The German and Polish constitutional courts and the Cypriot Supreme Court had taken challenges to the validity of the national implementation of the EAW framework decision as an occasion to reinforce their willingness to defy human rights infringements by Union law.[312] While the Polish Constitutional Court

[307] AG Mengozzi, in: Case C-355/04 P, *Segi* (n 8 above), para 99.

[308] ibid, para 110.

[309] Case 283/81, *CILFIT* [1982] ECR 3415.

[310] Jonathan Golub, 'The Politics of Judicial Discretion: Rethinking the Interaction between National Courts and the European Court of Justice', *West European Politics*, 19 (1996), pp 376–7.

[311] See the discussion of the *EAW* judgments in Chapter 2, Section 4.2 but see also Chapter 5, Section 5.2 on the German Constitutional Court and: GCC, judgment of the Second Senate of 30 June 2009 (Treaty of Lisbon), 2 BvE 2/08; 2 BvE 5/08; 2 BvR 1010/08; 2 BvR 1022/08; 2 BvR 1259/08; 2 BvR 182/09.

[312] Supreme Court of Cyprus, Judgment of 7 November 2005 (Case 294/2005); German Constitutional Court, AW Decision of 18 July 2005 (2 BvR 2236/04); Polish Constitutional Court, Judgment of 27 April 2005, No P 1/05; but see also: Czech Constitutional Court, Judgment of 3 May 2006 (Case 66/04).

allowed the implementation legislation to remain in force in order to avoid putting Poland immediately in breach of EU law obligations, the German Constitutional Court (GCC) simply ruled that '[a]s long as the legislature does not adopt a new Act [...] the extradition of a German citizen to a Member State of the European Union is not possible'[313] The Court hence demonstrated that obligations under Union law will not keep it from fully scrutinizing all national law as to its compatibility with the German Constitution.

In the *EAW* decision, the GCC did not rule on the complainant's allegations that the European framework decision itself was contrary to the German Constitution.[314] On the contrary, it ruled that the framework decision could have been incorporated in conformity with the German Constitution, but that the German legislator did not exhaust the margins afforded by the European legal instrument. Indirectly, however, the Court addressed the claim of the complainant that the framework decision lacked democratic legitimacy. It pointed out that the European Parliament is merely consulted during the law-making process and emphasized the role of the national parliaments in the implementation process.[315] The Court explicitly stated that the national parliaments' legal power to breach European law by not implementing it contributes to its legitimacy.[316] This is a warning to the EU that the national legislator is bound by the national Constitution and that the GCC will require the legislator to comply with the constitutional rules notwithstanding conflicting Union law.

While the German Government argued in line with the supremacy concept of the ECJ, namely that legal instruments of the EU, including framework decisions,[317] cannot be reviewed in the light of the German Constitution,[318] the GCC took a purely domestic view.[319] The GCC did *not* even consider the obligation of conform interpretation introduced under the third pillar by the ECJ's judgment in the case of *Pupino*[320] The

[313] GCC, *EAW Decision* of 18 July 2005 (2 BvR 2236/04), para 124.

[314] Applicant's claims: ibid, para 21; the Court's reply: para 60 et seq.

[315] ibid, para 81.

[316] Judge Lübbe-Wolf critically remarked that the freedom to infringe the law could not legitimately be an endorsement of democracy in the EU (ibid, para 177).

[317] The transfer of the principle of conform interpretation in Case C-105/03, *Pupino* (n 186 above) requires a form of supremacy of third pillar instruments.

[318] GCC, *EAW Decision* (n 313 above), paras 35 and 51.

[319] See criticism in Chapter 2, Section 4.2.

[320] Case C-105/03, *Pupino* (n 186 above); the majority did not mention the judgment, only Judge Gerhardt mentioned it in his dissenting opinion.

majority opinion did *not* mention the Maastricht decision either;[321] yet its argument demonstrated that it considered Union law from a different angle. While in the *Maastricht* decision the GCC reserved the competence to declare Community law contrary to the *core principles* of the German Constitution,[322] in the *EAW* decision the Court went even further and defended the *full standard* of protection provided by the German Constitution.

Without directly addressing the constitutionality of the framework decision, the Court discussed the possibility of national bodies breaching EU law obligations where compliance would be irreconcilable with the German Constitution. This implies that the Court places national constitutional standards above obligations arising from Union law. And, since it is the Court's constitutional duty to ensure that fundamental rights are respected within the German legal order, it might imply that the Court will declare Union law that breaches these rights inapplicable within the national legal order.

Moreover, on substance it is interesting to note that the GCC annulled the national act of implementation among other reasons because it infringed the fundamental right to effective judicial protection from acts of public authority in Article 19(4) of the German Constitution.[323] It must be conceded that the GCC ruled that the type of measure can require a margin of discretion on the part of the political bodies that results in 'differences regarding the completeness of judicial review'[324] However it also stated[325] that the examination of the severity of the sanction attached to the offence on which the request for extradition is based is

> not a question of freedom of assessment under foreign-policy aspects but one that very significantly affects the protection of the prosecuted person's fundamental rights and even the guarantee of his or her human dignity. To the extent that the legislature is constitutionally obliged to regulate other elements that are to be taken into account in a decision on extradition, Article 19.4 of the Basic Law also requests that the decision on extradition is subject to judicial review in this respect.

The Union listings have a significant impact on the legal interests of those affected, notwithstanding national measures of implementation.[326] The listing themselves are of course not acts of the German legislator but of the

[321] See Chapter 2, Section 4.2.
[322] See Chapter 5, Section 5.2.
[323] GCC, *EAW Decision* (n 313 above), para 102 et seq.
[324] ibid, para 105. [325] ibid, para 114. [326] Chapter 3, Sections 3.2.2 and 3.2.3.

EU Council. However, they are based on decisions of the competent national authorities, followed by a listing proposal of that Member State, and adopted following a unanimous decision of the representatives of the national governments in the Council. All three acts (decision of the competent national authority, the proposal and the voting) could be attributed to the Member State.

In the *EAW* decision the GCC ruled that the examination of the severity of the punishment that those extradited might face is a legally relevant act that must be subject to judicial review in the national courts. The same assessment could be made with regard to a listing proposal (that follows the decision of the competent national authorities) and possibly, albeit less likely, with regard to the voting behaviour of the national representatives in the Council. The decision to list someone as a terrorist suspect must be based on an examination of the factual and legal evidence.[327] This examination directly results in a measure having detrimental effect on the legal position of individuals. It can be expected that the GCC will not accept that those decisions remain outside the scope of judicial review.

Additionally, the exchange of information and other national implementation measures in the third pillar could be made subject to judicial review in the national courts. The GCC demonstrated in the *EAW* decision that it is not willing to accept implementation measures that do not satisfy national fundamental rights guarantees only because they are required by Union law.

4.2.3 Lists of Terrorist Suspects in National Courts

The GCC has ruled in settled case-law that public warnings give those affected a right to an effective remedy, not only when they entail a formal change of their legal position, but also when they impair rights of individuals in a factual, indirect manner.[328] In 2000 the GCC agreed to review

[327] This was confirmed in: Joined Cases T-110/03, T-150/03 and T-405/03, *Sison* (n 96 above).

[328] The GCC has ruled with regard to warnings of youth sects that being listed in a public document can infringe fundamental rights and must be subject to judicial control: GCC, BVerfG NJW 89, 3269; see also GCC, decisions of 26 June 2002, BvR 670/91 regarding youth sects and BvR 558/91 and 1428/91 regarding warning of poisoned wine. The German Federal Administrative Court considers the listing of religious groups by the government as being a legally relevant action and requiring judicial review: BVerwG NJW 89, 2272; see in particular GCC, BvR 670/91, para 70: 'Die genannten Äußerungen hatten in Bezug auf die Beschwerdeführer eine mittelbar faktische Wirkung. Als Beeinträchtigungen des Grundrechts aus art 4 Abs. 1 und 2 GG sind aber auch sie von Verfassungs wegen nur dann nicht zu beanstanden, wenn sie sich verfassungsrechtlich hinreichend rechtfertigen lassen.'

the constitutionality of public warnings against youth sects and poisoned wine. Even though the GCC confirmed its position in earlier – harshly criticized – judgments[329] and held that these public allegations were constitutional[330] these cases demonstrate that the GCC considers allegations published by the state a restriction of fundamental rights that must be subject to judicial scrutiny.[331] It is submitted that the German national courts would consider lists of terrorist suspects equally legally relevant and consequently find that those listed have a right to judicial review.[332]

Further, the fact that the warnings in the mentioned cases were justified does not have a high indicative value. The cases before the GCC were very different from Union lists of terrorist suspects. The main objective of the warnings in those cases was to inform the public. The warnings were published in order to prevent consumers from drinking the poisoned wine, to exculpate other participants in the wine trade indirectly from the allegations, and to prevent potential worshipers from joining the allegedly harmful sects. Publishing the information was indispensable in order to achieve the Government's objectives. Moreover, the listings were preliminary, further investigations were conducted, and those listed were informed about the allegations. All this stands in sharp contrast to how the Union lists individuals as terrorist suspects.

In France, several cases concerning registrations in the Schengen Information System (SIS) give an indication of the courts' view of public listings. In 1999 the decision to refuse a visa, because the person in question was registered in the SIS, was brought before the Conseil d'État (the

[329] Christoph Gusy, 'Richterliches Prüfungsrecht', *Juristenzeitung* (1989), p 1003; Friedrich Schoch, 'Staatliche Informationspolitik und Berufsfreiheit', *Deutsches Verwaltungsblatt* (1991), p 667; see in English: Reinhard Ruge, 'Between Law and Necessity: The Federal Constitutional Court Confirms the Right of the Federal Government to Warn the Public', *German Law Journal* (2002).

[330] GCC, decisions of 26 June 2000, BvR 670/91 and BvR 558/91 and 1428/91.

[331] It must be conceded that in the poisoned wine case the GCC found an intrusion into the freedom to practice a profession, as it is guaranteed by Art 12 of the German Constitution, which protects to a limited extend future economic prospects, and that this right does not find an equivalent in the ECHR.

[332] Agreeing with: Sandra Bartelt and Helge Elisabeth Zeitler, '"Intelligente Sanktionen" zur Terrorismusbekämpfung in der EU', *EuZW* (2003), p 714, fn 38. One difference between the warnings of religious groups and individual sanctions lies in the fact that the warnings have the only intention to inform the public about the dangers of these organizations, while the list in Common Position 2001/931/CFSP was addressed at the Member States and the institutions. In the latter case informing the public was claimed an unintended side effect. Despite this difference, however, the factual situation for the listed is very similar and the potential impairment of rights is comparable.

highest French Administrative Court). The Conseil d'État annulled the refusal for breach of procedural rights. It ruled that the person must be given all information necessary to challenge the decision of the designating state to report his or her details to the SIS, including a statement of reasons, which amongst other information sets out the country that reported them.[333] In a second case, delivered on the same day, the Conseil d'État even agreed reluctantly to assess the well-foundedness of the German administrative decision to report a Romanian national to the SIS for seeking asylum in Germany.[334] Of course, both cases were actions against French implementation measures. The issue at stake was not immediately the listing in the SIS. However, the decisions of the Conseil d'État demonstrate that it considers the consequences of the SIS sufficient to require access to justice against the original decision to report someone. Further, those cases show that the Conseil d'État might not be willing to give up jurisdiction simply because the national decision was motivated by compliance with international law.

4.3 Interplay between the Different Courts

The jurisdiction of the different courts in Europe is overlapping. Potentially all three – national courts, the EU courts, and the ECtHR – could have the mandate under their own constitutional foundation to review Union lists of terrorist suspects. This creates a situation in which the different courts act as (potential) watchdogs of each other by exercising mutual control that could strengthen the judicial protection of the individual.[335]

While the ECtHR rejected the applicants' case in the *Segi* case because they did not fulfil the standing requirements under the Convention, the national constitutional courts of Germany and Poland issued indirect warnings to the ECJ when reviewing the respective national implementation of the *EAW* framework decision. *Segi* demonstrated that the ECtHR is to a certain extent willing to go along with the reduction of fundamental rights protection when states fight 'international terrorism'. Even if the ECtHR did not rule on the substance of the case, *Segi* makes a ruling by the

[333] Conseil d'État, *Hamssaoui*, judgment of 9 June 1999.

[334] Conseil d'État, *Forabosco*, judgment of 9 June 1999, see at: Elspeth Guild, 'Adjudicating Schengen: National Judicial Control in France', *European Journal of Migration and Law*, 1 (1999), p 436.

[335] See Chapter 5, Section 5.3 with regard to the overlapping jurisdiction to review Community sanctions.

Strasbourg Court finding in favour of those listed less likely. Advocate-General Mengozzi correctly observed that this does not have implications for the assessment of Union lists in the EU courts in the light of general principles of EU law.[336] The ECHR purports to ensure a minimum level of fundamental rights protection, which does not always match the level of protection provided by domestic law. Yet, it could be argued that Advocate-General Mengozzi's position in *Segi* was influenced by the intention to avoid review of Union law by the ECtHR. After the ECtHR's judgment in the *Bosphorus* case, which the Advocate-General discussed in his opinion, review of Union lists of terrorist suspects by the ECtHR cannot be excluded.[337]

The role of national courts in providing fundamental rights protection from individual sanctions is problematic. National courts are obliged to comply with (and hence apply) European Union law,[338] including general principles of EU law, the ECHR as interpreted by the ECtHR, and finally they have to act in accordance with their mandate under domestic law. Will national courts apply European law if it does not satisfy the Convention standards as interpreted by the ECtHR or their national constitutions?

Review of Union law by national courts would harm the effectiveness of the European legal order in an unpredictable manner. Hence, the European legal order must find a way to accommodate the concerns of national courts in order to avoid this situation. In the past, the EU courts have demonstrated that they are cautious to avoid an open conflict. The mere threat that national courts exercise jurisdiction over European law can help to discipline them. Arguably the effects of the *EAW* judgments can already be seen in the ECJ's ruling in *Segi*. The multi-level-review structure of the ECtHR, the EU courts and the courts in the Member States suffers from certain limitations; however, in principle it has proven to strengthen judicial protection rather than to weaken it.

Conclusions

With regard to individual sanctions based on Union lists one must distinguish two different issues: first, judicial protection from Community measures, and, secondly, protection from Union listings. While the former

[336] AG Mengozzi, in: Case C-355/04 P, *Segi* (n 8 above), para 88.

[337] See Section 4.2.1 above.

[338] See Case C-355/04 P, *Segi* (n 8 above), para 52.

appears to be in place after a series of annulments by the CFI, the latter is not satisfactory.

Those sanctioned by the Community enjoy the rights of defence guaranteed by the European legal order and have access to full judicial review. In the *OMPI* cases the CFI has cautiously outlined the restrictions on the rights of individuals justified by security considerations and the need for international cooperation. Whether the procedural protection offered in principle allows those sanctioned to defend their rights in practice is a different issue. Not only security considerations but also the particularities of the two-staged listing procedure entail the risk that those affected are not able to access the relevant information and make their view known in an effective manner. The same is true for judicial review. The CFI has repeatedly found that it is simply not in the position to assess the well-foundedness of a particular listing because the Council is unwilling or unable to share the relevant information even with the judiciary.

In *Segi* the CFI came to the rather uneasy conclusion that the applicant does not have any remedy at its disposal against its Union listing as a terrorist suspect.[339] The ECJ explicitly rejected the CFI's assumption that there was no effective judicial remedy available to the applicant. However, it did not indicate a possibility of direct judicial review at the EU level, but extended the preliminary ruling procedure to Union lists. This alone does not provide sufficient protection. The Union lists remain excluded from direct substantive review notwithstanding that they gravely affect the legal position of those listed.

On different grounds both the ECtHR and the CFI have denied judicial protection from Union measures. National courts were called upon by Advocate-General Mengozzi to review the Union lists, but under European law they do not have the competences necessary to provide effective protection. They can only disapply Union law within their Member State. It is for the EU courts to ensure that the European legal order complies with the right of access to justice. However, the role of the ECJ as it is defined by the Treaties is not strong enough to control the adoption of lists

[339] Case T-338/02, *Segi* (n 8 above), para 38:

> Concerning the absence of an effective remedy invoked by the applicants, it must be noted that indeed probably no effective judicial remedy is available to them, whether before the Community Courts or national courts, with regard to the inclusion of Segi on the list of persons, groups or entities involved in terrorist acts.

of terrorist suspects under the Union pillars. Fundamental rights standards within the EU have begun to differ.[340]

The current judicial set-up was created on the premise that the decisions taken under the Union pillars are general policy decisions only. They were thought to be general norms that require application to the individual case and do not immediately impact on the individual. Judicial protection was afforded in a decentralized system because decisions directly affecting individuals were reserved to either the Community or the national level. By shifting the identification of individuals to the Union level fundamental rights dissolve in the pillar structure. The Union pillars fall short of providing the judicial protection needed for a decision to identify an individual as terrorist suspect. In the *Segi* case it would have been for the EU courts to ensure judicial protection in an area of law where, for the time being, the necessary judicial remedies are not yet codified in the Treaties. The CFI did not choose to address the existing gap. This is deplorable and not only infringes fundamental rights in the individual case but harms the general objective of promoting fundamental rights.[341] On appeal, the ECJ introduced some form of judicial protection; however, limited by the facts of the particular case, its ruling in *Segi* was not as principled as would have been needed to provide *effective* protection from Union lists of terrorist suspects. The task of ensuring the observance of the law requires the EU courts on occasion to look beyond the literal constraints of the relevant Treaty provisions[342] and read the Treaties – including their own competences – in the light of the rule of law and in the light of the general principles of EU law. These principles oblige the Court to 'correct [...] the rules which limit its powers' as it has done before.[343]

The warnings of the national constitutional courts in the *EAW* cases must be taken seriously. Even if national courts are not in the position to provide effective judicial protection from Union listings, they have the

[340] Filip Jasinski, 'EU Counter-Terrorist Policy after 11 March 2004', *The Polish Quarterly of International Affairs* (2004), p 72.

[341] '[...] the Union can only achieve the leadership role to which it aspires through the example it sets', see Philip Alston, and JHH Weiler, 'An "Ever Closer Union" in Need of a Human Rights Policy: The European Union and Human Rights', in Philip Alston (ed), *The EU and Human Rights* (Oxford: Oxford University Press, 1999), pp 4–5.

[342] See above all: C-2/88, *Zwartveld* [1990] ECR I-3365.

[343] AG Mancini, in C-294/83, *Les Verts* (n 9 above), para 7.

mandate to protect those within their judicial system. Scrutiny by national courts on the basis of national constitutional requirements is effective *within their legal order*; it should be at the disposal of the affected person whenever international judicial systems fail to provide sufficient protection. However, effective judicial protection by the EU courts from Member States' attempts to use the European legal order to do what they cannot do under national law is not only desirable but also possible.

7

What are the Alternatives? Adoption and Review

Introduction

The Parliamentary Assembly of the Council of Europe found the 'practices [of sanctioning individuals as terrorist suspects] unworthy of international bodies such as the United Nations and the European Union'.[1] This view is shared by numerous human rights lawyers.[2] The latter have strongly criticized both European sanctions against individuals giving effect to United Nations (UN) lists of terrorist suspects and those giving effect to European Union (EU) managed lists (autonomous sanctions). Besides arguments that they infringe substantive rights, a majority agrees that they do not comply with the procedural rights guaranteed in the European legal order.[3]

The Council has taken steps to improve the procedural rights of those sanctioned in response to this criticism, but even more directly in response to the repeated annulments of sanctions through the European Court of

[1] Resolution 1597 (2008) of the Parliamentary Assembly, Council of Europe, 23 January 2008, para 7.

[2] On both autonomous EU sanctions and EU sanctions based on UN lists of terrorist suspects: Sandra Bartelt et al, '"Intelligente Sanktionen" zur Terrorismusbekämpfung in der EU' (Intelligent sanctions to fight terrorism in the EU), (2003) *EuZW*, p 715 et seq; Iain Cameron, 'European Union Anti-Terrorist Blacklisting', 4 *Human Rights Law Review* (2004); see also: Dick Marty, Report of the Committee on Legal Affairs and Human Rights to the Council of Europe, Document 11454, of 16 November 2007, endorsed by the parliamentary assembly on 23 January 2008 in Recommendation 1824 (2008) and Resolution 1597 (2008); on sanctions based on UN lists: Iain Cameron, 'The European Convention on Human Rights, Due Process and United Nations Security Council Counter-Terrorism Sanctions', Report to the Council of Europe, of 6 February 2006, http://www.coe.int, visited: 28 March 2008; Piet Eeckhout, 'EC Law and UN Security Council Resolutions – In Search of the Right Fit', 3 *EuConst* (2007), p 183 et seq.

[3] See references in n 2 above.

Justice (ECJ) and the Court of First Instance (CFI).[4] However, further changes remain necessary. The sanctioning practice of the EU continues to fall short of procedural justice.

So far this book has sought to demonstrate the flaws of the current practice of listing and sanctioning individuals as terrorist suspects. Chapter 2 concluded that the Community does not have at present the competence to adopt counter-terrorist sanctions against individuals. Chapter 5 examined how the international origin of the sanctions giving effect to UN lists could strip individuals of well-established fundamental rights guarantees under domestic law. Chapter 6 focused on the autonomous European listing procedure and pointed out the lack of procedural protection of those listed (and sanctioned). This final chapter takes a practical and principled look into the future. It explores whether and how individual sanctions could lawfully and legitimately be adopted under European law.

The two different types of sanctions adopted by the EU must be distinguished: sanctions based on UN lists of terrorist suspects and autonomous EU-managed sanctions. Certain parallels can be drawn between the two sanction regimes: both fail to provide sufficient procedural and legal safeguards and both have similar detrimental consequences for the rights of those affected. Yet, the origins of the defects of the listing procedure are different and so are the changes required to address them.

The Security Council holds the monopoly to determine what constitutes a threat to international peace and security[5] and what measures are necessary to address such a threat.[6] Its decisions weigh heavily in a balancing exercise aiming to reconcile conflicting rights and interests. Yet, obligations under the UN Charter cannot alone justify displacing the general principles of EU law where implementation measures are concerned.[7] The European institutions are placed in a difficult position. Lack of information and lack of procedural safeguards at the UN level appear to make it impossible to comply with general principles of European law

[4] Case T-228/02, *Organisation des Modjahedines du peuple d'Iran v Council and UK (OMPI I)* [2006] ECR II-4665; Case T-256/07, *People's Mojahidin Organization of Iran v Council (OMPI II)*, judgment of 23 October 2008, not yet reported; appeal pending: Case C-576/08 P, *People's Mojahedin Organization of Iran* and Case T-284/08, *People's Mojahedin Organization of Iran v Council (OMPI III)*, judgment of 4 December 2008; Case T-47/03, *Jose Maria Sison v Council and Commission* [2007] ECR II-73 (sum pub); Cases C-402/05 P and C-415/05 P, *Kadi and al Barakaat*, judgment of 3 September 2008, not yet reported.

[5] Art 39 UN Charter.

[6] Arts 41 and 42 UN Charter.

[7] See Chapter 5.

when giving effect to UN sanctions. While the EU itself is not under an obligation to comply with obligations under the UN Charter, Member States are.[8]

By contrast, the autonomous European sanctions regime appears to be easier to bring into compliance with general principles of EU law, notwithstanding that it was adopted in order to comply with UN Security Council Resolution 1373.[9] The Member States, and as a consequence also the EU, are subject to fewer constraints under international law when they autonomously identify individuals as terrorist suspects. They take discretionary decisions and possess all the relevant information to grant effective remedies.[10]

Chapter 7 is structured as follows. Section 1 examines how autonomous sanctions against individuals could be adopted in compliance with procedural rights. The discussion starts with the changes introduced to the EU's sanctioning practice as a response to the successful court challenges. This includes consideration of the amendments under the Treaty of Lisbon. Despite certain improvements it has been argued that 'fundamental human rights remain unprotected'.[11] Further improvements of the listing procedure are suggested. This includes recommendations for reviewable listing criteria. Finally, the discussion turns to the crucial problem of disclosure of sensitive information.

Section 2 considers procedural protection from European sanctions giving effect to UN lists. The European institutions are confronted with an irresolvable dilemma. The ECJ required in *Kadi and al Barakaat*[12] compliance with the general principles of European law, including fundamental rights. However, the European institutions do not possess the information necessary to place those sanctioned in the position to exercise their rights of the defence.

The following two sections consider both sanction regimes together. Section 3 addresses the necessary level of *judicial* control over individual sanctions. It considers the role of the judiciary in determining the line that separates lawful counter-terrorist measures from unjustifiable human rights restrictions. Section 4 discusses the proportionality of individual sanctions.

[8] Arts 25 and 103 UN Charter, see also: Chapter 5, Section 2.

[9] See Chapter 1, Sections 3 and 4.

[10] See Chapter 6 and Section 1 below.

[11] Marty, Report of the Committee on Legal Affairs (n 2 above), para 22.

[12] Cases C-402/05 P and C-415/05 P, *Kadi and al Barakaat* (n 4 above).

1. Adopting Autonomous European Sanctions in Compliance with Procedural Rights

1.1 Reform of the Autonomous European Sanctions Regime

At the outset in 2001, the sanctioning procedure did not offer even the most basic legal safeguards. Those listed were not notified at all. They did not have the opportunity to address the Council with a request for review; nor were they able to obtain knowledge of the information that led to their listing. Since then some efforts have been made to introduce at least minimal procedural protection.

The CFI started annulling Community listings under the autonomous sanctions regime in December 2006.[13] It identified fundamental flaws in the autonomous listing procedure and developed tentative guidelines for a different approach.[14] This left the Council no other choice but to reform the adoption procedure of individual sanctions. At that time, individuals had been sanctioned as terrorist suspects pursuant to this flawed procedure for five years.

The need for improvement of the listing and delisting procedure was identified and discussed before the first annulments of autonomous sanctions.[15] In December 2003 the Council adopted Guidelines addressing issues surrounding the designing, implementing, enforcing, and monitoring of restrictive measures (sanctions).[16] It also adopted an 'EU Best Practices Paper'. Both documents have been amended several times.[17] They emphasize repeatedly the importance of complying with fundamental rights.[18] Yet, even basic procedural rights were introduced after and arguably in response to[19] the CFI's first annulment of a sanction measure against individuals in the case of *OMPI I*.[20]

[13] Case T-228/02, *OMPI I*; Case T-256/07, *OMPI II*; Case T-284/08, *OMPI III* (all n 4 above); see Chapter 6 for more details.

[14] See Chapter 6, Section 1.

[15] Council doc 10826/07 on the fight against the financing of terrorism – implementation of Common Position 2001/931/CFSP, of 21 June 2007, OJ 2003, L 16/68–70, para 2.

[16] Council doc 15579/03 of 8 December 2003.

[17] The guidelines were updated by doc 6749/05 and doc 15114/05; EU Best Practice Papers: doc 13851/4/04 REV 4, of 8 December 2004; doc 10533/06, Brussels, 14 June 2006.

[18] See eg: doc 15114/05, ibid, paras 10 and 17.

[19] See the specific reference to the case of *OMPI* at Council doc 11309/07, 29 June 2007, p 2.

[20] Case T-228/02, *OMPI I* (n 4 above).

Besides expressing a general intention to improve the adoption procedure,[21] the Council established a permanent Working Party (CP 931 WP) and introduced procedural safeguards.[22] Originally, an ad hoc forum constituted by the Member States, the Commission and the General Secretariat (the so-called 'clearing house')[23] was in charge of drawing up the lists of terrorist suspects. The clearing house was subordinate to the Committee of Permanent Representatives. In the reform of the procedure the clearing house was replaced by a new permanent Council Working Party in charge of (1) examining and evaluating information with a view to listing; (2) assessing whether the information meets 'the criteria in Common Position 2001/931/CFSP and in the Council's statement agreed when the Common Position was adopted'; (3) preparing the regular review; and (4) making recommendations for listings and delistings.[24] The clearing house had been judged as comparatively effective[25] but criticized for its lack of funds and continuity.[26] Other criticisms pointed out that there was no formal delisting or review procedure and that the listing criteria were not public.[27] This is a parallel to the UN Sanctions regime between 1999 and 2002 when the UN Sanctions Committee listed persons as terrorist suspects without offering any mechanism for delisting.[28]

Each person listed in an EC Council decision is now provided with a statement of reasons.[29] Those listed in an EC Council decision are notified

[21] Notice for the attention of the persons, groups and entities on the list provided for in Art 2(3) of Council Regulation (EC) No 2580/2001 on specific restrictive measures directed against certain persons and entities with a view to combating terrorism, OJ [2007] C 144/01, 29.6.2007.

[22] Council doc 10826/07 (n 15 above), Annex II, see in particular para 17 et seq.

[23] Council doc 11693/02, 3 September 2002, Annex I, 'Decision of the Permanent Representatives Committee of 7 December 2001'.

[24] See the Working Party's mandate at: Council doc 10826/07 (n 15 above), Annex I, page 4.

[25] Annegret Bendiek, 'EU Strategy on Counter-Terrorism–Steps Towards a Coherent Network Policy', SWP Research Paper, Stiftung Wissenschaft und Politik, German Institute for International and Security Affairs, November 2006, http://www3.swp-berlin.org/, pp 6 and 19.

[26] Robin Niblett and Derek Mix, 'Transatlantic Approaches to Sanctions: Principles and Recommendations for Action', October 2006, p 24 (available at: http://www.csis.org/).

[27] Frank Meyer, 'Lost in Complexity – Rechtsschutz gegen Smart Sanctions in der EU', (2007) *ZEUS*, Imelda Tappeiner, 'The fight against terrorism. The lists and the gaps.', 1 *Utrecht Law Review* (2005), p 97; Bill Bowring, 'Terrorist Designation with Regard to European and International Law: The Case of the PMOI', International Conference of Jurists in Paris on Wednesday, 10 November 2004.

[28] Chapter 1, Section 3.

[29] Council doc 10826/07 (n 15 above), Annex II, paras 17–19.

(1) of their listing,[30] (2) of the possibilities to submit a request for delisting, and (3) of the possibilities to bring a legal action before the CFI. The new statement of reasons must be 'sufficiently detailed to allow those listed to understand the reasons for their listing and to allow the Community Courts to exercise their power of review'.[31] In particular, it must contain information about the acts committed, the competent national authority, and the type of decision that was taken.[32] Each statement of reasons is discussed by the Working Party on a case-by-case basis.[33]

The 'working methods' of the Working Party have now been declassified and are publicly available.[34] The Working Party ensures that 'the information provided meets the criteria in Articles 1(3) and 1(4)' of Common Position 2001/931/CFSP.[35] Article 1(3) defines the meaning of 'terrorist act' and 'terrorist group'. Article 1(4) stipulates that listings are based on

> precise information or material in the relevant file which indicates that a decision has been taken by a competent [usually judicial] authority in respect of the persons, groups and entities concerned, irrespective of whether it concerns the instigation of investigations or prosecution for a terrorist act, an attempt to perpetrate, participate in or facilitate such an act based on serious and credible evidence or clues, or condemnation for such deeds.

Although the CFI held that the Council cannot examine whether the decision of the national authority is well-founded,[36] the working methods clarify that the Council Working Party must establish that the allegations raised by the competent national authority meet the criteria set out in Article 1(3). This is that the activity that the person allegedly supported is a 'terrorist act' within one of the categories in Article 1(3).

Moreover, after the CFI's ruling in the *OMPI* cases, and particularly in *OMPI III*,[37] the Working Party will have to verify that all relevant information has been made available to the Council. In the event of a legal challenge, the Council must be in the position to submit this

[30] ibid, paras 20–1.

[31] ibid, para 17.

[32] ibid, paras 17–18.

[33] ibid, para 19.

[34] See the working methods of the Working Party in: Council doc 10826/07 (n 15 above).

[35] ibid, Annex II, para 2.

[36] Case T-256/07, *OMPI II* (n 4 above), para 147, this section concerned the listing in Council Decision 2007/445/EC of 28 June 2007, OJ 2007 L 169/58.

[37] Case T-228/02, *OMPI I*, Case T-256/07, *OMPI II* and Case T-284/08, *OMPI III* (all n 4 above); see also Chapter 6, Section 1.

information to the court. Further, the working methods provide[38] for the possibility

> to invite a representative from EUROPOL or the Situation Centre to attend the meeting of the Working Party to make a presentation of background information in order to facilitate discussion on a particular subject.

Even though no information is available on how often this has happened in practice, the working methods appear to assume that the Working Party does indeed discuss the informational basis of the proposal.

The working methods also stipulate that the Working Party 'will check *in particular* whether the proposal complies with the fundamental principles and the rule of law' when the proposal was submitted by a third state.[39] This implies that, while the Working Party must pay particular attention to these principles when examining proposals from non-EU Member States, it will also check compliance when Member States proposes a listing. This task goes beyond what the CFI assumed to be the Council's role in *OMPI II*. The Court explicitly stated that any such scrutiny by the Council would be contrary to the principle of loyal cooperation.[40]

The adoption and publication of working methods and the establishment of a permanent body exercising the role of a 'European sanctions committee' is a positive development. Greater transparency and legal safeguards were imperatively needed in the listing procedure. Yet, in practice the adoption of autonomous European sanctions continues to be flawed. The cases of *OMPI II and III*[41] demonstrate that the Council does not (always) comply with the existing rules. In *OMPI II*, the CFI annulled the listing because the Council failed to give sufficient reasons as to why it had not taken into account the decision of a national quasi-judicial body ordering the removal of the applicant from the list (the British Proscribed Organisations Appeal Commission (POAC)).[42] In *OMPI III*, the CFI annulled the listing of the same organization because the Council was unwilling to submit the relevant information on which it had based its decision to the EU courts.[43]

[38] Council doc 10826/07 (n 15 above), Annex II, paras 13–14.

[39] Council doc 10826/07 (n 15 above), Annex II, para 4.

[40] Case T-256/07, *OMPI II* (n 4 above), para 133; Case T-228/02, *OMPI I* (n 4 above), para 122.

[41] Case T-256/07, *OMPI II* and Case T-284/08, *OMPI III* (both n 4 above).

[42] The POAC is the specialist body set up by the Parliament of the UK to hear and determine appeals brought against decisions proscribing, or refusing to lift the proscription of, organizations regarded as terrorist by the Home Secretary; see Case T-256/07, *OMPI II* (n 4 above), para 155 et seq, this section concerned the listing in Council Decision 2007/868/EC of 20 December 2007, OJ 2007 L 340/100.

[43] Case T-284/08, *OMPI III* (n 4 above), para 71–3.

Moreover, the existing rules, even if complied with, are insufficient to ensure the necessary procedural protection.[44]

If the Treaty of Lisbon enters into force, Articles 215 and 75 TFEU[45] will unequivocally give the Union the competence to adopt restrictive measures against natural and legal persons. The EU courts will have jurisdiction to review sanctions against natural and legal persons.[46] Both Articles 215 and 75 TFEU state explicitly that '[t]he acts referred to in this Article shall include necessary provisions on legal safeguards'[47] The European Parliament will have a more prominent role in the sanctioning procedure. Article 215 TFEU gives the European Parliament a right to be informed. Under Article 75 TFEU[48] a framework for administrative measures with regard to capital movements and payments is defined by the European Parliament and the Council in regulations adopted in accordance with the ordinary legislative procedure. Hence, even though the European Parliament is not involved in the adoption of operational measures against specific individuals, it has considerable powers to establish the overarching framework for the adoption of sanctions against internal European terrorists. Additionally, the Treaty of Lisbon will make the Charter of Fundamental Rights legally binding.[49]

The protection in practice will depend on the interpretation of the new Treaty provisions and of the mandate of the new Council Working Party. Yet, in any event, further changes remain necessary. The legal safeguards for those sanctioned will need to be determined in more detail in legally binding form. This cannot be done in rather vague and not legally binding

[44] See Section 1.2 below for suggestions for improvement

[45] Treaty on the Functioning of the European Union (TFEU); see also Chapter 2, Section 5.

[46] Article 275 TFEU.

[47] Article 215(3) and 75(3) TFEU.

[48] Article 75 TFEU (ex Art 60 TEC):

(1) Where necessary to achieve the objectives set out in Art 67, as regards preventing and combating terrorism and related activities, the European Parliament and the Council, acting by means of regulations in accordance with the ordinary legislative procedure, shall define a framework for administrative measures with regard to capital movements and payments, such as the freezing of funds, financial assets or economic gains belonging to, or owned or held by, natural or legal persons, groups or non-State entities.

(2) The Council, on a proposal from the Commission, shall adopt measures to implement the framework referred to in the first paragraph.

(3) The acts referred to in this Article shall include necessary provisions on legal safeguards.

[49] Article 6(1) of the consolidated version of the Treaty on European Union as amended by the Treaty of Lisbon.

recommendations of the Council on designation and identification[50] or Council statements accompanying legislation.[51]

1.2 Further Necessary Changes to the Autonomous Listing Procedure

The listing procedure for autonomous European sanctions against individuals has come a long way since its introduction in December 2001. However, the sanctioning practice of the European institutions continues to violate fundamental rights. Moreover, it damages basically and essentially the EU's legitimacy as a political entity.

In addition to the positive developments described in the previous section, this section argues in favour of three categories of interconnected changes: (1) legislative, (2) institutional, and (3) procedural. Some suggestions go beyond the legally required minimum protection.

1.2.1 Legislative Changes

At present, the most detailed legislation on the listing procedure is Common Position 2001/931/CFSP, a cross-pillar Union law instrument. The common position would have to be replaced by a Community law instrument, adopted by co-decision to ensure the involvement of the European Parliament. At the legislative level, the Community should set out, in a clear and precise manner:

(1) the objective(s) of the sanctioning regime;
(2) the listing criteria;
(3) the division of tasks between the Council and the competent national authorities, including the scope of the hearings both at the national and at the European level;
(4) the exact requirements that a proposal of a Member State has to meet on a standardized form;
(5) the legal safeguards provided in the national procedure;
(6) the delisting procedures that individuals can initiate, including the possibility to challenge the listing before the CFI;
(7) the conditions and procedures to obtain compensation for being wrongfully listed.

Clear objectives (1) are necessary to evaluate the effectiveness of individual sanctions[52] and to give guidance for their interpretation and

[50] Restrictive Measures – EU Best Practices for the effective implementation of restrictive measures 11679/07, Brussels, 9 July 2007; compare also the earlier version at: doc 10533/06 (n 17 above).

[51] See the reference in the Working Party's mandate at: Council doc 10826/07 (n 15 above), Annex I, p 4.

[52] See Chapter 1, Section 7.

application. The objective of each measure should be clearly stated and recalled in the introductory paragraphs of the sanctions legislation. Do individual sanctions (also) aim to change the conduct of those sanctioned? Or, do they exclusively aim to freeze money otherwise available for terrorist acts?

On 22 April 2009 the Commission proposed a draft Council regulation amending Regulation 881/2002/EC (currently governing the European sanctions regime giving effect to UN lists).[53] This draft regulation newly includes an explanation that its purpose is 'to prevent terrorist crimes, including terrorist financing, in order to maintain international peace and security'.[54] Regulation 881/2002/EC does not contain a purpose statement. However, the new purpose statement does not meet the requirements of a clear objective. 'Preventing terrorist crimes' is not sufficiently clear. Further, 'terrorist crime' is not a defined term similar to 'terrorist act' under the autonomous sanctions regime.[55]

Listing criteria (2) must ensure a sufficient level of precision and predictability as well as flexibility.[56] In line with the settled case-law of the ECtHR, restrictions of fundamental rights should be imposed 'in accordance with the law'. This requires not only some legal basis, but also imposes quality requirements. The legal basis should be accessible to the person concerned and foreseeable as to its effects.[57] This requires a public legal instrument. The (only recently) declassified working methods of the Council Working Party[58] and 'the Council's statement agreed when the Common Position [2001/931/CFSP] was adopted',[59] which is not publicly available, cannot ensure the necessary accessibility.

In double-staged procedures a transparent division of tasks (3) complies with the principle of loyal cooperation and allows those affected to exercise their procedural rights effectively.[60] The Union is an entity separate from the Member States. It takes its own autonomous decisions for which it is responsible. Even if the Union did not cause the potential flaws at the

[53] Commission proposal for amending Reg 881/2002/EC, of 22 April 2009, COM (2009) 187 final, 2009/0055 (CNS).

[54] ibid, recital 11.

[55] See below in Section 1.3.

[56] ibid.

[57] ECtHR, *Segerstedt-Wiberg v Sweden* (2006) 44 EHRR 14, para 76, referring to ECtHR, *Rotaru v Rumania*, No 28341/95, 4 May 2000, para 52.

[58] Council doc 10826/07 (n 15 above).

[59] See the Working Party's mandate at: Council doc 10826/07 (n 15 above), Annex I, p 4.

[60] See Chapter 6, Section 1 for both points.

national level, it cannot turn a blind eye to these flaws when attaching additional adverse consequences to national decisions. Listing someone as a terrorist suspect based on a national decision that *evidently* breaches fundamental procedural rights demonstrates disrespect for these rights. In the case of an *evidently* flawed decision the listing amounts to a deliberate perpetuation of that flaw and to a violation in itself.

The suggested standardized form[61] (4) should require clear information that identifies the terrorist suspect;[62] demonstrates which procedures were instigated at the national level; and explains the reasons for the listing request. This form should further allow Member States to indicate that certain information is classified and can only be shared with persons and institutions that comply with special security requirements. The Member State should also be required to set out the steps that will follow the listing. Standardized forms ensure a higher level of comparability and reduce procedural oversights. The assessment of the continuous justification of a listing (subsequent listing decision) will be done against the planned follow-up investigation.

Article 1(4) of Common Position 2001/931/CFSP provides:

> the list in the Annex shall be drawn up on the basis of precise information or material in the relevant file which indicates that a decision has been taken by a competent authority in respect of the persons, groups and entities concerned, irrespective of whether it concerns the instigation of investigations or prosecution for a terrorist act, an attempt to perpetrate, participate in or facilitate such an act based on serious and credible evidence or clues, or condemnation for such deeds. Persons, groups and entities identified by the Security Council of the United Nations as being related to terrorism and against whom it has ordered sanctions may be included in the list. For the purposes of this paragraph 'competent authority' shall mean a judicial authority, or, where judicial authorities have no competence in the area covered by this paragraph, an equivalent competent authority in that area.

The first sentence of Article 1(4) of Common Position 2001/931/CFSP was interpreted by the CFI in the *OMPI* cases. The CFI held that listing decisions fall within the discretion of the Council.[63] Yet, as was discussed in Chapter 6, the Court ruled that the Council's decision is limited to the

[61] Compare the Cover Sheet/Standard Form for listing submissions and the Guidance document at the UN level, at: http://www.un.org/sc/committees/1267/pdf/coversheet.pdf.

[62] See on the importance of the identifying information: doc 15114/05 (n 17 above), para 20 et seq.

[63] Case T-228/02, *OMPI I*; Case T-256/07, *OMPI II*; Case T-284/08, *OMPI III* (all n 4 above); see Chapter 6 for more details.

question of whether the decision of a competent national authority satisfies the conditions of Article 1(4) of Common Position 2001/931/CFSP. According to the CFI, the Council does not have the powers to review whether the national proceedings complied with procedural rights and access to judicial review. The Court found this contrary to the principle of loyal cooperation.

Article 1(4) of Common Position 2001/931/CFSP by its wording does not necessarily require this restraint. It refers to 'precise information or material in the relevant file which indicates that a decision has been taken by a competent authority... based on serious and credible evidence or clues'.[64] A crucial question is whether Article 1(4) requires the file to contain information or material that goes beyond the decision of the competent national authority, or whether information that such a decision was taken is sufficient. It is here argued that the former interpretation is not only more desirable, but also supported by the working methods of the Working Party. They set out an explicit mandate to check compliance with fundamental rights and appear to be based on the assumption that a discussion takes place on the substance of the individual case.[65]

1.2.2 Institutional Changes

At the institutional level, one basic change is proposed: lists of singled-out individuals, who have allegedly supported terrorism, should only be adopted in the first pillar. This conclusion was reached in Chapter 2. Decisions that impose far-reaching adverse effects on individuals, such as terrorist listings, can only legitimately be adopted in a legal framework that is vested with a sufficient level of democratic legitimacy and that provides the necessary procedural and judicial safeguards. At present, both the procedural rights and the judicial protection of those listed on Union lists remain uncertain. The working methods of the Working Party, for instance,

[64] See also the German version:

> Die Liste im Anhang wird auf der Grundlage genauer Informationen bzw. der einschlägigen Akten erstellt, aus denen sich ergibt, dass eine zuständige Behörde — gestützt auf ernsthafte und schlüssige Beweise oder Indizien — gegenüber den betreffenden Personen, Vereinigungen oder Körperschaften einen Beschluss gefasst hat...

and the French version:

> La liste à l'annexe est établie sur la base d'informations précises ou d'éléments de dossier qui montrent qu'une décision a été prise par une autorité compétente à l'égard des personnes, groupes et entités visés...basées sur des preuves ou des indices sérieux et crédibles.

[65] Council doc 10826/07 (n 15 above), Annex I, p 4, see also Section 1.1 above.

stipulate that the Council will issue a notification and a statement of reasons for those listed in the Community pillar.[66] This leaves open the question whether individuals, who are only included in a Union list, but not in a Community list,[67] also receive a notification and a statement of reasons. Judicial protection form Union lists is in practice equally uncertain.[68]

Additionally, an independent investigator should be designated who ensures compliance with human rights, oversees the handling of delisting, and exemption requests. Individuals should be able to address the investigator directly with any relevant information that they may want to submit. Besides acting as a contact person for those listed and sanctioned, the investigator should also attend to the rights of third parties affected by individual sanctions. The prohibition of any economic contact with those listed can have severe effects on the economic interests of others. Third parties should have the opportunity to address the independent investigator and draw attention to their position. In exceptional circumstances compensation might even be appropriate.

Finally, individual sanctions require institutional adaptations to ensure compliance with the rights of defence. Special procedures must apply where those listed cannot–for security reasons–access (all) the information relating to the case against them. This should include the automatic appointment of a special (vetted) advocate, who will represent the interests of those listed.[69]

1.2.3 Procedural Changes

The division of tasks between the Community and the Member States should avoid conflicting decisions as far as possible and require exchange of all relevant information. The existing distinction between the initial and subsequent listing decisions is useful. Moreover, the distinction between proposals from EU Member States and from third states[70] is sensible and should be retained.

For the initial listing decision it is particularly important that all relevant information is submitted to the Council. The CFI correctly ruled that the Council cannot base its decision to list an individual as a terrorist suspect

[66] Council doc 10826/07 (n 15 above), Annex II, paras 17–19.

[67] See Case T-338/02, *Segi and others* [2004] ECR II-1647 and Case C-355/04 P, *Segi v Council* [2007] ECR I-1657 and Chapter 6 for further explanation.

[68] See Chapter 6, Sections 2 and 3 for a critical discussion of status quo and an argument in favour of the necessary level of procedural and judicial protection.

[69] See Section 1.4 below for more details on the procedure.

[70] See Guidelines, doc 15579/03 (n 16 above).

on information that it does not share with the EU courts.[71] When submitting a listing request, Member States must consequently place the Council in the position to argue its case in court. This is notwithstanding whether the Council will actually assess the submitted information.

Moreover, Member States should be obliged to indicate explicitly that the decision of the competent national authority was adopted in compliance with fundamental rights at the national level (see (5) above). Making this demonstration an explicit requirement under the listing procedure has several advantages. It does not undermine the Member States' autonomy in conducting national criminal procedures pursuant to their domestic rules. At the same time, if national governments have to set out when and where those listed were given the opportunities to exercise their procedural rights this will guarantee a higher level of scrutiny within the national legal order. It will contribute to ensuring that the Union less easily attaches additional adverse effects to a faulty decision of national authorities.[72]

As provided in Article 2(3) of Regulation No 2580/2001 and Article 1(6) of Common Position 2001/931, subsequent listing decisions are based on review by the Council of the situation of the persons, groups, and entities covered.[73] For these subsequent decisions, the Council is competent to review whether there are reasons justifying the continued listing. The Council's competence would have to be interpreted to include verifying that national authorities have actually taken further action after the initial listing proposal. The principle of proportionality requires that the longer the freezing continues the stronger must be the evidence supporting the freezing decision. This should be explicitly stated as a condition of Article 1 (6) of Common Position 2001/931/CFSP and not only in the guidelines drawn up by the Council.[74] Normal rules and standards both of legal safeguards and of proof apply to measures that cannot any longer be considered preventive or temporary. But even for preventive and temporary measures national legal orders provide guidelines of the level of suspicion/information that is necessary to justify taking action.

It seems problematic that a person should be listed for years *without any action* by the national authorities. The CFI's statement that the Council

[71] Case T-284/08, *OMPI III* (n 4 above), para 73.

[72] This is in line with: ECJ 3 December 1992, Case C-97/91, *Oleificio Borelli v Commission* [1992] ECR I-6313.

[73] Held in: Case T-229/02, *PKK and KNK v Council* [2005] ECR II-539, para 44; confirmed in: C-229/05 P, *PKK and KNK v Council* [2007] ECR I-439, para 103.

[74] See eg: doc 15114/05 (n 17 above), para 9.

should verify '*the consequences of that decision* at the national level'[75] implies that the listing at the European level should *not* usually be renewed in that situation. Renewal would have to be particularly justified with reference to that inactivity.

After a person has been included on a terrorist list for a certain period of time further investigation must be undertaken. If those listed indeed support terrorism to a degree that justifies placing them on the lists of terrorist suspects in the first place this in itself cannot be sufficient. Where states allege that the listed person has committed a crime, they would have an obligation to initiate prosecution within a reasonable period of time; not only because indefinite listings infringe the rights of individuals, but also because states have an obligation under international law to prosecute terrorist acts.

While intelligence might be sufficient to justify the initial listing, evidence is necessary to justify keeping a person listed. Hence, even before a measure has been applied for a sufficiently long time to be considered permanent, states would have to demonstrate that they have initiated further investigation to the body that manages the listings. Courts will scrutinize both that an investigation was initiated and conducted and that the body managing the listings took note of it.

Proposals from third states must be complete and must contain sufficient relevant information to justify the suspicion that the person is a terrorist suspect. The principle of loyal cooperation does not apply in the relationship between the Council and third states.[76] This principle requires a particular level of deference to the factual assessment of the competent authorities of the EU Member States, which is not legally required with regard to the assessment of third states. Further, the division of tasks within the European Union is based on the principle of mutual trust, which is underpinned by the shared commitment to common constitutional values. These values are codified in Article 6 TEU and comprise commitment to the rule of law and fundamental rights.

1.2.4 Concluding Remarks

By way of conclusion, the identification of individuals as terrorist suspects must take place in the first pillar under the control of the European Parliament and the EU courts. Community legislation should set out, in a clear and precise manner the listing criteria and the listing procedure, including the

[75] Case T-47/03, *Sison* (n 4 above), para 164.

[76] The principle of loyal cooperation in Art 10 EC governs only the relationship between the Member States and the European institutions.

division of tasks between the Community and the Member States, and legal safeguards. The office of an independent investigator should be created.

1.3 Reviewable Listing Criteria

The substantive criteria that justify listing someone as a terrorist suspect are different from the 'conditions for listing' in Articles 1(4) and (6) of Common Position 2001/931/CFSP, which lead the EU to list someone. The former are the reasons–ie information–that substantiate the decision of the competent national authorities alleging that the person is involved in terrorist activities. The latter were restrictively interpreted by the CFI as relating to the listing procedure and the formal criterion that a decision of a competent national authority exists.[77]

Common Position 2001/931 sets out some substantive criteria. Article 1 (2) of Common Position 2001/931/CFSP describes the activity, in which a person has to engage in order to be considered a terrorist suspect. It provides

> 'persons, groups and entities involved in terrorist acts' shall mean: — persons who commit, or attempt to commit, terrorist acts or who participate in, or facilitate, the commission of *terrorist acts.*

Article 1(3) defines 'terrorist act' as an

> *intentional* act, which...may seriously damage a country or an international organization, as defined as *an offence under national law*, where committed *with the aim of*: (i) seriously intimidating a population, or (ii) unduly compelling a Government or an international organisation to perform or abstain from performing any act, or (iii) seriously destabilising or destroying the fundamental political, constitutional, economic or social structures of a country or an international organisation.

The article then exhaustively enumerates acts in three categories of offences: the first comprises conduct that directly endangers interests protected by law;[78] the second makes the threat of such conduct a

[77] See Chapter 6, Section 1.1.1.

[78] Article 1(3) (a)–(h):

> (a) attacks upon a person's life which may cause death; (b) attacks upon the physical integrity of a person; (c) kidnapping or hostage taking; (d) causing extensive destruction to a Government or public facility, a transport system, an infrastructure facility, including an information system, a fixed platform located on the continental shelf, a public place or private property, likely to endanger human life or result in major economic loss; (e) seizure of aircraft, ships or other means of public or goods transport; (f) manufacture, possession, acquisition, transport, supply or use of weapons, explosives or of nuclear, biological or chemical weapons, as well as research into, and development of, biological and chemical weapons; (g) release of dangerous substances, or causing fires, explosions or floods the effect of which is to endanger human life; (h) interfering with or disrupting the supply of water, power or any other fundamental natural resource, the effect of which is to endanger human life.

punishable offence;[79] and the third consists of conduct related to terrorist groups.[80]

The definition of 'terrorist acts' in Common Position 2001/931/CFSP requires that these acts must: (1) be intentional; (2) have a political aim; (3) *potentially* cause great damage; and (4) fall within the categories of offences above, criminalized under national law. Financing terrorism is a crime in all EU Member States.[81] Yet, in order for someone to be listed and sanctioned as a terrorist suspect, that person does not have to be found guilty of financing terrorism. At the UN level, the listing criteria require only that the person is 'associated' with Al-Qaida, Usama bin Laden or the Taliban.[82]

At the EU level, although the definition of 'terrorist act' requires that the act is an offence under national law, the activity of the listed person does not necessarily have to meet this requirement. The lower intensity of 'attempting to commit', 'participating in', or 'facilitating' the commission of terrorist acts does not necessarily have to be criminalized under national law.[83] Yet this does not exclude the fact that this ancillary conduct is a punishable offence under national law.[84]

In principle, this 'criminal law' approach to the fight against terrorism appears sensible. It links listing–albeit in a rather vague manner–to criminal offences. This draws the counter-terrorist lists and sanctions within the realm of criminal law. Given the criminal characteristics of these measures,[85] it appears justified to align them with criminal law. This leads to greater clarity and justifies requiring the necessary (higher) level of procedural protection.[86] Critical is the establishment of a clear link

[79] Article 1(3)(i): 'threatening to commit any of the acts listed under (a) to (h)'.

[80] Article 1(3)(j)–(k):

> (j) directing a terrorist group; (k) participating in the activities of a terrorist group, including by supplying information or material resources, or by funding its activities in any way, with knowledge of the fact that such participation will contribute to the criminal activities of the group.

[81] All EU Member States have ratified the International Convention for the Suppression of the Financing of Terrorism, UN doc A/RES/54/109 of 9 December 1999. It obliges them to make financing terrorism a punishable crime. See Chapter 1 for more details.

[82] See Chapter 1; compare also on the criterion of 'material support to terrorist organizations' in the US: David Cole, 'The New McCarthyism: Repeating History in the War on Terrorism', Georgetown University Law Center 2003 Research Paper Series in Public Law and Legal Theory Research Paper No 383660, p 38 et seq.

[83] Article 1(4) of Common Position 2001/931/CFSP.

[84] Compare Chapter 1, Section 6.2.2 on the UK Terrorism Act 2006.

[85] See Chapter 3, Section 3.2.2.

[86] See Chapter 3, Section 3.2.2 and Chapter 6, Section 1.

between those listed and the terrorist activity.[87] Such a link becomes particularly important where listing is attached to a broad (usually antecedent) ancillary conduct such as attempting, participating, or facilitating. The EU's criminal law approach can be contrasted with the approach of the UN, which hinges on the term 'associated with' the Taliban or Al-Qaida[88] that does not require demonstration of a criminal offence. This is not to say that individual sanctions are subject to the rules of criminal law. They take substantive and procedural shortcuts toward the end of reducing terrorist financing and are not aimed at bringing terrorist supporters to justice. Because of these shortcuts, individual sanctions cannot be considered to entail a judgment of the conduct of those listed, which is necessarily implied in criminal law.

The CFI ruled that the Council can keep someone listed and sanctioned if the sanctions are considered necessary to avoid money being made available for terrorist activities.[89] The person in question does not have to have engaged in fresh acts of terrorism since the initial listing. Yet, if the reason for freezing a person's assets is not criminal intent but the objective support given to terrorism, the listing procedure should include a *de minimis* rule. Where a person can demonstrate that the total amount of frozen funds and their economic activity in the past years is below a certain threshold, this alone should be sufficient to justify delisting. In these cases the objective contribution that the person *can make* to terrorism does not justify the draconian measures (or the resources spent to administrate the sanctions).

Finally, it is necessary to differentiate between natural persons and legal persons (group or organizations), because the former have different rights than the latter and because the listing has different consequences for the latter. Humanitarian exemption must be applied to natural persons to ensure compliance with the core of certain fundamental rights, such as right to life and physical integrity.

For organizations the consequences of being listed are similar to prohibition, even though strictly speaking the organization is not banned.[90]

[87] See also for the UN: Robert K Goldman, Report of the Independent Expert on the Protection of Human Rights and Fundamental Freedoms while Countering Terrorism, E/CN.4/2005/103, para 32.

[88] See Chapter 1, Section 3.1.1.

[89] For OMPI terrorist activity before 2001 was in principle considered sufficient to justify a subsequent listing decision in 2007, see: Case T-256/07, *OMPI II* (n 4 above), para 107 et seq.

[90] See however Art 2:20 of the Burgerlijke Wetboek, which stipulates that an organization listed either on a European or on a UN lists of terrorist suspects is *ipso jure* banned and unable to take legal action ('van rechtswege verboden en niet bevoegd tot het verrichten van rechtshandelingen').

The listing may result in dissolution. Hence, where sanctions are applied to legal persons, there is an even greater danger of politicization. Clarity and predictability lie at the heart of the rule of law. Clearly defined criteria lead to greater transparency and consequently strengthen the legitimacy of the adoption procedure. The more blurry the listing criteria are, the more careful people will be to avoid listing. They may become less inclined to participate in groups and organizations whose political activities might potentially lead to a label of 'terrorist organization'. Uncertainty is a powerful political tool. It places not only individuals in a Kafkaesque situation, but changes the political climate.

'Guilt by association is an attractive principle for law enforcement officials concerned about preventing future harms.'[91] The EU and the UN listing practices are both following this logic.[92] Intent is not a necessary criterion for the listing under European law. Hence, individuals might join, support, fund, or even participate in political organizations for reasons unrelated to any violent activity that the organization might occasionally engage in, but nonetheless end up on a terrorist list.

Although being a member of a designated 'terrorist group' is not a crime per se, members must fear being listed and sanctioned as terrorist suspects themselves, solely because of their membership and regardless of their intention or even knowledge of the activities of that group.[93] As was explained in Chapter 3, individual sanctions have sufficiently severe implications for those listed that they should be considered criminal charges, at least after a certain period of time.

The US Supreme Court effectively ended prosecutions of member of the Communist Party during the Cold War based on guilt by association with the words:[94]

> In our jurisprudence guilt is personal, and when the imposition of punishment on a status or on conduct can only be justified by reference to the relationship of that status or conduct to other concededly criminal activity ... that relationship must be sufficiently substantial to satisfy the concept of personal guilt in order to withstand attack under the Due Process Clause of the Fifth Amendment.

[91] David Cole, 'Terror Financing, Guilt by Association and the Paradigm of Prevention in the "War on Terror" ', in: Andrea Bianchi and Alexis Keller (eds), *Counterterrorism: Democracy's Challenge* (Oxford: Hart Publishing 2008), p 233.

[92] See above Section 1.3 and Chapter 1, Sections 3 and 4 and Chapter 6, Section 1.

[93] See Case T-306/01, *Ahmed Ali Yusuf and al Barakaat International Foundation v Council and Commission* [2005] ECR II-3533, see Chapter 1, Section 3.1.2.

[94] US Supreme Court, *Scales v United States*, 367 US 203 (1961), at 224–5.

It later extended the reasoning to exclude consequence under civil law based on the principle of guilt by association.[95] Today, the counter-communist pursuit of the 1950s/1960s is almost universally seen as a mistake.[96]

1.4 Disclosure of Information

Access to information is essential to the applicants' rights of defence.[97] In *Sison*, the CFI explicitly stated that:[98]

> the parties concerned can make genuine use of their right to a judicial remedy only if they have precise knowledge of the content of and the reasons for the act in question.

The EU courts exercise full jurisdiction over *Community* instruments sanctioning individuals. However, the Courts can only offer protection and test the soundness of the case against the applicants if they can access the relevant information supporting the allegation that the applicant is a terrorist. Both with regard to autonomous European sanctions and with regard to sanctions giving effect to UN lists, the CFI and the ECJ[99] have ruled that the applicants have not been placed in a position to make good use of their right of action before the Court[100] and that the Court itself was 'not in a position to carry out adequately its review of the lawfulness of the decision'.[101] Not only the applicants, but also the EU courts were refused access to information that substantiated the allegations.

In *OMPI I*, the CFI made clear that while the information shared with those sanctioned can be strictly limited for reasons of public security, it has

[95] See: Cole, 'Terror Financing, Guilt by Association and the Paradigm of Prevention' (n 91 above), referring to: Claiborne Hardware Co, 458 US at 932; *Elfbrandt v Russell*, 384 US 11, 19 (1966); *United States v Robel*, 389 US 258, 265–66 (1967); *Aptheker v Secretary of State*, 378 US 500, 510–12 (1964); *Healy v James*, 408 US 169, 186–87 (1972).

[96] See David Cole, 'The New McCarthyism' (n 82 above); see also for the media condemnation of left wing activists during the 'Deutscher Herbst': Sven Kramer, 'Demarcations and Exclusions: Terrorism, State Violence, and the Left in German Novels of 1970s and 1980s', in: Robert Weninger (ed), *Gewalt und kulturelles Gedächtnis. Repräsentationsformen von Gewalt in Literatur und Film seit 1945* (Tübingen: Stauffenberg, 2005), ss 255–65.

[97] See also Chapter 6, Section 1.1.2.

[98] Case T-47/03, *Sison* (n 4 above), para 137; the court here referred to ECJ 19 February 1998, Case C-309/95, *Commission v Council* [1998] ECR I-655, para 18 and Case T-89/96, *British Steel v Commission* [1997] ECR II-835, para 33.

[99] Cases C-402/05 P and C-415/05 P, *Kadi and al Barakaat* (n 4 above).

[100] Case T-47/03, *Sison* (n 4 above), para 219.

[101] ibid, para 225, see also: Case T-228/02, *OMPI I* (n 4 above), para 172.

to be shared with the courts.[102] In *OMPI III*, the CFI was even more explicit. It held that the Council cannot rely on information that it is not willing to share with the Court.[103]

The reluctance of the Council to share 'sensitive information' with the EU courts is a central obstacle to effective judicial protection from individual sanctions.[104] However, EU Member States have also shown a certain reluctance to share intelligence at the supranational level outside the Courts.[105] The recommended standardized form for listing proposals should require a level of information that justifies the imposed sanctions. Member States should not be allowed to request a listing based on evidence they do not share with the Council. However, they should be able to classify information on the standardized form as confidential and exclude disclosure to third parties, including those listed and sanctioned.[106]

In this event, there are ways to protect confidential information and allow at the same time for an effective judicial review. One possibility could be in-camera proceedings. In-camera hearings can be used in two different manners: either the information is concealed from the public but made accessible to the defendant, or even the defendant is excluded from the evidence and the secret information is only revealed to the court. In the first case the defendant could be present for the entire in-camera proceedings. In the second case the judge, after having reviewed the information behind closed doors, would only have to pronounce its judgment on limited reasons; yet, this would at least allow for a judicial review, albeit in secret.[107]

Moreover, where for security reasons defendants and their chosen lawyers must be excluded from parts of the legal process the strength of the government's case could be tested by a special vetted advocate, acting as an independent third person taking the role of the opposition.[108] Different

[102] Case T-228/02, *OMPI I* (n 4 above).

[103] See Case T-284/08, *OMPI III* (n 4 above), para 73.

[104] See ibid.

[105] Björn Müller-Wille, 'The Effect of International Terrorism on EU Intelligence Co-operation', *JCMS* (2008), vol 46.1, pp 49–73.

[106] This appears to be the practice at present: Case T-256/07, *OMPI II* (n 4 above), paras 11 and 91.

[107] With regard to UN sanctions: Biehler, Gernot, 'Individuelle Sanktionen der Vereinten Nationen und Grundrechte', *Archiv des Völkerrechtes*, 41 (2003), p 169 et seq, at 180.

[108] See above; see also Ian Leigh, 'National Legal Dimension of the Democratic Control of the Security Sector: Values and Standards in Developed Democracies', 2006, http://www.dcaf.ch/, p 9.

from the rules under the UK Anti-terrorism, Crime and Security Act 2001, the special advocate should be able to communicate with the applicant after receiving the classified information. Restricting the communication between the advocate and their client makes proper representation even more difficult and appears to be unnecessary if the advocate was vetted by security services.[109] This is not the place to outline the practical possibilities in further detail. It should only be noted that there are proved and tested ways of reconciling concerns of national security with effective judicial review.

2. European Sanctions against Individuals Giving Effect to UN Lists of Terrorist Suspects

Those targeted by European sanctions giving effect to UN lists of terrorist suspects (first sanctions regime) are in a position similar to those targeted by autonomous sanctions (second sanctions regime).[110] The adverse effects under the two sanctions regimes are comparable. As a matter of principle, the former should consequently have the same rights to procedural protection. Yet, it is even more difficult to provide those targeted by sanctions originating at the UN level with the opportunity to exercise their procedural rights. Neither the CFI nor the ECJ have so far addressed the necessary level of procedural protection from European sanctions giving effect to UN terrorist lists.[111]

A particular obstacle to procedural fairness under the first sanctions regime is lack of information. After the ECJ's appeal decisions in *Kadi* and *al Barakaat*, European sanctions giving effect to UN lists are subject to full judicial review.[112] Hence, the European institutions can no longer sanction individuals solely because they are included on a UN list of terrorist suspects. The ECJ did not elaborate how it will take into account that the

[109] See also the criticism of the rules under the UK Anti-terrorism, Crime and Security Act 2001 at: House of Lords, *Roberts v Parole Board* [2005] UKHL 45, judgment of 7 July 2005, HL, esp at paras 18–19 per Lord Bingham of Cornhill (dissenting).

[110] See Chapter 3, Sections 3.2.2 and 3.2.3 for the effects; Chapter 5, Section 1 for procedural protection from the first sanctions regime and Chapter 6, Sections 1 and 2 for procedural protection from the second sanctions regime.

[111] See critical for the ECJ's appeal decision in Cases C-402/05 P and C-415/05 P, *Kadi and al Barakaat* (n 4 above): Iain Cameron, 'Sökandet efter en rättvis lösning pa FN:s riktade sanctioner: ett sisyfosarbete', *Svensk Juristtidning* (2009), p 76.

[112] Cases C-402/05 P and C-415/05 P, *Kadi and al Barakaat* (n 4 above).

sanctions originate at the UN level. The Court did not indicate whether restrictions on procedural rights might be justified by the fact that sanctions are decided in international cooperation and therefore not (entirely) within the sphere of influence of the EU Member States or the European institutions.[113] Yet, with regard to the right to judicial protection, which is arguably the strongest procedural right,[114] the ECJ did not appear to allow for far-reaching restrictions.[115]

Thus, based on the assumption that both types of sanctions (those based on UN lists and those based on Union lists) give rise to the same procedural rights, the European institutions would have to be able–for both types of sanctions–to supply to the EU courts the relevant information on which the listing was based. The European institutions are left in a Catch-22 position. They are obliged to provide the same legal safeguards as in the autonomous listing procedure. At the same time, where a listing request to the UN Sanctions Committee is submitted by a third state (non-EU Member State) the European institutions do not have access to the relevant information.

The England and Wales Court of Appeal discussed this problem.[116] It readily admitted that a fair hearing could be granted only because the listing request had been filed by the UK itself, but that '[t]here may be greater difficulties in a case where HM T[reasury] knows nothing of the facts upon which the designation was made by the Committee'[117] For the time being, these difficulties are left to be decided in future challenges. Yet, they pose practical and real problems that courts will not be able to ignore forever.

From the perspective of European law, it appears impossible to implement UN lists of terrorist suspects in compliance with general principles of EU law unless they have access to the relevant information that substantiates the terrorist allegation. On 22 April 2009 the Commission proposed a draft Council regulation amending Regulation 881/2002, which

[113] In an argument parallel to ECtHR, *Soering v UK*, Application No 14038/88, judgment of 7 July 1989, see Chapter 3, Section 3.2.1.

[114] See the importance that the ECtHR gives to the right to fair trial: ECtHR, *Delcourt*, 17 January 1970, A.11, para 15; ECtHR, *Golder v UK*, of 21 February 1975, Series A No 18, para 27, 1 EHRR 524.

[115] Cases C-402/05 P and C-415/05 P, *Kadi and al Barakaat* (n 4 above), see Chapter 5.

[116] Court of Appeal, *G v HM Treasury; A and others v Same* [2008] EWCA Civ 1187, [2008] WLR (D) 339 (CA: Sir Anthony Clarke MR, Sedley and Wilson LJJ: 30 October 2008); see also: High Court, *A, K, M, Q & G v HM Treasury* [2008] EWHC 869 (Admin).

[117] ibid, para 120.

currently governs the first sanctions regime.[118] The proposal specifically addresses the lack of information communicated by the UN Sanctions Committee. First, it introduces a distinction between a 'provisional' and a 'final decision to freeze the funds and economic resources of the individual or entity concerned'.[119] The provisional decision is taken by the Commission alone. The final decision is taken in accordance with the advisory procedure for implementing powers exercised by the Commission.[120] Hence, the Commission is assisted by a committee consisting of the representatives of the Member States when taking the final decision.

Secondly, the draft Council regulation provides that the Commission shall take the decision to list and sanction a person 'as soon as a statement of reasons has been provided by the United Nations'.[121] This differs from Regulation 881/2002 where no such requirement is set out. However, much will depend on the quality of the statement of reasons. The publicly available summaries on the website of the UN Sanctions Committee do not contain sufficient information to enable those sanctioned to make effective use of their rights of defence. The statement of reasons should be distinguished from 'classified information'. The draft regulation sets out in Article 7(d) how the Commission should treat 'classified information' 'if' such information is submitted by the United Nations or a third state. However, this does not allow the conclusion that the Commission will in all cases be in the possession of information that goes beyond the publicly available statement of reasons. It also leaves open whether and how the European institutions will request any relevant information. It remains unclear whether the European institutions are actually able to obtain the relevant information substantiating the terrorist allegation. The fact that the draft regulation makes sanctioning within the EU conditional on the issuing of a statement of reasons by the UN allows the conclusion that it does not depend on the provision of any information going beyond this. After the ECJ's ruling in the *Kadi and al Barakaat* appeal,[122] however,

[118] Commission proposal for amending Reg 881/2002/EC, of 22 April 2009, COM(2009) 187 final, 2009/0055 (CNS).

[119] ibid, para 4 of the explanatory memorandum and Art 7a(1)–(3).

[120] Articles 3 and 7 of Decision 1999/468/EC, [1999] OJ L 184/23; see on Comitology eg: Alexander Ballmann, David Epstein and Sharyn O'Halloran, 'Delegation, Comitology, and the Separation of Powers in the European Union', *International Organization* (2002), 56:3, pp 551–74.

[121] ibid, Art 7a(1).

[122] Cases C-402/05 P and C-415/05 P, *Kadi and al Barakaat* (n 4 above); see also the new application in Case T-45/09 *al Barakaat v Commission* and T-85/09, *Kadi v Commission*, action brought on 26 February 2009, OJ 2009 C 90/37.

sanctions giving effect to UN lists of terrorist suspects are subject to full judicial scrutiny. In the CFI's rulings on sanctions adopted under the autonomous sanctions regime this requires the European institutions in the event of a legal challenge to share the information that substantiates the listing with the EU courts.[123]

The present analysis does not imply a judgment on the lawfulness of individual sanctions under the UN Charter. However, it implies that those targeted by European sanctions giving effect to UN lists of terrorist suspects continue to be able to challenge these measures in the EU courts with good prospects of success.

3. Judicial Review of European Sanctions against Individuals

The focus of this book is the right to fair trial. This right has a non-derogable core.[124] The most central element of the right to fair trial is that the review is carried out by an independent, impartial and regularly constituted tribunal. Article 6(1) ECHR requires a determination 'by an independent and impartial tribunal established by law'. Article 14(1) of the International Covenant of Civil and Political Rights (ICCPR) speaks of a 'competent, independent and impartial tribunal established by law.' Article 10 of the Universal Declaration of Human Rights (UDHR) refers to 'independent and impartial tribunal'.

The ECtHR has confirmed in its settled case-law that while other elements can be restricted (eg a trial can be held behind close doors, information shared with the parties can be limited), the independence and impartiality of the court cannot be compromised;[125] not even for reasons of national security.[126] Similarly, the Human Rights Committee has

[123] See in particular the OMPI cases: Case T-228/02, *OMPI I*, Case T-256/07, *OMPI II* and Case T-284/08, *OMPI III* (all n 4 above), and in particular *OMPI III*, para 73; see also the first case in which the CFI followed the ECJ's ruling in the Kadi appeal: Case T-318/01, *Omar Mohammed Othman v Council and Commission*, judgment of 11 June 2009, not yet reported.

[124] See the detailed study of the non-derogable aspects of Art 14 ICCPR: Evelyne Schmid, 'The Right to a Fair Trial in States of Emergencies: Non-Derogable Aspects of Article 14 of the International Covenant on Civil and Political Rights', 15 April 2008, available at http://fletcher.tufts.edu/research/2008/Schmid.pdf.

[125] See above all: ECtHR, *Demicoli*, Application No 13057/87, [1991] ECHR 37, judgment of 27 August 1991; see also Chapter 3, Section 3.2.2.

[126] See Chapter 4, Conclusions.

confirmed that this 'institutional dimension' of the fair trial guarantee is non-derogable.[127]

Independence from political pressures is what distinguishes the judiciary from the political branches. On the one hand, this independence incites criticism due to the lack of democratic legitimacy of court decisions.[128] On the other, independence equips the judiciary with a different type of legitimacy. The strength and the weakness of their judgment lie in the greater distance from daily public pressures. Courts take a rights-based approach.

3.1 Role of the Judiciary

Counter-terrorist policies require a delicate balance between fundamental values and principles followed by states committed to the rule of law. This substantive issue, however, is preceded by the question *who* should decide where the tipping line of this balance is to be placed. What is the role of courts in finding this balance? Which decisions should be reserved for the executive?[129]

For Ronald Dworkin, '[t]he responsibility of articulation is the nerve of adjudication'.[130] This responsibility weighs particularly heavy in the context of the counter-terrorist policies adopted after 11 September 2001. The adoption of these policies is strongly shaped by a discourse of 'security imperatives' that muffle all other considerations and perceptions.[131] This is where the role of judges in society goes beyond adjudicating the particular case brought before them. It goes beyond 'individual justice'. Judges also have the responsibility to take principled decisions of long-term

[127] Human Rights Committee, General Comment 13, Art 14 (Twenty-First Session, 1984), Compilation of General Comments and General Recommendations Adopted by Human Rights Treaty Bodies, UN doc HRI/GEN/1/Rev 1 at 14 (1994), para 4.

[128] See eg: Richard Ekins 'Judicial Supremacy and the Rule of Law' (2003) 119 *Law Quarterly Review* 127; House of Lords, *A (FC) and others; X (FC) and others v Secretary of State for the Home Department* [2004] UKHL 56 (Anti-terrorism, Crime and Security Act 2001: detention without charge – *Belmarsh detainees case*), submission of the Attorney-General and Lord Bingham's response para 37–42 (per Lord Bingham of Cornhill).

[129] Discussing this question in the context of the ECJ's ruling in *Kadi*: Deirdre Curtin and Christina Eckes, 'The Kadi Case: Mapping the Boundaries between the Executive and the Judiciary in Europe', *International Organizations Law Review* 5 (2008), p 1 et seq.

[130] Ronald Dworkin, 'The Judge's New Role: Should Personal Conviction Count?', *Journal of International Criminal Justice* 1 (2003), p 4.

[131] Explaining the powerful influence of 'the security ideational framework' on counter-terrorist legislation: Dora Kostakopoulou, 'How to do things with security post 9/11', *Oxford Journal of Legal Studies* (2008), p 317 et seq.

importance (constitutional justice).[132] Because of this contribution to the political discourse and to constitutional justice, there lies great danger in the judicial rationalization of the extreme. Judges must be aware of their particular responsibility. While an extreme measure ceases to exist at some point, the argument subsists that this measure was in compliance with human rights law.

While certain policy decisions arguably fall within the discretion of the political institutions,[133] it is the task of the judiciary to map the application of these policies to the particular case within the human rights framework.[134] Human rights law establishes a framework in which terrorism can be effectively countered without destroying traditional rights and political values of states committed to the rule of law.

The application of counter-terrorist policies in particular leads to far-reaching restrictions of human rights, such as the right to life, freedom from torture and other ill treatment, the right to non-discrimination, free speech, and the right to property, as well as the right to a fair trial and protection from arbitrary detention without charge.[135] It is argued that the assessment of the seriousness of the general threat is a matter of policy, which should be left to the government, because it is the democratically supported executive and because it has access to superior information that relates not only to the concrete situation before court but to the larger scale of things.[136] The proportionality of the means applied in the individual case, however, is not a matter of policy. It is for the courts to draw the line in the individual case and to show absolute limits that the executive cannot cross in its attempt to fight even greatest threat. The judiciary should identify what are necessary and proportionate means to fight a threat even of such magnitude as terrorism.

The judiciary might not be ideally equipped to take the difficult choices inherent in judging the lawfulness of counter-terrorist measures. The quality of judgment can be undermined by lack of information, capacity,

[132] Thomas Franck, 'The International Judge and the Principled Imperative', in: *Weltinnenrecht - Liber amicorum Jost Delbrück* (Berlin: Duncker & Humblot, 2005), p 267 et seq.

[133] See Chapter 3, Section 3.2.1 on the political question doctrine.

[134] See the intention (p 1) of the Digest of Jurisprudence of the United Nations and Regional Organizations on the Protection of Human Rights while Countering Terrorism (New York and Geneva, 2003), available at: http://www.ohchr.org/Documents/Publications/DigestJurisprudenceen.pdf.

[135] See the case-law discussed in Chapter 4, Sections 3, 4, and 5.

[136] See in particular the argument of the ECtHR at *Ireland v United Kingdom* (1978) 2 EHRR 25, para 207; and of the House of Lords in *Belmarsh detainees* case (n 128 above), para 29 per Lord Bingham of Cornhill, see Chapter 4, Section 2.

and to some extent also expertise, as well as the retroactive nature of judicial review and sometimes lack of support. Nonetheless, states guarantee certain rights to their citizens when they exercise public power. Courts are the best forum to ensure that these domestic standards are met when the domestic legislator acts.

The *ex-post* assessment of *ex-ante* decisions intended to prevent the realization of a future risk is not new to the judiciary. Of course, they have to take into account that the choices of the executive were made under different pressures, possibly within a tight timeframe and without all the information. In these circumstances, it cannot be right for courts, which have the benefit of ruling with hindsight, to ponder whether they would have opted for a different course of action. However, courts must be in the position to conduct a meaningful *ex-post* review of the measures imposed. For this purpose they must have full access to the relevant information, including the information that the executive had at the moment of application but also any information obtained after the sanctions were applied.

If any organ of an international organization or a state can restrict fundamental rights in a secret procedure and without having to fear independent judicial control, the values that constitute the very essence of the rule of law are at danger.[137] This, however, is not to say that those listed as terrorist suspects should have access to interim proceedings to stop the listing from day one. It is not the role of the judiciary to replace the decision of the political branches. Decisions of the executive enjoy protection not only within a core of substantive discretion but also in time. The executive must have sufficient time to obtain and examine the (partially highly sensitive) information that might have led to the listing. The right of access to justice is not excluded from considerations of proportionality. The longer a measure is in place, the less justifiable becomes an exclusion of judicial review.

In the particular context of the EU, there are additional challenges. Good arguments suggest that EU courts do not have the necessary competence to rule on criminal law decisions.[138] Yet, the greatest problem does not lie in the EU courts' limited competence for criminal law, but in the

[137] Jürgen Habermas, *Faktizität und Geltung: Beiträge zur Diskurstheorie des Rechts und des demokratischen Rechtsstaats* (Frankfurt am Main: Suhrkamp, 1992) (English translation as *Between facts and norms: contributions to a discourse theory of law and democracy*, tr William Rehg).

[138] See GCC, judgment of the Second Senate of 30 June 2009 (Treaty of Lisbon), 2 BvE 2/08; 2 BvE 5/08; 2 BvR 1010/08; 2 BvR 1022/08; 2 BvR 1259/08; 2 BvR 182/09.

blacklisting itself. Blacklisting is not the outcome of a criminal procedure. Those listed and sanctioned do not infringe laws.[139]

Courts are not concerned with the merits of the exercise of public power but with its legality.[140] The court is not called on to express agreement or disagreement with a particular policy or measure. They must solely assess whether the challenged act falls within the band of lawfulness. This does not entail a judgment of whether the executive has taken the *correct* decision, but it does entail a judgment of whether the executive has had a *correct understanding of the law and the limits it imposes* when reaching its decision.

The CFI stated correctly and unambiguously that it will not substitute the Council's decision for its own decision.[141] Yet, a combination of procedural and substantive restraints, which fall within the competence of the judiciary, defines the line between lawful and wrongful acts. Judicial review of individual sanctions raises questions of whether and to what extent departure from the rule of law, including from the ordinary rules of judicial protection, can be justified. Can such departure be justified because of the overwhelming importance of containing terrorism, or because decisions are agreed in international cooperation?

3.2 *The Struggle for the Last Word*

'[I]t is the tasks of the judges to protect every individual's human rights against excessive demands for security.'[142] It is the primary responsibility of the legislator and the executive to address the popular demand for security. Autonomous European sanctions against individuals exemplify how the political branches and the judiciary can struggle for the final word on what is possible and acceptable in the fight against terrorism. The case of *OMPI* is the most illustrative in this regard.[143] The EC Council's decisions to list OMPI as a terrorist suspect were annulled three times by the CFI.

[139] See Section 1.3 above the discussion of reviewable listing criteria.

[140] See also the opinion of Lord Nicholls of Birkenhead in: House of Lords, *Belmarsh detainees* case (n 128 above), para 74 et seq.

[141] Case T-228/02, *OMPI I* (n 4 above), para 159.

[142] See Jutta Limbach, 'Human Rights in Times of Terror – Is Collective Security the Enemy of Individual Freedom?', *Göttingen Journal of International Law* 1 (2009), p 23.

[143] Case T-228/02, *OMPI I*, Case T-256/07, *OMPI II* and Case T-284/08, *OMPI III* (all n 4 above); see also Chapter 6, Section 1; see also the case of Sison: Case T-47/03, *Sison* (n 4 above); Case T-341/07, *Sison v Council*, application of 10.11.2007, OJ [2007] C 269/58, oral hearing of 20 April 2009.

OMPI,[144] the main opposition group to the current regime in Iran, was listed by the UK under the Terrorism Act 2000 as a 'proscribed organization' in 2001.[145] In the same year, the organization renounced all military operations. On 2 May 2002, OMPI was for the first time included on a European list of terrorist organizations.[146] This listing was based on the decision of the UK Home Secretary. The consequences of the listing for OMPI were dramatic. All of OMPI's assets were frozen. Those supporting OMPI financially were threatened with criminal charges. Additionally, supporters would have to fear being considered terrorist suspects and, as a consequence, being listed and sanctioned themselves. European governments revoked the political asylum status and denied visas to Iranian exiles associated with OMPI. The Iranian Government made use of the terrorist organization label to justify detention and suppression in Iran.[147] On 26 July 2002, OMPI brought the first action against the listing before the CFI.[148] At this stage OMPI had not received any notification, statement of reasons, or been given the opportunity to make its views known. In June 2006, 35 Members of Parliament made an application to the UK Home Secretary to remove OMPI from the list.[149]

On 12 December 2006, the CFI for the first time annulled the decision to sanction OMPI.[150] It essentially did so because the measure infringed the applicant's rights to defence and 'even at the end of the oral procedure, the Court did not find itself to be in a position to review the lawfulness of

[144] OMPI is the acronym for Organisation des Modjahedines du people d'Iran or People's Mojahedin of Iran; see for background information on OMPI and its listing as a terrorist group: http://euobserver.com/9/27472; http://euobserver.com/9/24393; http://euobserver.com/9/25123; http://euobserver.com/9/25521; http://euobserver.com/9/25917; http://euobserver.com/22/24165; http://euobserver.com/9/24028; http://euobserver.com/9/27316; http://euobserver.com/9/26315; http://euobserver.com/9/26990/?rk=1; http://euobserver.com/9/27234; http://euobserver.com/9/25698; http://euobserver.com/9/23497.

[145] Case T-228/02, *OMPI I* (n 4 above), para 2.

[146] Council Decision 2002/334of 2 May 2002 implementing Article 2(3) of Regulation (EC) No 2580/2001 on specific restrictive measures directed against certain persons and entities with a view to combating terrorism and repealing Decision 2001/927/EC, OJ 2002 L 116/33–4 (3.5.2002).

[147] Marc Henzelin, 'Anti-Terrorismusrechtsprechung des EuGH: Von den Segi und Gestoras Pro Amnistía zu den Yusuf and Kadi Urteilen', ERA, *Anti-Terrorismus-Recht und Rechtsprechung im Bereich des Europäischen Strafrechts*, Trier, 7 November 2008.

[148] Case T-228/02, *OMPI I* application, OJ [2002] C 247/20.

[149] Statement by the British Parliamentary Committee for Iran Freedom on the House of Commons Foreign Affairs Committee's 2007–08 annual report on Iran released 2 March 2008; avaiable at: http://iran-freedom.org/index.php?option=com_content&task=view&id=162&Itemid=28.

[150] Case T-228/02, *OMPI I* (n 4 above): annulment of Council Decision 2005/930/EC.

the contested decision'[151] In these first proceedings the Council had merely stated that it was 'desirable' to list OMPI.[152] On 28 June 2007, the Council adopted a new decision that listed OMPI as a terrorist organization,[153] again based on the request of the UK Home Secretary.[154] On 30 November 2007, the British Proscribed Organisations Appeals Commission (POAC) concluded that it would be 'perverse' to maintain the terrorist designation for OMPI.[155] The POAC further ordered the Home Secretary to take action to delist OMPI.[156] On 7 May 2008, the Court of Appeal denied the Government the right to appeal against the POAC's decision. On 15 July 2008, the Council adopted a new decision,[157] still listing OMPI; this time based on a request of the French Government.

On 23 October 2008, the CFI for the second time annulled a Council decision listing OMPI. The Court confirmed that, in principle, the Council could relist OMPI if it ensured 'that subsequent fund-freezing measures adopted after that judgment were not vitiated by the same defects'. In *OMPI II*, the CFI dismissed the application for annulment of Decision 2007/445/EC (first decision),[158] but annulled Council Decision 2007/868/EC (second decision).[159] The Court found with regard to the first decision that the Council had observed the applicant's rights to the defence. With regard to the second Council decision, the CFI found that there was no remaining national decision to keep OMPI on the list.

This is because the first listing decision of the Council was adopted before the POAC's decision (quasi-judicial national body finding the national listing 'perverse') and the second listing decision thereafter. The CFI's discussion of the lawfulness of the first Council decision[160] indicates that the CFI will settle for a low level of procedural protection under Community law. It will accept that only very limited information is shared

[151] Case T-228/02, *OMPI I* (n 4 above), para 173.

[152] Case T-228/02, *OMPI I* (n 4 above), para 164; OMPI knew that the UK had requested its listing, other people on the lists did not even know which country had proposed their name, see Case T-47/03 *Sison* (n 4 above), para 209.

[153] Council Decision 2007/445/EC (n 36 above).

[154] Case T-157/07 *OMPI II* (n 4 above), para 6.

[155] ibid, paras 22 and 157.

[156] ibid, para 22.

[157] Council Decision 2008/583/EC, OJ 2008 L 188/21–5.

[158] Council Decision 2007/445/EC (n 36 above).

[159] Council Decision 2007/868/EC, OJ 2007 L 340/100.

[160] Council Decision 2007/445/EC (n 36 above); see discussion at: Case T-157/07, *OMPI II* (n 4 above), para 129 et seq.

with those listed and hence that far-reaching restrictions are imposed on their rights to defence.

On 4 December 2008[161] the CFI for the third time annulled an EC Council decision listing OMPI as a terrorist suspect. In an unprecedented speedy procedure (the judgment was given one day after the oral hearing) the CFI annulled a decision that was still in force.[162] The CFI ruled that:[163]

> the Council is not entitled to base its funds-freezing decision on information or material in the file communicated by a Member State, if the said Member State is not willing to authorise its communication to the Community judicature whose task is to review the lawfulness of that decision.

Finally, on 26 January 2009, after six years and eight months the Council removed OMPI from the Union list of terrorist suspects.[164]

In the *OMPI* saga, it is interesting to see that even though the CFI left the Council a considerable margin of discretion and explicitly did not substitute the Council's decision with its own judgment, the Council defended every inch and continued to adopt sanctions against OMPI in breach of its procedural rights. The Council continued to list terrorist suspects in defiance of the CFI's rulings. The case of *Sison* appears to have taken a similar course to *OMPI*. On 10 September 2007, Mr Sison brought a new action[165] for annulment of the new Council decision listing him.[166] This new listing decision had been adopted between the oral hearing and the pronouncement of the judgment declaring the earlier listing unlawful. Hence, the declaration had no practical consequences for Mr Sison's situation. He remained on the counter-terrorist list.

The European institutions and the judiciary have started a similar struggle under the European sanctions regime that gives effect to UN lists. The cases of *Kadi and al Barakaat* however demonstrate that the developments are comparable under the latter.[167] Only, Member States are subject to an additional pressure: they are obliged under the UN Charter to sanction those listed by the UN Sanctions Committee.

[161] Case T-284/08, *OMPI III* (n 4 above).

[162] Council Decision 2008/583/EC (n 157 above).

[163] Case T-284/08, *OMPI III* (n 4 above), para 73.

[164] Euobserver of 26 January 2009, available at: http://euobserver.com/9/27472.

[165] Case T-341/07, *Sison v Council*, OJ C 269/105, 10.11.2007, oral hearing on 30 April 2009, see abbreviated defence application, available at: http://www.statewatch.org/; see also: Case T-157/07 *OMPI II* (n 4 above).

[166] Council Decision 2007/445/EC (n 36 above).

[167] Cases C-402/05 P and C-415/05 P, *Kadi and al Barakaat* (n 4 above); see also the new application in Case T-45/09, *al Barakaat v Commission* and T-85/09, *Kadi v Commission*, action brought on 26 February 2009, OJ 2009 C 90/37; compare also the first case in which the CFI

Mr Kadi and al Barakaat remain listed and sanctioned under European law, despite the ECJ's ruling in their favour.[168] The UN Sanctions Committee identified Mr Kadi and al Barakaat as terrorist suspects shortly after the attacks of 11 September 2001.[169] As a consequence of their listing at the UN level, the Community adopted a regulation freezing all their financial assets within the EU.[170] In December 2001, Mr Kadi and al Barakaat challenged this regulation.[171] Seven years later, on 3 September 2008, the ECJ finally annulled the measures, holding that they infringed the applicants' fundamental rights.[172] Yet, the applicants' assets have remained frozen even after the ECJ's rulings.[173] The Commission has continued copying the terrorist list of the UN Sanctions Committee.[174] The Commission explicitly reacted to the ECJ's ruling by pointing out[175] that it:

> has communicated the narrative summaries of reasons provided by the UN Al-Qaida and Taliban Sanctions Committee, to Mr Kadi and to Al Barakaat International Foundation and given them the opportunity to comment on these grounds in order to make their point of view known.

Individual sanctions are a particularly illustrative example of expanding executive power because they combine the substantive area of counter-terrorism policy–an area in which executive powers have most prominently increased in recent years–with the formal context of externalization and Europeanization of this policy area.[176]

followed the ECJ's ruling in the *Kadi* appeal: Case T-318/01, *Omar Mohammed Othman v Council and Commission*, judgment of 11 June 2009, not yet reported.

[168] See Chapter 5, Section 1 on the CFI's and the ECJ's rulings in these cases.

[169] On 17 October 2001 and on 9 November 2001, respectively.

[170] EC Regulation 467/2001 of 6 March 2001 (OJ 2001 L 67/1), amended by Commission Regulation 2199/2001 of 12 November 2001 (OJ 2001 L 295/16) and repealed by EC Regulation 881/2002 of 27 May 2002 (OJ 2002 L 139/9).

[171] See besides the rulings in the main proceedings: Cases C-402/05 P and C-415/05 P, *Kadi and al Barakaat* (n 4 above), Case T-315/01, *Yassin Abdullah Kadi v Council and Commission* [2005] ECR II-3649 and Case T-306/01, *Yusuf and al Barakaat* (n 93 above), the order of 7 May 2002 in the interim proceedings in T-306/01 R, *Aden and others v Council and Commission* [2002] ECR II-2387.

[172] Cases C-402/05 P and C-415/05 P, *Kadi and al Barakaat* (n 4 above), see Chapter 5, Section 1.

[173] The ECJ granted the institutions a grace period of three months delaying the immediate consequences of the annulment by virtue of Art 231 EC, see Cases C-402/05 P and C-415/05 P, *Kadi and al Barakaat* (n 4 above), para 375 et seq.

[174] Commission Regulation (EC) No 1109/2008 of 6 November 2008, OJ 2008 L 229/23 (8.11.2008) and Commission Regulation (EC) No 1190/2008 of 28 November, OJ 2008 L 322/25 (2.12.2008).

[175] Commission Regulation (EC) No 1190/2008, ibid, recital 3.

[176] Deirdre Curtin, *Executive Power of the European Union: Law, Practice, and the Living Constitution* (Oxford: Oxford University Press, 2009).

Even if the Security Council can suspend the application of fundamental rights where (and to the extent that) this is necessary to maintain international peace and security,[177] this power has to be subject to limits, which can be patrolled by an independent judiciary. International cooperation must remain rooted in national constitutional systems, at least in a world without a universal constitution. Anything else would place international cooperation in a constitutional 'vacuum' outside of the domestic legal framework and with no forum able to hold political actors to account *ex post* for their actions. Indeed, the Special Rapporteur concluded for individual sanctions that 'if there is no proper or adequate international review available, national review procedures–even for international lists–are necessary'[178]

Courts have taken different approaches to legal obligations resulting from international cooperation. Most show a high level of deference in one way or another.[179] In the *Kadi* appeal, the ECJ offered a clear vision of the role of courts in ensuring boundaries of externalized executive power. Hence, if the EU courts are to show deference to the Security Council, they will do so from an informed position.

3.3 Political Solutions – or a Right to Diplomatic Protection?

'Political control' over individual sanctions has been advocated as the only 'realistic solution' for individual sanctions originating at the UN level.[180] Indeed, the Swiss Supreme Court ruled that this is the only option for

[177] Luis Hinojosa Martinez, 'Las Sanciones del Consejo de Seguridad Contra al Qaeda y los Talibanes:? Son realmente inteligentes?', *REDI*, Vol LVIII (2006), 756.

[178] Robert K Goldman, Report of the Independent Expert on the Protection of Human Rights and Fundamental Freedoms while Countering Terrorism, E/CN.4/2005/103, para 38; see Chapter 5.

[179] ECtHR, *Behrami v France*; *Saramati v France, Germany and Norway*, Application Nos 71412/01 and 78166/01. For a discussion on the cases see, A Sari, 'Jurisdiction and international responsibility in peace support operations: the Behrami and Saramati cases', *Human Rights Law Review* 8 (2008), 151–70; see also the line of cases dismissed by the ECtHR after *Behrami:* ECtHR, *Beric and others v Bosnia and Herzegovina*, Application Nos 36357/04, 36360/04, 38346/04, 41705/04, 45190/04, 45578/04, 45579/04, 45580/04, 91/05, 97/05, 100/05, 101/05, 1121/05, 1123/05, 1125/05, 1129/05, 1132/05, 1133/05, 1133/05, 1169/05, 1172/05, 1175/05, 1177/05, 1180/05, 1185/05, 20793/05 and 25496/05, 16 October 2007; ECtHR; *Gejic v Germany*, Application No 31446/02, 28 August 2007; *Kasumaj v Greece*, Application No 6974/05, 5 July 2007; see also: Swiss Supreme Court (Schweizer Bundesgericht), *Youssef Mustapha Nada v SECO*, Staatssekretariat für Wirtschaft, judgment of 14 November 2007, 1A.45/2007/daa; District Court in The Hague of 10 September 2008 (Case number/cause-list number: 265615 / HA ZA 06–1671); see also Chapter 5, Section 5.2.2.

[180] Thomas Meerpohl, *Individualsanktionen des Sicherheitsrates der Vereinten Nationen: Das Sanktionsregime gegen die Taliban und al Qaida vor dem Hintergrund des Rechts der VN und der Menschenrechte* (München: Herbert Utz Verlag, 2008), Part 4, p 249 et seq.

Switzerland since anything else would put Switzerland in breach of its UN Charter obligations.[181]

Several states[182] have tried to improve fundamental rights protection at the UN level through diplomatic channels; others have demonstrated a considerable level of disobedience by introducing their own humanitarian exemptions.[183] Both political pressure and limited compliance were seen to form part of the reasons for the adoption of Security Council Resolutions 1542, 1617, 1730, and 1735, which were all intended to improve the situation of those listed.[184] These resolutions introduced humanitarian exemptions, a definition of what is meant by 'associated with Al-Qaida', and a so-called focal point, which allows the individual to address the Sanction Committee with any exculpating evidence.[185] Hence, political pressure has shown some results.

Yet, the UN defends every inch. The focal point is no more than a mailbox. No consideration on the part of the UN is guaranteed. The humanitarian exemption provides for the most basic human needs, such as food and clothing, and medical emergencies, but they do not address the problem that individuals are alleged to be terrorist suspects without any chance to challenge this allegation.[186]

For several reasons 'political control' will not be enough to reach a reasonable level of compliance with human rights as quickly as possible. The enormous time delays in introducing even the most basic exemptions, and the fact that procedural rights at the UN level remain largely window-dressing, demonstrate the limited effectiveness of political solutions. Even states committed to the rule of law, such as the EU Member States,[187] have only a limited political will to make it a priority that counter-terrorist sanctions are brought into compliance with fundamental rights. This was amply demonstrated by the adoption of autonomous European sanctions and the

[181] Swiss Supreme Court (Schweizer Bundesgericht), *Youssef Mustapha Nada* v *SECO*, Staatssekretariat für Wirtschaft, judgment of 14 November 2007, 1A.45/2007/daa (Chapter 5, Section 5.2.2).

[182] In particular Austria, Germany, Sweden and Switzerland, see ibid.

[183] See Chapter 1, Section 5.

[184] Eg: Meerpohl, *Individualsanktionen* (n 180 above), p 260.

[185] See Chapter 1, Section 3.

[186] This assessment differs from the assessment of Thomas J Biersteker and Sue E Eckert, *Strengthening Targeted Sanctions Through Fair and Clear Procedures*, White Paper prepared by the Watson Institute Targeted Sanctions Project, Brown University, 30 March 2006, 26, p 26 available at: http://watsoninstitute.org/pub/Strengthening_Targeted_Sanctions.pdf. They state: 'Since 1999, there has been consistent, incremental movement toward addressing procedural concerns—a form of institutional learning within the 1267 Committee.'

[187] See Chapter 3, Section 1 and Chapter 5, Section 4.

failure to provide for a sufficient level of procedural protection 'at home', even after the EU courts started annulling individual sanctions.

The CFI came close to establishing under European law, a *right* to have a delisting request presented to the UN Sanctions Committee.[188] The Court held that those sanctioned had a right to present their case to their government of nationality or residence and that this right did not only result from the guidelines of the UN Sanctions Committee but also from Community law.[189] The Court stated further that Member States must take into account the particular 'difficulties that the [listed] persons encounter',[190] and that:[191]

> the Member States would not be justified in refusing to initiate the review procedure provided for by the Guidelines solely because the persons concerned could not provide precise and relevant information.

A lack of precision in defending their innocence can almost be expected in the light of the fact that those listed have no means to find out the precise reasons for their listing. Finally the CFI stated that if applicants are not granted diplomatic protection, they can bring an action in national courts, which then have to apply the European law principles of equivalence and effectiveness.[192] In the UK Court of Appeal's ruling in the case of *A, K, M, Q & G v HM Treasury*, Sir Anthony Clarke MR appeared to follow the CFI's reasoning. He argued[193] that if

> it were held that G [one of the appellants] should not have been listed, I see no reason why HMT (or the relevant Government body) should not, as the judge put it, be bound to support delisting. I feel sure that, if it were so held, HMT would wish to have G delisted and take appropriate steps to that end.

If this 'European right to diplomatic protection' is an attempt by the CFI to improve the individual's legal position, it falls short. The delisting procedure at the UN level does not provide an effective remedy.[194] Consequently, a right to have this (ineffective) procedure initiated cannot provide an effective remedy either. The Court's ruling in the case of *Ayadi* was given on 12 July 2006. On 19 December 2006, the Security Council

[188] The latter was mentioned already in Case T-315/01, *Kadi* (n 171 above), para 270.

[189] Case T-253/02, *Chafiq Ayadi v Council* [2006] ECR II-2139; appealed: C-403/06 P, *Ayadi v Council*, OJ 2006 C 294/32, paras 144–5.

[190] ibid, para 147.

[191] ibid, para 148.

[192] ibid, para 151.

[193] Court of Appeal, *G v HM Treasury; A and others v Same* [2008] EWCA Civ 1187, [2008] WLR (D) 339 (CA: Sir Anthony Clarke MR, Sedley and Wilson LJJ: 30 October 2008); see also: High Court, *A, K, M, Q & G v HM Treasury* [2008] EWHC 869 (Admin), para 119.

[194] Chapter 1, Section 3.

adopted Resolution 1730, which introduced a new body to the delisting procedure, the so-called focal point, allowing individuals to address their requests directly to an administrative body at the UN level.[195] Hence, the Court's introduction of a right to diplomatic protection has lost part of its relevance, because individuals are no longer entirely dependent on their government in order to submit a delisting request. Even if the use of diplomatic channels might be considered more effective at the international level than actions of individuals, it seems doubtful whether the submission through a reluctant government compelled by court judgment is more helpful than a request directly brought by the individual to the focal point.

More importantly, the right to diplomatic protection can only be as effective as the diplomatic protection itself. The possibility to judicially enforce the state's obligation to submit a delisting request does not offer any more protection than the delisting procedure itself; and this procedure remains inadequate.[196]

The difference between a delisting request to the Sanctions Committee and judicial protection from listing requests of the national authorities in national courts is that the EU courts have the power and authority to require national courts to comply with certain procedural rights and standards, while the UN Sanctions Committee lies outside the sphere of influence of the EU courts. The CFI timidly attempted to exercise some influence on the 'law-making' at the UN level by pointing out that the Member States when acting as representatives in the Sanctions Committee have to act in good faith.[197] Yet, this is not enough.

4. Proportionality of Individual Sanctions

The principle of proportionality plays an important role when reconciling rival interests, all the more in the context of human rights. It is widely accepted that a test of proportionality is conducted as part of judicial review.[198] However, the question of *how* this test is conducted and *what factors* should be taken

[195] SC Res 1730 (S/RES/1730 (2006)), para 1; see also Chapter 1, Section 3.1.2.

[196] Chapter 1, Section 3.

[197] Case T-253/02, *Ayadi* (n 189 above), para 142.

[198] See case-law of the ECtHR, the ECJ and the GCC at nn 206–8 below; see also: Evelyn Ellis, *The Principle of Proportionality in the Laws of Europe* (Oxford: Hart, 1999); Matthias Maslaton, *Notstandsklauseln im regionalen Menschenrechtsschutz. Eine vergleichende Untersuchung der Artikel 15 EMRK and 27 AMRK* (Frankfurt am Main: Peter Lang, 2002), Chapter 4; the Council guidelines on restrictive measures explicitly emphasize, besides compliance with fundamental rights, the necessity to comply with the principle of proportionality: doc 15114/05 (n 18 above), para 9.

into account requires further examination. The criteria and application of the test of proportionality are vital to the result.

The present discussion cannot reach any final decisions on the proportionality of individual sanctions. Neither the use of individual sanctions, nor the listing and sanctioning of any particular person can be finally assessed in the present discussion. The aim must be far more modest: conclusions are drawn on how the proportionality of individual sanctions should be assessed and what considerations should be taken into account.

Judges are not in the luxurious position where they can 'restrict themselves to describing the conflict of values between security and freedom in nice-sounding phrases. They must solve the conflict and in doing so, they must specify their criteria'.[199] A balancing point cannot be found in the abstract. It is not constant but depends on the circumstances of the individual case. Each case is an expression of a specific balancing exercise and in particular judges take the rights of the applicant as the starting point of the examination. It is one of the key functions of the principle of proportionality to safeguard the essence of fundamental rights. Aharon Barak, the President (Emeritus) of the Israeli Supreme Court stated[200] that the test of proportionality

> carries on its shoulders the constitutional view that the ends do not justify the means. It is a manifestation of the idea that there is a barrier of values which democracy cannot surpass, even if the purpose whose attainment is being attempted is worthy.

Yet, beyond excluding the extreme, proportionality requires a balancing exercise that ensures the justice or fairness of acts.[201]

Although the principle of proportionality plays an important role in the case-law of national constitutional courts, as well as of the ECJ,[202] courts do not always attach the same meaning to the proportionality principle. The ECJ, for instance, sometimes distinguishes three elements, (1) suitability/appropriateness, (2) necessity of the measures, and (3) absence of disproportionate character (proportionality *sensu stricto*). Sometimes

[199] Limbach, 'Human Rights in Times of Terror' (n 142 above), p 22.

[200] Supreme Court of Israel, HCJ 8276/05 *Adalah – The Legal Center for Arab Minority Rights in Israel v The Minister of Defense* (unpublished), para 30.

[201] In its early case-law the ECJ referred to the 'principle of justice', see eg: Cases 17 and 20/61, *Klöckner-Werke AG and others/ECSC High Authority* [1962] ECR 325, at 340; Case 19/61, *Mannesmann AG/ECSC High Authority* [1962] ECR 357, p 371.

[202] See for the ECJ's case-law and for German and French Public Law: Nicholas Emiliou, *The principle of proportionality in European law: a comparative study* (London: Kluwer Law International, 1996), pp 23–115 and Walter van Gerven, 'The Effects of Proportionality on the Actions of Member States of the European Community: National Viewpoints from Continental Europe', in: Evelyn Ellis, *The Principle of Proportionality in the Laws of Europe* (Oxford: Hart, 1999), p 37 et seq.

however, the Court examines only two elements.[203] In certain cases the ECJ directly addresses (3) the proportionality *sensu stricto*. Yet, this rather means that the Court assumes implicitly that the measures challenged in these cases were (1) suitable/appropriate and (2) necessary to achieve a legitimate aim.[204] The ECtHR, by contrast, examines whether the imposition on the Convention right is necessary in a democratic society or, in emergency situations, whether it is necessary in the exigencies of the situation.[205]

Based on the case-law of the ECJ,[206] the German Constitutional Court (GCC),[207] and the ECtHR,[208] a four-step proportionality review can be

[203] Van Gerven, 'The Effects of Proportionality on the Actions of Member States', ibid, p 37 referring to: AG Van Gerven, Opinion in Case C-159/90, *Society for the Protection of Unborn Children Ireland Ltd v Grogan* [1991] ECR I-4685.

[204] Van Gerven, 'The Effects of Proportionality on the Actions of Member States', ibid, p 39 with regard to Case 44/79, *Hauer v Rheinland-Pfalz* [1979] ECR 3727; as the conclusion of a broader examination of the ECJ's case-law on proportionality: Emiliou, *The principle of proportionality in European law* (n 202 above), ch 5, in particular p 191 et seq.

[205] Jeremy McBride, 'Proportionality and the European Convention on Human Rights', in: Evelyn Ellis, *The Principle of Proportionality in the Laws of Europe* (Oxford: Hart 1999), p 23 et seq.

[206] Eg: Case C-331/88, *R v Minister of Agriculture, Fisheries and Food and Secretary of State for Health, ex p Fedesa and others* [1990] ECR I-4023, para 13:

> The Court has consistently held that the principle of proportionality is one of the general principles of Community law. By virtue of that principle, the lawfulness of the prohibition of an economic activity is subject to the condition that the prohibitory measures are appropriate and necessary in order to achieve the objectives legitimately pursued by the legislation in question; when there is a choice between several appropriate measures recourse must be had to the least onerous, and the disadvantages caused must not be disproportionate to the aims pursued.

Equally explicit: Cases C-133/93, 300/93 and 362/93, *Crispoltoni* [1994] ECR I-4863. For step four see also: Case 11/70, *Internationale Handelsgesellschaft mbH/Einfuhr- und Vorratsstelle für Getreide und Futtermittel* [1970] ECR 1125, para 16:

> The costs involved in the deposit do not constitute an amount disproportionate to the total value of the goods in question and of the other trading costs. It appears therefore that the burdens resulting from the system of deposits are not excessive and are the normal consequence of a system of organization of the markets conceived to meet the requirements of the general interest, defined in Art 39 of the Treaty, which aims at ensuring a fair standard of living for the agricultural community while ensuring that supplies reach consumers at reasonable prices.

[207] Eg: GCC, BVerfGE 7, 377; GCC, BVerfGE 16, 194 (202); GCC, BVerfGE 26, 215 (222); GCC, BVerfGE 31, 275 (290); GCC, BVerfGE 42, 263 (295).

[208] Eg: ECtHR, *Open Door Counselling Ltd & Cublin Well Woman Centre v Ireland* (1993) 15 EHRR (1) 244, Series A Vol 246-A, para 70:

> ...the Court must examine the question of 'necessity' in the light of the principles developed in its case-law (see, inter alia, the Observer and Guardian v the United Kingdom judgment

identified: (1) Does the measure have a legitimate objective, ie does it protect a legitimate interest? (2) Are the employed means appropriate or suitable? (3) Was the means necessary, ie was there no less intrusive way of reaching the same result? (4) Is the restriction proportionate *sensu stricto* (ie not disproportionate)? While step one entails a general evaluation of the policy objective, steps two, three and four introduce a specific dimension. Both suitability and necessity considerations require an evaluation of how much of a contribution a particular restriction can make towards securing a given objective.[209]

Individual sanctions have the primary objective to reduce the financial support of terrorism. Fighting terrorism is a legitimate objective. Terrorist activities pose a real threat to the human rights of large groups of people and to the foundations of the rule of law. This appraisal finds widespread support among policy makers at the international, European, and national level.[210] Fighting terrorism is the legitimate objective both of individual sanctions as a policy and of each individual sanctioning measure adopted against a particular person.

The appropriateness, necessity, and proportionality in *sensu stricto* are more difficult to test given the lack of precise information on individual sanctions. In *Kadi and al Barakaat*, Advocate-Genreal Maduro made a strong point, namely that 'the Court has no way of knowing' whether the measures against the appellant are 'disproportionate or even misdirected' and that 'the mere existence of that possibility is anathema in a society that respects the rule of law'.[211]

The lack of information and the disagreement on the effectiveness of individual sanctions as a policy[212] raises doubts whether they could

of 26 November 1991, Series A No 216, pp 29–30, para 59). It must determine whether there existed a pressing social need for the measures in question and, in particular, whether the restriction complained of was 'proportionate to the legitimate aim pursued' (ibid.).

[209] McBride, 'Proportionality and the European Convention on Human Rights' (n 205 above), p 24.

[210] Chapter 1, Section 6 and Conclusions.

[211] Opinion of AG Maduro in: Cases C-402/05 P and C-415/05 P, *Kadi and al Barakaat* (n 4 above), para 53.

[212] See: National Commission on Terrorist Attacks on the US, The 9/11 Commission Report, 2004, http://govinfo.library.unt.edu/911/report/911Report.pdf, p 382; House of Lords Select Committee on Economic Affairs, Report on 'The Impact of Economic Sanctions', 2007: '"Targeted" financial sanctions have been relatively ineffective. They have often been imposed on people and entities selected on non-transparent or dubious grounds.'; see also: report of the Sanction Committee in 2004, S/2004/1039, and the reports of the Monitoring Team, S/2005/572 and S/2005/761. For an evaluation of the effectiveness of the fight against terrorist financing: John Howell & Co, The EU's Efforts in the Fight Against Terrorist Financing in the Context of the

constitute an appropriate and suitable means to contribute to containing the treat of terrorism. Yet, judges are called upon to rule on the proportionality in individual cases. They must decide whether it was appropriate, necessary, and proportionate to list and sanction the specific person before them. Critical for this assessment is the likelihood that that person is actually involved with terrorism and that their financial resources would have actually been available for terrorist activities if they had not been frozen. This assessment should be made by the political branches when adopting sanctioning measures against an individual person. The courts should then test the reasonableness of this assessment. Yet, in none of the discussed cases have the EU courts been placed in the position to judge whether the assessment of the political branches was reasonable with regard to the applicant.

Assuming that individual sanctions as a policy are a suitable means to reduce the financial support for terrorism, the question remains whether they are also necessary. Are they the least intrusive means to reduce the

Financial Action Task Force's Nine Special Recommendations and the EU Counter Terrorist Financing Strategy, Final Report, 1 February 2007, Independent Scrutiny, European Commission Directorate-General Justice Freedom and Security, available at: http://ec.europa.eu/justice_home/doc_centre/terrorism/docs/report_01_02_07_with_appendix_en.pdf; The most recent examination of European sanctions, and the only large study focused on efficacy, came to a very negative conclusion on autonomous European sanctions targeting government officials. However, this study did not include the here discussed sanctions against terrorist suspects: C Portela, 'The Efficacy of Sanctions of the European Union: When and why do they work?' EUI Florence, unpublished PhD dissertation, 2008. Iain Cameron, 'Respecting Human Rights and Fundamental Freedoms and EU/UN Sanctions: State of Play', October 2008, Study requested by the European Parliament's Subcommittee on Human Rights, EXPO/B/DROI/2008/34, p 34: evaluates the effectiveness of individual sanctions to be 'most likely zero'; very different: S Dewulf and D Pacquée, 'Protecting Human Rights in the War on Terror: Challenging the Sanctions Regime Originating from Res 1267 (1999)', *Netherlands Quarterly of Human Rights*, 24/4 (2006), p 616 et seq, p 608, generally speak of 'the great value this list has proven to be'. Obviously, the effectiveness depends on the definition of the objective of individual sanctions; see also however: Sixth report of the Analytical Support and Sanctions Monitoring Team, UN S/2007/132 (8 March 2007), para 17:

> This lack of confidence in the List is unfortunate as it is in fact potentially one of the most useful operational tools in the whole panoply of international measures against al Qaida-related terrorism. It brings individuals, groups and entities to the attention of all States and obliges all States to take action against them. But even States that are currently or have recently been members of the Committee, and so know the potential of the List, do not submit names that would seem both to represent key elements of the threat and also might be vulnerable to the measures. At the very least, States might reckon to find benefit from the United Nations-Interpol special notices of listed individuals that are issued after listing and are circulated internationally to law enforcement agencies.

See also paras 18–20: 'the presence on the List of names of people who are widely believed to be dead, or whose identity cannot be established, reinforces doubts about the List's credibility and purpose'; see for more details Chapter 1, Section 7.

financial resources available to terrorists? Generally, it can be acknowledged that other means used in the fight against terrorism, such as detention or the confiscation of funds, have more far-reaching effects on the fundamental rights of terrorist suspects. Asset freezing *initially* constitute a limited interference with economic rights. Yet, individual sanctions can have far-reaching adverse effects depending on their duration and on the circumstances of stigmatizing someone as terrorist.[213]

Further, the necessity of imposing sanctions does not mean that the restrictions on procedural rights during the adoption procedure are also necessary. It is important to distinguish between the proportionality of individual sanctions (both the public allegation to have supported terrorism and the asset freezing) on the one hand, and the proportionality of the restrictions imposed on judicial review of these measures on the other. The latter have to be justified by a strict necessity of the restrictions to protect confidential information and the relationship to third states. With regard to the former, it will be argued that it demands balancing the intensity of the interference with the terrorist suspect's rights, depending on factors such as duration, with the contribution of individual sanctions to reducing the terrorism threat. However, the proportionality of individual sanctions and the restrictions imposed on judicial review are not disconnected. As the ECtHR has repeatedly pointed out, the lack of an effective remedy can make an otherwise proportionate measure disproportionate.[214]

Proportionality *sensu stricto* examines whether the particular measure has not posed a disproportionate burden on the applicant. Particularly in the context of counter-terrorist measures this specific dimension is crucial. Otherwise an abstract balancing exercise would allow the primary objective of maintaining international peace and security and protecting the public from terrorist attacks to cancel out the procedural rights of terrorist suspects. In the abstract, the procedural rights of a limited number of listed individuals might appear relatively insignificant in comparison with the right to life of potentially a multitude of people. This, however, would ultimately result in establishing an absolute abstract hierarchy between values. When policies are applied to particular individuals and specific situations, this application must be proportionate with regard to each individual person. Anything else would challenge the subjectivity of the

[213] See Chapter 3, Sections 3.2.2 and 3.2.3.

[214] See eg the considerations in ECtHR, *Lawless v Ireland*, judgment of 1 July 1961, A 3, p 58, para 36.

individual as a rights holder. It would reduce individuals to an objective factor in the calculation.[215]

A much cited statement of the ECJ concerning the impact of trade embargoes (state sanctions) illustrates this point well. The Court remarked that state sanctions have, *by definition*, consequences that affect the rights of individuals.[216] Individual sanctions, by contrast, are specifically targeted at those identified as terrorist suspects. Legal measures can either be abstract or concrete with regard to their factual scope. They can apply either in general to everybody or to a particular group of persons (personal scope). State sanctions determine a factual situation, but remain general in their personal scope. Trade embargoes imposed on a specific state concern all traders in this state. National traders must refrain from trading with this state, but by doing so they avoid further interference with their economic activity. Individual sanctions, by contrast, apply to a specifically defined group of people: it is clear from the instrument itself who is targeted by primary sanctions. Only with regard to secondary sanctions one could argue that sanctions against individuals are more similar to state sanctions in that they target anybody who trades with those subject to primary sanctions. With regard to the factual scope, individual sanctions are more similar to state sanctions; they cover any form of economic activity of those sanctioned. If we leave aside secondary sanctions for a moment, individual sanctions affect only those listed as terrorist suspects. Thus, they do not affect anybody *by definition*, but only those deliberately targeted. Indeed, the intention to reduce violations of the rights of innocent persons, particularly within the targeted states, was one of the main reasons why individual sanctions were introduced.[217] Those wrongly listed and sanctioned cannot be considered 'collateral damage' of the sanctions regime in the same way as those affected by state sanctions.

In the case of individual sanctions, fundamental interests are at stake on both sides. As Aharon Barak stated:[218]

[215] Compare: GCC, *Aviation Security Act*, para 121 (119 in the English translation):

> 'the obligation to respect and protect human dignity generally precludes making a human being a mere object of the state. What is thus absolutely prohibited is any treatment of a human being by public authority which fundamentally calls into question his or her quality of a subject ... by its lack of the respect of the value which is due to every human being for his or her own sake, by virtue of his or her being a person.'

See also Chapter 4.

[216] Case C-84/95, *Bosphorus Airways* [1996] ECR I-3953, para 22.

[217] See Chapter 1, Section 1.

[218] Aharon Barak, 'Introduction: The Supreme Court and the Problem of Terrorism', in: Israel Supreme Court (ed), *Judgments of the Israel Supreme Court: Fighting Terrorism within the Law* (2005), p 5.

Fighting against terrorism in an effective manner entails finding the right balance between security and public interests, on the one hand, and the need to safeguard human rights and basic freedoms, on the other.

Yet, secondary questions arise: (1) How do additional objectives and side-effects influence the balance? (2) How important is the probability that the security risk materializes?

The ECtHR takes a number of factors into account:[219] It considers the overall effect of a particular restriction,[220] including whether it extinguishes the right entirely or whether it leaves some room for its exercise. The ECtHR also pays attention to the likelihood/evidence that the legitimate interest was in peril.[221]

For the overall effects of the restriction the duration of the listing and of the freezing of asset is crucial. If the measures last for too long,[222] they become not only illegitimate but arguably also illegal. Not only is a higher level of proof required after the measures have been in place for a period of time,[223] but also the balance between the involved interests might change.

The enormous harm that might occur if the terrorist threat materializes cannot render futile all assessment of the *probability* that such harm occurs and the *suitability* and *cost* of counter-terrorism measures. By definition a threat requires a different evaluation than an attack. The former is a danger that has not yet materialized.

The proportionality review of individual sanctions can and should be decided following well-established and tried methods. A complete test of

[219] See McBride, 'Proportionality and the European Convention on Human Rights' (n 205 above) on Convention rights referring to necessity.

[220] Compare ECtHR, *Jacubowski v Germany* (1995) 19 EHRR 64 (proportionate restriction) with ECtHR, *Hertel v Switzerland*, judgment of 25 August 1998 (disproportionate).

[221] ECtHR, *Hertel* (n 220 above); ECtHR, *Vereinigung Demokratischer Soldaten Österreichs and Gubi v Austria* (1995) 20 EHRR 56; see also Chapter 4, Section 5.1 on US Supreme Court, *Hamdi*, 124 SCt 2633; US Supreme Court, *Hamdan v Rumsfeld*, 548 US 557 (2006); US Supreme Court, *Boumediene v Bush*, doc O6-1195, 553 US (2008), 128 SCt 2229 and above all on US District Judge Joyce Hens Green in *Re Guantanamo Detainee* Cases, holding that the detainees had a right to fair process and that the military courts set up to determine their status as 'enemy combatants' did not meet that standard. She conducted a detailed balancing test assessing what due process means in the light of the significant interest of safeguarding security and identified the factors that need consideration in defining the exact contours of the right (District Court for the District of Columbia, *Re Guantanamo Detainee* Cases, judgment of 31 January 2005, 355 F Supp 2d 443 (DDC 2005), in particular 465–6).

[222] Hinojosa Martinez, 'Las Sanciones del Consejo de Seguridad' (n 177 above), p 767 mentions six years.

[223] Thomas Franck suggested at the NYU Kadi panel discussion on 14 October 2008 to consider 'probable cause' sufficient.

proportionality requires a specific risk assessment. What was the threat posed by the person listed? This requires identifying how the person was 'supporting terrorism', including the likelihood that any of the frozen assets would actually have been used for terrorist activities. The substantive question of whether restrictive measures were proportionate in the individual case will then depend on the intensity of the interference with the rights of those targeted and on their (potential) contribution to terrorism. Further, the scope of the economic activity of those listed, ie the amount of money owned or handled, has to be taken into account.[224]

In particular the evidential standard necessary to justify restrictive measures against individuals is controversial. Hard choices are inevitable. The burden of proof for freezing somebody's assets lies with the public body. The question remains at what point does suspicion harden sufficiently to allow taking and maintaining measures against that suspect? The case-law analysed in Chapter 4 comes to very different conclusions on this matter.

Finally, it is important to acknowledge that assessing the proportionality of counter-terrorist measures usually requires a 'balancing exercise' that weighs the majority's security against the liberty of a small minority, to which the greater part of the majority will (in all probability) never belong. The House of Lords ruled that section 4 of the Anti-terrorism, Crime and Security Act 2001, which established executive powers to detain someone indefinitely, infringed human rights, inter alia because it considered the law to be discriminatory in that it applied to foreign nationals only.[225] Individual sanctions against terrorist suspects are not by law limited to a certain group of people. Yet, the fact that they are used disproportionately often against persons of a certain nationality, race, and ethical origin is an additional argument in support independent judicial review in order to avoid even the appearance of discrimination.

The ECJ has not specifically addressed the proportionality of individual sanctions. However, it did not reject the UN sanctions against private individuals as a matter of principle. On the contrary, the ECJ showed its understanding for the necessity to limit fundamental rights for the purpose of fighting terrorism. Indeed, it ruled that the right to property of the applicant was infringed only because of the lack of procedural protection.[226] The Court further acknowledged that because of the factual

[224] See also above the recommendation to introduce a general *de minimis* requirement.

[225] House of Lords, *Belmarsh detainees* case (n 128 above), para 68 (per Lord Bingham of Cornhill); para 132 (per Lord Hope of Craighead).

[226] Cases C-402/05 P and C-415/05 P, *Kadi and al Barakaat* (n 4 above), para 368 et seq.

circumstances of the contested asset-freezing the hearing of those listed can take place after their names were included for the first time,[227] but that the regulation infringed the appellants' rights to fair trial because the evidence used against them was not communicated to them either when they were listed or during a reasonable period of time afterwards.[228] The ECJ specifically mentioned the possibility to remedy the failure to communicate the incriminating evidence to the appellants by allowing the Community judicature to investigate the evidence.[229] These differentiated considerations on substance give an indication of the factors that the ECJ would take into account when assessing the lawfulness of individual sanctions.

By way of conclusion, assessing the proportionality of counter-terrorist measures is not a simple 'balancing exercise' by which security is increased when freedom is diminished. The policy decision of adopting sanctions must be distinguished from imposing sanctions on a particular person and other interests and factors that play important roles have to be considered. Restricting procedural rights in the adoption procedure requires justification separate from the justification of imposing sanctions. At the same time, procedural rights must be taken into account when assessing the proportionality in *senso strictu*. Moreover, a proportionality review also entails considering the duration of the measure, the likelihood that the frozen funds would have actually been used for terrorist activities, as well as the danger of discrimination.

Conclusions

Justice requires that all persons enjoy relatively uncontroversial basic rights.[230] Any restriction of these uncontroversial basic rights, including where the restriction serves the objective of fighting terrorism, must be justified.

This book has not rejected the adoption of sanctions against individuals as a matter of principle. It has rejected European sanctions against individuals in their current form. While it is *possible* to adopt individual sanctions in compliance with general principles of EU law, there is little doubt that

[227] ibid, para 341.
[228] ibid, para 348.
[229] ibid, para 350.
[230] Allen Buchanan, *Justice, Legitimacy, and Self-Determination – Moral Foundations for International Law* (Oxford: Oxford University Press, 2004), Chapter 5.

in the past the Union has adopted these measures *without* offering the necessary procedural safeguards.

Chapters Six and Seven Seven further argued that the EU continues to infringe the rights of those it lists and sanctions. The adoption procedure of individual sanctions has been improved after the EU courts have repeatedly annulled European sanctions for breaching the rights of the defence. Those sanctioned are now notified, receive a statement of reasons, and are informed of their rights to a fair hearing and to judicial protection. However, the adoption procedure remains obscure and those sanctioned cannot make effective use of their rights of defence because they are denied access to the relevant information on their case. Further changes to the adoption procedure will be necessary, such as the automatic appointment of a special (vetted) advocate representing those sanctioned when information can only be shared with the latter.

European sanctions giving effect to UN lists also breach fundamental rights. They also cause additional difficulties, which appear to be even more difficult to resolve. The European institutions do not possess the information necessary to place those sanctioned in the position to exercise their rights of defence. However, the ECJ held correctly that they cannot simply hide behind the supremacy of international legal obligations of the Member States to justify departure from fundamental principles of European law.[231] The EU is here confronted with an irresolvable dilemma that supports the conclusion that terrorist suspects should only be identified in a legal framework that complies with the rule of law and meets a certain standard of legal protection.

It is the role of judges not only to deliver individual justice but to play the principled philosopher to the king.[232] It is the task of the political branches to decide that a particular individual should be listed and their assets should be frozen. Courts, however, must determine the legal limits of this political action and strike down measures that violate human rights. This requires placing the judiciary in the position to know all the relevant information that allows the judge to determine whether the listing decision was reasonable. Individuals cannot be listed and sanctioned as terrorist suspects solely because the political branches say so, either at the European or at the UN level. The relevant information must be subject to a test of reasonableness by an independent judge, who is in the position to strike

[231] Cases C-402/05 P and C-415/05 P, *Kadi and al Barakaat* (n 4 above).

[232] Franck, 'Principled Imperative' (n 132 above), p 278.

down the contested measure. This leads to the conclusion that the European institutions cannot lawfully give effect to UN terrorist lists. They do not possess the relevant information and the listings are not subject to review at the UN level either.[233] Nor can individuals be listed as terrorist suspects in the Union pillars where procedural and judicial protection remains uncertain.

The question of whether individual counter-terrorist measures were suitable, necessary, and proportionate must be answered by a court of law. Existing criminal law offers a wide range of tested punitive but also preventive measures to fight crime.[234] It requires additional justification to go above and beyond these tested means to fight terrorist financing at an earlier stage and with evidence that would be deemed insufficient in a criminal procedure. Indeed, neither in international nor in domestic law does the end of fighting terrorism sweepingly justify all means.

Hans Kelsen argued that any value judgment is subjective, but that striving to rationalize decisions is the basic human pursuit of justice.[235] Where individuals are listed and sanctioned as terrorist suspects without any attempt for rationalization before an independent third party, be it as part of an internal control mechanism or before a judge, this basic human pursuit of justice is not satisfied.

[233] Chapter 1, Section 3.

[234] The argument was made that criminal law is sufficient to fight terrorism: Cameron, 'Respecting Human Rights and Fundamental Freedoms' (n 212 above).

[235] Hans Kelsen, *Was ist Gerechtigkeit?* (Reclam: Ditzingen, 2000), Section II, pp 16–20.

CONCLUSIONS

International terrorism is perceived to be one of the most pressing challenges that the international community faces at present. Irrespective of whether one agrees that it is new and different from earlier forms of terrorism and earlier threats to international peace and security, a strong willingness to take action against international terrorism can be observed. Sanctions against private individuals, in the form in which they are currently adopted at the United Nations (UN) level and the European Union (EU) level, are one of the counter-terrorist measures that were made possible by this willingness.

Counter-terrorist sanctions against individuals directly affect the rights of individuals without offering the necessary procedural and judicial safeguards. The adoption of individual sanctions in this form is possible because, both at the international and at the European level, they are adopted as general legal instruments pursuant to mechanisms that have been set up to adopt state sanctions. At the same time however, individual sanctions instruments are construed as narrowly as executive decisions within the domestic legal sphere. They immediately set out a clearly determined circle of persons to whom they apply. It is reasonable to assume that sanctions against private individuals, in the form in which they are currently adopted by the UN and by the EU, would face difficulties to be lawfully adopted within the domestic legal order of many countries.[1]

European sanctions adopted to give effect to UN lists of terrorist suspects further illustrate how international legal cooperation, which has traditionally been used to discipline states and to enhance fundamental rights protection, increases executive powers over citizens and can result in circumventing domestic protection mechanisms. The Court of First Instance (CFI) suggested redefining the relationship between the UN Charter and the European legal order.[2] The European Court of Justice

[1] Eg: Art 19(1) GG prohibits the adoption of 'Einzelfallgesetze' (individualized decisions disguised as measures of general application).

[2] Case T-306/01, *Ahmed Ali Yusuf and al Barakaat International Foundation v Council and Commission* [2005] ECR II-3533; Case T-315/01, *Yassin Abdullah Kadi v Council and Commission* [2005] ECR II-3649.

(ECJ) repealed the CFI's decisions and defended the autonomy of the European legal order.[3] However, the European institutions continue to give effect to UN lists of terrorist suspects without having access to the information on which the listings are based.[4]

This book sought to demonstrate that the current way of adopting European sanctions against private individuals threatens the protection of the individual and the functioning of the European legal order. First, both the EU and the Community lack the necessary competences to adopt individual sanctions.[5] Secondly, those listed and sanctioned do not have at their disposal effective procedural and judicial protection.[6] Although Community sanctions are now in principle subject to full judicial review in the EU courts, the well-foundedness of the allegation cannot be reviewed. Neither the affected individuals nor the EU courts are provided with the necessary information.[7] Further, the relationship between the European legal order and the UN Charter is fundamentally different from the relationship between the national legal orders of the Member States and the EU.[8] The EU courts cannot show the same deference to the Security Council as national constitutional courts do to the EU courts. Finally, the adoption procedure of individual sanctions would have to be (further) improved.[9] The identification of the individual terrorist suspect and the proportionality of the individual measure would have to be subject to judicial review.[10]

Chapter 1 set out the context in which individual sanctions are adopted in the EU. It introduced the two UN sanctions regimes. The first sanctions regime is governed by Resolutions 1267, 1333, and 1390. These resolutions mandated a Sanctions Committee to draw up lists of alleged terrorist suspects and obliged the UN member states to freeze the assets of these persons. UN lists cannot be challenged at the UN level. Even after the introduction of the so-called focal point by Resolution 1730, there is no effective remedy against the listing. The delisting procedure remains based on traditional means of diplomatic protection, and only the same body that

[3] Cases C-402/05 P and C-415/05 P, *Kadi and al Barakaat*, judgment of 3 September 2008, not yet reported.

[4] See Chapter 7, Sections 1.4 and 2.

[5] See Chapter 2, Section 1.

[6] See Chapter 6, Sections 1 and 2.

[7] See Chapter 7, Sections 1.4 and 2; most recently: Case T-318/01, *Omar Mohammed Othman v Council and Commission*, judgment of 11 June 2009, not yet reported, paras 87–8.

[8] Chapter 5, Section 4.

[9] Chapter 7, Section 1.2.

[10] See Chapter 7, Sections 3 and 4.

has taken the original listing decision can remove a person from the list by unanimous decision. The second sanctions regime was established by Resolution 1373. Here, the UN member states are required to set up their own sanctioning mechanisms, in which they identify and freeze the assets of alleged terrorist supporters. The EU set up an autonomous listing procedure to comply with the Member States' obligations under the UN Charter.

The two different UN sanctions regimes are mirrored by two different types of European implementation measures: on the one hand, the EU adopts asset freezes against those listed by the UN; and, on the other, it draws up its own autonomous lists of terrorist suspects and freezes the financial funds of those listed. The adoption procedure as well as the impact on the fundamental rights of those listed and sanctioned is nearly identical under both regimes. Both types of sanctions are adopted pursuant to the two-tier procedure in Article 301 EC. First, a common position is adopted under the second pillar (Common Foreign and Security Policy – CFSP). This common position contains a list of individuals suspected to have supported terrorism (Union list). Secondly, a Community regulation imposes the actual operative measures (asset freezes).

Article 301 TEU was introduced for sanctions against states. However, it was argued that individual sanctions differ fundamentally from state sanctions. In particular, the identification of the target is much more difficult and important in the latter case. Further, when individual sanctions are adopted, already the legal instrument containing the list of names directly impinges on the fundamental rights of those listed. State sanctions, by contrast, interfere with the rights of individuals not at the legislative level but at the level of implementation.

Sanctions against individuals were compared and contrasted with other counter-terrorist policies at the international, European, and domestic level. Most counter-terrorist policies within the EU are based on cooperation rather than harmonization. Individual sanctions constitute in this regard an exception. They are adopted in directly applicable regulations. It was argued that the recourse to preventive administrative measures should be strictly limited to avoid circumvention of well-established protection mechanism. In principle, the fight against terrorism should rely on criminal law instruments that provide the necessary legal safeguards.

Chapter 2 argued that both the Community and the Union lack the competence to adopt individual sanctions. In the European legal order individual sanctions are adopted on the joint legal basis of Articles 301, 60 and 308 EC. Both the CFI and the ECJ confirmed that this joint legal basis allows for the adoption of individual sanctions. However, even if such a competence might be desirable both for political reasons and with regard to the division of competences between the EU and the Member States, it goes against the clear wording of Article 301 EC and is not justifiable on legal grounds.

Article 301 EC requires a decision under the second pillar that Community action is necessary in order to pursue political goals by interrupting economic relations with a third country. This form of joint action by the Union and the Community is an exception in the EU. As a general rule, Article 47 TEU separates Union and Community law. Article 308 EC allows the Community to take action that is *necessary* to attain *Community* objectives where no specific provision confers the required competences. It does not enable the Community to pursue *Union* objectives.

In order to enable the EU to adopt individual sanctions, the CFI interpreted Article 301 EC to build a general 'bridge' between Union and Community competence[11] and accepted that the addition of Article 308 EC heals the problem that Article 301 EC by its wording does not allow for the adoption of individual sanctions. This construction effectively allows the Union to make use of Community competences in order to attain the objectives of the TEU. However, Article 301 EC *exceptionally* allows for cross-pillar action in order to adopt state sanctions. It has to be interpreted narrowly and cannot be stretched to cover individual sanctions, either by its wording or by its purpose. State sanctions and individual sanctions are fundamentally different and the rationale behind Article 301 EC does not extend to individual sanctions. The adoption of state sanctions is a political decision to employ trade embargoes that fall within the Community competence for the Common Commercial Policy (CCP). The coordination of embargoes is highly relevant for the functioning of the internal market. Individual sanctions, on the other hand, are the specific application of a general policy to particular individuals. They are much closer to criminal measures and they do not have a great impact on the internal market. Consequently, neither the political dimension nor the trade dimension of Article 301 EC applies to individual sanctions. As confirmed by the ECJ in Opinion 2/94, Article 308 EC is strictly limited to *Community* action required to achieve *Community* objectives and the fight against

[11] Case T-306/01, *Yusuf and al Barakaat* (n 2 above); Case T-315/01, *Kadi* (n 2 above).

terrorism does not form part of the Community objectives. Consequently, adding Article 308 EC cannot extend the Community's competence under Article 301 EC to comprise all action necessary to attain CFSP objectives. This is confirmed by an analysis of the past use of Article 308 EC as part of a combined legal basis.

The ECJ rejected the CFI's construction of competence, but it equally accepted that the Community had the competence to adopt individual sanctions based on Articles 301, 60, and 308 EC. Only, the ECJ found in Article 301 EC a Community objective 'of making it possible to adopt [economic] measures [in order to implement CFSP decisions] through the efficient use of a Community instrument'.[12] This 'functional objective' is equally unconvincing. The clear wording of Article 301 EC does not cover individual sanctions; nor does it vest the Community with a blank competence to implement all CFSP decisions.

Further, allowing the Community to use a mechanism created to adopt state sanctions in order to adopt measures as specific as counter-terrorist sanctions endangers the division of competences between the pillars. The adoption of individual sanctions pursuant to the procedure in Article 301 EC allows the Union to determine the actions of the Community. It puts the latter in a situation where it has to choose to either breach general principles of EU law, or reject the Union's request to take action and thereby threaten the coherency of European law.

Moreover, within the Union pillars, individual sanctions are adopted under the second pillar because Article 301 EC requires a CFSP decision in order to allow the Community to take action. The fight against terrorism is not a CFSP objective, and substantively individual sanctions appear to belong rather under the third pillar (Police and Judicial Cooperation in Criminal Matters) than under the second pillar. However, neither of the two Union pillars offers the necessary judicial remedies to justify the adoption of measures that impinge on fundamental rights in such a direct manner as individual sanctions.

Chapter 3 examined in detail in which way European sanctions against private individuals clash with the right of access to justice under the European Convention of Human Rights (ECHR) and under EU law. The ECHR is relevant not only for judicial protection in Strasbourg, but also in Luxembourg. Article 6 ECHR requires the Contracting Parties to provide judicial protection from criminal charges and measures determining the

[12] Cases C-402/05 P and C-415/05 P, *Kadi and al Barakaat* (n 3 above), para 226.

civil rights and obligations of individuals. Chapter 3 sought to demonstrate that Article 6 ECHR is applicable to Union lists of terrorist suspects (adopted in CFSP common positions) and to EC regulations imposing the actual asset freezes. Both measures determine the civil rights and obligations of those listed and sanctioned. While the exact scope of civil rights depends on domestic law this book predominantly referred to Community law as an example of the core of the civil rights protected by the Member States. Union lists of terrorist suspects and Community asset freezes interfere in particular with the right to an unharmed reputation and to property.

However, it was shown that both the Union lists and the Community asset freezes have clear criminal implications. The European Court of Human Rights (ECtHR) determines whether a measure qualifies as a criminal charge by means of three criteria: the classification of the proceedings in domestic law, the nature of the offence or conduct in question and the severity of any possible punishment. All three apply to a certain extent to the legal instruments used to adopt individual sanctions in the EU. In particular the last criterion is increasingly satisfied the longer the public listings as terrorist suspects and the asset freezes go on. And, even if it remains uncertain whether the ECtHR would consider both Union lists of terrorist suspects and Community asset freezes as criminal charges within the meaning of Article 6 ECHR, it was shown that both measures have characteristics of criminal law. These criminal characteristics require a strict application of Article 6 ECHR, which is interpreted by the ECtHR practically rather than schematically as having the ultimate objective to ensure fairness.

Chapter 4 discussed how far fundamental rights restrictions can be justified because they pursue the aim to fight terrorism. It considered to what extent terrorism creates an exceptional situation and how far this can justify exceptional limitation of fundamental rights. The threat of terrorism in the abstract cannot justify a derogation under Article 15 ECHR. This, however, does not exclude that a country can make a derogation if the abstract terrorist threat has intensified in a particular place and for a specific period of time. Chapter 4 analysed the case-law of the ECtHR and a selection of national courts concerning the compatibility of counter-terrorist measures with fundamental rights. Although the particular measures challenged in the discussed cases differ from individual sanctions, the courts' reasonings give some guidance on how to reconcile the fight against terrorism with fundamental rights protection.

The selection of case-law was chosen to demonstrate that national courts acknowledge the need to restrict fundamental rights in the fight against terrorism, but that they also emphasize the importance of judicial protection through an independent court. The ECtHR, for instance, while accepting that in criminal proceedings some information cannot be shared with the accused, attaches particular importance to the role of independent judges in determining whether it is necessary to conceal specific information. This decision cannot be taken by the executive outside the realm of judicial scrutiny.

The US courts gave principled rulings on the importance of *habeas corpus* and extended this writ to those detained in Guantanamo. In particular, Judge Green examined in detail that detainees were not provided with a meaningful opportunity to challenge the case against them in the Combatant Status Review Tribunals.[13] She found fault with the fact that the detainees could not access the relevant information. Hence, in essence, they were not given the opportunity to have their side argued. The House of Lords gave a similarly principled ruling in cases concerning the indefinite detention of foreign nationals (*Belmarsh detainee case*).[14] However, in other cases the House of Lords was less principled. In particular in the *Torture Evidence* case, the House of Lords limited the implications of its ruling by requiring a high level of evidence that a statement was obtained through torture.[15] On the balance of things, this will allow the executive to make use of statements obtained in countries that are thought to use coercive interrogation methods. This is a blow to the fairness of the British judiciary system. The Israeli Supreme Court has repeatedly ruled on fundamental rights restrictions imposed by counter-terrorist policies. In a ruling on 'pre-emptive strikes' or 'targeted killings' the Supreme Court rejected with strong words a political doctrine approach to counter-terrorist policies and emphasised the need to ensure the proportionality of individual measures.[16] By way of conclusion, the examination of selected case-law concerning the compatibility of counter-terrorist policies with

[13] District Court for the District of Columbia, *Re Guantanamo Detainees* case, judgment of 31 January 2005, 355 F Supp 2d 443 (DDC 2005).

[14] House of Lords, *A (FC) and others; X (FC) and others v Secretary of State for the Home Department (Belmarsh Detainees* case) [2004] UKHL 56, [2005] 2 AC 68.

[15] House of Lords, *A and Others v Secretary of State for the Home Department (Torture Evidence case*), [2005] UKHL 71.

[16] Supreme Court of Israel, HCJ 769/02 [2006] HCJ 769/02, *Public Committee against Torture in Israel et al v Government of Israel et al*, 13 December 2006; available in English at: http://elyon1.court.gov.il/Files_ENG/02/690/007/a34/02007690.a34.pdf.

human rights sought to demonstrate that even though far-reaching human rights restrictions have been considered justifiable, particular importance was attached to judicial protection.

Chapters 5 and 6 examined in detail the case-law of the EU courts on individual sanctions and its consequences for individuals and for the European legal order. Chapter 5 discussed judicial protection from European sanctions giving effect to UN lists of terrorist suspects (as opposed to the autonomous European sanctions regime). In 2005, in the cases of *Yusuf* and *Kadi*[17] the CFI rejected applying the general principles of EU law to European legal instruments implementing UN terrorist lists. Essentially, the Court argued that this would indirectly subordinate the decisions of the Security Council to European standards. Instead, the CFI found the *Community bound by decisions of the Security Council by virtue of the European Treaties*. The CFI further ruled that Security Council resolutions enjoy unconditional primacy over European law. However, Chapter 5 sought to demonstrate that neither the European Treaties nor the case-law of the ECJ justify the conclusion that the Community itself is bound by decisions of the Security Council. The ECJ's reasoning in *International Fruit Company*[18] is not transferable to the UN. Further, Article 103 of the UN Charter is a conflict norm only and addresses conflicts between obligations flowing from the UN Charter and other international legal obligations. Finally, even *if* the Community were bound by the obligations under the UN Charter, this would not allow the assumption that Security Council resolutions prevail over European primary law, including general principles of EU law.

On 3 September 2008, the ECJ ruled in the appeal decisions of *Kadi and al Barakaat* that the EU courts must take the perspective of European law. This perspective is built on the understanding that the European legal order, and in particular the Community, is autonomous from international law. International legal obligations are external to the domestic European legal order and have to comply with European primary law in order to become binding by virtue of the Treaties. They cannot therefore be understood to prevail over European primary law. The argument in Chapter 5 supports the ECJ's basic position, including the Court's rejection of a future possibility to show deference to the Security Council in an approach similar to the German Constitutional Court's *Solange* decisions. The Security Council is a political and not an independent judicial body.

[17] Case T-306/01, *Yusuf and al Barakaat* (n 2 above); Case T-315/01, *Kadi* (n 2 above).

[18] Cases 21-24/72, *International Fruit Company* [1972] ECR 1219.

Moreover, the UN system takes a fundamentally different view on individuals and their participation rights. Despite the fact that the UN system shares many of the basic values of the EU, it lacks the mechanisms that are necessary to ensure fundamental rights *within the UN system in practice*.

Chapter 6 finally focussed on procedural and judicial protection from European sanctions based on autonomous European lists of terrorist suspects. It distinguishes between Community and Union instruments. Judicial protection from Community sanctions appears to be largely in place after the CFI's ruling in the case of *OMPI I*.[19] However, the cases of *Sison*,[20] and in particular the repeated successful challenges of *OMPI*,[21] demonstrate that in practice the adoption procedure continues to infringe the rights of those sanctioned. Individuals do not (yet) have access to a court that can take an informed decision on the merits.

Today, those sanctioned by the Community are notified; they receive a statement of reasons; and they have a right to a hearing at the EU level. However, individual sanctions are adopted in a double-staged administrative procedure, where the tasks are divided between the European institutions and national authorities. In these procedures the right to be heard is exercised where the actual decision is taken. This is generally speaking where discretion is exercised. In the adoption procedure of individual sanctions (under the autonomous European regime), the Council cannot examine the substance of the decision of a competent national authority. This limits the hearing at the EU level to the finding that a national decision existed, which met the necessary requirements of the listing legislation. The Council attaches significant adverse effects to the decision of national authorities in a separate procedure (eg the decision to instigate investigations) without hearing the individual on the reasons why these additional consequences (terrorist listing and asset freezes) are not justified. Chapter 6 argued that the Council, when it takes the discretionary decision to list and sanction a person, must hear that person on why–considering the personal circumstances of that person–the listing decision

[19] Case T-228/02, *Organisation des Modjahedines du peuple d'Iran v Council and UK (OMPI I)* [2006] ECR II-4665.

[20] Case T-47/03, *Jose Maria Sison v Council and Commission* see also: Case T-341/07, *Sison v Council*, OJ 2007 C 269/58 (10.11.2007).

[21] Case T-228/02, *OMPI I* (n 19 above); Case T-256/07, *People's Mojahidin Organization of Iran v Council (OMPI II)*, judgment of 23 October 2008, not yet reported; appeal pending: Case C-576/08 P, *People's Mojahedin Organization of Iran* and Case T-284/08, *People's Mojahedin Organization of Iran v Council (OMPI III)*, judgment of 4 December 2008, not yet reported.

was taken. It is not sufficient to indicate the existence of a decision of a national authority in separate proceedings. Finally, access to information remains the greatest difficulty to ensure effective protection both at the procedural and at the judicial level. This was also discussed in Chapter 7.

Moreover, finding protection from Union listings remains even more problematic than protection from Community measures. In *Segi*, both Advocate-General Mengozzi[22] and the ECJ[23] pursued parallel – albeit different – strategies: both turned to the national legal orders for fundamental rights protection. The CFI found in *Segi*[24] that the applicants did not have any effective remedy at their disposal. On appeal, Advocate-General Mengozzi argued that the Union pillars are not sufficiently integrated to be submitted to the jurisdiction of the EU courts and that it is for the national courts to provide *direct* judicial review. The ECJ, by contrast, interpreted Article 35 TEU very extensively. It imposed on the national courts an obligation to refer a *preliminary question* where they consider Union instruments to infringe fundamental rights.

The CFI's conclusion that EU law does not allow for judicial protection from Union lists is incorrect. Review by national courts must be rejected as alien to the European legal order and as a threat to its functioning. The extension of the preliminary ruling procedure to allow requests regarding common positions improved the legal protection from Union lists of terrorist suspects. However, it does not provide sufficient protection from measures as intrusive as terrorist lists. Chapter 6 set out three additional ways to obtain full or partial review of Union lists. First, those listed can bring an action for infringement of their procedural rights. Not only the right of access to documents, but also the right to a statement of reasons are judiciable in the Union pillars. Secondly, the EU courts must exercise jurisdiction in order to protect Community law based on Articles 46(b) and 47 TEU. The exact predetermination of Community regulations by CFSP decisions allows the Union in practice to make use of Community instruments. This is contrary to the horizontal competence division within the European legal order. Finally, the EU courts have the mandate to uphold the rule of law within the EU. They should review Union lists of terrorist suspects because these lists have significant adverse effects on the legal

[22] AG Mengozzi, in Case C-355/04 P, *Segi v Council* [2007] ECR I-1657.

[23] Case C-355/04 P, *Segi v Council* [2007] ECR I-1657.

[24] Case T-338/02, *Segi and others* [2004] ECR II-1647.

position of individuals and go beyond the legal effects that can be adopted in common positions (based on the principle of wider jurisdiction).

Both Chapters 5 and 6 sought to demonstrate that not only the EU courts but also the ECtHR and the courts of the Member States have in principle jurisdiction to provide protection from European sanctions against individuals. The interplay between the three different judiciaries in Europe has already played a role with regard to individual sanctions and will continue to do so. While an open rebellion of the courts of the Member States could threaten the functioning of the European legal order, more careful warning signals, which have already been flagged up by the constitutional courts in Germany and Poland, might strengthen the judicial protection in the EU courts.

Chapter 7 discussed possible changes that could ensure that individual sanctions are adopted within the European legal order without breaching fundamental rights. The starting point of the discussion are the changes that the Council has introduced to the autonomous European sanctions regime in response to the repeated annulments of Community measures. The Council set up a permanent working group that verifies that the information provided by the Member State meets the requirements of the sanctioning legislation. Those listed and sanctioned under the first pillar are now notified, provided with a statement of reasons, and informed of the possibility to challenge the measures before the CFI. However, the information disclosed to the parties and the courts in practice remains insufficient to allow for a fair trial. Further, the listing criteria would have to be formulated sufficiently clearly and precisely to allow for meaningful judicial review. In particular, a clear link with the violent activities of a 'terrorist organization' would have to be demonstrated to justify listing and sanctioning one of its members. Also, a special advocate should be automatically appointed to argue the side of the applicants where relevant information cannot be disclosed to those affected.

Further, Chapter 7 complemented the argument in Chapters 1 and 2 that the identification of terrorist suspects must take place within a system that is governed by the rule of law and that offers *effective judicial protection*. In Chapter 1, it was submitted that the first sanctions regime established by Resolutions 1267, 1333, and 1390 was irreconcilable with widely accepted fundamental rights standards, because the UN system does not offer the necessary legal safeguards. Chapter 7 took this further by arguing that the European institutions cannot lawfully give effect to UN terrorist lists within the European legal order if these measures cannot be made subject to judicial review. The European institutions do not possess the relevant information on which the allegations are based and consequently cannot disclose this information to the EU courts. Finally, Chapter 7 argued that the judiciary has a role in controlling the exercise of executive powers in the fight against terrorism. Judges are mandated to ensure the proportionality of specific measures affecting individuals and to contribute to the human rights discourse. This is particularly relevant where extraordinary restrictions are imposed as it is the case in the fight against terrorism.

Throughout the book a number of broader conclusions were drawn from the above analyses. Judicial protection from individual sanctions remains below the standard required by the European legal order. Chapter 3 sought to demonstrate that the different legal instruments used to adopt European sanctions against individuals directly impinge on fundamental rights and give those affected a right to full judicial review in the EU courts. However, Chapters 6 and 7 showed that those listed in Union law instruments do not enjoy sufficient procedural or judicial protection. In *OMPI I*[25] the CFI in fact ruled that the listing procedure in the first pillar infringes general principles of EU law. This assessment is transferable both to the Community sanctions based on UN lists[26] and to the Union lists of terrorist suspects. As the repeated successful challenges of OMPI[27] have shown in practice, the adoption procedure still does not offer effective protection, despite certain changes.[28] Access to the relevant information is in practice one of the greatest obstacle to effective procedural and judicial protection. No procedural safeguards, such as a special advocate, are in place that could compensate for the fact that individuals do not know the case against them.

Fundamental rights in general, and the right of access to justice in particular, are based on the understanding that individuals are subjects with their own rights, rather than mere objects whose rights are governed by law. While individuals have been recognized as subjects under national law for a long time, they have not traditionally had the position of original rights holders under international law. The latter has more recently changed to some extent. However, international sanctions against private individuals are an example of a trend to the opposite: individuals are again

[25] Case T-228/02, *OMPI I* (n 19 above).
[26] See also Cases C-402/05 P and C-415/05 P, *Kadi and al Barakaat* (n 3 above).
[27] Case T-256/07, *OMPI II* and Case T-284/08, *OMPI III* (n 21 above).
[28] Chapter 7, Section 1.1.

treated as mere objects in the cooperation between actors of international law. The implementation of international law carries this view even into the domestic sphere. Individuals are listed and sanctioned because they are thought to constitute a threat to international peace and security. They are treated as factors in an equation of what could improve security. They are not considered as legal subjects with rights and interests. Hence, individual sanctions symbolize a trend away from the micro-perspective of individual rights holders, back to the formerly prevailing macro-perspective of states as interacting legal structures. From this perspective the states have the power to determine the rights of individuals. Individual sanctions are adopted both under international law and under European law. As a consequence, individuals are denied their subjectivity not only at the international level, but also under domestic law. This strips individuals of their well-established fundamental rights protection.

From the point of view of the affected individual both European sanctions regimes have similar effects. They should therefore enjoy the same procedural rights. Within the EU legal order it is accepted practice that procedural and judicial protection is divided between the national and the European level. However, with regard to the UN the situation is very different. While the EU courts can compel national authorities to offer procedural rights, they have no power to even influence UN bodies. Referring individuals to the UN level, where procedural protection remains window-dressing only (at least for the moment), translates into denying individuals their procedural rights altogether. Further, the level of judicial protection cannot legitimately depend on the pillar in which a measure is adopted either: again from the perspective of the individual, the protection should depend on the gravity of the interference and not on the formal choice of means.

If sanctions against private individuals should be adopted in international cooperation at all, some changes would have to be introduced to make them comply with fundamental rights. Sanctioning private individuals is not a policy decision. Individual sanctions are particular enforcement measures of the underlying general policy decision to stop the financing of terrorism. From the perspective of the individual the listings directly impinge on fundamental rights. The listings have strong criminal implications and therefore cannot be taken by political institutions acting within a law-free zone, but only at a level that offers adequate review mechanisms. This leads in fact to two conclusions: they can neither be taken at the UN level, nor at the Union level (as opposed to the Community level) – at least not *de lege lata*.

The UN Security Council could continue to adopt the underlying political decisions. It could set up sanctions committees charged with the task of outlining listing criteria, monitoring Member States' compliance and providing technical assistance. These criteria could be drawn up with much precision and detail, so that the Security Council retains some political influence on who is sanctioned without immediately targeting particular persons. Arguably, sanctions against well-known political figures and government officials might be different. Since these are utterly political decisions they might be acceptable at the UN level. This, however, goes beyond the subject of this book.

Identifying all alleged terrorists within the EU, instead of within the UN, would have major advantages both for the effectiveness of the sanctioning process and for the human rights protection of those sanctioned. The level of mutual trust between the EU Member States is much higher than the level of trust between the UN member states. *All* EU Member States are committed to the rule of law, democratic representation, and human rights. Moreover, these basic principles can actually be enforced against the EU Member States by the EU courts and by the ECtHR. This makes the EU a much better forum for the exchange of information on which basis an independent body could examine the listing decisions. While it appears almost impossible to obtain the relevant information at the UN level,[29] within the EU the sharing and controlled release of information appears more workable. Based on the principle of mutual trust the EU Member States already cooperate (closely) in certain areas of criminal law.[30]

However, while in the first pillar, the EU courts have a strong role and a convincing record of fundamental rights protection, their jurisdiction is strictly limited in the Union pillars.[31] Both the CFI and Advocate-General Mengozzi criticized in *Segi* that those listed in Union law did not have an effective remedy at their disposal at the European level. There seem to be two solutions to the lack of judicial control in the Union pillars. First, a better judicial control could be offered and, secondly, parallel to the above

[29] See: Chapter 1, Section 3.

[30] See ie: Guy Stessens, 'The Principle of Mutual Confidence between Judicial Authorities in the Area of Freedom, Justice and Security', in Gilles de Kerchove and Anne Weyembergh (eds), *L'espace pénal européen: enjeux et perspectives* (Brussels: ULB 2002), 93–103; with regard to terrorism: Jan Wouters and Frederik Naert, 'Of Arrest Warrants, Terrorist Offences and Extradition Deals: An Appraisal of the EU's Main Criminal Law Measures against Terrorism after "11 September"', *CML Rev* 41 (2004), 909–35.

[31] Article 46 TEU.

argument against UN lists of terrorist suspects, it could be concluded that the Union pillars are simply not the right forum to list individuals. Advocate-General Mengozzi's suggestion that national courts should step in and review Union lists endangers the constitutional structure of the EU. The ECJ correctly rejected this. The ECJ's suggestion of relying on the preliminary ruling procedure improves the legal protection of those listed; yet the improvement is not sufficient to justify the adoption of Union lists. In Chapter 6 it was concluded that the European legal order in fact allows for (some) judicial review of Union lists. However, already the *uncertainty* of whether there is a judicial remedy excludes the Union pillars as a legitimate forum for the adoption of lists of terrorist suspects.

Advocate-General Mengozzi acknowledged in *Segi* that if effective judicial review is denied 'situations may arise in which [...] the action of the Union may in fact infringe with impunity all the other rights [...] which the Union professes to respect'.[32] And, indeed, this is what is happening in the area of European sanctions against private individuals. Thus, if lists of terrorist suspects were to be adopted in the Union pillars the jurisdiction of the Court would have to be formally extended. However, it is very doubtful whether it would in fact be desirable to extend the jurisdiction of the EU courts to the Union pillars, including the Common Foreign and Security Policy.[33] *De lege lata*, if the EU was to adopt individual sanctions it is for the Community to draw up lists of those who are targeted. This appears to be a better solution than submitting the second pillar under the jurisdiction of the EU courts.

Based on an argument similar to the preceding conclusion, the EU courts must not allow Security Council resolutions to directly shape EU law. The UN might share the fundamental values of the EU to the extent that it commits its member states to comply with them. However, at the UN level itself these values are insufficiently well-rooted for the EU courts to adopt a *Solange* approach to decisions of the Security Council. The UN lacks the independence and legitimacy necessary to justify the recognition of its decisions without further judicial control. It does not commit to the same subjectivity of individuals as the EU. This is irrespective of certain improvements of the sanctioning procedure at the UN level.

32 AG Mengozzi, in C-355/04 P, *Segi* (n 22 above), para 82.

33 See Chapter 2, Section 2; see also: Daniel Thym, 'Beyond Parliament's Reach? The Role of the European Parliament in the CFSP', *European Foreign Affairs Review*, 11 (2006), p 113 et seq, at 121 et seq.

Additionally, from the perspective of the EU courts, national courts would be prevented from reviewing *national* law adopted to implement UN obligations so far as the European institutions implement it without further scrutiny. The German Constitutional Court's *Solange* reasoning was based on shared values and their effective protection in practice. It places on the EU courts the responsibility to defend these values for the European legal order. If the EU courts pass this responsibility on to the UN level where fundamental rights are currently insufficiently protected in practice, the German Constitutional Court may decide to challenge the authority of the ECJ and ultimately the primacy of European law. A *Solange* chain is only as strong as its weakest link.

National courts and the ECtHR have a judicial mandate to step in and offer fundamental rights protection where EU courts do not live up to the necessary standard. They have the power to discipline the EU courts. Yet, national courts should further feel the obligation to defend the integrity of the European legal order to the outside and fundamental rights standards under European law – although it must be conceded that these two obligations might be difficult to reconcile at times.

This book sought to demonstrate that the quote of the song of the Lord High Executioner in *The Mikado of Japan*, which was cited at the very beginning,[34] quite accurately describes the practice of listing private individuals as terrorist suspects. However, it also sought to demonstrate that the EU courts have not endorsed this practice but forced the Council to reconsider the blatant disregard for procedural and judicial rights. European sanctions against terrorist suspects are an example where, against a high level of political agreement on the desirability of these measures, the EU courts have – at least to some extent – taken the role of a principled guardian of justice.

On a final note, it is submitted that Lord Hoffmann's remarks on indefinite detention also hold true for counter-terrorist sanctions against private individuals:[35]

> The real threat to the life of the nation ... comes not from terrorism but from laws such as these. That is the true measure of what terrorism may achieve.

[34] Introduction, n 1:

> But it really doesn't matter whom you put upon the list,
> For they'd none of 'em be missed – they'd none of 'em be missed!

[35] House of Lords, *Belmarsh Detainees* case (n 14 above), para 97 per Lord Hoffmann; see Chapter 4, Sections 2 and 4.

BIBLIOGRAPHY

Adviesraad Internationale Vraagstukken (Advisory Council on International Affairs), *Counterterrorism from an International and European Perspective* (The Hague: Advisory Council on International Affairs, 2007).

Albors-Llorens, Albertina, *Private Parties in European Community Law: Challenging Community Measures* (Oxford: Clarendon Press, 1996).

Alexander, Yonah and Nanes, Allan S (eds), *Legislative Responses to Terrorism* (Dordrecht, Martinus Nijhoff Publishers, 1986).

Alland, Denis, 'Jurisprudence en matière de droit international public', *RGDIP* (1998), 203.

Alnasrawi, Abbas, *Iraq's Burdens: Oil, Sanctions and Underdevelopment* (Westport: Greenwood Press, 2002).

Alston, Philip and Weiler, JHH, 'An "Ever Closer Union" in Need of a Human Rights Policy: The European Union and Human Rights', in Philip Alston (ed), *The EU and Human Rights* (Oxford: Oxford University Press, 1999).

Alvarez, José, 'Judging the Security Council', *AJIL*, 90 (1996), 1–39.

—— 'Hegemonic International Law Revisited', *AJIL*, 97 (2003), 873.

—— 'The Security Council's War on Terrorism: Problems and policy options', in Erika de Wet and André Nollkaemper, *Review of the Security Council by Member States* (Antwerp: Intersentia, 2003).

Andersson, Torbjörn, Cameron, Iain and Nordback, Kenneth, 'EU Listing: The Renaissance of Imperial Power, but on a Global Scale', *European Business Law Review* (2003), 111.

Angelet, Nicolas, 'Vers un renforcement de la prévention et la répression du terrorisme par de moyens financiers et économiques?', in Karine Bannelier et al (eds), *Le droit international face au terrorisme: après le 11 septembre 2001* (Paris: Pedone, 2003), 219.

d'Appollonia, Ariane Chebel and Reich, Simon (eds), *Immigration, Integration and Security: America and Europe in Comparative Perspective* (Pittsburgh: University of Pittsburgh Press, 2008).

Arnull, Anthony, 'The Treaty of Amsterdam and the Court of Justice', in David O'Keeffe and Patrick Twomey (eds), *Legal issues of the Amsterdam Treaty* (Oxford: Hart Publishing, 1999).

—— 'Private Applicants and the Action for Annulment since Codorníu', *CML Rev*, 38 (2001).

—— *The European Union and its Court of Justice* (Oxford: Oxford University Press, 2006).

—— 'When is an Act not an Act', *ELR*, 32 (2007), 1.

—— et al, *Wyatt and Dashwood's European Union Law* (London: Sweet & Maxwell, 2006).

Aspremont, Jean d' and Dopagne, Frédéric, 'The European Endeavors To Constitutionalize: The International Legal Order', draft paper presented at GARNET Conference on 'The European Union in International Affairs', Brussels 24–26 April 2008.

Avbelj, Matej, 'European Court of Justice and the Question of Value Choices: Fundamental Human Rights as an Exception to the Freedom of Movement of Goods', *Jean Monnet Working Papers*, 6/04 (2004), http://www.jeanmonnetprogram.org/papers/04/040601.html.

Babier de La Serre, Eric, 'Procedural Justice in the European Community Case-Law Concerning the Rights of the Defence: Essentialist and Instrumentalist Trends', *European Public Law* 12.2 (2006), 225 et seq.

Bailey, Sydney D and Daws, Sam, *The Procedure of the UN Security Council* (Oxford: Clarendon Press, 1998).

Ballmann, Alexander, Epstein, David and O'Halloran, Sharyn, 'Delegation, Comitology, and the Separation of Powers in the European Union', *International Organization*, 56:3 (2002), 551–74.

Barak, Aharon, 'Introduction: The Supreme Court and the Problem of Terrorism', in Israel Supreme Court (ed), *Judgments of the Israel Supreme Court: Fighting Terrorism within the Law* (2005).

Baratta, Roberto, 'Overlaps between European Community Competence and European Union Foreign Policy Activity', in Enzo Cannizzaro (ed), *The European Union as an Actor in International Relations* (The Hague: Kluwer Law International, 2002), 51.

Bartelt, Sandra and Zeitler, Helge Elisabeth, '"Intelligente Sanktionen" zur Terrorismusbekämpfung in der EU', *EuZW* (2003), 715.

Bates, Ed, 'Anti-Terrorism Control Orders: Liberty and Security still in the Balance', *Legal Studies*, 29:1 (2009), 99–126.

Becher, Klaus, 'Has-been, Wannabe, or Leader: Europe's Role in the World after the 2003 European Security Strategy', *European Security*, 13:4 (2003), 345–59.

Beck, Ulrich, *Weltrisikogesellschaft* (Frankfurt am Main: Suhrkamp Verlag, 2007).

Becker, Tal, *Terrorism and the State: Rethinking the Rules of State Responsibility* (Oxford: Hart Publishing, 2006).

Bedjaoui, Mohammed, *Nouvel ordre mondial et contrôle de la légalité des actes du Conseil de Sécurité* (Brussels: Bruylant, 1994).

Benda, Ernst, 'Deutsche Außenpolitik vor Gericht-Bundesverfassungsgericht und auswärtige Gewalt', *Internationale Politik*, 12 (1995), 39.

Bendiek, Annegret, 'EU Strategy on Counter-Terrorism: Steps Towards a Coherent Network Policy', *SWP Research Paper*, Stiftung Wissenschaft und Politik/German Institute for International and Security Affairs, November 2006, http://www3.swp-berlin.org/.

Benitez, Rafael A, 'Administrative Justice in a World in Transition: Pan-European Values in Administrative Justice', *Common Law World Review, 30* (2001), 434.

Ben-Naftali, Orna, 'A Judgment in the Shadow of International Law', *Journal of International Criminal Justice*, 5:2 (2007), 322.

—— and Michaeli, Keren, 'Public Committee Against Torture in Israel et al. v. Government of Israel', *AJIL*, 101:2 (2007), 459.

Benoit, Loick, 'La lutte contre le terrorisme dans le cadre du deuxième pilier: un nouveau volet des relations extérieures de l'Union Européenne', *Revue du Droit de l'Union Européenne* (2002), 283.

Bernhardt, Rudolf, 'Article 103', in Bruno Simma (ed), *The Charter of the United Nations: A Commentary* (Oxford: Oxford University Press, 2002).

Berrod, Frédérique and Mariatte, Flavien, 'Le pourvoi dans l'affaire Unión de Pequeños Agricultores c/Conseil: le retour de la procession d'Echternach', *Europe*, Editions du Juris-Classeur, 12/10 (October 2002).

Bianchi, Andrea, 'Enforcing International Law Norms Against Terrorism: Achievements and Prospects', in Andrea Bianchi (ed), *Enforcing International Law Norms Against Terrorism* (Oxford: Hart Publishing, 2004), 491.

—— 'Assessing the Effectiveness of the UN Security Council's Anti-terrorism Measures: The Quest for Legitimacy and Cohesion', *EJIL*, 17 (2007).

Bieber, Roland, Epiney, Astrid and Haag, Marcel, *Die Europäische Union: Europarecht und Politik* (Baden-Baden: Nomos, 2005).

Biehler, Gernot, 'Individuelle Sanktionen der Vereinten Nationen und Grundrechte', *Archiv des Völkerrechtes*, 41 (2003), 169.

Biersteker, Thomas J, Eckert, Sue E, *Strengthening Targeted Sanctions Through Fair and Clear Procedures*, White Paper prepared by the Watson Institute Targeted Sanctions Project, Brown University, 30 March 2006, 26, http://watsoninstitute.org/pub/Strengthening_Targeted_Sanctions.pdf.

—— Halegua, Aaron and Romaniuk, Peter, 'Consensus from the Bottom Up? Assessing the Influence of the Sanctions Reform Processes', in Peter Wallensteen and Carina Staibano (ed), *International Sanctions: Between Words and Wars in the Global System* (London: Routledge, 2005), 15.

Bindreiter, Uta, *Why Grundnorm? A Treatise on the Implications of Kelsen's Doctrine* (The Hague: Kluwer Law International, 2002).

Blakesley, Christopher L, *Terrorism and Anti-terrorism: A Normative and Practical Assessment* (Ardsley-on-Hudson, NY: Transnational Publishers, 2006).

Blekxtoon, Rob and Ballegooij, Wouter FW van (eds), *Handbook on the European Arrest Warrant* (Hague: TMC Asser Press, 2004).

Bogdandy, Armin von, 'The European Union as a Human Rights Organization? Human Rights and the Core of the European Union', *CML Rev*, 37 (2000), 1307.

—— 'The Legal Case for Unity: The European Union as a Single Legal System', *CML Rev*, 36 (1999), 887.

Bono, Ricardo Gosalbo, 'Some Reflections on the CFSP Legal Order', *CML Rev*, 43 (2006), 337.

Bothe, Michael, 'Les limites des pouvoirs du Conseil de Sécurité' in: Rene-Jean Dupuy (ed), *Le Dévelopement de la rôle du Conseil de Sécurité* (Dordrecht: Martin Nijhoff Publishers, 1993), 67 et seq.

Bowett, Derek, 'The Impact of Security Council Decisions on Dispute Settlement Procedures', *EJIL*, 5 (1994), 93.

Bowring, Bill, 'Terrorist Designation with Regard to European and International Law: The Case of the PMOI', paper presented at the International Conference of Jurists in Paris on Wednesday, 10 November 2004.

Bray, Robert (ed), *Procedural Law of the European Union* (London: Sweet & Maxwell, 2006).

Brown, Christopher and Morijn, John, 'Case C-263/02 P, Commission v. Jégo-Quéré & Cie SA', *CML Rev*, 41 (2004), 1639.

Brownlie, Ian, *The Rule of Law in International Affairs* (The Hague: Nijhoff, 1998).

Brzoska, Michael (ed), *Smart Sanctions: The Next Steps. The Debate on Arm Embargoes and Travel Sanctions within the 'Bonn-Berlin Process'* (Baden-Baden: Nomos, 2001).

Buchanan, Allen, *Justice, Legitimacy, and Self-Determinatio: Moral Foundations for International Law* (Oxford: Oxford University Press, 2004).

——, Keohane, Robert O, 'The Legitimacy of Global Governance Institutions', *Ethics and International Affairs*, 20/4 (2006), 405–37.

Buck, Carsten, *Über die Auslegungsmethoden des Gerichtshofs der Europäischen Gemeinschaft* (Frankfurt am Main: P Lang, 1998).

Bulterman, Mielle, 'Fundamental Rights and the United Nations Financial Sanction Regime: The Kadi and Yusuf Judgments of the Court of First Instance of the European Communities', *Leiden Journal of International Law*, 19 (2006), 753–72.

Búrca, Gráinne de, 'Europe's Judicial Resolution and the UN Security Council', paper presented at the Harvard Law School faculty workshop on 27 October 2008, 2, http://www.law.harvard.edu/.

——, 'The European Court of Justice and the International Legal Order after Kadi Europe's Judicial Resolution and the UN Security Council', *Jean Monnet Working Paper* 01/09.

Callies, Christian, 'Article 297', in Christian Callies and Matthias Ruffert (eds), *Kommentar zum EU-/EG-Vertrag* (Neuwied: Luchterhand, 2002).

—— and Ruffert, Matthias (eds), *Kommentar zum EU-Vertrag und EG Vertrag* (Neuwied: Luchterhand, 2002).

Cameron, Iain, *National Security and the European Convention on Human Rights* (The Hague: Kluwer Law International, 2000).

—— 'Report to the Swedish Foreign Office on Legal Safeguards and Targeted Sanctions' (2002), http://resources.jur.uu.se/repository/5/PDF/staff/sanctions.pdf.

—— 'UN Targeted Sanctions, Legal Safeguards and the European Convention on Human Rights', *Nordic Journal of International Law*, 72 (2003), 166.

—— 'European Union Anti-Terrorist Blacklisting', *Human Rights Law Review*, 4 (2004).

—— 'Protecting Legal Rights: On the (In)Security of Targeted sanctions', in Peter Wallensteen and Carina Staibano (eds), *International Sanctions: Between Words and Wars in the Global System* (London: Routledge, 2005), 181–206.

—— 'Skyddet för Mänskliga Rättigheter inom EU: Någon Annans Problem?', *Europarättslig tidskrift*, 2005, 631.

—— 'The European Convention on Human Rights: Due Process and United Nations Security Council Counter-Terrorism Sanctions', Report to the Council of Europe, of 6 February 2006, http://www.coe.int/.

—— 'Rapports: European Court of Human Rights. January 2005–March 2006', *EPL*, 13 (2007), 8.

—— 'Respecting Human Rights and Fundamental Freedoms and EU/UN Sanctions: State of Play', October 2008, Study requested by the European Parliament's Subcommittee on Human Rights, EXPO/B/DROI/2008/34.

—— 'Sökandet efter en rättvis lösning pa FN:s riktade sanctioner: ett sisyfosarbete', *Svensk Juristtidning* 2009, 64–83.

Cananea, Giacinto della, 'The European Union's Mixed Administrative Proceedings', *Law and Contemporary Problems*, 68 (2004), 197 et seq.

Cannizzaro, Enzo, 'Machiavelli, the UN Security Council and the Rule of Law', Hauser Global Law School Program, *Global Law Working Paper* 11/05, http://www1.law.nyu.edu/nyulawglobal/workingpapers/glwp_0106.htm.

Canor, Iris, '"Can Two Walk Together, Except They be Agreed?": The Relationship Between International Law and European Law. The Incorporation of United Nations Sanctions Against Yugoslavia Into European Community Law Through the Perspective of the European Court of Justice', *CML Rev*, 35 (1998), 172.

Cassese, Antonio, 'Terrorism is Also Disrupting Some Crucial Legal Categories of International Law', *EJIL*, 12 (2001), 993.

—— *International Law* (Oxford: Oxford University Press, 2005).

—— 'On Some Merits of the Israeli Judgment on Targeted Killings', *Journal of International Criminal Justice*, 5:2 (2007), 339.

—— Clapham, Andrew and Weiler, Joseph (eds), *European Union: The Human Rights Challenge*, vols I–III (Baden-Baden: Nomos, 1991).

Cassese, Sabino, 'European Administrative Proceedings', *Law and Contemporary Problems*, 68:21 (2004), 21 et seq.

Chalmers, Damian, Hadjiemmanuil, Christos, Monti, Giorgio and Tomkins, Adam, *European Union Law* (Cambridge: Cambridge University Press, 2006).

Charney, Jonathan, 'Universal International Law', *AJIL*, 87 (1993), 529.

Charters, David (ed), *Democratic Responses to International Terrorism* (London: Cavendish Publishers, 1991).

Chayes, Abram and Handler Chayes, Antonia, *The New Sovereignty: Compliance with International Regulatory Agreements* (Cambridge, MA: Harvard University Press, 1996).

Cohen, Amichai, and Shany, Yuval, 'A Development of Modest Proportions: The Application of the Principle of Proportionality in Targeted Killings Case', *Journal of International Criminal Justice*, 5:2 (2007), 310.

Cole, David, 'The New McCarthyism: Repeating History in the War on Terrorism', *Research Paper Series in Public Law and Legal Theory*, Georgetown University Law Center, Research Paper No. 383660 (2003), 38 et seq.

—— 'Terror Financing: Guilt by Association and the Paradigm of Prevention in the "War on Terror"', in Andrea Bianchi and Alexis Keller (eds), *Counterterrorism: Democracy's Challenge* (Oxford: Hart Publishing, 2008), 233–50.

Constantinesco, Vlad, 'The ECJ as a Law-maker: Praetor Aut Contra Legem?', in David O'Keeffe and Antonio Bavasso, *Judicial Review in European Union Law: Liber Amicorum in Honour of Lord Slynn of Hadley* (The Hague: Kluwer Law International, 2000), 73–9.

—— and Simon, Denys, 'Quelques problèmes des relations extérieures des Communautés européennes', *RTDE*, 11 (1975), 432.

Cortright, David and Lopez, George A, *Smart Sanctions: Targeting Economic Statecraft* (Lanham: Rowman & Littlefield, 2002).

—— 'A Sanctions Coordinator: Options for Enhancing Compliance', in Peter Wallensteen and Carina Staibano (eds), *International Sanctions: Between Words and Wars in the Global System* (London: Routledge, 2005), 65–74.

—— 'Assessing Smart Sanctions: Targeting Sanctions. Lessons from the 1990s', in Michael Brzoska, *Smart Sanctions: The Next Stops. The Debate on Arm Embargoes and Travel Sanctions within the 'Bonn-Berlin Process'* (Baden-Baden: Nomos, 2001), 20 et seq.

Council of Europe, *Principles of Administrative Law Concerning the Relations Between Administrative Authorities and Private Persons: The Administration and you. A Handbook* (Strasbourg: Council of Europe Publishing, 1996).

Couzigou, Irene, 'La lutte du Conseil de Sécurité contre le terrorisme international et les droits de l'homme', *Revue Générale de Droit International Public* (2008), 49–84.

Craig, Paul, *EU Administrative Law* (Oxford: Oxford University Press, 2006).

—— and Búrca, Gráinne de, *EU Law – Text, Cases and Materials* (Oxford: Oxford University Press, 2008).

Cramér, Per, 'Recent Swedish Experience with Targeted UN Sanctions: The Erosion of Trust in the Security Council', in Erika de Wet and André Nollkaemper, *Review of the Security Council by Member States* (Antwerp: Intersentia, 2003), 85–106.

Craven, Matthews, 'Humanitarianism and the Quest for Smarter Sanctions', *EJIL*, 13 (2002), 46.

Cremer, Wolfram, 'Article 230', in Christian Callies and Matthias Ruffert (eds), *Kommentar zum EU-/EG-Vertrag* (Neuwied: Luchterhand, 2002).

Cremona, Marise, 'External Relations of the EU and the Member States: Competence, Mixed Agreements, International Responsibility, and Effects of International Law', *EUI Law working papers*, 22 (2006).

Curtin, Deirdre, 'The Constitutional Structure of the Union: A Europe of Bits and Pieces', *CML Rev*, 30 (1993), 17.

—— 'The Right to Fair Procedures in Administrative Law' in James O'Reilly (ed), *Human Rights and Constitutional Law: essays in honour of Brian Walsh* (Dublin: The Round Hall Press, 1992), 293 et seq.

—— 'The Developing Right of Citizen Access to Information on Asylum and Immigration Decision-Making', in Elspeth Guild and Carol Harlow (eds), *Implementing Amsterdam: Immigration and Asylum Rights* (Oxford, Portland: Hart Publishing, 2001).

—— *Executive Power of the European Union: Law, Practice, and the Living Constitution* (Oxford: Oxford University Press, 2009).

—— and Dekker, Ige, 'The EU as a "Layered" International Organisation: Institutional Unity in Disguise', in Paul Craig and Gráinne de Búrca (eds), *The Evolution of EU Law* (Oxford: Oxford University Press, 1999).

—— 'The Constitutional Structure of the European Union: Some Reflections on Vertical Unity-in-Diversity', in Paul Beaumont, Carole Lyons and Neil Walker (eds), *Convergence and Divergence in European Public Law* (Oxford: Hart Publishing, 2002).

—— and Eckes, Christina, 'The Kadi Case: Mapping the Boundaries between the Executive and the Judiciary in Europe', *International Organizations Law Review*, 5 (2008), 1 et seq.

—— and Ooik, Ronald H van, 'Revamping the European Union's Enforcement Systems with a View to Eastern Enlargement', Working Document W 110, Scientific Council for Government Policy, The Hague, October 2000.

Dagtoglou, Prodromos D, 'The Legal Nature of the European Community', in Commission of the European Communities, *Thirty Years of Community Law* (Luxembourg: Office for Official Publications of the European Communities, 1982).

Dahme, Gudrun, *Terrorismusbekämpfung durch Wirtschaftssanktionen*, Schriftenreihe des Europäischen Forums für Außenwirtschaft, Verbrauchsteuern und Zoll e. V an der Westfälischen Wilhelms-Universität Münster (Witten: Mendel, 2007).

Dawes, Anthony and Kunoy, Bjørn, 'Plate tectonics in Luxembourg: The ménage à trois between EC law, international law and the European Convention on Human Rights following the UN sanctions cases', *Common Market Law Review*, 46 (2009), 73–104.

Denza, Eileen, *The Intergovernmental Pillars of the European Union* (Oxford: Oxford University Press, 2002).

Dewulf, Steven and Pacquée, Didier, 'Protecting Human Rights in the War on Terror: Challenging the Sanctions Regime Originating from Res 1267 (1999)', *Netherlands Quarterly of Human Rights*, 24/4 (2006), 616.

Di Fabio, Udo, 'Das Bundesverfassungsgericht und die internationale Gerichtsbarkeit', in Andreas Zimmermann (ed), *Deutschland und die internationale Gerichtsbarkeit* (Berlin: Duncker & Humblot, 2004), 107 et seq.

Dicey, Albert, *Introduction to the Study of the Law of the Constitution* (London: MacMillan, 1885).

Dickson, Brice, 'Law versus Terrorism: Can Law Win?', *EHRLR*, 1 (2005), 11 et seq.

Dijk, Pieter van and Hoof, Godefridus JH van, *Theory and Practice of the European Convention on Human Rights* (The Hague: Kluwer Law International, 1998).

Dillon, Sara, 'Looking for the Progressive Empire: Where is the European Union Foreign Policy?', *Connecticut Journal of International Law*, 19 (2003), 280.

Doehring, Karl, 'Unlawful Resolutions of the Security Council and their Legal Consequences', in Jochen A Frowein and Rüdiger Wolfrum (eds), *Max Planck Yearbook of United Nations Law*, vol 1 (The Hague: Kluwer Law International, 1997), 91.

Douglas-Scott, Sionaidh, 'The Rule of Law in the European Union: Putting the Security into the EU's Area of Freedom, Security and Justice', *ELR*, 29/2 (2004), 219–42.

Doxey, Margaret P, *International Sanctions in Contemporary Perspective* (London: Macmillan, 1996).

Duffy, Helen, *The "War on Terror" and the Framework of International Law* (Cambridge: Cambridge University Press, 2005).

Dumitriu, Eugenia, 'The EU's Definition of Terrorism: The Council Framework Decision on Combating Terrorism', *German Law Journal*, 5 (2004), 585.

Dupuy, Pierre-Marie, 'The Law After the Destruction of the Towers', *European Journal of International Law* series on Legal Responses to 'The Attack on the World Trade Center' (2002).

Düx, Heinz, 'Globale Sicherheitsgesetze und weltweite Erosion von Grundrechten: Statt "Feindstrafrecht" globaler Ausbau demokratischer Rechte', *ZRP* (2003).

Dworkin, Ronald, 'The Judge's New Role: Should Personal Conviction Count?', *Journal of International Criminal Justice*, 1 (2003), 4.

Eaton, Mary, 'Common Foreign and Security Policy', in David O'Keeffe and Patrick Twomey (eds), *Legal Issues of the Maastricht Treaty* (London: Chancery Law Publishing, 1994), 224 et seq.

Eckes, Christina, 'How not Being Sanctioned by a Community Instrument Infringes a Person's Fundamental Rights: The Case of Segi', *King's College Law Journal* (2006), 144.

Eckes, Christina, 'Does the European Court of Human Rights Provide Protection from the European Community? The Case of Bosphorus Airways', *European Public Law*, 13 (2007), 47.
—— 'Judicial Review of European Anti-Terrorism Measures: The Yusuf and Kadi Judgments of the Court of First Instance', *European Law Journal* (2008), 74–92.
—— 'Sanctions Against Individuals: Fighting Terrorism within the European Legal Order', *European Constitutional Law Review*, (2008), 205–24.
——, 'International Sanctions against Individuals: A Test Case for the Resilience of the European Union's Constitutional Foundations', *European Public Law* (2009), 351–78.
—— 'UN Mandated Military Operations: Orientations of State Responsibility and the Hierarchy of International Law', *EuConst* (2010), forthcoming.
Eeckhout, Piet, 'The EU Charter of Fundamental Rights and the Federal Question', *CML Rev*, 39 (2002), 945.
—— *External Relations of the European Union: Legal and Constitutional Foundations* (Oxford: Oxford University Press, 2004).
—— 'EC Law and UN Security Council Resolutions: In Search of the Right Fit', *European Constitutional Law Review*, 3 (2007), 183.
Eek, Hilding, Bring, Ove and Hjerner, Lars, *Folkrätten* (Stockholm: Norstedts, 1987).
Ekins, Richard, 'Judicial Supremacy and the Rule of Law', *Law Quarterly Review*, 119 (2003), 127.
Ellis, Evelyn, *The Principle of Proportionality in the Laws of Europe* (Oxford: Hart Publishing, 1999).
Emiliou, Nicholas, *The Principle of Proportionality in Europe Law: A Comparative Study* (London: Kluwer Law International, 1996).
Everling, Ulrich, 'Reflections on the Structure of the European Union', *CML Rev* 29 (1992), 1053–77.
—— 'The Maastricht Judgment of the German Federal Constitutional Court and its Significance for the Development of the European Union', *YEL*, 14 (1994), 1.
Fallon, Richard, '"The Rule of Law" as a Concept in Constitutional Discourse', *Columbia Law Review*, 97 (1997), 1.
Fassbender, Bardo, *UN Security Council Reform and the Right of Veto: A Constitutional Perspective* (The Hague: Kluwer Law International, 1998).
—— 'The United Nations Charter as Constitution of the International Community', *Columbian Journal of Transnational Law*, 36 (1998), 531–619.
—— 'Targeted Sanctions and Due Process', study commissioned by the United Nations, 20 March 2006 (final), http://www.un.org/law/counsel/Fassbender_study.pdf.
Feinaeugle, Clemens, 'Die Terroristenlisten des Sicherheitsrates: Endlich Rechtsschutz des Einzelnen gegen die Vereinten Nationen?', *ZRP*, 3 (2007), 75 et seq.

Feldman, David, 'Terrorism, Human Rights and their Constitutional Implications: Case Note on *A and others v Secretary of State for the Home Department*, Judgment of 16 December 2004', *European Constitutional Law Review*, 1 (2005), 531–52.

—— 'Deprivation of Liberty in Anti-Terrorism Law', *Cambridge Law Journal*, 67:1 (2008), 4.

Fenrick, William J, 'The Targeted Killings Judgment and the Scope of Direct Participation in Hostilities', *Journal of International Criminal Justice*, 5:2 (2007), 332.

Fenwick, Helen, 'The Reaction of Great Britain's Legal Order to September 11, 2001', in Bernd Rill (eds), *Terrorismus und Recht: Der wehrhafte Rechtsstaat* (Hanns Seidel Stiftung, 2003), 57 et seq.

Fikentscher, Wolfgang, *Methoden des Rechts in vergleichender Darstellung* (Tübingen: Mohr, 1977).

Fink-Hooijer, Florika, 'The Common Foreign and Security Policy of the European Union', *EJIL*, 5 (1994), 175.

Finnie, Wilson, 'Anti-Terrorist Legislation and the European Convention on Human Rights', *Modern Law Review*, 54:2 (1991), 288–93.

Fitzgerald, Peter, 'Managing "Smart Sanctions" against Terrorism Wisely', *New England Law Review*, 36 (2002), 957.

—— 'Compliance Issues Associated with Targeted Economic Sanctions', in House of Lords, Select Committee on Economic Affairs, 2nd Report of Session 2006–07, 'The Impact of Economic Sanctions', Vol II: Evidence (2007).

Forsyth, Christopher, 'Control Orders, Conditions Precedent and Compliance with Article 6(1)', *Cambridge Law Journal*, 67:1 (2008), 1–4.

Franchini, Claudio, 'European Principles Governing National Administrative Proceedings', *Law And Contemporary Problems*, 68:21 (2004), 183 et seq.

Franck, Thomas M, *The Power of Legitimacy Among Nations* (New York: Oxford University Press, 1990).

—— *Political Question/Judicial Answers* (Princeton, NJ: Princeton University Press, 1992), 31.

—— *Fairness in International Law and Institutions* (Oxford: Clarendon Press, 1995).

—— *The Empowered Self: Law and Society in the Age of Individualism* (New York: Oxford University Press, 1999).

—— 'Individuals and Groups of Individuals as Subjects in International Law', in Rainer Hofmann and Nils Geissler (eds), *Non-State Actors as New Subjects of International Law* (Berlin: Duncker & Humblot, 1999).

—— 'The International Judge and the Principled Imperative', in: *Weltinnenrecht: Liber amicorum Jost Delbrück* (Berlin: Duncker & Humblot, 2005), 267 et seq.

Frowein, Jochen, 'Implementation of Security Council Resolutions taken under Chapter VII in Germany', in Eibe Riedel (ed), *German Reports on Public Law* (Baden-Baden: Nomos, 2002).

Garbagnati Ketvel, Maria-Gisella, 'The Jurisdiction of the European Court of Justice in Respect of the Common Foreign and Security Policy', *ICLQ*, 55 (2006), 82.

Garde, Amadine, 'Is it Really for the European Community to Implement Anti-Terrorism UN Security Council Resolutions?', *Cambridge Law Journal*, 65/2 (2006), 281.

Garfield, Richard, 'Morbidity and Morality among Iraq's Children from 1990 to 1998: Assessing the Impact of Economic Sanctions', *Occasional Paper Series* University of Notre Dame, 16/3 (1999).

Gattini, Andrea, 'Joined Cases C-402/05 P & 415/05 P, Yassin Abdullah Kadi, Al Barakaat International Foundation v. Council and Commission, judgment of the Grand Chamber of 3 September 2008, nyr', *Common Market Law Review*, 46 (2009), 213–39.

Geck, Wilhelm Karl, 'Diplomatic Protection', in Rudolf Bernhardt (ed), *Encyclopedia of Public International Law*, vol I/2 (Max Planck Institute for Comparative Public Law, 1992).

Geiger, Rudolf, *Grundgesetz und Völkerrecht* (München: Beck, 2002).

Geiss, Robin, 'Humanitarian Safeguards in Economic Sanctions Regimes: A Call for Automatic Suspension Clauses, Periodic Monitoring, and Follow-Up Assessment of Long-Term Effects', *Harvard Human Rights Journal*, 18 (2005), 183.

Gerven, Walter van, 'The Effects of Proportionality on the Actions of Member States of the European Community: National Viewpoints from Continental Europe', in Evelyn Ellis, *The Principle of Proportionality in the Laws of Europe* (Oxford: Hart Publishing, 1999), 37 et seq.

Gill, Terry Douglas, 'Legal and Some Political Limitations of the Power of the UN Security Council to Exercise its Enforcement Powers under Chapter VII of the Charter', *Netherlands Yearbook of International Law* (1995), 33.

Giraldo, Jeanne K and Trinkunas, Harold A, *Terrorism Financing and State Responses: A Comparative Perspective* (Stanford University Press, 2007).

Goldsmith, Jack and Posner, Eric, *The Limits of International Law* (New York: Oxford University Press, 2005).

Golub, Jonathan, 'The Politics of Judicial Discretion: Rethinking the Interaction between National Courts and the European Court of Justice', *WEP*, 19 (1996), 360.

Goodrich, Leland M, Hambro, Edvard, and Simons, Anne Patricia (eds), *Charter of the United Nations: Commentary and Documents* (3rd ed, 1969).

Govaere, Inge, 'The *Supra*national Courts and the Application of Community Law: Positive and Negative Aspects', in Deisy Ventura (ed), *Direito Communitario do Mercosul* (Porto Alegre: Livraria do Advogado Editoria, 1997), 139.

—— Capiau, Jeroen and Vermeersch, An, 'In-Between Seats: The Participation of the European Union in International Organisations', *European Foreign Affairs Review*, 9 (2004), 155.

Gowlland-Debbas, Vera, 'Comments', in Harry Post (ed), *International Economic Law and Armed Conflict* (Dordrecht: Nijhoff, 1994), 163–73.

—— 'Sanctions Regimes under Article 41 of the UN Charter', in Vera Gowlland-Debbas (ed), *National Implementation of Non-Military Security Council Sanctions: A Comparative Study* (Leiden: Brill Publishers, 2004), 1–31.

—— (ed), *National Implementation of Non-Military Security Council Sanctions: A Comparative Study* (Leiden: Brill Publishers, 2004).

Graulich, Kurt (ed), *Terrorismus und Rechtsstaatlichkei: Analysen, Handlungsoptionen, Perspektiven*, Interdisziplinäre Arbeitsgruppen – Forschungsberichte, vol 17 (juro230; jurp905; jurp905; jurp106) (Berlin: Akademie-Verl, 2007).

Guild, Elspeth, 'Adjudicating Schengen: National Judicial Control in France', *European Journal of Migration and Law*, 1 (1999), 436.

Guillaume, HE Gilbert, 'Terrorism and International Law', Grotius Lecture at the British Institute of International and Comparative Law, 13 November 2003.

Gusy, Christoph, 'Richterliches Prüfungsrecht', *Juristenzeitung* (1989), 1003.

Gutherie, Peter, 'Security Council Sanctions and the Protection of Individual Rights', *NYU Ann Surv Am L*, 60 (2004), 491.

Habermas, Jürgen, *Faktizität und Geltung: Beiträge zur Diskurstheorie des Rechts und des demokratischen Rechtsstaats* (Frankfurt am Main: Suhrkamp, 1992); Eng trans as *Between facts and norms: contributions to a discourse theory of law and decmocracy*, tr William Rehg.

Hailbronner, Kay, 'The European Union from the Perspective of the German Constitutional Court', *GYIL*, 37 (1994), 93.

Halberstam, Daniel and Stein, Eric, 'The United Nations, the European Union, and the King of Sweden: Economic sanctions and individual rights in a plural world order', *Common Market Law Review*, 46 (2009), 13–72.

Happold, Matthew, 'Security Council Resolution 1373 and the Constitution of the United Nations', *Leiden Journal of International Law*, 16 (2003), 593.

Harpaz, Guy, 'The European Court of Justice and its Relations with the European Court of Human Rights: The quest for enhanced reliance, coherence and legitimacy', *Common Market Law Review*, 46 (2009), 105–41.

Hartley, Trevor, *Constitutional Problems of the European Union* (Oxford: Hart Publishing, 1999).

Hayek, Friedrich von, *The Road to Serfdom* (London: Routledge, 1944).

Heiskanen, Veijo, *International Legal Topics* (Helsinki: Finnish Lawyers' Publishing Company, 1992).

Hemke, Katja, *Methodik der Analogiebildung im öffentlichen Recht* (Berlin: Duncker & Humblot, 2006).

Henkin, Louis, *International Law: Politics and Values* (Dordrecht: Nijhoff, 1995).

—— Crawford Pugh, Richard, Schachter, Oscar and Smit, Hans, *International Law: Cases and Materials* (St Paul, Minn: West Publishing, 1993).

Herdegen, Matthias, 'Maastricht and the Constitutional Court: Constitutional Restraints for an Ever Closer Union', *CML Rev*, 31 (1994), 235.

Herik, Larissa van der and Schrijver, Nico, 'Section Two: Human Rights Concerns in Current Targeted Sanctions Regimes from the Perspective of International and European Law', in Thomas J Biersteker and Sue E Eckert, *Strengthening Targeted Sanctions Through Fair and Clear Procedures*, White Paper prepared by the Watson Institute Targeted Sanctions Project, Brown University, 30 March 2006, 26.

Herlin-Karnell, Ester, 'Commission v. Council: Some Reflections on Criminal Law in the First Pillar', *European Public Law*, 13:1 (2007), 69–84.

—— 'An Exercise in Effectiveness?', *European Business Law Review* (2007), 1181–91.

Hernández-López, Ernesto, '*Boumediene v. Bush* and Gantánamo: Cuba: Does the "Empire Strike Back"?', *SMU Law Rev*, 61 2009, 117–200.

Hess, Henner, 'Like Zealots and Romans: Terrorism and Empire in the 21st Century', *Crime, Law and Social Change*, 39 (2003), 339.

Hilf, Meinhard and Hörmann, Saskia, in Pierre-Marie Dupuy (ed), *Völkerrecht als Wertordnung: Festschrift für Christian Tomuschat: essays in honour of Christian Tomuschat* (NP Engel Verlag 2006).

Hinarejos Parga, Alicia, 'Bundesverfassungsgericht (German Constitutional Court), Decision of 18 July 2005 (2 BvR 2236/04) on the German European Arrest Warrant Law', *CML Rev*, 43 (2006), 583.

Hobe, Stephan, 'The German State in Europe after the Maastricht Decision of the German Constitutional Court', *GYIL*, 37 (1994), 113.

—— 'Individuals and Groups as Global Actors', in Rainer Hofmann and Nils Geissler (ed), *Non-State Actors as New Subjects of International Law* (Berlin: Duncker & Humblot, 1999).

Hoffmann-Becking, Gerhard, *Normaufbau und Methode. Eine Untersuchung zur Rechtsprechung des Gerichtshofs der Europäischen Gemeinschaften* (Tübingen: Mohr, 1973).

Hörmann, Saskia, 'Völkerrecht bricht Rechtsgemeinschaft? Zu den rechtlichen Folgen einer Umsetzung von Resolutionen des UN-Sicherheitsrates durch die EG', *AVR*, 44 (2006), 267.

House of Lords, Select Committee on Economic Affairs, 2nd Report of Session 2006–07, 'The Impact of Economic Sanctions', Vol I: Report, published 9 May 2007, Chapter 5: Targeted Financial Sanctions on Individuals and Groups; the United Nations, the IMF, the Swiss Federal Office for Foreign Economic Affairs.

Howell, John et al, 'The EU's Efforts in the Fight Against Terrorist Financing in the Context of the Financial Action Task Force's Nine Special Recommendations and the EU Counter Terrorist Financing Strategy', Final Report, 1 February 2007, Independent Scrutiny, European Commission Directorate-General Justice

Freedom and Security, http://ec.europa.eu/justice_home/doc_centre/terrorism/docs/report_01_02_07_with_appendix_en.pdf.

Hufbauer, Gary Clyde, Schott, Jeffrey J and Elliott, Kimberly Ann, *Economic Sanctions Reconsidered* (Washington DC: Peterson Institute, 1985).

Human Security Report Project, Simon Fraser University, Vancouver, *Human Security Brief 2007, Featuring A Special Report: Dying To Lose. Explaining The Decline In Global Terrorism*, see in particular Overview and Chapter 1, 1–21, http://www.humansecuritybrief.info/.

Jacobs, Francis Geoffrey, 'Is the Court of Justice of the European Communities a Constitutional Court?', in Deirdre Curtin and David O'Keeffe (eds), *Constitutional Adjudication in European Community and National Law* (Dublin: Butterworth, 1992).

—— 'Necessary Changes to the System of Judicial Remedies', Working Group II, Working Document 20 (2002), http://european-convention.eu.int/docs/wd2/3222.pdf.

—— 'The question of effective judicial remedies and access of individuals to the European Court of Justice', Working Group II, Working Document 21, (2002), http://european-convention.eu.int/docs/wd2/3299.pdf.

Jacqué, Jean-Paul, *Droit institutionnel de L'Union Européenne* (Paris: Dalloz, 2004).

Jasinski, Filip, 'EU Counter-Terrorist Policy after 11 March 2004', *The Polish Quarterly of International Affairs* (2004), 72.

Jennings, Robert and Watts, Arthur (eds), *Oppenheim's International Law*, vol I, Peace: Introduction and Part 1 (London: Longman, 1992).

Jørgensen, Nina H B, *The Responsibility of States for International Crimes* (Oxford: Oxford University Press, 2000).

Kaddous, Christine, 'L'arrêt France c. Commission de 1994 (accord concurrence) et le contrôle de «légalité» des accords externes en vertu de l'article 173 CE: la difficile réconciliation de l'orthodoxie communautaire avec l'orthodoxie internationale', *CDE* (1996), 629.

Karayigit, Mustafa, 'The Yusuf and Kadi Judgments: The Scope of the EC Competences in Respect of Restrictive Measures', *Legal Issues of Economic Integration*, 33 (2006), 393.

Kauff-Gazin, Fabienne, 'L'arrêt Bosphorus de la CEDH: quand le juge de Strasbourg décerne au système communautaire un label de protection satisfaisante des droits fondamentaux', *Les Petites Affiches* no 234 (2005), 13.

Keller, Helen and Forowicz, Magdalena, 'A Tightrope walk between Legality and Legitimacy: An analysis of the Israeli Supreme Court's judgment on targeted killing', Case Comment, *Leiden Journal of International Law* (2008).

Kelsen, Hans, 'The Pure Theory of Law', *Law Quarterly Review*, 50 (1934), 474, 477–85 and *Law Quarterly Review*, 51 (1935), 517–22.

—— *Was ist Gerechtigkeit?* (Ditzingen: Reclam, 2000).

Kirschbaum, Stanislav J (ed), *Terrorisme et sécurité internationale* (Brussels: Bruylant, 2004).

Klabbers, Jan, 'Presumptive Personality: The European Union in International Law', in Martti Koskenniemi (ed), *International Law Aspects of the European Union* (The Hague: Kluwer Law International, 1998), 231.

—— *An Introduction to International Institutional Law* (Cambridge: Cambridge University Press, 2002).

Kley-Struller, Andreas, *Art 6 EMRK als Rechtsschutzgarantie gegen die öffentliche Gewalt: Die aktuelle Praxis der Konventionsorgane zur Anwendung des Art 6 EMRK in der Verwaltungsrechtspflege* (Zürich: Schulthess, 1993).

Köck, Heribert Franz, 'On the Unity of European Law: European Law as a Separate Body of Law and as an Independent Subject of Legal Doctrine', in Jost Delbrück (ed), *New Trends in International Lawmaking: International 'Legislation' in the Public Interest* (Berlin: Duncker & Humblot, 1997).

Kokott, Juliane, 'German Constitutional Jurisprudence and European Integration II', *EPL*, 2 (1996), 413.

Komárek, Jan, 'European Constitutionalism and the European Arrest Warrant: In Search of the Limits of "Contrapunctual Principles"', *CMLRev* 44 (2007), 9–40.

Koskenniemi, Martti, 'The Place of Law in Collective Security', *Michigan Journal of International Law*, 17 (1995–96), 477.

—— and Leino, Päivi, 'Fragmentation of International Law? Postmodern Anxieties', *Leiden Journal of International Law*, 15 (2002), 553.

Kostakopoulou, Dora, 'How to do Things with Security Post 9/11', *Oxford Journal of Legal Studies*, 28:2 (2008), 317–42.

Kotzur, Markus, 'Eine Bewährungsprobe für die Europäische Grundrechtsgemeinschaft: Zur Entscheidung des EuG in der Rs Yusuf ua gegen Rat', *EuGRZ*, 33 (2006), 21.

Koutrakos, Panos, *Trade, Foreign Policy and Defence in EU Constitutional Law* (Oxford: Hart Publishing, 2001).

—— *EU International Relation Law* (Oxford: Hart Publishing, 2006).

Krajewski, Markus, 'Foreign Policy and the European Constitution', *YEL*, 23 (2004), 435.

Kramer, Sven, 'Demarcations and Exclusions: Terrorism, State Violence, and the Left in German Novels of 1970s and 1980s', in Robert Weninger (ed), *Gewalt und kulturelles Gedächtnis: Repräsentationsformen von Gewalt in Literatur und Film seit 1945* (Tübingen: Stauffenberg, 2005), 255–65.

Krenzler, Horst G and Schneider, Henning C, 'Die Gemeinsame Außen- und Sicherheitspolitik der Europäischen Union', *EuR* (1994), 144.

Krisch, Nico, 'The Rise and Fall of Collective Security: Terrorism, US Hegemony, and the Plight of the Security Council', in Christian Walter, Silja Vöneky, Volker Röben, and Frank Schokopf (eds), *Terrorism as a Challenge for National and International Law: Security versus Liberty?* (Berlin, Heidelberg: Springer 2003).

—— and Frowein, Jochen, 'Chapter VII: Action with respect to the Peace, Breaches of the Peace and Acts of Aggression. Introduction', in Bruno Simma (ed), *The Charter of the United Nations: A Commentary* (Oxford: Oxford University Press, 2002).

Kunoy, Bjørn and Dawes, Anthony, 'Plate Tectonics In Luxembourg: The Ménage À Trois Between Economic Law, International Law and the European Convention On Human Rights Following the UN Sanctions Cases', *Common Market Law Review*, 46 (2009), 73–104.

Lachmann, Per, 'The Treaty of Maastricht vs. the Danish Constitution', *Nordic Journal of International Law*, 67 (1998), 365.

Lavranos, Nikolaos, 'Concurrence of Jurisdiction between the ECJ and other International Courts and Tribunals', EUSA Ninth Biennial International Conference, 31 March– 2 April 2005, Austin, Texas, 30, http://aei.pitt.edu/3016/01/EUSA_paper_LAVRANOS_FINAL-1.txt.

—— 'The Scope of the Exclusive Jurisdiction of the Court of Justice' *ELR*, 32(1) (2007), 84.

—— 'UN Sanctions and Judicial Review', *Nordic Journal of International Law*, 76 (2007), 12.

Leigh, Ian, 'National Legal Dimension of the Democratic Control of the Security Sector: Values and Standards in Developed Democracies', 2006, http://www.dcaf.ch/.

Lenaerts, Koen and Smijter, Eddy de, 'The EU as an Actor under International Law', *YEL*, 19 (1999–2000), 97.

Liivoja, Rain, 'The Scope of the Supremacy Clause of the United Nations Charter', *ICLQ*, 57 (2008), 583–612.

Limbach, Jutta, 'Human Rights in Times of Terror: Is Collective Security the Enemy of Individual Freedom?', *Göttingen Journal of International Law*, 1 (2009), 23.

Llorente, Francisco Rubio, 'Mostrar los derechos sin destruir la Unión', in: Eduardo García de Enterría and Ricardo Alonso García (eds), *La encrucijada constitucional de la Unión Europea* (Madrid: Civitas, 2002), 113–50.

Lorinser, Barbara, *Bindende Resolutionen des Sicherheitsrates* (Baden-Baden: Nomos, 1996).

Loughlin, John P and Aja, Eliseo (eds), *Subnational Democracy in the European Union: Challenges and Opportunities* (Oxford: Oxford University Press, 2001).

Lutter, Marcus, 'Die Auslegung angeglichenen Rechts', *Juristenzeitung* (1992), 599.

Lysén, Göran, 'Targeted UN Sanctions: On the Issue of Legal Sources and their Application and also some Procedural Matters', Swedish Institute of International Law, Uppsala University, 2003, http://www-hotel.uu.se/webbtjanster/hotell.php.

—— *Att Studera Folkrätt och EG/EU* (Uppsala: Iustus, 2005).

MacLeod, Iain, Hendry, Ian and Hyett, Stephen, *The External Relations of the European Communities* (Oxford: Clarendon Press, 1996).

Malanczuk, Peter, *Akehurst's Modern Introduction to International Law* (London: Routledge, 1997).

Malloy, Michael, *United States Economic Sanction: Theory and Practice* (The Hague: Kluwer Law International, 2001).

Martenczuk, Bernd, 'The Security Council, the International Court and Judicial Review: What Lessons to Learn from Lockerbie?', *EJIL*, 10 (1999), 517.

Martin, Lisa L and Laurenti, Jeffrey, *The United Nations and Economic Sanctions: Improving Regime Effectiveness* (New York: United Nations Association of the United States of America, 1997).

Martinez, Luis Hinojosa, 'Las Sanciones del Consejo de Seguridad Contra al Qaeda y los Talibanes: ¿Son realmente inteligentes?', REDI, vol LVIII (2006), 756.

Marty, Dick, 'Report of the Committee on Legal Affairs and Human Rights to the Council of Europe', Document 11454, of 16 November 2007.

Maslaton, Matthias, *Notstandsklauseln im regionalen Menschenrechtsschutz: Eine vergleichende Untersuchung der Artikel 15 EMRK and 27 AMRK* (Frankfurt am Main: Peter Lang, 2002).

Maunz, Theodor, Düring, Günter und Herzog, Roman, *Kommentar zum Grundgesetz* (München: Beck Verlag, 2005).

McBride, Jeremy, 'Proportionality and the European Convention on Human Rights', in: Evelyn Ellis, *The Principle of Proportionality in the Laws of Europe* (Oxford: Hart Publishing, 1999), 23 et seq.

McGhee, Derek, 'Deportation, Detention & Torture by Proxy: Foreign National Terror Suspects in the UK', *Liverpool Law Journal* 29 (2008), 99–115.

McGoldrick, Dominic, *International Relations Law of the European Union* (London: Longman, 1997).

Meerpohl, Thomas, *Individualsanktionen des Sicherheitsrates der Vereinten Nationen: Das Sanktionsregime gegen die Taliban und Al-Qaida vor dem Hintergrund des Rechts der VN und der Menschenrechte* (München: Herbert Utz Verlag, 2008).

Meessen, Karl M, 'The Application of Rules of Public International Law within Community Law', *CML Rev*, 13 (1976), 485.

Mendes, Joana, 'Participation and Participation Right in EU Law and Governance', in Herwig Hofmann and Alexander Türk (eds), *The Move to an Integrated Administration: Legal Challenges in EU Administrative Law* (Cheltenham: Edward Elgar, 2008).

Meron, Theodor, *The Humanization of International Law* (Leiden: Brill Publishers, 2006).

Meyer, Frank, 'Lost in Complexity: Rechtsschutz gegen Smart Sanctions in der EU', *ZEuS* (2007).

Milano, Enrico, 'Diplomatic Protection and Human Rights Before the International Court of Justice: Re-Fashioning Tradition?', *NYIL* (2004), 85.

Miller, Elin, 'The Use of Targeted Sanctions in the Fight Against International Terrorism: What about Human Rights?', in American Society of International Law, *An Imperial Security Council? Implementing Security Council Resolutions 1373 and 1390. Proceedings of the Annual Meeting* (Washington DC: American Society of International Law, 2003), vol 97, 41.

Mitsilegas, Valsamis and Gilmore, Bill, 'The EU legislative framework against money laundering and terrorist finance: a critical analysis in the light of evolving global standards', *International and Comparative Law Quarterly* 56 (2007), 119–41.

Möllers, Christoph, 'Das EuG konstitutionalisiert die Vereinten Nationen', *Europarecht*, 3 (2006), 426.

—— 'European Governance: Meaning and Value of a Concept', *CML Rev*, 43 (2006), 313.

Monar, Jörg, 'Common Threat and Common Response? The European Union's Counter-Terrorism Strategy and its Problems', *Government and Opposition*, 42.3 (2007), 292–313.

Moran, Jon, 'State power in the war on terror: A comparative analysis of the UK and USA', *Crime, Law & Social Change*, 44 (2005) 335–59.

Müller, Erwin (ed), *Die Europäische Union im Kampf gegen den Terrorismus: Sicherheit vs. Freiheit?* (Baden-Baden: Nomos, 2006).

Müller-Wille, Björn, 'The Effect of International Terrorism on EU Intelligence Co-operation', Journal of Common Market Studies, 46.1 (2008) 49–73.

Murphy, James M, *Sanctions in Transition* (London: David Davies Memorial Institute of International Studies, 2000).

Naske, Nina and Nolte, Georg, '"Aerial Security Law." Case No. 1 BvR 357/05. 115 BVerfGE 118', *American Journal of International Law*, vol 101, No. 2 (Apr 2007), 466–71.

National Commission on Terrorist Attacks on the United States, 'The 9/11 Commission Report', http://www.9-11commission.gov/report/911Report.pdf.

Nehl, Hanns Peter, *Principles of Administrative Procedure in EC Law* (Oxford: Hart Publishing, 1999).

Nettesheim, Martin, 'UN Sanctions Against Individuals: A Challenge to the Architecture of European Union Governance', *CML Rev*, 44 (2007), 567.

Neuwahl, Nanette and Rosas, Allan (eds), *The European Union and Human Rights* (Martinus Nijhoff Publishers, The Hague, 1995).

Niblett, Robin, and Mix, Derek, 'Transatlantic Approaches to Sanctions: Principles and Recommendations for Action', October 2006, (available at: http://www.csis.org/).

Nkala, Jericho, *The United Nations, International Law and the Rhodesia Independence Crisis* (Oxford: Clarendon Press, 1985).

O'Boyle, Harris and Warbrick, Colin, *Law of the European Convention on Human Rights* (London: Butterworths, 1995).

O'Brian, John Lord, *National Security and Individual Freedom* (Cambridge: Harvard University Press, 1955).

O'Connell, Mary Ellen, *International Law and the 'Global War on Terror'*, Cours et travaux/Institut des Hautes Etudes Internationales de Paris (Paris: Pedone, 2007).

Oeter, Stefan, 'Terrorismus und Menschenrechte', *AVR*, 40 (2002), 424.

Oette, Lutz 'A Decade of Sanctions against Iraq: Never Again! The End of Unlimited Sanctions in the Recent Practice of the UN Security Council', *EJIL*, 13 (2002), 93.

Ohler, Christoph, 'Die Verhängung von smart sanctions durch den UN-Sicherheitsrat: Eine Herausforderung für das Gemeinschaftsrecht', *EuR* (2006).

Olivier, Clementine, 'Human Rights Law and International Fight against Terrorism: Could Security Council Regulations Impact on States' Obligations under International Human Right Law?', *NJIL*, 73 (2004), 410.

Opi, Sergio Baches and Floyd, Ryan, 'A Shaky Pillar of Global Stability: The Evolution of the European Union's Common Foreign and Security Policy', *Columbian Journal of European Law*, 9 (2003), 300.

Orakhelashvili, Alexander, 'The Impact of Peremptory Norms on the Interpretation and Application of United Nations Security Council Resolutions', *EJIL*, 16 (2005), 86.

Ortino, Federico *Basic Legal Instruments for the Liberalisation of Trade* (Oxford: Hart Publishing, 2004).

Osteneck, Kathrin, *Die Umsetzung von UN-Wirtschaftssanktionen durch die Europäische Gemeinschaft* (Berlin: Springer-Verlag, 2004).

Österdahl, Inger, *Threat to the Peace* (Uppsala: Iustus, 1998).

Ovey, Clare and White, Robin CA, *Jacobs and White: The European Convention on Human Rights* (Oxford: Oxford University Press, 2002).

Paasivirta, Esa, 'Human Rights, Diplomacy and Sanctions: Aspects to "Human Rights Clauses" in the External Agreements of the European Union', in Jarna Petman and Jan Klabbers (eds), *Nordic Cosmopolitanism: Essays in International Law for Martti Koskenniemi* (Boston, Mass: Nijhoff, 2003), 174.

Parker, Richard W, 'The Problem with Scorecards: How (and How not) to Measure the Cost-Effectiveness of Economic Sanctions', *Michigan Journal of International Law*, 21/2 (2000), 235.

Paulus, Andreas, *Die internationale Gemeinschaft im Völkerrecht: Eine Untersuchung zur Entwicklung des Völkerrechts im Zeitalter der Globalisierung* (München: Beck, 2001).

Pavoni, Riccardo, 'UN Sanctions in EU and National Law: The Centro Com Case', *ICLQ*, 48 (1999), 582.

Payandeh, Mehrdad, 'Rechtskontrolle des UN-Sicherheitsrates durch staatliche und überstaatliche Gerichte', *Zeitschrift für Ausländisches Öffentliches Recht und Völkerrecht*, 66 (2006), 41.

Peers, Steve, 'EU Responses to terrorism', *International and Comparative Law Quarterly* 52 (2003), 227–43.

Pernice, Ingolf, 'Multilevel Constitutionalism and the Treaty of Amsterdam: European Constitution-Making Revisited?', *CML Rev*, 36 (1999), 703.

Pernice, Ingolf, 'Art. 24, 32 GG', in Horst Dreier (ed), *Grundgesetz Kommentar* (Commentary on the German Basic Law), vol II (Tübingen: Mohr Siebeck, 2004).

Pescatore, Pierre, 'External Relations in the Case-Law of the Court of Justice of the European Communities', *CML Rev*, 16 (1979), 615.

—— 'Opinion 1/94 on "Conclusion" of the WTO Agreement: Is there an Escape from a Programmed Disaster?', *CML Rev*, 36 (1999), 387.

Peters, Anne, 'Global Constitutionalism in a Nutshell', in: Dicke, Klaus, Hobe, Stephan, Meyn, Karl-Ulrich, Peters, Anne, Riedel, Eibe, Schütz, Hans-Joachim, Tietje, Christian (eds), *Weltinnenrecht, Liber amicorum Jost Delbrück*, (Berlin: Duncker & Humblot, 2005).

Petersman, Ernst-Ulrich, 'Darf die EG das Völkerrecht ignorieren?', *EuZW* (1997), 325.

Poole, Thomas, 'Harnessing the Power of the Past? Lord Hoffmann and the Belmarsh Detainees Case', *Journal of Law and Society*, Vol 32.4 (2005), 534–61.

Poole, Thomas, 'Courts and conditions of uncertainty in "times of crisis" ', *Public Law* (2008), 234–59.

Portela, Clara, 'The Efficacy of Sanctions of the European Union: When and why do they work?' EUI Florence, unpublished PhD dissertation, 2008.

Powell, Rhonda Louise, 'The Right to Security of Person in European Court of Human Rights Jurisprudence', *European Human Rights Law Review*, 6 (2007), 649 et seq.

Prantl, Heribert, *Der Terrorist als Gesetzgeber. Wie man mit Angst Politik macht* (Droemer Knaur, 2008).

Prechal, Sacha, 'Does Direct Effect Still Matter?', *CML Rev*, 37 (2000), 1047.

Rabinowitz, Itai, *The Fundamental Right to Be Heard in the Administrative Procedures of the European Union*, unpublished PhD at King's College London awarded on 1 August 2008.

Ragolle, Filip, 'Access to Justice for Private Applicants in the Community Legal Order: Recent (R)Evolutions', *ELR*, 29 (2003), 90.

Rausch, Rolf, *Die Kontrolle von Tatsachenfeststellungen und -würdigungen durch den Gerichtshof der Europäischen Gemeinschaften* (Berlin: Duncker & Humblot, 1994).

Raz, Joseph, 'The Rule of Law and its Virtue', in *The Authority of Law: Essays on Law and Morality* (Oxford: Oxford University Press, 1979).

Recker, Sebastian, 'European Court of Justice Secures Fundamental Rights from UN Security Council Resolutions', *Göttingen Journal of International Law* 1 (2009), 159–78.

Reid, Karen, *A Practitioners Guide to the ECHR* (London: Thomson/Sweet & Maxwell, 2004).

Reinisch, August, 'The Action of the European Union to Combat International Terrorism' in: Bianchi, Andrea (ed), *Enforcing International Law Norms Against Terrorism* (Oxford: Hart Publishing, 2004), 119 et seq.

Reisman, Michael, 'The Constitutional Crisis in the United Nations', *AJIL*, 87 (1993), 83.

Richardson, Louise, *What Terrorists Want: Understanding the Enemy, Containing the Threat* (Random House, 2006).

Rigaux, François, 'Hans Kelsen on International Law', *EJIL*, 9 (1989), 325.

Rosand, Eric, 'The Security Council's Efforts to Monitor the Implementation of Al Qaeda/Taliban Sanctions', *AJIL*, 98 (2004), 749.

Ruge, Reinhard, 'Between Law and Necessity: The Federal Constitutional Court Confirms the Right of the Federal Government to Warn the Public', *German Law Journal* (2002).

Rummel, Reinhardt and Wiedemann, Jörg, 'Identifying Institutional Paradoxes of CFSP', *EUI Working Paper RSC* No 97/67 (1997).

Russell, Meg and Sciara, Maria, 'The Policy Impact of Defeats in the House of Lords', *BJPIR* 10 (2008), 571–589.

Santulli, Carlo, *Le statut international de l'ordre juridique étatique: étude du traitement du droit interne par le droit international* (Paris: Pedone, 2001).

Sari, Aurel, 'Jurisdiction and international responsibility in peace support operations: the Behrami and Saramati cases', *Human Rights Law Review* 8 (2008), 151–70.

Sarooshi, Danesh, *The United Nations and the Development of Collective Security: The Delegation by the UN Security Council of its Chapter VII Powers* (Oxford: Oxford University Press, 1999).

Schabas, William A, *Introduction to the International Criminal Court* (Cambridge: Cambridge University Press, 2007).

Scharpf, Fritz W, 'Reflections on Multilevel Legitimacy', *Max-Planck-Institut für Gesellschaftsforschung Working Paper* 07/3 (2007).

Schermers, Henry, 'Community Law and International Law', *CML Rev*, 12 (1975), 77.

—— and Waelbroeck, Denis, *Judicial Protection in the European Union* (The Hague: Kluwer Law International, 2001).

Schilling, Theodor, 'Die "neue Weltordnung" und die Souveränität der Mitglieder der Vereinten Nationen', *AVR* (1995).

Schmalenbach, Kirsten, 'Der internationale Terrorismus: Ein Definitionsversuch', *NZWehrR*, 42 (2000), 15.

—— 'Terrorismus: Der Vorrang des UN-Rechts vor EU-Recht', *Juristenzeitung* (2006), 352.

Schmid, Evelyne, 'The Right to a Fair Trial in Times of Terrorism: A Method to Identify the Non-Derogable Aspects of Article 14 of the International Covenant on Civil and Political Rights', *Göttingen Journal of International Law*, 1 (2009), 29–44.

Schneckener, Ulrich (ed), *Chancen und Grenzen multilateraler Terrorismusbekämpfung* (Berlin: Stiftung Wiss. und Politik, Dt Inst für Internat. Politik und Sicherheit, 2007) (33: sozr511.s358).

Schoch, Friedrich, 'Staatliche Informationspolitik und Berufsfreiheit', *Deutsches Verwaltungsblatt* (1991), 667.

Schondorf, S, 'The Targeted Killings Judgment: A Preliminary Assessment', *Journal of International Criminal Justice*, 5.2 (2007) 301 et seq.

Schütze, Robert, 'Organized Change towards an "Ever Closer Union": Article 308 EC and the Limits to the Community's Legislative Competence', *YEL*, 22 (2003), 79.

Schwarze, Jürgen, *European Administrative Law* (London: Sweet & Maxwell, 1992).

—— 'The Procedural Guarantees in the Recent Case-Law of the European Community', in Deirdre Curtin and Ton Heukels (eds), *Institutional Dynamics of European Integration: Essays in Honour of Henry G Schermers* (Dordrecht: Nijhoff, 1994), 488.

Schwarzenberger, Georg, *International Law as Applied by International Courts and Tribunals*, vol II, The Law of Armed Conflict (London: Stevens, 1968).

Schweigmann, David, *The Authority of the Security Council under Chapter VII of the UN Charter: Legal Limits and the Role of the International Court of Justice* (Berlin: Springer, 2001).

Shah, Sangeeta, 'The UK's Anti-Terror Legislation and the House of Lords: The First Skirmish', *Human Rights Law Review*, 5 (2005), 403–21.

—— 'The UK's Anti-Terror Legislation and the House of Lords: The Battle Continues', *Human Rights Law Review* 6:2 (2006), 416–34.

—— 'Seeking Remedies for Violations of International Humanitarian Law: Markovic v Italy', *Human Rights Law Review*, 7 (2007), 417.

Shaw, Jo, 'Postnational Constitutionalism in the European Union', *Journal of European Public Policy*, 6 (1999), 579.

Shaw, Malcolm, *International Law* (Cambridge: Cambridge University Press, 5th ed, 2003).

Shelton, Dinah, 'International Law and "Relative Normativity"', in Evans, Malcolm (ed), *International Law* (Oxford: Oxford University Press, 2nd ed, 2006).

Simma, Bruno (ed), *The Charter of the United Nations: A Commentary* (Oxford: Oxford University Press, 2002).

Slaughter, Anne-Marie, 'Rogue Regimes and the Individualization of International Law', *New England Law Review*, 36 (2002), 815.

Sliedregt, Elisabeth van, *The Criminal Responsibility of Individuals for Violations of International Humanitarian Law* (The Hague: TMC Asser Press, 2003).

Snyder, Francis, 'Institutional Development in the European Union: Some implications of the Third Pillar', in Joerg Monar and Roger Morgan (eds), *The Third Pillar of the European Union* (Brussels: European Interuniversity Press, 1995), 85.

Sorel, Jean-Marc, 'Some Questions About the Definition of Terrorism and the Fight Against Its Financing', *EJIL*, 14 (2003), 366.

Sottiaux, Stefan *Review of Terrorism and the Limitation of Rights: The ECHR and the US Constitution* (Oxford, UK: Hart Publishing, 2008).

Spiegel (Hamburg: Spiegel-Verlag), issue no 14/2006.

The Stanley Foundation, 'The United Nations and Multilateral Sanctions: New Options of US Policy?', Report of the 33rd Strategy for Peace, US Foreign Policy Conference, 22–24 October 1992.

Starmer, Keir, 'European Human Rights Law: The Human Rights Act 1998 and the European Convention of Human Rights' (London: Legal Action Group, 1999).

Statens Öffentliga Utredninga, *Internatinalla Sanktioner: Betänkande av Sanktionslagutredningen* (Stockholm: SOU, 2006).

Stein, Eric, 'Collective Enforcement of International Organisations', *Zeitschrift für ausländisches öffentliches Recht und Völkerrecht*, 47 (1987).

—— 'Application and Enforcement of International Organization Law by National Authorities and Courts', in Stephen Schwebel (ed), *The Effectiveness of International Decisions* (Leyden: Sijthoff, 1971), 68.

Stein, Torsten, 'Außerpolitisch motivierte (Wirtschafts-)Sanktionen der Europäischen Union: Nach wie vor eine rechtliche Grauzone', in Ulrich Beyerlin, Michael Bothe, Rainer Hofmann and Ernst-Ulrich Petersmann (eds), *Recht zwischen Umbruch und Bewahrung. Festschrift für R Bernhardt* (Berlin: Springer 1995), 1129.

Stenhammar, Fredrik, 'Swedish State Practice 2004–05: United Nations Targeted Sanctions', *Nordic Journal of International Law*, 75 (2006), 317.

Stessens, Guy, 'The Principle of Mutual Confidence between Judicial Authorities in the Area of Freedom, Justice and Security', in Gilles de Kerchove and Anne Weyembergh (eds), *L'espace pénal européen: enjeux et perspectives* (Brussels: ULB 2002), 93–103.

Steyn, Johan, 'Guantanamo Bay: The Legal Hole', *ICLQ* 53 (2004), 1–15.

Stone Sweet, Alec, *The Judicial Construction of Europe* (Oxford: Oxford University Press, 2004).

Strömholm, Stig, *Rätt, rättskällor och rättstillämpning* (Stockholm: Norstedts Juridik, 1996).

Suy, Erik, 'Unilateral Acts of States as a Source of International Law: some New Thoughts and Frustrations', in: Olivier Corten (ed), *Droit du pouvoir, pouvoir du droit: mélanges offerts à Jean Salmon* (2007), 631–42.

Swart, Bert, 'Human Rights and the Abolition of Traditional Principles', in: Albin Eser and Otto Lagony (eds), *Principles and Procedures for a New Transnational*

Criminal Law: Documentation of an International Workshop in Freiburg (Freiburg i Br: Max-Planck-Institut für Ausländisches und Internationales Strafrecht, 1992), 505.

Szasz, Paul C, 'Notes and Comments: The Security Council starts Legislating', *AJIL*, 96 (2002), 901.

Tappeiner, Imelda, 'The Fight against Terrorism: The Lists and the Gaps', *Utrecht Law Review*, 1 (2005), 97.

Taylor, Paul, 'The New Dynamics of EC Integration in the 1980s', in Juliet Lodge (ed), *The European Community and the Challenge of the Future* (London: Pinter, 1989), 3.

Temple Lang, John, 'Actions for Declarations that Community Regulations are Invalid: The Duties of National Courts under Article 10 EC', *ELR*, 28 (2003), 102.

Tesauro, Guiseppe, 'The Effectiveness of Judicial Protection and Co-operation between the Court of Justice and the National Courts', *YEL* (1993), 1.

Thies, Anne, 'Biret and beyond: The status of WTO rulings in EC Law', *CML Rev*, 41 (2004), 1661.

—— 'Case annotation on the judgements of 14 December 2005, Court of First Instance in Cases T-69/00, T-151/00, T-301/00, T-320/00, T-383/00 and T-135/01 FIAMM et al.', *CML Rev*, *43* (2006), 1145.

Thony, Jean-Francis and Png, Cheong-Ann 'FATF Special Recommendations and UN Resolutions on the Financing of Terrorism: A Review of the Status of Implementation and Legal Challenges faced by Countries', *Journal of Financial Crime*, vol 14(2) (2007), 150–69.

Thym, Daniel, 'Beyond Parliament's Reach? The Role of the European Parliament in the CFSP', *European Foreign Affairs Review*, 11 (2006), 113.

Tietje, Christian and Hamelmann, Sandy, 'Gezielte Finanzsanktionen der Vereinten Nationen im Spannungsverhältnis zum Gemeinschaftsrecht und zu Menschenrechten', *JuS* (2006), 299.

Timmermans, Christiaan, The Constitutionalization of the European Union', 31 *Yearbook of European Law* (2001–02), 1.

Tobler, Christa, 'Case C-176/03, Commission v Council, Judgement of the Grand Chamber of 13 September 2005, nyr, Commentary', *CML Rev*, 43 (2006), 840.

Tomuschat, Christian, 'Peace Enforcement and Law Enforcement: Two Separate Chapters of International Law?', in *Studi di diritto internazionale in onore di Gaetano Arangio-Ruiz* (Napoli: Editoriale Scientifica, 2004).

—— 'Case law: Case T-306/01, Ahmed Ali Yusuf and Al Barakaat International Foundation v Council and Commission, Judgment of the Court of First Instance of 21 September 2005; Case T-315/01, Yassin Abdullah Kadi v. Council and Commission, judgment of the Court of First Instance of 21 September 2005, nyr', *CML Rev*, 43 (2006), 537.

Tomuschat, Christian, Internationale Terrorismusbekämpfung als Herausforderung für das Völkerrecht', Vortrag anlässlich der Eröffnung des Wintersemesters 2005/2006, Speyer, 15. November 2005, Speyer, Deutsche Hochschule für Verwaltungswissenschaften 2006.

Tranholm-Mikkelsen, Jeppe, 'Neo-Functionalism: Obstinate or Obsolete? A Reappraisal in the Light of the New Dynamism of the EC', *Millennium*, 20 (1991), 1.

Tridimas, Takis, 'Knocking on Heaven's Door: Fragmentation, Efficiency and Defiance in the Preliminary Reference Procedure', *CML Rev*, 40 (2003), 9.

—— *General Principles of EU Law* (Oxford: Oxford University Press, 2nd ed, 2006).

—— and Eeckhout, Piet, 'The External Competence of the Community and the Case-Law of the Court of Justice: Principle versus Pragmatism', *YEL*, 14 (1995), 143.

—— and Gutierrez-Fons, Jose A, 'EU Law, International Law and Economic Sanctions Against Terrorism: The Judiciary in Distress?', *Fordham International Law Journal* (2009).

Turpin, Colin and Tomkins, Adam, *British Government and the Constitution* (New York: Cambridge University Press, 6th ed, 2007).

Uerpmann, Robert, 'International Law as an Element of European Constitutional Law: International Supplementary Constitutions', *Jean Monnet Working Papers* 9/03 (2003), http://www.jeanmonnetprogram.org/papers/03/030901-02.html.

—— 'Internationales Verfassungsrecht', *Juristenzeitung*, 56 (2001), 565.

Usher, John, 'Direct and Individual Concern: An Effective Remedy or a Conventional Solution?', *ELR*, 28 (2003), 575.

Vennemann, Nicola, 'Country Report on the EU', in Christian Walter, Silja Vöneky, Volker Röben and F Schorkopf (eds), *Terrorism as a challenge for national and international law: security versus liberty?*, Beiträge zum ausländischen öffentlichen Recht und Völkerrecht, vol 169 (Berlin: Springer, 2004).

Verdugo-Yepes, Concepcion, 'Enhancing International Cooperation in the Fight Against the Financing of Terrorism', *Journal of Global Change and Governance*, vol I, No 3 (2008).

Verhoeven, Joe, 'Souveraineté et mondialisation: Libres propos', in Eric Loquin and Catherine Kessedjian (eds), *La mondialisation du droit* (Paris: Litec, 2000).

Vervaele, John A E, 'Terrorism and information sharing between the intelligence and law enforcement communities in the US and the Netherlands: emergency criminal law?', *Utrecth Law Review*, vol 1.1 (2005), available at: http://www.utrechtlawreview.org/.

Vitzthum, Nikolaus Graf, 'Les compétences législatives et juridictionnelles de la Communauté européenne dans la lutte contre le terrorisme – l'affaire « Kadi »', *ZEuS* (2008), 375–429.

Vitzthum, Wolfgang Graf, 'Article 2(6)' in: Bruno Simma (ed), *The Charter of the United Nations: A Commentary* (Oxford: Oxford University Press, 2002).
Waelbroeck, Denis, 'Editorial: Le droit au recours juridictionnel effectif du particulier. Trois pas en avant, deux pas en arrière', *Cahiers de Droit Européen*, 38 (2002), 3.
Walker, Clive, 'Clamping Down on Terrorism in the United Kingdom', *Journal of International Criminal Justice* 4 (2006), 1137–51.
Warbrick, Colin, 'The Principles of the European Convention on Human Rights and the Response of States to Terrorism', *EHRLR* (2002), 287.
Ward, Angela, *Judicial Review and the Rights of Private Parties in EC Law* (Oxford: Oxford University Press, 2000).
—— 'National and EC Remedies under the EU Treaty', in: Catherine Barnard and Okeoghene Odudu (eds), *The Outer Limits of European Union Law* (Oxford: Hart Publishing, 2009).
Ward, Curtis A, 'The CTC and Targeted Sanctions', in Peter Wallensteen and Carina Staibano (ed), *International Sanctions: Between Words and Wars in the Global System* (London: Routledge, 2005), 167.
Watson, Geoffrey R, 'Constitutionalism, Judicial Review, and the World Court', *Harvard International Law Journal*, 34 (1993), 1–45.
Watson, JS, 'State Consent and the Sources of International Obligation', *Proceedings of the American Society of International Law* (1992), 108 et seq.
Watts, Arthur, 'The International Rule of Law', *GYIL*, 36 (1993), 15.
Wedgewood, Ruth, 'Responding to Terrorism: The Strikes against Bin Laden', *YJIL*, 24 (1999), 559.
Wennerström, Erik, *The Rule of Law and the European Union* (Uppsala: Iustus, 2007).
Wessel, Ramses A, 'The UN, The EU And Jus Cogens', *International Organizations Law Review*, 3 (2006), 1–6.
Wessel, Ramses, 'Good Governance and EU Foreign Security and Defence Policy', *CES Working Paper*, No 2/04 (2004).
Wet, Erika de, 'Human Rights Limitations to Economic Enforcement Measures under Article 41 of the United Nations Charter and the Iraqi Sanctions Regime', *Leiden Journal of International Law*, 14 (2001), 278.
—— *The Chapter VII Powers of the United Nations Security Council* (Oxford: Hart Publishing, 2004).
—— 'The International Constitutional Order', *International and Comparative Law Quarterly*, 55 (2006), 51 et seq.
—— and Nollkaemper, André, 'Review of Security Council Decisions by National Courts', *GYIL*, 45 (2002), 166.
—— (eds), *Review of the Security Council by Member States* (Antwerp: Intersentia, 2003).

Wet, Erika de and Nollkaemper, André, 'Review of the Security Council by Member States', in Vera Gowlland-Debbas (ed), *National Implementation of Non-Military Security Council Sanctions: A Comparative Study* (Leiden: Brill Publishers, 2004).

Wieland, Joachim, 'Germany in the European Union: The Maastricht Decision of the Bundesverfassungsgericht', *EJIL*, 5 (1994), 259.

Witte, Bruno de, 'The Pillar Structure and the Nature of the European Union: Greek Temple or French Gothic Cathedral?', in Ton Heukels, Niels Blokker and Marcel Brus (eds), *The European Union after Amsterdam* (The Hague: Kluwer Law International, 1998), 66.

Woods, Lorna, 'The European Union and Human Rights', in: Raija Hanski and Markku Suksi (eds), *An Introduction to the International Protection of Human Rights: A Textbook* (Turku/Åbo: Åbo Akademi University, Institute for Human Rights, 1999), 283–300.

Wouters, Jan and Naert, Frederik, 'Of Arrest Warrants, Terrorist Offences and Extradition Deals: An Appraisal of the EU's Main Criminal Law Measures against Terrorism after "11 September" ', *CML Rev* 41 (2004), 909–35.

Wyngaert, Christine van den, 'Rethinking the Law of International Criminal Cooperation: Restrictive Function of International Human Rights Through Individual-Oriented Bars', in Albin Eser and Otto Lagony (eds), *Principles and Procedures for a New Transnational Criminal Law: Documentation of an International Workshop in Freiburg*, May 1991 (Freiburg i. Br.: Max-Planck-Institut für Ausländisches und Internationales Strafrecht, 1992), 491.

Yearbook of the International Law Commission (1979), Vol II, Part One.

Zagel, Gudrun Monika, 'Article 301 TEC (Economic Sanctions)', in Hans Smit and Peter E Herzog, *Law of the European Union – a Commentary* (New York: LexisNexis, 2006).

Zöller, Verena, 'Liberty Dies by Inches: German Counter-Terrorism Measures and Human Rights', *German Law Journal* 5.5 (2004), 469.

INDEX

9/11
effect on counter-terrorist measures, 1
general call to fight terrorism, 37
globalisation of fight against terrorism, 57
UN resolutions following attacks, 26

Access to information
autonomous European sanctions, 320–1
European sanctions based on UN lists, 391–3
improvements to European sanctions regime, 375–7
non-disclosure of evidence, 197–200
publication of first list by UN Security Council, 26
role of judiciary, 399
statement of reasons, 322–4, 354–6
UN listings published on internet, 29

Access to justice. *see also* **Fair trial**
alternative interpretations of the rule of law, 130–1
Article 6 ECHR, 139–80
EU's commitment to rule of law
case law of the ECJ, 129–30
European Treaties, 132–3
guarantees under ECHR, 131–2
EU law, 183–4
fair trial
administrative measures, 140–1
applicability to civil and criminal cases, 140
civil rights and obligations, 166–80
criminal charges, 150–65
effective remedy distinguished, 138–9
international cooperation, 145–9
political question doctrine, 141–5
provisional measures, 170, 174–5, 375
unrestrictive interpretation, 139
general recognition, 183–4
relevance of ECHR to EU law, 133–8
right to effective remedy
applicability, 180–3
fair trial distinguished, 138–9

Administrative measures, 140–1

Adoption procedure. *see also* **Listing practice**
autonomous European sanctions, 22–3, 47–51
Commission, role in adoption procedure, 43–4
competence to adopt Community sanctions, 81–100
Council, role in adoption procedure, 47–51, 80, 82
double-staged administrative procedure, 309–310, 314–6, 322
effect on pillar division, 107, 110–2
need for change, 380–6, 418
Proposed changes
access to information, 391–3
identification of terrorists, 386–7
institutional changes to listing procedure, 383–4
legislative changes to listing procedure, 380–3
procedural changes to listing procedure, 384–6
reviewable listing criteria, 387–391
reform of the autonomous sanctions regime, 375–80
sanctions giving effect to UN lists, 44–6
sanctions giving effect to Union lists, 46–52
state and individual sanctions distinguished, 20–1

Al-Qaida
criteria for listing, 27–8
effectiveness of asset freezing, 72–3
first UN Security Council list, 26
reasons for listing published on internet, 29
review of freezing order by national courts, 291
role of UN Sanctions Committee, 15
state and individual sanctions distinguished, 20–1
Taliban distinguished, 86–7

Al-Qaida (cont.)
- UN listing procedure, 24–31

Approximation of EU pillars, 105–14
Articles. *see* **respective Treaty**
Asset freezing. *see also* **Community sanctions**
- criminal law implications, 150–65, 425
- dependence on prior CFSP decision, 101
- effectiveness, 72–6
- exemptions and qualifications to UN listing, 36
- fair hearing, 313–4
- fair trial guarantees, 150–1
- implementation of Resolution 1373 by EU, 46–7
- national implementation of Security Council resolutions, 52–6
- as part of the international fight against terrorism, 58
- review by national courts, 291, 293
- Security Council Resolution 1373, 37
- statement of reasons, 323, 354–6
- UN statistics, 23–4

Autonomous European sanctions
- adoption procedure, 22–3, 47–51
- avenues of judicial review, 327–33
- classification as criminal charges
  - classification in domestic law, 151–5
  - importance of classification, 150–1
  - nature of offence or conduct, 155–7
  - severity of penalties, 157–64
- conflict between judiciary and political branches, 400–3
- determination of civil rights, 166
- division of tasks between EU and national courts, 358–67, 432
- double-staged administrative procedure, 309–10, 314–6, 322
- effects, 12–13
- EU-internal and external terrorist suspects distinguished, 327–28
- EU sanctions giving effect to UN lists distinguished, 22–3, 43–4, 303–4
- exemptions and qualifications, 51
- fair trial guarantees, 150–1
- identification of terrorists, 22
- impact on individual rights, 13, 150–76
- implementation of Resolution 1373, 46–7
- initial listing, 305, 310–2, 319, 322–3, 325, 327
- judicial protection, 428–30
- judicial review by national courts
  - European Arrest Warrant rulings, 362–5
  - interplay between different courts, 367–8
  - public warnings, 365–7
  - review of third pillar instruments, 358–62
- judicial review of Union law
  - defence rights, 353–4
  - direct action against Union lists, 351–3
  - indirect review, 334–8
  - preliminary rulings procedure, 347–51
  - statement of reasons, 354–6
  - support for, 333–4
  - wider jurisdiction principle, 338–47
- legal basis
  - European Treaties, 81–90
  - joint basis of Arts 60, 301, and 308 EC, 90–100
- limited jurisdiction of EU courts, 23, 327
- procedural protection, 306–24, 353
- proposals for adoption in compliance with procedural rights
  - access to information, 391–3
  - identification of terrorists, 386–7
  - institutional changes to listing procedure, 383–4
  - legislative changes to listing procedure, 380–3
  - procedural changes to listing procedure, 384–6
  - reviewable listing criteria, 387–91
- protection by ECtHR, 357–8
- protection from Community sanctions
  - access to information, 320–2
  - fair hearing, 308–20
  - judicial review, 324–7
  - leading case, 306–8
  - statement of reasons, 322–4
  - Union listing distinguished, 368–71
- reform of the sanctions regime, 375–80
- repeated annulment, 303, 400–5
- sanctions giving effect UN lists distinguished, 77
- sanctions giving effect UN lists distinguished by CFI, 303–5
- subsequent listing, 304–5, 311–2, 323, 325
- updating of Union lists, 47–9

Autonomy of the European legal order, 253–9

***Belmarsh detainees* case**, 192, 195, 202
Bin Laden. *see* **Usama bin Laden**
Binding force of Security Council resolutions
absence of specific provisions in European Treaties, 234–5
International Fruit Company case, 235–41
under national law, 244–5
national security considerations of CFI, 242–3
Bundesverfassungsgericht, *see* **German Constitutional Court**

Changes. *see* **Reform**
Civil rights
applicability of fair trial, 139–41, 150, 176–7
Article 6 ECHR, 139–80
asset freezing, 167
autonomous definition applied by ECtHR, 166
consequences of being listed, 170–2
core protection, 425
direct impact of Union lists, 172–3
procedural protection, 166–7
reputation, 159, 167–70, 174, 176, 178, 180, 183
right to property, 141, 156, 162–6
rubber-stamping UN lists, 173–6
stigmatization, 167–70
Classification of sanctions as criminal charges
classification of proceedings in domestic law, 151–55
importance of classification, 150–1
nature of offence or conduct, 155–7
severity of penalties, 157–64
Clues, 326 *see also* **Standard of proof**
Co-decision procedure, 105
Collateral damage
individual and state sanctions distinguished, 16, 18–9
Common Foreign and Security Policy (CFSP)
adoption of Union lists, 51, 81
approximation of EU pillars, 105–14
autonomous sanctions and sanctions giving effect to UN list distinguished, 305
changes effected by Lisbon Treaty, 123
common positions containing Union lists, 49, 327
compromise solution between international and Community law, 333
different avenues of judicial review, 327–33
implementation of Resolution 1373, 47
lack of judicial review, 327
preliminary rulings procedure, 332
relative merits of adoption under PJCC, 100–5
relevance of ECHR to EU law, 135
Common Positions
CP 931/2001/CFSP, 47–50
as cross-pillar instruments, 49–50
Community sanctions. *see also* **Asset freezing**
Article 301 EC as bridge to TEU, 92–6
insufficient legal basis, 82–90, 96–100
joint legal basis, 90–2
protection from sanctions giving effect to UN lists, 223–8
protection from sanctions giving effect to Union lists
access to information, 320–2
annulment by CFI, 306–8
fair hearings, 308–20
judicial review, 324–7
statement of reasons, 322–4
review standards, 219–20
Competences
Article 301 EC as bridge to TEU, 92–6
changes effected by Lisbon Treaty, 121–4, 126, 379
EU-internal and external terrorist suspects distinguished, 332
horizontal division, 105–14
inadequacies of existing law, 124–5
individual sanctions and state sanctions distinguished, 125–6
insufficient legal basis, 82–90, 96–100
joint legal basis of EC Articles, 90–2
lack of competences, 422–4
Opinion 2/94, 93–6
pragmatic approach of EU courts, 125
state sanctions, 238
vertical division, 114–21

Competences (cont.)
Community law, 115–7
EU law, 117–21
overview, 114–6
Conflict rule. *see* **UN Charter, Article 103**
Constitutional legal order
different approaches by CFI and ECJ, 221–2
duty of state to protect against terrorism, 187–9
European *Solange* criteria, 263–8
German application of *Solange* criteria, 265–6
political questions doctrine, 141–5
potential challenges to authority of ECJ, 435
primacy of Security Council resolutions over European law, 245–60
primacy of Security Council resolutions over national law, 289–90
Rechtsstaatsprinzip, 269–71
UN law as world constitution, 231
Control orders, 202–4
Cooperative procedure. *see* **Double-staged administrative procedure**
COREPER, 48
Counter-Terrorism Implementation Task Force (CTITF), 58
Counter-terrorist policies
European Union
differences between Member States, 64–5
effectiveness as security actor, 65–7
Europeanization of problem, 68
increased momentum, 64
limited operational success, 68–9
individual sanctions compared to other counter-terrorist policies, 422
international fight against terrorism, 57–63
need for proportionality, 76
new human rights approach, 1
Resolution 1373 as 'next step', 40
Court of First Instance (CFI)
autonomous Union lists and UN lists distinguished, 303–5
deferent approach to Security Council, 262–3, 278
duty to apply *jus cogens*, 253
interplay with other courts, 295–8
primacy of Security Council resolutions, 224–5
protection from Community sanctions giving effect to Union lists
access to information, 320–2
avenues of judicial review, 327–33
fair hearing, 308–20
judicial review, 324–7
leading case, 306–308
statement of reasons, 322–4
relationship between EU law and UN Charter, 221–2
attempts to redefine, 224–5, 420
derogation for national security considerations, 242–3
EU law standpoint, 234–59
review of Security Council resolutions, 181, 224–6
Courts. *see* **Court of First Instance (CFI); European Court of Justice (ECJ); European Court of Human Rights (ECtHR); International Court of Justice (ICJ); International Criminal Court (ICC); National courts**
Criminal charge, individual sanctions as
classification of proceedings in domestic law, 151–5
importance of classification, 150–1
nature of offence or conduct, 155–7
severity of penalties, 157–64
Criminal law
competence of EU courts, 319, 326
effect of Resolution 1373, 43
Environmental Crime case, 92, 96, 108, 153–4, 335–6
EU competence, 96
European counter-terrorist policies, 66, 69
implementation of Security Council resolutions, 55
implications of asset freezing, 425
implications of listings, 150–64
individual sanctions as part of the international fight against terrorism, 59–61
politicization by anti-terrorist measures, 13
role of judiciary, 399–400
sensible approach to listing criteria, 388–9
Criteria. *see* **Listing criteria**
Cross-pillar instruments, 49–50

Deference. *see* **Judicial deference**
Delisting procedure
at the EU level, 77
at the UN level
absence of procedural protection, 35–6
adverse comments by ECJ, 34–5
continuing fundamental rights concerns, 77
decision of listing state, 41
direct petition to UN Security Council, 32–3
government petition, 31–2
focal point, 32–3, 253
improvements through Resolutions 1730 and 1735, 32
inadequate remedy, 35, 421–2
lack of successful applications, 33–4
Derogation. *see* **Emergency**
Detention, 186, 192, 199–200
Diplomatic protection
delisting procedure, 32, 421–2
inadequacy of political control over UN lists, 405–8
UN delisting, 32
Direct action under Union law
position of ECJ, 356
review of Union lists, 351–3
Direct effect of common positions, 149–150, 172–3
Discretion. *see also* **Margins of appreciation**
autonomous European sanctions and sanctions giving effect to UN lists distinguished by CFI, 303–5
fair hearing, 304, 311–3, 315–7
Double-staged administrative procedure, 309–19
Duration, 167. *see also* **Provisional measures; Temporary measures**
Duty to protect, 187–9

EC Treaty
Article 10, 111–2
Article 60, 82–4, 90–93, 100–1, 122
Article 301, 79–98, 100–1, 109–14, 116, 122–4
Article 308, 90–91, 93–96
Ecowas judgment, 92, 108, 111, 335–6
Effective remedy
applicability, 180–1
fair trial distinguished, 138–9
independent and impartial authority, 182–3
relevance of ECHR to EU law, 133
Effectiveness of individual sanctions, 72–6
Effet utile, 92–3
Embargoes. *see* **State sanctions**
Emergency
'actual' or 'imminent' requirement, 193–4
adoption of measures by Germany, 56
approach of national courts, 189–91
Belmarsh detainee case, 192–3
derogation criteria
appropriateness, 218
consistency with international law, 195
determination, 189–95
necessity, 195
hearing restrictions, 312
requirement for balanced approach, 198–9
role of Security Council, 281
rulings of ICJ, 191
temporariness of threat, 174, 191–2
European Arrest Warrant
as EU counter-terrorist policy, 65
rulings of national courts
importance of views expressed by national courts, 370–1
review of Union law in national courts, 362–5
European Convention on Human Rights (ECHR)
Article 6, 139–80
Article 13, 180–3
Article 15, 189–96
Minimum protection, 137–8, 296
European Court of Human Rights (ECtHR). *see also* **Fundamental rights**
civil rights
asset freezing, 167
autonomous definition applied by ECtHR, 166
procedural protection, 166–7
reputation, 167–70, 174, 176, 178, 180, 183
right to property, 166
stigmatization, 167–70
criminal charge

European Court of Human Rights (ECtHR) (cont.)
classification of proceedings in domestic law, 151–5
importance of classification, 150–1
nature of offence or conduct, 155–7
severity of penalties, 157–64
determination of criminal law implications, 425
duty of state to protect against terrorism, 187
influence of case law on EU courts, 282
interplay with national courts, 367–8
interplay with other EU courts, 295–8
mandate to protect fundamental rights, 435
non-disclosure of evidence, 197–200
perspective on terrorism, 200–1
primacy of Security Council resolutions, 284–7
proportionality, 409–11, 413, 415
protection from Community law, 282–4
protection from Community and Union law distinguished, 369
protection from Union listing, 357–8
Segi case, 127–8, 135, 153, 160–2, 169, 175, 357–8, 367
threshold for judicial review, 128
European Court of Justice (ECJ), 420
access to justice
limitations on jurisdiction, 135
relevance of ECHR, 136
binding force of Security Council resolutions, 235–41
classification of criminal charges, 154–5
commitment to rule of law, 129–30
competence to review Community sanctions, 330
defence of EU constitutional framework, 266–7
defensive approach to Security Council, 261, 278
extension of preliminary rulings procedure, 331
failure to identify hierarchy of norms, 280
influence of ECtHR case law, 282
interplay with other EU courts, 295–8
legal basis of Community sanctions
dangers of using first pillar instruments, 98–9
joint basis of Arts 60, 301, and 308 EC, 93–6
rejection of Arts 60 and 301 EC alone, 83
position on direct review, 356
potential challenges to authority, 435
protection from Community measures and Union listing distinguished, 369
protection from sanctions implementing Union lists
attempts to extend powers, 345–7
courts mandate and imitations, 339–40
direct action against Union lists, 351–3
interplay with other courts, 367–8
Les Verts case, 340–4
preliminary rulings procedure, 347–51
primacy of Security Council resolutions
ECJ's defence of EU's autonomy, 253–9, 298–301, 420–1
International Fruit Company case, 245–6
relationship between EU law and UN Charter, 221–2
review of European sanctions implementing UN lists
amending European treaties, 260–1
autonomy of European legal order, 253–9
force of Security Council resolutions, 245–6
individual sanctions, 252–3
International Fruit Company case, 235–41
interplay between different courts, 295–8
review of Security Council Resolutions, 227–8
state sanctions, 246–9
UN delisting procedure, 34–5
wider jurisdiction principle, 338–9
Les Verts case, 340–4
European Parliament, 90, 98–9, 101, 105
European Security Strategy, 65
Evidence, 139, 153, 185, 415. *see also* **Clues; Standard of proof**
Executive powers, 19, 42, 52, 54, 56, 397–400, 404–5
Exemptions
autonomous European sanctions, 51

continuing fundamental rights concerns, 77
UN sanctions, 36–7

Fair hearing. *see also* **Access to information**
Community sanctions giving effect to UN lists,
Community sanctions giving effect to Union lists, 308–20
discretion, 304, 311–3, 315–7
double-staged administrative procedure, 309–10, 314–6
improvement to adoption procedures, 418
limitations on grounds of security, 220
limited right, 204, 220
presumption of innocence, 162
Fair trial. *see also* **Access to justice**
administrative measures, 140–1
applicability
civil and criminal cases, 140
determination of civil rights, 139–41, 150, 176–7
international cooperation, 145–9
provisional measures, 170, 174–5, 375
delisting procedure, 35
effective remedy distinguished, 138–9
Habeas corpus, 186, 207, 210, 212–4
House of Lords approach to terrorism, 203–4
political questions doctrine, 141–5
non-derogable core, 396–7
non-derogable rights, 190
non-disclosure of evidence, 197–200
right to be heard by independent and impartial tribunal, 177–80
unrestrictive interpretation, 139
US courts approach, 208
Financial Action Task Force (FATF), 59–60
Financing of terrorism
criminal money, 57, 59–60, 67
effectiveness of asset freezing, 76
European counter-terrorist policies, 67
Financial Action Task Force (FATF), 59–61
individual sanctions as part of the international fight, 63
justifications for fight against, 419
money laundering, 57, 59–60, 67
shift in EU focus, 67
Fundamental rights. *see also* **Access to justice; Fair hearing; Fair trial; Procedural protection; Property rights**
compliance at national level, 385–6
constitutional basis within the European legal order, 244
defensive approach of ECJ, 261
difficulties of comparison between state and individual sanctions, 21–2
duty of state to protect against terrorism, 187–9
emergency, 193–5
EU commitment to rule of law, 129–33
exemptions and qualifications to UN listing, 36–7
fair trial and effective remedy distinguished, 138–9
focus on exercise of public power, 76
as foundations of EU, 266
hierarchy of institutions and substantive values distinguished, 279–82
human rights distinguished, 16
individual sanctions unworthy of international bodies, 372
limitations justified in the fight against terrorism, 425–7
accepted by national courts, 201–17
primacy of Security Council resolutions over national law, 289
proportionality
appropriateness and necessity of sanctions, 411–3
differing interpretations, 409–11
importance in judicial review, 408–9
Israeli decisions on limitation of rights, 215–6
minority interests, 416–7
objective approach, 413–4
secondary considerations, 415–6
shift in counter-terrorism policies, 62
state sanctions, 414
protection from Community law by ECtHR, 282–4
protection under EU law, 137–8
protection by international law, 268–9
relationship between EU law and UN Charter, 221–2
relevance of ECHR to EU law, 133–8
relevance of Resolution 1373, 40–1
relevance to UN Security Council, 24

Fundamental rights. (cont.)
review by German Constitutional Court, 115, 263–5
role of judiciary, 398
role of Monitoring Team, 29–30
state and individual sanctions distinguished, 88
status of ECHR in EU law, 257
terrorism as exceptional circumstances, 189–93

GATT, 235–8, 240–1, 245–8
German Constitutional Court,
European Arrest Warrant case, 362–6
Lisbon Treaty decision, 114–5, 128, 362, 399
Maastricht decision, 263–5
Public warnings, 365–7
Solange cases, 258, 261, 263–5
***Guantanamo Bay* cases**, 206–15
Guilt by association, 390

Habeas corpus, 186, 206–8, 210, 212–4
Hierarchy
of institutions and substantive values distinguished, 279–82
Solange rulings, 223, 258, 261, 263–5, 267, 279, 282, 298
House of Lords
Belmarsh detainees case, 192, 195, 202
on control orders, 202–4
Torture evidence case, 204–6
Human rights. *see* **Fundamental rights**
Humanitarian exemptions. *see* **Exemptions**

Identification of terrorists
general fight against terrorism, 37–40
individual and state sanctions distinguished, 21, 422
proposals for compliance of autonomous European lists, 386–7
rule of law, 430–1
UN listings and autonomous Union listings distinguished, 22
Implementation of Security Council resolutions,
by UN member states, 52–6
by the EU, 44–6
Independence and impartiality of courts
fair trial, 177–80
no compromise even for national security, 396
right to an effective remedy, 182–3
Indirect review of Union law, 334–8
Information. *see* **Access to information**
Initial listing, 305, 310–2, 319, 322–3, 325, 327
Intelligence, 28
'Intelligent sanctions', 17
International Convention for the Suppression of the Financing of Terrorism, 39, 41, 57–60, 67
International cooperation
avoidance of judicial scrutiny, 253
exclusion of access to justice, 140, 145–9
need for, 369
political institutions, 125
recognition as public interest, 290
reliance on external value choices, 182–3
requirement of individual sanctions, 101
restriction of procedural rights, 319, 394, 400
role of domestic courts, 297–9
sacrifice of well-established rights, 18
International Court of Justice, 191, 229–30, 232–3, 262–3, 271–2, 274
International Criminal Court, 13
***International Fruit Company* case**, 235–42, 245–6
International law
approach to individuals, 156, 431–2
CFSP as compromise with Community law, 333
classical approach to adoption of treaties, 39
compliance to avoid state sanctions, 20
condemnation of torture, 205
direct impact on individuals, 77
discrepancies between effects on individual rights and legal redress, 18, 89
ECJ approach in *International Fruit Company* case, 240–1
legal personality of EU, 134
motivation for national decisions, 367
obligation to prosecute terrorists, 386
primacy of UN Security Council resolutions over domestic law, 274–8

protection of fundamental rights through state cooperation, 147
relationship between EU law and UN Charter, 228–34, 427
relationship with EU law, 106
relevance for judicial review in national courts, 13
requirement to protect fundamental rights, 268–9
rule of law, 269–72

International peace and security, 11, 37, 57–8, 93, 141, 155, 191–2, 231, 235, 249, 281, 289, 373, 405, 413, 381, 420, 431

Iraq
ineffectiveness of state sanctions, 15

Israel
decisions on limitations on rights, 215–7
duty of state to protect citizens, 186–7
justifications for limitations on rights, 426
test of proportionality, 409

Judicial deference
European *Solange* approach, 264
German Constitutional Court, 263–5, 362–6
review of European sanctions based on UN lists, 222
Security Council resolutions, 247

Judicial review *see also* **Review mechanisms**
appropriateness for derogations, 218
central element of fair trial, 396
defence rights, 353–4
different degrees for different European measures, 184
direct action against Union lists, 351–3
ECJ's defence of Community's autonomy, 254
excluded by primacy of Security Council resolutions, 277
inadequate standard of protection, 421, 431
indirect review of Union law, 334–8
jurisdiction over UN lists, 22
national courts
European Arrest Warrant rulings, 362–5
interplay between different courts, 367–8
public warnings, 365–7
review of Union law, 358–62
political questions doctrine, 144–5
preliminary rulings procedure, 347–51
protection from Community measures and Union listing distinguished, 368–71
protection from Community sanctions giving effect to reviewable listing criteria, 387–91
statement of reasons, 322–4, 354–6
threshold in ECtHR, 128
Union lists
avenues for review, 327–3
competence of EU courts to review fundamental procedural rights, 319
fair hearing, 318–9
lack of effective protection, 324–7
Union lists and UN lists distinguished, 303–305
wider jurisdiction principle, 338–47

Judiciary
assessment of proportionality, 409
conflict with political branches, 400–5
role, 397–400, 418

Jurisdiction of EU Courts
binding force of Security Council resolutions, 236
ECJ's defence of Community's autonomy, 253–9
interplay between different courts, 295–8
review of defence rights in Union pillars, 353–4
Union law, 345–7
wider jurisdiction principle
EU commitment to fundamental rights and rule of law, 338–9
extension of EU court powers under Union Pillars, 345–7
interpretation and application of EC Treaty, 339–40
Les Verts case, 340–4

Jus cogens, 9, 35, 181, 219, 225–7, 253, 263, 271, 273, 277, 281, 287, 292, 299

***Kadi* case**
CFI
access to justice, 128, 140, 148, 174, 181
competences, 78–9, 81, 83, 87, 90–3, 96, 99, 100, 106–7, 110, 114

Kadi case (cont.)
relationship EU law and UN Charter, 221, 223–5, 227, 233–5, 242–3, 245, 250–3, 261–2, 264, 267, 273, 275, 278, 281, 287, 290–1, 296–7, 299,
ECJ
competences, 78, 79, 81, 83, 86, 88, 93–4, 98–100, 108, 110–1, 124,
access to justice, 128, 141–2, 144, 148, 181, 184,
relationship EU law and UN Charter, 221, 224, 226–7, 233, 244, 247, 251–5, 257–8, 261–4, 266–7, 273, 276, 280, 287, 290–1, 296–8, 300–2

Legal basis, 81–99
***Les Verts* case (*Parti Ecologiste and 'Les Verts' v EP*)**, 340–4
Limitations on rights
case law of ECtHR
non-disclosure of evidence, 197–200
overview, 196–7
perspective on terrorism, 200–1
duty of state to protect against terrorism, 187–9
emergency
'actual' or 'imminent' requirement, 193–4
overview, 194–5
justification on grounds of security, 220
justifications in the fight against terrorism, 425–7
national courts
House of Lords approach, 201–6
Supreme Court of Israel, 215–7
US courts, 206–15
terrorism as exceptional circumstances
approach of national courts, 189–91
Belmarsh detainees case, 192–3
rulings of ICJ, 191
temporariness, 191–2
Lisbon Treaty
Article 75 TFEU, 121–3, 379
Article 215 TFEU, 121–3, 379
Article 352 TFEU, 98
general, 121–4, 379
Listing criteria
EU listing criteria
initial listing, 305, 310–2, 319, 322–3, 325, 327
subsequent listing, 304–5, 311–2, 323, 325
UN listing criteria
lack of clear evidential requirements, 31
Usama bin Laden, 27–8
Listing practice
EU
adoption of common position, 81–2
EC as bridge to TEU, 92–96
initial listing, 305, 310–2, 319, 322–3, 325, 327
joint legal basis of EC Articles, 90–92
missing competences, 82–90, 96–100
subsequent listing, 304–5, 311–2, 323, 325
UN
Sanctions Committee, 15, 23–33
listings on the internet, 29
Lists. *see* **UN lists Union lists**

Maastricht Treaty, 78, 82
Margins of appreciation. *see also* **Discretion**
case law from ECtHR, 196
emergencies, 193
Mixed procedure. *see* **Double-staged administrative procedure**
Money laundering, 57, 59–60, 67
Monitoring Team, 29–30

National courts
classification of sanctions as criminal charges, 151–5
competence to review EU law, 330
competence to review fundamental procedural rights, 319
determination of rights by ECHR, 138
duty of state to protect against terrorism, 187–9
effect of interplay between different courts, 297–8
German Constitutional Court, 114–5, 128, 258, 261, 262–5, 362, 365–7, 399
House of Lords on terrorism, 201–6
importance of views on European Arrest Warrant, 370–1
limitations on rights
House of Lords approach, 201–6

Supreme Court of Israel approach, 215–7
US courts approach, 206–15
mandate to protect fundamental rights, 435
need to restrict fundamental rights, 426
power balance between EU and Member States
Community law, 115–7
EU law, 117–21
overview, 114–6
primacy of Security Council resolutions, 288–90
protection from Union lists
European Arrest Warrant rulings, 362–5
interplay between different courts, 367–8
public warnings, 365–7
review of third pillar instruments, 358–62
reluctance to offer judicial protection from Community sanctions, 224
review of individual sanctions, 290–5
stricter standards imposed by EU courts, 350
Supreme Court of Israel on terrorism, 215–7
Swiss Supreme Court, 34–5, 53, 128, 223, 261, 291–2, 297, 405–6
terrorism as exceptional circumstances, 189–91
US courts on terrorism, 206–15

National emergency, *see* **Emergency**
National measures implementing UN lists, 244–5
National security. *see also* **Emergency; International peace and security**
EU focus on terrorism, 68
relationship between EU law and UN Charter, 242–3
Non-disclosure of evidence
ECtHR approach, 197–200
House of Lords approach, 203–4

Obligation of loyal cooperation. *see* **EC Treaty, Article 10**
Obligation to state reasons. *see* **Statement of reasons**
Ombudsman, 139, 183
Opinion 2/94, 93–6

Pacta tertiis non nocent, 231
Pillars
approximation, 105–14
CFSP, 44, 45, 47–51, 77, 80–1, 86, 92–4, 97, 100–5, 107, 109–14, 118, 123, 126, 135, 141, 153, 155, 161, 164, 170, 172–6, 180, 304–5, 310, 326–56
delimitation, 92, 111–12, 138, 154, 334–6, 354
PJCC, 4, 9, 51, 80, 100–4, 135, 305
Police and Judicial Cooperation in Criminal Matters (PJCC)
adoption procedure for Union lists, 51
approximation of EU pillars, 105–14
autonomous European sanctions and European sanctions giving effect to UN lists distinguished, 305
common positions containing Union lists, 49
implementation of Resolution 1373 by EU, 47
protection from Union lists, 305, 358–68
relative merits of adopting Union lists under CFSP, 100–5
relevance of ECHR to EU law, 135
review by national courts, 358–62
Policies. *see* **Counter-terrorist policies**
Political questions doctrine, 141–5
Power balance between EU and Member States, 117–21
Preliminary rulings procedure
limitations on access to justice, 219
Segi case, 219, 331–2
under Union pillars, 331–2, 347–51
Primacy of Security Council resolutions
amendment of European treaties, 259–61
ECJ approach in *International Fruit Company* case, 245–46
ECJ's defence of Community's autonomy, 253–9, 298–301, 420–1
review of European sanctions giving effect to UN lists, 250–9
review of state sanctions, 246–9
Procedural protection
absence of effective protection, 421
defence rights, 353–4
delisting procedure, 35–6
derogation because of terrorism, 189–90
from Community sanctions giving effect to Union lists

Procedural protection (cont.)
access to information, 320–2
fair hearing, 308–20
judicial review, 324–7
leading cases, 306–8
statement of reasons, 322–4
from Union lists, 353–6
proposals for compliance of autonomous European sanctions
access to information, 391–3
identification of terrorists, 386–7
institutional changes to listing procedure, 383–4
legislative changes to listing procedure, 380–3
procedural changes to listing procedure, 384–6
reviewable listing criteria, 387–91
proposals for compliance of European sanctions giving effect to UN lists, 393–6
reform of the sanctions regime, 373–380
scope of ECHR rights, 138–9
statement of reasons, 322–4, 354–6
Proof. *see* **Standard of proof**
Property rights, 141, 153, 162–7, 183, 189, 194, 267, 283, 387, 398, 407
Proportionality
Belmarsh prison detainees case, 192
counter-terrorist policies, 76
individual sanctions, 408–17
individual sanctions as a policy tool, 63
international cooperation, 146
protection of confidential information, 220
state sanctions, 414
test of, 409
Proposed changes
autonomous European sanctions
access to information, 391–3
identification of terrorists, 386–7
institutional changes to listing procedure, 383–4
legislative changes to listing procedure, 380–3
necessary changes listing procedure, 380
procedural changes to listing procedure, 384–6
reform of the sanctions regime, 375–80
reviewable listing criteria, 387–91
sanctions giving effect to UN lists, 393–6
Provisional measures, 170, 174–5, 375. *see also* **Duration; Temporary measures**
Public warnings, 365–7

Reasons. *see* **Statement of reasons**
Rechtstaatprinzip. 269–72 *see also* **Rule of law**
Reform of adoption procedure, 375–80 *see also* **Proposed changes**
Reputation, 159, 167–70, 174, 176, 178, 180, 183
Review mechanisms. *see also* **Judicial review**
absence of effective remedy at UN level, 223–4, 301–2
CFI's findings in respect of Security Council resolutions, 224–6
ECJ's findings in respect of Security Council resolutions, 227–8
German Constitutional Court, 115–6
national courts, 290–5
ranking of Security Council resolutions in the European legal order
individual sanctions, 250–9
state sanctions, 246–9
US Review Tribunals, 210–3
Role of judiciary, 397–400
Rule of law
alternative concepts, 130–1
analogy for individual sanctions excluded, 89
ECHR, 131–2
ECJ affirmations, 129–30
European law, 132–3
foundations of EU, 266
identification of terrorists, 430–1
international law, 269–72
limitations on powers, 272
recognition by UN, 269–72
terrorist aims to destroy, 187
wider jurisdiction principle, 338–9

Sanctions Committee
administration of lists, 25
changes since first implementation, 15
criteria for listing, 27–8
delisting procedure, 32–3
focus on 'international terrorists', 23
lack of clear evidential requirements, 31

listing of Al-Qaida as 'international terrorists', 23
publication of first list, 26–7
role, 15
statistics on frozen assets, 23–4
Schengen Information System, 64, 366
Secondary sanctions, 44, 55, 153, 171, 173, 414
Security Council
compliance with human rights, 24
compliance with rule of law, 269–72
as legislator, 41–2
limitations on powers, 272–4
Security Council resolution 1267, 14, 19, 21, 24–7, 29, 33, 37, 40–1, 43–5, 50, 52–3, 60, 224, 258–9, 267–8, 271 291, 294, 303, 382, 406, 412, 421, 430
Security Council resolution 1373, 14, 19, 26, 37–43, 46, 60, 293, 304, 326, 374, 422
Security Council resolutions
absolute primacy, 300–1
binding effect on EU Member States, 232
binding effect on non-members of UN, 230
binding force under European law
absence of specific provisions, 234–5
annulment of national measures, 244–5
ECJ approach in *International Fruit Company* case, 235–41
reliance on derogation for national security considerations, 242–3
CFI's approach to review, 181, 224–6
criteria for listing, 27–8
determination of status
CFI, 262–3
ECJ, 227–8, 261, 278–9
national courts, 288–94
evaluation of fundamental rights threats, 40–1
following 9/11, 26
general call to fight terrorism, 37–40
improvements to delisting procedure, 32
national implementation, 52–6
need for changes to international cooperation, 432–4
presumption of legality, 229
primacy and effectiveness, 274–8
primacy over ECtHR, 284–7
primacy over primary EU law
amendment of European treaties, 259–61
ECJ approach in *International Fruit Company* case, 245–6
ECJ's defence of Community's autonomy, 253–9, 298–301, 420–1
review of individual sanctions, 250–9
review of state sanctions, 246–9
primacy over international treaties, 233
primacy over national law, 288–90
Resolution 1373 as 'next step', 40
review by national courts, 291
***Segi* case**
CFI, 7, 10, 50–1, 80, 123, 128, 143, 156, 175–6, 305, 328–30, 333, 335, 338, 340, 360, 369, 384, 429
ECJ, 7, 10, 50–1, 102, 104, 112–3, 123, 128–9, 131–3, 135, 138, 172, 219, 284, 298, 305–6, 330–4, 337, 339, 343–50, 352–3, 355–62, 368, 384, 429, 433–4
ECtHR, 127–8, 135, 153, 160–2, 169, 175, 357–8, 367
Separation of powers, 142
'Smart sanctions', 17
***Solange* rulings**, 263–6. *see also* **German Constitutional Court; Hierarchy**
Special advocate, 393
Special Rapporteur, 30, 63
Standard of proof, 87, 139, 153, 205, 385, 415–6. *see also* **Clues; Duration**
Standing, 35, 46, 168, 347–8
State of emergency, *see* **Emergency**
State sanctions
based on general policy decisions under CFSP, 109
exclusive Community competence, 238
fair hearing, 313
impact on human rights, 88
individual sanctions distinguished
adoption procedure, 20–1
difficulties with identification of target, 21, 422
economic and political issues, 18–20
impact on target, 20
political questions doctrine, 143
proportionality, 414

State sanctions (cont.)
 reconsideration because of limited effectiveness, 15
 review by ECJ, 246–9
Statement of reasons
 changes effected by EU, 21
 Community sanctions giving effect to Union lists, 322–4
 improvements to autonomous European sanctions regime, 376–7
 UN listings, 29, 395
 Union law, 354–6
Stigmatization
 breaches of civil rights, 167–70
 effect of listing, 12–3
 no challenge of Union lists, 328
 right to be heard by independent and impartial tribunal, 178
Subsequent listing, 304–5, 311–2, 323, 325
Swiss Supreme Court, 34–5, 54, 128, 223, 261, 291–2, 405–6

Taliban
 criteria for listing, 27–8
 effectiveness of asset freezing, 72
 inclusion in UN Security Council lists, 23, 26
 reasons for listing published on internet, 29
 role of UN Sanctions Committee, 15
 UN resolutions following US embassy attacks, 25
Temporary measures, 30, 174, 190–1, 385. *see also* **Provisional measures**
Terrorism
 as European problem, 64–8
 different focuses of UN and autonomous European listings, 23
 duty of state to protect against, 187–9
 ECtHR approach to limitations on rights, 200–1
 emergency
  'actual' or 'imminent' requirement, 193–4
  approach of national courts, 189–91
  designation and necessity of Belmarsh prison detentions, 192–3
  rulings of ICJ, 191
  temporariness, 191–2
 EU counter-terrorist policy, 64–71
 House of Lords approach, 201–6
 individual sanctions as part of the international fight, 57–63
 international fight against terrorism, 57–63
 justifications for limitations on rights, 218–9, 425–7
 pressing international challenge, 420
 Security Council resolution 1373 calling for general fight against, 37–40
 threat to core values, 76
 US courts approach, 206–15
Terrorists
 Al-Qaida
  criteria for listing, 27–8
  effectiveness of asset freezing, 72–3
  legal basis for European sanctions, 83, 87
  listing by UN Security Council, 23, 26
  reasons for listing published on internet, 29
  review of freezing orders by national court, 291
  role of UN Sanctions Committee, 15
  UN resolutions following US embassy attacks, 25
 identification of terrorists
  general fight against terrorism, 37–40
  individual and state sanctions distinguished, 21, 422
  proposals for compliance of Union lists, 386–7
  rule of law, 430–1
  UN listings and Union listings distinguished, 22
 Taliban
  criteria for listing, 27–8
  effectiveness of asset freezing, 72
  listing by UN Security Council, 23, 26
  reasons for listing published on internet, 29
  role of UN Sanctions Committee, 15
  UN resolutions following US embassy attacks, 25
***Torture evidence* case**, 205–6
Trade embargoes. *see* **State sanctions**
Transparency, 28, 381
Travel bans, 4, 12, 15, 25, 31, 41, 97
Treaty Establishing the European Community. *see* **EC Treaty**

Treaty of Lisbon. *see* **Lisbon Treaty**
Treaty of Maastricht. *see* **Maastricht Treaty**
Treaty on European Union
Article 47, 92, 111–2, 138, 154, 334–6, 354

UN Charter
Article 103, 224, 230–1, 233, 273, 285–6, 288
CFI attempts to redefine relationship with, 223–6, 420
Community law obligations to give effect to, 242–3
EU law standpoint on binding force and status, 234–61
international law standpoint, 228–34
not binding on EU or Community, 259
references to rule of law, 270–2
relationship with ECHR, 285–6
relationship with EU law, 228–34
UN lists
absence of effective remedy at UN level, 223–4, 301–2
autonomous European sanctions distinguished by CFI, 303–5
circumvention of protective measures, 420, 432
classification of sanctions as criminal charges
classification of proceedings in domestic law, 151–5
importance, 150–1
nature of offence or conduct, 155–7
severity of penalties, 157–64
conflict between judiciary and political branches, 403–4
criteria for listing, 27–8
delisting procedure
absence of procedural protection, 35–6
adverse comments by ECJ, 34–5
direct petition to UN Security Council, 32–3
government petition, 31–2
improvements effected by Resolutions 1730 and 1735, 32
lack of successful applications, 33–4
violations of fair trial guarantees, 35
effect, 12–3
European sanctions giving effect to UN lists
difficulties of complying with EU law, 373
ECtHR case law, 282–8
EU law approach, 234–61
international law approach, 228–34
overview, 44–6
proposals for compliance with procedural rights, 393–6
exemptions and qualifications, 36–7
exercise of executive function, 42–3
fair hearing for autonomous European sanctions distinguished, 312–3
identification of terrorists, 22
impact of Resolution 1373, 41–2
impact on human rights, 18
inadequacy of political control, 405–8
information sources for listing, 28
jurisdiction for judicial review, 22
lack of clear evidential requirements, 31
lower level of fundamental rights protection, 128
political implications of review, 252
political questions doctrine, 141
primacy of UN Council resolutions, 261–82
publication of first list by UN Security Council, 26–7
publication on internet, 29
relevance of human rights guarantees, 24
review by national courts, 288–98
right to an effective remedy, 181–2
role of UN Sanctions Committee, 15
sanctions regimes mirrored by EU, 22, 43–52, 422
Union lists compared, 22, 373
United Nations. *see also* **UN lists; Security Council resolutions; Union lists**
Charter. *see* **UN Charter**
Global Counter-Terrorism Strategy, 57
Sanctions Committee
administration of lists, 25
changes since first implementation, 15
criteria for listing, 27–8
delisting procedure, 32–3
focus on 'international terrorists', 23
lack of clear evidential requirements, 31
listing of Al-Qaida as 'international terrorists', 23

United Nations. (cont.)
- publication of first list, 26–7
- role, 15
- statistics on frozen assets, 23–4

Union lists. *see also* **UN lists**
- adoption under CFSP or PJCC, 100–5
- approximation of EU pillars, 105–14
- defence rights, 353–4
- determination of civil rights, 166
- direct action, 351–3
- indirect review, 334–8
- listing practice under European Treaties
  - adoption of common position, 81–2
  - missing competences, 96–100
- obligation to state reasons, 354–5
- preliminary ruling procedure, 347–51
- protection—status quo, 327–33
- protection from Community sanctions implementing Union lists
  - access to information, 320–2
  - annulment by CFI, 306–8
  - fair hearings, 308–20
  - indirect review, 334–8
  - judicial review, 324–7
  - obligation to state reasons, 322–4
- updating, 47–9
- wider jurisdiction principle, 338–47

United States
- 9/11
  - effect on counter-terrorist measures, 1
  - general call to fight terrorism, 37
  - globalisation of fight against terrorism, 57
  - UN resolutions following attacks, 26
- Courts' approach to terrorism, 206–15
- decisions to limit rights, 206–15
- duty of state to protect citizens, 186–7
- effectiveness of individual sanctions, 73–4
- ending of guilt by association, 390–1
- justifications for limitations on rights, 426

Usama bin Laden
- criteria for listing, 27–8
- UN resolutions following US embassy attacks, 25

Vienna Convention on the Law of Treaties, 224, 228, 233, 260

Wider jurisdiction principle
- direct action, 353
- EU commitment to fundamental rights and rule of law, 338–9
- extension of EU court powers under Union Pillars, 345–7
- interpretation and application of EC Treaty, 339–40

Working Party, 376–81, 383

World Trade Organisation, 240, 245, 248–9